Lecture Notes in Computer Science 5524

Commenced Publication in 1973
Founding and Former Series Editors:
Gerhard Goos, Juris Hartmanis, and Jan van Leeuwen

W0235497

Helder Araujo   Ana Maria Mendonça
Armando J. Pinho   María Inés Torres (Eds.)

Pattern Recognition and Image Analysis

4th Iberian Conference, IbPRIA 2009
Póvoa de Varzim, Portugal, June 10-12, 2009
Proceedings

 Springer

Volume Editors

Helder Araujo
University of Coimbra–Pólo II
Department of Electrical and Computer Engineering
Institute of Systems and Robotics
3030-290 Coimbra, Portugal
E-mail: helder@isr.uc.pt

Ana Maria Mendonça
University of Porto
Faculty of Engineering
Institute of Biomedical Engineering
Rua Dr. Roberto Frias, 4200-465 Porto, Portugal
E-mail: amendon@fe.up.pt

Armando J. Pinho
University of Aveiro
DETI/IEETA
Signal Processing Lab
3810–193 Aveiro, Portugal
E-mail: ap@ua.pt

María Inés Torres
Universidad del País Vasco (UPV/EHU)
Facultad de Ciencia y Tecnología
Departamento de Electricidad y Electrónica
Apartado 644, 48080 Bilbao, Spain
E-mail: manes.torres@ehu.es

Library of Congress Control Number: Applied for

CR Subject Classification (1998): I.4, I.5, I.7, I.2.10, I.2.7

LNCS Sublibrary: SL 6 – Image Processing, Computer Vision, Pattern Recognition, and Graphics

ISSN   0302-9743
ISBN-10   3-642-02171-9 Springer Berlin Heidelberg New York
ISBN-13   978-3-642-02171-8 Springer Berlin Heidelberg New York

springer.com

© Springer-Verlag Berlin Heidelberg 2009
Printed in Germany

Typesetting: Camera-ready by author, data conversion by Scientific Publishing Services, Chennai, India
Printed on acid-free paper   SPIN: 12693948   06/3180   5 4 3 2 1 0

Preface

IbPRIA 2009 (Iberian Conference on Pattern Recognition and Image Analysis) was the fourth edition of a series of conferences jointly organized by APRP (Associação Portuguesa de Reconhecimento de Padrões) and AERFAI (Asociación Española de Reconocimiento de Formas y Análisis de Imágenes). This year, IbPRIA was held in Póvoa de Varzim, Portugal, June 10–12, 2009, and was a local joint organization of ISR (Instituto de Sistemas e Robótica), INEB (Instituto de Engenharia Biomédica) and IEETA (Instituto de Engenharia Electrónica e Telemática de Aveiro). It followed the three successful previous editions hosted by the Universitat de les Illes Balears (2003), Instituto de Sistemas e Robótica and Centro de Geo-Sistemas of Instituto Superior Técnico (2005), and the Institute of Informatics and Applications of the University of Girona (2007).

A total of 106 manuscripts, from 18 countries, were received. Each of these submissions was reviewed in a blind process by at least two reviewers, resulting in 62 accepted papers, 33 for oral presentation and 29 for poster presentation.

We were very honored to have as invited speakers such internationally recognized researchers as Samy Bengio from Google Inc., USA, Joachim Weickert from Saarland University, Germany, and Nando de Freitas from the University of British Columbia, Canada.

We would like to thank all the authors for submitting their papers and thus making these proceedings possible. We address special thanks to the members of the Program Committee and the additional reviewers for their great work, which contributed to the high quality of these proceedings. We are also grateful to the members of the Local Organizing Committee, for their substantial contribution of time and effort.

Finally, our thanks go to IAPR (International Association for Pattern Recognition), for sponsoring the Best Paper Award at IbPRIA 2009, and also to FCT (Fundação para a Ciência e a Tecnologia), for providing a key support to this event.

The next edition of IbPRIA will be held in Spain in 2011.

June 2009

Helder Araújo
Ana Maria Mendonça
Armando J. Pinho
María Inés Torres

Organization

IbPRIA 2009 was jointly organized by APRP (Associação Portuguesa de Reconhecimento de Padrões) and AERFAI (Asociación Española de Reconocimiento de Formas y Análisis de Imágenes), and was a local joint organization of ISR (Instituto de Sistemas e Robótica), INEB (Instituto de Engenharia Biomédica) and IEETA (Instituto de Engenharia Electrónica e Telemática de Aveiro).

General Conference Co-chairs

Helder Araújo	ISR/University of Coimbra, Portugal
Ana Maria Mendonça	INEB/University of Porto, Portugal
Armando J. Pinho	IEETA/University of Aveiro, Portugal
María Inés Torres	University of the Basque Country, Spain

Invited Speakers

Samy Bengio	Google Inc., USA
Nando de Freitas	University of British Columbia, Canada
Joachim Weickert	Saarland University, Germany

Local Organizing Committee

Jorge Alves da Silva	INEB/University of Porto
Miguel Pimenta Monteiro	INEB/University of Porto
Gabriela Afonso	INEB/University of Porto
Pedro Quelhas	INEB/University of Porto
Ana Maria Tomé	IEETA/University of Aveiro
Gonçalo Monteiro	ISR/University of Coimbra

Program Committee

Ana Fred	Technical University of Lisbon, Portugal
Ana Maria Tomé	University of Aveiro, Portugal
Andrew Gee	University of Cambridge, UK
Aurélio Campilho	University of Porto, Portugal
Colin de la Higuera	Jean Monnet University, France
Edwin R. Hancock	University of York, UK
Fabio Roli	University of Cagliari, Italy
Fadi Dornaika	Institut Geographique National, France
Filiberto Pla	University Jaume I, Spain

Gabriella Sanniti di Baja	Istituto di Cibernetica CNR, Italy
Hans Burkhard	University of Freiburg, Germany
Hans du Buf	University of Algarve, Portugal
Hermman Ney	RWTH-Aachen, Germany
Hervé Bourlard	EPFL, Switzerland
Horts Bunke	University of Bern, Switzerland
Ioannis Pitas	University of Thessaloniki, Greece
Joachim Weickert	Saarland University, Germany
Jordi Vitrià	University of Barcelona, Spain
Jorge Batista	University of Coimbra, Portugal
Jorge Marques	Technical University of Lisbon, Portugal
Jorge Padilha	University of Porto, Portugal
Laurent Heute	Université de Rouen, France
Luís Alexandre	University of Beira Interior, Portugal
Luis Baumela	Polytechnic University of Madrid, Spain
Luís Corte-Real	University of Porto, Portugal
Majid Mirmehdi	University of Bristol, UK
Marcello Federico	FBK-irst Trento, Italy
María Luisa Micó	University of Alicante, Spain
Maria Petrou	Imperial College, UK
María Vannrell	Autonomous University of Barcelona, Spain
Massimo Tistarelli	University of Sassari, Italy
Nicolás Pérez de la Blanca	University of Granada, Spain
Pedro Pina	Technical University of Lisbon, Portugal
Peter Sturm	INRIA Rhone-Alpes, France
Philipp Koehn	University of Edinburgh, UK
Pierre Soille	Joint Research Centre, Italy
Renato de Mori	Université d'Avignon, France
Reyerz Zwiggelaar	University of Wales, UK
Roberto Paredes	Polytechnic University of Valencia, Spain
Wiro Niessen	University of Utrech, The Netherlands

Additional Reviewers

Jorge Barbosa	University of Porto, Portugal
Laurent Boyer	University of Saint-Etienne, France
Jorge Calera Rubio	Universidad de Alicante, Spain
Alicia Fornes	Universitat Autònoma de Barcelona, Spain
Maria Frucci	Istituto di Cibernetica CNR, Italy
Marcos Gestal	Facultad de Informatica, UDC, Spain
Diego Giuliani	Fondazione Bruno Kessler - FBK, Italy
Jose Manuel Iñesta	Universidad de Alicante, Spain
Jacopo Grazzini	Joint Research Centre, Italy
Paulo Miguel Jesus Dias	University of Aveiro, Portugal
Ciro Martins	University of Aveiro, Portugal
Jose Oncina	Universidad de Alicante, Spain

Pedro Quelhas   University of Porto, Portugal
Giuliana Ramella   Istituto di Cibernetica CNR, Italy
Rui Rocha   Polytechnic Institute of Porto, Portugal
Jorge Silva   University of Porto, Portugal
Vitor Silva   DEE - FCTUC / IT, Portugal
Eduard Vazquez   Universitat Autònoma de Barcelona, Spain

Sponsoring Institutions

IAPR (International Association for Pattern Recognition)
FCT (Fundação para a Ciência e a Tecnologia)

Table of Contents

Image Analysis and Processing

Pattern Recognition

Inference and Learning for Active Sensing, Experimental Design and Control

Hendrik Kueck, Matt Hoffman, Arnaud Doucet, and Nando de Freitas

Department of Computer Science, UBC, Canada
{kueck,hoffmanm,arnaud,nando}@cs.ubc.ca

Abstract. In this paper we argue that maximum expected utility is a suitable framework for modeling a broad range of decision problems arising in pattern recognition and related fields. Examples include, among others, gaze planning and other active vision problems, active learning, sensor and actuator placement and coordination, intelligent human-computer interfaces, and optimal control. Following this remark, we present a common inference and learning framework for attacking these problems. We demonstrate this approach on three examples: (i) active sensing with nonlinear, non-Gaussian, continuous models, (ii) optimal experimental design to discriminate among competing scientific models, and (iii) nonlinear optimal control.

1 The Principle of Maximum Expected Utility

Broadly speaking, *utility* reflects the preferences of an agent. That is, if outcome o_1 is preferred to o_2 (*i.e.* $o_1 \succ o_2$), we say that o_1 has higher utility than o_2. More formally, let $o_1 \succeq o_2$ denote weak preference, $o_1 \succ o_2$ denote strong preference and $o_1 \sim o_2$ denote indifference. Define a *lottery* to be a random set of outcomes with corresponding probabilities: $l = [(o_1, p_1), (o_2, p_2), \ldots, (o_k, p_k)]$, where the probabilities satisfy $p_i \geq 0$ and $\sum_i^k p_i = 1$ as usual. Now consider the following axioms:

1. **Completeness:** $\forall o_1, o_2$, we have $o_1 \succ o_2$, $o_2 \succ o_1$ or $o_1 \sim o_2$.
2. **Transitivity:** If $o_1 \succeq o_2$ and $o_2 \succeq o_3$, then $o_1 \succeq o_3$.
3. **Substitutability:** If $o_1 \sim o_2$, then for all sequences of outcomes $o_3, \ldots, o_k$ and sets of probabilities $p, p_3, \ldots, p_k$ for which $p + \sum_{i=3}^k p_i = 1$, we have $[(o_1, p), (o_3, p_3), \ldots, (o_k, p_k)] \sim [(o_2, p), (o_3, p), \ldots, (o_k, p_k)]$.
4. **Decomposability:** Let $P_l(o_i)$ be the probability that outcome o_i is selected by lottery l. If for all o_i: $P_{l_1}(o_i) = P_{l_2}(o_i)$, then $l_1 \sim l_2$.
5. **Monotonicity:** If $o_1 \succ o_2$ and $p > q$, then $[(o_1, p), (o_2, 1-p)] \succ [(o_1, q), (o_2, 1-q)]$.
6. **Continuity:** If $o_1 \succ o_2$ and $o_2 \succ o_3$ then $\exists p \in [0, 1]$ such that $o_2 \sim [(o_1, p), (o_3, 1-p)]$.

Using these axioms, von Neumann and Morgenstern [16] proved the following fundamental result showing the existence of utility:

H. Araujo et al. (Eds.): IbPRIA 2009, LNCS 5524, pp. 1–10, 2009.

Theorem 1. *If a preference relation $\succeq$ satisfies axioms 1 to 6 above, then there exists a function u mapping outcomes to the real line with the properties that:*

1. $u(o_1) \geq u(o_2)$ *iff* $o_1 \succeq o_2$
2. $u([(o_1, p_1), (o_2, p_2), \ldots, (o_k, p_k)]) = \sum_{i=1}^{k} u(o_i) p_i$.

Expected utility does therefore arise as a rational consequence of fairly unassailable axioms. An agent expecting to behave optimally must maximize its expected utility; see [14] for a more comprehensive treatment.

Following this result, it is reasonable that our goal in decision making under uncertainty be one of finding an optimal strategy π^* that maximizes the *expected utility* $U(\pi)$ of the agent:

$$\pi^* = \arg\max_{\pi} U(\pi), \text{ with } U(\pi) = \int u(x, \pi) p(x|\pi) \, dx \tag{1}$$

Note, we are integrating over all possible unknown states x (that is we are considering all *possible worlds* and weighting them according to how likely we deem them). $U(\pi)$ then describes how useful we expect the outcomes of adopting a policy to be based on the current beliefs encoded in $p(x|\pi)$. In the MEU view, we are assuming that we can solve the joint maximization and integration problem. In general we can't do this and are forced to make approximations. Theories that take into account these approximations have appeared under the umbrella of *bounded rationality*. The application domain of the MEU principle is very broad. The principle can be used to guide the placement and control of a network of sensors in a changing environment, to decide what data must be gathered to improve a classifier, to plan a sequence of gazes to dynamically understand a visual scene, to plan the trajectory of a robot so as to minimize resources, and so on. In this paper, we will present an inference and learning approach for solving MEU problems. This single approach will suffice to solve difficult nonlinear, non-Gaussian problems arising in myopic and sequential (multi-stage) decision making. We discuss these two problems in the following subsections.

1.1   Myopic Decision Making

We will illustrate myopic decision making in the context of Bayesian experimental design. We don't lose much generality doing this because Bayesian experimental design is a broad field of study that is applicable to many problems, including active vision, sensor network management and active learning. We assume that we have a measurement model $p(y|\theta, \pi)$ of experimental outcomes $y \in \mathcal{Y}$ given a design π as well as a prior $p(\theta)$ on the model parameters $\theta \in \Theta$. The prior could be based on expert knowledge or previous experiments. We recover the general model presented in the previous section by noting that $x = \{y, \theta\}$.

The model parameters as well as future observations are unknown so we have to integrate out over their probability distributions. (In the simple case of learning a regression function or a classifier, which is widely studied in active learning,

π would correspond to the predictors (inputs) and y to the corresponding covariates (outputs).) The general goal is then to choose the optimal design $\pi^* \in \mathbb{R}^p$, which maximizes the expected utility

$$U(\pi) = \iint u(y, \pi, \theta) \, p(\theta) p(y|\theta, \pi) \, dy \, d\theta \tag{2}$$

with respect to some measure of utility $u(y, \pi, \theta)$. When the model parameters are the objects of interest, which will be the case in Section 3.1, the negative posterior entropy is commonly chosen as the utility function. That is, one aims to maximize

$$u(y, \pi, \theta) = \int p(\theta'|y, \pi) \log p(\theta'|y, \pi) d\theta'.$$

This measures how concentrated the belief distribution over the parameters is after conducting an experiment with design π and observing outcome y. Note the difference between θ and θ' here. θ represents the true model parameters of the possible world under consideration in which the hypothetical experiment is conducted. The outcome y is generated according to $p(y|\theta, \pi)$. $p(\theta'|y, \pi)$ then is the belief distribution over the model parameters that we would have after observing y. Note that this particular utility function does not actually depend on θ. It merely measures how peaked the posterior belief $p(\theta'|y, \pi)$ is, not how close it is to the 'real' θ. In the case of a linear-Gaussian model, this entropy based utility function is referred to as Bayesian D-optimality [1].

In general, the choice of utility function should reflect the objective of the experiment as well as costs and risks related to the experiment as well as possible. For example in a medical trial the goal might be to gain the maximum amount of information about the effects of a new drug while at the same time keeping the risk of people dying (or suffering severe side effects) to a minimum and also minimizing the monetary cost of the trial. The utility function would then consist of several terms representing these (possibly conflicting) objectives. Another interesting choice of utility is given in Section 3.2 of this paper.

1.2   Sequential Decision Making

In the previous section, we only considered integrating over the outcome at the next step of decision making. In general, we would like to plan several steps ahead. This type of planning can be modeled with a Markov decision process (MDP); illustrated in Figure 1. Here we are integrating over an infinite sequence $z_{0:\infty} = \{z_0, z_1, \dots\}$, where each $z_n = (s_n, a_n, r_n)$ represents a tuple of state, action, and reward at time n.

The design parameter π in this setting determines a policy for choosing an action a_n based on the current state s_n according to $p(a_n|s_n, \pi)$. Given a policy, the states and rewards of the Markov process evolve according to an initial-state model: $s_0 \sim \mu(s_0)$, a transition model: $s_{n+1} \sim p(s_{n+1}|s_n, a_n)$, and rewards: $r_n \sim p(r_n|s_n, a_n)$. We can then define the utility function for a single trajectory as its discounted reward, $u(z_{0:\infty}) = \sum_{n=0}^{\infty} \gamma^n r_n$. Intuitively the discount factor

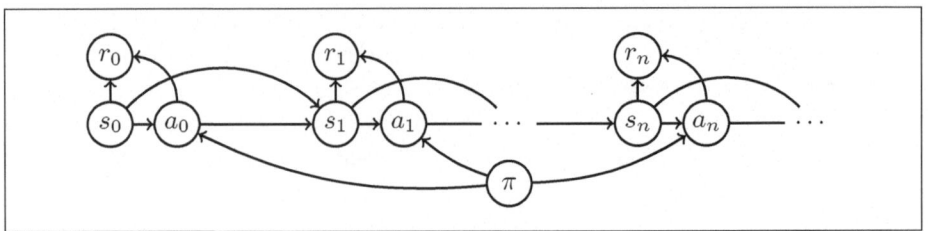

Fig. 1. A graphical model depicting the random variables for an MDP

$\gamma \in [0,1]$ emphasizes immediate rewards over more distant future rewards. Our goal is then to find the policy π^* which maximizes this expected utility:

$$U(\pi) = \int \left[\sum_{n=0}^{\infty} \gamma^n\, r_n \right] p(z_{0:\infty}|\pi)\, dz_{0:\infty}.$$

This integration problem is made difficult, however, by the fact that $z_{0:\infty}$ is an infinite dimensional object.

Following [15], it is possible to move the expectation *inside the summation* and rewrite the expected utility as

$$U(\pi) = (1-\gamma)^{-1} \sum_{n=0}^{\infty} \int r_n\, p(n, z_{0:n}|\pi)\, dz_{0:n}$$

where this expectation is taken with respect to the trans-dimensional distribution

$$p(n, z_{0:n}|\pi) = (1-\gamma)\, \gamma^n\, p(z_0|\pi) \prod_{j=1}^{n} p(z_j|z_{j-1}, \pi). \tag{3}$$

With this formulation we are still integrating[1] over an infinite-dimensional quantity, but now we have broken this into a joint integral where one of our random variables is the dimensionality n. Note, however, that the general form of Equation (1) can be recovered by letting $x = (n, z_{0:n})$ and defining our utility as the final reward in each finite-length trajectory $u(n, z_{0:n}) = r_n$.

It is also possible to further generalize this model to take into account situations where the states s_n are not visible, and instead some observations $y_n \sim p(y_n|s_n)$ are given. This model, known as a partially observable MDP (POMDP), is a much more difficult problem and is not one currently tackled by this framework.

2   A Common Solution Framework

The joint optimization and nested integration problem in equation (1) is computationally challenging. For this reason, much of the research in experimental

---

[1] We note that the sum over n is really an integral over the natural numbers.

design and control has focused on the simple linear-Gaussian models, for which closed form solutions exist [2,3]. Recently, however, there has been a flurry of work applying inference and learning techniques to more difficult nonlinear problems. In the context of control this seems to have originated with [4], although only immediate rewards are considered, thus making it perhaps more applicable to the setting of myopic experimental design. In this section we will focus on a promising sample-based technique originating in the experimental design literature [10].

One possible strategy for solving these problems involves sampling policies π and hidden states x from the artificial target distribution

$$h(\pi, x) \propto u(x, \pi) \, p(x|\pi). \tag{4}$$

We can see by marginalizing over x that this produces a distribution

$$h(\pi) \propto \int u(x, \pi) \, p(x|\pi) \, dx = U(\pi)$$

proportional to the expected utility. In order to sample from this distribution we must assume that $u(x, \pi)$ is positive and finite but this is easy to ensure so long as the utility is bounded. We may also be required to introduce a prior $p(\pi)$ to ensure that this distribution is well defined, but typically a uniform distribution over some bounded region is sufficient.

If $U(\pi)$ happens to have a strongly dominant and highly peaked mode around the global maximum π^*, we can justify sampling from (4) and deriving a point estimate by averaging these samples. In the context of sequential decision making this is the approach taken in [6]. However, in general the assumption of such a favorable $U(\pi)$ is unrealistic, and applying this strategy to a multimodal or fairly flat utility landscape will yield poor estimates.

Other strategies involve discretizing the policy space $\mathbb{R}^p$ and approximating the integrals with direct Monte Carlo methods. However, these approaches are expensive and inadequate for high dimensional spaces. To eliminate the need for discretization, Müller et al. [10] proposed a Markov chain Monte Carlo annealing technique for simultaneous maximization and integration. They define the following artificial target distribution

$$h_J(\pi, x_{1:J}) \propto \prod_{j=1}^{J} u(\pi, x_j) p(x_j|\pi)$$

Marginalizing this distribution over the unknown outcomes and parameters gives

$$h_J(\pi) = \iint h_J(\pi, x_{1:J}) \, dx_{1:J} = \iint \prod_{j=1}^{J} u(\pi, x_j) p(x_j|\pi) \, dx_{1:J}$$

$$= U(\pi) \iint \prod_{j=2}^{J} u(\pi, x_j) p(x_j|\pi) \, dx_{2:J} = \prod_{j=1}^{J} U(\pi) = U^J(\pi).$$

For large exponents J, the probability mass of this distribution will concentrate on the global maximum for π^*. However, because the modes of this distribution will typically be narrow and widely separated for large J, sampling from this distribution using Markov chain Monte Carlo techniques directly is difficult. We must therefore take a simulated annealing approach in which we start sampling from $U^J(\pi)$ for $J = 1$ and slowly increase this exponent over time according to some annealing schedule. Increasing J slowly enough allows the chain to efficiently explore the whole parameter space before becoming more constrained to the major modes.

In order to apply this technique to problems of sequential decision making we must use reversible jump MCMC [5] to sample from trans-dimensional distributions such as (3); see [6,7] for more details on applying these ideas to control problems. In the myopic experimental design setting we advise the use of sequential Monte Carlo samplers [8] (see also Figure 2).

3   Demonstrations

3.1   Active Sensing Example

As a first example we study a synthetic problem that, despite its apparent simplicity, exhibits complex multi-modality. In particular, we address the problem of inferring the parameters of a sine wave. This non-linear experimental design example is motivated by the problem of scheduling expensive astronomical observations [9]. The sine wave is parameterized by $\theta = \{A, \omega, \rho\}$ where A is the amplitude, ω the frequency and ρ the phase

$$y = f(\pi; A, \omega, \rho) + \epsilon = A \sin(\pi \omega + \rho) + \epsilon.$$

Here ϵ denotes the normally distributed measurement noise. The objective is to find the optimal location π^* along the x-axis at which to make the next noisy y measurement in order to maximally reduce uncertainty about the parameters θ. In the example shown in Figure 2, two prior observations have already been made and the design problem consists of choosing the optimal third measurement. That is, the prior belief $p(\theta)$ here is actually the posterior parameter distribution after these first two measurements. Figure 2(a) shows some sine waves corresponding to samples from this $p(\theta)$, visualizing the belief about possible sine waves.

The corresponding expected utility function $U(\pi)$ shown in Figure 2(b) is proportional to the uncertainty about y at a given point π along the x-axis. This function is highly multi-modal, with most of the modes having similar magnitudes. However exponentiating this function to a power of 50 concentrates most of the probability mass on the major mode, so that samples distributed proportional to this function provide a good basis for estimating π^*. When using a single MCMC chain using the approach of [10], the chain often gets trapped in the minor modes, as can be seen in Figure 2(c). The interaction between multiple particles in the SMC samplers algorithm we proposed in [8] helps avoid this and yields a much better estimate as shown in Figure 2(d).

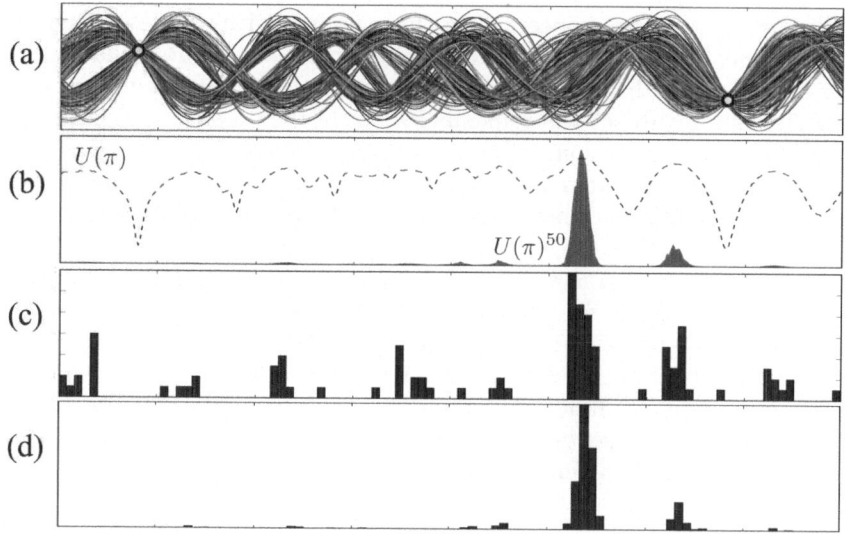

Fig. 2. Plot (a) shows sine waves visualizing the belief after 2 initial observations. The corresponding expected utility $U(\pi)$ for the maximum entropy criterion from Equation 1.1 is shown as a dashed blue line in (b) while $U(\pi)^{50}$ is displayed in solid red. Plot (c) presents a histogram of the final samples of 100 independent MCMC chains using the approach of [10] when annealing to $U(\pi)^{50}$, while (d) shows the result achieved using 100 interacting particles using our SMC samplers algorithm proposed in [8].

3.2 Experimental Design to Choose among Scientific Models

Often in science and economics, several mathematical models are proposed for describing a common phenomenon. It is therefore important to have a sound mechanism for gathering evidence so as to validate the various model options and assess their merits. For example, in mathematical psychology — a branch of psychology concerned with the mathematical modeling of various aspects of human cognitive performance — researchers have proposed the use of automatic experimental design techniques to find the most plausible model from a set of model alternatives [11]. In this domain, the goal is to choose an optimal experiment for maximally discriminating among several given models. Since such experiments tend to be very costly and work intensive, it is crucial to carefully design them to gain the most information from them and make the most efficient use of the resources involved.

There exists a large body of research in psychology on how we remember and/or forget things. Typically this research involves experiments in which subjects initially memorize some material (such as word lists) and are subsequently tested for recall after several different time intervals. A survey of many such studies is presented in [13]. The percentage of recalled items monotonically decreases over time according to a function of roughly logarithmic shape. The question that researchers in mathematical psychology are interested in is exactly which mathematical function best describes human retention performance.

Following [11], we are concerned in this example with differentiating among two previously proposed models. More specifically, we assume that a trial in which a single item has to be recalled after time t is repeated n times. The probability that a subject will remember k out of the possible n objects is given by the Binomial distribution: $p(k|n, \rho) = \binom{n}{k}\rho^k(1 - \rho)^{n-k}$.

The two models considered for predicting the probability of retention ρ after elapsed time t have 2 parameters $\phi = \{a, b\}$. The first is an exponential model, $\rho_{M_e}(t, \phi) = a\,e^{-bt}$, while the second one is a power model $\rho_{M_p}(t, \phi) = a\,(t+1)^{-b}$.

In our example, the goal will be to compute the optimal 2 point design $\pi \equiv t_{1:2} = \{t_1, t_2\}$. That is, we need to choose the two time lags after which the subject's retention will be tested. We are seeking the design that will allow us to best distinguish between the two models. We adopt a Bayesian model comparison criterion for our utility function. The utility of an experiment with design $t_{1:2}$ and experiment outcomes $k_{1:2}$ is given by the posterior marginal probability of the true model M which generated the data

$$u(t_{1:2}, k_{1:2}, M) = p(M|t_{1:2}, k_{1:2}) \propto \int \prod_{j=1}^{2} p(k_j|n, \rho_M(t_j, \phi))\, p(\phi|M)\, d\phi$$

where $p(\phi|M)$ is the prior on the parameters for the model under consideration; In our experiments we used an empirical prior based on data from a previously conducted study [12]. Intuitively, an experiment is of high utility if we strongly favor the true model after observing the experiment outcome.

To compute the expected utility according to Equation (2) we need to integrate over the unknown model parameters θ, wich in this case consist of $\{M, \phi\}$ as well as over the possible experiment outcomes $y \equiv k_{1:2}$. The expected utility of an experiment design $t_{1:2}$ is then

$$U(t_{1:2}) = \frac{1}{2} \sum_{M \in \{M_e, M_p\}} \int u\,(t_{1:2}, k_{1:2}, M)\, p\,(k_{1:2}|n, \rho_M(t_{1:2}, \phi))\, p\,(\phi|M)\, dk_{1:2}\, d\phi$$

As in Section 3.1 we are using an SMC samplers approach, employing a system of interacting particles to efficiently sample from $U(t_{1:2}|n)^{100}$. The resulting samples as well as the derived optimal design are shown in Figure 3.

3.3 Control Example: Particles with Force-Fields

Consider a physical system consisting of particles moving in a 2-dimensional space. The particles are released from some stochastic start region, fall downwards under the force of gravity, and are slowed by a frictional force resisting movement. At each discrete time step the particles receive some reward based on their current position and the position and velocity are then updated using a simple forward simulation. The goal is to direct the particles, using additional forces, through high reward regions of the state space in order to maximize their expected utility.

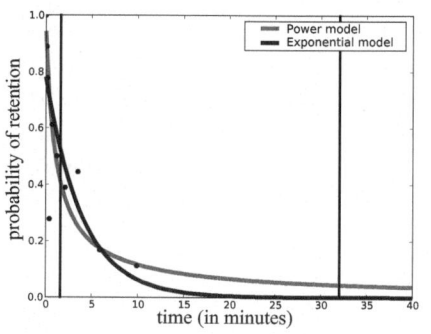
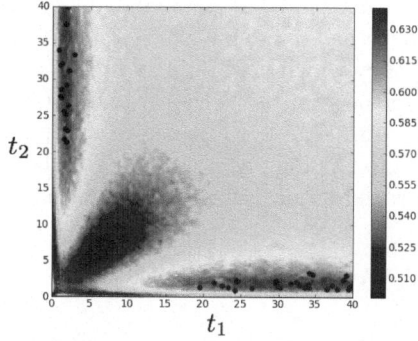

(a) example model fits and optimal design   (b) $U(t_{1:2})$ and final particle locations

Fig. 3. Figure (a) shows the computed optimal design for discriminating between the power and exponential model for explaining human memory performance; the two black bars are the optimal time points for testing a subject's retention. For illustration we show fits of the two models (red and blue curve) to an example subject's data from a previous study [12] (black dots). Figure (b) visualizes both $U(t_{1:2}|n)$ (background colors) as well as the final samples from $U(t_{1:2}|n)^{100}$ (black points) that the optimal design in (a) was derived from.

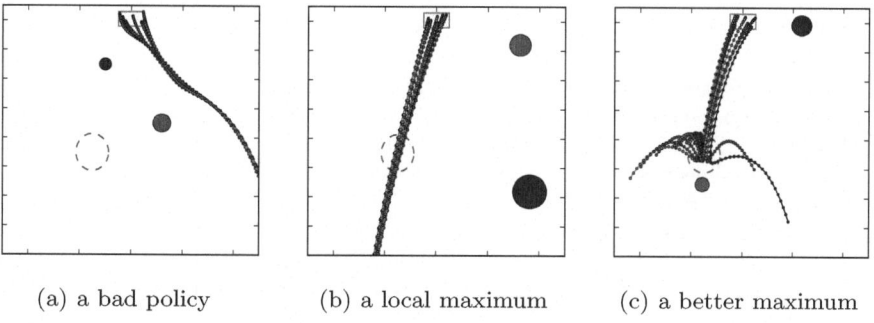

(a) a bad policy   (b) a local maximum   (c) a better maximum

Fig. 4. Example trajectories from the repellers model. The two colored circles denote the repellers' location and strength, the dotted circle denotes the reward region, and the yellow rectangle is the initial state region. Shown are (a) a low utility policy, (b) a low utility local maximum, and (c) a higher utility maximum.

The four-dimensional state-space in this problem consists of a particle's position and velocity $s_n = (p, \dot{p})$ for $p \in \mathbb{R}^2$, and actions a_n consist of external forces acting on the particles. In particular, we will use a policy defined by a set of "repellers" which push each particle directly away from themselves with a force inversely proportional to their distance from the particle. More precisely, the force acting on a particle at position p is given by $a_n = f_\pi(p) = \sum_i w_i \frac{p - c_i}{\|p - c_i\|^3}$, where this policy is parameterized by $\pi = \{(c_1, w_1), \dots\}$ for repeller centers c_i and strengths w_i. Example trajectories for different policies are shown in Figure 4. In these examples rewards r_n are defined using a simple Gaussian defined over the particles' position p.

This model is particularly interesting because it is highly multimodal with large flat regions in the expected utility surface. In Figure 4(b) we can see one policy which very quickly moves particles into the reward region. A better policy can be seen in 4(c), in which one repeller is used to direct particles towards the reward region while another repeller slows particles so that they stay in this region as long as possible. This better policy is the one ultimately found by the procedure described in this paper.

References

1. Bernardo, J.: Expected information as expected utility. The Annals of Statistics 7(3), 686–690 (1979)
2. Bertsekas, D.P.: Dynamic Programming and Optimal Control. Athena Scientific (1995)
3. Chaloner, K., Verdinelli, I.: Bayesian experimental design: A review. Statistical Science 10(3), 273–304 (1995)
4. Dayan, P., Hinton, G.E.: Using EM for reinforcement learning. Neural Computation 9, 271–278 (1997)
5. Green, P.: Reversible jump Markov Chain Monte Carlo computation and Bayesian model determination. Biometrika 82(4), 711–732 (1995)
6. Hoffman, M., Doucet, A., de Freitas, N., Jasra, A.: Bayesian policy learning with trans-dimensional MCMC. In: NIPS (2007)
7. Hoffman, M., Doucet, A., de Freitas, N., Jasra, A.: On solving general state-space sequential decision problems using inference algorithms. Technical Report TR-2007-04, University of British Columbia, Computer Science (2007)
8. Kueck, H., de Freitas, N., Doucet, A.: SMC samplers for Bayesian optimal nonlinear design. Nonlinear Statistical Signal Processing (2006)
9. Loredo, T.J.: Bayesian adaptive exploration. Bayesian Inference And Maximum Entropy Methods In Science And Engineering, 330–346 (2003)
10. Müller, P., Sansó, B., de Iorio, M.: Optimal Bayesian design by inhomogeneous Markov chain simulation. Journal of the American Statistical Association 99, 788–798 (2004)
11. Myung, J.I., Pitt, M.A.: Optimal experimental design for model discrimination (under review)
12. Rubin, D., Hinton, S., Wenzel, A.: The precise time course of retention. Journal of experimental psychology. Learning, memory, and cognition 25(5), 1161–1176 (1999)
13. Rubin, D.C., Wenzel, A.E.: One hundred years of forgetting: A quantitative description of retention. Psychological review 103, 734–760 (1996)
14. Shoham, Y., Leyton-Brown, K.: Multiagent Systems: Algorithmic, Game-Theoretic, and Logical Foundations. Cambridge University Press, Cambridge (2009)
15. Toussaint, M., Storkey, A.: Probabilistic inference for solving discrete and continuous state Markov Decision Processes. In: ICML (2006)
16. von Neumann, J., Morgenstern, O.: Theory of Games and Economic Behaviour. Princeton University Press, Princeton (1947)

Large Scale Online Learning of Image Similarity through Ranking

Gal Chechik[1], Varun Sharma[1], Uri Shalit[2], and Samy Bengio[1]

[1] Google
Mountain View, CA, USA
{gal,vasharma,bengio}@google.com
[2] Hebrew University
Jerusalem, Israel
uri.shalit@mail.huji.ac.il

Abstract. Learning a measure of similarity between pairs of objects is a fundamental problem in machine learning. Pairwise similarity plays a crucial role in classification algorithms like nearest neighbors, and is practically important for applications like searching for images that are similar to a given image or finding videos that are relevant to a given video. In these tasks, users look for objects that are both visually similar and semantically related to a given object.

Unfortunately, current approaches for learning semantic similarity are limited to small scale datasets, because their complexity grows quadratically with the sample size, and because they impose costly positivity constraints on the learned similarity functions. To address real-world large-scale AI problem, like learning similarity over all images on the web, we need to develop new algorithms that scale to many samples, many classes, and many features.

The current abstract presents OASIS, an *Online Algorithm for Scalable Image Similarity* learning that learns a bilinear similarity measure over sparse representations. OASIS is an online dual approach using the passive-aggressive family of learning algorithms with a large margin criterion and an efficient hinge loss cost. Our experiments show that OASIS is both fast and accurate at a wide range of scales: for a dataset with thousands of images, it achieves better results than existing state-of-the-art methods, while being an order of magnitude faster. Comparing OASIS with different symmetric variants, provides unexpected insights into the effect of symmetry on the quality of the similarity. For large, web scale, datasets, OASIS can be trained on more than two million images from 150K text queries within two days on a single CPU. Human evaluations showed that 35% of the ten top images ranked by OASIS were semantically relevant to a query image. This suggests that query-independent similarity could be accurately learned even for large-scale datasets that could not be handled before.

1 The Similarity Learning Model and Algorithm

We focus on a similarity learning problem that only assumes a supervised signal about the *relative similarity* of image pairs. Given a set of images, each

H. Araujo et al. (Eds.): IbPRIA 2009, LNCS 5524, pp. 11–14, 2009.

represented as a vector of features $p_i \in \mathbb{R}^d$, we assume that for every image p_i, we have access to images that are similar to p_i and images that are less similar. Formally, for a small fraction of image pairs we have a relevance measure available $r_{ij} = r(p_i, p_j) \in \mathbb{R}$, which states how strongly p_j is related to p_i. This relevance measure could encode the fact that two images share the same label or match the same query. We do not assume that values of r are precise but only that they correctly capture ordering among pairs. Our goal is to learn a similarity measure $S_{\mathbf{W}}$ with the form:

$$S_{\mathbf{W}}(p_i, p_j) \equiv p_i^T \mathbf{W} p_j \tag{1}$$

with parameters $\mathbf{W} \in \mathbb{R}^{d \times d}$. Importantly, if image vectors p_i are sparse, then $S_{\mathbf{W}}$ can be computed very efficiently even when d is large. We propose an online algorithm based on the Passive-Aggressive (PA) family of learning algorithms introduced by [1]. Here we consider an algorithm that uses triplets of images p_i, p_i^+, p_i^- that obey $r(p_i, p_i^+) > r(p_i, p_i^-)$. We define the hinge loss function for all triplets:

$$L_{\mathbf{W}} = \sum_{(p_i, p_i^+, p_i^-)} l_{\mathbf{W}}(p_i, p_i^+, p_i^-) \quad \text{with} \quad l_{\mathbf{W}}(p_i, p_i^+, p_i^-) = \\ = \max\left\{0, 1 - S_{\mathbf{W}}(p_i, p_i^+) + S_{\mathbf{W}}(p_i, p_i^-)\right\}. \tag{2}$$

To minimize $L_{\mathbf{W}}$, we apply the Passive-Aggressive algorithm iteratively to optimize $\mathbf{W}$. First, $\mathbf{W}$ is initialized to some value $\mathbf{W}^0$. Then, at each training iteration i, we randomly select a triplet (p_i, p_i^+, p_i^-), and solve the following convex problem with soft margin:

$$\mathbf{W}^i = \underset{\mathbf{W}}{\mathrm{argmin}} \frac{1}{2}\|\mathbf{W} - \mathbf{W}^{i-1}\|_{Fro}^2 + C\xi \quad \text{s.t.} \quad l_{\mathbf{W}}(p_i, p_i^+, p_i^-) \leq \xi \quad \text{and} \quad \xi \geq 0 \tag{3}$$

where $\|\cdot\|_{Fro}$ is the Frobenius norm. At each iteration i, $\mathbf{W}^i$ optimizes a trade-off between remaining close to the previous parameters $\mathbf{W}^{i-1}$ and minimizing the loss on the current triplet $l_{\mathbf{W}}(p_i, p_i^+, p_i^-)$. The *aggressiveness* parameter C controls this trade-off. Eq. 3 can be solved analytically and yields a very efficient parameter update rule. Unlike previous approaches for similarity learning, OASIS does not enforce positivity or even symmetry during learning, since projecting the learned matrix onto the set of symmetric or positive matrices *after training* yielded better generalization (not shown). The intuition is that positivity constraints help to regularize small datasets but harm learning with large data.

2   Experiments

We have first compared OASIS with small-scale methods over the standard *Caltech256* benchmark. Fig. 1 compares the performance of OASIS to other recently proposed similarity learning approaches over 20 of the 256 Caltech classes. All hyper-parameters of all methods were selected using cross-validation. OASIS outperforms the other approaches, achieving higher precision at the full range of first to top-50 ranked image. Furthermore, OASIS was faster by 1-4 orders of magnitude than competing methods (Fig. 1B). For the purpose of a fair comparison with competing approaches, we tested both a Matlab implementation and a C implementation of OASIS for this task. Finally, Fig. 1C compares the runtime of OASIS with a clever fast implementation of LMNN [2], that maintains smaller active set of constraints, but still scales quadratically. OASIS scales linearly on a web-scale dataset described below.

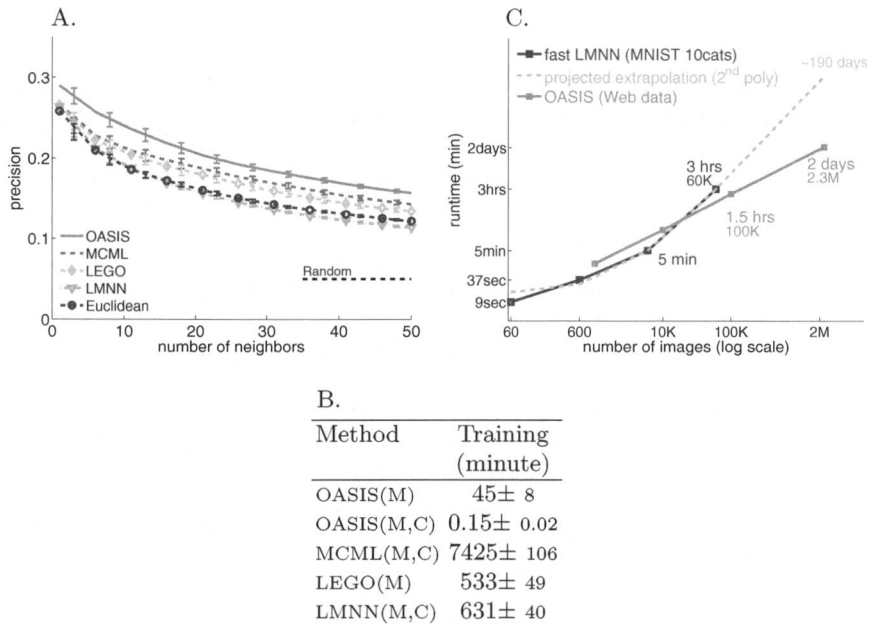

Fig. 1. A. Comparison of the precision of OASIS, LMNN [3], MCML [4], LEGO [5] and the Euclidean metric in feature space. Each curve shows the precision at top k as a function of k neighbors. Results are averages across 5 train/test partitions (40 training images, 25 test images). **B.** Run time in minutes for methods on panel A. M means Matlab, while M,C means core components implemented in C. **C.** Run time as a function of data set size for OASIS and a fast implementation of LMNN [2].

Our second set of experiments is two orders of magnitude larger than the previous experiments. We collected a set of ∼150K text queries submitted to the Google Image Search system. For each of these queries, we had access to a set of relevant images, each of which associated with a numerical relevance score. This yielded a total of ∼2.7 million images, which we split into a training set of 2.3 million images and a test set of 0.4 million images. Overall, training took ∼3000 minutes (2 days) on a single CPU. Fig. 2 shows the top five images as ranked by OASIS on two examples of query-images in the test set.

Fig. 2. Examples of successful cases from the Web dataset using OASIS

References

1. Crammer, K., Dekel, O., Keshet, J., Shalev-Shwartz, S., Singer, Y.: Online passive-aggressive algorithms. Journal of Machine Learning Research (JMLR) 7, 551–585 (2006)
2. Weinberger, K., Saul, L.: Fast Solvers and Efficient Implementations for Distance Metric Learning. In: Proc. of 25th International Conference on Machine Learning (ICML) (2008)
3. Weinberger, K., Blitzer, J., Saul, L.: Distance Metric Learning for Large Margin Nearest Neighbor Classification. Advances in Neural Information Processing Systems 18, 1473 (2006)
4. Globerson, A., Roweis, S.: Metric Learning by Collapsing Classes. Advances in Neural Information Processing Systems 18, 451 (2006)
5. Jain, P., Kulis, B., Dhillon, I., Grauman, K.: Online metric learning and fast similarity search. Advances in Neural Information Processing Systems 22 (2008)

Inpainting Ideas for Image Compression

Joachim Weickert

Faculty of Mathematics and Computer Science
Saarland University, Building E1.1
66041 Saarbruecken, Germany
weickert@mia.uni-saarland.de
http://www.mia.uni-saarland.de/weickert

Abstract. In the last decade, partial differential equations (PDEs) have demonstrated their usefulness for so-called inpainting problems, where missing image information is recovered by interpolating data from the neighbourhood. For inpainting problems, however, usually a large fraction of the image data is available.

We extend these ideas to a much more challenging task, namely PDE-based lossy image compression. To this end, only a very small amount of data are kept, and the remaining data are restored using PDE-based interpolation. This gives rise to three interdependent questions: (1) What are the most useful PDEs for this task? (2) Which are the best points for being kept? (3) How can these data be encoded in an efficient way?

In this talk, recent results from our group will be presented. For the linear diffusion operator, a method for optimal point selection is described. In the anisotropic diffusion setting, a tree-based subdivision method is used to encode relevant pixels in a compact way. Our experiments demonstrate that PDE-based image compression may give better results than JPEG and even JPEG2000, in particular if images are not dominated by texture and high compression rates are required.

H. Araujo et al. (Eds.): IbPRIA 2009, LNCS 5524, p. 15, 2009.
© Springer-Verlag Berlin Heidelberg 2009

Improving Scene Recognition through Visual Attention

Fernando López-García[1], Anton García-Díaz[2], Xose Ramon Fdez-Vidal[2],
Xose Manuel Pardo[2], Raquel Dosil[2], and David Luna[2]

[1] Universidad Politécnica de Valencia, Grupo de Visión por Computador,
Departamento de Informática de Sistemas y Computadores, Camino de Vera s/n,
46022 Valencia, Spain
flopez@disca.upv.es

[2] Universidade de Santiago de Compostela, Grupo de Visión Artificial,
Departamento de Electrónica e Computación, Campus Sur s/n,
15782 Santiago de Compostela, Spain
{anton.garcia,xose.vidal,xose.pardo,raquel.dosil,david.luna}@usc.es

Abstract. In this paper we study how the use of a novel model of
bottom-up saliency (visual attention), based on local energy and color,
can significantly accelerate scene recognition and, at the same time, pre-
serve the recognition performance. To do so, we use a mobile robot-like
application where scene recognition is performed through the use of SIFT
features to characterize the different scenarios, and the Nearest Neighbor
rule to carry out the classification. Experimental work shows that important reductions in the size of the database of prototypes can be achieved
(17.6% of the original size) without significant losses in recognition performance (from 98.5% to 96.1%), thus accelerating the classification task.

1 Introduction

Visual attention is related with the process by which the human visual system
is able to select [from a scene] regions of interest that contain salient information, reducing the amount of information to be processed and therefore the
complexity of viewing [1,2]. In the last decade, several computational models
biologically inspired have been released to implement visual attention in image
and video processing [3-5]. Visual attention has also been used to improve object
recognition and scene analysis [6,7].

In this work, we study the utility of using a recently presented model of
bottom-up saliency [3] to improve a scene recognition application by reducing
the amount of prototypes needed to carry out the classification. The application
is based on mobile robot-like video sequences taken in an indoor university area
formed by several rooms and halls. The aim is to recognize the different scenarios
in order to provide a mobile robot system with general location data.

The visual attention approach that we use [3] is a novel model for the implementation of the Koch & Ullman [2] architecture of bottom-up saliency for static
images. Two features are used to measure the saliency: local energy and color.

H. Araujo et al. (Eds.): IbPRIA 2009, LNCS 5524, pp. 16–23, 2009.

From them, we extract local maxima of variability through the decorrelation of responses and the measurement of statistical distance, followed by a non-linear local maxima excitation process; to deliver a final map of saliency. With this method we obtain saliency areas in images that point out to relevant regions from the point of view of visual attention. In addition, saliency is not measured in a binary manner (salient or not) but scaled from 0 to 255, which permits to determine different levels of relevance by simply thresholding the saliency map.

Scene recognition is performed using the SIFT features [8] and the Nearest Neighbor rule. SIFT features are distinctive image features that are invariant to image scale and rotation, and partially invariant to change in illumination and 3D viewpoint. They are fast [to compute] and robust to disruptions due to occlusion, clutter or noise. SIFT features have proved to be useful in many object recognition applications and currently they are considered the state of the art for general purpose real-world object learning and recognition.

Results of experimental work have shown that the use of saliency maps permits to drastically reduce the size of the database of prototypes, used in the 1-NN recognition process, without significant losses in performance. Thus, the computing costs of classification are reduced proportionally to the database size and the scene recognition application is accelerated. The database was reduced to 17.6% of its original size achieving a recognition performance of 96.1%, only a drop of 2.4% from the original performance. Also, we carried out several experiments using random patches to test the utility and sense of saliency maps.

The outline of the paper is the following. In Section 2, we overview the visual attention model used to obtain salient regions in static images. Section 3 is devoted to the scene recognition application. Section 4 shows the experimental work and its results. And finally, conclusions are presented in Section 5.

2 Visual Attention

In this model, following the standard model of V1, we use a decomposition of the image by means of a gabor-like bank of filters. We employ two feature dimensions: color and local energy. By decorrelating responses and extracting local maxima of variability we obtain a unique, and efficient, measure of saliency.

Local Energy and Color Maps. Local energy is extracted through the convolution of the intensity, the average of the three channels r, g and b, with a bank of log Gabor filters [9], which besides a number of advantages against Gabor filters, have complex valued responses. Hence, they provide in each scale and orientation a pair of filters in phase quadrature [10], an even filter and its Hilbert transform, an odd filter; allowing us to extract local energy as the modulus [11] of the response to this filter vector. A more detailed description of our approach to local energy extraction can be found in [3]. With regards to Color Maps, we extract first two color opponent components: r/g and b/y. From them we obtain a multi-scale center-surround representation obtained from the responses of the two double opponent components to high-pass logarithmic Gaussian filters.

By subtracting large scales from small scales (1-3, 1-4, 2-4, 2-5), we obtain a pyramid of four center-surround maps for each color component, r/g and b/y.

Measurement of Variability. Difference and richness of structural content have been proven as driving attention in psychophysical experiments [12]. Observations from neurobiology show decorrelation of neural responses, as well as an increased population sparseness in comparison to what can be expected from a standard Gabor-like representation [13][14]. Hence, we use decorrelation of the responses to further measure the statistical distance of local structure from the average structure. To decorrelate the multi-scale information of each sub-feature (orientations and color components) we perform a PCA on the corresponding sets of scales. From the decorrelated responses, we extract the statistical distance at each point as the T2 of Hotelling.

Excitation of Local Maxima. Once the structural distance within each sub-feature has been measured, we force a spatial competition exciting local maxima in a non-linear approach already described in [3]. Next, we fuse the resultant sub-feature maps simply gathering the surviving maxima, with a max() operation, in a local energy saliency map, and in a color saliency map. Finally, we repeat the process, with these two maps to extract a final measure of salience. All the process is illustrated in Figure 1.

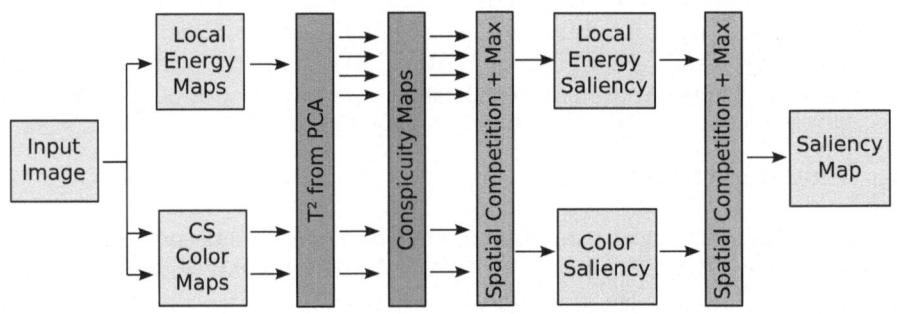

Fig. 1. Saliency computation using the bottom-up model of visual attention

3   Scene Recognition

Scene recognition or classification is related with the recognition of general scenarios rather than local objects. This approach is useful in many applications such as mobile robot navigation, image retrieval, extraction of contextual information for object recognition, and even provide access to tourist information using camera phones. In our case, we are interested in recognize a set of different areas which are part of the facilities of the Electronics and Computer Science Department of the University of Santiago de Compostela. These facilities are formed by four class rooms and three halls that connect them. The final aim is to provide general location data useful for the navigation of a mobile robot system.

Scene recognition is commonly performed using generic image features that try to collect enough information to be able to distinguish the different scenarios. In our case, we chose SIFT features [8] to achieve this aim. We used Lowe's algorithm which is applied to each image [or frame] and works as follows. To identify candidate keypoint locations, scale space extrema are found in a difference-of-Gaussian (DoG) function convolved with the image. The extremas are found by comparing each point with its neighbors in the current image and adjacent scales. Points are selected as a candidate keypoint locations if they are the maximum or minimum value in their neighborhood. Then image gradients and orientations, at each pixel of the Gaussian convolved image at each scale, are computed. For each key location an orientation, determined by the peak of a histogram of previously computed neighborhood orientations, is assigned. Once the orientation, scale, and location of the keypoints have been computed, invariance to these values is achieved by computing the keypoint local feature descriptors relative to them. Local feature descriptors are 128-dimensional vectors obtained from the precomputed image orientations and gradients around the keypoints.

To carry out the classification task we used the 1-NN rule, which is a simple classification approach but fast [to compute] and robust. For this approach, we need to previously build a database of prototypes that will collect the recognition knowledge of the classifier. These prototypes are in fact a set of labeled SIFT keypoints obtained from training frames. The class (or label) of the SIFT keypoints computed for a specific training frame will be that previously assigned to this frame in an off-line supervised labeling process. This database is then incorporated into the 1-NN classifier, which uses the Euclidean distance in the 128-D space to select the closest prototype to the test SIFT keypoint being classified. The class of the test keypoint will be assigned to the class of the closest prototype in the database, and finally, the class of the test frame will be that of the majority of its test keypoints. Although the scene recognition application is an important part of the present work, and other improvements could be introduced, we have to point out that in this work we have focus onto the advantages that visual attention can provide to accelerate the recognition process by reducing the size of the original database of prototypes.

4   Experiments and Results

Experimental work consisted in a set of experiments carried out using two video sequences taken in a robot-navigation manner. These video sequences were grabbed in an university area covering several rooms and halls. Both sequences were taken at 5 fps collecting a total number of 2,174 frames (7:15 minutes) for the first sequence and 1,816 for second one (6:03 minutes). In all the experiments, the first sequence was used for training and the second one for testing.

In the first experiment we computed the SIFT keypoints for all the frames of the first video sequence. Then, we labeled these keypoints with the corresponding frame class. The labels that we used were: room-1, room-2, room-3, room-4, hall-1, hall-2 and hall-3. The whole set of labeled keypoints formed itself the database of prototypes to be used by the 1-NN classifier to carry out classification on the second sequence. For each frame of the second sequence its corresponding SIFT keypoints were computed and classified. The final frame class was set to the majority class within its keypoints. This experiment achieved very good recognition performance, 98.5% of correct frame classification, though, an important drawback was the high computing costs of classification, despite the fact that the 1-NN is a simple classifier. It is was due to the very large size of the knowledge database of prototypes formed by 588,826 samples.

Although there are well known techniques for NN classifiers to optimize the database of prototypes (e.g. feature selection, feature extraction, condensing, editing) and also for the acceleration of the classification computation (e.g. kd-trees), at this point we are interested in the utility of using the saliency maps derived from the visual attention approach shown in Section 2. The idea is to achieve a significant reduction of the original database by selecting in each training frame only those SIFT keypoints that are included within the saliency map computed for this frame. Also, in recognition, only those SIFT keypoints lying within the saliency maps, computed for the testing frames, will be considered for classification. Once the database is reduced that way, optimizing techniques could be used to achieve even further improvements.

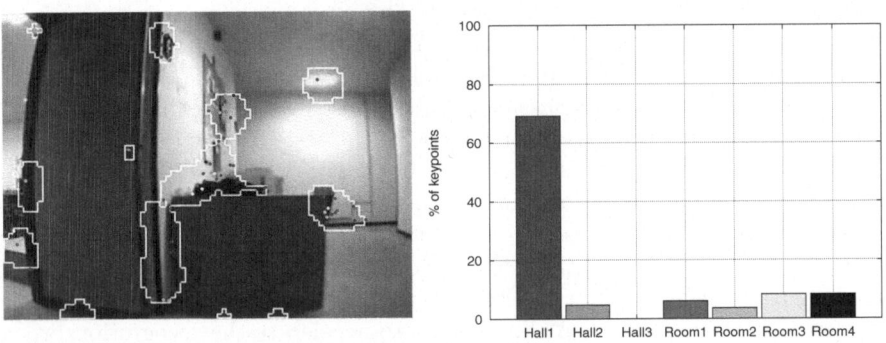

Fig. 2. A frame being processed using its saliency map at threshold 64

In the second experiment we carried out the idea exposed in previous paragraph. Nevertheless, we wanted to explore more in-depth the possibilities of saliency maps. As it was commented, saliency measures are set in a range between 0 and 255, thus, we can choose different levels of saliency by simply using thresholds. We will be the less restrictive if we choose a saliency > 0, and more restrictive if we choose higher levels (e.g. 16, 32, etc). We planed to use 7 different saliency levels or thresholds: 0, 16, 32, 64, 128, 192 and 224. For each of these levels we carried out the recognition experiment (see Figure 2). Two were the results obtained: percentage of recognition performance for each

Table 1. Results achieved in the original and saliency maps experiments

	Recognition %	Database Size	Database Size %
original	98.5	588,826	100.0
saliency > 0	98.6	441,204	74.9
saliency > 16	97.6	241,021	40.9
saliency > 32	97.2	175,352	29.8
saliency > 64	96.1	103,428	17.6
saliency > 128	89.3	39,565	6.7
saliency > 192	77.2	12,453	2.1
saliency > 224	67.8	4,895	0.83

saliency level, and size reduction of the original database. Results are shown in Table 1.

These results show that by using saliency maps we can achieve great reductions in the database size while the recognition performance is held. The best choice would be to use saliency maps at threshold 64 (saliency > 64). In this case, the recognition percentage with regards to the first experiment only drops 2.4% points, from 98.5% to 96.1%, while the database is reduced to a 17.6% of its original size. If we want to reach one order of magnitude in size reduction, we could choose a threshold slightly greater than 64 and also maintain a recognition performance over 90%.

In order to further test the utility and sense of saliency maps, we carried out another experiment. In this case we used for each frame, in training and testing sequences, patches randomly generated. The area of the image covered by the patches at each frame and threshold was the same that the corresponding saliency map at the specific threshold. That way, we wanted to point out the relevance of using a visual attention approach. Results of this experiment are shown in Figure 3. We observe that recognition in random patches is always worst than using saliency maps, although the first thresholds achieve good results. This is because low thresholds lead to sets of areas in the image that can cover a big portion of it (until 50% of image), thus, though in a random manner, enough keypoints to perform a correct classification are selected. However, from level 32, recognition performance using random patches achieves important drops with regards to saliency maps. With regards to the database sizes achieved using random patches, in all cases, they are more or less the half of those achieved using saliency maps. This underlines the qualities of saliency maps which prove good skills locating the SIFT keypoints. If we have to select a result in random patches similar to that achieved by saliency maps at threshold 64, we should choose the threshold 0 or 16. However, in the first case, though we obtain a 96.7% of recognition performance, the achieved database size is more than the double, and, in the second case, the database size is similar but recognition performance drops four points to 92.0%.

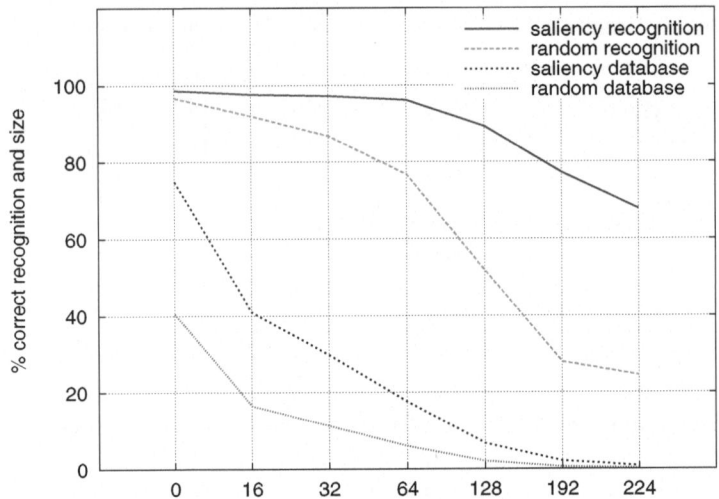

Fig. 3. Results using saliency maps and random patches

5   Conclusions

In this paper [1], we have studied the utility of using a visual attention approach to improve a scene recognition application. We have used a recently presented model of bottom-up saliency to extract the relevant areas in images, from a visual attention point of view, which have permitted to drastically reduce the amount of prototypes used to carry out classification. We used this approach in the context of an application which aim is to provide a navigation robot system with general location data. In this application, SIFT features were used as descriptors and the 1-NN rule as classifier. In a first experiment, without using saliency maps, a 98.5% of correct classification was achieved, though, computing costs of classification were very expensive due to the large size of the database of prototypes used as the recognition knowledge in the 1-NN classifier.

Experiments using saliency maps, at different thresholds of saliency, led to important reductions on the database size while recognition performance was held, thus, underlying the utility of using a visual attention approach. The best result, taking into account a balance between recognition performance and database size, was obtained using a saliency threshold of 64. In this case, a 96.1% of recognition performance was achieved while the database size was reduced to 17.6% of its original size. A reduction in the database size of one order of magnitude could be achieved, holding a recognition performance over 90%, using a saliency threshold slightly greater than 64. Finally, to further test the visual attention approach, we carried out a set of experiments using random patches instead of saliency maps. The results from these experiments reinforced the utility and sense of using the saliency maps derived from the visual attention approach.

[1] Work financially supported by the Ministry of Education and Science of the Spanish Government (research projects AVISTA TIN2006-08447 and DPI2007-66596-C02-01), and the Government of Galicia (research project PGIDIT07PXIB206028PR).

References

1. Treisman, A., Gelade, G.: A feature integration theory of attention. Cognitive Psychologhy 12, 97–136 (1980)
2. Koch, C., Ullman, S.: Shifts in selective visual attention: towards the underlying neural circuitry. Human Neurobiology 4(4), 219–227 (1985)
3. García-Díaz, A., Fdez-Vidal, X.R., Dosil, R., Pardo, X.M.: Local Energy Variability as a Generic Measure of Bottom-Up Salience. In: Yin, P.-Y. (ed.) Pattern Recognition Techniques, Technology and Applications, In-Teh, Vienna, ch. 1, pp. 1–24 (2008)
4. Itti, L., Koch, C.: A saliency-based search mechanism for overt and covert shifts of visual attention. Vision Research 40, 1489–1506 (2000)
5. Milanese, R., Gil, S., Pun, T.: Attentive mechanisms for dynamic and static scene analysis. Optical Engineering 34(8), 2428–2434 (1995)
6. Bonaiuto, J.J., Itti, L.: Combining attention and recognition for rapid scene analysis. In: Proceedings of the 2005 IEEE Computer Society Conference on Computer Vision and Pattern Recognition (CVPR 2005), vol. (III)90, p. 90 (2005)
7. Walther, D., Rutishauser, U., Koch, C., Perona, P.: Selective visual attention enables learning and recognition of multiple objects in cluttered scenes. Computer Vision and Image Understanding (100), 1–63 (2005)
8. Lowe, D.G.: Distinctive image features from scale-invariant keypoints. International Journal of Computer Vision 60(2), 91–110 (2004)
9. Field, D.J.: Relations Between the Statistics of Natural Images and the Response Properties of Cortical Cells. Journal of the Optical Society of America A 4(12), 2379–2394 (1987)
10. Kovesi, P.: Invariant Measures of Image Features from Phase Information. Ph.D. Thesis, The University or Western Australia (1996)
11. Morrone, M.C., Burr, D.C.: Feature Detection in Human Vision: A Phase-Dependent Energy Model. Proceedings of the Royal Society of London B 235, 221–245 (1988)
12. Zetzsche, C.: Natural Scene Statistics and Salient Visual Features. In: Itti, L., Rees, G., Tsotsos, J.K. (eds.) Neurobiology of Attention, ch. 37, pp. 226–232. Elsevier Academia Press, Amsterdam (2005)
13. Vinje, W.E., Gallant, J.L.: Sparse coding and decorrelation in primary visual cortex during natural vision. Science 287, 1273–1276 (2000)
14. Weliky, M., Fiser, J., Hunt, R.H., Wagner, D.N.: Coding of natural scenes in primary visual cortex. Neuron 37, 703–718 (2003)

Smoothed Disparity Maps for Continuous American Sign Language Recognition

Philippe Dreuw, Pascal Steingrube, Thomas Deselaers, and Hermann Ney

Lehrstuhl für Informatik 6– Computer Science Department,
RWTH Aachen University – D-52056 Aachen, Germany
surname@cs.rwth-aachen.de

Abstract. For the recognition of continuous sign language we analyse whether we can improve the results by explicitly incorporating depth information. Accurate hand tracking for sign language recognition is made difficult by abrupt and fast changes in hand position and configuration, overlapping hands, or a hand signing in front of the face. In our system depth information is extracted using a stereo-vision method that considers the time axis by using pre- and succeeding frames. We demonstrate that depth information helps to disambiguate overlapping hands and thus to improve the tracking of the hands. However, the improved tracking has little influence on the final recognition results.

1 Introduction

Sign language recognition and translation to spoken languages is an important task to ease the cohabitation of deaf and hard of hearing people with hearing people.

Only few studies consider the recognition of continuous sign language. Most of the current sign language recognition systems use specialised hardware [3,16] and are person dependent [13], i.e. can only recognise the one signer it was designed for. Furthermore, most approaches focus on the recognition of isolated signs or on the even simpler case of recognising isolated gestures [14], which can often be characterised just by their movement direction. Ong et al. [9] give a review on recent research in sign language and gesture recognition.

In contrast to these approaches, our aim is to build a person independent system to recognise sentences of continuous sign language. We use a vision-based approach which does not require special data acquisition devices, e.g. data gloves or motion capturing systems which restrict the natural way of signing.

In our system, the manual features are extracted from the dominant hand (i.e. the hand that is mostly used for one-handed signs such as finger spelling). However, in some sequences, the tracking confuses the hands after frames in which both hands were overlapping. An example for such a sequence is shown in Figure 1. It can be observed that in the frame before the hands are overlapping, the speaker's right hand is further away from the camera than his left hand. However, this knowledge is obvious only to human observers. Here, we analyse the usage of depth features on the one hand within our hand tracking framework, and on the other hand within our continuous sign language recognition system.

H. Araujo et al. (Eds.): IbPRIA 2009, LNCS 5524, pp. 24–31, 2009.

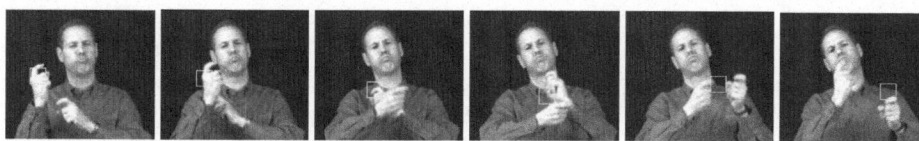

Fig. 1. Tracking error due to rotary overlapping hand movements: the tracker (yellow rectangle) switches from tracking the correct and dominant right hand to the incorrect non-dominant left hand

Apart from the possible advantages of depth information within the tracking frame-work, there are other advantages that motivate the use of depth information in sign language recognition: discourse entities like persons or objects can be stored in the sign language space, i.e. the 3D body-centred space around the signing signer, by executing them at a certain location and later just referencing them by pointing to the space. Furthermore this virtual signing space is used to express past, present, or future tenses e.g. by signing a verb in a backward direction, just in front of the signer, or in a forward direction, respectively [15]. Due to only small changes of hand configuration but large depth changes, stereo-vision and the extraction of depth information is a helpful knowledge cue for sign language recognition, e.g. for the (simpler) recognition of isolated sign language words [4,6].

Stereo vision and the extraction of depth information from images is an active area of research. Although in principle approaches exist that allow to extract depth information from monocular sequences by incorporating prior information such as human body models, in this work, we will use depth information extracted from a camera pair mounted in front of the signer. As the video corpus that we are using was not recorded using a calibrated set of stereo cameras with unknown camera parameters, we follow the idea to use two cameras, which are not calibrated and rectify the images later [10,5], which allows us to create a dense depth map by scanline-wise matching, which we do using the standard dynamic programming scanline matching algorithm [8].

2   System Overview

For purposes of linguistic analysis, signs are generally decomposed analytically into hand shape, orientation, place of articulation, and movement (with important linguistic information also conveyed through non-manual gestures, i.e., facial expressions and head movements). In a vision-based, at every time-step $t := 1, \ldots, T$, tracking-based features are extracted at unknown positions $u_1^T := u_1, \ldots, u_T$ in a sequence of images $x_1^T := x_1, \ldots, x_T$.

In an automatic sign language recognition (ASLR) system for continuous sign language, we are searching for an unknown word sequence w_1^N, for which the sequence of features $x_1^T = f(x_1^T, u_1^T)$ best fits to the trained models. Opposed to a recognition of isolated gestures, in continuous sign language recognition we want to maximise the posteriori probability $\Pr(w_1^N | x_1^T)$ over all possible word sequences w_1^N with unknown number of words N. This can be modeled by Bayes' decision rule:

$$x_1^T \longrightarrow \hat{w}_1^N = \arg\max_{w_1^N} \left\{ \Pr(w_1^N | x_1^T) \right\} = \arg\max_{w_1^N} \left\{ \Pr(w_1^N) \cdot \Pr(x_1^T | w_1^N) \right\} \quad (1)$$

where $\Pr(w_1^N)$ is the a-priori probability for the word sequence w_1^N given by the language model (LM), and $\Pr(x_1^T | w_1^N)$ is the probability of observing features x_1^T given the word sequence w_1^N, referred to as visual model (VM).

The baseline system uses hidden Markov models a trigram language model. In subsequent steps, this baseline system is extended by features accounting for the hand configuration and depth. In the following, we describe our recognition and tracking system [2] which will be extended to incorporate depth information.

2.1   Vision-Based Features

Non-Manual Features. In our baseline system we use image features only, i.e. thumbnails of video sequence frames. These intensity images scaled to 32×32 pixels serve as good basic features for many image recognition problems with homogenous background, and have already been successfully used for gesture and sign language recognition. They give a global description of all (manual and non-manual) features proposed in linguistic research.

Manual Features. To describe the appearance or shape of the dominant hand, the tracked hand patch itself can be used as a feature, too. These hand patches are extracted at these positions and scaled to a common size of e.g. 40×40 pixels, in order to keep enough information about the hand configuration. Given the hand position $u_t = (x, y)$ at time t in signing space, hand trajectory features as presented in [2] can easily be extracted.

2.2   Stereo Vision-Based Features

Since the available data is neither calibrated nor synchronised, we rectify the images using the described procedure. The synchronisation was done manually by temporal alignment of the sequences and thus might be not absolutely precise.

Figure 2a gives an overview of this process. The left most frames are the original video frames. Then, we find corresponding points in two images of each signer (second column), from these we obtain an affine transformation to align the corresponding scanlines of the images of each video sequence (third column) and finally we apply the standard dynamic programming stereo matching algorithm to determine the disparity map for each pair of frames [8] (the depth maps are segmented for visualisation purposes).

Since all signers in the database were recorded with a different camera setup, we created different transformations for the rectification of video sequences for the individual signers. To determine this transformation, we semi-automatically specify SIFT key points on the signers' bodies (c.f. Figure 2b) and determine a speaker dependent alignment transformation. Note, that this alignment has to be done only once per camera setup and if a calibrated camera setup was used it would not be necessary.

It is well known that the dynamic programming algorithm to determine depth maps leads to visible artifacts in the depth maps between succeeding scanlines. This effect is commonly reduced by using a local neighbourhood of say 7×3 pixels to determine the matching costs. Here, additionally these artifacts occur between succeeding frames and

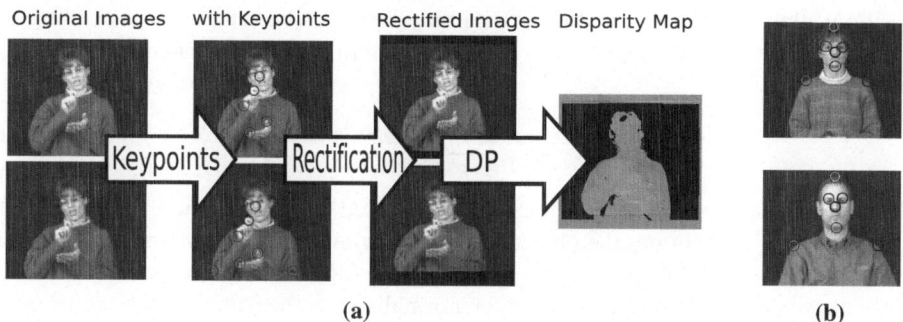

Fig. 2. (a) Obtaining depth maps from uncalibrated sequences, and (b) frames for aligning the non-aligned signer sequences

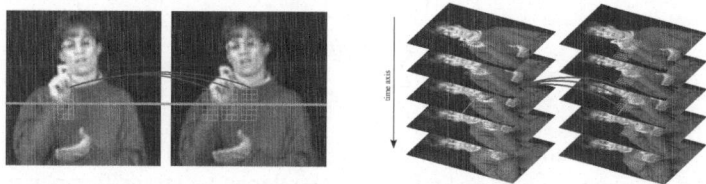

Fig. 3. Conventional calculation of matching cost and extension of the matching cost calculation over the time axis to obtain smoother disparity maps

their corresponding scanlines. Novel in our approach is the use of temporal information from pre- and succeeding frames to obtain smooth and dense disparity maps. This extension is schematically shown in Figure 3.

These disparity maps are directly used as appearance-based image features and they are additionally used as a second cue in the tracking framework to disambiguate after hands were overlapping in an image frame. Note that under occlusion obviously there is no depth information for the occluded hand but the optimization over time allows for recovering the correct path even with missing depth information over longer periods.

2.3 Extending Hand Tracking with Stereo Features

The task of tracking one object in an image sequence $x_1^T = x_1, \ldots, x_T$ can be formulated as an optimization problem. Expressed in a probabilistic framework, the path of object positions $u_1^T = u_1, \ldots, u_T$, with $u = (x, y) \in \mathcal{R}^2$, is searched that maximises the likelihood of this path given the image sequence x_1^T:

$$[u_1^T]_{opt} = \arg\max_{u_1^T} \left\{ p(u_1^T | x_1^T) \right\} = \arg\max_{u_1^T} \left\{ \prod_{t=1}^{T} p(u_t | u_1^{t-1}, x_1^t) \right\} \qquad (2)$$

The advantage of this approach is the optimization over the complete path, which avoids possibly wrong local decisions. Assuming a first-order Markov process for the path, meaning a dynamic model where an object position depends only on the previous position, allows an easier modeling of the object behavior, because only succeeding object positions have to be rated. Applying the logarithm, Equation 2 can be reformulated as:

$$[u_1^T]_{opt} = \arg\max_{u_1^T} \left\{ \sum_{t=1}^{T} \log p(u_t|u_{t-1}, x_{t-1}^t) \right\} \quad (3)$$

The probability $p(u_t|u_{t-1}, x_{t-1}^t)$ can be expressed by a relevance score function $\tilde{q}(u_{t-1}, u_t; x_{t-1}^t)$ that rates the object position u_t with a score depending on the previous position u_{t-1} and the images x_{t-1}^t. In order to fulfill the requirements of a probability density function, the score has to be normalised by the sum over the scores of all possible object positions. The logarithm can be omitted due to its monotonicity:

$$[u_1^T]_{opt} = \arg\max_{u_1^T} \left\{ \sum_{t=1}^{T} \log \frac{\tilde{q}(u_{t-1}, u_t, x_{t-1}^t)}{\sum_{u'} \tilde{q}(u_{t-1}, u'; x_{t-1}^t)} \right\} \quad (4)$$

$$= \arg\max_{u_1^T} \left\{ \sum_{t=1}^{T} \frac{\tilde{q}(u_{t-1}, u_t, x_{t-1}^t)}{\sum_{u'} \tilde{q}(u_{t-1}, u'; x_{t-1}^t)} \right\} \quad (5)$$

The relevance score function $\tilde{q}(u_{t-1}, u_t; x_{t-1}^t)$ is split into a function $q(u_{t-1}, u_t; x_{t-1}^t)$ depending on the image sequence, and an image independent transition penalty function $T(u_{t-1}, u_t)$ to control properties of the path.

Here we extended the tracking framework proposed in [1], by using the obtained depth information not only as features for the models to be trained but also as scoring function $q(u_{t-1}, u_t; x_{t-1}^t)$ to determine a likelihood for the tracked hand being still the correct one. In particular, after hands were overlapping, the tracker often confused the hands afterwards (c.f. Figure 1), with the additional depth information, the tracker has a cue to decide which hand to follow in the remaining frames.

For each of these tracked positions, we look up the corresponding depth information from the smoothed disparity maps, for later use in the recognition framework.

3   Experimental Results

For our experiments, we use a publicly available Boston-104 database, which has been used in several other works [2,11] and consits of 201 American Sign Language sentences performed by 3 different signers (161 are used for training and 40 for testing [2]). On the average, these sentences consist of 5 words out of a vocabulary of 104 unique words. In particular, four camera views are available therefrom two for stereo vision. Unfortunately, calibration sequences or exact camera settings are not available and require the above mentioned methods.

Hand Tracking Performance Measurement. For the evaluation of the hand tracking methods, the ground truth positions of both hands in the test sequences are used to evaluate the effect of the depth information on the tracking performance. For an image sequence x_1^T and corresponding annotated hand positions u_1^T, the tracking error rate (TER) of tracked positions $\hat{u}_1^T$ is defined as the relative number of frames where the

Table 1. Hand tracking results for different tracking features and tolerances

Features	$TER\,[\%]$	
	$\tau = 20$	$\tau = 15$
appearance-based	28.61	39.06
+ stereo-vision	21.54	28.45

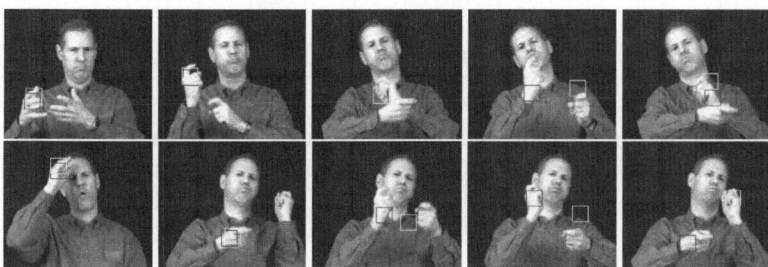

Fig. 4. Comparison of vision-based tracking (yellow) and joint vision- and stereo-vision-based tracking (red) of the dominant hand performing rotating and overlapping hand movements (first row) and fast asynchronous upward and downward movements (second row)

Euclidean distance between the tracked and the annotated position is larger than or equal to a tolerance τ, with $TER = \frac{1}{T}\sum_{t=1}^{T}\delta_\tau(u_t, \hat{u}_t)$ and $\delta_\tau(u, v) := 0$ iff $\|u - v\| < \tau$, $\delta_\tau(u, v) := 1$ otherwise.

For $\tau = 20$ (i.e. approximately the half of the hand's palm size), the baseline TER of 28.61% using only appearance-based tracking features can be strongly improved to 21.54% TER when using the depth information as additional cue. In average, the tracking accuracy of the system is improved by ± 5 pixels in Table 1 by combining appearance-based and stereo-vision based tracking features.

A few example sequences with visualised tracking results when appearance only (yellow) and both, depth and appearance, is used (red) are shown in Figure 4. It can be observed that after hands were overlapping, often the yellow, purely appearance-based tracker, confuses the dominant and non-dominant hands, but the tracker which additionally uses the depth information is able to follow the correct dominant hand.

Continuous Sign Language Recognition. Recognition experiments are evaluated using the word error rate (WER) in the same way as it is currently done in speech recognition, i.e. we measure the amount of insertion (INS), deletion (DEL), and substitution (SUB) errors.

First, we analyse different appearance-based and depth-based features for our baseline system. Table 2 gives an overview of results obtained with the baseline system for image, depth, and manual features alone, as well as for various combinations of these. It can be seen that the original intensity images as well as the disparity images scaled down to 32×32 pixels already lead to reasonable results.

Combining the original image with depth features has so far not led to a performance improvement (c.f. (1) in Table 2). Using the improved tracking framework, the

Table 2. Baseline results using appearance-based features

Features	DEL	INS	SUB	errors	WER %
Frame (32x32)	43	6	16	65	35.62 (1)
Frame + tracking trajectory	14	10	19	43	24.16 (2)
Depth-Hand	33	15	54	102	57.30
PCA-Depth-Hand	28	13	54	95	53.37
Frame + PCA depth hand	27	13	31	71	39.89 (1)
Frame + tracking trajectory + PCA depth-Hand	12	8	15	35	19.66 (2)

combination of the original image with the trajectory, which consists only of x and y coordinates extracted from succeeding tracking positions, leads to a WER of 24.1% which can be improved to 19.66% when the PCA reduced hand patch from the depth image is used additionally (c.f. (2) in Table 2).

4   Summary

We have presented an approach to incorporate depth information into our automatic continuous sign language recognition system. We have shown that the use of the additional depth cue leads to a clear improvement of the tracking results and to minor improvements in the recognition of sign language sentences. For the tracking we have shown that the depth information helps to disambiguate between different hands after these have overlapped. The recognition results have shown small improvements although the tracking was improved because on the one hand, the tracking is sufficiently good for continuous sign language recognition without stereo information and on the other hand, the signs to be distinguished cannot better be discriminated using depth information than without.

It will be interesting to analyse the impact of the depth information when recognising more complicated sentences with a stronger focus on future and past tenses under more adverse imaging conditions.

Acknowledgements. This work was partly realised as part of the Quaero Programme, funded by OSEO, French State agency for innovation.

References

1. Dreuw, P., Deselaers, T., Rybach, D., Keysers, D., Ney, H.: Tracking using dynamic programming for appearance-based sign language recognition. In: FG, pp. 293–298. IEEE, Los Alamitos (2006)
2. Dreuw, P., Rybach, D., Deselaers, T., Zahedi, M., Ney, H.: Speech recognition techniques for a sign language recognition system. In: Interspeech, Antwerp, Belgium, August 2007, pp. 2513–2516 (2007)
3. Fang, G., Gao, W., Zhao, D.: Large-vocabulary continuous sign language recognition based on transition-movement models. IEEE Trans. on Systems, Man, and Cybernetics 37(1) (January 2007)

4. Fujimara, K., Liu, X.: Sign recognition using depth image streams. In: FG, Southampton, UK, April 2006, pp. 381–386 (2006)
5. Kolmogorov, V., Criminisi, A., Crogs, G., Blake, A., Rother, C.: Probabilistic fusion of stereo with color and contrast for bi-layer segmentation. PAMI (2006)
6. Lichtenauer, J., ten Holt, G., Hendriks, E., Reinders, M.: 3d visual detection of correct ngt sign production. In: Annual Conf. of the Advanced School for Computing and Imaging (2007)
7. Neidle, C.: Signstream^{TM} Annotation: Conventions used for the American Sign Language Linguistic Research Project and addendum. Technical Report 11 and 13, American Sign Language Linguistic Research Project, Boston University (2002) (2007)
8. Ohta, Y., Kanade, T.: Stereo by intra- and inter-scanline search using dynamic programming. PAMI 7(2), 139–154 (1985)
9. Ong, S., Ranganath, S.: Automatic sign language analysis: A survey and the future beyond lexical meaning. PAMI 27(6), 873–891 (2005)
10. Robertson, D., Ramalingam, S., Fitzgibbon, A., Criminisi, A., Blake, A.: Learning priors for calibrating families of stereo cameras. In: ICCV, Rio de Janeiro, Brazil (October 2007)
11. Ruiduo Yang, S.S., Loeding, B.: Enhanced level building algorithm to the movement epenthesis problem in sign language. In: CVPR, Minneapolis, MN, USA (June 2007)
12. Viola, P., Jones, M.J.: Robust real-time face detection. IJCV 57(2), 137–154 (2004)
13. Vogler, C., Metaxas, D.: A framework for recognizing the simultaneous aspects of american sign language. CVIU 81(3), 358–384 (2001)
14. Wang, S.B., Quattoni, A., Morency, L.-P., Demirdjian, D., Darrell, T.: Hidden conditional random fields for gesture recognition. In: CVPR, New York, USA, June 2006, vol. 2, pp. 1521–1527 (2006)
15. Wrobel, U.R.: Referenz in Gebärdensprachen: Raum und Person. Institut für Phonetik und Sprachliche Kommunikation, Universität München 37, 25–50 (2001)
16. Yao, G., Yao, H., Liu, X., Jiang, F.: Real time large vocabulary continuous sign language recognition based on op/viterbi algorithm. In: ICPR, Hong Kong, vol. 3, pp. 312–315 (August 2006)

Human Action Recognition Using Optical Flow Accumulated Local Histograms

Manuel Lucena[1], Nicolás Pérez de la Blanca[2], José Manuel Fuertes[1], and Manuel Jesús Marín-Jiménez[2]

[1] Departamento de Informática, Escuela Politécnica Superior, Universidad de Jaén
Campus de las Lagunillas, 23071. Jaén, Spain
{mlucena,jmf}@ujaen.es
[2] Departamento de Ciencias de la Computación e Inteligencia Artificial,
ETSII, Universidad de Granada
C/ Periodista Daniel Saucedo Aranda s/n, 18071 Granada, Spain
nicolas@ugr.es

Abstract. This paper addresses the human action recognition task from optical flow. We develop a non-parametric motion model using only the image region surrounding the actor making the action. For every two consecutive frames, a local motion descriptor is calculated from the optical flow orientation histograms collected from overlapping regions inside the bounding box of the actor. An action descriptor is built by weighting and aggregating the estimated histograms along the temporal axis. We obtain a promising trade-off between complexity and performance compared with state-of-the-art approaches. Experimental results show that the proposed method equals or improves on the performance of state-of-the-art approaches using these databases.

1 Introduction

The human action recognition process from video sequences is a particularly relevant challenge at the moment due to its high impact on numerous technical and social applications: visual surveillance, human-machine multimedia interfaces, social robot building, video-interactive games, etc. In recent years different parametric and non-parametric approaches have been proposed in order to obtain good video sequence classifiers for human action recognition (see [1]).

The study of human motion in the last decade has given birth to a large number of techniques for characterizing, learning and recognizing complex 3D motions from 2D image features [1,2,3,4]. We consider an action as a continuous motion identifiable when a substantial part of it has been observed, and characterizable from the aggregation of local motions. In this way, our proposal does not follow the common strategy of preprocessing the full sequence looking for features before classifying them, but we build and improve the set of optical flow features on the fly, with each new incoming image. In recent years, fast and accurate algorithms have been proposed for optical flow, (see [5,6]), but at the cost of increasing the implementation complexity significantly. To evaluate the

H. Araujo et al. (Eds.): IbPRIA 2009, LNCS 5524, pp. 32–39, 2009.

accuracy of the estimate in our motion descriptor two different algorithms with different accuracies have been used: the Lucas-Kanade algorithm (LK) [7] and the algorithm proposed by Farnebäck (FAR) [8].

In human action classification tasks the most relevant motion information is obtained from inside the bounding box (BB) enclosing the subject performing the action. For each image we focus our interest on this area. To do this we build a new sequence from the BB regions extracted from each image. The idea of using optical flow features from the interior of the bounding box is not new and it was first suggested in [9] for 3D poses characterization. Our approach is reminiscent of this one, but in our case we propose a new way of representing the motion information as a new action descriptor.

The paper is organized as follows: In section 2 the feature extraction process and the development of the new action descriptor are presented. Section 3 shows the experimental set up with the obtained results. In section 4 the discussion and conclusions are presented.

2 Features and Action Descriptor

Let us assume a sequence of t images $I = \{I_1, I_2, \ldots, I_t\}$, containing one actor playing the action of interest. The first step of our approach is to compute the sequence of bounding boxes of the actor on each frame, I'. Simple thresholding methods approximating size and mass center have been used with satisfactory results [10].

The next step of the proposed algorithm involves the computation of the optical flow F of the whole sequence, F_k being the optical flow between two consecutive images I'_k and I'_{k+1}. We denote by $m(x, y; k)$ the norm of the velocity vector of F_k located at (x, y), and by $\theta(x, y; k)$ its rotation angle. We have chosen two algorithms in order to evaluate the influence of the quality of the estimations on our experiments, the classical Lucas-Kanade's algorithm (LK) [7] and the algorithm proposed by Farnebäck (FAR) [8], that provides a dense and more stable estimation with a reasonable computational cost.

2.1 Oriented Histograms Computation

In order to get stable and robust information regarding the whole motion, we summarize the instantaneous motion between every two frames in a set of $d-$bins spatial histograms. Different samples of the same type of action should activate the same regions of the image. Let $\mathbf{p}_i, i = 1, \cdots, N$ denote the set of selected points inside of the BB. In order to extract the stable information we compute histograms, $h_i, i = 1, \cdots, N$, from areas centered on the set of points $\mathbf{p}_i$. These areas represent the image parts in which the motion is most active. Let $W_i(x, y)$ be a function defining the contribution from each image point (x, y) to each one of the histograms h_i. We assume $0 \leq W_i(x, y) \leq 1$, $\sum_i W_i(x, y) = 1$. Let us remark that these normalization conditions on each pixel (x, y) imply a redistribution of its estimation.

For each point $\mathbf{p}_i$ and each orientation bin b, h_i^b is computed as:

$$h_i^b = \sum_{(x,y;k)\in I'} W_i(x,y)m(x,y;k)\delta(\theta(x,y;k),b) \tag{1}$$

where $m(x,y;k)$ and $\theta(x,y;k)$ are the norm and the angle respectively of the estimated optical flow at (x,y) and

$$\delta(\theta,b) = \begin{cases} 1 & \text{if} \quad b-1 \leq \theta\frac{d}{2\pi} < b \\ 0 & \text{in other case} \end{cases} \tag{2}$$

Each h_i^b represents the contribution of the orientation b to the full motion associated to the region surrounding the ith point. The contribution to several histograms from each pixel makes the full estimate robust to bounding box shifting errors and to random local motions of the actor. Once the histograms h_i have been calculated on all frames, we accumulate the value along the temporal axis on each region $H_i = \alpha_i \sum_t h_i(t)$ weighting the result according with our prior belief on the importance of the region i in the motion definition. Concatenating the aggregated histograms, we obtain a vector, denoted AD, of $N \times d$ coefficients defining the action descriptor,

$$AD = \frac{1}{C}\{H_1,\dots,H_N\} \tag{3}$$

where C is a normalization constant so that $\sum_{i=1}^N H_i = 1$,. The weight values α_i can be estimated according to the motion activity measured along the sequence. In our experiments we fix $\alpha_i = 1$ for all i.

In this work, simple choices for the point location, distribution function and importance weights have been used. A grid of fixed k points $x_i, i = 1,\cdots,k$ in the horizontal dimension of I', and l points $y_j, j = 1,\cdots,l$ in the vertical axis define the points p_i. That is, we fix a set of $k \times l$ two-dimensional points, $\mathbf{p}_{ij} = (x_i, y_j)$, with $1 \leq i < k$ and $1 \leq j < l$. Then a local oriented histogram H_{ij} is associated to each point. Here we restrict the influence of each optical flow vector to its first nearest neighborhood of $\mathbf{p}_{ij}$ points. The kernel functions $W_{ij}(x,y)$ are all the same and defined by the tensorial product of two one-dimensional functions.

$$W_{ij}(x,y) = \omega_i^{\mathsf{x}}(x)\omega_j^{\mathsf{y}}(y). \tag{4}$$

Assuming n points $\mathbf{p} = \{p_1,\dots p_{n-1}\}$ along a dimension, the set of function $\omega_i^{\mathbf{P}}$ is defined as follows:

$$\omega_i^{\mathbf{P}}(z) = \begin{cases} 1 - \dfrac{(p_i - z)}{(p_i - p_{i-1})} & \text{if } i > 1 \text{ and } p_{i-1} \leq z < p_i \\ 1 - \dfrac{(z - p_i)}{(p_{i+1} - p_i)} & \text{if } i < n \text{ and } p_i \leq z < p_{i-1} \\ 1 & \text{if } i = 1 \text{ and } 0 \leq z < p_1 \\ 1 & \text{if } i = n \text{ and } p_n \leq z \leq 1 \\ 0 & \text{in other case.} \end{cases} \tag{5}$$

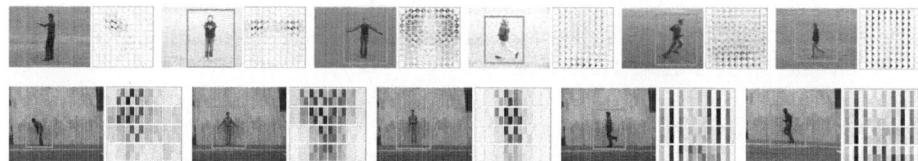

Fig. 1. First row corresponds to the KTH database, second row to the Weizmann database. The darker the gray level in a cell of the descriptor the higher the intensity of the accumulated optical flow on it.

3 Experiments

In order to be able to compare with reported results, two well-known action video sequence databases, *WeizmannDB* [11] and *KTH Database* [12], have been selected to run the experiments.

3.1 Methodology

The experiments have been performed using the Nearest Neighbor classifier (NNC) jointly with a leave-one-out cross-validation technique. Each cross-validation round uses the set of sequences containing one specific actor as a test set, and the rest of the sequences as the training set, so we have 9 rounds on WeizmannDB and 25 on KTHDB. In addition and for comparison purposes k-NNC with n-fold cross-validations has also been used. On both databases the actor BB was calculated automatically using the algorithm proposed in [10] assuming constant speed and orientation in the local motion. All the BB images are normalized to the same size of 40×40 pixels using bilinear interpolation. Figure 1 shows descriptors calculated for different sequences from both databases.

3.2 Classification Results

In order to select the best number of $\mathbf{p}_{ij}$ points and orientation bins, d, on each database have carried out leave-one-out classification experiments with different value combinations of k, l and d. We found that different combinations of number of points and bins provide similar results. For the KTHDB we select $k = 10, l = 10, d = 8$ for both optical flow algorithms. In the WeizmannDB case we select $k = 8, l = 4, d = 4$ for LK and $k = 10, l = 2, d = 8$ for FAR.

KTH Database: Table 1 shows the confusion matrices obtained with each one of the two algorithms. If we look at the individual actions, we can see that our method classifies all the categories with a success rate of over 91%, except *running* and *jogging*. The average score is 89.38% and 90.51% for LK and FAR respectively. In order to evaluate how much is gained by the use of local histograms, we ran the same experiments using only one histogram per image. The average score obtained was 67.29% and 70.95% for LK and FAR respectively. As expected, the use of several histograms improves the classification score quite a lot.

Table 1. Classification results over the KTH database. Descriptor: Local orientation histograms ($h = 10, v = 10, d = 8$) (see section 2.1). Overall recognition rate: 89.38% using LK and 90.51% using Farnebäck .

(a)

Lucas-Kanade Optical Flow

	Walking	Jogging	Running	Handclapping	Handwaving	Boxing
Walking	94.2	4.8	0.8	0.2	0.0	0.0
Jogging	14.4	78.6	6.8	0.0	0.0	0.2
Running	3.2	22.5	73.6	0.5	0.0	0.1
Handclapping	0.0	0.0	0.0	91.2	5.1	3.8
Handwaving	0.0	0.0	0.0	0.5	99.5	0.0
Boxing	0.3	0.0	0.0	0.3	0.3	99.2

(b)

Farnebäck Optical Flow

	Walking	Jogging	Running	Handclapping	Handwaving	Boxing
Walking	95.1	4.1	0.8	0.0	0.0	0.0
Jogging	14.6	81.2	4.1	0.0	0.0	0.0
Running	5.5	18.9	75.4	0.2	0.0	0.0
Handclapping	0.0	0.0	0.0	94.2	2.3	3.5
Handwaving	0.0	0.0	0.0	0.5	99.2	0.3
Boxing	0.8	0.0	0.0	0.5	0.8	98.0

Table 2. This table shows a comparison of our classifier with the current state-of-the-art one on the KTH database. Rows 1-4 show the following: r1) compared methods, r2) sceneries considered in the experiments, r3) strategy used in training+testing according to the number of actors used on each stage, r4) classification score (see text for comments).

Method	Dollar et col.	Laptev et col.	Ahmad&Lee	Our		
Scenery	s1,s3	s1-s4	s1,s3,s4	s1-s4	s1,s3,s4	s1,s3
Exper. Design	24+1	8+8+9	8+11	24+1	24+1	24+1
Score	81%	91.8%	88.55%	90.51%	92.13%	93.08%

A comparison of our results with the state-of-the-art results on this database is given in the Table 2. We show some of the best results reported to date Dollar et al. [13], Laptev et col. [14], Ahmad and Lee [15]. This table shows global results and the details about the training and testing set. In [14] the four sceneries are considered using 8 actors for training 8 for validation and 9 for testing. In this case the inclusion of the difficult s2 scenery can be a load on the global score. In [15] a complex classifier is proposed combining different information and techniques. They do not use all the actors on the database but 8 actors for training and 11 for testing. In [13] only half of the database is considered. Although these results are not directly comparable they provide a raw overview of the current achievements. According to these results our proposal provides very encouraging indications especially since we achieve the state-of-the-art level with a very simple descriptor.

Weizmann Database: Table 3 shows the results using our proposal. We obtained a recognition rate of 98.92% for both databases.

For this database we have also implemented the technique described in Zelnik-Manor and Irani [16] and we applied it to the I' sequences obtained after the subject localization step. The overall recognition rate is 92.47% (with descriptors of 1152 coefficients), which is clearly below our results.

If we remove the *skip* action from this database, we can compare our results with the ones shown in [17], which reach 100% in some cases, with the same database and similar methodology. In our case we obtain an overall recognition

Table 3. Classification results on the WeizmannDB. Descriptor: local orientation histograms with ($k = 8, l = 4, d = 4$) for LK, and ($k = 10, l = 2$, $d = 8$) for Farnebäck (see section 2.1). Classification algorithm: *Nearest Neighbor* with χ^2 distance. Overall recognition rate: 98.92% using LK, 98.92% using Farnebäck.

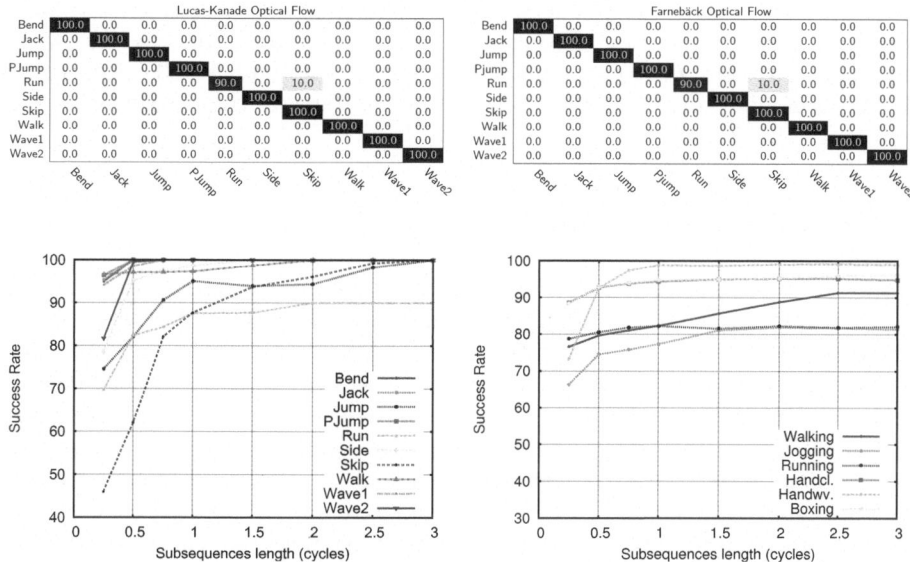

Lucas-Kanade Optical Flow

	Bend	Jack	Jump	P.Jump	Run	Side	Skip	Walk	Wave1	Wave2
Bend	100.0	0.0	0.0	0.0	0.0	0.0	0.0	0.0	0.0	0.0
Jack	0.0	100.0	0.0	0.0	0.0	0.0	0.0	0.0	0.0	0.0
Jump	0.0	0.0	100.0	0.0	0.0	0.0	0.0	0.0	0.0	0.0
P.Jump	0.0	0.0	0.0	100.0	0.0	0.0	0.0	0.0	0.0	0.0
Run	0.0	0.0	0.0	0.0	90.0	0.0	10.0	0.0	0.0	0.0
Side	0.0	0.0	0.0	0.0	0.0	100.0	0.0	0.0	0.0	0.0
Skip	0.0	0.0	0.0	0.0	0.0	0.0	100.0	0.0	0.0	0.0
Walk	0.0	0.0	0.0	0.0	0.0	0.0	0.0	100.0	0.0	0.0
Wave1	0.0	0.0	0.0	0.0	0.0	0.0	0.0	0.0	100.0	0.0
Wave2	0.0	0.0	0.0	0.0	0.0	0.0	0.0	0.0	0.0	100.0

Farnebäck Optical Flow

	Bend	Jack	Jump	Pjump	Run	Side	Skip	Walk	Wave1	Wave2
Bend	100.0	0.0	0.0	0.0	0.0	0.0	0.0	0.0	0.0	0.0
Jack	0.0	100.0	0.0	0.0	0.0	0.0	0.0	0.0	0.0	0.0
Jump	0.0	0.0	100.0	0.0	0.0	0.0	0.0	0.0	0.0	0.0
Pjump	0.0	0.0	0.0	100.0	0.0	0.0	0.0	0.0	0.0	0.0
Run	0.0	0.0	0.0	0.0	90.0	0.0	10.0	0.0	0.0	0.0
Side	0.0	0.0	0.0	0.0	0.0	100.0	0.0	0.0	0.0	0.0
Skip	0.0	0.0	0.0	0.0	0.0	0.0	100.0	0.0	0.0	0.0
Walk	0.0	0.0	0.0	0.0	0.0	0.0	0.0	100.0	0.0	0.0
Wave1	0.0	0.0	0.0	0.0	0.0	0.0	0.0	0.0	100.0	0.0
Wave2	0.0	0.0	0.0	0.0	0.0	0.0	0.0	0.0	0.0	100.0

Fig. 2. Average success rate for classifying subsecuences of variable length belonging to WeizmannDB and KTHDB. Descriptor: $k = 10, l = 10, d = 8$ for KTH and $k = 10, l = 2, d = 8$ for Weizmann . Optical Flow Algorithm: Farnebäck.

rate of 98.8%, with $k = 8, l = 4, d = 4$ (128 coefficients) using LK, and $k = 10, l = 2, d = 8$ (160 coefficients) using FAR.

3.3   The Shortest Sequence to Recognize an Action

In this experiment we analyze the minimum information required by our descriptor in order to recognize the playing action. In order to do this we run experiments testing the classifiers with sequences of different lengths measured in cycles of the motion. Fig. 2 shows the average recognizing rate on the full set of actions in terms of the number of times that the action is present in the test sequence. It can observed that from one cycle ahead the classification is very stable for most of the actions. For some of the actions one half of one cycle is even sufficient to obtain very good score. This results show that the descriptor codes the relevant information of the motion.

3.4   Recognizing Activity Changes

We have carried out experiments on sequences of images composed by pieces of the original sequences, in order to test the capability of our proposal for detecting activity changes. That is, for each actor in the database we generate 10 new sequences comprising random concatenations of all his sequences. Then we classify each image in the new sequences using a sliding window of 15 images long, where we assign the result of the classification of the window to the image in the window center. We use a leave-one-out cross-validation technique, training with all the actors except one and testing the new sequences from this one. The whole score is 86.73% for the WeizmannDB and 80.87% for the KTHDB. Applying a 15 length median filter to the class sequence we improve the classification rate by 3% in both cases.

4   Discussion and Conclusions

In this work we have presented an optical flow-based motion descriptor, suitable for characterizing spatio-temporal dynamic patterns with special emphasis in human actions recognition. The proposed descriptor is defined using optical flow oriented histograms calculated from the video sequences. In the spatial domain we have characterized the local area around the subject by a set of optical flow local histograms. In doing so we get invariance to local deformations of the viewpoint and reduce as much as possible the background contribution. In the temporal domain we aggregate the estimated values making the descriptor invariant to performance changes and estimation noise, at the same time as bringing out the relevant motions defining the full action. Our proposal in this sense is simple but effective. The only free parameter in our proposal is the number of histograms to collect on each image. The experiments with two well-known video databases have shown encouraging results. It is important to remark that our proposal needs a detection stage to localize the BB of the actor, but this is a reasonable strategy since the BB information can be extracted from the image gradients, and these are part of the optical flow estimation process.

We think that the proposed descriptor achieves a clear improvement in the action recognition task. We have also shown that aggregated optical flow is an important source from which to decode motion information.

Acknowledgements

This work has been financed by the Spanish Minister of Education under grants TIN2005-01665 and Consolider Ingenio MIPRCV2007.

References

1. Moeslund, T., Hilton, A., Krüger, V.: A survey of advances in vision-based human motion capture and analysis. Computer Vision and Image Understanding 104, 90–126 (2006)
2. Aggarwal, J., Cai, Q.: Human motion analysis: A review. Computer Vision and Image Understanding 73(3), 428–440 (1999)

3. Gavrila, D.: The visual analysis of human movement: A survey. Computer Vision and Image Understanding 73(1), 82–98 (1999)
4. Moeslund, T., Granum, E.: A survey of computer vision-based human motion capture. Computer Vision and Image Understanding 81(3), 231–268 (2001)
5. Bruhn, A., Weickert, J., Schnörr, C.: Lucas/Kanade meets Horn/Schunck: Combining local and global optic flow methods. International Journal of Computer Vision 61(3), 211–231 (2005)
6. Brox, T., Bruhn, A., Papenberg, N., Weickert, J.: High accuracy optical flow estimation based on a theory for warping. In: Pajdla, T., Matas, J(G.) (eds.) ECCV 2004. LNCS, vol. 3024, pp. 25–36. Springer, Heidelberg (2004)
7. Lucas, B., Kanade, T.: An iterative image registration technique with an application to stereo vision. In: Proceedings of DARPA IU Workshop, pp. 121–130 (1981)
8. Farnebäck, G.: Two-frame motion estimation based on polynomial expansion. In: Bigun, J., Gustavsson, T. (eds.) SCIA 2003. LNCS, vol. 2749, pp. 363–370. Springer, Heidelberg (2003)
9. Efros, A., Berg, A., Mori, G., Malik, J.: Recognizing action at a distance. In: IEEE International Conference on Computer Vision, vol. 2, pp. 726–733 (2003)
10. Otsu, N.: A threshold selection method from gray level histograms. IEEE Trans. Systems, Man and Cybernetics 9, 62–66 (1979)
11. Blank, M., Gorelick, L., Shechtman, E., Irani, M., Basri, R.: Actions as space-time shapes. In: Proceedings of the IEEE International Conference on Computer Vision (ICCV 2005), vol. 2, pp. 1395–1402 (2005)
12. Schüldt, C., Laptev, I., Caputo, B.: Recognizing human actions: A local SVM approach. In: International Conference on Pattern Recognition, Cambridge, U.K., vol. 3, pp. 32–36 (2004)
13. Dollar, P., Rabaud, V., Cottrell, G., Belongie, S.: Behavior recognition via sparse spatio-temporal features. In: 2nd Joint IEEE International Workshop on Visual Surveillance and Performance Evaluation of Tracking and Surveillance, pp. 65–72 (2005)
14. Laptev, I., Marszalek, M., Schmid, C., Rozenfeld, B.: Learning realistic human actions from movies. In: Intern. Conference on Computer Vision and Pattern Recognition (2008)
15. Ahmad, M., Lee, S.: Human action recognition using shape and clg-motion flow from multi-view image sequences. Pattern Recognition 41, 2237–2252 (2008)
16. Zelnik-Manor, L., Irani, M.: Statistical analysis of dynamic actions. IEEE Transaction on Pattern Analysis and Machine Intelligence 28(9), 1530–1535 (2006)
17. Ikizler, N., Duygulu, P.: Human action recognition using distribution of oriented rectangular patches. In: Elgammal, A., Rosenhahn, B., Klette, R. (eds.) Human Motion 2007. LNCS, vol. 4814, pp. 271–284. Springer, Heidelberg (2007)

Trajectory Modeling Using
Mixtures of Vector Fields⋆

Jacinto C. Nascimento, Mário A.T. Figueiredo, and Jorge S. Marques

Instituto de Sistemas e Robótica and Instituto de Telecomunicações
Instituto Superior Técnico
1049-001 Lisboa,
Portugal

Abstract. Trajectory analysis plays a key role in human activity recognition and video surveillance. This paper proposes a new approach based on modeling trajectories using a bank of vector (velocity) fields. We assume that each trajectory is generated by one of a set of fields or by the concatenation of trajectories produced by different fields. The proposed approach constitutes a space-varying framework for trajectory modeling and is able to discriminate among different types of motion regimes. Furthermore, the vector fields can be efficiently learned from observed trajectories using an expectation-maximization algorithm. An experiment with real data illustrates the promising performance of the method.

1 Introduction

Motion analysis is a central block in many computer vision systems, namely those designed for human activity recognition and video surveillance. When the camera is close to the subject(s) being observed, a wide variety of cues characterizing human activities can be retrieved, *e.g.*, silhouette, head and hands, spatio-temporal templates, color histograms, or articulated models. However, when the camera is far away and has a wide field of view, it is not possible to obtain a detailed description of the subjects. In this case, only trajectory information can be reliably acquired. Motion cues such as velocities and trajectories are therefore a key source of information.

Different trajectory analysis problems (such as classification and clustering) have been addressed using pairwise (dis)similarity measures; these include Euclidean [8] and Hausdorff [11,18] distances, and dynamic time warping [15]).

Another class of methods adopts probabilistic generative models for the trajectories [7,12,14,17], usually of the hidden Markov model (HMM) family. These approaches have the important advantage of not requiring trajectory alignment/registration; moreover, they provide a solid statistical inference framework, based on which model parameters may be estimated from observed data.

⋆ This work was supported by Fundação para a Ciência e a Tecnologia (ISR/IST pluri-anual funding) through the POS Conhecimento Program which includes FEDER funds.

H. Araujo et al. (Eds.): IbPRIA 2009, LNCS 5524, pp. 40–47, 2009.

2   Overall Idea

This paper describes a novel approach for modeling object (e.g., pedestrian) trajectories in video sequences. We assume that the object motion is characterized by a set of vector fields, which are learned from observed trajectories. The use of multiple velocity fields aims to describe a variety of behaviors which can be observed in a scene. The system should be able to select the most appropriate velocity field for each sequence.

Two models are considered in this paper. The first model (*M1*) assumes that each object trajectory is generated by one vector field (we don't know which). This leads to a generative model based on a mixture of velocity fields which is flexible enough to represent many types of trajectories. The second model (*M2*) assumes that each trajectory is obtained by the concatenation of segments, each of them generated by one velocity field. Therefore, switching between velocity fields is allowed. Furthermore, it is assumed that the switching mechanism, follows a probabilistic distribution which can be location-dependent.

To illustrate the concept consider two intersecting roads, as depicted in Fig. 1. Given a set of trajectories (Fig. 1 left) we wish to estimate the vector fields which describe the trajectory of cars in the image. Fig. 1 (center and right) shows the expected solution if the problem is addressed using model *M2* (which includes switching). At the intersection, cars have a significant probability of changing direction, whereas far from it, the switching probability is low.

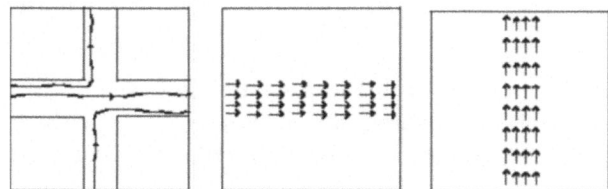

Fig. 1. Cross road example. Set of trajectories (left) and two vector fields modeling to the trajectories (center and right)

Both models are flexible enough to represent a wide variety of trajectories and allow space-varying behaviors without resorting to non-linear dynamical models which are infamously hard to estimate from observed data.

3   Generative Motion Model

For the sake of simplicity, we assume that objects may move freely in the image domain. The object position at time t is represented by a vector $\mathbf{x}_t$ in $\mathbb{R}^2$.

Let $\mathcal{T} = \{\mathbf{T}_1, \ldots, \mathbf{T}_K\}$, with $\mathbf{T}_k : \mathbb{R}^2 \to \mathbb{R}^2$, for $k \in \{1, \ldots, K\}$, be a set of K vector (velocity) fields. The velocity vector at point $\mathbf{x} \in \mathbb{R}^2$ of the k-th field is denoted as $\mathbf{T}_k(\mathbf{x})$. At each time instant, one of these velocity fields is *active*, *i.e.*, is driving the motion. Formally, each object trajectory is generated according to

$$\mathbf{x}_t = \mathbf{x}_{t-1} + \mathbf{T}_{k_t}(\mathbf{x}_{t-1}) + \mathbf{w}_t, \quad t = 2, \ldots, L, \tag{1}$$

where $k_t \in \{1, ..., K\}$ is the label of the active field at time t, $\mathbf{w}_t \sim \mathcal{N}(0, \sigma_{k_t}^2 \mathbf{I})$ is a realization of white Gaussian noise with zero mean and variance $\sigma_{k_t}^2$ (which may be different for each field), and L is the length (number of points) in the trajectory. The initial position follows some distribution $p(\mathbf{x}_1)$.

The conditional probability density of a trajectory $\mathbf{x} = (\mathbf{x}_1, ..., \mathbf{x}_L)$, given the sequence of active models $\mathbf{k} = \{k_1, ..., k_L\}$ is

$$p(\mathbf{x}|\mathbf{k}, \mathcal{T}) = p(\mathbf{x}_1) \prod_{t=2}^{L} p(\mathbf{x}_t|\mathbf{x}_{t-1}, k_t),$$

where $p(\mathbf{x}_t|\mathbf{x}_{t-1}, k_t) = \mathcal{N}(\mathbf{x}_t|\mathbf{x}_{t-1} + \mathbf{T}_{k_t}(\mathbf{x}_{t-1}), \sigma_{k_t}^2 \mathbf{I})$ is a Gaussian density.

The sequence of active fields $\mathbf{k} = (k_1, ..., k_L)$ is modeled as a realization of a first order Markov process, with some initial distribution $P(k_1)$, and a space-varying transition matrix, *i.e.*, $P(k_t = j|k_{t-1} = i, \mathbf{x}_{t-1}) = \mathbf{B}_{ij}(\mathbf{x}_{t-1})$. This model allows the switching probability to depend on the location of the object. The matrix-valued field $\mathbf{B}$ can also be seen as a set of K^2 fields with values in $[0, 1]$, under the constraint that $\sum_j \mathbf{B}_{ij}(\mathbf{x}) = 1$, for any $\mathbf{x}$ and any i. If we want to forbid switching between vector fields (as in model *M1*) all we have to do is to assume that $\mathbf{B}(\mathbf{x}) = \mathbf{I}$ (the identity matrix), for any $\mathbf{x}$.

The joint distribution of a trajectory and the underlying sequence of active models, is given by

$$p(\mathbf{x}, \mathbf{k}|\mathcal{T}, \mathbf{B}) = p(\mathbf{x}_1)P(k_1) \prod_{t=2}^{L} p(\mathbf{x}_t|\mathbf{x}_{t-1}, k_t)P(k_t|k_{t-1}, \mathbf{x}_{t-1}). \qquad (2)$$

Of course, $P(k_t|k_{t-1}, \mathbf{x}_{t-1})$ is a function of $\mathbf{B}$ and $p(\mathbf{x}_t|\mathbf{x}_{t-1}, k_t)$ is a function of $\mathcal{T}$; to keep the notation lighter, we abstain from explicitly including these dependencies. Finally, a graphical model representation of our generative process is depicted in Fig. 2.

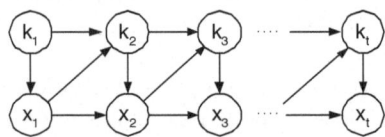

Fig. 2. Graphical model of the trajectory generation process

4   Learning the Fields

In this section we address the problem of learning, from a set of trajectories, the set of velocity fields $\mathcal{T}$, the field of transition matrices $\mathbf{B}$, and the set of noise variances $\boldsymbol{\sigma} = \{\sigma_1^2, ..., \sigma_K^2\}$. Consider a training set of S independent trajectories $\mathcal{X} = \{\mathbf{x}^{(1)}, ..., \mathbf{x}^{(S)}\}$, where $\mathbf{x}^{(j)} = (\mathbf{x}_1^{(j)}, ..., \mathbf{x}_{L_j}^{(j)})$ is the j-th observed trajectory, assumed to have length L_j. Naturally, we assume that the corresponding set of sequences of active fields, $\mathcal{K} = \{\mathbf{k}^{(1)}, ..., \mathbf{k}^{(S)}\}$, is not observed (it's hidden).

In this paper, we focus on model *M1*; *i.e.*, we fix the matrix field $\mathbf{B}$ equal to identity everywhere, $\mathbf{B}(\mathbf{x}) = \mathbf{I}$, thus it does not have to be estimated. In this case, all the elements of each label sequence are identical, *i.e.*, $\mathbf{k}^{(j)} = (k^{(j)}, ..., k^{(j)})$, so we represent the active field of each trajectory simply by $k^{(j)} \in \{1, ..., K\}$. The missing set of labels is thus $\mathcal{K} = \{k^{(1)}, ..., k^{(S)}\} \in \{1, ..., K\}^S$. Finally, we denote the set of the fields and parameters to estimate as $\boldsymbol{\theta} = (\mathcal{T}, \boldsymbol{\sigma})$.

4.1   Estimation Criterion: Marginal MAP

The fact that the active field labels $\mathcal{K}$ are missing suggests the use of an EM algorithm to find a *marginal maximum a posteriori* (MMAP) estimate of $\boldsymbol{\theta}$ under some prior $p(\boldsymbol{\theta}) = p(\mathcal{T})p(\mathbf{B})p(\boldsymbol{\sigma})$; formally,

$$\widehat{\boldsymbol{\theta}} = \arg \max_{\boldsymbol{\theta}} \; p(\boldsymbol{\theta}) \prod_{j=1}^{S} \sum_{k^{(j)}=1}^{K} p(\mathbf{x}^{(j)}, \mathbf{k}^{(j)} | \boldsymbol{\theta}), \tag{3}$$

where each factor $p(\mathbf{x}^{(j)}, \mathbf{k}^{(j)} | \boldsymbol{\theta})$ has the form in (2), with $\mathbf{k}^{(j)} = (k^{(j)}, ..., k^{(j)})$. Next, we derive the E and M steps of the EM algorithm for solving (3). For simplicity, we assume that the initial distributions $p(\mathbf{x}_1)$ and $P(k_1)$ are known.

4.2   The E-step

As is well known, the E-step consists in computing the conditional expectation of the complete log-likelihood, given the current estimates $\widehat{\boldsymbol{\theta}}$ and the observations $\mathcal{X}$. The complete log-likelihood is given by

$$\log p(\mathcal{X}, \mathcal{K} | \boldsymbol{\theta}) = \sum_{j=1}^{S} \log p(\mathbf{x}^{(j)}, \mathbf{k}^{(j)} | \boldsymbol{\theta}) \tag{4}$$

where each $p(\mathbf{x}^{(j)}, \mathbf{k}^{(j)} | \boldsymbol{\theta})$ has the form (2), with $\mathbf{k}^{(j)} = (k^{(j)}, ..., k^{(j)})$. The conditional expectation, usually called the Q-function and denoted as $Q(\boldsymbol{\theta}; \widehat{\boldsymbol{\theta}}) \equiv \mathbb{E}\left[\log p(\mathcal{X}, \mathcal{K} | \boldsymbol{\theta}) \middle| \mathcal{X}, \widehat{\boldsymbol{\theta}}\right]$, can thus be written as

$$Q(\boldsymbol{\theta}; \widehat{\boldsymbol{\theta}}) = \sum_{j=1}^{S} \sum_{t=2}^{L_j} \sum_{l=1}^{K} \bar{y}_l^{(j)} \log \mathcal{N}(\mathbf{x}_t^{(j)} | \mathbf{x}_{t-1}^{(j)} + \mathbf{T}_l(\mathbf{x}_{t-1}^{(j)}), \sigma_l^2 \mathbf{I}) \tag{5}$$

where $\bar{y}_l^{(j)}$ is the posterior probability that the j-th trajectory was generated by field l, given by

$$\bar{y}_l^{(j)} = P\left[k^{(j)} = l \middle| \mathbf{x}^{(j)}, \widehat{\boldsymbol{\theta}}\right] = \frac{p(\mathbf{x}^{(j)}, \mathbf{k}^{(j)} = (l, ..., l) | \widehat{\boldsymbol{\theta}})}{\displaystyle\sum_{m=1}^{K} p(\mathbf{x}^{(j)}, \mathbf{k}^{(j)} = (m, ..., m) | \widehat{\boldsymbol{\theta}})}. \tag{6}$$

4.3   The M-step

In the M-step, the field and parameter estimates are updated according to

$$\widehat{\boldsymbol{\theta}}_{\text{new}} = \arg\max_{\boldsymbol{\theta}} Q(\boldsymbol{\theta}; \widehat{\boldsymbol{\theta}}) + \log p(\boldsymbol{\theta}). \tag{7}$$

This section describes this maximization in detail, as well as the adopted priors, by looking separately at the maximization with respect to $\mathcal{T}$ and $\boldsymbol{\sigma}$.

Updating $\widehat{\boldsymbol{\sigma}}$. Adopting flat priors, $i.e.$, looking for the usual maximum likelihood noise variance estimates, computing the partial derivative of $Q(\boldsymbol{\theta}; \widehat{\boldsymbol{\theta}})$ with respect to each component σ_k^2 of $\boldsymbol{\sigma}$, and equating to zero, yields

$$(\widehat{\sigma}_k^2)_{\text{new}} = \left(\sum_{j=1}^{S} \sum_{t=2}^{L_j} \bar{y}_k^{(j)} \, \|\mathbf{x}_t^{(s)} - \mathbf{x}_{t-1}^{(s)} - \mathbf{T}_k(\mathbf{x}_{t-1}^{(s)})\|^2 \right) \left(\sum_{j=1}^{S} \sum_{t=2}^{L_j} \bar{y}_k^{(j)} \right)^{-1},$$

for $k = 1, ..., K$.

Updating $\widehat{\mathcal{T}}$. Estimating the velocity fields requires some sort of regularization. Moreover, these fields live in infinite dimensional spaces (if we ignore the discrete nature of digital images), thus optimization with respect to them constitute a difficult variational problems. We sidestep this difficulty by adopting a finite dimensional parametrization, in which each velocity field is written as a linear combination of basis functions, $i.e.$,

$$\mathbf{T}_k(\mathbf{x}) = \sum_{n=1}^{N} \mathbf{t}_k^{(n)} \, \phi_n(\mathbf{x}), \tag{8}$$

where each $\mathbf{t}_k^{(n)} \in \mathbb{R}^2$ and $\phi_n(\mathbf{x}) : \mathbb{R}^2 \to \mathbb{R}$, for $n = 1, \ldots, N$, is a set of basis functions (scalar basis fields). Collecting all these vector coefficients in $\boldsymbol{\tau}_k \in \mathbb{R}^{N \times 2}$, defined according to $\boldsymbol{\tau}_k^T = [\mathbf{t}_k^{(1)}, ..., \mathbf{t}_k^{(N)}]$ and letting $\boldsymbol{\Phi}(\mathbf{x}) = [\phi_1(\mathbf{x}), ..., \phi_N(\mathbf{x})] \in \mathbb{R}^N$, we can write

$$\mathbf{T}_k(\mathbf{x}) = \boldsymbol{\Phi}(\mathbf{x})\, \boldsymbol{\tau}_k, \tag{9}$$

thus estimating $\mathbf{T}_k$ becomes equivalent to estimating the coefficient vector $\boldsymbol{\tau}_k$.

To encourage smoothness of each velocity field $\mathbf{T}_k$, we adopt a zero mean Gaussian prior, with a covariance function chosen to assign low probability to large velocity differences between nearby locations

$$p(\boldsymbol{\tau}_k) \propto \exp\{-\frac{1}{2\,\alpha^2} \, \boldsymbol{\tau}_k^T \, \boldsymbol{\Gamma}^{-1} \boldsymbol{\tau}_k\}, \tag{10}$$

where α^2 is a global variance factor that allows controlling the "strength" of the prior. The covariance $\boldsymbol{\Gamma}$ and the basis functions ϕ_i determine the covariance function of $\mathbf{T}_k$; for details, see [16].

The term of $Q(\boldsymbol{\theta};\widehat{\boldsymbol{\theta}}) + \log p(\boldsymbol{\tau}_k)$ which is a function of $\boldsymbol{\tau}_k$ is (apart from a $1/2$ factor) equal to

$$\sum_{j=1}^{S}\sum_{t=2}^{L_j} \bar{y}_k^{(j)} \|\mathbf{x}_t^{(j)} - \mathbf{x}_{t-1}^{(j)} - \Phi(\mathbf{x}_{t-1}^{(j)})\boldsymbol{\tau}_k\|^2 + \boldsymbol{\tau}_k^T \boldsymbol{\Gamma}^{-1}\boldsymbol{\tau}_k \tag{11}$$

Computing the gradient with respect to $\boldsymbol{\tau}_k$ and equating to zero, leads to a linear system of equations,

$$\left(\mathbf{R}_k + \frac{\boldsymbol{\Gamma}^{-1}}{\alpha^2}\right)\boldsymbol{\tau}_k = \mathbf{r}_k \tag{12}$$

where

$$\mathbf{R}_k = \sum_{j=1}^{S}\sum_{t=2}^{L_j} \bar{y}_k^{(j)} \left(\Phi(\mathbf{x}_{t-1}^{(j)})\right)^T \Phi(\mathbf{x}_{t-1}^{(j)}) \tag{13}$$

and

$$\mathbf{r}_k = \sum_{j=1}^{S}\sum_{t=2}^{L_j} \bar{y}_k^{(j)} \left(\Phi(\mathbf{x}_{t-1}^{(j)})\right)^T (\mathbf{x}_t^{(j)} - \mathbf{x}_{t-1}^{(j)}). \tag{14}$$

Notice that since $\Phi(\mathbf{x}_{t-1}^{(j)})$ is $1 \times N$, matrix $\mathbf{R}_k$ is $N \times N$ and $\mathbf{r}_k$ is $N \times 2$ (as is $\boldsymbol{\tau}_k$). Solving (12), yields $(\widehat{\boldsymbol{\tau}}_k)_{\text{new}}$, for $k = 1,...,K$, which in turn define $\widehat{\mathcal{T}}_{\text{new}} = (\widehat{\mathbf{T}}_1, ..., \widehat{\mathbf{T}}_K)_{\text{new}}$.

5   Experimental Results

The proposed algorithm was applied to several synthetic and real data sets. We present here only an example showing the ability of the proposed method to separate different types of trajectories, according to their structure, and to estimate a space-varying model for the trajectories of each group.

Fig. 3 (left, center) shows the trajectories of points of interest in two video sequences often used in multi-point tracking (rotating disk and golf ball). We applied the proposed method to a data set containing all the trajectories extracted from both video sequences. It was assumed that the number of vector fields is

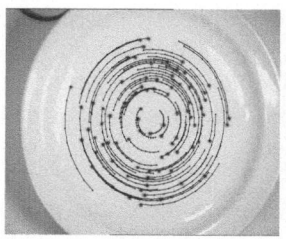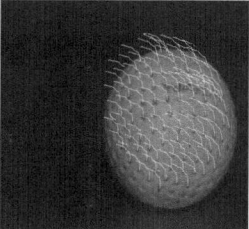

Fig. 3. Data set: original velocity fields (left, center) and their superposition (right)

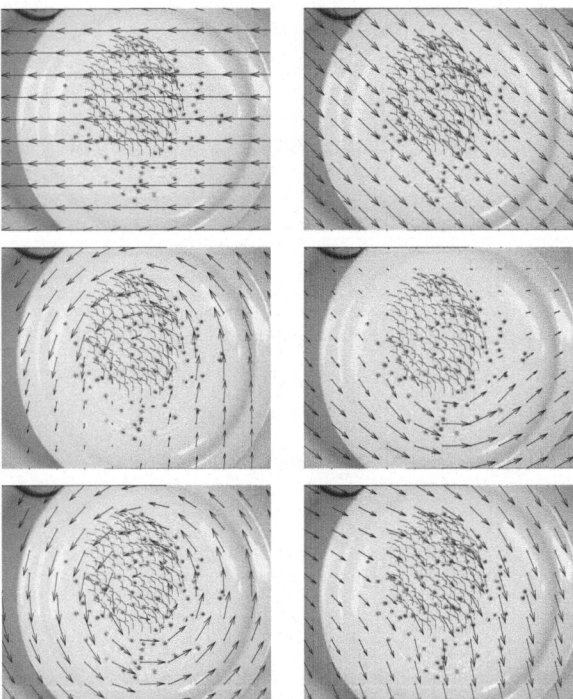

Fig. 4. Left and right columns: the two velocity field estimates, shown in blue. Top row: initialization. Second row: intermediate estimates. Bottom row: final estimates.

known to be equal to 2. Fig. 4 shows the velocity fields estimates obtained by the EM algorithm. It is clear that the proposed algorithm successfully separated the two sets of trajectories and estimated the motion fields explaining each of them. This approach has also been applied to surveillance videos obtained in a university campus with success. Those results will be presented in a forthcoming paper due to lack of space.

6   Conclusions

This paper described probabilistic models for trajectories in video sequences using multiple velocity fields. Two models were considered: (i) each trajectory is generated by a single velocity field, randomly selected (M1); (ii) switching among vector fields during the trajectory is allowed (M2). We have described in detail an EM algorithm to estimate the fields under model M1. A proof-of-concept experiment with real data was presented, giving evidence of the adequacy of the proposed approach.

The implementation of the second scenario, which involves the estimation of a field of stochastic matrices, as well as a comprehensive experimental evaluation in video surveillance tasks will be presented in a forthcoming paper.

Acknowledgement. The image sequences used in this paper were kindly provided by K. Shafique.

References

1. Agarwal, A., Triggs, B.: Tracking articulated motion with piecewise learned dynamical models. In: Pajdla, T., Matas, J(G.) (eds.) ECCV 2004. LNCS, vol. 3023, pp. 54–65. Springer, Heidelberg (2004)
2. Ali, S., Shah, M.: A Lagrangian particle dynamics approach for crowd flow segmentation and stability analysis. In: IEEE Conf. Comp. Vision and Patt. Rec., Minneapolis (2007)
3. Boiman, O., Irani, M.: Detecting irregularities in images and in video. In: IEEE Int. Conf. on Comp. Vision, Beijing, China (2005)
4. Boult, T., Micheals, R., Gao, X., Eckmann, M.: Into the woods: Visual surveillance of non-cooperative camouflaged targets in complex outdoor settings. Proc. of the IEEE 89(10), 1382–1402 (2001)
5. Dierchx, P.: Curve and Surface Fitting with Splines. Oxford University Press, Oxford (1993)
6. Duchi, J., Shalev-Shwartz, S., Singer, Y., Chandra, T.: Efficient projections onto the ℓ_1-ball for learning in high dimensions. In: Int. Conf. on Machine Learning, Helsinki, Finland (2008)
7. Duong, T., Bui, H., Phung, D., Venkatesh, S.: Activity recognition and abnormality detection with the switching hidden semi-Markov model. In: IEEE Conf. Comp. Vision and Patt. Rec., San Diego, CA (2005)
8. Fu, Z., Hu, W., Tan, T.: Similarity based vehicle trajectory clustering and anomaly detection. In: IEEE Int. Conf. on Image Proc., Genoa, Italy (2005)
9. Hu, W., Tan, T., Wang, L., Maybank, S.: A survey on visual surveillance of object motion and behaviors. IEEE Trans. Systems, Man, and Cybern. (Part C) 34(3), 334–352 (2004)
10. Johnson, N., Hogg, D.C.: Learning the distribution of object trajectories for event recognition. Image and Vision Computing 14, 583–592 (1996)
11. Junejo, I., Javed, O., Shah, M.: Multi feature path modeling for video surveillance. In: Int. Conf. on Patt. Rec., Cambridge, UK (2004)
12. Nascimento, J., Figueiredo, M., Marques, J.: Independent increment processes for human motion recognition. Comp. Vision & Image Underst. 109(2), 126–138 (2008)
13. Nocedal, J., Wright, S.: Numerical Optimization. Springer, New York (2006)
14. Oliver, N., Rosario, B., Pentland, A.: A Bayesian computer vision system for modeling human interactions. IEEE Trans. Patt. Anal. Mach. Intell. 22(8), 831–843 (2000)
15. Pierobon, M., Marcon, M., Sarti, A., Tubaro, S.: Clustering of human actions using invariant body shape descriptor and dynamic time warping. In: IEEE Conf. on Adv. Video and Sig. Based Surv., pp. 22–27 (2005)
16. Rasmussen, C., Williams, C.: Gaussian Processes for Machine Learning. The MIT Press, Cambridge (2006)
17. Wang, X., Ma, K., Ng, G., Grimson, E.: Trajectory analysis and semantic region modeling using a nonparametric Bayesian model. In: IEEE Conf. on Comp. Vision and Patt. Rec., Anchorage (2008)
18. Wang, X., Tieu, K., Grimson, E.: Learning semantic scene models by trajectory analysis. In: Eur. Conf. on Comp. Vision, Graz, Austria (2006)

High-Speed Human Detection Using a Multiresolution Cascade of Histograms of Oriented Gradients

Marco Pedersoli, Jordi Gonzàlez, and Juan José Villanueva

Departament de Ciències de la Computació and Computer Vision Center
Campus UAB, Edifici O, 08193, Bellaterra, Spain
marcopede@cvc.uab.es

Abstract. This paper presents a new method for human detection based on a multiresolution cascade of Histograms of Oriented Gradients (HOG) that can highly reduce the computational cost of the detection search without affecting accuracy. The method consists of a cascade of sliding window detectors. Each detector is a Support Vector Machine (SVM) composed by features at different resolution, from coarse for the first level to fine for the last one.

Considering that the spatial stride of the sliding window search is affected by the HOG features size, unlike previous methods based on Adaboost cascades, we can adopt a spatial stride inversely proportional to the features resolution. This produces that the speed-up of the cascade is not only due to the low number of features that need to be computed in the first levels, but also to the lower number of detection windows that needs to be evaluated.

Experimental results shows that our method permits a detection rate comparable with the state of the art, but at the same time a gain in the speed of the detection search of 10-20 times depending on the cascade configuration.

Keywords: Support Vector Machine, Human Detector, Multiresolution Analysis.

1 Introduction

Human detection represents one of the most difficult challenges in the field of object category detection. This is due to the fact that, differently than many other categories, humans are not rigid bodies and, furthermore, they can wear every kind of dress with different shapes, dimensions and colors. This means that humans have a very high intra-class visual variation that still makes their detection a difficult problem. Restricting the problem to standing people (but still observed from every possible direction: frontal, side, backward) makes possible to tackle the problem.

A common method for human detection is the use of a sliding window to search for the possible detection in all the possible positions and scales. In this way

H. Araujo et al. (Eds.): IbPRIA 2009, LNCS 5524, pp. 48–55, 2009.
© Springer-Verlag Berlin Heidelberg 2009

the detection problem is transformed in a classification problem, and standard techniques like Support Vector Machine (SVM) ([6],[5]) and Adaboost ([9],[8]) can be used.

A step ahead in human detection was done with the work of Dalal and Triggs [1]. They used grids of HOGs which are a dense collection of local histograms of gradients. Studying influences of the binning on scale, orientation and position they yield excellent categorization by a linear SVM classifier. Our baseline detector will be based on this technique which has shown bright results.

Another human detector with very good performances is introduced by Tuzel et al [7]. This work boost an ensemble of covariance descriptors that are analysed in a Reinmannian manifold geometry, which actually makes the method quite slow. It is also worth to mention the work of Felzenszwalb et al,[3], where the authors obtain excellent results using the same idea of several years ago [2] of modeling the human body as a deformable tree of parts, but this time using SVMs and HOG features.

The main characteristic common to the previous methods is the fact that they are not real-time. This is due to the high computational time necessary to scan the full image at all the possible scales looking for features that reveal the presence of humans. However, real-time performance is a really important feature for real applications, where in most of the cases the reaction to certain visual stimuli has to be as fast as possible.

Considering that in sliding window approaches the number of positive samples is far less the number of negative ones, the use of a system that can calibrate its computational time based on the difficulty of the samples can highly speed-up the full process. This is applied in the cascade of detectors, where a chain of detectors with increasing accuracy but also higher computational cost is used to discard easy examples.

One of the first works based on cascade of classifiers that was able to run in real-time has been presented in [4]. The authors performed human detection based on the matching of a tree of silhouette images leaned from a set of exemplars using Chamfer distance. A more recent approach to real-time human detection was presented by Viola and Jones [8], who built a Adaboost cascade of Haar-like features for pedestrian detection. However, Haar-like features alone provide too poor accuracy for human detection, so they also included temporal information in the feature descriptors.

An attempt to speed-up the Dalal and Triggs method comes from Zhu et al. [11], where they adapted the integral image to compute HOG features and used it in an Adaboost cascade. The method has similar detection performances of the original, but the use of Adaboost for features selections permits real-time detection. However, the features selection process makes the training time much longer, which is an important issue when many parameters need to be optimized in the training phase.

A work similar to our has been recently presented by Zhang [10], who also presented a cascade of detectors with different feature resolution. However, in our formulation, the different way we use the multiresolution allows to further reduce the computational costs and at the same time to increase the localization accuracy as it will be explained in section 2.

The rest of the paper is divided in the following parts: section 2 is dedicated to the concept of multiresolution Cascade highlighting the advantages that provides. Experiments comparing the performances of the framework with the state of the art are presented in section 3. Finally, section 4 states some concluding remarks.

2 Description of the Method

A typical cascade model is based on Adaboost classifiers, where for each stage of the cascade a classifier with more features is used. In case of using SVM, they are not based on feature selection, thus another element has to be used for implementing the speed-accuracy trade-off. A possible way could be the use of different SVM kernels, starting from the faster linear until the slower Gaussian one. However, as shown in [1], the use of a non linear kernel does not improve very much the results but it makes the computation much slower.

Another possibility would be to select only a subset of the features in the first level, and then add more and more features for each following level, until all the relevant features are considered. This solution has two problems. First, there is not a clear way on how to select the features. Second, selecting sparse features provokes loosing the global and dense representation of the object, which can be useful in many circumstances (i.e. detection of occlusions).

2.1 Multiresolution Cascade

Our method consists on representing the object that we aim to detect using several feature resolutions that represent the stages of the cascade: from few big features which are representing all the object, to many small features, where each one is representing only a small portion of the object.

The fact that no feature selection has been applied in the cascade implies three important consequences: (i) the feature size of every level is known and this is used to decide the sliding window stride: in this way in the first level it is possible to use a high stride of the sliding window which reduces the number of window to scan, while in the last level is used a small sliding window stride which allows higher detection accuracy. (ii) the training time is highly reduced (from days to minutes) because the time expensive process of Adaboost feature selection has been substituted by a faster SVM training optimization; (iii) the features always keep a lattice distribution which can be used for additional reasoning, like observing the feature response distribution looking for possible partial occlusions or also neighbourhood coherence.

2.2 HOG Features Pyramid

Differently than in [10], where each feature resolution level needs to be calculated as a supplementary step, we use the same features for both scale-search and multiresolution cascade. In fact, constraining the resolution levels and the sliding windows scale-search to the same scaling stride or even a multiple makes possible to adopt the same features for both processes. This means a high saving of computational time considering that feature computation in this kind of system is one of the most time-expensive tasks.

In practice, to speed up the detection process, the features computation is pre-calculated for each scale, resulting on a pyramid of features, as represented in Fig. 1. The pyramid is used for scanning the image at different scale space, as well as for the different resolutions of the cascade process. If we move through the levels keeping the same number of features per detection window, we are move over the scale-space, while if we move through the pyramid varying the number of feature per detection window, we are moving over the multiresolution cascade.

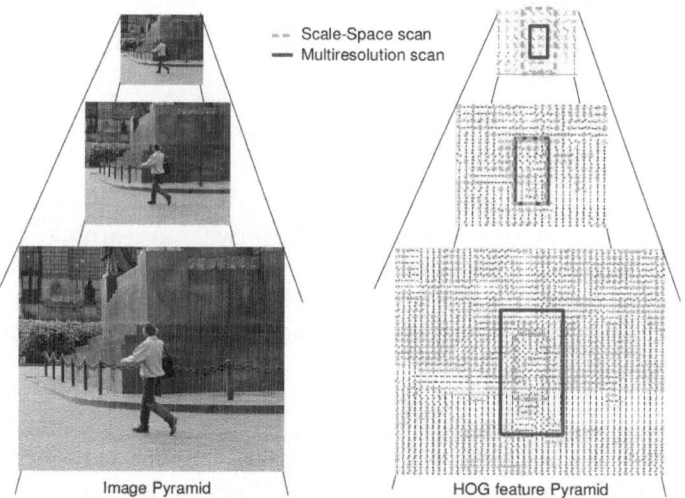

Fig. 1. HOG feature pyramid. It is used for both Scale-space search (green dashed detection window) and Multiresolution Cascade (red continuous detection window).

The basic block of the pyramid is the HOG feature which has reveled very effective for object class detection tasks (see [1],[3]). The use of orientation histograms over image gradients allows capturing local contour information, that is the most characteristic information of a local shape. Translations and rotations do not influence HOGs as long as they are smaller than the local spatial and orientation bin size respectively. Finally, local contrast normalization contributes another key component: affine illumination invariance that allows detection in a high range of illumination conditions.

To make the HOG computation faster, we decide to use an approach similar to [11] in which the Gaussian smoothing is dropped. However, differently than there, we already know the position and size of the features that is necessary to compute. So, instead of using the integral histogram which needs a time of $2N$ (where N is the number of pixels of the image) memory access per bin for the integral propagation, and 4 memory access per bin for the feature computation, we used a direct feature computation which takes a similar time for the pre-computation, but it needs only 1 memory access per bin for the use.

Table 1. Detection algorithm using the Multiresolution Cascade. Up-sample operation is used for propagating the detections to the next resolution level and is defined in Equation 1.

> **Given** image I, resolution levels R, SVM classifier g_r, threshold t_r at resolution r
> Calculate the HOG pyramid H of I as explained in section 2.2
> **for each** scale s
>   resolution $r \leftarrow 1$
> $W_s \leftarrow$ valid detection windows of $H(s)$
>   **while** $r < R$ **and** $W_s \neq \emptyset$
> $W_s \leftarrow g_r(W_s) > t_r$
> $W_s \leftarrow upsample(W_s)$ (see Equ. 1)
> $r \leftarrow r + 1$
> W_s are the final detection windows per scale s

2.3   Training and Detection

The training of the multiresolution cascade consists on learning separately the linear SVM detectors. Differently than [10], where each detector receives as negative training data the false positives of the previous level, in our case each detector is trained totally independently from the previous one, making possible an on-line tuning of the detector's thresholds t_r (where r is the stage of the cascade). The training strategy is similar to [3]. Each detector is initially trained using cropped and resized images of humans as positive examples and randomly cropped and resized image regions not containing humans as negative examples. After that, the learned detector is used to select more representative negative examples (hard examples), which can help to improve the detection performances. The training process is repeated until no further improvements are obtained.

The algorithm for the detection search using the multiresolution is shown in Table 1. For each scale s all the possible window positions W_s at the lowest resolution are scanned to evaluate the SVM classification raw response $g_r(W_s)$. Those windows that have a raw value higher than the threshold t_r will be propagated to the $r + 1$ level of the cascade. This is done using the function $upsample(W_s)$ defined as:

$$upsample(W_s)[2h, 2k] = W_s[h, k]$$
$$upsample(W_s)[2h + 1, 2k] = W_s[h, k] \qquad (1)$$
$$upsample(W_s)[2h, 2k + 1] = W_s[h, k]$$

which is a nearest neighbour up-sampling by a factor two of the set of valid windows so that it is possible to map them in the next feature resolution.

3   Experimental Results

To be able to compare our results, the experiments have been tested on the INRIA human database with the same configuration proposed in [1]. The images are separated into training and test images. Training images have been used for training the linear SVM detector and for the selection of the hard examples, while test images have been used for evaluate the detection performances.

Fig. 2 summarizes the characteristics of the three detectors used in the multiresolution cascade. Each column represents a detector, from left to right, from the coarser to the finer one. The first row shows an example image of the cascade process, where in each stage the valid windows are drawn with different colors until reaching the final detection. The second row shows the HOG feature weight distribution learned in the SVM training process for each detector level. Finally, the detection performances are represented in the third column using the ROC curve which represents the number of false positives per window in the x axis and the percentage of correct detections in the y axis.

Experiments of different configurations of the cascade of detectors are shown in Table 2. The first row in the table represents the use of the higher resolution detector without any cascade, which corresponds to the original human detector presented in [1]. The detection rate of this detector is slightly lower than the original one because in our implementation we did not use Gaussian smoothing in the features computation, which makes the features slightly less discriminative, but faster to compute. This detector is taken as reference to verify the increment of speed that one can get using exactly the same configuration but substituting the single detector with the multiresolution cascade. It is important to remark that the gain in the scanning time presented in the last column of the Table 2 is only taking into account the gain in speed due to the cascade model and not the one due to the faster feature computation neither the fact that we do not need any further feature computation for the multiresolution level (differently than [10]).

Table 2. Multiresolution Configurations. The examples show three different trade-off between speed and detection performances: *Config. 1* is the detector without using the cascade, *Config. 2* is using the cascade with high detection rates and *Config. 3* is using the cascade with lower detection rates. *Det.* is the percentage of detection rate of each detector at 10^{-4} false positive per window; *Rej.* is the rejection rate; *Cost* is the percentage of time used for each detector; *T./W.* is the average time in μs necessary to scan a window; *Gain* is the estimated gain in speed to scan an entire window considering that the configuration 1 is taken as reference.

Config.	Level 1			Level 2			Level 3			Cascade		
	Det.	Rej.	Cost	Det.	Rej.	Cost	Det.	Rej.	Cost	Det.	T./W.	Gain
1	-	-	-	-	-	-	83	99.99	100	83	135	1
2	99.5	56	2.3	99.5	88	28.8	85	99.95	68.9	82	21.2	13.1
3	95	64	4.2	95	93	40	90	99.9	55.8	80	6.87	23.4

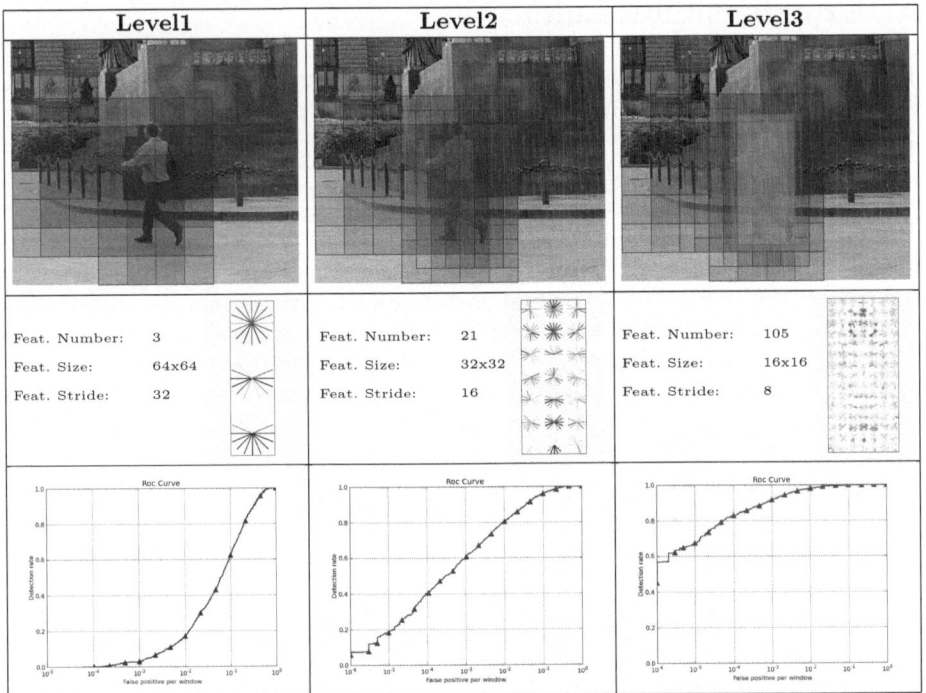

Level1	Level2	Level3
Feat. Number: 3	Feat. Number: 21	Feat. Number: 105
Feat. Size: 64x64	Feat. Size: 32x32	Feat. Size: 16x16
Feat. Stride: 32	Feat. Stride: 16	Feat. Stride: 8

Fig. 2. The three detectors composing the multiresolution cascade (better to see with colors). Each column is representing a level of the multiresolution cascade: from left to right from the coarser to the finer resolution. The first row shows an example image, where the detection windows that passed the detector threshold are drawn; the second row represents the feature distribution of the detector and the weight that every gradient orientation has received from the linear SVM training; the third row shows the ROC curve of the corresponding detector.

The second and Third row of Table 2 show two configurations of the multiresolution cascade with different thresholds t_r values. *Config. 2* represents the conservative case, where the detectors thresholds are very loose, which corresponds to make the detectors less selective and it allows most of the the positive cases to reach the final detector. This cascade configuration obtains a gain in speed of the scanning process of around 13 times the original one with a reduced detection rate of around 1% at 10^{-4} false positives per window. In the third row (*Config. 3*) of the table, the detectors are tuned with a more restrictive threshold which allows to reach an increase of gain of more than 23 times with a reduction of the detection rate of around 3% at 10^{-4} false positives per window.

Table 2 (*Cost* column) also shows that differently than in [10], the computational load of the three detectors is not uniformly distributed. This is due to the constrain that we imposed in the use of the multiresolution; fixing the resolution factor to two (every feature level has a resolution size that is the double of the previous one) does not allow to choose the computational load of each detector, but it allows to use a varying spatial stride of the detection window, which is high for coarse feature resolution permitting high speed search, and it is low for fine feature resolution allowing higher localization.

4   Conclusions

The present work shows that it is possible to build a high-speed and robust human detector using a multiresolution cascade. To reach this objective we defined a new model of cascade of detectors where the trade-off between speed and accuracy is achieved varying the distribution of the extracted features, from few and big features to many and small. Experimental results show that our method increments the speed of the detection search of around 10-20 times depending on the tuning of the detectors' thresholds, maintaining at the same time comparable detection rates.

Acknowledgements

This work is supported by EC grants IST-027110 for the HERMES project and IST-045547 for the VIDI-video project, and by the Spanish MEC under projects TIN2006-14606 and CONSOLIDER-INGENIO 2010 MIPRCV CSD2007-00018.

References

1. Dalal, N., Triggs, B.: Histograms of oriented gradients for human detection, Washington, DC, USA, June 2005, vol. 1, pp. 886–893 (2005)
2. Felzenszwalb, P., Huttenlocher, D.: Efficient matching of pictorial structures. In: CVPR, Hilton Head Island, SC, USA, pp. 66–73 (June 2000)
3. Felzenszwalb, P., Mcallester, D., Ramanan, D.: A discriminatively trained, multi-scale, deformable part model. In: CVPR, Anchorage, Alaska (June 2008)
4. Gavrila, D., Philomin, V.: Real-time object detection for smart vehicles. In: CVPR, Ft. Collins, CO, USA, June 1999, pp. 87–93 (1999)
5. Mohan, A., Papageorgiou, C., Poggio, T.: Example-based object detection in images by components. PAMI 4, 349–361 (2001)
6. Papageorgiou, C., Poggio, T.: A trainable system for object detection. IJCV 38(1), 15–33 (2000)
7. Tuzel, O., Porikli, F., Meer, P.: Human detection via classification on riemannian manifolds. In: CVPR, Minneapolis, Minnesota, June 2007, vol. 1 (2007)
8. Viola, P., Jones, M.J., Snow, D.: Detecting pedestrians using patterns of motion and appearance. IJCV 63(2), 153–161 (2005)
9. Wu, B., Nevatia, R.: Detection of multiple, partially occluded humans in a single image by bayesian combination of edgelet part detectors. In: ICCV, Beijing, China, October 2005, vol. 1, pp. 90–97 (2005)
10. Zhang, W., Zelinsky, G., Samaras, D.: Real-time accurate object detection using multiple resolutions, Rio de Janeiro, Brazil (October 2007)
11. Zhu, Q., Yeh, M.C., Cheng, K.T., Avidan, S.: Fast human detection using a cascade of histograms of oriented gradients. In: CVPR, Washington, DC, USA, June 2006, pp. 1491–1498 (2006)

Face-to-Face Social Activity Detection Using Data Collected with a Wearable Device

Pierluigi Casale[1,2], Oriol Pujol[1,2], and Petia Radeva[1,2]

[1] Computer Vision Center, Campus UAB, Edifici O, Bellaterra, Barcelona, Spain
[2] Dep. of Applied Mathematics and Analysis, University of Barcelona, Spain
pierluigi@cvc.uab.es
http://www.cvc.uab.es, http://www.maia.ub.es

Abstract. In this work the feasibility of building a socially aware badge that learns from user activities is explored. A wearable multisensor device has been prototyped for collecting data about user movements and photos of the environment where the user acts. Using motion data, *speaking* and other activities have been classified. Images have been analysed in order to complement motion data and help for the detection of social behaviours. A face detector and an activity classifier are both used for detecting if users have a social activity in the time they worn the device. Good results encourage the improvement of the system at both hardware and software level.

Keywords: Socially-Aware Sensors, Wearable Devices, Activity Classification, Social Activity Detection.

1 Introduction

Computation is packaged in a variety of devices. Nowadays, personal organizers and mobile phones are really networked computers. Interconnected computing devices using various sensing technologies, from simple motion sensors to electronic tags to videocameras are invading our personal and social activities and environments. This kind of technologies is moving the site and style of human-computer interaction from desktop environments into the larger real world where we live and act. Nevertheless, they are not yet able to understand social signaling and social context.

At MIT Media Labs, three socially aware communications systems incorporating social signaling measurements have been developed (Pentland, 2005 [2]). The *Uberbadge* is a badge-like platform, *GroupMedia* is based on the Sharp Zaurus PDA and *Serendipity* is based on the Nokia 6600 mobile telephone. In each system the basic element of social context is the identity of people in the users immediate presence. The systems use several sensors, including Bluetooth-based proximity detection, infrared or radio-frequency tags, and vocal analysis. At Microsoft Research, Hodges *et al.*, 2006 [3] presented a sensor augmented wearable stills camera, the *SenseCam*, designed to capture a digital record of

H. Araujo et al. (Eds.): IbPRIA 2009, LNCS 5524, pp. 56–63, 2009.

the wearers day, by recording a series of images and capturing a log of sensor data.

In this work, we explore the feasibility of building a socially aware device that learns from user's activities. The novelty of the work consists in presenting a device able to acquire multi-modal data, recognize several activities and if a social interaction occurs. The wearable multisensor device, *TheBadge*, has been prototyped to collect data for detecting face-to-face social activities of people wearing it. Using data collected by a LIS3LV02DQ accelerometer, *speaking* and others coarse activities as "walking", "climbing stairs" or "moving" have been classified. In addition, a face detector working on the photos automatically taken by a C628 Camera Module, is used in combination with the activity classifier for helping the detection of a social activity.

This document is organized as follows. In Section 2, a description of TheBadge at hardware level is given. In Section 3, the classification techniques, the overall classification system architecture and the single components of the system are explained. Section 4 describes which features have been used for classifying data and Section 5 report the results of the experiments we perform. Conclusions and improvements are discussed in Section 6.

2   TheBadge

TheBadge prototype consists of a PIC16F680 managing a LIS3LV02DQ triaxial accelerometer and a C628 Enhanced JPEG Camera Module. The device can be worn by a lanyard around the neck as shown in Figure 1.a. The block diagram of TheBadge is shown in Figure 1.b. The digital camera takes photos automatically, without user intervention, whilst the device is being worn. In addition, the tri-axial accelerometer estimates the acceleration of the user movements along the x, y, z axes. Photos and acceleration values are stored in a Secure Digital (SD) Card for offline processing. Communication with the camera via UART protocol has been programmed directly in PIC Assembler in order to properly manage the baudrate and overcome the differences between the clock of the microcontroller and the clock of the camera. Communication with accelerometer and SDcard via SPI bus has been written in C. Every 100 ms, the values of the acceleration on the x, y, z axis are read and stored in a buffer in the RAM. At most 240

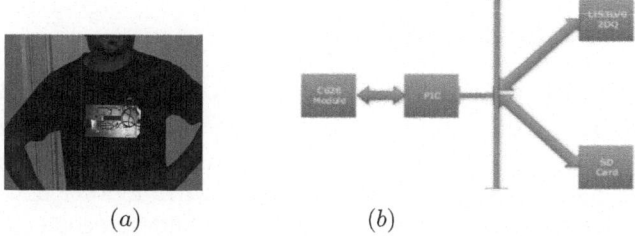

(a) (b)

Fig. 1. a) TheBadge worn by an Experimenter; b) Block Diagram of TheBadge

bytes of data can be stored in the PIC RAM, that means 4 seconds of motion data. When the buffer is full, the command for taking a photograph is sent to the camera and a routine for managing datatransfer runs. With taking a photo, motion data are complemented with a visual information of the environment.

3   Features Extraction

In order to classify data related to user's activity, a sliding windows technique with 50% of ovelap has been used, as described in Dietterich, 2002 [4]. Overlapping demostrated success in the classification of accelerometer data (Bao and Intille, 2004 [7]). Features for activity classification have been computed on a motion data frame composed by 40 acceleration samples of each of x, y, and z axes, with 20 samples overlapping between consecutive windows. Each window represents 4 seconds of motion data. Features have been extracted using wavelet analysis. Wavelets have advantages over traditional windowed Fourier transforms in analyzing physical situations where the signal contains discontinuities and sharp spikes. From wavelet decomposition using Haar bases, features have been computed as the subband energy of the wavelet coefficients, for data in each axes of the accelerometer. In addition, standard deviation and covariance between all pairwise combinations of the three axes have been computed. Features measuring the degree of coupling between axes can help to discriminate between activities like walking and climbing stairs, having same energy but different behaviours in the axes.

Gabor filters based features have been used for detecting faces. Gabor filters have been considered as a very useful tool in computer vision and image analysis due to its optimal localization properties in both spatial analysis and frequency domain. The Gabor filter banks, whose kernels are similar to the 2D receptive fields of the mammalian cortical simple cells, exhibit desirable characteristics of spatial locality and orientation selectivity. Gabor filter based features have been used for face recognition on different illumination variations, facial expression classication etc. and reported to achieve great successes. For the face detector, Gabor filters with seven orientations on three scales have been used, obtaining 21 filters. The face image is convolved with each filter. Each filtered image is subdivided in 4x4 no-overlapped regions and the integral image of every region is computed obtaining a 336 dimensional feature vector.

4   The Classification System

Data collected with TheBadge have been used for learning user's social activity. A face-to-face social activity might not be evaluated taking into account only one single source of data. For istance, a person speaking at phone could exhibit the same motion patterns than a person speaking with another one. On the other side, a face detector should detect a face of unknown people staying in front of us who is not speaking with us. The block diagram of the software system developped is shown in Figure 2.

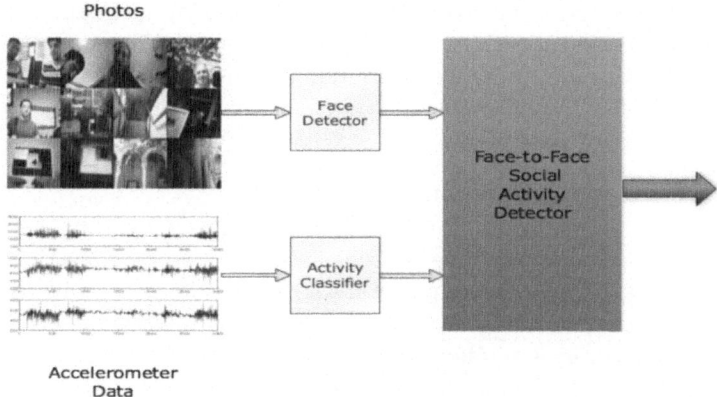

Fig. 2. System Architecture

The overall system has been built as a stacked architecture, as proposed by Wolpert,1992 [5]. The activity classifier and the face detector are the Level-0 classifiers. The activity classifier uses motion data to classify user's activities. The face detector detects if people are present in the photos. The output of both classifiers, with in addition position and distance of faces in consecutive images, is given as input of the Level-1 classifier, that perform the final prediction about the social activity. In next subsections, every block of the classification system is described in detail.

Activity Classifier: A multiclass GentleBoost classifier has been used for activity classification. GentleBoost performs better than AdaBoost on the noisy data collected with accelerometer. The multiclass extension of GentleBoost has been performed via ECOC technique as proposed by Allwein *et al.*, 2001 [6]. Activity with strong movements on two or three axis, such as working at computer or moving on chair, have been taken into account together and labeled as a "Moving" activity. On the other side, activities involving slow movements on two axis have been labeled as a "Stopped" activity. Standing still or waiting for the elevator are examples of activities belonging to this class. A social activity has been labeled into a "Speaking" class. It has been choosen to keep togheter climbing up or down stairs activities in a general "Climbing Stairs" class . Finally, a "Walking" class has been also taken into account.

Face Detector: Images from the real world have been collected with The-Badge. In order to detect faces in such images, a technique able to overcome problems like strong luminance contrast or images quite moved is needed. A face detector has been trained using an AdaBoost classifier working on Gabor filters based features, as proposed by Huan *et al.*, 2004 ([8]) able to detect faces with different poses and illumination conditions assuring, at the same time, very high detection rates and very low false positive rate. The face detector gives as output a boolean value and the position of the face when a face in found in the image.

Face-to-Face Social Activity Detection: A GentleBoost classifier takes care of the detection of a face-to-face social activity. The detector works on windows of three consecutive outputs of both the activitiy classifier and the face detector. Three outputs has been arbitrarly choosen from taking into account that a face-to-face social activity does not last less than 15 seconds. In addition, when a face in consecutive images is found, the euclidean distance between the position of the face is computed and passed as input to the final classifier.

5   Experiment and Results

TheBadge has been worn by five persons acting in two circumscribed environments. Each person was asked to perform a sequence of activity with, at least, activities like walking, climbing stairs and speaking with a person. Experimenters performed activites in a random order selected by themself. The experiments had a duration of 10/15 minutes. Another person annoting the time sequence of the activity, always accompained who wore TheBadge. At the end of each session, data were downloaded from SD memory and labeled. A total of thirteen data sequences have been collected. Ten of thirteen motion data sequences have

Table 1. 10-fold Cross Validated Confusion Matrix for Activity Classifier

—	Climbing	Speaking	Moving	Stopped	Walking
Climbing	**211**	1	6	5	30
Speaking	1	**287**	13	15	25
Moving	0	14	**506**	90	28
Stopped	14	9	75	**663**	13
Walking	33	19	25	12	**387**

Table 2. Confusion Matrix for Activity Classifier evaluated by 10-fold Cross Validation on the Exploitation Set

—	Climbing	Speaking	Moving	Stopped	Walking
Climbing	**39**	0	0	0	21
Speaking	0	**98**	2	4	2
Moving	0	0	**13**	13	6
Stopped	0	0	0	**158**	5
Walking	5	4	8	2	**276**

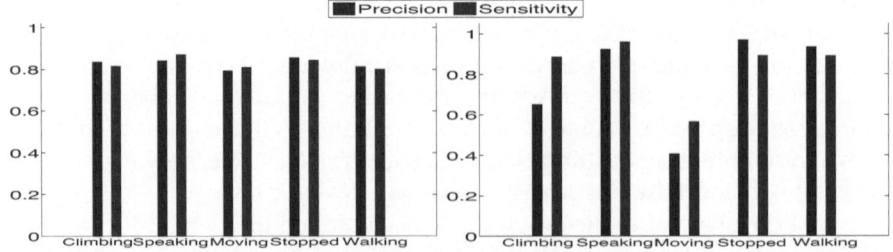

Fig. 3. Precision and Sensitivity for Activity Classifier evaluated on the Training Set, on the right, and on the Exploitation Set, on the left

Table 3. Performaces of Face Detector

Confusion Matrix			Performance Metrics		
—	Face	No Face	—	Precision	Sensitivity
Face	**289**	7	Face	0.9763	0.9829
No Face	5	**474**	No Face	0.9895	0.9854

Table 4. Performaces of Social Activity Classifier

Confusion Matrix			Performance Metrics		
—	Interaction	No Interaction	—	Precision	Sensitivity
Interaction	**197**	57	Interaction	0.6502	0.8239
No Interaction	67	**976**	No Interaction	0.9151	0.9471

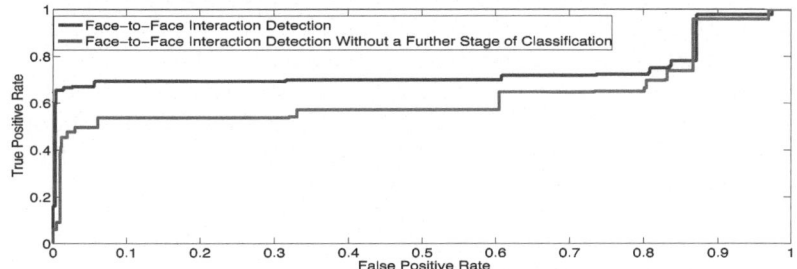

Fig. 4. Roc Curve of Face-to-Face Social Activity Classifier, in blue, and Roc Curve obtained taking the logic "and" of the outputs of the Level-0 classifiers without a further stage of classification, in red

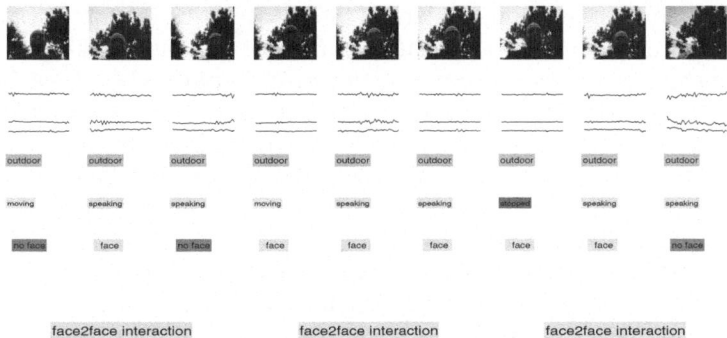

Fig. 5. Example of Classification Results on Data Collected with TheBadge

been used for training the activity classifier, three sequences have been used for exploitation. Table 1 reports the confusion matrix obtained by 10-fold cross validation on the training set. Table 2 reports the confusion matrix obtained by 10-fold cross-validation on the exploitation set. Performance metrics evaluated on both training set and exploitation set are reported in Figure 3. The face detector has been trained on a set of 294 faces taken from the Yale Face Database ([9]) and 481 no face images. Confusion matrix obtained by 10-fold cross validation on the training set and performance metrics are reported in Table 3. The detector has a false positive rate of 0.01%. The detector has been tested on 100 images taken with TheBadge, 50% containing faces and 50% not containing faces. True positive detections occur in 32 images. False negatives occur in 16 images. In only four images, false positives have been detected.

The Face-to-Face Social Activity Classifier has been trained using the entire dataset and validated by 10-fold cross validation. Confusion matrix and performances of the detector are shown in Table 4. The detector has a classification rate of 0.928. Figure 4 shows the ROC curve of the face-to-face social activity detector, in blue. The area under ROC curve is 0.7398. In the same figure, it has been shown that the detection of a Face-to-Face Social activity using only the logic "and" between the outputs of the Level-0 classifiers, without a further stage of calssificaton, is worst than using a subsequent stage of classification. In this case, the area under the red ROC curve equals to 0.6309.

In Figure 5, a sequence of classified data is shown. The activity classifier correctly classifies six of nine motion data frame. The interaction detector operating on windows, despite some confusion of the base classifiers, correctly detects that an interaction is occurring.

6   Conclusions and Future Works

In this work, the feasibility of building a socially-aware wearable device has been evaluated. Results show that a system being aware of a user's social activity is feasible using a camera and an accelerometer. Data collection from two sensors has been usefull for avoiding the lack of information due to store data after every acquisition frame. From motion data, coarse activities as speaking, walking and climbing stairs have been successfully detected. In particular, it has been shown that a speaking activity can be recognized and separated from general moving patterns using only data related to the user's motion. Analyzing the images, the presence of a person in front of the user confirms that user had a social activity in that time. Furthermore, using a second level of classification enanches the predition of a social activity.

Many improvements have to be taken into account in our system. At hardware level, passing from the prototyped version to a more robust system is necessary for optimizing power consumption and operating time with the aim to perform experiments on long time and to use TheBadge in many real life situations. In addition, social activities involve comunication. For that reason, adding audio capabilities able to get data about user's conversations must be considered a necessary and immediate evolution of TheBadge. At software level, using different sequential machine learning techniques will improve the detection of activities based on the inherently sequential motion data. Finally, some non technichal issues related to privacy and safenees of data collected have to be taken into account. In our experiments, all the people wearing TheBadge give their consent for using data collected. The aim of future works will be to develop a system able to process data in real-time without the need to store personal data. In this way, the system will not invade privacy of people wearing TheBadge.

Acknowledgments. This work is partially supported by a research grant from projects TIN2006-15308-C02, FIS-PI061290 and CONSOLIDER- INGENIO 2010 (CSD2007-00018), MI 1509/2005.

References

1. Moran, T.P., Dourish, P.: Introduction to Special Issue on Context-Aware Computing. Human-Computer Interaction (HCI) 16(2-3), 87–96 (2001)
2. Pentland, A.: Socially Aware Media. In: MULTIMEDIA 2005: Proceedings of the 13th annual ACM international conference on Multimedia, vol. 1, pp. 690–695 (2005)
3. Hodges, S., Williams, L., Berry, E., Izadi, S., Srinivasan, J., Butler, A., Smyth, G., Kapur, N., Wood, K.: SenseCam: A Retrospective Memory Aid. In: Dourish, P., Friday, A. (eds.) UbiComp 2006. LNCS, vol. 4206, pp. 177–193. Springer, Heidelberg (2006)
4. Dietterich, T.G.: Machine Learning for Sequential Data: A Review. In: Caelli, T.M., Amin, A., Duin, R.P.W., Kamel, M.S., de Ridder, D. (eds.) SPR 2002 and SSPR 2002. LNCS, vol. 2396, pp. 15–30. Springer, Heidelberg (2002)
5. Wolpert, D.H.: Stacked generalization. Neural Netw. 5(2), 241–259 (1992)
6. Allwein, E.L., Schapire, R.E., Singer, Y.: Reducing multiclass to binary: a unifying approach for margin classifiers. JMLR 1, 113–141 (2001)
7. Bao, L., Intille, S.S.: Activity recognition from user-annotated acceleration data. In: Proc. Pervasive, Vienna, Austria, vol. 1, pp. 1–17 (2004)
8. Huang, L., Shimizu, A., Kobatake, H.: Classification-based face detection using Gabor filter features. Automatic Face and Gesture Recognition 21(9), 849–870 (2004)
9. Georghiades, A.S., Belhumeur, P.N., Kriegman, D.J.: From Few to Many: Illumination Cone Models for Face Recognition under Variable Lighting and Pose. IEEE Trans. Pattern Anal. Mach. Intell. 23(6), 643–660 (2001)

Estimating Vehicle Velocity Using Image Profiles on Rectified Images

Cristina Maduro, Katherine Batista, and Jorge Batista

ISR-Institute of Systems and Robotics, Department of Electrical Engineering,
FCTUC, University of Coimbra, Coimbra, Portugal
{cristina.maduro,katbatista}@gmail.com, batista@isr.com
http://www.isr.uc.pt

Abstract. In this paper a technique is presented to estimate vehicle velocity using intensity profiles. This technique does not require background estimation or even the identification and tracking of individual vehicles. On the other hand, it requires the estimation of virtual images that represent a bird eye view of the scenario. This is achieved estimating an homography assuming that each lane on the image is parallel on the ground plane. To each rectified lane, an intensity profile is computed along the traffic flow direction for each frame, obtaining an image that represents the displacement as a time function. The main idea is to search for the best matching profile for different times and spaces on each lane, consequently obtaining the velocity profile.

Keywords: Intensity Profile, image rectification, lane detection and vehicle velocity estimation.

1 Introduction

Technological advances in scientific areas, such as computer vision, have lead to the development of new algorithms and methods that automatically estimate highway traffic parameters such as vehicle velocity. However, this task is rather complex due to the loss of some geometric properties, such as parallelism between lines and length ratios, that occur in the image formation process. To restore these properties, the captured images are rectified in order to obtain a top view of the highway. By doing this, the vehicle's movement throughout the image becomes linear and its velocity is consequently simpler to estimate. This rectification is achieved using an homographic matrix, which could be acquired by using the intrinsic and extrinsic camera parameters. Unfortunately, the surveillance cameras are uncalibrated and therefore, these parameters are unknown. Consequently, several methods have been developed in order to automatically restore geometric properties to objects moving on the image plane. Namely, D. Dailey [1] presents a method that estimates the location of one vanishing point in order to calibrate the surveillance camera. However, this method presupposes the knowledge of one of the angles of orientation of the surveillance camera. estimated. In [4] we successfully employed a method based in [7], presented by

H. Araujo et al. (Eds.): IbPRIA 2009, LNCS 5524, pp. 64–71, 2009.

D. Liebowitz and A. Zisserman, to rectify images. This technique requires the estimation of two vanishing points and the prior knowledge of two angles on the ground plane and can only be applied to highways that are fairly straight near the surveillance camera.

In this paper we propose a method based on [2] that does not have this restriction, considering only that the road width is constant on the ground plane. To do so, the number of lanes and polynomial functions that describe the central regions of these lanes are automatically estimated using a method proposed in [8]. There is a wide range of methods to estimate traffic speed, where great part of these depend on vehicle tracking. Most methods, such as [1], [3], [4] and [5], estimate the average lane velocity by tracking all detected vehicles or their features, throughout the image sequence, and establishing the distance traveled between frames. The main problems of these methods are related to occlusion situations and when the vehicles move a large distance between frames, which is the case at low frame rate. Also, if the image has poor resolution the vehicles may not be detected and tracking fails, leading to an imprecise velocity estimation. The algorithm presented here is based in [6] and estimates each lane's average velocity using an intensity profile. Basically, this method assumes that one intensity profile at a given x, will be repeated in a consecutive time interval at a different displacement, allowing the estimation of velocity without relying on the accuracy of segmentation and tracking systems.

2 Image Rectification

The problem of vehicle velocity estimation can be simplified by linearizing the vehicle's movement throughout the image. To do so, a camera calibration process could be employed using a set of points on the image and their correspondents on the ground plane. However, these points are unknown which complicates the estimation of the required homographic matrix. Nevertheless, this matrix can be obtained considering that the road has a constant width and that it is viewed through a pinhole camera that is oriented at a tilt angle θ and at a very small or no pan angle. This reduces the problem to one unknown (θ) by approximating the image to ground plane transformation to a rotation according to the image X-axis. For further information see [2]. In order to fit the lane centers by a polynomial function we must guarantee that for each x coordinate value, there is only and only one correspondent y coordinate. To assure this, the image is rotated $-90°$ according to its Y-axis. The image to ground plane transformation can then be approximated to a rotation (R) according to the Y-axis. Figure 1 represents a top view of the road, where it is visible that the lane boundaries are parallel and hence, the road width (K) is constant. From this figure we can also infer the following relation, between the two represented points P_l and P_r:

$$K = \frac{D}{\cos \psi} \tag{1}$$

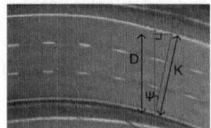

Fig. 1. Top view of the road morphology

where D is the Y-axis component of the distance between those points and ψ the angle on the ground plane. Therefore, D can be defined as $D = y_l'' - y_r''$, where y_l'' and y_r'' are the Y components of P_l and P_r, that represent the points resultant from applying the ideal projective transformation to the correspondent points on the image plane ((x_l, y_l) and (x_r, y_r)). To obtain the ground plane transformation's unknown, θ, it is necessary to consider the relation between the ground plane points and some constraints mapped into the image plane, which can be given by:

$$\frac{y_l}{-x_l \sin\theta + \cos\theta} - \frac{y_r}{-x_r \sin\theta + \cos\theta} = K \cos\psi \qquad (2)$$

Seeing as ψ or $|x_l - x_r|$ are small when compared with x_l or x_r, they can be approximated by $(x_l + x_r)/2$. In spite the fact that the value of ψ is unknown on the ground plane, it can be approximated by its correspondent on the image plane (ψ_{img}). Using these approximations and equation 2 we can obtain the following expression:

$$\frac{y_l - y_r}{-0.5(x_l + x_r)\sin\theta + \cos\theta} = K \cos\psi_{img}. \qquad (3)$$

Since the values of K and θ are unknown, at least two pairs of points on the image plane are required in order to solve this equation system. Nonetheless, a better estimation is achieved applying the least-squares method to more sets of points. Hence, an automatic method is used to obtain these sets of points. This is achieved by estimating polynomial functions that describe lane centers.

To do so, a method in [8] is used. This method is more robust to light changes or noisy scenarios seeing as it uses a higher amount of information and is able to discard erroneous data. It also doesn't require the prior knowledge of the lane's geometry. This method uses information from a Kalman based vehicle tracking system to estimate a polynomial function that describes the vehicle's trajectory throughout the image plane. More precisely, once known a vehicle's position, (x, y), on the image plane for each instance, it is possible to use this information to estimate a polynomial function using the least-squares method. This information is then used in a modified K-means clustering algorithm, [8], which automatically estimates the number of lanes (K) and also the polynomial coefficients that describe the lane centers. Seeing as information provided from the tracking system can be noisy, a RANSAC [9] based algorithm is used in the estimation of the required polynomial coefficients. Figure 2 shows the evolution of this process, since the initial identification of the number of lanes (left image),

Fig. 2. Evolution of the lane detection algorithm

following the association and clustering of trajectories to a given initial estimation (middle image), until the final estimated polynomial functions that describe each lane (rightmost image). For more information regarding this method see [8]. These polynomial function can then, be used in the proposed rectification process.

Algorithm 1: θ angle estimation algorithm.

Read the cluster points
for $n = 1$ *to* $NUM\_ITERATIONS$ **do**

1. Estimate the polynomial functions (p_l, p_m and p_r) that fit those cluster points;
2. **for** *Point* $(x_{m,i}, y_{m,i}) = (x_{m,1}, y_{m,1})$ *to* $(x_{m,f}, y_{m,f})$, $\in p_m$ **do**
   (a) Compute the line t_i, which is orthogonal to p_m and passes through $(x_{m,i}, y_{m,i})$;
   (b) Determine the points $(x_{l,i}, y_{l,i})$ and $(x_{r,i}, y_{r,i})$ resultant of the intersection of t_i with the polynomials p_l and p_r;
3. Define the following system:

$$\begin{pmatrix} y_{l,1} - y_{r,1} \\ y_{l,2} - y_{r,2} \\ \vdots \\ y_{l,f} - y_{r,f} \end{pmatrix} = \begin{pmatrix} -0.5(x_{l,1} + x_{r,1})\cos\psi_{img_1}\ \cos\psi_{img_1} \\ -0.5(x_{l,2} + x_{r,2})\cos\psi_{img_2}\ \cos\psi_{img_2} \\ \vdots \qquad \vdots \\ -0.5(x_{l,f} + x_{r,f})\cos\psi_{img_f}\ \cos\psi_{img_f} \end{pmatrix} \begin{pmatrix} K\sin\theta_n \\ K\cos\theta_n \end{pmatrix} \quad (4)$$

4. Compute the θ_n angle: $\theta_n = \arctan\left(\frac{K\sin\theta_n}{K\cos\theta_n}\right)$
5. Correct θ_{n+1}: $\theta_{n+1} = \theta_n + \alpha\delta\theta_{n+1}$
6. Determine the transformation matrix R.
7. Apply this transformation to the initial points of the clusters.

Apply the transformation matrix to the image.

The unknown parameter θ can then be obtained once these polynomial functions are known. To do so, algorithm 1 can be used. The value of θ is an approximation of the real value, since ψ is an approximated value. A more precise estimation can be acquired using this process iteratively. In each iteration the value of θ is estimated using the equation present in algorithm 1, where $\delta\theta_{n+1}$ is the estimated value of θ for the $n+1$ iteration and α is a damp factor to prevent overcorrection/oscillations in the final iterations ($\theta_0 = 0$).

This algorithm was applied to the left image of Figure 3 and the resulting image is represented on the right.

 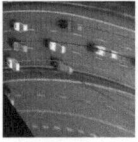

Fig. 3. Example of a captured image and its corresponding rectified image

3   Intensity Profile

Vehicle segmentation is highly dependent on the quality of the images provided by the camera, which in most outdoor surveillance systems have poor resolution. This fact allied to adverse weather conditions may lead to sudden variations of the vehicle's dimension or even to the lack of its identification. Therefore, these factors affect the precision of the estimated velocity by methods that rely on the accuracy of the segmentation system (such as [1], [3], [4] and [5]).

This method overcomes this problem by assuming that one intensity profile at a given x, will be repeated in a consecutive time interval at a different displacement. For each lane the mean intensity of the three rgb channels is computed, acquiring a gray scale image. Afterwards, the mean value of each column (orthogonal direction to the traffic flow) is estimated, obtaining the intensity profile at that instant, see bottom right image of Figure 4. This process is repeated for all frames, and this profile added to the profile image which relates the movement of space as a time function (see Figure 4). On the resulting image (upper right image of Figure 4), the traffic movement throughout the highway can be observed. More precisely, each vehicle can be represented by one or more lines, or two vehicles that circulate very close to each other can be represented by one line. It is also important to state that vehicles that possess similar color to the highway may not be perceptible. Due to the rectification process, the vehicle's shape is distorted which leads to an enlargement of its intensity profile while it moves away from the camera, which can also be seen on the same image of Figure 4.

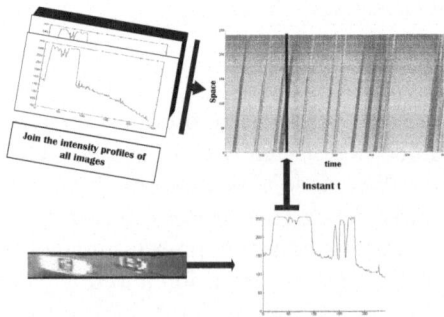

Fig. 4. Representation of the intensity profile as a time function

4   Velocity Estimation

To estimate vehicle velocity at a given time and location (t, x), two windows are chosen with size w_t by w_x, where one is centered at $(t + \tau, x)$ while the other centered at $(t - \tau, x)$.

One window is moved up (window centered at $t + \tau$) and the other moved down (window centered at $t - \tau$), so that the information from these regions can be used to determine the sum of the absolute difference using the following expression:

$$D(d) = \sum_{t=t_0-w_t}^{t_0+w_t} \sum_{x=x_0-w_x}^{x_0+w_x} |I(t + \tau, x + d) - I(t - \tau, x - d)|, \qquad (4)$$

where $I(t, x)$ represents the intensity of the (t, x) pixel on the time-space domain and d represents the distance between each pair of windows that are moved up or down. This distance $(d = 0, \ldots, m)$, covered by the profile corresponds to the minimal norm distance. Seeing as the shifts on the image are discrete, to find the interpolated distance that minimizes this norm (d_0), the norm values are approximated near the minimum by a quadratic function.

The velocity value corresponds to the ratio between the shift distance calculated and the τ value (equation 5), which is equivalent to the slope between the pairs of windows that best match.

$$\hat{v}(t, x) = d_0/\tau. \qquad (5)$$

In order to obtain a better speed estimation, a combination of multiple estimations of $\hat{v}(t, x)$ are taken into account, so that the effect of the outliers are minimized. This procedure is possible, seeing as the vehicle's velocity is assumed to follow a normal distribution with mean v_0 and standard deviation σ_0. For a more detailed description see [6]. This algorithm does two simultaneous shifts of two squared windows (centered shifting), instead of fixing one and moving the other (forward or backward shifting). Given the fact that this process requires the determination of the sum of absolute differences of two windows, it is computationally heavy. Thus, to speed up this process, MMX instructions are used in the implementation of this algorithm. At this point, the estimated velocities are given in pixels per frame. To determine the desired velocities one must calculate a scale factor that relates pixels in the image with the corresponding distances on the ground plane. This scale factor can be obtained by estimating the ratio between the imaged highway stripe period and the genuine stripe period on the ground plane, which is known. For more information on how this scale factor is achieved see [4].

5   Results

This method has been subject to several tests and some of the results are presented in this section. For instance, the following figure presents results achieved throughout different parts of the algorithm. The rectification process was applied to the first image of this figure, resulting in the second image. The third one corresponds to the intensity profile of the leftmost lane of rectified highway, which corresponds to the lane with highest traffic intensity. The last image of this figure presents the estimated velocities for this same lane.

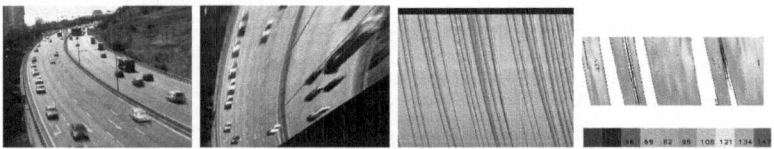

Fig. 5. Stages of this algorithm applied to an image sequence

Table 1. Estimated velocities of several vehicles

	Velocity (km/h)								Average Error (km/h)
Ground Truth	129	120	78	93	49	108	118	126	
Method 1	**133**	**125**	**79**	**96**	**46**	**100**	**115**	**125**	**3.5**
Method 2	127	119	76	96	44	101	114	116	4.25
Method 3	127	137	91	91	49	112	100	120	7.75
Method 4	128	125	79	108	46	103	120	126	3.75

In order to correctly evaluate the velocity estimation's precision, this method was applied to a video sequence with several vehicles that traveled at known velocities measured with a GPS system. Their velocities were also estimated using two different methods, as can be seen in table 1. The results obtained by the first method were achieved using the method presented in this paper. As can be observed, the results achieved by this method are quite precise, seeing as it presents the smallest average error of all the referred methods. The second method was proposed by H. Palaio *et. al* in [5] and the estimation of the vehicles velocity is made using a swarm particle filter. This method produced acceptable results, however the process is computationally heavy. The second method presented in this table is an approach of the method proposed by M. Litzenberger *et. al* [10], being its accuracy mainly dependent on the location and size of the velocity sensors. We propose the last method in [4] and the accuracy of the velocity estimations given by this method are mainly dependent on the performance of the segmentation process.

6   Conclusions

A simple and efficient solution to rectify and estimate vehicle velocity on traffic scenarios is here presented. The rectification method considers that the road has constant width and is flat. This method can be applied to different types of scenarios, such as curved or straight laned highways. Once the image is rectified, the information is condensate on a time-space image. The system estimates the mean velocity speed for all vehicles on each lane, without identifying any particular vehicle. As future work this system needs to improve its performance and to be tested on several scenarios which present different types of conditions. The referred time-space image could also be used to attain an idea of the traffic intensity in the observed scenario. Nonetheless, this method has achieved very accurate results.

References

1. Dailey, D.J., Cathey, F.W.: A Novel Technique to Dynamically Measure Vehicle Speed using Uncalibrated Roadway Cameras. Proceeding IEEE (2005)
2. Magee, D.R.: Tracking multiple vehicles using foreground, background and motion models. Image and Vision Computing 22, 143–155 (2004)
3. Beymer, D., McLauchlan, P., Coifman, B., Malik, J.: A real-time computer vision system for measuring traffic parameters. In: IEEE International Conference on Computer Vision and Pattern Recognition (CVPR 1997), pp. 495–501 (1997)
4. Maduro, C., Batista, K., Peixoto, P., Batista, J.: Estimation of vehicle velocity and traffic intensity using rectified images. In: IEEE International Conference on Image Processing (ICIP), p. 777 (2008)
5. Palaio, H., Maduro, C., Batista, K., Batista, J.: Ground plane velocity estimation embedding rectification on a particle filter multi-target tracking. In: IEEE International Conference on Robotics and Automation, ICRA (2009)
6. Cho, Y., Rice, J.: Estimating Velocity Fields on a Freeway from Low Resolution Video. IEEE Transactions on Intelligent Transportation Systems (2005)
7. Liebowitz, D., Zisserman, A.: Metric rectification for perspective images of planes. In: Proceedings of Computer Vision and Pattern Recognition (1998)
8. Melo, D.J., Naftel, A., Bernardino, A., Santos-Vitor, J.: Detection and classification of highway lanes using vehicle motion trajectories. IEEE Transactions on Intelligent Transportation Systems (2006)
9. Fischler, M.A., Bolles, R.C.: Random sample consensus: A paradigm for model fitting with applications to image analysis and automated cartography. Comm. Assoc. Comp. Mach. (1981)
10. Litzenberger, M., Belbachir, A., Donath, N., Gritsch, G., Garn, H., Kohn, B., Posch, C., Schraml, S.: Estimation of vehicle speed based on asynchronous data from a silicon retina optical sensor. In: Proceedings of the 2006 IEEE Intelligent Transportation Systems Conference (2006)

Kernel Based Multi-object Tracking Using Gabor Functions Embedded in a Region Covariance Matrix

Hélio Palaio and Jorge Batista

ISR-Institute of Systems and Robotics
DEEC-FCTUC, University of Coimbra, Portugal

Abstract. This paper presents an approach to label and track multiple objects through both temporally and spatially significant occlusions. The proposed method builds on the idea of object permanence to reason about occlusion. To this end, tracking is performed at both the region level and the object level. At the region level, a kernel based particle filter method is used to search for optimal region tracks. At the object level, each object is located based on adaptive appearance models, spatial distributions and inter-occlusion relationships. Region covariance matrices are used to model objects appearance. We analyzed the advantages of using Gabor functions as features and embedded them in the RCMs to get a more accurate descriptor. The proposed architecture is capable of tracking multiple objects even in the presence of periods of full occlusions.

1 Introduction

The task we address in this paper is a dynamic scene analysis from a fixed camera (e.g. Visual Surveillance Systems). The aim is to successfully detect, label and track targets in image sequences, despite the presence of background clutter or occlusions.

To accomplish this goal two major components can be distinguished in the proposed approach: *Target Representation* and *Detection, Filtering* and *Data Association*. *Target Representation* and *Detection* is mostly a bottom-up process which has also to cope with the changes in the appearance of the targets. *Filtering* and *Data Association* is mostly a top-down process dealing with the dynamics and occlusions of the tracked objects.

In what concerns *Target Representation* salience and uniqueness are the most important characteristics. RCM-based algorithms with feature mapping functions have achieved good results in people detection, object tracking, and texture classification [9][13] [12][7]. The RCM, proposed by Tuzel *et al.* [12], is a matrix of covariance of several image statistics computed inside a region defining a target. The RCM is considered as a feature descriptor of the region and classification is conducted based on these RCMs. The RCM is a covariance of simple features including coordinate, color, the first and second-order gradient.

H. Araujo et al. (Eds.): IbPRIA 2009, LNCS 5524, pp. 72–79, 2009.

Though these features are relatively effective for tracking and detecting objects, their discriminating ability is not strong enough for crowded scenes, which is generally a more difficult and demanding task from the classification point of view. To overcame this limitation, we analyzed the advantages of using Gabor functions [6][4] as features and embedded them in the RCMs to get a more accurate descriptor. Gabor features exhibit strong characteristics of spatial locality, scale and orientation selectivity. This enables Gabor features to carry more important information than the first-and-second gradients. By embedding Gabor features in the RCMs, the descriptiveness, as well the discriminating ability of the RCM, has proven to be significantly enhanced.

For the purpose of *Filtering* and *Tracking*, a kernel based approach is proposed for visual tracking in image sequences. A kernel particle filter (KPF) is presented that invokes kernels to form a continuous estimate of the posterior density function [5][1]. KPF estimates the gradient of the kernel density and moves particles toward the modes of the posterior, leading to a more effective allocation of the particles. The gradient estimation and particle allocation is implemented by the mean-shift algorithm.

Our goal was to develop a complete system which gathered the advantages of the tracking based on a kernel approach with those of the regions covariance descriptors, resulting in a very effective system. Using real data from an outdoor scenario, the effectiveness of the proposed approach was evaluated, by comparing the performance of the KPF with respect to the standard PF [11][3] and also with respect to a kernel based tracking. Results showed that KPF performs robust visual tracking with improved sampling efficiency.

2   Region Covariance Descriptor

The RCMs present several advantages as region descriptors, providing a natural way of fusing multiple features. RCMs can be categorized as a matrix-form feature. The RCM is a covariance of simple features including coordinate, color, the first and second order gradient. Let I be a three dimensional color image, and J a $w \times h \times d$ dimensional feature image, extracted from I: $J(x,y) = \Phi(I, x, y)$ where $\Phi(I, x, y) = [x \ y \ I_r \ I_g \ I_b \ I_x \ I_y \ I_{xy}]$ represents the mapping such as intensity, color, gradients, etc. If we define a region R in image J, so that, $R \subset J$ and assuming $\{r_i\}$ be the feature points of R, then this region could be represented by a covariance matrix $\mathbf{C}_R = \frac{1}{S-1} \sum_{i=1}^{S} (r_i - \mu)(r_i - \mu)^T$ where C_R is a $d \times d$ matrix, S the number of points of R and μ the mean of these points.

RCM Gabor Features. In order to improve the discrimination capability of the RC descriptor, Gabor functions are added to the feature space. Spatial frequencies and their orientations are important characteristics of textures in images. Gabor functions act as low-level oriented edge and texture discriminators and are sensitive to different frequencies and scale information [6] [4].

Mathematically, a 2D Gabor function, g, is the product of a 2D Gaussian and a complex exponential function. Assuming that the Gaussian part is symmetric, we can express the resulting isotropic Gabor function as:

$$g_{\theta,\sigma,\gamma}(x,y) = exp\{-\frac{x^2+y^2}{2\sigma^2}\}exp\{\frac{j\pi}{\gamma\sigma}(xsin\theta - ycos\theta)\} \qquad (1)$$

where θ represents the orientation, σ is the standard deviation of the Gaussian representing the scale and $\gamma = \lambda/\sigma$ with λ being the wavelength. The variation of θ changes the sensitivity to edge and texture orientations. The variation of σ will change the "scale" at which we are viewing the world. In order to cover the principal orientations at various scales we define $\Phi_{gabor}(x,y)$ as:

$$\Phi_{gabor}(x,y) = [g_{\theta(0),\sigma(0),\gamma}(x,y),\ g_{\theta(0),\sigma(1),\gamma}(x,y),\ ...\ ,\ g_{\theta(6),\sigma(5),\gamma}(x,y)] \qquad (2)$$

where γ is constant, $\theta(i) = \{0\ \pi/6\ \pi/3\ \pi/2\ -\pi/3\ -\pi/6\}$ and $\sigma = [6\ 8\ 10\ 12\ 14]$. To select the best value for γ a coefficient of impact is tested. This coefficient of impact is computed as $\zeta = -exp(mean\{\rho_d(i)\}/mean\{\rho_e(j)\})$ where ρ_d is the dissimilarity value between two different targets and ρ_e is the dissimilarity value between the same target in different frames. In table 1 the results computed with different γ are shown. If we start with a small value and increase it, we can see that it is possible to improve the impact factor. However, when γ is to high the impact factor begins to deteriorate. From this analysis we can conclude that the best value for γ is $\gamma = 3/4$. Figure 1 shows the real part of the Gabor functions used as features (6 orientations in 5 different scales).

Table 1. Impact Factor for different values of γ

	$\gamma = 1/2$	$\gamma = 3/4$	$\gamma = 3/2$	$\gamma = 5/2$
ζ	0.4426	0.6217	0.5145	0.4942

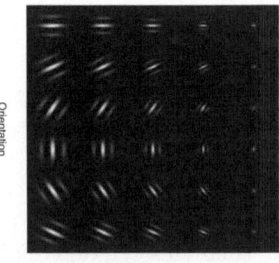
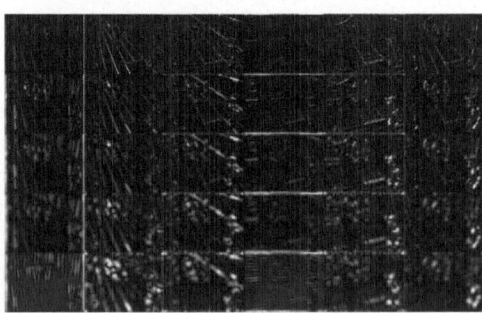

Fig. 1. Left: Real part of Gabor Functions - $\sigma = [6\ 8\ 10\ 12\ 14]$, $\theta = [0\ \pi/6\ \pi/3\ \pi/2\ -\pi/3\ -\pi/6]$; Right: The Gabor function applied to a scene

2.1 Descriptors Dissimilarity and Update

In a tracking process, the objects appearance changes over time. This dynamic behavior requires a robust temporal update of the region covariance descriptors and the definition of a dissimilarity metric for the regions covariances. The important question here is: how to measure the dissimilarity between two regions covariance matrices and how to update the regions covariance matrix in the next time slot. Note that the covariance matrices do not lie on Euclidean space. For example, the space is not closed under multiplication with negative scalars. So it is necessary to get the dissimilarity between two covariances in a different space. To overcome this problem a Riemannian Manifold is used.

Riemannian Manifolds. A Manifold is a topological space which locally can be seen as an Euclidean space. A Riemannian manifold is a manifold with a Riemannian metric. This allows to generalize notions from Euclidean geometry. The Riemannian metric is a continuous collection of inner products at each tangent space at a point of the Manifold. In general Riemannian Manifolds invariance properties lead to a natural choice for the metric. In the present work we use a metric proposed in [10] which is an invariant metric for the tangent space for symmetric positive definite matrices (e.g. covariance matrices) and is given by $< \mathbf{y}, \mathbf{k} >_{\mathbf{X}} = tr(\mathbf{X}^{-\frac{1}{2}}\mathbf{y}\mathbf{X}^{-1}\mathbf{k}\mathbf{X}^{-\frac{1}{2}})$ where capital letters denote the points on the Manifold and small letters correspond to vectors on the tangent space, which are also matrices. We refer the readers to [8] for a detailed discussion on Riemannian Geometry with this metric.

Dissimilarity Metric. The dissimilarity between two regions covariance matrices can be given by the distance between two points of the manifold M, considering that those points are the two regions covariance matrices.

That distance on a Manifold M is the length of the curve with the minimum length which connects them. This curve lives on a geodesic. Let $\mathbf{y} \in T_{\mathbf{x}}M$, where $T_{\mathbf{x}}M$ is the tangent space at point $\mathbf{X} \in M$. There is a unique geodesic starting at $\mathbf{X}$ with tangent vector $\mathbf{y}$. The exponential map, $exp_{\mathbf{X}} : T_{\mathbf{X}}M \mapsto M$, maps the vector $\mathbf{y}$ to a point $\mathbf{Y}$ belonging to the previous geodesic. We denote by $log_{\mathbf{X}}$ its inverse. The distance between $\mathbf{X}$ and $\mathbf{Y}$ is given by $d^2(X, Y) = \|y\|_{\mathbf{X}}^2$. Like above we use the exponential map proposed in [10] with the same metric,

$$\mathbf{Y} = exp_{\mathbf{X}}(\mathbf{y}) = \mathbf{X}^{\frac{1}{2}}exp(\mathbf{X}^{-\frac{1}{2}}\mathbf{y}\mathbf{X}^{-\frac{1}{2}})\mathbf{X}^{\frac{1}{2}} \tag{3}$$
$$\mathbf{y} = log_{\mathbf{X}}(\mathbf{Y}) = \mathbf{X}^{\frac{1}{2}}log(\mathbf{X}^{-\frac{1}{2}}\mathbf{Y}\mathbf{X}^{-\frac{1}{2}})\mathbf{X}^{\frac{1}{2}} \tag{4}$$

If we use the definition of the geodesic distance and substituting (4) into our metric we have,

$$d^2(\mathbf{X}, \mathbf{Y}) = tr(log^2(\mathbf{X}^{-\frac{1}{2}}\mathbf{Y}\mathbf{X}^{-\frac{1}{2}})) \tag{5}$$

Regions Covariance Matrix Update. In this paper, we propose a novel solution for the covariance matrix update, that is based on the mean of the new covariance matrix and the last covariance updated. If $\mathbf{y}$ is the velocity that takes us from X to Y, $\mathbf{y}/2$ will take us half the distance to point $\overline{\mathbf{C}}$. Using equations (3) and (4), we have $\overline{\mathbf{C}} = \mathbf{X}^{\frac{1}{2}}exp(\mathbf{X}^{-\frac{1}{2}}(\frac{1}{2}\mathbf{y})\mathbf{X}^{-\frac{1}{2}})\mathbf{X}^{\frac{1}{2}}$ which after some mathematical simplification turns into,

$$\overline{\mathbf{C}} = (\mathbf{X}^{\frac{1}{2}}\mathbf{Y}\mathbf{X}^{\frac{1}{2}})^{\frac{1}{2}} \tag{6}$$

where $\overline{\mathbf{C}}$ is the average distance between two points on a Riemannian Manifold (the updated covariance matrix).

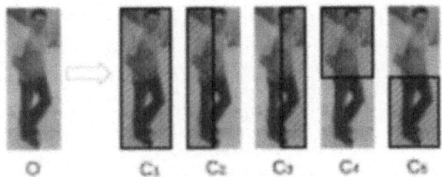

$$O \qquad C_1 \quad C_2 \quad C_3 \quad C_4 \quad C_5$$

Fig. 2. Object representation. Construction of the five covariance matrices from over-lapping regions of an object feature image.

2.2   Improvement to Occlusion

One way to improve the capacity of matching even with occlusions [12] consists in representing the object with five RCMs, extracted from five different regions. By combining global and part-based representations, the robustness towards possible occlusions and large illumination variations is increased. Figure 2 shows the five part-regions associated to each RCM. The covariance matrices are computed as described above and the dissimilarity between two objects is, now, defined by

$$\rho(O_1, O_2) = \sum_{i=1}^{5} d^2(\mathbf{C}_i^{O_1}, \mathbf{C}_i^{O_2}) \tag{7}$$

where $\mathbf{C}_i^{O_1}$ and $\mathbf{C}_i^{O_2}$ are the five regions covariance matrices of object 1 and object 2, respectively.

3   Kernel Particle Filter Tracking

Multi-object tracking using region covariance descriptors embedded on a PF framework has already been proposed by the authors in the past [3]. In this paper, we proposed the extension of the PF to a KPF [1]. KPF estimates the gradient of the kernel density and moves the particles toward the modes of the posterior, leading to a more effective allocation of particles.

Kernel Density Estimation (KDE) is used in this work to form a continuous estimate of the posterior in order to facilitate gradient estimation. Given a particle set at time t: $S_t = \left(S_t^{(n)}\right)_{n=1}^{N}$ and associated weights $\left(w_t^{(n)}\right)_{n=1}^{N}$, the kernel density estimation of the posterior with kernel K can be formulated as

$$\hat{p}(x_t|Y_t) = \frac{1}{Nh^d} \sum_{n=1}^{N} K\left(\frac{x_t - s_t^{(n)}}{h}\right) w_t^{(n)} \tag{8}$$

where h is the kernel width, denoting x_t the target state at time t, where $x_t \in \Re^d$. Y_t represents the history of observations up to time t.

The probability density function of the joint feature-spatial spaces can be estimated from the sample points by the kernel density estimation, with each particle contributing to the estimate in accordance with its distance from x_t and also in accordance with the dissimilarity obtained from eq.7.

Given the posterior estimation, we estimate its gradient, and an mean-shift procedure is used to move the particles along the gradient direction toward the modes of the posterior. In this procedure, each particle is moved to its sample mean determined by

$$m(s_t^{(n)}) = \frac{\sum_{l=1}^{N} G\left(s_t^{(n)} - s_t^{(l)}\right) w_t^{(l)} s_t^{(l)}}{\sum_{l=1}^{N} G\left(s_t^{(n)} - s_t^{(l)}\right) w_t^{(l)}} \tag{9}$$

where G is an arbitrary kernel. The mean-shift vector $m(x) - x$ using kernel G would be in the gradient direction if the kernel profile g and k satisfy $h(r) = -ck'(r)$ for all $r \in [0, \inf)$ and some $c > 0$ [2]. In these work, a Gaussian Kernel was used since the derivative of the normal profile remain normal.

The mean-shift can be applied repeatedly to a particle set. A problem arises when particles change their positions. In this case, the new particles do not follow the posterior distribution anymore. This is compensated in KPF by reweighting the particles. Representing the particle set after the ith mean-shift procedure at time t as $s_{t,i}^{()}$, after each mean-shift procedure, the weight is recomputed as the posterior density evaluated at the new particle positions, adjusted by a balancing factor $w_{t,i}^{(n)} = \frac{p(s_{t,i}^{(n)}|Y_t)}{q_{t,i}(s_{t,i}^{(n)})}$, where the denominator is the new proposal density that captures the non-uniformity of the new particle set $q_{t,i}(x_t) = \frac{1}{Nh^d} \sum_{l=1}^{N} K(\frac{x_t - s_{t,i}^{(l)}}{h})$ and the posterior density is given by $p(s_{t,i}^{(n)}|Y_t) \propto p(y_t|s_{t,i}^{(n)}) \sum_{l=1}^{N} p(s_{t,i}^{(n)}|s_{t-1}^{(l)}) w_{t-1}^{(l)}$.

In our solution, the likelihood is evaluated as $p(y_t|s_{t,i}^{(n)}) \propto exp(-\rho(O_1, O_2))$ and a constant velocity model was used as system dynamics: $x_t^{(n)} = x_{t-1}^{(n)} + v_t + \eta$, being $v_t = \frac{1}{k} \sum_{n=t-k}^{t} \|x_n - x_{n-1}\|$ and $\eta : N(0, \Sigma)$ is gaussian noise. The estimate, $\hat{x}_t \sim p(x_t|x_{t-1})$, is approximated by the sample with the higher weight, $\hat{x} = x^{(n)}|_{w^{(n)}=max(w)}$.

Performing mean-shift on S_t causes the next generation of particles to concentrate more on the approximated density modes, but the weights will contain a factor that offsets this effect, allowing the next mean-shift iteration to follow the correct posterior gradient.

4   Results

In order to correctly evaluate the solution hereby proposed two different types of tests were performed: RCMs features descriptiveness evaluation and object tracking performance evaluation. The performance was evaluated in a very challenging scenario, where five people are walking and severe occlusion occurs. Three set of features were used to build the RCM descriptor of an object (see table 2) and its discrimination ability was evaluated. The best feature set was also used for tracking purposes, using a PF and the KPF proposed on the paper.

To evaluate the robustness of the different features we tested three characteristics: the correct labelling, the factor of impact and the RMS object tracking

Table 2. Test Features to evaluate the system

	Feature
Test 1	$\Phi_1 = [x \ y \ I_r \ I_g \ I_b \ I_x \ I_y \ I_{xy}]$
Test 2	$\Phi_2 = [x \ y \ I_r \ I_g \ I_b \ g_{\theta(0),\sigma(0),\gamma}, \ \cdots, \ g_{\theta(6),\sigma(5),\gamma}]$
Test 3	$\Phi_3 = [g_{\theta(0), \ \sigma(0), \ \gamma}, \ \cdots, \ g_{\theta(6),\sigma(5),\gamma}]$

Table 3. Features evaluation results - Five people scenario

	Correct Labelling	Factor of impact ζ	Average RMS error
Test 1	63 %	0.4168	20,93
Test 2	81 %	0.5327	14,33
Test 3	85 %	0.5792	9,25

error in a scenario with five people interacting with one another. The objects position of this dataset was manually set to get the ground truth. The results were obtained by just changing the features set, which means that each tracking method was evaluated with the same conditions.

Table 3 shows the results of the three set of features. From the results on table 3 we can conclude that the Gabor features alone obtain the better results. This is due to the fact that the object sometimes presents similar colors (eg. gray shirts). From these tests we can state that by embedding Gabor features in the RCMs, the descriptiveness, as well the discriminating ability of the RCM, can be significantly enhanced.

In order to test the proposed tracking method, the third set of features is used, Φ_3, to evaluate the performance of a particle filter with a fine tuning given by the kernel tracking (KPF) *vs.* a particle filter method and a kernel based tracking.

The graphics in figure 3 shows the RMS tracking error of the three tracking solutions under evaluation. It is possible to observe that the performance of these

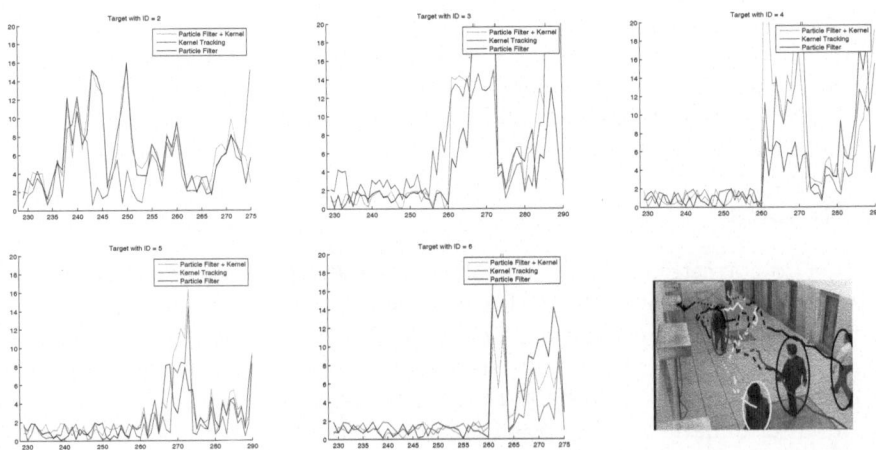

Fig. 3. Image position RMS error per person. Bottom right: The estimated tracking paths of the five people using the KPF

three solutions are equivalent. However, it is important to remark that the KPF, that performs a coarse-to-fine approach, allows to reduce the number of particles up to 20 instead of the usual 150 or more used with the PF solution.

5 Conclusions

The performance of the proposed solution proved its effectiveness even in a very clutter scene with multiple occlusions. The kernel based tracker showed that it has a similar performance to other tracker systems (eg. Particle Filter). Moreover, this kernel based method can be integrated on a particle filter to reduce the number of particles and consequently improve the sampling efficiency.

Regarding the features, it is proven that by embedding Gabor features in the RCMs, the descriptiveness, as well the discriminating ability of the RCM, is significantly improved.

References

1. Chang, C., Ansari, R.: Kernel particle filter for visual tracking (2005)
2. Cheng, Y.: Mean shift, mode seeking, and clustering. IEEE PAMI, 17(8) (1995)
3. Batista, J., Palaio, H.: Multi-object tracking using an adaptative transition model particle filter with region covariance data association. In: ICPR (2008)
4. Kälviäinen, H., Kamarainen, J.K., Kyrki, V.: Fundamental frequency gabor filters for object recognition. In: ICPR (2002)
5. Maggio, E., Cavallaro, A.: Hybrid particle filter and mean shift tracker with adaptive transition model. In: Proc. of IEEE Signal Processing Society International Conference on Acoustics, Speech, and Signal Processing (ICASSP), Philadelphia, PA, USA, March 19–23 (2005)
6. Santos-Victor, J., Moreno, P., Bernardino, A.: Gabor parameter selection for local feature detection. In: Marques, J.S., Pérez de la Blanca, N., Pina, P. (eds.) IbPRIA 2005. LNCS, vol. 3522, pp. 11–19. Springer, Heidelberg (2005)
7. Yuan, Y., Pang, Y., Li, X.: Histograms of oriented gradients for human detection, vol. 18 (2008)
8. Pennec, X., Fillard, P., Ayache, N.: A riemannian framework for tensor computing. In: IJCV (2006)
9. Porikli, F., Kocak, T.: Robust licence plate detection using covariance descriptor in a neural network framework. In: Proc. AVSS (2006)
10. Porikli, F., Tuzel, O., Meer, P.: Covariance tracking using model update based on means on riemannian. In: Proc. IEEE CVPR (2006)
11. Tao, H., Sawhney, H.S., Kumar, R.: A sampling algorithm for tracking multiple objects. In: Workshop on Vision Algorithms (1999)
12. Tuzel, O., Porikli, F., Meer, P.: Region covariance: A fast descriptor for detection and classification. In: Leonardis, A., Bischof, H., Pinz, A. (eds.) ECCV 2006. LNCS, vol. 3952, pp. 589–600. Springer, Heidelberg (2006)
13. Tuzel, O., Porikli, F., Meer, P.: Human detection via classification on riemannian manifolds. In: Proc. IEEE CVPR (2007)

Autonomous Configuration of Parameters in Robotic Digital Cameras

António J.R. Neves, Bernardo Cunha, Armando J. Pinho, and Ivo Pinheiro

Signal Processing Lab, DETI / IEETA
University of Aveiro, 3810–193 Aveiro, Portugal
an@ua.pt, mbc@det.ua.pt, ap@ua.pt, pinheiro@ua.pt

Abstract. In the past few years, the use of digital cameras in robotic applications has been increasing significantly. The main areas of application of these robots are the industry and military, where these cameras are used as sensors that allow the robot to take the relevant information of the surrounding environment and making decisions. To extract information from the acquired image, such as shapes or colors, the configuration of the camera parameters, such as exposure, gain, brightness or white-balance, is very important. In this paper, we propose an algorithm for the autonomous setup of the most important parameters of digital cameras for robotic applications. The proposed algorithm uses the intensity histogram of the images and a black and a white area, known in advance, to estimate the parameters of the camera. We present experimental results that show the effectiveness of our algorithms. The images acquired after calibration show good properties for further processing, independently of the initial configuration of the camera.

1 Introduction

Vision is an extremely important sense for both humans and robots, providing detailed information about the environment. A robust vision system should be able to detect objects reliably and present an accurate representation of the world to higher-level processes, not only under ideal conditions, but also under changing lighting intensity and color balance.

To extract information from the acquired image, such as shapes or colors, the camera calibration procedure is very important. If the parameters of the camera are wrongly calibrated, the image details are lost and it may become almost impossible to recognize anything based on shape or color.

The work that we present in this paper[1] is related to the Middle Size League (MSL) of Robocup. The MSL competition of RoboCup is a standard real-world test for autonomous multi-robot control. The ultimate goal of the RoboCup project is, by 2050, to develop a team of fully autonomous humanoid robots that can win against the human world champion soccer team. It means that, in a near future,

---

[1] This work was partially supported by project ACORD (Adaptive Coordination of Robotic Teams), FCT/PTDC/EIA/70695/2006.

H. Araujo et al. (Eds.): IbPRIA 2009, LNCS 5524, pp. 80–87, 2009.

the robots will have to play under natural lighting conditions and in outdoor fields. This introduces many obstacles to the robots because they must be able to play either under controlled lighting conditions, as is the case of artificial illumination, as well as in non-controlled lighting conditions, such as in outdoor fields. In outdoor fields the illumination can change slowly during the day, due to the movement of the sun, as well as fast in short periods of time due to a partial and temporally covering of the sun by clouds. Consequently, the robots have to adjust, in real time, its color segmentation values as well as its camera parameters according to the lighting conditions [1].

As far as we can understand from the published work made by the other teams of RoboCup MSL, most of them don't have any software in the robots to autonomous calibrate the most important parameters of the digital cameras, which means that their cameras are only adjusted manually at the beginning of each game. Some of the teams have tried to solve the problem by developing algorithms for run-time color calibration (see for example [2]).

In this work, we show that the problem can be solved by adjusting the parameters of the camera in order to guarantee the correct colors of the objects, allowing the use of the same color classification independently of the light conditions. In the team description papers of Brainstormers Tribots [3], NuBot [4], Tech United [5] and Robofoot PM [6], some auto-calibration algorithms of the camera parameters are mentioned, although they don't present any details about them.

We propose an algorithm to configure the most important parameters of the cameras, namely exposure, white-balance, gain and brightness without human interaction. We use the histogram of intensities of the images acquired and a black and a white area, known in advance, to estimate the referred parameters of the camera. This approach differs from the well known problem of photometric camera calibration (a survey can be found in [7]), since we are not interested in obtaining the camera response values but only to configure its parameters according to some measures obtained from the acquired images in robotic applications. The self-calibration process for a single robot requires a few seconds, including the time necessary to interact with the application, which is considered fast in comparison to the several minutes needed for manual calibration by an expert user.

The algorithms proposed in this paper have been tested in the CAMBADA MSL soccer team of the University of Aveiro. The general architecture of the CAMBADA robots has been described in [8]. The vision system of the CAMBADA robots is based on an hybrid vision system, formed by an omnidirectional vision sub-system (Point Grey Flea 2 camera) and a perspective vision sub-system (Unibrain Fire-i camera), that together can analyze the environment around the robots, both at close and long distances [9].

2   Configuration of the Camera Parameters

The configuration of the parameters of digital cameras is crucial for object detection and has to be performed when environmental conditions change. The calibration procedure should be effective and fast. The proposed calibration algorithm processes the image acquired by the camera and analyzes a white area in the image to calibrate the white-balance, a black area to calibrate the brightness and the histogram of the intensities of the image to calibrate the exposure and gain. The black and white areas are known in advance.

The histogram of the intensities of an image is a representation of the number of times that each intensity value appears in the image. For an image represented using 8 bits per pixel, the possible values are between 0 and 255. Image histograms can indicate if the image is underexposed or overexposed.

The assumptions used by the proposed algorithm are:

- the white area should be white – in the YUV color space this means that the average value of U and V should be 127. If the white-balance is not correctly configured, these values are different from 127 and the image does not have the correct colors;
- the black area should be black – in the RGB color space, this means that the average values of R, G and B should be close to zero. If the brightness is too high, it is observed that the black region becomes blue, resulting in a degradation of the image;
- the distribution of the intensity histogram should be centered around 127. Dividing the histogram into regions, the left regions represent dark colors, while the right regions represent light colors. An underexposed image will have the histogram be leaning to the left, while an overexposed image will have the histogram leaning to the right (for an example see the Fig. 4 a)).

Statistical measures can be extracted from digital images to quantify the image quality [10,11]. A number of typical measures used in the literature can be computed from the image gray level histogram, namely, the mean (μ), the entropy (E), the absolute central moment (ACM) and the mean sample value (MSV):

$$\mu = \sum_{i=0}^{N-1} iP(i) \qquad E = -\sum_{i=0}^{N-1} P(i)\log(P(i))$$

$$ACM = \sum_{i=0}^{N-1} |i - \mu|P(i) \qquad MSV = \frac{\sum_{j=0}^{4}(j+1)x_j}{\sum_{j=0}^{4} x_j},$$

where N is the number of possible gray values in the histogram (typically, 256), $P(i)$ is the probability of each gray value and $x(j)$ is the sum of the gray values in region j of the histogram (in the proposed approach we divided the histogram into five regions). When the histogram values of an image are uniformly distributed in the possible values, then $\mu \approx 127$, $E \approx 8$, $ACM \approx 60$ and $MSV \approx 2.5$. In Section 3 we use these measures to analyze the images acquired by the camera and to characterize the performance of the proposed calibration algorithm. Moreover, we use the information of MSV to calibrate the exposure and the gain of the camera.

The algorithm configures the most important parameters of the camera: exposure, gain, white-balance and brightness. For each one of these parameters, a

PI controller was implemented. PI controllers are used instead of proportional controllers as they result in better control having no stationary error. The constants of the controller have been obtained experimentally for both cameras, guaranteeing the stability of the system and an acceptable time to reach the desired reference [12].

The algorithm (see Fig. 1) configures one parameter at a time, iterating between them when the convergence of the parameter under analysis has been attained. The algorithm stops when all the parameters have converged. This procedure solves the problem of the correlation that exists between the parameters. After configuring one parameter, the others are configured taking into account the new values.

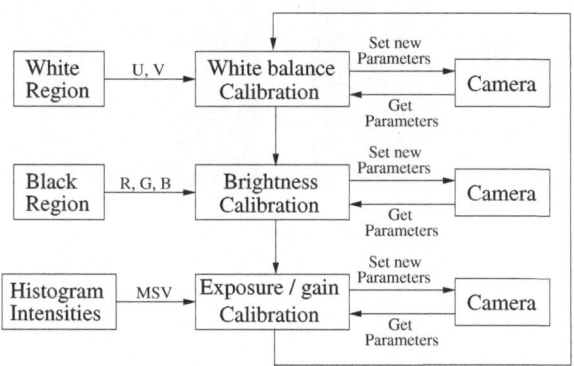

Fig. 1. Overview of the automated calibration procedure. The algorithm executes one module at a time, changing between them when the convergence of the parameter under analysis has been attained.

3   Experimental Results

To measure the performance of this calibration algorithm, tests have been conducted using the camera with different initial configurations. In Fig. 2, the experimental results are presented both when the algorithm starts with the parameters of the camera set to zero as well as when set to the maximum value. As it can seen, the configuration obtained after using the proposed algorithm is approximately the same, independently of the initial configuration of the camera. Moreover, the algorithm converges fast (it takes between 60 and 70 frames to converge).

In Fig. 3 we present an image acquired with the camera in auto mode. The results obtained using the camera with the parameters in auto mode are overexposed and the white balance is not correctly configured. This is due to the fact that the camera analyzes the entire image and, as can be seen in Fig. 2, there are large black regions corresponding to the robot itself. Our approach uses a mask to select the region of interest, in order to calibrate the camera using only the valid pixels. Moreover, and due to the changes in the environment around the robot as it moves, leaving the camera in auto mode leads to undesirable

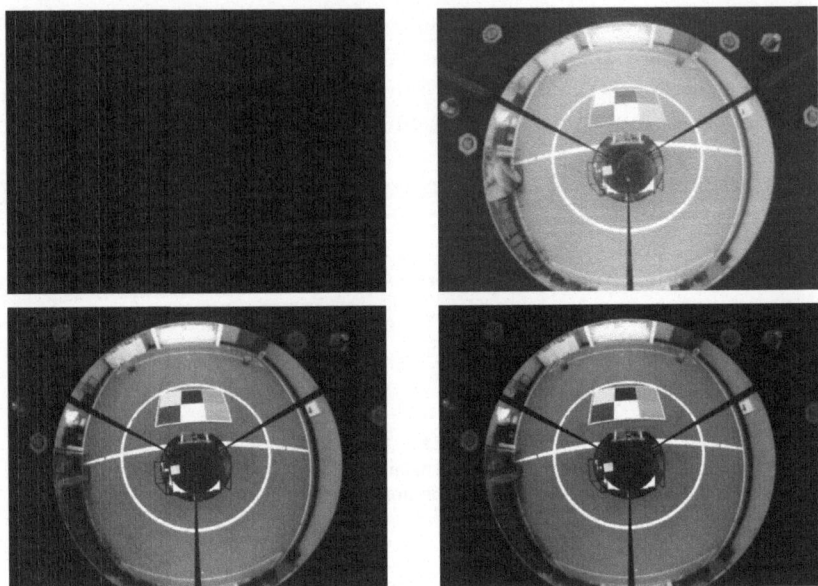

Fig. 2. Some experiments using the automated calibration procedure. On the left, results obtained starting with all the parameters of the camera set to zero. On the right, results obtained with all the parameters set to the maximum value. At the top, the initial image acquired. In the last row, the image obtained after applying the automated calibration procedure.

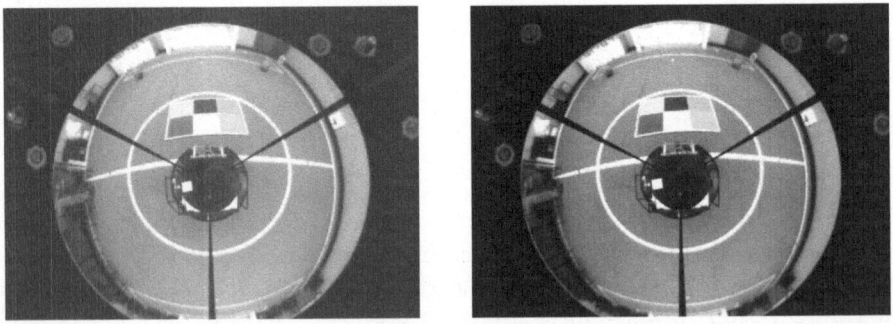

Fig. 3. On the left, an example of an image acquired with the camera parameters in auto mode. On the right, an image acquired after applying the automated calibration algorithm.

changes in the parameters of the camera, causing problems to the correct color classification.

Table 1 presents the value of the statistical measures described to evaluate the quality of digital images, regarding the experimental results presented in Fig. 2. These results confirm that the camera is correctly configured after applying the

Table 1. Statistical measures obtained for the images presented in Figs. 2 and 3. The initial values refer to the images obtained with the camera before applying the proposed automated calibration procedure. The final values refer to the images acquired with the cameras configured with the proposed algorithm.

Experiment	—	ACM	Average	Entropy	MSV
Parameters	Initial	111.00	16.00	0.00	1.00
set to zero	Final	39.18	101.95	6.88	2.56
Parameters.	Initial	92.29	219.03	2.35	4.74
set to maximum	Final	42.19	98.59	6.85	2.47
Camera in	Initial	68.22	173.73	6.87	3.88
Auto Mode	Final	40.00	101.14	6.85	2.54

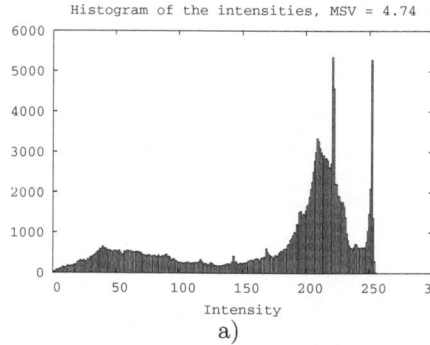 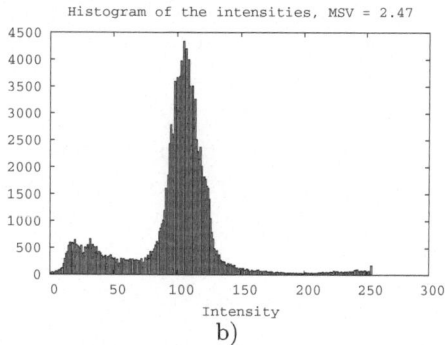

a)   b)

Fig. 4. The histogram of the intensities of the two images presented in Fig. 2. a) shows the histogram of the image obtained with the camera parameters set to maximum. b) shows the histogram of the image obtained after applying the automated calibration procedure.

automated calibration procedure, since the results obtained are near the optimal. Moreover, independently of the initial configuration, we obtain images with the same characteristics.

According to the experimental results presented in Table 1, we conclude that the MSV measure is the best one in classifying the quality of an image. This measure can distinguish between two images that have close characteristics, as the case when the camera is used in auto mode. This observation led us to use it in the calibration procedure.

The good results of the automated calibration procedure can also be confirmed by the histograms presented in Fig. 4. The histogram of the image obtained after applying the proposed automated calibration procedure (Fig. 4b) is centered near the intensity 127, which is a desirable property, as visually confirmed in Fig. 2. The histogram of the image acquired using the camera in auto mode (Fig. 4a) shows that the image is overexposed, leading to the majority of the pixels to have saturated values.

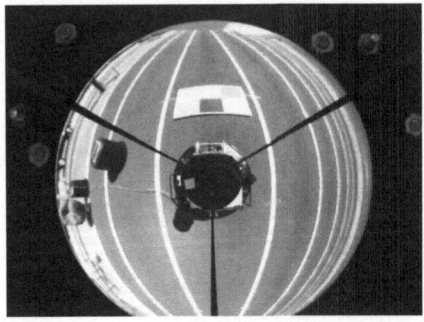 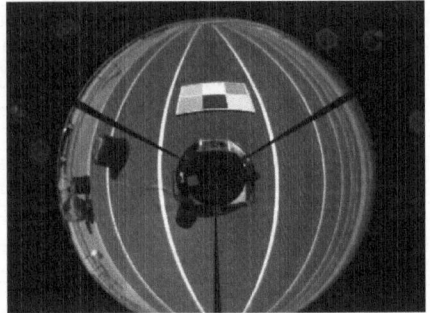

Fig. 5. On the left, an image acquired outdoors using the camera in auto mode. As it is possible to observe, the colors are washed out. That happens because the camera's auto-exposure algorithm tries to compensate the black around the mirror. On the right, the same image with the camera calibrated using the implemented algorithm. As can be seen, the colors and their contours are much more defined.

This algorithm has also been tested outdoors, under natural light. Figure 5 shows that the algorithm works well even with different light conditions. It confirms that the algorithm could be used in non-controlled lighting conditions and under different environments.

4   Conclusions

We propose an algorithm to autonomously configure the most important parameters of a digital camera. This procedure requires a few seconds for a single robot, which is much faster than the manual calibration performed by an expert user. The experimental results obtained show that the algorithm converges independently of the initial configuration of the camera. Moreover, we have analyzed the images obtained after the proposed calibration algorithm using statistical measures and we concluded that the images have the desired characteristics. These results allow the use of the same color classification independently of the lighting conditions.

The calibration algorithm is also used in run-time in order to adjust the camera parameters during a game, because the illumination along the field could not be constant and the nature of the light and its intensity could change during a game. This algorithm contributed to success of the CAMBADA team during the RoboCup2008, allowing it to distinctively achieve the 1st place.

References

1. Mayer, G., Utz, H., Kraetzschmar, G.: Playing robot soccer under natural light: A case study. In: Polani, D., Browning, B., Bonarini, A., Yoshida, K. (eds.) RoboCup 2003. LNCS, vol. 3020, pp. 238–249. Springer, Heidelberg (2004)
2. Heinemann, P., Sehnke, F.S.F., Zell, A.: Towards a calibration-free robot: The act algorithm for automatic online color training, pp. 363–370 (2007)

3. Hafner, R., Lange, S., Lauer, M., Riedmiller, M.: Brainstormers tribots team description. Technical report, Institute of Computer Science, Institute of Cognitive Science, University of Osnabru, Germany (2008)
4. Zhang, H., Lu, H., Wang, X., Sun, F., Ji, X., Hai, D., Liu, F., Cui, L., Zheng, Z.: Nubot team description paper, Technical report, College of Mechatronics and Automation, National University of Defense Technology, China (2008)
5. Lunenburg, J.J.M., Ven, G.v.d.:Tech united team description. Technical report, Control Systems Technology Group, Eindhoven University of Technology, Netherlands (2008)
6. Bouchard, B., Lapensée, D., Lauzon, M., Pelletier-Thibault, S., Roy, J.C., Scott, G.: Robofoot Épm team description paper, Technical report, Mechatronics Laboratory, École Polytechnique de Montréal, Canada (2008)
7. Krawczyk, G., Goesele, M., Seidel, H.: Photometric calibration of high dynamic range cameras. Research Report MPI-I-2005-4-005, Max-Planck-Institut für Informatik, Stuhlsatzenhausweg 85, 66123 Saarbrücken, Germany (April 2005)
8. Azevedo, J.L., Lau, N., Corrente, G., Neves, A., Cunha, M.B., Santos, F., Pereira, A., Almeida, L., Lopes, L.S., Pedreiras, P., Vieira, J., Martins, D.A., Figueiredo, N., Silva, J., Filipe, N., Pinheiro, I.: CAMBADA 2008: Team description paper. Technical report, Universidade de Aveiro, Portugal (2008)
9. Neves, A.J.R., Martins, D.A., Pinho, A.J.: A hybrid vision system for soccer robots using radial search lines. In: Proc. of the 8th Conference on Autonomous Robot Systems and Competitions, Portuguese Robotics Open - ROBOTICA 2008, Aveiro, Portugal, pp. 51–55 (April 2008)
10. Shirvaikar, M.V.: An optimal measure for camera focus and exposure. In: Proc. of the IEEE Southeastern Symposium on System Theory, Atlanta, USA (March 2004)
11. Nourani-Vatani, N., Roberts, J.: Automatic camera exposure control. In: Proc. of the 2007 Australasian Conference on Robotics and Automation, Brisbane, Australia (December 2007)
12. D'Azzo, J.J., Houpins, C.H., Sheldon, S.N.: Linear Control System Analysis and Design with Matlab. CRC Press, Boca Raton (2003)

Facial Reconstruction and Alignment Using Photometric Stereo and Surface Fitting

Gary A. Atkinson, Abdul R. Farooq, Melvyn L. Smith, and Lyndon N. Smith

University of West England, Bristol BS16 1QY, UK
Gary.Atkinson@uwe.ac.uk
www.uwe.ac.uk/cems/research/groups/mvl

Abstract. This paper presents a novel 3D face shape capture device suitable for practical face recognition applications. A new surface fitting based face alignment algorithm is then presented to normalise the pose in preparation for recognition. The 3D data capture consists of a photometric stereo rig capable of acquiring four images, each with a different light source direction, in just 15ms. This high-speed data acquisition process allows all images to be taken without significant movement between images, a previously highly restrictive disadvantage of photometric stereo. The alignment algorithm is based on fitting bivariate polynomials to the reconstructed faces and calculating the pitch, roll and yaw from the resulting polynomial parameters. Successful experiments are performed on a range of faces and pose variations.

1 Introduction

Face recognition has become one of the most widely studied areas of computer vision. A huge range of different approaches have been adopted for the detection, processing, analysis and recognition of faces within images [1]. A recent trend in the field has been to incorporate three-dimensional data into the techniques [2]. As with 2D methods, reliable data capture and processing (feature extraction, face alignment etc.) are essential steps that must be performed prior to recognition.

In this paper, we describe a 3D facial geometry capture device that uses photometric stereo [3]. We then describe a face alignment method that fits a bivariate polynomial to the faces for normalisation purposes. In doing so, we advance the state-of-the-art in 3D facial geometry capture and processing, thus improving the potential robustness of general 3D face recognition systems.

The contributions of this paper are threefold:

1. The construction of 3D data capture hardware suitable for practical face recognition environments.
2. The development of a face alignment algorithm based on surface fitting.
3. Detailed experiments to test the device on a variety of faces.

The device that we have constructed is shown in Fig. 1. The construction uses four-source photometric stereo with the lights placed evenly around an

H. Araujo et al. (Eds.): IbPRIA 2009, LNCS 5524, pp. 88–95, 2009.
© Springer-Verlag Berlin Heidelberg 2009

archway. A high-speed camera acquires one image of the face per light source with a total capture time of approximately 15ms. This very short acquisition time overcomes one major disadvantage of photometric stereo: that the images tend to be misaligned due to target object motion between frame captures.

The method of alignment uses bivariate polynomial fitting to correct for variations in the yaw, pitch and roll angles of the face. Yaw and pitch correction is an important aspect of face recognition as, even for co-operative applications, people do not always face directly towards the camera. We found that fitting a second order polynomial to the reconstructed face allows for rapid and robust correction of these two angles. The roll angle tends to be less problematic for face recognition as people seldom *tilt* their heads. Nevertheless, we show that a fourth order polynomial can be used to correct the roll angle if necessary. Our alignment method is faster than standard ICP-based methods [4] and, unlike ICP, does not require a mean face, or other fixed model, to align with.

In our experiments, we test the method on a range of faces. We are particularly interested in practical uses of the device. All tests were therefore performed with the subject casually passing through the archway, as they would do in a working environment. We demonstrate the performance of the device under several difficult situations including where the subject is wearing spectacles and is greatly misaligned with the camera.

Of the vast amount of research into automatic face recognition during the last two decades [1], relatively little work has involved photometric stereo. Kee et al. [5] investigate the use of 3-source photometric stereo under dark room conditions. They were able to determine the optimal light source arrangement and demonstrate a working recognition system. Zhou, Chellappa and Jacobs apply rank, integrability and symmetry con-

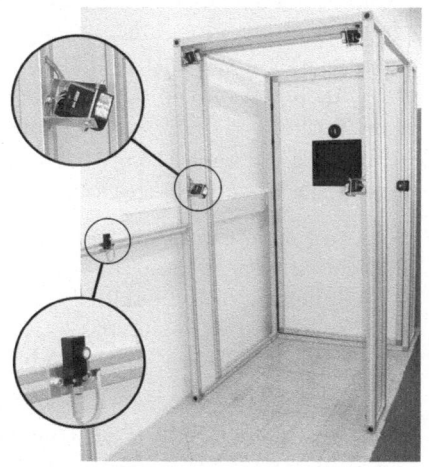

Fig. 1. Photograph of the geometry capture device. One of the light sources and an ultrasound trigger are shown to the left. The camera is located on the back panel.

straints to adapt photometric stereo to face-specific applications [6]. Zhou et al. extended a photometric stereo approach to unknown light sources [7]. Georghiades, Belhumeur and Kriegman show how reconstructions from photometric stereo can be used to form a generative model to synthesise images under novel pose and illumination [8].

Our hardware offers several advantages over many other on-site face shape capture devices. Firstly, it is cheaper and faster than laser triangulation and projected pattern devices. It is also able to rapidly analyse the fine details of a face. The device is simple to construct and is able to simultaneously extract both reflectance and topographical information. It is also easy to calibrate and is relatively robust to light source position error and ambient illumination.

2   Image Acquisition

Our device, shown in Fig. 1, is designed for practical 3D face geometry capture and recognition. Individuals walk through the archway towards the camera located on the back panel and exit through the side. This arrangement makes the device suitable for usage at the entrance to buildings, high security areas, airports etc. The presence of an individual is detected by an ultrasound proximity sensor placed before the archway. This can be seen in Fig. 1 on the horizontal beam towards the left-hand side of the photograph.

The sensor triggers the sequence of high speed synchronised frame grabbing and light source switching. We found experimentally that for people casually passing through the device, a minimum frame rate of approximately 150fps was necessary to avoid significant movement between frames. Our device currently operates at 200fps. Our four light sources are Jessops M100 flashguns. A monitor is included on the back panel to indicate whether the face has been recognised/authorised or to display other information.

For each person passing through the device, the following sequence of events takes place to capture the four images:

1. Await signal from ultrasound sensor.
2. Send trigger to camera.
3. Await integration enabled signal from camera.
4. Discharge first flashgun.
5. Await end of integration enabled signal.
6. Repeat from step 2 for the remaining light sources.

All interfacing code is written in NI LabVIEW. The ultrasonic sensor is a highly directional Baumer proximity switch. When its beam is broken within a distance of 70cm, it transmits a signal to an NI PCI-7811 DIO card fitted to a computer. When this signal is received, a trigger is sent to the camera. This is a Basler 504kc camera with a 55mm, $f5.6$ Sigma lens. The trigger is transmitted to the camera from a frame grabber via Camera Link®. The frame grabber is an NI PCIe-1429, which communicates with the DIO card via a RTSI bus for triggering purposes.

To ensure that the signal has reached the camera, and that the camera has commenced frame capture (i.e. is integrating), we have added a second connection from the camera to the DIO card. This connection is TTL-high while the camera is integrating. When the computer receives this signal, the first light source is to be immediately illuminated. A flashgun is discharged by making a short circuit between its input pins. This is achieved here by sending a short pulse from the DIO card to the input pins via a phototransistor opto-isolator IC. This electrically isolates the sensitive DIO card from the high voltages of the flashgun terminals. Finally, the DIO card awaits the falling edge of the camera integration enabled signal before moving on to the next light source.

3   Photometric Stereo

Figure 2 shows an example of four raw images of an individual. The person was slowly ($\approx$ 1m/s), but casually, walking through the device. Each image has pixel dimensions of 500×400 and there was at most one pixel length misaligment between the first and last images.

Fig. 2. Four raw input images and the resulting reconstruction, $H(x, y)$

The flashguns were located approximately 75cm from the head of the subject at evenly spaced angles. The camera was 2m away from the head. Before any processing was performed, we applied the face detection method of Lienhart and Maydt [9] to extract the face from the background of the image. This was a relatively simple task as the high intensity flashes, coupled with the short camera exposure, means that the background of the images is almost black. The four intensity images were processed using a MATLAB implementation of a standard photometric stereo method [10, §5.4]. This results in a dense field of surface normals, which we then integrate to form height maps using the well-known Frankot and Chellappa method [11]. For future reference, we shall refer to the recovered height map as $H(x, y)$.

4   Image Alignment

This section explains the method we have devised to align the 3D face reconstruction, $H(x, y)$, so that they face forward. We perform the alignment not with the whole reconstruction (i.e. not the entire surface in Fig. 2) but with the actual face region. This is extracted by first applying the 3D nose detection method of Mian et al. [12] and then cropping the image to a fixed region surrounding the nose tip. This region is a square of 300×300 pixels, or about 15×15cm.

The orientation of the face has three degrees of freedom: yaw (shaking the head left or right), pitch (nodding the head up and down) and roll (tilting the head to the left or right). For most 3D facial geometry capture devices, and face recognition applications, only the first two of these are typically varied. We therefore primarily concentrate on these two degrees of freedom.

The first stage of the alignment process is to fit a bivariate polynomial, $z(x, y)$, to the reconstructed height map, $H(x, y)$. The polynomial that we use for yaw and pitch correction is:

$$z_2(x, y) = ax^2 + bx + cy + d \tag{1}$$

Here, the quadratic term allows the surface to wrap around the face, the linear term in y allows for variance in pitch and the other two terms add generality. Figure 3 shows an example of fitting polynomial (1) to a reconstructed face.

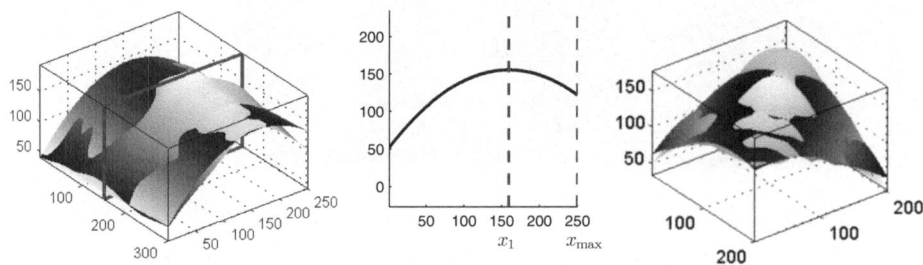

Fig. 3. Left: result of fitting polynomial (1) to a face reconstruction. Centre: cross-section of the fitted surface corresponding to the highlighted rectangle and the definition of x_1. Right: result of applying a fourth order polynomial (4) to a tilted face.

The pitch angle, θ_p, is then obtained by differentiating the surface in the y direction:

$$\frac{\partial z_2}{\partial y} = \cot \theta_p \quad \Longrightarrow \quad \theta_p = \cot^{-1} c \tag{2}$$

There is no obvious analytic means to determine the yaw angle, θ_y, from the parameters of (1). Instead, we form a lookup table solution based on the value of x_1, which is defined as the x-position peak in z_2 (see Fig. 3). This value is given by differentiating z_2 in the x direction and setting the result to zero, i.e. $x_1 = -b/2a$.

An expression is then needed to relate x_1 to θ_y. The expression is acquired by repetitively reconstructing a mannequin head placed at precisely measured yaw angles. Of course, we are making the assumption here, that the mannequin well represents a typical face shape. It turned out that the relation between x_1 and θ_y is very close to linear and is given by

$$\theta_y = 0.7 + \frac{1.4}{x_{\max}} x_1 \quad = 0.7 - \frac{1.4b}{2ax_{\max}} \tag{3}$$

Together, (2) and (3) allow the reconstructed surfaces, $H(x, y)$, to be rotated so that they are aligned, via the formation of a 3×3 rotation matrix with parameters θ_p and θ_y. We present some results of this procedure in the next section.

For cases where the roll must be incorporated into the algorithm we add extra terms to the fitting polynomial. By experimentation, we found that a fourth order polynomial was necessary but that not all possible terms are required. A good compromise was found to be

$$z_4(x, y) = ax^2y^2 + bx^2 + cy^2 + dxy + ex + fy + g \tag{4}$$

Figure 3 shows an example of such a polynomial and its fitting to a face reconstruction. The roll angle, θ_r, can then be extracted using the method of moments on the region of $z_4(x, y)$ that overlaps with the face [13, §14.5]. This results in the principle direction of the surface over the region, which corresponds to the vertical axis of the face.

5 Results

Figure 4 shows a series of reconstructions from the method. The device was placed at the entrance to a workplace to ensure casual (and thus realistic) usage. The general 3D structure of the faces have clearly been well estimated. Note however, that the spectacles of one of the subjects have been "blended" into the face. This is a combined consequence of the rim of the spectacles being non-Lambertian and the surface being non-integrable for this region of the image [11]. The blending effect can potentially be beneficial to face recognition algorithms because it means that such details have a lesser impact on the 3D shape of the face.

In order to quantify the height error, we have compared the results to the height data acquired using a commercial projected pattern range finder [14]. The root-mean-square (RMS) errors for the faces in Fig. 4 were (clockwise from top-left) 26px, 9px, 23px and 13px. This RMS value is computed from the square region of the face, centred on the nose, that is just large enough to contain the

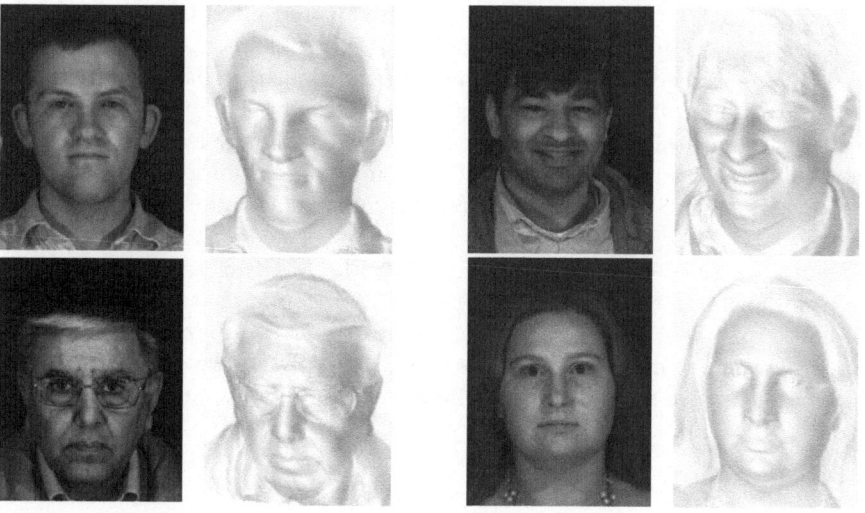

Fig. 4. Estimated geometry of four different subjects

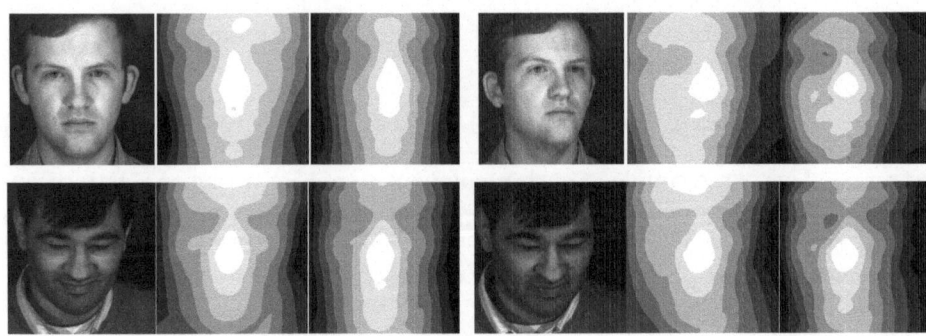

Fig. 5. Results of face alignment. For each face, the original height map (left) and the re-aligned height map (right) are shown.

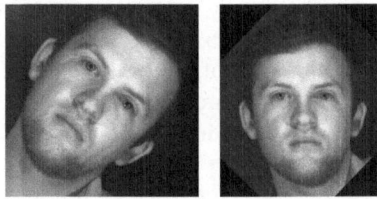

Fig. 6. Example of roll re-alignment

eyebrows and mouth. For reference, the dimensions of this square are typically 200×200 pixels, depending on the size of the head. For the face in Fig. 2, the RMS error was 15px.

Figure 5 shows results of aligning non-frontal faces. The top two images show a face with a small pitch (left) and a large yaw (right). The lower two images show a face with large pitch (left) and both yaw and pitch (right). The original height maps, also in Fig. 5, clearly indicate the problems caused by non-frontal faces. The re-aligned height maps show that the algorithm has been successful in rotating the faces towards their frontal position. This is particularly successful for the faces with pitch misalignment. The yaw is slightly less successful due to errors introduced into the symmetry from imperfect photometric stereo reconstruction. However, all four rotated reconstructions are much more frontal than the originals.

Results for roll realignment are shown in Fig. 6. Clearly, the method is very successful for large roll angles. Unfortunately, we found that the accuracy of the calculated roll angle was slightly inconsistent with errors up to approximately five degrees. For fine tuning, it may prove useful to apply an eye detection algorithm and rotate the face so that the eyes lie on the same horizontal line.

6   Conclusion

The first achievement of this work was the construction a novel 3D facial geometry capture device based on photometric stereo. The device is easily deployable in industrial and commercial settings. We conducted experiments on a range of examples, which yielded good results overall. Our alignment algorithm shows good results for yaw and pitch correction and promising results for the less important roll correction. Using a typical specification modern computer, the reconstructions take approximately 3 seconds to compute and the alignment takes 1.5 seconds without roll correction and 6 seconds with roll correction.

In the next stage of our work, we intend to incorporate more advanced shape recovery methods. We will also allow for person-specific light source calibration. That is, the light source directions used in the photometric stereo algorithm, will be adjusted depending on the position of the detected face within the image.

References

1. Zhao, W., Chellappa, R. (eds.): Face Processing: Advanced Modeling and Methods. Elsevier, Amsterdam (2006)
2. Bowyer, K.W., Chang, K., Flynn, P.: A survey of approaches and challenges in 3D and multi-modal 3D+2D face recognition. Comp. Vis. Im. Understanding 101, 1–15 (2006)
3. Woodham, R.J.: Photometric method for determining surface orientation from multiple images. Optical Engineering 19, 139–144 (1980)
4. Besl, P.J., McKay, N.D.: A method for registration of 3D shapes. IEEE Trans. Patt. Anal. Mach. Intell. 14, 239–256 (1992)
5. Kee, S.C., Lee, K.M., Lee, S.U.: Illumination invariant face recognition using photometric stereo. In: IEICE Trans. Inf. and Syst., vol. E83-D, pp. 1466–1474 (2000)
6. Zhou, S., Chellappa, R., Jacobs, D.: Characterization of human faces under illumination variations using rank, integrability, and symmetry constraints. In: Pajdla, T., Matas, J(G.) (eds.) ECCV 2004. LNCS, vol. 3021, pp. 588–601. Springer, Heidelberg (2004)
7. Zhou, S., Aggarwal, G., Chellappa, R., Jacobs, D.: Appearance characterization of linear lambertian objects, generalized photometric stereo, and illumination-invariant face recognition. IEEE Trans. Patt. Anal. Mach. Intell. 29, 230–245 (2007)
8. Georghiades, A.S., Belhumeur, P.N., Kriegman, D.J.: From few to many: illumination cone models for face recognition under variable lighting and pose. IEEE Trans. Patt. Anal. Mach. Intell. 23, 643–660 (2001)
9. Lienhart, R., Maydt, J.: An extended set of Haar-like features for rapid object detection. In: IEEE ICIP, pp. 900–903 (2002)
10. Forsyth, D.A., Ponce, J.: Computer Vision, A Modern Approach. Prentice-Hall, Upper Saddle River (2003)
11. Frankot, R.T., Chellappa, R.: A method for enforcing integrability in shape from shading algorithms. IEEE Trans. Patt. Anal. Mach. Intell. 10, 439–451 (1988)
12. Mian, A.S., Bennamoun, M., Owens, R.: An efficient multimodal 2D-3D hybrid approach to automatic face recognition. IEEE Trans. Patt. Anal. Mach. Intell. 29, 1927–1943 (2007)
13. Watt, A.H., Policarpo, F.: The Computer Image. Addison-Wesley, Reading (1998)
14. http://www.3dmd.com/3dmdface.html (February 26, 2009)

Facial Feature Extraction and Change Analysis Using Photometric Stereo

Gary A. Atkinson and Melvyn L. Smith

University of West England, Bristol BS16 1QY, UK
Gary.Atkinson@uwe.ac.uk
www.uwe.ac.uk/cems/research/groups/mvl

Abstract. This paper presents a new technique for three-dimensional face analysis aimed towards improving the robustness of face recognition. All of the 3D data used in the paper are obtained from a high-speed photometric stereo arrangement. First, a nose detection algorithm is presented, which is largely based on existing work, before a novel method for finding the nasion is described. Both of these methods rely solely on the 3D data. A new eye detection method is then described that uses a combination of 3D and 2D information with adaptive thresholding applied to the region of the image surrounding the eyes. The next main contribution of the paper is an analysis of the effects of makeup and facial hair on the success of the reconstruction and feature detection. We found that our method is very robust to such complications and can also handle spectacles and pose variation in many cases.

1 Introduction

A central aspect of many face recognition algorithms is the need for feature detection. Features are useful for many different reasons including image alignment, image normalisation, feature matching, stereo correspondence detection, biometric analysis and expression analysis [1]. As explained below, a great range of techniques have been proposed in the literature for the detection of eyes, noses, mouth corners etc. Most of this work relies on 2D image processing. Recently, face recognition research has began to incorporate 3D data. This is in effort to overcome limitations of 2D recognition caused by pose and illumination variations and other reasons.

In this paper, we present a novel method for the detection of the nose, nasion (the saddle-point located midway between the eyes) and eyes, using the relative strengths of both 2D and 3D methods. Essentially the nose and nasion are textureless features which have a well defined 3D topology. We therefore rely on 3D information to detect these features. The eyes however, have distinctive 2D attributes and so we use texture information for their detection after narrowing down the search using the nasion location. Our 3D data capture is based on photometric stereo [2].

For our nose tip detection algorithm, we call upon previous work by Mian et al. [3], where the "pointedness" of the face is calculated at various points.

H. Araujo et al. (Eds.): IbPRIA 2009, LNCS 5524, pp. 96–103, 2009.

The most pointed part is then assumed to be the nose tip. The nasion is then found using a new technique that fits a tangent line between the nose tip and the forehead. It assumes that the deepest valley under the tangent line corresponds to the nasion. The eyes are found by segmenting a horizontal portion of the image and applying a multilevel adaptive thresholding technique. The eyes are then taken as the centroid locations of the pixel regions falling below the lower thresholds. Photometric stereo is well suited to this work as it provides high resolution 2D texture data in addition to the recovered 3D shape. We present our results on a range of challenging situations including pose variation, spectacles and occlusion. We also consider the effects of heavy makeup and facial hair on both feature detection and the reconstruction accuracy.

Research into facial feature detection has previously adopted a wide variety of approaches. These include template matching [4], neural networks [5], infrared and physiological analysis [6], flesh tone filtering [7], wavelets [8], adaptive thresholding [9], regression [10], probabilistic analysis [11] and contour methods for the chin and eyebrows [12]. Of the above methods, the one most closely related to this work was carried out by Sankaran et al. [9]. Their method first estimates the pose of the face using multi-view classifiers before applying an adaptive thresholding technique to an area suspected of containing the eyes.

The method proposed in this paper offers the following advantages over most previous work. The computation time for our method is short, taking only a few seconds for combined reconstruction and feature detection using MATLAB; the method usually works when spectacles are worn; and the method is reasonably robust to occlusion and pose variation (especially in the non-spectacled case). The main disadvantage is the requirement for multiple light sources.

2   Nose and Nasion Detection

The nose and nasion detection methods that we use are based on 3D data captured using photometric stereo. We adopt a basic experimental arrangement involving four Jessops 100M flashguns positioned at equally spaced angles around the face. The images are captured at high speed by a Basler A504kc camera, such that the reflection of the flashgun light completely swamps any ambient illumination. Figure 1 shows some sample images and a resulting reconstruction [13, §5.4].

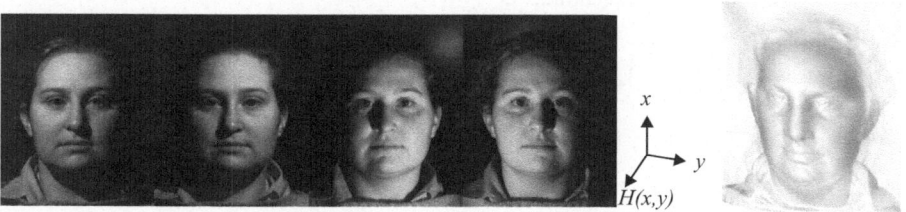

Fig. 1. Four raw input images and a 3D reconstruction

For the nose detection, we adopt the existing method of Mian et al. [3]. The method assumes that the nose tip is, essentially, the most projected part of the face. This is detected by fitting horizontal triangles to slices of the face height data, $H(x, y)$. One vertex of each triangle is given by the candidate point for the nose tip. The other two are defined by the intersections of the slice of the face height data with a horizontal circle, which is centred on the first vertex. The nose tip is assumed to be located where the distance between the first vertex and the bisector of the line connecting the other two vertices is greatest.

For the nasion detection, consider Fig. 2, which shows a profile outline of a face (ground truth). We define the nasion as follows. Assume that the head is vertical and facing the camera (a pose correction method will be incorporated for future work). First define a straight line, $L(x)$, that forms a tangent to the face at the nose and forehead as shown in the figure. The line therefore satisfies the following conditions:

$$L(x = x_{\text{nose}}) = h(x = x_{\text{nose}}) \qquad L(x = x_{\text{fore}}) = h(x = x_{\text{fore}}) \qquad (1)$$

$$\frac{dL(x)}{dx} = \frac{dh(x)}{dx}\bigg|_{x=x_{\text{fore}}} = \frac{dh(x)}{dx}\bigg|_{x=x_{\text{nose}}} \qquad (2)$$

where $h(x)$ is the profile extracted from the height map $H(x, y)$ and x_{fore} and x_{nose} are the two points where $h(x) = L(x)$. The variable x_{fore} is defined as the nearest point on $h(x)$ that allows a tangent line to satisfy (1) and (2). The nasion is given by the point between x_{fore} and x_{nose} where the distance between $L(x)$ and $h(x)$ is greatest, i.e.

$$x_{\text{nasion}} = \underset{x \in (x_{\text{fore}}, x_{\text{nose}})}{\operatorname{argmax}} (L(x) - h(x)) \qquad (3)$$

Our experimental tests showed that our nasion detection method based on (1) – (3) was very robust except when used on subjects wearing spectacles. The problem caused by spectacles is illustrated by Fig. 3. It is apparent that a spike in the reconstruction occurs due to the bridge of the spectacles. This is exaggerated in Fig. 3 for clarity. We overcome this by noting that the bridge of the spectacles forms only a small part of the profile and by fitting a cubic, $h_2(x)$ to the height data above the nose tip. The cubic is illustrated by the broken line in Fig. 3. The constraints supplied by the limited parameters of the cubic mean that the high frequency data caused by the spectacles are removed.

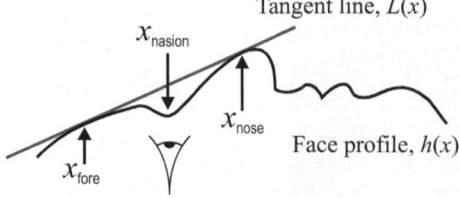

Fig. 2. Definition of the nasion

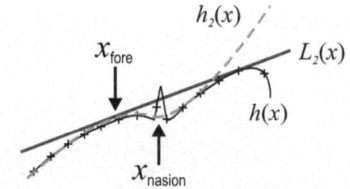

Fig. 3. Fitting the profile height data above the nose tip to a cubic

A new straight line $L_2(x)$ is then formed, which is tangent to $h(x)$ at x_{nose} and to $h_2(x)$ at x_{fore}:

$$L_2(x = x_{\mathrm{nose}}) = h(x = x_{\mathrm{nose}}) \qquad L_2(x = x_{\mathrm{fore}}) = h_2(x = x_{\mathrm{fore}}) \qquad (4)$$

$$\frac{dL_2(x)}{dx} = \left.\frac{dh_2(x)}{dx}\right|_{x=x_{\mathrm{fore}}} = \left.\frac{dh(x)}{dx}\right|_{x=x_{\mathrm{nose}}} \qquad (5)$$

The final estimate of the nasion location is then

$$x_{\mathrm{nasion}} = \operatorname*{argmax}_{x \in (x_{\mathrm{fore}}, x_{\mathrm{nose}})} (L_2(x) - h_2(x)) \qquad (6)$$

3   Eye Detection

The proposed eye detection method uses the nasion location as a starting point, and applies 2D image processing techniques to locate the eyes. The first step in our eye detection algorithm is to perform "rolling ball" erosion [14] on the mean greyscale image, $\mathcal{I}_\mu$, to give a new image, $\mathcal{I}_e$ (Fig. 4). The eyes have been clearly highlighted compared to the original image (Fig. 1), which greatly aids in their detection.

We know that the eyes will have approximately the same vertical position as the nasion, so we extract a horizontal band from the image, which we shall call $\mathcal{I}'_e \subset \mathcal{I}_e$. Our technique then makes use of a thresholding algorithm developed by Otsu [15]. Otsu's original method was designed to segment an input image into n classes using thresholds based on minimising the within-class variance. Denote the operation of Otsu thresholding by $\mathcal{S} = O(\mathcal{I}, n)$, which classifies pixels in image $\mathcal{I} = \{I_i; i = 1, 2, \ldots |\mathcal{I}|\}$ according to nonlinearly spaced thresholds $\{T_1, T_2, \ldots T_{n-1}\}$. In other words, $\mathcal{S}$ is defined by

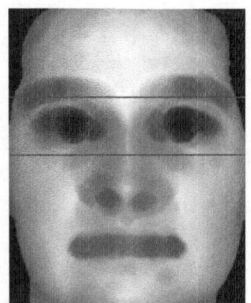

Fig. 4. Result of applying "rolling ball" erosion to the face in Fig. 1 and selection of the eye band

$$\mathcal{S} = \{s_i; i = 1, 2, \ldots |\mathcal{I}|\} \quad \text{where} \quad s_i = \begin{cases} 0 & \text{if} & I_i < T_1 \\ 1 & \text{if } T_1 \leq I_i < T_2 \\ \vdots \\ n-1 & \text{if } T_{n-1} \leq I_i \end{cases} \qquad (7)$$

We apply this algorithm to $\mathcal{I}'_e$, as shown in Fig. 5. This emphasises the eyes and gives optimal thresholds for the iterative method described below. Initially, the Otsu thresholding algorithm was applied with $n = 10$, although sometimes higher values of 20 or 30 were found to give better results. Use of the Otsu

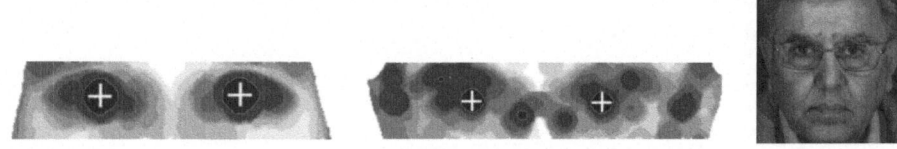

Fig. 5. Result of applying Otsu thresholding on the eye band (the left example corresponds to the highlighted region of Fig. 4, the right example corresponds to the image shown here). The calculated eye centre positions are shown and the highlighted regions indicate $\mathcal{S}'(j^*)$.

$$\mathcal{I}_\mu \qquad \mathcal{I}_e \qquad \mathcal{S} \qquad \mathcal{S}'(j^*) \qquad \mathcal{S}''(j^*)$$

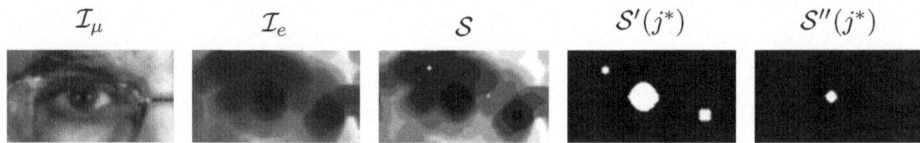

Fig. 6. The various stages involved in isolating the final eye candidates

method is particularly useful for spectacle wearers because the frames of the spectacles tend to be classified differently to the eyes.

Let the result of thresholding the image $\mathcal{I}'_e$ be $\mathcal{S}$ and the thresholds be $\{T_1, T_2, \ldots T_{n-1}\}$. In the final stage of our method, we iteratively select subsets of $\mathcal{S}$ that are defined by

$$\mathcal{S}'(j) = \{s'_i, i = 1, 2, \ldots |S'(j)|\} \subset \mathcal{S} : s'_i \leq j \,\forall\, i \tag{8}$$

where j is incremented from zero in steps of unity between each iteration. The process halts when regions of $\mathcal{S}'(j)$ are found each side of the nasion. This is the optimum value of j, which we shall call

$$j^* = \min j : (\mathcal{S}'_L(j) \neq \emptyset \,\wedge\, \mathcal{S}'_R(j) \neq \emptyset) \tag{9}$$

where $\mathcal{S}'_L(j)$ is the subset of $\mathcal{S}'(j)$ containing pixels to the left of the nasion and $\mathcal{S}'_R(j)$ contains the pixels to the right. The pixels in $\mathcal{S}'(j^*)$ should then correspond to the eyes. The eye centres are taken as the centroids of each region in $\mathcal{S}'(j^*)$.

Algorithm 1 summarises the eye detection procedure. There are three simple additional steps that we have added to improve robustness. Firstly, for each $\mathcal{S}'(j)$ we apply a morphological *close* operation followed by an *erosion*. This removes holes and unreliable regions. Secondly, we discard regions that are exceptionally close to the nasion. We denote the modified version of $\mathcal{S}'(j)$ after these two additional steps by $\mathcal{S}''(j)$. The final step applies to cases where more than one region of $\mathcal{S}''(j^*)$ is present on either side of the nasion (after the iterative procedures are complete). For these cases the the pair of regions that are most symmetric about the nasion is assumed to correspond to the the eyes.

Figure 6 illustrates the stages in the eye detection process. The figure shows a portion of the mean image, $\mathcal{I}_\mu$, the eroded image, $\mathcal{I}_e$, the Otsu segmented image, $\mathcal{S}$, the set of pixels below the optimum threshold, $\mathcal{S}'(j^*)$, and the pixels after the basic morphological processing, $\mathcal{S}''(j^*)$.

Algorithm 1. Eye Detection.

Perform rolling ball erosion on $\mathcal{I}_\mu \to \mathcal{I}_e$
Extract eye band $\to \mathcal{I}'_e$
Perform segmentation on $\mathcal{I}'_e \to \mathcal{S}$
$j \leftarrow 0$
while $[\mathcal{S}'_L(j) = \emptyset \ \vee \ \mathcal{S}'_R(j) = \emptyset]$ **do**
    $j \leftarrow j + 1$
    Extract regions up to current threshold (8) $\to \mathcal{S}'(j)$
    Perform morphological image processing on $\mathcal{S}'(j) \to \mathcal{S}''(j)$
    Calculate centroid of regions of $\mathcal{S}''(j)$.
    Discard regions that are exceptionally close to nasion.
Optimum value of j is found: $j^* \leftarrow j$
if more than one eye candidate on either side of nasion **then**
    use the pair of candidates with closest symmetry

4   Results

Figure 7 shows the locations of the detected features for a range of faces. Clearly, the method has been successful here for the majority of both non-spectacled and spectacled faces. Some of the faces would have benefited slightly from allowing the nasion detection algorithm to permit some horizontal freedom. We found that the method copes very well with loose hair close to the eyes, as shown in top centre image of Fig. 7. The method only becomes less reliable when the hair blocks the centre of an eye, as shown in the next example in the figure. Figure 7 also shows a successful example of a non-spectacled face at a wide angle to the camera (top-right).

Fig. 7. Examples of detected features. In the bottom-right image, the algorithm incorrectly predicted that the nose was located at the circle. When the nose position was set manually, the nasion and eyes were approximately correctly located.

For the final contribution of this paper, we consider the effects of typical changes to facial appearance caused by makeup and facial hair. Figure 8 shows a comparison of the 3D reconstruction with ground truth and the effects of uniform skin makeup (facial expression has been studied in detail elsewhere in the literature, e.g. [16]). The figure shows that makeup has a relatively small impact on the recovered shape and practically no impact at all on feature detection. The makeup used was intended to give the most matte and most shiny skin likely to be encountered within the general public.

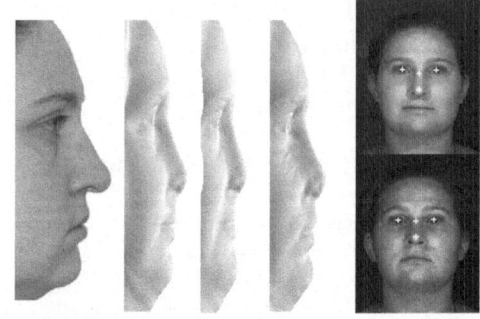

Fig. 8. Profile view photograph of a subject (left) followed by reconstructions with bare skin, heavy matte makeup and extra shiny makeup. Raw images of the matte and shiny faces are shown to the right, with the detected features indicated.

Figure 9 demonstrates the effect of facial hair on the reconstructed surface. Facial hair was left to grow for four weeks and the reconstructions before and after were compared. In fact, there is very little difference between the two reconstructions. This is mainly a result of smoothing introduced by the normal map to depth conversion process [17]. The graphs compare the results to ground truth obtained using a commercial projected pattern range finder [18]. Surprisingly, the reconstruction is marginally more accurate in the presence of facial hair.

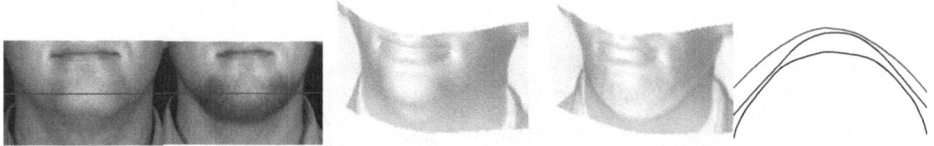

Fig. 9. Effects of facial hair (raw images to the left) on the reconstructed height (centre). The right-hand graph shows a comparison of horizontal slice reconstructions of the chin with facial hair (top) and clean shaved (middle) with ground truth (bottom). The vertical offset here is arbitrary.

5   Conclusion

This paper has presented a new method for facial geometry analysis using photometric stereo for data acquisition. The paper has shown how 3D face data, combined with texture information, can be used for robust detection of the nose tip, nasion and eye centres. The nose tip detection (based on an existing method) and nasion detection are found with reference to the 3D relief map. The process then narrows down the search for the eyes, before a novel 2D method finds the pupils. The method has shown robustness to spectacles and limited pose variation. The paper has also shown the effects of makeup and facial hair on the shape reconstruction and feature detection. Neither of these seriously affect the feature detection and have little effect on the recovered geometry. In the next stage of our work, we intend to use surface curvature analysis based on the raw surface normals to aid in the feature detection.

References

1. Zhao, W., Chellappa, R. (eds.): Face Processing: Advanced Modeling and Methods. Elsevier, Amsterdam (2006)
2. Woodham, R.J.: Photometric method for determining surface orientation from multiple images. Optical Engineering 19, 139–144 (1980)
3. Mian, A.S., Bennamoun, M., Owens, R.: An efficient multimodal 2D-3D hybrid approach to automatic face recognition. IEEE Trans. Patt. Anal. Mach. Intell. 29, 1927–1943 (2007)
4. Yuille, A.L.: Deformable templates for face recognition. J. Cognitive Neurosci. 3, 59–70 (1991)
5. Rowley, H.A., Baluja, S., Kanade, T.: Rotation invariant neural network-based face detection. In: Proc. CVPR, pp. 38–44 (1998)
6. Haro, A., Flickner, M., Essa, I.: Detecting and tracking eyes by using their physiological properties, dynamics, and appearance. In: Proc. CVPR, pp. 163–168 (2000)
7. Sirohey, S., Rosenfeld, A.: Eye detection in a face image using linear and nonlinear filters, pattern recognition. Pattern Recognition 34, 1367–1391 (2001)
8. Feris, R.S., Gemmell, J., Toyama, K., Krüger, V.: Hierarchical wavelet networks for facial feature localization. In: Proc. Intl. Conf. Automatic Face and Gesture Recognition, pp. 125–130 (2002)
9. Sankaran, P., Gundimada, S., Tompkins, R.C., Asari, V.K.: Pose angle determination by face, eyes and nose localization. In: Proc. CVPR Workshops, pp. 161–167 (2005)
10. Everingham, M., Zisserman, A.: Regression and classification approaches to eye localization in face images. In: Proc. Int. Conf. Autom. Face and Gesture Recog., pp. 441–446 (2006)
11. Wang, P., Ji, Q.: Multi-view face and eye detection using discriminant features. Comp. Vis. Im. Understanding 105, 99–111 (2007)
12. Chen, Q., Chama, W.K., Lee, K.K.: Extracting eyebrow contour and chin contour for face recognition. Pattern Recognition, 2292–2300 (2007)
13. Forsyth, D.A., Ponce, J.: Computer Vision, A Modern Approach. Prentice-Hall, Englewood Cliffs (2003)
14. Parker, J.R.: Algorithms for Image Processing and Computer Vision. Wiley, Chichester (1997)
15. Otsu, N.: A threshold selection method from gray-level histograms. IEEE Trans. Sys. Man. Cyber. 9, 62–66 (1979)
16. Kakadiaris, I.A., Passalis, G., Toderici, G., Murtuza, M.N., Lu, Y., Karampatziakis, N., Theoharis, T.: Three-dimensional face recognition in the presence of facial expressions: An annotated deformable model approach. IEEE Trans. Patt. Anal. Mach. Intell. 29, 640–649 (2007)
17. Frankot, R.T., Chellappa, R.: A method for enforcing integrability in shape from shading algorithms. IEEE Trans. Patt. Anal. Mach. Intell. 10, 439–451 (1988)
18. http://www.3dmd.com/3dmdface.html (February 26, 2009)

Match Selection in Batch Mosaicing Using Mutual Information

Armagan Elibol, Nuno Gracias, and Rafael Garcia

Computer Vision and Robotics Group,
University of Girona, 17071, Spain
{aelibol,ngracias,rafa}@eia.udg.edu

Abstract. Large area photo-mosaics are widely used in many different applications such as optical mapping, panorama creation and autonomous vehicle navigation. When the trajectory of the camera provides an overlap between non-consecutive images (closed-loop trajectory), it is essential to detect such events in order to get globally coherent mosaics. Recent advances in image matching methods allow for registering pairs of images in the absence of prior information on orientation, scale or overlap between images. Owing to this, recent batch mosaicing algorithms attempt to detect non-consecutive overlapping images using exhaustive matching of image pairs. This paper proposes the use of *Observation Mutual Information* as a criterion to evaluate the benefit of potential matches between pairs of images. This allows for ranking and ordering a list of potential matches in order to make the loop-closing process more efficient. In this paper, the *Observation Mutual Information* criterion is compared against other strategies and results are presented using underwater imagery.

1 Introduction

One of the most important steps in building a mosaic is image matching [1]. In absence of other sensor data, time consecutive images are generally assumed to have an overlapping area. This overlap allows to register the images and to obtain an initial estimate of the camera trajectory over time. This initial estimate suffers from rapid accumulation of registration errors and can be very far from the real trajectory. However, it provides useful information to predict the non-time consecutive overlapping images. Matching those images helps to refine the topology by using global alignment methods [2,3]. With the refined topology, new non-time consecutive overlapping images can be predicted and attempted to match. This iterative matching and optimization process continues until no new overlapping images occur. Topology estimation was first argued in [4] where iterative topology inference was proposed assuming that time-consecutive images have an overlapping area.

Recent advances in image matching techniques such as the Scale Invariant Feature Transform (SIFT) [5], allow for registering pairs of images in the absence of prior information on orientation, scale or overlap between images. Such

H. Araujo et al. (Eds.): IbPRIA 2009, LNCS 5524, pp. 104–111, 2009.

techniques are behind the recent widespread of panorama creation algorithms, since they allow creating panoramas with minimal user input [6,7]. In several approaches attempt to match all images against all or rely upon manually selection of spatially overlapping images [8,9]. While this is feasible for small sets, it becomes impractical for larger problems, such as creating underwater mosaics where useful surveys may comprise many thousand images.

The objective of this work is to study different strategies for selecting the image pairs to be matched and get the best estimation of the topology of the surveyed area by exploring the contributions of image matchings, and by choosing which images to be matched first. We assume that all images have already been acquired and time consecutive images have an overlapping area. Therefore, we are free to choose the order of the image pairs to be matched.

2 Topology Estimation Using Extended Kalman Filter

Our approach is inspired by image mosaicing methods based on the Extended Kalman Filter(EKF), which have been studied over the last decade especially in the context of mosaic based navigation [10,11,12].

As matching non-consecutive image pairs provides more information about the topology and improves the trajectory estimation, it is essential to detect them while estimating the topology of the surveyed area. In this context, it is important to measure the contribution of matching one image pair in terms of how much information it will provide about the topology. In this work, the potential gain of matching image pairs is predicted by considering image matching between potential overlapping images as an observation or measurement. Then, the predicted gain is calculated as the amount of information the observation provides to the information matrix of the whole system. This is obtained by calculating the *Observation Mutual Information* (OMI). As our interest is batch mosaicing, we do not require any control input and do not use the state prediction equations. Only observation update equations are used. As a design option, each image is used once (at most), in each iteration of the algorithm. This ensures the independence among the observation elements and allows us to adapt the existing methods for sensor fusion, selection and management.

2.1 Definitions

The *state vector*, $\mathbf{x}$, is composed of absolute homographies, $^m\mathbf{H}_i = mat(\mathbf{x}_i)$, which relate all images to the mosaic frame. We use similarity homographies [13] which have 4 degrees of freedom (Scaling, Rotation and Translation in both x and y axis). Let $\mathbf{P}$ be the covariance matrix of $\mathbf{x}$. $\mathbf{x}_i = [a_i, b_i, c_i, d_i]^T$ $i = 1, 2, 3, ..., N$ where N is the total number of images.

A new measurement (*observation*) is obtained when two images, i and j, are successfully matched. The observation is represented by the homography between corresponding images at iteration k, $\mathbf{z}_k = ^i\mathbf{H}_m \cdot ^m\mathbf{H}_j + \mathbf{v}_k$ where $\mathbf{v}_k$ is the observation noise vector and m denotes the mosaic frame. We follow the usual assumption that observation noise is Gaussian and not correlated with state noise. The covariance matrix of the observation noise is denoted by $\mathbf{R}_k$ and can be estimated from points and matches[14].

A *potential observation* is a non time-consecutive overlapping image pair, which has not been attempted to match and for which there is predicted overlap. The predicted overlap is computed using state vector and its covariance matrix.

OMI score is calculated for each potential observation. This OMI score is the Predicted Information Gain of the observation.

$$I_{(k,z_k)} = \frac{1}{2} \log \left[\frac{|\mathbf{Y}_{(k|k)}|}{|\mathbf{Y}_{(k|k-1)}|} \right] \tag{1}$$

where $\mathbf{Y}$ is the information matrix [15].

The OMI score requires the knowledge of $\mathbf{R}_k$. For potential observations (where image matching has not been attempted yet), a generic $\mathbf{R}_k$ is used. This generic $\mathbf{R}_k$ was experimentally obtained from matches among consecutive image pairs by selecting the one with the highest uncertainty from this set. Each matched image pair allow for estimating one $\mathbf{R}_k$.

2.2   Implementation

Our algorithm is composed of five blocks: Initialization, Potential Observation List Generation, Selection, Image Matching and Filter update. The pipeline is illustrated in Fig. 1. In the initialization block, the initial values of $\mathbf{x}$ and $\mathbf{P}$ are computed from correspondences between time consecutive images pairs. The first image frame is chosen as a global (reference) frame. The absolute homography of image i, $^1\mathbf{H}_i$, is calculated by accumulating the relative homographies, $^1\mathbf{H}_i = {}^1\mathbf{H}_{i-1} \cdot {}^{i-1}\mathbf{H}_i$ $i = 2, 3, ..., N$. As the first image is chosen as a global frame, its covariance matrix is set to zero. The uncertainties of relative homographies are calculated from the point and matches by using the first order propagation [14]. Covariance matrices of initial absolute homographies are also obtained by using the first order approximation of the accumulation, assuming that covariances of time consecutive homographies are not correlated.

Once the initial covariance matrix is computed, a *Potential Observation List* can be generated. For every possible image pair, the overlapping area is computed using a numerical approximation. If the overlap is bigger than a given threshold,

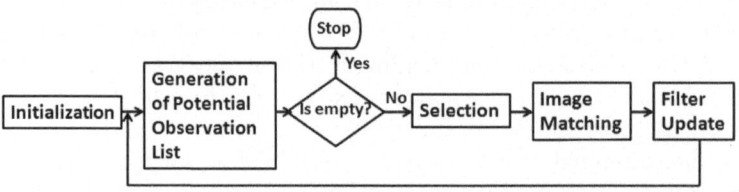

Fig. 1. Pipeline of EKF based topology estimation framework

the image pair is considered as an overlapping image pair and it is added to potential observation list.

After generating the list, the *Selection* step starts. For each possible observation in the list, which has not been processed in the previous iterations, different scores can be calculated depending on the tested strategy. The aim of the *Selection* step is to choose the subset of observations in such a way that maximizes the score. The selection step is modeled as a linear assignment problem [16].

The maximum number of observations to be selected is equal to $\frac{N}{2}$ as one image can only be used in one observation.

After generating and choosing the list of potential observations, image matching starts. The image matching step is composed of two sub-steps: SIFT [5] is used to detect the features in images and RANSAC [13] is used to reject outliers and estimate the homography. Each image pair is attempted to be matched only once. If it is successful, noise covariance is calculated from the correspondences by using the first order noise propagation [14].

The final filter update step updates the state and covariance by using EKF equations.

3   Experimental Results

Several criteria can be devised to order the pairs of potential image matches, so that the most relevant ones are attempted first. We propose and test the following criteria: (1) Expected Overlap (2) OMI, (3) Overlap Weighted OMI, and (4) Random Order. The Expected Overlap criterion selects the pairs which have higher overlap, and thus a higher chance of being successfully matched. This criterion takes into account the uncertainty in the trajectory (using a numerical approximation to compute the overlap under uncertainty) and has been used before in the context of underwater mosaicing [17]. The OMI criterion selects the pairs that contribute the most in terms of Mutual Information with the aim of quickly reducing the uncertainty on the trajectory. The Overlap Weighted OMI combines the first two. Finally the Random Order criterion selects the pairs randomly. It is included a comparison baseline to assess the performance of the other criteria.

The data set is an underwater image sequence that consists of 169 images of size 512×384 pixels. In order to compare the results, we computed the set of homographies using a standard iterative bundle adjustment approach [2]. Bundle adjustment minimizes the reprojection error over the trajectory parameters. The result of applying bundle adjustment iteratively is given at the last line of Table 1. Fig. 2 shows the resulting trajectory. The resulting homography set is used as a reference to compare the results of EKF based topology estimation strategies. Our comparison criteria is the average reprojection error over all correspondences that were previously found by employing iteratively bundle adjustment and image matching. Table 1 gives the summary of the results. Tested strategies are listed in the first column. The second column shows the total number of image pairs that have been matched successfully. The third column

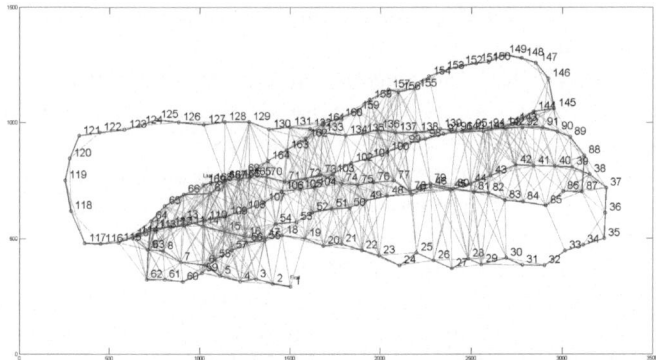

Fig. 2. Final topology with bundle adjustment. Numbers correspond to the image centers and lines denote the overlapping image pairs which were successfully matched.

Table 1. Summary of Results

Strategy	Number of Successful Obs.	Number of Unsuccessful Obs.	Total Number of Obs.	Iterations	Avg. Error in pixels
Expected Overlap	869	967	1836	38	11.04
OMI	870	1036	1906	40	9.58
Overlap Weighted OMI	871	1011	1882	40	9.54
Random Order	870.3	1022.3	1892.7	38	10.67
Bundle Adjustment	872	2141	3013		8.78

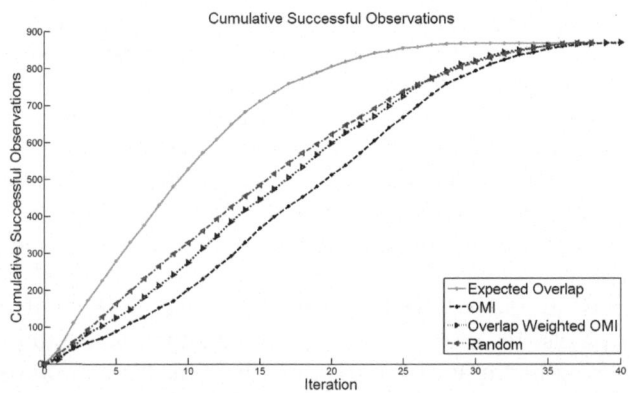

Fig. 3. Cumulative number of successful observation for each iteration. X axis shows iterations and Y axis shows the number of successful observations in cumulative order.

contains the total number of image pairs that were not matched successfully, referred to as unsuccessful observations. Adding the second and the third column gives the total number of matching attempts which is illustrated in the fourth column. The fifth column denotes how many iterations have been executed. The

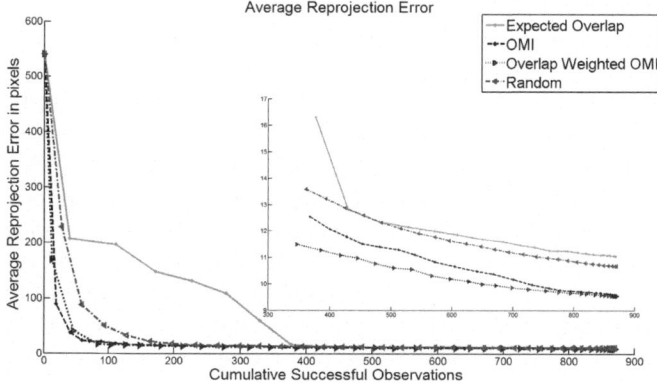

Fig. 4. Average Reprojection Error for all correspondences for tested selection strategies. X axis shows the number of successful observations in cumulative order and Y axis shows the Average Reprojection Error in Pixels. The small plot contains a zoomed area of the bigger plot between 300 and 900 cumulative successful observations.

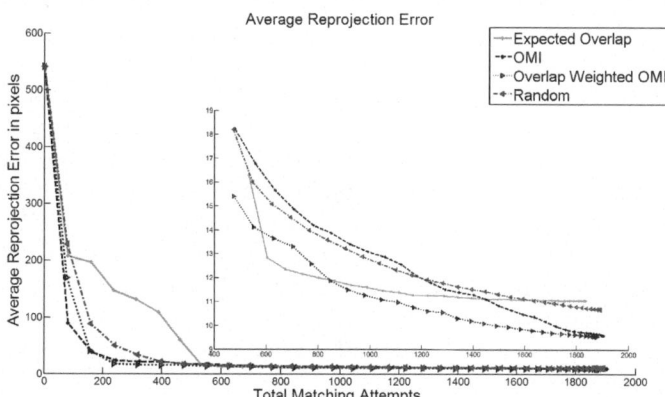

Fig. 5. Average Reprojection Error for all correspondences for tested selection strategies. X axis shows the total number of matching attempts in cumulative order and Y axis shows the Average Reprojection Error in Pixels. The small plot contains a zoomed area of the bigger plot between 500 and 2000 cumulative total matching attempts.

last column shows the average reprojection error in pixels calculated by using all correspondences with the resulting set of homographies for each tested strategy.

To assess the performance of the random strategy, we have run our algorithm 10 times and computed the average values. From Table 1, one can conclude that OMI Based observation selection produces the minimum reprojection error among all strategies and also the closest to the bundle adjustment. Plots of the total number of successful observation and total matching attempts vs. reprojection error are given in Figs. 4 and 5. It can be noted that the order of observations makes a difference and has an effect on the resulting trajectory. OMI based selection strategy has the biggest total number of image matching attempts. Especially after the initialization step, the generated potential observation list has several entries which actually do not have overlap because of the high uncertainty of the state. During the first iterations, the total number of successful observations in OMI based selection strategy is low. This can be seen in Fig. 3. OMI selects the observations that provide the most information to the system and this reduces the reprojection error rapidly. This is clearly illustrated in Fig. 4. It is worth noting that random selection has produced relatively good results in terms of total matching attempts. This is partly due to the characteristics of the data set where trajectory lines are very close each other (see Fig. 2). This leads to a high probability of having overlap between any two images.

4   Discussion

When there is no a *priori* information on the topology, a conceptually simple strategy is to use exhaustive matching "all against all". If there is a priori information such as consecutive images having overlap, then iterative Bundle adjustment approach can be employed, as it is shown in the previous section. For the test data set (169 images) all-against-all matching strategy would try to match 14, 196 image pairs. If the prior information that time consecutive images have an overlap is available, then initial estimation about trajectory can be computed by accumulating. Non-consecutive overlapping pairs can be estimated by using this initial estimation. As this initial estimation is far from the real trajectory, finding non-consecutive image pairs could generate several false image pairs. Total number of matching attempts can be seen in the last row of Table 1. Using priori information helps to reduce the total matching attempts compared to the all-against-all. In our EKF based framework, we were able to reduce the total matchings attempts even more by incorporating the covariances on the image position while generating the potential observation list. This eliminates several non-overlapping image pairs.

5   Conclusions

In this paper, we have proposed a ranking criterion to evaluate the benefit of potential matches between pairs of images of a sequence. Proper ordering of these matches makes loop-closing more efficient in building large area photomosaics. All successfully matched image pairs contribute differently in terms of reducing uncertainty and reprojection error. An important conclusion of this study is that the order of matching overlapping images plays an important role when trying to reduce the reprojection error of the trajectory while taking into account uncertainties of the parameters. Although all tested strategies had nearly the same number of observations, the resulting reprojection errors are not the same. This emphasizes the importance of the proper selection of pairs to be matched and their order. In this context, different strategies for ordering of image matching have been tested and their performance have been compared.

Acknowledgments. This work has been partially funded by the Spanish Ministry of Education and Science(MEC) under grant CTM2007-64751 and the FREESUBNET EU project MRTN-CT-2006-036186. Nuno Gracias has been supported by Ramon y Cajal program and Armagan Elibol has been funded by Generalitat de Catalunya under grant 2004FI-IQUC1/00130.

References

1. Zitová, B., Flusser, J.: Image registration methods: A survey. Image and Vision Computing 21(11), 977–1000 (2003)
2. Triggs, B., McLauchlan, P., Hartley, R., Fitzgibbon, A.: Bundle adjustment – A modern synthesis. In: Triggs, B., Zisserman, A., Szeliski, R. (eds.) ICCV-WS 1999. LNCS, vol. 1883, pp. 298–375. Springer, Heidelberg (2000)
3. Gracias, N., Zwaan, S., Bernardino, A., Santos-Victor, J.: Mosaic based navigation for autonomous underwater vehicles. IEEE Journal of Oceanic Engineering 28(3), 609–624 (2003)
4. Sawhney, H., Hsu, S., Kumar, R.: Robust video mosaicing through topology inference and local to global alignment. In: Burkhardt, H., Neumann, B. (eds.) ECCV 1998. LNCS, vol. 1407, pp. 103–119. Springer, Heidelberg (1998)
5. Lowe, D.: Distinctive image features from scale-invariant keypoints. International Journal of Computer Vision 60(2), 91–110 (2004)
6. Yao, J., Chamb, W.K.: Robust multi-view feature matching from multiple unordered views. Pattern Recognition 40(11), 3081–3099 (2007)
7. Brown, M., Lowe, D.G.: Automatic panoramic image stitching using invariant features. International Journal of Computer Vision 74(1), 59–73 (2007)
8. Szeliski, R.: Image mosaicing for tele-reality applications. In: IEEE Workshop on Applications of Computer Vision, pp. 44–53 (1994)
9. Can, A., Stewart, C., Roysam, B.: Robust hierarchical algorithm for constructing a mosaic from images of the curved human retina. In: IEEE Conference on Computer Vision and Pattern Recognition, vol. 2, p. 292 (1999)
10. Richmond, K., Rock, S.M.: An operational real-time large-scale visual mosaicking and navigation system. In: MTS/IEEE OCEANS Conference, Boston, USA (2006)
11. Garcia, R., Puig, J., Ridao, P., Cufí, X.: Augmented state Kalman filtering for AUV navigation. In: IEEE International Conference on Robotics and Automation, Washington D.C., vol. 3, pp. 4010–4015 (2002)
12. Caballero, F., Merino, L., Ferruz, J., Ollero, A.: Homography based Kalman filter for mosaic building. applications to UAV position estimation. In: IEEE International Conference on Robotics and Automation, pp. 2004–2009 (2007)
13. Hartley, R., Zisserman, A.: Multiple View Geometry in Computer Vision, 2nd edn. Cambridge University Press, Cambridge (2004)
14. Haralick, R.: Propagating covariance in computer vision. In: Proceedings of the Theoretical Foundations of Computer Vision, TFCV on Performance Characterization in Computer Vision, Germany, pp. 95–114 (1998)
15. Grocholsky, B.: Information-Theoretic Control of Multiple Sensor Platforms. PhD thesis, University of Sydney (2002)
16. Boyd, S., Vandenberghe, L.: Convex Optimization. Cambridge University Press, Cambridge (2004)
17. Gracias, N., Victor, J.: Underwater mosaicing and trajectory reconstruction using global alignment. In: MTS/IEEE OCEANS Conference, vol. IV, pp. 2557–2563 (2001)

Space Carving Acceleration Using Uncertainty Measurements

M. Claudia Pérez, Miquel Casamitjana, and Enric X. Martín

Department of System Engineering
Universitat Politècnica de Catalunya
08028 Barcelona, Spain
{maria.claudia.perez,miquel.casamitjana,
enric.xavier.martin}@upc.edu

Abstract. This paper presents a method for obtaining a fast but rough 3D object reconstruction. This reconstruction will contain enough information to determine a minimum complementary view set that can refine it more accurately. Thus it is possible to take advantage of the space carving algorithm simplicity. This algorithm is fast and easy to accelerate by means of hardware and software techniques, but cannot easily manage the uncertainty derived from the segmentation process. In the proposed method, uncertainty is projected onto the voxels and computed with them when new views are processed. In this way, a measure of the reconstruction certainty is obtained, identifying the regions where more information is needed in order to be resolved.

Keywords: space carving, uncertainty measure, 3D reconstruction.

1 Introduction

Three-dimensional reconstruction of objects and/or scenes is still a fundamental problem for computer vision researchers. Several techniques have been developed in the last decades: multi-view stereo matching techniques [1], deformable surfaces that fit the scene or the objects with strong mathematical basis [2] or a plenoptic modeling from multiple images [3] and others [4]. Nevertheless, in order to achieve real time 3D inference from scene views it is necessary to use a few views and simple algorithms, where improvements can easily be done to take advantage of present day hardware acceleration possibilities.

Space carving methods are fast and good enough for recovering 3D structure. In these methods a structure of voxels is projected into the two-dimensional views of the scene and carved (removed) if they are related to the background segmentation. Originally they have a minimal set of constraints [5] because these methods can fail when dealing with concavities, specularity or transparency. Other volumetric representations like voxel coloring [6] and generalized voxel coloring [7] determine whether, or not, to remove a voxel using its visibility property.

Some authors are working in three-dimensional reconstruction methods based on probabilistic schemes. [8] suggest a probabilistic framework for space carving, where each voxel is assigned a probability using Gaussian model and classified using a

H. Araujo et al. (Eds.): IbPRIA 2009, LNCS 5524, pp. 112–119, 2009.

Bayes theorem, which is computed by comparing the likelihoods for the voxel existing and not existing. [9] extends previous carving methods for non-Lambertian objects from arbitrary set of calibrated images, using reflectance models and statistics on the photo-consistency criterion. [10] works about a probabilistic theory based on visibility, occupancy, emptiness and photo-consistency of the Photo Hull distribution. [11] proposes "Roxel reconstruction algorithm" able to reconstruct volumetric representations of 3D space from a collection of observed images. They use a probabilistic framework to represents objects with partial opacity.

With a few views, space carving can quickly achieve a good initial object reconstruction. If, at this point, it were possible to have an idea of the certainty of the reconstruction for every voxel, it could be a trigger for a more accurate refinement process like space carving with a precise selection of views in an area or a refinement with stereo matching techniques [12]. This is the main idea of this paper. As it will be shown, this can be helpful when dealing with shadows or imprecision in image segmentation. The following sections will explain the basic features of the proposed method.

2   Some Space Carving Algorithm Problems

Space Carving [5] method represents volume by an array of n^3 identical voxels enclosing the interest area (scene/object) of processed images.

Originally, the three dimensional model is obtained by the projection of the image set into the array of voxels. Those voxels related to the image foreground are maintained, while those related to the background are removed. However, space carving difficulties are presented if images have an incorrect segmentation because a voxel could be removed by mistake and then it cannot be retrieved. It means that in final 3D reconstruction there could be holes that aren't in the real scene/object.

Figure 1 shows the result of applying carving algorithm to temple set images [13], as illustrated, some holes have appeared in the object. There are regions where voxels have been eliminated but they are actually part of the object (A). On the other hand, there is an image region belonging to the background that has not been eliminated (B). Changing binarization threshold for the image can resolve one problem but raises the other.

Fig. 1. Original image, binarized image and 3D reconstruction

These problems reflect the strict nature of the space carving algorithm, where a single image can significantly affect the result of the 3D reconstruction.

3 Sources of Uncertainty

As seen, space carving requires performing a binarization of the image. Determining the appropriate thresholds will be a source of uncertainty for the reconstruction. The geometric errors due to camera calibration process must also be accounted for. For these reasons it was decided to be less restrictive when assuming pixel membership to the background, which in the algorithm of carving means the voxel elimination.

Binarization can be preceded by an image smoothing in order to eliminate image noise that can erroneously create holes in the reconstructed object. Despite all, if an object has relatively large shadows, it will be needed a larger smoothing operator which will lose necessary information about object's shape.

With tested data sets, binarization is performed using the distance between the brightness of pixel and the reference brightness of the background (black). In other sets, distance between pixel and background color in the Hue-Saturation plane, can be used as a measure for binarization.

In this paper, pixel-background distance (either in luminosity or in the HS plane) is not used for binarization but to obtain certainty indicators of pixel membership to the object or to the background regions.

4 Proposed Algorithm

The algorithm proposed has two steps: in the first, a sparse and reduced set of views is used to eliminate a majority of voxels and mark the areas where the result is not certain. In the second, the voxels marked as "uncertain" are used to determine the next best views to continue the carving process. Figure 2 describes the first step, where a dark tone remarks some processes to be studied: object membership function, background membership function, the aggregation function and the decision rule.

For the proposed algorithm the following definitions must be assumed:

N, i	Number of images and image index. $i \in \{1 \dots N\}$
x,y	pixel coordinate index
k,l,m	Voxel index
P_i	Projection matrix for image I_i
$R_{x,y}^i$	Area surrounding $pixel_{xy}$ for image I^i
MFO, MFB	Membership function to object/background
$\mu_{o(xy)}^i, \mu_{b(xy)}^i$	Certainty value of $pixel_{xy}$ is object/background
$\mu_{o(klm)}^i, \mu_{b(klm)}^i$	Certainty value of $voxel_{klm}$ is object/background

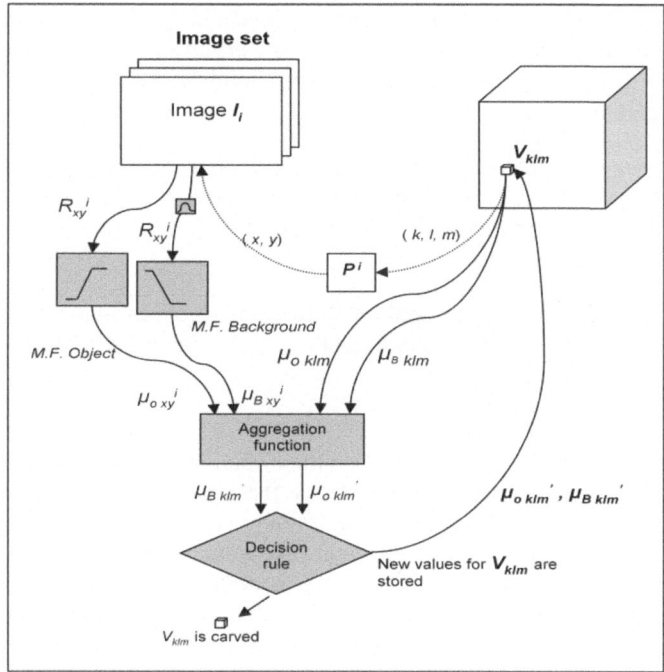

Fig. 2. Diagram showing the first step for the proposed algorithm

Step 1: For a sparse set of images, we apply the following algorithm:

Certainty values of voxels are initialized using the identity element of aggregation function.

1. Each $Voxel_{k,l,m}$ is projected on the image I_i to which it has previously applied a Gaussian function of diameter d to reduce noise in the background.
2. Using the object membership function and background membership function, certainty is calculated for each corresponding pixel, where:
    $\mu^i_{o(xy)}$: Certainty of $pixel_{xy}$ belongs to object
    $\mu^i_{b(xy)}$: Certainty of $pixel_{xy}$ belongs to background
3. Applying aggregation function to certainty values of $pixel^i_{x,y}$ and $voxel^i_{k,l,m,}$, it obtained new values of certainty of $voxel^{i+1}_{k,l,m}$ (for the ith image)
4. Comparing the values of certainty achieved, it is decided whether the voxel is removed (positively belongs to the background) or whether a new iteration it is necessary to obtain new values of certainty.

Step 2: Use the remaining voxels to find a subset of views that minimizes the uncertainty.

At this point, the following iteration is applied: while carving is useful (it carves more than a number of voxels per iteration: thr1) and it can reduce uncertainty (number of uncertain voxels is greater than a threshold thr2), a suitable view is obtained and used to update the certainty values. The criterion tested to choose this view is to find a projection (graphical) of the voxel model where a majority of voxels marked as uncertain were visible.

> *while (number_of_voxels_carved >thr1) and (number_of_voxels_uncertain> thr2)*
>   *Find_a_view_with_maximum_visibility_on_uncertain_voxels( )*
>   *Apply_space_carving_with_this_view( )*
> *endwhile*

Alternatively it is possible to apply a third step, when an algorithm able to deal with concavities like stereo vision could make a final refinement of the model [12].

4.1 Membership Functions

Object/background membership functions allow obtaining a continuous value of certainty for a pixel. These certainty values are in the interval [0, 1]. Membership functions are studied because background (*valRef*) and pixel color (*p(x,y)*) distance can be transformed into certainty value by different functions: sigmoid, linear, cubic, etc. In this algorithm linear functions are proposed to define the membership function to object / background. Threshold values have been determined manually to values 0 and 0.2 for background (*threshold$_{b1}$*, *threshold$_{b2}$*) and 0 and 0.4 for the object (*threshold$_{o1}$*, *threshold$_{o2}$*). These threshold values of uncertainty have been empirically verified and correspond to shadows that are generating problems in binarization process.

$$\mu^i_{b(xy)} = \begin{cases} 1 & \textbf{\textit{if }} dist(p(x,y), valRef) < threshold_{b1} \\ 0 & \textbf{\textit{if }} dist(p(x,y), valRef) > threshold_{b2} \\ 1 - \dfrac{dist(p(x,y), valRef) - threshold_{b1}}{threshold_{b2} - threshold_{b1}} & \textbf{\textit{otherwise}} \end{cases}$$

$$\mu^i_{o(xy)} = \begin{cases} 0 & \textbf{\textit{if }} dist(p(x,y), valRef) < threshold_{o1} \\ 1 & \textbf{\textit{if }} dist(p(x,y), valRef) > threshold_{o2} \\ \dfrac{dist(p(x,y), valRef) - threshold_{o1}}{threshold_{o2} - threshold_{o1}} & \textbf{\textit{otherwise}} \end{cases}$$

4.2 Aggregation Function

Given an uncertainty pixel value and an uncertainty voxel value, a new value of the voxel certainty must be calculated for the object and the background. Uncertainty values for pixel and voxel can be combined in different ways by using methods like the maximum, median, minimum, and so on. In this case the following functions have been used for the background and the object respectively:

$$\mu^{i+1}_{b(klm)} = \max\left(\mu^i_{b(klm)}, \mu^i_{b(xy)}\right)$$

$$\mu^{i+1}_{o(klm)} = \frac{i * \mu^i_{o(klm)} + \mu^i_{o(xy}}{i + 1}$$

Aggregation function that has been chosen to find the new certainty value of background is the maximum function because it allows a simple view to strongly influence the background value, like in the original carving algorithm. On the contrary, the object aggregation function requires that many views to influence the final value. This allows the regions to be seen as an object from most views whilst background for some of them are classified as regions with uncertainty.

4.3 Decision Rule

Finally, a decision rule makes possible to determine whether the voxel should be removed. This allows the fast elimination of a majority of voxels without increasing significantly the carving computing time.

When enough views have been used ($i > Th_v$), voxel background belonging certainty is greater than a threshold $Th1$ and voxel object belonging certainty is lower than a threshold $Th2$, it can be assumed that this voxel belongs to the background and can be eliminated. In the experiments these values have been set to:

$Th_v = 5$, $Th1 = 0.9$ and $Th2 = 0.1$.

5   Results

The image set named "Temple Ring" located in Middlebury University computer vision resources [13] has been used for testing the algorithm.

Figure 1 (right) shows the result of applying the original space carving algorithm on these images and some errors in the three-dimensional object reconstruction occur. The same set of images has been used to test the refined algorithm. Figure 3 shows some views of the 3D model obtained. Black voxels belong to the object and transparent voxels are part of the background. Gray voxels show uncertainty regions. The level of gray is calculated by the difference between $\mu^i_{o(klm)}$ and $\mu^i_{b(klm)}$, so a neutral gray indicates an absolute uncertainty and as it turns white (or black) indicates that it belongs to the background (or object) with more certainty.

Left side of figure 3, shows the result of the algorithm after sixteen images (randomly taken) were used to carve the voxel volume. It can be seen how after first step of the proposed algorithm is done the uncertain regions are marked in gray color. On the right side, the refinement after twelve more views were projected is shown. The majority of uncertain voxels has been removed and only those voxels corresponding to concavities in the object that produce shadows in the image projections remain. Selection of views for refinement has been made using a criterion based on uncertain voxels visibility (i.e. views where the projection of voxels marked as uncertain is maximum). Remaining uncertain voxels could be resolved by using other techniques like stereovision.

Figure 4 shows a comparison between the number of remaining voxels while projecting images into the voxel volume with a random selection of views and an uncertainty-guided selection of views. As it can be seen, the second method obtains a faster and better convergence into the model.

Fig. 3. Reconstruction after 16 random sparse views (left) and after 28 views (16 plus 12 chosen to reduce uncertainty; right). Gray points identify uncertainty, black points identify actual voxels and transparent points are the eliminated voxels.

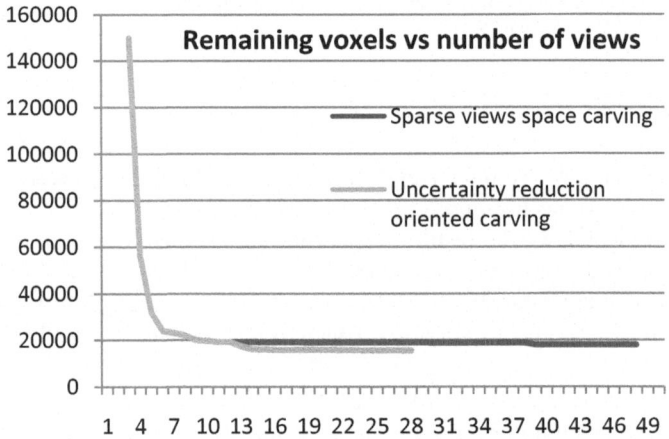

Fig. 4. Acceleration in the convergence of the model reconstruction

6   Conclusions and Future Work

The method presented reduces considerably the number of views needed to obtain an accurate reconstruction of an object, allowing the acceleration of the space carving process. It's clear for the authors that space carving is an optimal algorithm for the purpose of achieving a very fast 3D object reconstruction: it is simple and easy to accelerate by hardware using platforms like CUDA [14]. This is one of the tasks in which work is being done. At the moment of publication of this paper, the whole process is done in 200 ms per a 128^3 voxel set.

The capacity to manage the uncertainty reduces some typical errors of the space carving process. However, several tasks should be done: to find an optimal definition and automatic thresholds for the membership function, to experiment with several aggregation functions, to optimize the decision rule and so forth. In this way, some alternatives can be tested: usage of probabilistic methods, usage of fuzzy systems and, in data sets where the 3D model is known *a priori*, parametrization of the different algorithm steps and use neural networks techniques to adjust these parameters.

References

1. Kanade, T.: Virtualized Reality Home Page. Robotic Institute, Carnegie Mellon,
   `http://www.cs.cmu.edu/afs/cs/project/VirtualizedR/www/`
   `VirtualizedR.html` (accessed 12 9, (2008)
2. Faugeras, O.D., Keriven, R.: Variation Principles, surface evolution, pde's level set methods and the stereo problem. IEEE Trans. Image Processing 7, 336–344 (1998)
3. McMillan, L., Bishop, G.: Plenoptic Modeling: An Image-Based Rendering System. In: Proceedings of SIGGRAPH 1995 (1995)
4. Slabaugh, G., Culbertson, B., Malzbender, T., Schafer, R.: Methods for Volumetric Reconstruction of Visual Scenes. International Journal of Computer Vision 57(3), 179–199 (2004)
5. Kutulakos, K.N., Seitz, S.M.: A theory of shape by space carving. International Journal of Computer Vision, 198–218 (2000)
6. Seitz, S., Dyer, C.M.: Photorealistic scene reconstruction by voxel coloring. International Journal of Computer Vision, 1067–1073 (1999)
7. Culbertson, B., Malzbender, T., Slabaugh, G.: Generalized Voxel Coloring. In: Proceedings of the International Workshop on Vision Algorithms: Theory and Practice, pp. 100–115. Springer, Heidelberg (1999)
8. Broadhurst, A., Drummond, T.W., Cipolla, R.: A Probabilistic Framework for Space Carving. In: International Conference on Computer Vision, pp. 388–393 (2001)
9. Zeng, G., Paris, S., Quan, L.: Robust Carving for Non-Lambertian Objects. In: International Conference on Pattern Recognition, ICPR 2004 (2004)
10. Bhotika, R., Fleet, D., Kutulakos, K.N.: A probabilistic theory of occupancy and emptiness. In: Heyden, A., Sparr, G., Nielsen, M., Johansen, P. (eds.) ECCV 2002. LNCS, vol. 2352, pp. 112–130. Springer, Heidelberg (2002)
11. De Bonet, J.S., Viola, P.: Roxels: Responsability Weighted 3D Volumen Reconstruction. In: International Conference on Computer Vision, pp. 418–425 (1999)
12. Martín, E.X., Aranda, J., Martinez, A.: Refining 3D recovering by carving through View Interpolation and Stereovision. In: Perales, F.J., Campilho, A.C., Pérez, N., Sanfeliu, A. (eds.) IbPRIA 2003. LNCS, vol. 2652, pp. 486–493. Springer, Heidelberg (2003)
13. Seitz, S., Curless, B., Diebel, J., Scharstein, D., Szeliski, R.: Multi-view stereo page,
    `http://vision.middlebury.edu/mview/data/` (accessed 12 11, 2008)
14. The resource for CUDA developer. Hosted by nVidia corp.,
    `http://www.nvidia.com/object/cuda` (accesed 12 16, 2008)

Mean Shift Parallel Tracking on GPU

Peihua Li and Lijuan Xiao

School of Computer Science and Technology, Heilongjiang Univesity
Harbin, Heilongjiang Province, China, 150080
peihualj@hotmail.com

Abstract. We propose a parallel Mean Shift (MS) tracking algorithm on Graphics Processing Unit (GPU) using Compute Unified Device Architecture (CUDA). Traditional MS algorithm uses a large number of color histogram, say typically 16x16x16, which makes parallel implementation infeasible. We thus employ K-Means clustering to partition the object color space that enables us to represent color distribution with a quite small number of bins. Based on this compact histogram, all key components of the MS algorithm are mapped onto the GPU. The resultant parallel algorithm consist of six kernel functions, which involves primarily the parallel computation of the candidate histogram and calculation of the Mean Shift vector. Experiments on public available CAVIAR videos show that the proposed parallel tracking algorithm achieves large speedup and has comparable tracking performance, compared with the traditional serial MS tracking algorithm.

Keywords: Mean Shift tracking; Parallel algorithm; GPU; CUDA.

1 Introduction

Object tracking is an important research topic in the field of the computer vision. In recent years, the increasing demand for automated video analysis together with the advent of high quality, inexpensive video cameras and computers motivates more researchers to pay a great deal of attention to object tracking issues.

Mean Shift (MS) based tracking [1] is well known for its efficiency and performance. The MS tracking algorithm uses color histogram combined with spatial kernel to represent object distribution, and Bhattacharrya coefficient is used as similarity function that is optimized by Mean Shift iteration. Following [1], many researchers propose diverse algorithms for improving its performance. Collins solves the problem of kernel scale selection that exists in traditional MS tracking algorihtm [2]. In [3, 4], more rich spatial information is incorporated into object representation to increase robustness of the tracking algorithm. Tracking of objects with similarity or affine information are handled in [5, 6, 7]. Review of other MS tracking algorithms are omitted due to page limit.

A visual task of automated video analysis generally comprises object detection, object tracking, and recognition or encoding. A real time implementation of the visual task demands that each process should consume as little time as

H. Araujo et al. (Eds.): IbPRIA 2009, LNCS 5524, pp. 120–127, 2009.

possible. It is the most desirable that the intermediate process such as object tracking should be highly efficient. Hence, we develop a parallel MS tracking algorithm on GPU using CUDA that is implemented on GeForce 8800 GTS. The parallel algorithm solves the key issues concerned with computation of the candidate histogram and the mean shift vector. The resulting parallel MS consists of six kernel functions that corresponds to the principal components of its serial version.

Our paper is organized as follows. Section 2 reviews the serial MS tracking algorithm. The parallel tracking algorithm on GPU using CUDA is detailed in the section 3. In the section , The experiments are given in section 4 followed by the concluding remarks in section 4.

2   Serial Mean Shift Tracking Algorithm

In this section, we briefly review the traditional, serial MS tracking algorithm [1].

2.1   Target Model Representation

The target is represented by the rectangle region of width h_x and height h_y, centered on the origin. The target model is computed as

$$p_u = C \sum_{i=1}^{n} k \left(\frac{(x_i^*)^2}{h_x^2} + \frac{(y_i^*)^2}{h_y^2} \right) \delta_{ui}, \quad u = 0, \cdots, m-1 \tag{1}$$

where n is the number of pixels in the reference image, m is the number of bins, $k(\cdot)$ is the kernel function [1], and C is the normalization constant so that $\sum_{u=0}^{m-1} p_u = 1$.

2.2   Candidate Model Representation

The candidate model is defined by the following equation

$$q_u(\mathbf{z}) = C_h \sum_{i=1}^{n_h} k \left(\frac{(x - x_i)^2}{h_x^2} + \frac{(y - y_i)^2}{h_y^2} \right) \delta_{ui}, \quad u = 0, \cdots, m-1 \tag{2}$$

where the candidate image is centered on $\mathbf{z} = (x, y)$ that has n_h pixels with the spatial coordinates (x_i, y_i), C_h is the normalization constant and $\delta_{ui} = 1$ if the pixel with spatial coordinate $\mathbf{z}_i = (x_i, y_i)$ belongs to the uth bin, otherwise $\delta_{ui} = 0$.

2.3   Similarity Function (SF)

In our paper, we use Bhattacharyya coefficient as the similarity metric between the target model and the candidate model and it is defined by

$$S(\mathbf{p}, \mathbf{q}(\mathbf{z})) = \sum_{u=0}^{m-1} \sqrt{p_u q_u(\mathbf{z})} \tag{3}$$

2.4   Mean Shift Vector

The traditional MS tracking algorithm evaluates the object center position in a new frame by computing the MS vector $\Delta \mathbf{z}$ iteratively until convergence or a prescribed maximum iteration number reaches. The formula for computing $\Delta \mathbf{z}$ is as follows:

$$\Delta \mathbf{z} = \frac{\sum_{i=1}^{n_h} (\mathbf{z}_i - \mathbf{z}) \omega_i g(\cdot)}{\sum_{i=1}^{n_h} \omega_i g(\cdot)} \tag{4}$$

where $g(\cdot) = k(\cdot)'$ and ω_i is given by $\omega_i = \sum_{u=0}^{m-1} \sqrt{\frac{p_u}{q_u(\mathbf{z}_k)}} \delta_{ui}$.

3   Parallel MS Tracking Algorithm on GPU

Compute Unified Device Architecture (CUDA) [8] is a new hardware and software architecture for managing computation on the GPU, which consists of extension of C Language for programming that makes it unnecessary to access graphics APIs. For the developers who are not acquainted with GPGPU, CUDA provides more flexibility and smooth transition from the serial algorithms to the parallel algorithms. In our experiments, we utilize the GPU card GeForce 8800 GTS manufactured by NVIDIA's corporation.

3.1   Color Space Partition

The color space in the traditional MS tracking algorithm is uniformly partitioned into m bins, typically 16x16x16, which makes parallel algorithm infeasible. Noticing that object color is usually compact and distributed only in some small regions in the whole color space, as done in [9], we use K-Means clustering method to partition the color space and then construct lookup table.

3.2   Parallel Tracking Algorithm with CUDA

Before invoking kernel functions, we first compute the bin indices of candidate pixels according to lookup table with CPU. In order to avoid frequent data transfer between CPU memory and GPU memory, we compute the bin indices of a sub-image that is centered at the object center and that is double size of the object. Then we bind (copy) the 2D index array to the texture memory on GPU. The advantage of texture memory is that its access is optimized for 2D spatial locality by GPU.

Kernel #1. The purpose of the kernel is to calculate the n sub-histograms and n stands for the number of blocks. Each thread loads one bin index u from the texture memory. During computation of the candidate histogram, when different threads simultaneously write data into the same shared memory address, memory collision is inevitable. In order to solve the problem, we follow the tactic that one thread maintains its own sub-histogram $[q'_{(i,0)}(\mathbf{z}), q'_{(i,1)}(\mathbf{z}), \cdots, q'_{(i,m-1)}(\mathbf{z})]$,

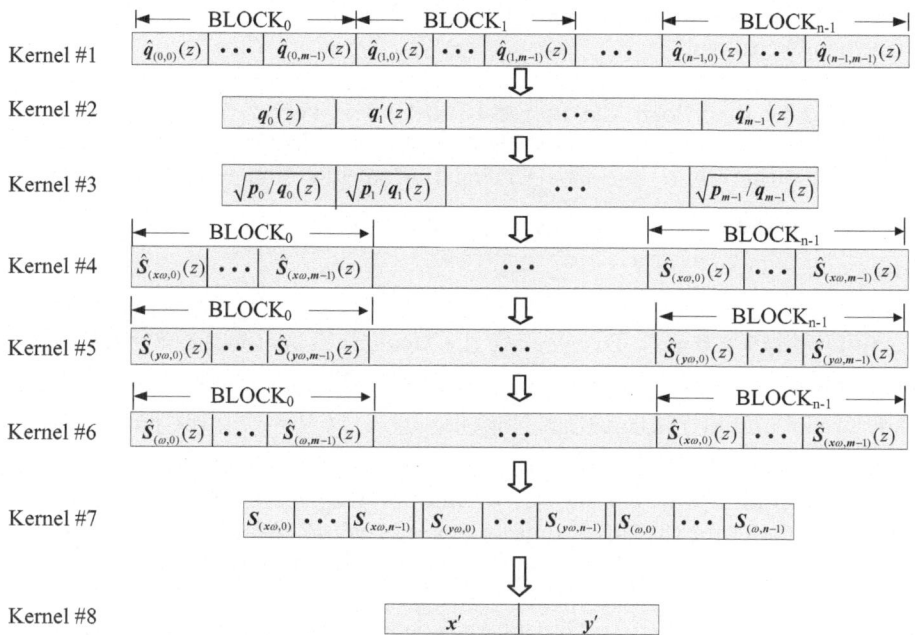

Fig. 1. Six kernels results in global memory

$i = 0, \cdots, l - 1$, where l is the number of threads in a block. At this time, all the computed sub-histograms are written into the shared memory. The advantage of this method is that each thread writes data into different shared memory addresses and there is no memory collision. Then we merge the sub-histograms within block. For the jth block, $j = 0, 1, \cdots, n-1$, we have $\hat{q}_{(j,u)}(\mathbf{z}) = \sum_{i=0}^{l-1} q'_{(i,u)}(\mathbf{z}), (u = 0, 1, \cdots, m - 1)$. And then the n sub-histograms $[\hat{q}_{(j,0)}(\mathbf{z}), \hat{q}_{(j,1)}(\mathbf{z}), \cdots, \hat{q}_{(j,m-1)}(\mathbf{z})]$ are written into the global memory, which are seen in the Fig. 1.

Remark. The size of the shared memory in CUDA is limited by $16KB$, which is a big challenge for the developers. In our experiments, we empirically set the number of bins to 13. So, noticing that the data type in histogram is single-precision floating number, if the number of threads per block is set to 256, we can only have one active block per multiprocessor ($\lfloor (16 * 1024)/(13 * 256 * 4) \rfloor = 1$), which greatly impacts the parallelism of the tracking algorithm.

Kernel #2. The kernel aims at merging the n sub-histograms produced by the kernel #1, into the complete m candidate histograms without being normalized (CHWN) $\mathbf{q}'(\mathbf{z}) = [q'_0(\mathbf{z}), q'_1(\mathbf{z}), \cdots, q'_{m-1}(\mathbf{z})]$. Load the n sub-histograms into the shared memory and for the jth block, the uth CHWN is produced by $q'_u(\mathbf{z}) = \sum_{j=0}^{n-1} q'_{(j,u)}(\mathbf{z})$, using the parallel sum reduction algorithm, which is introduced below. But the algorithm demands that the data must be a power of two. To handle non-power-of-two data, while loading the sub-histograms from the global memory, the kernel pads the shared memory array and initializes the extra memory to zero.

Kernel #3. First load the m results from the kernel #2 into the shared memory. To obtain the candidate histogram $\mathbf{q}(\mathbf{z}) = [q_0(\mathbf{z}), q_1(\mathbf{z}), \cdots, q_{m-1}(\mathbf{z})]$, we compute the $C_h = \frac{1}{\sum_{u=0}^{m-1} q'_u(\mathbf{z})}$ using the parallel sum reduction algorithm and then caculate $\mathbf{q}(\mathbf{z}) = [C_h q'_0(\mathbf{z}), C_h q'_1(\mathbf{z}), \cdots, C_h q'_{m-1}(\mathbf{z})]$, and $\sqrt{\frac{p_u}{q_u(\mathbf{z})}}$, $(u = 0, 1, \cdots, m-1)$.

Kernel #4 #5 #6 #7. To calculate the Mean Shift vector $\Delta \mathbf{z} = \frac{\sum_{i=1}^{n_h}(\mathbf{z}_i - \mathbf{z})\omega_i}{\sum_{i=1}^{n_h}\omega_i}$, we must first compute $\sum_{i=1}^{n_h} x_i\omega_i$, $\sum_{i=1}^{n_h} y_i\omega_i$ and $\sum_{i=1}^{n_h}\omega_i$, where we use Epanechnikov profile and $g(\cdot)$ is constant. Noticing $\omega_i = \sqrt{\frac{p_u}{q_u(\mathbf{z}_k)}}\delta_{ui}$, the pattern of the above three summations is similar to the pattern of CHWN $q'_u(\mathbf{z}) = \sum_{i=1}^{n_h} k(\cdot)\delta_{ui}$. Hence, in a similar way, Kernel #4, #5 and #6 respectively produce the n sub-sums of m entries for the three summations. Kernel #7 merges the n sub-sums to get $[S_{(x\omega,0)}, \cdots, S_{(x\omega,n-1)}]$, $[S_{(y\omega,0)}, \cdots, S_{(y\omega,n-1)}]$, and $[S_{\omega_0}, \cdots, S_{\omega_{n-1}}]$.

Kernel #8. Using the parallel sum reduction algorithm, we can compute the new object center $\mathbf{z}' = (x', y')$, where $x' = \frac{\sum_{j=0}^{n-1} S_{(x\omega,j)}}{\sum_{j=0}^{n-1} S_{\omega_j}}$ and $y' = \frac{\sum_{j=0}^{n-1} S_{(y\omega,j)}}{\sum_{j=0}^{n-1} S_{\omega_j}}$.

The new center $\mathbf{z}' = (x', y')$ is transferred from GPU to CPU and the latter can determine whether iteration process should continue, by verifying whether $\|\mathbf{z} - \mathbf{z}'\| < \varepsilon_{\mathbf{z}}$, or maximum iteration number N reaches.

4   Experiments

The proposed parallel tracking algorithm is implemented on GPU card GeForce 8800 GTS, which is installed on a PC with 3.0GHz Intel Pentium(R) 4 CPU and 2G Memory. In all experiments, the 16x16x16 color histogram is used in the serial MS algorithm and the cluster number K is set to 13 in the parallel algorithm.

4.1   Data Set and Performance Comparision

We use publicly available benchmark data sets of CAVIAR project [10], where ground truth has been labeled. Two video clips of OneStopEnter2cor.mpg (OSE) and ThreePastShop1cor.mpg (TPS) are used in which six objects are tracked. Please see Fig. 2 for reference.

In Table 1, the 4th and 5th columns give average distance error and average overlapping region error [11] in the format of mean plus/minus standard variance (mean ± std), which shows that the two algorithm are comparable in performance. The 6th column lists the average tracking time of CPU and GPU respectively, and the speedups are provided in the last column of Table 1.

| (a) ID3 in OSE | (b) ID4 and ID6 in OSE | (c) ID0 in TPS | (d) ID1 and ID4 in TPS |

Fig. 2. Six objects that are tracked in our experiments

Table 1. Comparison between GPU and CPU

Scenarios	Object ID	Algorithm	Distance error (pixel)*	Overlapping region error(%)*	Tracking time (ms)	SpeedUp
OSE	ID3	CPU	18.47±11.23	0.361±0.221	5.69	2.44
		GPU	12.28±06.38	0.345±0.210	2.33	
	ID4	CPU	12.68±04.63	0.446±0.221	5.49	2.52
		GPU	15.21±07.12	0.478±0.185	2.18	
	ID6	CPU	07.10±03.61	0.351±0.179	6.38	2.44
		GPU	8.58±02.49	0.456±0.153	2.61	
TPS	ID0	CPU	15.43±08.20	0.246±0.165	8.98	2.79
		GPU	15.05±06.75	0.232±0.164	3.22	
	ID1	CPU	12.96±13.29	0.182±0.117	9.01	3.36
		GPU	07.21±06.41	0.183±0.114	2.68	
	ID4	CPU	08.00±06.25	0.266±0.100	5.88	2.77
		GPU	06.57±02.53	0.362±0.165	2.12	

* The format of data is mean±std.

4.2 Effect of Bandwidth between CPU and GPU on the Parallel Algorithm

It is well-known that data transfer between CPU and GPU is the bottleneck for many GPGPU applications. In our algorithm, we first need to bind (copy) to the texture the bin index array of three times the size of the object. Take ID4 in TPS sequence as an example, this operation takes 0.406ms. During mean shift iterations, we have to transfer the object position $\mathbf{z}' = (x', y')$ from GPU to CPU so that the latter can determine whether to halt the iteration, which takes 0.0188*5=0.094ms, assuming that average iterative number is 5. Finally, to compute the $S(\mathbf{p}, \mathbf{q}(\mathbf{z}))$, we must copy the candidate histogram from GPU to CPU as well that takes 0.0181ms. To sum up, data transfer between GPU and CPU takes 0.518ms. And the speedup will reach 3.67 if the data transfer cost is neglected.

5 Conclusions

The paper proposes a parallel MS tracking algorithm on GPU using CUDA. Using K-Means clustering to partition the object color space, we can represent object distribution with quite a very small number of bins which makes parallel MS algorithm possible. Then we map the major components in serial MS tracking algorithm onto the GPU, which involves primarily computation of the candidate histogram and the calculation of the MS vector. Experimental results show that the proposed parallel algorithm achieves large speedups. Meanwhile, it has comparable tracking performance with the traditional serial MS tracking method.

In the kernel functions (#1, #4, #5, #6), the number of active blocks per multiprocessor is severely limited by the $16KB$ shared memory that results in low parallelism of the algorithm. It is our concern to think about effective technique to increase the parallelism. In our experiments the number of histogram bins is empirically chosen. It is necessary in future work to determine adaptively the number of bins for better performance of the parallel algorithm.

Acknowledgment

The work was supported by the National Natural Science Foundation of China under Grant 60673110 and Natural Science Foundation of Heilongjiang Province (F200512), supported in part by Program for New Century Excellent Talents of Heilongjiang Province (1153-NCET-002), Sci. & Tech. Research Project of Educational Bureau of Heilongjiang Province (1151G033), the Scientific Research Foundation for the Returned Overseas Chinese Scholars, State Education Ministry and Ministry of Personnel of China, Sci. and Tech. Innovation Research Project (2006RFLXG030) of Harbin Sci. & Tech. Bureau.

References

1. Comaniciu, D., Ramesh, V., Meer, P.: Real-time Tracking of Non-rigid Objects Using Mean Shift. In: Proc. IEEE Conf. Comp. Vis. Patt. Recog., pp. 142–149. Hilton Head Island, South Carolina (2000)
2. Collins, R.T.: Mean-shift Blob Tracking Through Scale Space. In: Proc. IEEE Conf. Comp. Vis. Patt. Recog., Madison, Wisconsin, pp. 234–241 (2003)
3. Birchfield, S.T., Rangarajan, S.: Spatiograms versus Histograms for Region-based Tracking. In: Proc. IEEE Conf. Comp. Vis. Patt. Recog., San Diego, CA, USA, pp. 1158–1163 (2005)
4. Zhao, Q., Tao, H.: Object Tracking using Color Correlogram. In: IEEE Workshop on Visual Surveillance and Performance Evaluation of Tracking and Surveillance (VS-PETS) in conjunction with ICCV, pp. 263–270 (2005)
5. Yilmaz, A.: Object Tracking by Asymmetric Kernel Mean Shift with Automatic Scale and Orientation Selection. In: Proc. IEEE Conf. Comp. Vis. Patt. Recog., Minneapolis, Minnesota, pp. 1–6 (2007)

6. Zhang, H., Huang, W., Huang, Z., Li, L.: Affine object tracking with kernel-based spatial-color representation. In: Proc. IEEE Conf. Comp. Vis. Patt. Recog., San Diego, CA, USA, pp. 293–300 (2005)
7. Leichter, I., Lindenbaum, M., Rivlin, E.: Visual Tracking by Affine Kernel Fitting Using Color and Object Boundary. In: Proc. Int. Conf. Comp. Vis., Rio de, Janeiro, Brazil, pp. 1–6 (2007)
8. NVIDIA CUDA Homepage, http://developer.nvidia.com/object/cuda.html
9. Li, P.: A clustering-based color model and integral images for fast object tracking. Signal Processing: Image Communication, 676–687 (2006)
10. EC funded CAVIAR project/IST 2001 37540 (2004), http://homepages.inf.ed.ac.uk/rbf/CAVIAR/
11. Bajramovic, F., Grabl, C., Denzler, J.: Efficient Combination of Histograms for Real-Time Tracking Using Mean-Shift and Trust-Region Optimization. In: Proc. 27th DAGM Symposium on Pattern Recognition, Vienna, Austria, pp. 254–261 (2005)

Local Boosted Features for Pedestrian Detection[*]

Michael Villamizar[1,2], Alberto Sanfeliu[1,2], and Juan Andrade-Cetto[1]

[1] Institut de Robòtica i Informàtica Industrial, CSIC-UPC
[2] Department of Automatic Control, UPC

Abstract. The present paper addresses pedestrian detection using local boosted features that are learned from a small set of training images. Our contribution is to use two boosting steps. The first one learns discriminant local features corresponding to pedestrian parts and the second one selects and combines these boosted features into a robust class classifier. In contrast of other works, our features are based on local differences over Histograms of Oriented Gradients (HoGs). Experiments carried out to a public dataset of pedestrian images show good performance with high classification rates.

1 Introduction

Recently, several techniques based on Histograms of Oriented Gradients (HoG) have been developed showing successful results in object detection and categorization [1,2,3,4,5,6]. These type of features have demonstrated robustness and reliability for representing local image features. The keypoint in using HOG descriptors is to capture or encode feature layout where each histogram cell contains an oriented gradient distribution for pixels within this cell.

Dalal and Triggs [1] proposed to use HOG descriptors for pedestrian detection in static images and in videos. They use an overlapping local contrast normalization in order to improve detection performance giving a certain invariance to illumination and shadows. In Bosch *et al.* [2] pyramidal Histograms of Oriented Gradients (PHoGs) are used for object categorization. These pyramidal descriptors encode features and their spatial layout in several resolution levels, allowing robustness to small feature shifts. Finer histogram levels are weighted more than coarser ones, since finer resolutions have more a detailed feature shape description. This idea is inspired by image pyramid representation of scenes [3]. This spatial pyramidal representation is an extension to the Dalal and Triggs method where Histograms of Oriented Gradients are restricted to finer resolutions. In the same way, SIFT features [4] compute fixed HoG descriptors in a grid of 4x4 cells and 8 gradient orientations around interest points.

A cascade of HoG features has been proposed using the Adaboost algorithm to construct a fast and accurate human detector [5]. This idea is similar to addressed by Viola and Jones [7], but using HoGs instead of Haar-like features. The method selects features

---

[*] This research was partially supported by the Spanish Ministry of Innovation and Science under projects Consolider Ingenio 2010 CSD2007-00018, and projects DPI 2007-614452 and DPI 2008-06022; by the URUS project IST-045062 of the European Union; and by the Technical University of Catalonia (UPC) to MV.

H. Araujo et al. (Eds.): IbPRIA 2009, LNCS 5524, pp. 128–135, 2009.

of several sizes, finding in early cascade stages larger features. This fact is suitable for rapid detection and for discarding background image locations but it might have problems when pedestrians are partially occluded. A similar method is proposed by Laptev [6] for object class detection. This method aims to find what HoG features to use and where to compute them. For this, training information is used to determine the local HoG features, and HoG feature selection is carried out using random regions and selecting the best boosting over Weighted Fischer linear discriminant weak learners.

Our contribution is to learn reliable features inside HoG instead of using the whole HoG descriptor to detect human parts. In contrast to previous methods that use whole local HoG descriptors, we propose to use the training information to seek out the most discriminant HoG-based features using a boosting algorithm. These boosted features focus on histomgram's bins with high occurence and discard those whose contribution to object detection is lower. This learning process is carried out in all image locations in order to determine which are the most relevant pedestrian parts. Once the boosted features are learned a final boosting step is performed to select and combine the most discriminant.

2 Approach

We present boosted features computed on Histograms of Oriented Gradients in order to have faster and robust features with which to describe human parts and to face up intraclass variations present in class images (Figure 1). These local features are learned in a first training step and combined in a second one. This last step rejects some initial boosted features because they are not discriminant enough and tend to favor the background. Unlike Laptev's work, our boosted features are not computed in random

(a) Positive images

(b) Negative images

Fig. 1. Positive and negative images

locations but computed exhaustively over the whole image with the aim to determine which image locations are human parts and which ones are background. The training is carried out using the well-known Adaboost algorithm that has successful results in object detection [6,7,8].

Given that pedestrian HoGs are corrupted by background, we propose HoG-based features instead of whole HoG descriptors in order to concentrate on HoG parts with high reliability. Although these type of features have been used for keypoint classification and segmentation in intensity images [9,10], we use them over histograms of oriented gradients, combining the simplicity of these features with the robustness of HoGs.

The paper is organized as follows, Section 3 explains the local boosted feature computation using training data and simple features over histograms of oriented gradients. In Section 4 the boosted feature selection is described. The implementation details and experiments performed on a public pedestrian dataset are shown in Sections 5 and 6, respectively.

3   Boosted Features

Histograms of oriented gradients are used to capture local feature layout over images. Each histogram cell has a local distribution of features (gradient orientations). The proposed work aims to seek out the image locations, corresponding to human parts, that have high similarities across positive images and are discriminant to negative ones. These image locations are selected via a local boosting step where HoG-based features are computed.

Given that the input images have pedestrians segmented and aligned, it is possible to learn a classifier for each image location that allows to recognize it. This classifier is called boosted feature because of it consists of a weighted combination of simple HoG-based features. Boosted features measure similarity across positive and negative images. Positive histograms have strong similarities across images. Such similarities are learned using boosting of simple features over histograms. Figure 2 shows a local HoG

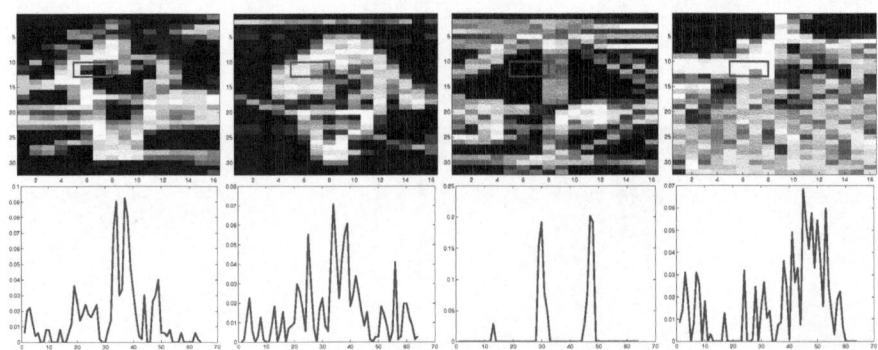

Fig. 2. Local HoG similarities. Positive and negative gradient images (first row), and their local HoGs (second row).

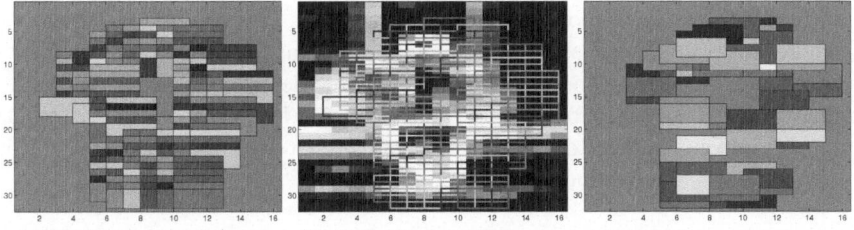

(a) Initial boosted features   (b) Initial boosted features   (c) Final boosted features

Fig. 3. Boosted features. Color boxes correpond to locations where boosted features have a high similarity across positive images.

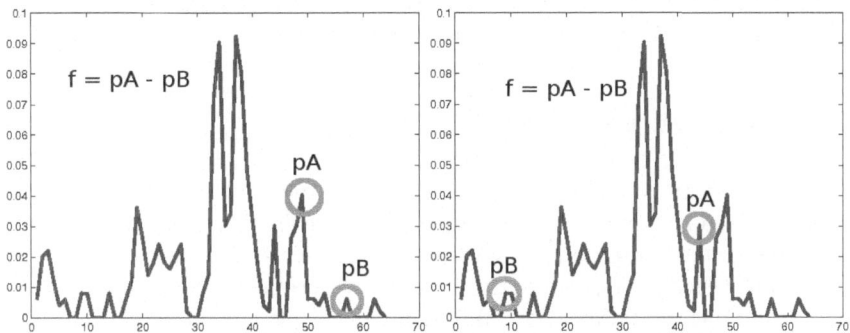

Fig. 4. HoG-based feature instances

and its similarities across images. Regions where it is possible to get a boosted feature classifier are selected as initial human parts. As background locations do not have strong similarities, the method can not find a classifier for those locations and therefore such locations are discarded. Figures 3a and 3b show initial boosted features. As we can see, the boosted features are localized on human contours and some background regions that present certain similarities such as ground edges.

The boosted features consist of combinations of simple and rapid features. These simple HoG-based features are defined as the difference between values of histogram bins

$$f_i(HoG) = HoG(pA) - HoG(pB),\tag{1}$$

where pA and pB are bin indexes. The boosted combination of these features gives a boosted feature classifier that represents those features which better classify the training data for current image location :

$$bof(HoG) = \sum_{i=1}^{n} \alpha_i f_i(HoG)\tag{2}$$

Parameter α_i is the weight associated to each feature and is obtained with the Adaboost algorithm, according to its classification error. Some illustrative feature instances are shown in Figure 4. These simple features resemble to features used for keypoint classification and for image categorization and segmentation. However, in this work they are computed over HoG descriptors. To increase robustness to image and intraclass variations, multiple boosted features are computed for the same image location and their outputs combined. This idea is inspired from randomized decision forests where each tree is trained on small random subsets from training images [10]. This technique speeds up the training time and reduces over-fitting problems. Therefore our local boosted feature is a combination of simple boosting iterations :

$$bof(HoG) = \sum_{j=1}^{m} \sum_{i=1}^{n} \alpha_{i,j} f_{i,j}(HoG) \tag{3}$$

Although each boosted feature has to be computed for each image location, by a window convolution over the image, the process is rapid lasting few seconds per region (in our case 2 seconds using 50 positive and 500 negative training images).

4   Boosted Feature Selection

In this step a second boosting process is applied to select the most accurate and discriminant boosted features over a validation set of images. The aim is to choose those boosted features that correspond to human parts in order to form the whole pedestrian detector while rejecting boosted features with low discriminant power against negative or background images. Furthermore, this step reduces the amount of boosted features that is suitable for a rapid detection. In spite of the reduced number of features and their simplicity, the proposed method achieves high detection rates in our experiments. This is because the method is focused on selecting what features to use and where to compute them. Figure 3c shows the final boosted features after the boosting selection step. The boosted features are localized on pedestrian contours.

5   Implementation Details

5.1   Histogram of Oriented Gradients

Gradient computation is applied to input images to form HoG images. The input image size is $256x128$ pixels both for positive and negative images. 4 gradient orientations are chosen to this work. A spatial binning of $8x8$ pixels is done to obtain a HoG image of $32x16x4$ cells. The boosted features are computed in small regions of $4x4x4$ cells using a sliding window over whole HoG image.

5.2   Boosted Features

The initial HoG-based features are selected randomly. In our experiments 150 features per location have been chosen. Boosting selects the 8 (n) more discriminant HoG-based features and uses 5 (m) boosting iterations to have finally a boosted Feature formed by 40 difference features. These parameters are chosen by the user according to object class. The number of images per set is 50% of all training images.

5.3   Detection Images

For each detection image an image pyramid is built, and for each level a HoG image is computed using the previous implementation details. The number of pyramid levels is 6 for an input image size of 640x854 pixels.

6   Experiments

The proposed method has been tested in a public pedestrian dataset [13]. This dataset contains people segmented but with a large amount of background. Moreover, people in images have a high class varitions because of different clothes and illumination conditions, see Figure 1. Negative images are extracted from several images which do not have people and have a high gradient content. Since the proposed method requires training, validation and test sets of images, the pedestrian dataset is split up randomly. For training, 50 positive and 500 negative images are chosen. In the same way, 200 and 200 images for validation and 300 and 300 for test, respectively.

In spite of the small set of positive training images (50) the proposed method performs well in image classification both in validation and test sets. These results can be seen in the ROC curve (Figure 5a).These results show how our approach using the learned boosted features generalizes the pedestrian class classification. Figures 5b and

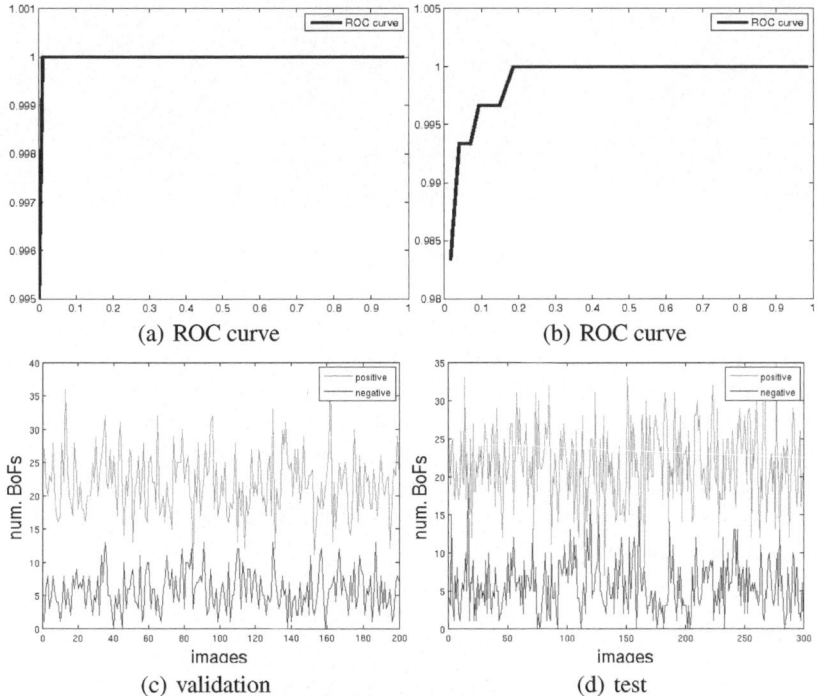

(a) ROC curve   (b) ROC curve

(c) validation   (d) test

Fig. 5. Detection curves

Fig. 6. Pedestrian detection

5c show boosted feature detection in validation and test images. We can see that positive images have more detected features than negative ones. However, negative images contain a considerable amount of features because they have local image representations like edges, corners, etc. One second test was to perform the pedestrian detector over outdoor scenes (Figure 6). The top images are input images and in each column appears detections in some HoG pyramid levels for each image. The first column shows how pedestrians are detected across several levels unlike image 3. The second column shows one false negative.

7   Conclusions

This paper proposes a detection method using learned boosted features that can be used for object categorization under high intraclass variation. The approach finds out the most significant local parts while rejecting background regions. These HoG-based features allow a robust and rapid image detection with high classification rates. The approach generalizes the pedestrian class using a reduced number of training images.

References

1. Dalal, N., Triggs, B.: Histograms of oriented gradients for human detection. In: IEEE Computer Society Conference on Computer Vision and Pattern Recognition, San Diego, California, vol. 1, pp. 886–893 (2005)
2. Bosch, A., Zisserman, A., Muoz, X.: Image Classification Using ROIs and Multiple Kernel Learning. International Journal of Computer Vision (2008)
3. Lazebnik, S., Schmid, C., Ponce, J.: Beyond bags of features: Spatial pyramid matching for recognizing natural scene categories. In: IEEE Computer Society Conference on Computer Vision and Pattern Recognition, New York, vol. 2, pp. 2169–2178 (2006)
4. Lowe, D.: Distinctive image features from scale invariant keypoints. International Journal of Computer Vision 60(2), 91–110 (2004)
5. Zhu, Q., Avidan, S., Ye, M., Cheng, K.-T.: Fast human detection using a cascade of Histograms of Oriented Gradients. In: IEEE Computer Society Conference on Computer Vision and Pattern Recognition, New York, vol. 2, pp. 1491–1498 (2006)
6. Laptev, I.: Improvements of object detection using boosted histograms. In: British Machine Vision Conference, vol. 3, pp. 949–958 (2006)
7. Viola, P., Jones, M.: Rapid object detection using a boosted cascade of simple features. In: IEEE Computer Society Conference on Computer Vision and Pattern Recognition, Kauai, Hawaii, vol. 1, pp. 511–518 (2001)
8. Villamizar, M., Sanfeliu, A., Andrade-Cetto, J.: Computation of rotation local invariant features using the integral image for real time object detection. In: IAPR International Conference on Pattern Recognition, Hong Kong, pp. 81–85 (2006)
9. Ozuysal, M., Fua, P., Lepetit, V.: Fast Keypoint Recognition in Ten Lines of Code. In: IEEE Computer Society Conference on Computer Vision and Pattern Recognition, Minneapolis, pp. 1–8 (2007)
10. Shotton, J., Johnson, M., Cipolla, R.: Semantic Texton Forests for Image Categorization and Segmentation. In: IEEE Computer Society Conference on Computer Vision and Pattern Recognition, Anchorage, Alaska, pp. 1–8 (2008)
11. Grauman, K., Darrell, T.: The pyramid match kernel: Discriminative classification with sets of image features. In: International Conference on Computer Vision, Beijing, vol. 2, pp. 1458–1465 (2005)
12. Chum, O., Zisserman, A.: An exemplar model for learning object classes. In: IEEE Computer Society Conference on Computer Vision and Pattern Recognition, Minneapolis, pp. 1–8 (2007)
13. Papageorgiou, C., Poggio, T.: A trainable system for object detection. International Journal of Computer Vision 38(1), 15–33 (2000)

Plane Filtering for the Registration of Urban Range Laser Imagery

Xavier Mateo[1] and Xavier Binefa[2]

[1] Universitat Autònoma de Barcelona,
Department of Computing Science, Barcelona, Spain
javier.mateo@uab.es
[2] Universitat Pompeu Fabra,
Department of Information and Communication Technologies, Barcelona, Spain
xavier.binefa@upf.edu

Abstract. A method for the registration between pairs of range images is proposed, taking advantage of the typical structures of an urban scene. The detection of large planes representing walls of buildings is the main step in the proposed method. Following steps are based on the use of descriptors for every image and the posterior matching between them.

Keywords: range scanner, pairwise registration, plane estimation, ICP.

1 Introduction

Registration of laser range images is a current topic in modern literature. The typically used variant is the so-called pairwise registration, where two range images taken from unknown positions are registered to each other. Often the registration is carried out using the whole range images and their corresponding 3D structures, without considering the particularities of the specific environment.

In this paper we introduce the possibility of achieving the registration assuming that the images are captured in an urban environment, and therefore looking for specific structures typical in urban scenarios. For these reasons, we first make a filtering in order to find planes with a minimum area, which will correspond to the walls of buildings. After this pre-processing, typical methods using already existing methods can be applied achieving an improved result.

2 State of the Art

The typical method for the pairwise registration of 3D points sets is the so-called Iterative Closest Point (ICP) [1], which performs an iterative process in order to minimize the mean square distance between two sets. Some modifications of the ICP algorithm have been appeared since its publication, achieving better results and advantages [2]. Nonetheless, the main problem of this family of algorithms is the necessity of having a good initialization, otherwise the registration could converge to a local minimum and not to a global minimum.

H. Araujo et al. (Eds.): IbPRIA 2009, LNCS 5524, pp. 136–143, 2009.

For this reason usually the main topic on the 3D registration literature is focused on the obtaining of this initial approximation. The most usual method is the combination of a GPS and an Inertial Measurement Unit (IMU) [3] in order to detect position and orientation of the range scanner in both scan images. Since the two 3Ds are expressed from the coordinates system with origin in the scanner, it is easy to register afterwards the 3D points sets.

Other possibilities make use of descriptors for specific points which, afterwards, are compared to find the possible matchings between the images. Most of them are based on the use of the SIFT descriptor [4], which analyzes 2D feature pixels and evaluates their relationship with the neighboring pixels. Main problem is that usually SIFT descriptor is able to cope with small differences in the point of view, but not with high differences as could be our case. For this reason different methods are proposed in the literature [5], estimating the surface normal at the 3D coordinate and performing an homography of the visible image as it would be seen from the front side of the keypoint. After applying this method, the SIFT descriptor is applied.

Also in the field of descriptors we can include the Spin Images [6], which create a 2D image for every specific 3D point. These 2D images encode the neighborhood of the 3D point within a defined distance, and have the particularity that are invariant to rotation and to the density of the 3D points set.

In this paper we want to show a previous pre-processing of the data, where later can be applied the algorithms that have been referenced. The idea is to detect the structures that are similar to a plane, which in a second step are used as a filter for the rest of the method.

3   Introduction to the Problem

Using traditional methods the first step in order to achieve the registration is the detection of keypoints in the associated visible images. Anyway, depending on the nature of the scene, and specially in the cases of urban environment, traditional techniques of keypoint detection will find a huge number of keypoints in places with low interest for the registration. As an example, see the image shown in Fig. 1, where the keypoints detected with a DoG detector [4] are shown. As can be seen, element with low importance for the registration as could be the autos have most of the detected keypoints. On the other side, the wall of the building, which should have the higher importance, does not have any keypoints by itself and only thanks to the presence of windows some keypoints are detected.

Anyway, as we have also access to the 3D structure of the scene thanks to the range image, we could use this information to have a pre-processing of the data and filter only the parts of the scene that are plane or near to plane. In this way, once the possible planes are detected, we can in a second step do the keypoint detection and obtain only the significant information.

Fig. 1. Keypoints detected in an image using DoG detector

4 Proposed Method

As mentioned, basis of our method is the processing of the scanner data in order
to find planes with large area. Some methods exist for this plane detection, as the
one explained by Cantzler in [7]. In our case we estimate the surface normal for
every 3D point and afterwards a grouping process of normal vectors is computed.
An easy way for the normal vector estimation in every 3D point is by computing
the SVD for the covariance in the neighborhood of the point and select as normal
vector $\overrightarrow{N}$ the eigenvector $\overrightarrow{V_i}$ corresponding to the smallest eigenvalue λ_j.

$$UDV^T = \frac{1}{n} \sum_{i=1}^{n} (\overrightarrow{X_i} - \widetilde{X}) \cdot (\overrightarrow{X_i} - \widetilde{X})^T, \qquad (1)$$

where $\widetilde{X} = \frac{1}{n} \sum_{i=1}^{n} \overrightarrow{X_i}$ is the mean position of the neighborhood points.

$$N = V_i \mid i = argmin_j(\lambda_j). \qquad (2)$$

The collection of all the normals for every range image can be expressed in polar coordinates and grouped together creating a 2D graph, where every normal is
represented as a coordinate indicating angles θ and ϕ with respect to the axes. Result can be seen in Fig. 2. Applying a clustering method (e.g. gaussian mixtures
[8]) to this result it can be detected that exist different groups of normals with
similar orientation. According to the definition of the angles θ and ϕ, should be
taken into account during the clustering phase that the value of θ does not have
importance when ϕ has a value around $\Pi/2$ or $-\Pi/2$, so that is the reason of the
expanded point cloud at the top side of Fig. 2. Often, and assuming that the laser
scanner can capture the scene in a pivoted position, all the points in the 2D graph
will be formed by two groups of points sets, separated $\Pi/2$ in the ϕ angle between
them. The first group, the one with higher ϕ value and usually with a higher number of normal vectors, correspond to the 3D points belonging to the floor of the
scene. The second group, which can have different subgroups along the θ value,
correspond to the different walls of the scene.

Once the different groups have been filtered, we should determine where are
the different walls by checking that every 3D point present after the filtering

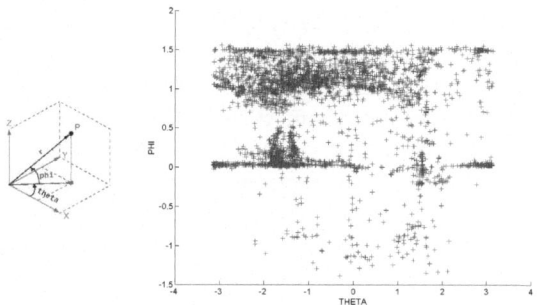

Fig. 2. Accumulation of normal vectors expressed in polar coordinates

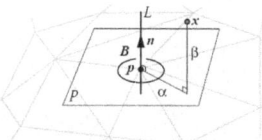

Fig. 3. Generation of Spin Image at oriented point p

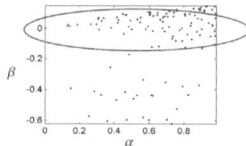

Fig. 4. Spin map and checking of neighboring points with low distance to the plane

should have at least 8 neighbors in the proximity with a maximum distance to the plane defined by its normal, and also with a similar normal orientation. The proximity size and the maximum distance to the plane depend on the resolution of the scanning process. The idea is to filter the 3D points that, even having a surface normal with an orientation similar to the selected, are isolated points or belonging to little walls. In order to find the distance of the neighbor points it can be used a concept similar to the one used in Spin Images, where, once the surface normal has been found out, two variables are defined in order to create an image: a radial coordinate α and an elevation coordinate β. α defines the distance of every point in the proximity to the line defined by the oriented point, and β defines the distance of every point to the tangent plane defined by the oriented point. Their graphical and mathematical representation are shown in Fig. 3 and in equations (3), where p represents the 3D point that we want to create the spin image, n its normal vector and x one of its proximity neighbors.

$$\beta = (x - p) \cdot n \qquad \alpha = \sqrt{(x - p)^2 - \beta^2}. \qquad (3)$$

Once all the points in the proximity have been projected we obtain a 2D image with a set of dots. As previously defined, at least 8 points should have a maximum distance to the plane defined by the current 3D point and its normal, that is, at least 8 points in the Spin Image should have a small value of β.

After this filtering of 3D points it is time to project them to the associated visible image in order to process them with 2D image techniques. As we should known the extrinsic orientation of the visible camera with respect to the laser scanner [9] it is easy to find this projection to the 2D image. The resulting image should contain a set of nearly-equispatiated points at the zones where a wall is detected. A postprocess based on morphology methods is required in order to join these separated points forming areas. An example can be seen in Fig. 5.

Fig. 5. Visible image with projected points and generation of the filter image

With all the planes of the scan image detected, it is now possible to apply the methods described in the state of the art (SIFT descriptor, Spin Images, etc...), but now with the advantage of the filtering of possible disturbance elements. Another advantage in case we want to use the SIFT descriptor is that it is not necessary to do an homography of the image as explained in [5], as SIFT works well applied on planes even if there is a high change in the point of view.

5   Experimental Results

The proposed method has been applied to different pairs of range images and their associated visible images. The images have been captured in a university campus, at different dates and times. The presence of buildings allows a probable good function of the method, but also exists a variety of vehicles, vegetation, humans and other element which could hinder a good registration of the scans.

The experiments have been carried out using a laser scanner Riegl LMS-Z420i with an attached camera Nikon D100, which was previously calibrated with the laser scanner. The three used scans are shown in Fig. 6, Fig. 7 and Fig. 8. Also, for a better scene understanding, their associated visible images are shown.

The registration process for the three possible combinations of the scannings were successful and achieve a good approximation of the registration, which afterwards can be refined by applying the ICP algorithm. The detection of the walls, after applying the method explained in this paper, is shown in Fig. 9.

The registration was achieved by searching keypoints using the DoG detector only to places where a plane is detected, and applying afterwards the SIFT descriptor. An euclidean distance was used in order to find the closest descriptors

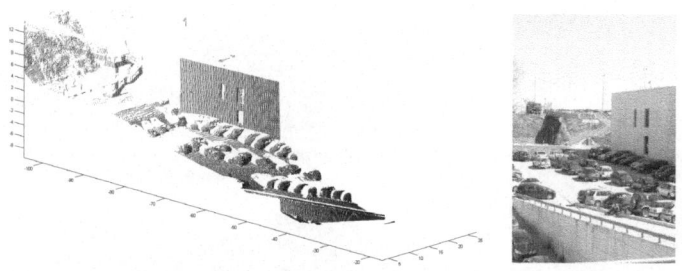

Fig. 6. First laser scan and associated visible image

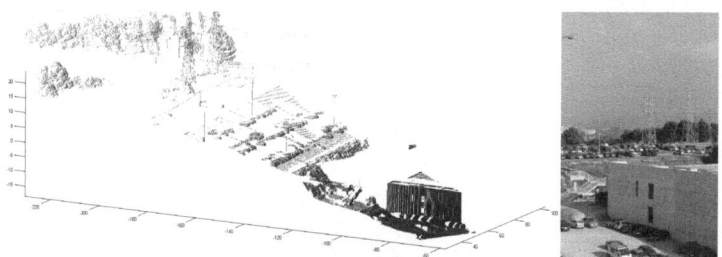

Fig. 7. Second laser scan and associated visible image

Fig. 8. Third laser scan and associated visible panorama

between the images, and a possible match is established only if the distance of the second closest pair is at least two times the distance of the closest pair. Finally, among all the possible matches detected a RANSAC method [10] is applied in order to find the rigid transformation between the scans. The registration achieved with two of the range images already presented is shown on Fig. 10.

Fig. 9. Filter images after applying the plane detection

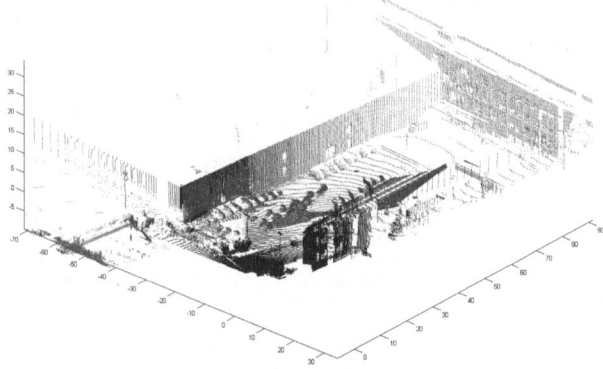

Fig. 10. Registration between two images after applying the presented method

6   Conclusions and Future Work

Pairwise registration of range images is a complex topic that has been studied for a long time. The most usual method to achieve the registration is the detection of keypoints in the associated visible images and the posterior matching between them using different descriptors. The main problem is that usually most of the keypoints are detected in parts of the scene that are not significant and often changing in time. For this reason a pre-processing before applying this method is proposed, using first of all the 3D obtained from the range image in order to detect possible walls of large area.

The filtering produced by the search of keypoints only in these detected planes allows a better matching between the keypoints of both scenes and thus achieving a faster and more accurate registration.

In the future it is expected to further investigate the possibility of applying this method but without the necessity of using the visible image. When a range image is captured by the scanner also a reflectance image is created thanks to the reflection of the laser in the objects. This reflectance image is quite similar to a visible image, and the idea is to use this additional image to obtain keypoints and descriptors, making unnecessary the image obtained by the visible camera.

Acknowledgements

This work was produced thanks to the support of the Universitat Autònoma de Barcelona and the Centro de Investigación y Desarrollo de la Armada (CIDA).

References

1. Besl, P.J., McKay, N.D.: A Method for the Registration of 3-D Shapes. Transactions on Pattern Analysis and Machine Intelligence 14, 239–256 (1992)
2. Rusinkiewicz, S., Levoy, M.: Efficient Variants of the ICP Algorithm. In: International Conference on 3-D Digital Imaging and Modeling, pp. 145–152 (2001)
3. Madhavan, R., Medina, E.: Iterative Registration of 3D LADAR Data for Autonomous Navigation. In: Proceedings of the IEEE Intelligent Vehicles Symp., pp. 186–191 (2003)
4. Lowe, D.G.: Distinctive Image Features from Scale-Invariant Keypoints. International Journal of Computer Vision 60, 91–110 (2004)
5. Smith, E.R., King, B.J., Stewart, C.V., Radke, R.J.: Registration of Combined Range-Intensity Scans: Initialization through Verification. Computer Vision and Image Understanding 110, 226–244 (2008)
6. Johnson, A.E., Hebert, M.: Using Spin Images for Efficient Object Recognition in Cluttered 3D Scenes. Transactions on Pattern Analysis and Machine Intelligence 21, 433–449 (1999)
7. Cantzler, H.: Improving architectural 3D reconstruction by constrained modelling. PhD Thesis, University of Edinburgh (2003)
8. McLachlan, G.J., Basford, K.E.: Mixture Models: Inference and Applications to Clustering. Editorial Marcel Dekker (1988)
9. Zhang, Q., Pless, R.: Extrinsic calibration of a camera and laser range finder. In: Int. Conference on Intelligent Robots and Systems, vol. 3, pp. 2301–2306 (2004)
10. Fischler, M.A., Bolles, R.C.: Random Sample Consensus: A Paradigm for Model Fitting with Applications to Image Analysis and Automated Cartography. Comm. of the ACM 24, 381–395 (1981)

Real-Time Motion Detection for a Mobile Observer Using Multiple Kernel Tracking and Belief Propagation

Marc Vivet[1], Brais Martínez[1], and Xavier Binefa[2]

[1] Universitat Autónoma de Barcelona,
Department of Computing Science, Barcelona, Spain
{marc.vivet,brais.martinez}@uab.cat
[2] Universitat Pompeu Fabra, Department of Information and Communication
Technologies, Barcelona, Spain
xavier.binefa@upf.edu

Abstract. We propose a novel statistical method for motion detection and background maintenance for a mobile observer. Our method is based on global motion estimation and statistical background modeling. In order to estimate the global motion, we use a Multiple Kernel Tracking combined with an adaptable model, formed by weighted histograms. This method is very light in terms of computation time and also in memory requirements, enabling the use of other methods more expensive, like belief propagation, to improve the final result.

Keywords: Real-time, Motion Detection, Background Subtraction, Mobile Observer, Multiple Kernel Tracking, Mosaicing, Belief Propagation, Markov Random Field.

1 Introduction

Motion Detection is used as a first step in many computer vision application and is needed to be very fast in order to let computation time to other more high level problems, like classification, tracking or also action recognition.

Using static cameras, there exist several Motion Detection methods, starting with the most naive ones, which use an statistical method to model each pixel from the background separately, like [1] which obtain the background like the average or the median for each pixel. Other more complex approaches, that also work at pixel level, like the generative method proposed in [2] which uses a Gaussian Mixture Models for each pixel; In Kernel Density Estimators methods [3], the background PDF is obtained by using the histogram of the n most recent pixel values, each one smoothed with a Gaussian kernel; Mean-shift based background estimation [4] uses a gradient-ascent method to find the modes and covariance of that PDF; And a Hidden Markov Model (HMM) approach, proposed in [5], impose temporal continuity to the classification of a pixel as background or foreground.

H. Araujo et al. (Eds.): IbPRIA 2009, LNCS 5524, pp. 144–151, 2009.

Another family of methods used in static cameras, in contrast to the previous ones, exploits the spatial consistency, like Eigen-background [6], Wallflower [7] and Markov Random Fields (MRF) based methods. In the first one, principle component analysis (PCA) is used to model the static background. Wallflower processes images at various spatial levels, pixel level, region level and frame level. Finally the MRF based methods use a Markov network to introduce the spatial information to the previous methods. [8] uses MRF to introduce spatial and temporal information to frame differencing.

In order to use the previous Motion Detection methods for non-static camera some background compensation is required. In [9], the author proposes an affine transformation, using an Iterated Re-weighted Least Squares method on a multi-resolution image pyramid. Other works use point correspondences calculated by optical flow for image coordinates on a regular grid [10]. To reduce the computation time, alternative methods are proposed like: tracking only the corner regions that belong to the background, instead of tracking the whole image [11] or improving the computation time by using the GPU to compute the alignment of feature points between frames using RANSAC (RANdom SAmple Consensus) [12].

In this work our aim is to obtain real time performance. We propose a novel method for computing the global motion which can work at over 150 frames[1] per second. The results of the proposed method are comparable to those obtained using other approaches but the computation reduction in this first step let us to use a more complex background model to improve the final result.

In section 2 we expose our global motion estimation approach, in section 3 we propose our background subtraction model. Then section 4 are presented the result that we have obtained in different scenarios. Finally in section 5 are shown the conclusion and the future of our work.

2   Global Motion Estimation

In order to estimate the global motion, we uniformly select some regions over the whole image and track them together using Multiple Kernel Tracking. We opt for Kernel-based Tracking methods because they are computationally efficient, they can handle non perfect matches and they don't have parameters manually tuned.

In subsection 2.1 we review the basic concepts of Kernel Tracking and finally in subsection 2.2 we expose our global motion estimation.

2.1   Kernel Tracking with SSD

This method represents the target region as a spatially weighted intensity histogram. Using the terminology and notation similar to [13] here we review the basics concepts of Kernel Tracking with the sum of squared differences (SSD).

---

[1] The test was done using a 640x512 Gray scale video, using 50 Kernels and a video sequence pre-loaded in memory. With this frame rate the main restriction is done by the capture time of our camera.

We denote r as the target region and $\{x_i\}_{i=1..n}$ the pixels positions that forms r. Let $K(x)$ be a function differentiable and summing one, called kernel. This function assigns smaller weights to pixels farther from the center. Let $b(x_i, t)$ be the bin that corresponds to x_i at time t. q denote the spatial weighted histogram of r, our target model, and q_u represents the value of the bin u. q is computed as,

$$q_u = \sum_{i=1}^{n} K(x_i - c)\delta(b(x_i, t), i) \tag{1}$$

where δ is the Kronecker delta function and c is the center of the region. Using the vector notation proposed in [13] function (1)Bevilacqua05 can be rewritten as,

$$q = U^t K(c) \tag{2}$$

where U is an n by m matrix $U = [u_1, u_2, ..., u_m]$ where $u_i = u_i(t) = \delta(b(x_i, t), i)$. The candidate region models at time t' would be modeled as,

$$p(c) = U^t(t')K(c) \tag{3}$$

To obtain the new position we have to find a location c' that minimize the difference between this two models using some metric. In our model we use SSD.

$$O(c) = ||\sqrt{q} - \sqrt{p(c)}||^2 \tag{4}$$

In order to solve this optimization we derive a Newton-style iterative procedure using the approximation of $\sqrt{p(c)}$ in a Taylor series,

$$\sqrt{p(c + \triangle c)} = \sqrt{p(c)} + \frac{1}{2}d(p(c))^{-\frac{1}{2}}U^t J_K(c)\triangle c = \sqrt{p(c)} + M\triangle c \tag{5}$$

where J_K is the jacobian matrix of the vector K, $d(p(c))$ is the diagonal matrix with values $p(c)$ and $M = \frac{1}{2}d(p(c))^{-\frac{1}{2}}U^t J_K(c)$. By substituting in 5 we obtain the linearized objective function, $||\sqrt{q} - \sqrt{p(c)} - M\triangle c||^2$, leading to a standard least square solution:

$$\triangle c = (M^t M)^{-1}M^t(\sqrt{q} - \sqrt{p(c)}) \tag{6}$$

2.2   Global Tracking Model and Maintenance

It is not possible to use a single target region, that covers the whole image, to estimate the global motion between two consecutive frames. Imprecision and computation time is proportional to the size of the target region. Besides, a priori we do not know which regions belong to the background and which ones belongs to the foreground. However we can assume that the major part of the image belongs to the background. This allows us to determine the global motion by uniformly selecting target regions to track, so that the whole image is covered. Then the global motion can be found by solving all of this target regions together using the Multi Kernel approach, i.e.: we have k regions denoted by

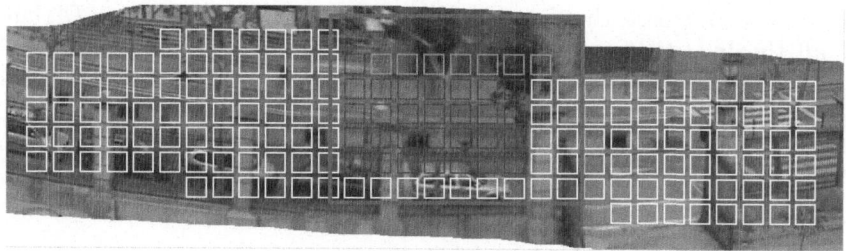

Fig. 1. Example of target regions configuration. The pink rectangle represents the position of the current frame, white rectangles represents the target regions in our model which are not used, the red rectangles represents the target regions which are used to compute the global motion (and which will be updated) and finally the green regions represent the new target regions which are added to the model in this iteration.

$R = \{r^1, r^2, ..., r^k\}$, for each region r^j we obtain its representation q^j. The joint representation Q is obtained by stacking in single vector all q^j, $P(c)$ and W is obtained equivalently using the individuals p^j and M^j. Then we can obtain the global motion of two consecutive frames by using the next function,

$$\triangle c = (W^t W)^{-1} W^t (\sqrt{Q} - \sqrt{P(c)}) \tag{7}$$

Our approach uses an adaptable model Q to deal with light changes and also to avoid accumulating errors. Each bin $q_u^j \in Q$ is represented by a gaussian $\eta_u^j(\mu_u^j, \sigma_u^j)$ computed iteratively using a gaussian modeling method proposed in [1]. This method uses two learn factors α_1 and α_2 where $\alpha_1 \gg \alpha_2$. It uses α_1 if the bin fits with the current model and it uses α_2 in other case. This minimizes the problem of learning from foreground and the model becomes adaptable to light changes. The adapted equations for our purpose are,

$$\mu_u^j = \mu_u^j + (\alpha_1(1 - B_t) + \alpha_2 B_t)(p(c')_u^j - \mu_u^j) \tag{8}$$

$$\sigma_u^{j\,2} = \sigma_u^{j\,2} + (\alpha_1(1 - B_t) + \alpha_2 B_t)((p(c')_u^j - \mu_t)^2 - \sigma_u^{j\,2}) \tag{9}$$

where c' is the final region center and B is the mask that determines if the bin fits in our model or not, obtained by using the Mahalanobis distance. If the distance is bigger than a parameter l then it means that the bin doesn't fits in our model.

When the accumulated displacement increases, it is necessary to add new target models to our global model in order to cover all new regions in our mosaic. To add this new regions it is important to save the global position of each model q^j, because we only can obtain a subset of $P(c)$ denoted by $P'(c)$ and constructed by concatenating the $p^j(c)$ which are included inside the current frame position. This forces to generate a set of q^j called Q' depending on the global position of the current frame and example is shown in figure 1. Note that we don't need too memory requirements, because we only have to save for each target model: the relative position, the number of iterations used to update the model and the mean and the variance for each bin.

In order to increase the accuracy of our system we use a mask D that set to 0 all the bins that have a variance bigger than a parameter d. The bins with a bigger variance means that this information belongs to regions which color changes like parts of the foreground. Using this mask, only the bins more probable to belong to the foreground are used. The final equation comes to,

$$\triangle c = (W^t W)^{-1} W^t (\sqrt{BQ'} - \sqrt{BP'(c)}) \qquad (10)$$

3   Local Motion Detection Using Belief Propagation

Our local motion detector is based on a background substraction method that uses a simple 3-dimensional gaussian for each pixel that form the mosaic. Then we use the information given by the global motion estimator to estimate the mobile regions in the current frame. In order to improve the results of this method we construct a 3D Markov Random Field (MRF) inspired in [8]. This MRF is represented by a 4-partite graph $G = (X, D, F, H, E)$ where there are two types of variables nodes and two types of factors nodes. First type of variable nodes $X_i \in X$ represents a binary discrete-valued random variable corresponding to static and dynamic states that each pixel can take in an image I_i and x_i represents its possible realizations. The second type of variable nodes are defined as $D_i \in D$, where D_i represents a binary discrete-valued random variable obtained by observation data and d_i its possible realizations.

Each node D_i is related to each X_i by a factor node $h(x_i, d_i) \in H$ which is the *local evidence*. X_i also have six relations with its neighborhood variable nodes X_j. Four of them connecting the neighbors in the same time layer (in order to add spatial information) and two connecting to the previous and next time layer (in order to add temporal information). This relations are called *compatibility functions* and denoted by $f_{ij} \in F$. The joint probability distribution for this model is defined as,

$$P(x, d) = \frac{1}{Z} \prod_{n=1}^{N} h(x_n, d_n) \prod_{m=1}^{M} f_m(x_m) \qquad (11)$$

We use Belief Propagation (BP) [14] for computing the marginals in our graphical model. Although this method is only exact in graphs that are cycle-free, it is empirically proved that, even in these cases, BP provides a good approximation of the optimal state. In some cases, BP algorithms are focused in finding the maximum posterior probability for all the graph like *Max-Product* BP algorithm. In other cases, the aim is to obtain the most probable state for each node, like the *Sum-Product* BP algorithm. We have selected the *Sum-Product* BP algorithm because it perfectly suits our needs. BP algorithms work by passing messages around the graph. The sum-product version will involve messages of two types: messages $q_{n \rightarrow m}$ from variable nodes to factor nodes, for our model this messages are defined as,

$$q_{n \to m}(x_n) = h(x_n, d_n) \prod_{m' \in M(n) \setminus m} r_{m' \to n}(x_n) \qquad (12)$$

where $M(n)$ is the set of factors in which variable X_n participates. And messages $r_{m \to n}$ from factor nodes to variable nodes, defined as

$$r_{m \to n}(x_n) = \sum_{x_m \setminus n} \left(f_m(x_m) \prod_{n' \in N(m) \setminus n} q_{n' \to m}(x_{n'}) \right) \qquad (13)$$

where $N(m)$ is the set of variables that the f_m factor depends on. Finally a *belief* $b_n(x_n)$, that is an approximation of the marginal $P_n(x_n)$, is computed for each node by multiplying all the incoming messages at that node,

$$b_n(x_n) = \frac{1}{Z} h(x_n, d_n) \prod_{m \in M(n)} r_{m \to n}(x_n) \qquad (14)$$

Note that $b_n(x_n)$ is equal to $P_n(x_n)$ if the MRF has no cycles.

Fig. 2. The top image is the mosaic and the from left to right represents: the mosaic generated, the original frame, the result obtained using a naive background method, the result obtained applying Belief Propagation to this naive background method and the last image is the final result

Fig. 3. Example of outdoor and indoor motion detection using a mobile observer

4   Experimental Results

We have applied our method in indoor and outdoor scenarios in order to determine its usability. The tests show that the background mosaic obtained is not perfectly aligned. Using a simple Background Subtraction model like compute a gaussian for each pixel is not enough, because the noise generated by this miss alignment is too big. However we have observed that this noise is different for each frame. This fact encourage us to apply the proposed method of belief propagation to reduce the noise without adding too many computation time. This combination improve the results in an incredible form. In figure 2 it is possible to see and example of this improvement.

Figures 3 show two sequences corresponding to the indoor and outdoor scenes, where the camera is in movement. The method proposed is able to do a correct segmentation of the mobile regions despite of the global motion.

5   Conclusions Future Work

We have presented a novel approach for global motion compensation which is light in term of computation time and memory requirements. This method combined with a naive statistical background subtraction improved by a MRF adding spatial and temporal information, enables to segment the foreground regions when the camera is not static.

The next step of our future work could be to improve the segmentation by adding more information to the belief propagation model, as the use for some kind blob detector and feature extractor.

References

1. Koller, D., Weber, J., Malik, J.: Robust multiple car tracking with occlusion reasoning. In: European Conference on Computer Vision (ECCV), pp. 189–196 (1994)
2. Stauffer, C., Grimson, W.E.L.: Adaptive Background Mixture Models for Real-Time Tracking. In: IEEE Computer Society Conference on Computer Vision and Pattern Recognition, vol. 2, p. 2246 (1999)

3. Elgammal, A., Harwood, D., Davis, L.: Non-parametric Model for Background Subtraction. In: Vernon, D. (ed.) ECCV 2000. LNCS, vol. 1843, pp. 751–767. Springer, Heidelberg (2000)
4. Han, B., Comaniciu, D., Zhu, Y., Davis, L.: Incremental density approximation and kernel-based bayesian filtering for object tracking. In: Proc. IEEE Conf. on Computer Vision and Pattern Recognition, Washington DC, pp. 638–644 (2004)
5. Rittscher, J., Kato, J., Joga, S., Blake, A.: A Probabilistic Background Model for Tracking, pp. 336–350 (2000)
6. Oliver, N., Rosario, B., Pentland, A.: A bayesian computer vision system for modeling human interactions. IEEE Transactions on Pattern Analysis and Machine Intelligence 22, 831–843 (2000)
7. Toyama, K., Krumm, J., Brumitt, B., Meyers, B.: Wallflower: principles and practice of background maintenance. In: The Proceedings of the Seventh IEEE International Conference on Computer Vision (ICCV), vol. 1, pp. 255–261 (1999)
8. Yin, Z., Collins, R.: Belief Propagation in a 3D Spatio-temporal MRF for Moving Object Detection. In: CVPR 2007, Conference on Computer Vision and Pattern Recognition (2007)
9. Winkelman, F., Patras, Y.: Online globally consistent mosaicing using an efficient representation. SMC (4), 3116–3121 (2004)
10. Unger, M., Asbach, M., Hosten, P.: Enhanced Background Subtraction using Global Motion Compensation and Mosaicing. In: ICIP (2008)
11. Bevilacqua, A., Di Stefano, L., Azzari, P.: An effective real-time mosaicing algorithm apt to detect motion through background subtraction using a PTZ camera. In: IEEE Conference on Advanced Video and Signal Based Surveillance, 2005. AVSS 2005, pp. 511–516 (2005)
12. Yu, Q., Medioni, G.: A GPU-based implementation of Motion Detection from a Moving Platform. IEEE Xplore (2008)
13. Hager, G., Dewan, M., Stewart, C.: Multiple kernel tracking with SSD. In: CVPR 2004, vol. 147, pp. 790–797 (2004)
14. Yedidia, J., Freeman, W., Weiss, Y.: Constructing Free Energy Approximations and Generalized Belief Propagation Algorithms. IEEE Transactions on Information Theory 51, 2282–2312 (2005)

Robust and Efficient Multipose Face Detection Using Skin Color Segmentation

Murad Al Haj, Andrew D. Bagdanov, Jordi Gonzàlez, and Xavier F. Roca

Departament de Ciències de la Computació and Computer Vision Center
Campus UAB, Edifici O, 08193, Bellaterra, Spain
{malhaj,bagdanov}@cvc.uab.es, {Jordi.Gonzalez,xavier.roca}@uab.es

Abstract. In this paper we describe an efficient technique for detecting faces in arbitrary images and video sequences. The approach is based on segmentation of images or video frames into skin-colored blobs using a pixel-based heuristic. Scale and translation invariant features are then computed from these segmented blobs which are used to perform statistical discrimination between face and non-face classes. We train and evaluate our method on a standard, publicly available database of face images and analyze its performance over a range of statistical pattern classifiers. The generalization of our approach is illustrated by testing on an independent sequence of frames containing many faces and non-faces. These experiments indicate that our proposed approach obtains false positive rates comparable to more complex, state-of-the-art techniques, and that it generalizes better to new data. Furthermore, the use of skin blobs and invariant features requires fewer training samples since significantly fewer non-face candidate regions must be considered when compared to AdaBoost-based approaches.

Keywords: Multiview Face Detection, View-Invariant Face Features Classification.

1 Introduction

Face detection is a crucial step in many applications in computer vision. These include automatic face recognition, video surveillance, human-computer interface and expression recognition. Face detection also plays an important role in video coding where data must be transmitted in real-time over low bandwidth networks [3]. The better the face detection system performs, the less post-processing will be needed and all the previously mentioned applications will perform better. A survey of face detection is presented in [11] where the different methods are classified into four, sometimes overlapping, categories: knowledge-based methods, feature invariant approaches, template matching methods, and appearance based methods.

However, Face detection is an expensive search problem. To properly localize a face in an image, all regions should be searched at varying scales. Usually, a sliding window approach is implemented to classify the regions in an image

H. Araujo et al. (Eds.): IbPRIA 2009, LNCS 5524, pp. 152–159, 2009.

at different scales. This naturally produces many more windows corresponding to background objects than windows corresponding to actual face positions.
The ratio of non-face regions produced to actual face regions can be as high as
100000:1. This high ratio calls for a very well trained classifier that will produce
a low number of false positives - especially that face detection, as mentioned
earlier, is a first step in many applications which will suffer from false positives.
Furthermore, intra-class variations of non-rigid objects like faces make detection a challenging problem. These variations are mainly caused by changes in
expression and pose. While classifiers aiming at frontal faces work well, training
a classifier to detect a multipose faces is not an easy task.

Frontal face detection has been extensively studied. Early work includes that
of Sung and Paggio [6] were the difference between the local image pattern
and a distribution based model was computed and used to build a classifier.
Papageorgiou used an over-complete wavelet representation of faces to achieve
detection [4]. Today, the most commonly used techniques for frontal upright
face detection are that of Rowley et al. [7] that uses neural networks and that of
Viola and Jones [9] that uses Haar-like features accompanied by Adaboost. Some
attempts were made to extend the Viola and Jones method to multiview faces
such as in [2]. However, fast multiview face detection is still an open problem
since the methods are either computationally expensive, such as in the previously
mentioned paper, or they produce a large number of false positives [10], or both.

In this paper, an efficient and robust face detection method is presented. Our
method starts by detecting skin blobs, then a small number of invariant features
are extracted from them. Those features are used to learn a statistical model of
faces vs. non-faces. The rest of the paper is divided as follows, section 2 introduces our skin color model, section 3 describes the different invariant features, in
section 4 the experimental results of training and detection are presented, while
finally concluding remarks are discussed in section 5.

2   Skin Color Model

Skin is an effective cue for face detection since color is highly invariant to geometric variations of the face and allows fast processing. By eliminating non-skin
regions, the search space is reduced significantly. Trying to model skin color,
around 800,000 skin pixels were sampled from 64 different images of people with
different ethnicities and under various lighting conditions. Studying the distribution of these pixels, we concluded that a pixel with (R,G,B) should be classified
as skin if:

$R > 75$ **and** $20 < R - G < 90$ **and** $R/G < 2.5$

The advantages of this method are its simplicity and computational efficiency,
especially that no colorspace transformation is needed. The distribution of R is
shown in Fig. 1.(a), while that of R-G is shown in Fig. 1.(b), and that of R/G
is shown in Fig. 1.(c). Our experiments revealed that 96.9% of the skin pixels
have their R value greater than 75, see Fig. 1.(a), 94.6% of them have their
R-G values between 20 and 90, see Fig. 1.(b), which supports the observation in

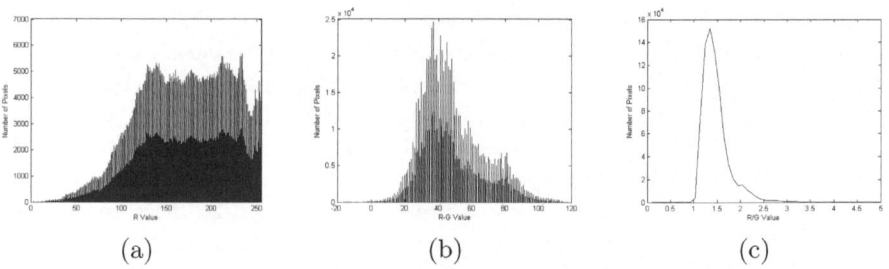

(a)   (b)   (c)

Fig. 1. (a) The distribution of R values in skin pixels. (b) The distribution of R-G values in skin pixels. (c) The distribution of R/G in skin pixels.

Fig. 2. The original image and its corresponding skin segmented blobs

[1], and 98.7% of them have their R/G values less than 2.5 see Fig. 1.(c). After skin-colored blobs are detected, a Sobel edge detector is applied in an attempt to separate any face blob from a background blob that might have the same color. A dilation process is then employed to further separate the edges. In Fig. 2 an example of this segmentation process is shown, where in Fig. 2.(a) the original image is shown, and in Fig. 2.(b) the skin segmented image is shown after edge detection and dilation are applied.

3   Invariant Features

Once the skin blobs are detected, a small number of view-invariant scale-independent features are extracted. Unlike the Viola and Jones method, where hundreds of Haar-like features are used for only frontal face detection, we use 16 features for multipose face detection. These features are listed below.

Aspect Ratio: The ratio of the bounding box longer side to the shorter.

Eccentricity: Fitting the whole blob under an ellipse which has the same second-moments as the blob, eccentricity is defined as the distance between the foci of this ellipse and its major axis.

Euler Number: The number of objects in the region minus the number of holes in those objects.

Extent: The area of the blob divided by the area of the bounding box.

Orientation: The angle between the x-axis and the major axis of the ellipse having the same second-moments as the blob.

Solidity: The proportion of the pixels in the convex hull that are also in the region.

Roundness: The ratio of the minor axis of the ellipse to its major axis.

Centroid Position: Two features encoding the distance between the centroid of the blob and the center of its bounding box in both x and y directions.

Hu Moments: Hu moments are very useful for our problem since they are invariant under translation, rotation, and changes in scale. They are computed from normalized centralized moments up to order three as shown below:

$$I_1 = \eta_{20} + \eta_{02}$$
$$I_2 = (\eta_{20} - \eta_{02})^2 + 4\eta_{11}^2$$
$$I_3 = (\eta_{30} - 3\eta_{12})^2 + (3\eta_{21} - \eta_{03})^2$$
$$I_4 = (\eta_{30} + \eta_{12})^2 + (\eta_{21} + \eta_{03})^2$$
$$I_5 = (\eta_{30} - 3\eta_{12})(\eta_{30} + \eta_{12})[(\eta_{30} + \eta_{12})^2 - 3(\eta_{21} + \eta_{03})^2] + (3\eta_{21} - \eta_{03})(\eta_{21} + \eta_{03})[3(\eta_{30} + \eta_{12})^2 - (\eta_{21} + \eta_{03})^2]$$
$$I_6 = (\eta_{20} - \eta_{02})[(\eta_{30} + \eta_{12})^2 - (\eta_{21} + \eta_{03})^2 + 4\eta_{11}(\eta_{30} + \eta_{12})(\eta_{21} + \eta_{03})]$$
$$I_7 = (3\eta_{21} - \eta_{03})(\eta_{30} + \eta_{12})[(\eta_{30} + \eta_{12})^2 - 3(\eta_{21} + \eta_{03})^2] + (\eta_{30} - 3\eta_{12})(\eta_{21} + \eta_{03})[3(\eta_{30} + \eta_{12})^2 - (\eta_{21} + \eta_{03})^2]$$

4   Experimental Results

Having generated the corresponding features of each skin-color blob in a certain image, what remains is to classify which of these blobs correspond to a face. For that purpose several different classifiers have been evaluated. The first part of this section describes the training process where four classifiers were trained on faces from the CVL database, while the second part shows the classification results on an independent sequence we recorded, where the face varies under pose and expression.

4.1   Results on CVL Database

The face images used in this section have been provided by the Computer Vision Laboratory (CVL), University of Ljubljana, Slovenia [5],[8]. The CVL database contains color images of people under seven different poses with variations in the expressions. The database contains around 800 faces (positive examples for the face class). For the non-face class, many images that do not contain any faces

     (a)   (b)   (c)

Fig. 3. (a) A sample face from the CVL database along with the segmented face blob. (b) Negative examples corresponding to body parts. (c) Negative examples not corresponding to body parts.

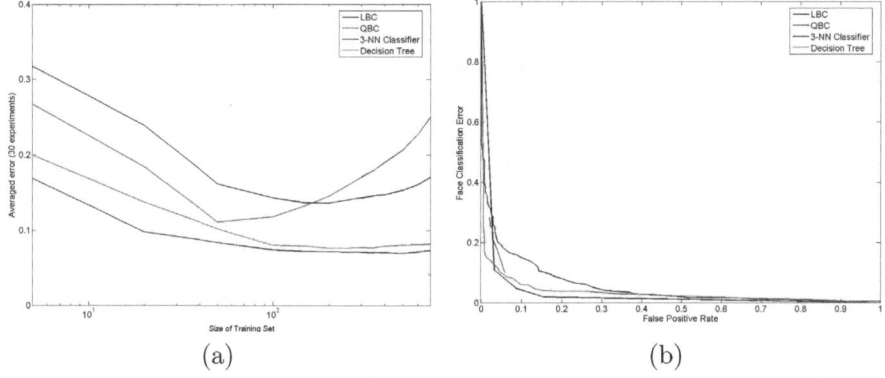

           (a)   (b)

Fig. 4. (a) The learning curves. (b) The ROC curves.

but do contain skin-colored regions have been collected from various sources. A total of around 1600 non-face blobs were detected in this independent test set. Examples of faces blobs and non-face blobs are shown in Fig. 3, where it can be noted that the negative examples contained body parts as well as non-body regions. We generated the invariant features on the faces and the non-faces blobs and used them to train several classifiers.

The classifiers we tested are the following:

- **Linear Bayes Classifier:** minimum Bayes risk classifier assuming normally distributed classes and equal covariance matrices.
- **Quadratic Bayes Classifier:** minimum Bayes risk classifier assuming normally distributed classes, trying to separate classes by a quadratic surface.
- **K Nearest Neighbor:** classifies objects based on closest training examples in the feature space. An object is classified by a majority vote of its neighbors, with the object being assigned to the class most common amongst its k nearest neighbors. In our experiments, k was set to 3.
- **Decision Tree Classifier:** is a hierarchically based classifier which compares the data with a range of automatically selected features. The selection of features is determined from an assessment of the spectral distributions or separability of the classes.

The learning curves for the different classifiers are shown in Fig. 4.(a), with a semi-log scale. The learning curves were computed by varying the size of the training set. For each training set size, the classification error was estimated by averaging over 30 trials (i.e. 30 randomly selected training sets for each size). It should be noted that at the end of the learning process, the error for the Decision Tree classifier and the K Nearest Neighbor is less than 10%. However, the Linear Bayes Classifier and Quadratic Bayes Classifier behave differently where the error start decreasing to a certain point and then it starts increasing, probably due to over-fitting. The ROC curves are shown in Fig. 4.(b), where half of the data was used for training while the other half was used for testing. It can be seen that low error rates are obtained while maintaining a reasonably low false-positive rate and that the Decision Tree classifier has the highest precision among the four.

4.2   Classification on a Video Sequence

In order to test the classification rate of our classifiers, we have recorded a sequence where the face of the agent is varying in terms of pose and expression. We generated the various blobs from the sequence using our skin color segmentation method, in this process all small blobs whose area is less than 2% of the image area are dropped. The sequence contained 541 face blob and 2012 non-face blobs. The classifiers, that were trained on the faces from the CVL database and the non-faces we collected, were used to classify these blobs. The results of the various classifiers on these blobs is shown in Table 1.

Table 1. Classification Results

	Face Detection Rate	Non-Face Detection Rate	Overall Detection Rate
LBC	97.23%	87.38%	89.46%
QBC	100%	46.17%	57.58%
kNN	72.83%	94.04%	89.54%
Decision Tree	95.75%	89.76%	91.03%

Fig. 5. The output of the Viola and Jones detector on one of our images

It is important to mention that we were able to achieve a high classification rate despite the fact that the testing sequence is completely unrelated to the training samples. The classifier with the best precision turned out to be the

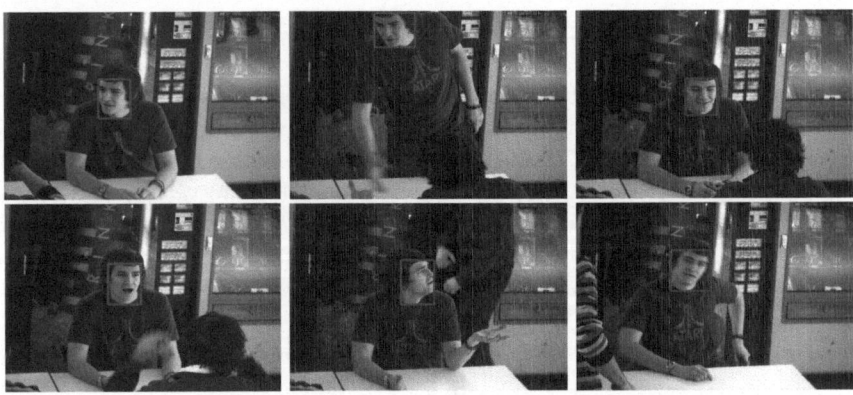

Fig. 6. Some of the experimental results of the decision tree classifier

Decision Tree, as it was suggested in the ROC curve in Fig. 4.(b). To compare with Viola and Jones method, we ran their detector on our sequence and we detected only 386 faces out of the 541 (around 69%) with a huge number of false positives, 470 false positives in 541 images. A sample output image of the Viola and Jones detector is shown in Fig. 5, while some experimental results of the Decision Tree classifier are shown in Fig. 6.

5   Conclusions

In this paper we described an efficient and robust technique for face detection in arbitrary images and video sequences. Our approach is based on segmentation of images into skin-colored blobs using a pixel-based heuristic described in section 2. Identified skin blobs are then analyzed to extract scale- and view-invariant features. These features are used to train a statistical pattern classifier to discriminate face blobs from non-face blobs.

The use of scale-invariant features, particularly the Hu-moments characterizing the spatial distribution of skin pixels in a candidate blob, is key to the success of our algorithm. The use of invariant features on segmented blobs obviates the need to scan all possible regions of an image at multiple scales looking for candidate faces. This results in a more efficient algorithm and reduces the need to use a weak classifier with a vanishingly small false-positive rate as is needed for AdaBoost approaches.

A strong advantage of our approach is its ability to generalize to new data. The Viola and Jones face detector is known to be highly sensitive to the illumination and imaging conditions under which it is trained, and consequently it often does not generalize well to new situations without retraining. With our experiments we show that with our invariant feature space representation of skin blobs we can train a classifier on one dataset and it is able to accurately detect faces on an independent sequence it has never seen before (see table 1). The decision tree and k-NN classifiers consistently performed best, which is not surprising given the limited training data and their known optimality. The Bayes classifiers succumb to overtraining before they reach respectable classification rates. The Bayesian classifiers would be preferable due to their simplicity, and we plan to address this problem by investigating feature reduction techniques in the near future. Of interest also is the uncorrelated performance of the four classifiers in table 1. This indicates that classifier combination could be used to effectively improve overall accuracy. Finally, the skin detection algorithm described in this work will be improved to further reduce the number of false skin blob detections.

Acknowledgements

This work is supported by EC grants IST-027110 for the HERMES project and IST-045547 for the VIDI-video project, and by the Spanish MEC under projects TIN2006-14606 and CONSOLIDER-INGENIO 2010 MIPRCV CSD2007-00018.

References

1. Al-Shehri, S.A.: A simple and novel method for skin detection and face locating and tracking. In: Masoodian, M., Jones, S., Rogers, B. (eds.) APCHI 2004. LNCS, vol. 3101, pp. 1–8. Springer, Heidelberg (2004)
2. Huang, C., Ai, H., Wu, B., Lao, S.: Boosting nested cascade detector for multi-view face detection. In: Proceedings of the 17th Intl. Conf. on Pattern Recognition (ICPR 2004), vol. 2, pp. 415–418 (August 2004)
3. Menser, B., Brunig, M.: Face detection and tracking for video coding applications. In: The 34th Asilomar Conference on Signals, Systems and Computers, vol. 1, pp. 49–53. IEEE, Los Alamitos (2000)
4. Papageorgiou, C.P., Oren, M., Poggio, T.: A general framework for object detection. In: Proceedings of the 6th International Conference on Computer Vision, vol. 2, pp. 555–562 (January 1998)
5. Peer, P.: Cvl face database, http://www.lrv.fri.uni-lj.si/facedb.html
6. Poggio, T., Sung, K.K.: Example-based learning for view-based human face detection. In: Proceedings of ARPA Image Understanding Workshop, vol. 2, pp. 843–850 (1994)
7. Rowley, H.A., Baluja, S., Kanade, T.: Nueral network-based face detection. IEEE Trans. on Pattern Analysis and Machine Intelligence (PAMI) 20, 22–38 (1998)
8. Solina, F., Peers, P., Batagelj, B., Juvan, S., Kovac, J.: Color-based face detection in '15 seconds of fame' at installation. In: Mirage 2003, Conference on Computer Vision / Computer Graphics Collaboration for Model-Based Imaging, Rendering, Image Analysis and Graphical Special Effects, INRIA Rocquencourt, France, Wilfried Philips, Rocquencourt, INRIA, March 10-11 2003, pp. 38–47 (2003)
9. Viola, P., Jones, M.: Robust real-time object detection. In: Proceedings of IEEE Workshop on Statistical and Computational Theories of Vision (July 2001)
10. Wang, P., Ji, Q.: Multi-view face detection under complex scene based on combined svms. In: Proceedings of the 17th Intl. Conf. on Pattern Recognition (ICPR 2004), vol. 4, pp. 179–182 (2004)
11. Yang, J., Kriegman, D.J., Ahuja, N.: Detecting faces in images: A survey. IEEE Trans. on Pattern Analysis and Machine Intelligence (PAMI) 24(1), 34–58 (2002)

Contour Regularity Extraction Based on String Edit Distance

José Ignacio Abreu Salas[1] and Juan Ramón Rico-Juan[2]

[1] Universidad de Matanzas, Cuba
jose.abreu@umcc.cu
[2] Dpto Lenguajes y Sistemas Informáticos, Universidad de Alicante, Spain
juanra@dlsi.ua.es

Abstract. In this paper, we present a new method for constructing prototypes representing a set of contours encoded by Freeman Chain Codes. Our method build new prototypes taking into account similar segments shared between contours instances. The similarity criterion was based on the Levenshtein Edit Distance definition. We also outline how to apply our method to reduce a data set without sensibly affect its representational power for classification purposes. Experimental results shows that our scheme can achieve compressions about 50% while classification error increases only by 0.75%.

1 Motivation

Finding a set of representative prototypes from a group of contour instances is often useful for improving a classifier response time and to simplify data to be analysed by a human interpreter [1]. Different approaches have been proposed in the literature, such as [1] [2] and [4], based on the computation of the mean shape or inferring prototypes by some *ad-hoc* procedure [9].

However, there are contexts where getting good prototypes are not sufficient because the lack of an understandable criterion about its constitution and performance. For example, with forensic purposes its important to construct a model characterising an individual handwriting style not in a black box sense but taking into account about the relations among different handwriting constitutive elements.

In this work, we present a new model for computing a set of contour prototypes based on the identification of contour segments satisfying some similarity criterion which can be controlled by the user. In section 2, we explain some related techniques which have been used by our method. Section 3 describes our approach, first an algorithm to construct a prototype from two contour instances and latter the application of this algorithm to construct prototypes from a set of contour instances. Finally, some experimental results are showed in section 4.

H. Araujo et al. (Eds.): IbPRIA 2009, LNCS 5524, pp. 160–167, 2009.

2   Background and Notation

2.1   Extended Freeman Chain Codes

The classical chain codes can be used to represent a contour by traversing it to produce a string of codes which describes the direction to the next point on the contour. When images are represented as a square grid, usually eight codes are defined to describe a square neighbourhood.

In our work, contours where encoded by an extension of classic Freeman chain codes [6]. To represent a contour, we have not defined a fixed number of codes, instead, we consider an infinite set of directions at range $0 \leq d < 8$ and the symbol "?" to denote an undefined direction. This modifications allow us to avoid a discretization process at definition of the String Fusion Operation explained below. Also, the inclusion of symbol "?" will be useful to encode dissimilar regions at prototype construction stage.

2.2   Edit Distance

As a distance function for strings we take the Levenshtein string edit distance. Let Σ be an alphabet and $S_1 = \{S_{11}, S_{12}..S_{1m}\}$, $S_2 = \{S_{21}, S_{22}..S_{2n}\}$ two strings over Σ where $m, n \geq 0$, the edit distance between S_1 and S_2, $D(S_1, S_2)$, is defined in terms of elementary edit operations which are required to transform S_1 into S_2. Usually three edit operations are considered:

- *substitution* of a symbol $a \in S_1$ by a symbol $b \in S_2$, denoted as $w(a, b)$
- *insertion* of a symbol $b \in \Sigma$ in S_1, denoted as $w(\varepsilon, b)$
- *deletion* of a symbol $a \in S_1$, denoted as $w(a, \varepsilon)$.

where ε denotes an empty string. Let $E = \{e_1, e_2, ..., e_k\}$ be a sequence of edit operations transforming S_1 into S_2, if each operation have cost $c(e_i)$ the cost of E is $c(E) = \sum_{i=1}^{k} c(e_i)$ and the edit distance $D(S_1, S_2)$ is defined as:

$$D(S_1, S_2) = argmin\{ c(E) | \text{E an edit sequence to transform } S_1 \text{ into } S_2\}. \quad (1)$$

In our case, cost are computed as follows:

$$c(w(a, b)) = \begin{cases} min\{|a - b|, 8 - |a - b|\} & \text{if } a, b \neq \text{"?"}. \\ 2 & \text{in other case.} \end{cases} \quad (2)$$

The number 2, corresponding to insertion and deletion operations, is an half of the maximum substitution operation. The same fixed number is used in [10]. The dynamic programming algorithm exposed by Wagner and Fisher [5] lets to compute $D(S_1, S_2)$ in $O(n \times m)$ time.

3   Problem Definition and Solution Outline

Let two contours encoded by the chain codes S_1 and S_2, we address to construct a prototype S_3 by finding two sets (C_S, C_T) of pairs $(S_1(k, l) \in S_1, S_2(g, h) \in$

S_2) where C_S contains pairs encoding contour segments that fulfill a similarity criterion while C_T holds dissimilar regions. Each element at C_S or C_T determines a S_3 contour region and by merging all together we build the prototype. Next subsections explain how we get S_3 segment from $S_1(k,l)$ and $S_2(g,h)$ (*fusion operation*) and the way to construct C_S and C_T.

3.1   String Fusion Operation

Let S_1 and S_2 strings encoding two contour sections, the *fusion operation* can be defined as $F(S_1, S_2) = S_3$, where S_3 satisfies:

$$D(S_1, S_2) \geq D(S_1, S_3) \wedge D(S_1, S_2) \geq D(S_2, S_3) . \tag{3}$$

Thus, if we consider $D(S_k, S_l)$ be a measure how well represented is a string S_k by S_l, this is, if $D(S_k, S_j) < D(S_k, S_l)$ holds, it means S_j represent better S_k than S_l, we can say that fusion operation ensures S_3 describe S_1 and S_2 as well they represent each other or even better.

Let examine how to define $F(S_1, S_2)$. Be S_1, S_2 two strings with respective lengths L_1 and L_2, S_3 length are fixed by:

$$L_3 = \left\lfloor \frac{(L_1 + L_2)}{2} \right\rfloor . \tag{4}$$

If $L_1 = L_2$, a simple way to construct S_3 is computing its first symbol $S_3[1]$ as the mean of $S_1[1]$ and $S_2[1]$, and so on, this procedure ensures S_3 satisfies constrains (3).

However, a more general scheme must be consider to compute S_3, since most times $L_1 \neq L_2$, so the simple criterion used above can not be applied. Without lost of generality, lets $L_1 > L_2$, so $L_2 \leq L_3 < L_1$. It means that S_3 symbols can't be determined by the mean of only two symbols at S_1 and S_2. Now, a symbol $S_3[i]$ is computed voting over all $S_1[h]$ and $S_2[k]$, where the weight W_j for the j-esime symbol of S_1 or S_2 are determined by:

$$W_j = \begin{cases} 1 & \text{if } j \geq i\frac{L_1}{L_3} \wedge (j+1) \leq (i+1)\frac{L_1}{L_3} . \\[2mm] (i+1)\frac{L_1}{L_3} - j & \text{if } i\frac{L_1}{L_3} \leq j \leq (i+1)\frac{L_1}{L_3} \wedge (j+1) > (i+1)\frac{L_1}{L_3} . \\[2mm] \frac{L_1}{L_3} & \text{if } j < i\frac{L_1}{L_3} \wedge (j+1) \geq (i+1)\frac{L_1}{L_3} . \\[2mm] j+1 - i\frac{L_1}{L_3} & \text{if } j < i\frac{L_1}{L_3} \wedge (j+1) < (i+1)\frac{L_1}{L_3} . \end{cases} \tag{5}$$

Since a symbol from S_1 or S_2 represent a direction d, have no sense multiplying by its weight W_d and sum all of them, so we consider pairs $< d, W_d >$ like vectors with direction d and magnitude W_d, this way S_3 symbols can be computed as the direction of a vector obtained by the sum of each $< d, W_d >$.

Fig. 1 shows the result string S_3 when applied the fusion procedure over $S_1 = \{0, 0, 0, 0\}$ and $S_2 = \{2, 2\}$.

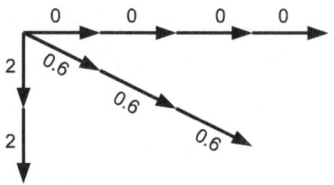

Fig. 1. Result of fusion operation over two strings

3.2 Finding Similar Regions

The algorithm to compute Edit Distance explained in section 2.2 from two strings S_1 and S_2 determines the minimum cost edit sequence (Q) to transform S_1 in S_2. Substitutions at Q maps a S_1 symbol to other at S_2, deletions denotes a S_1 symbol without image at S_2 and insertions symbols at S_2 that are not the image of any S_1 symbol. Thus, given a subsequence of edit operations $Q(k,l)$ from Q , it maps a contour segment $S_1^{k,l}$ from S_1 to other $S_2^{k,l}$ on S_2 and we can compute the cost $E_{Q(k,l)}$ which represent those edit operations involved at $Q(k,l)$ over the edit distance.

To select similar regions from S_1 and S_2, we fix a parameter T called *tolerance factor*, $0 \leq T \leq 1$, which determines a set C_S of non-overlapping subsequences from Q satisfying the following constraint:

$$\sum E_{Q(k,l)} \leq D(S_1, S_2)T \mid Q(k,l) \in C_S . \qquad (6)$$

We can see, there are multiples sets satisfying constraints (6). Since information from those $C_S \in Q(h,g)$ will be partially ignored, we are also interested finding a C_S subject to:

$$argmax\{\sum L(Q(k,l)) \mid Q(k,l) \in C_S\} . \qquad (7)$$

where $L(S)$ denotes the length of a string S. This constraint aims to find a set of similar regions covering as contour length as possible. Finally, we prefer solutions where C_S contains a few long length regions instead a large set of short regions.

Searching a set satisfying such conditions became a computational expensive problem, thus, defining:

$$P_{Q(k,h)} = \begin{cases} 2 \text{ if } Q(n, k-1) \wedge Q(h+1, m) \in C_S. \\ 1 \text{ if } Q(n, k-1) \in C_S \wedge Q(h+1, m) \ni C_S \text{ or viceversa} . \\ 0 \text{ if } Q(n, k-1) \ni C_S \wedge Q(h+1, m) \ni C_S. \end{cases} \qquad (8)$$

we applied a heuristic approach to get C_S that is good enough, by the greedy procedure outlined below:
Let:

- C_T a set of all subsequences $Q(k,k) \mid k = 0..L(Q)$
- $C_S = \emptyset$

while $C_T \neq \emptyset$ **and** $\sum E_Q(k,l) \leq D(S_1, S_2)T \mid Q(k,l) \in C_S$

- **get** $Q(g,g) = argmin\{E_{Q(k,k)}|Q(k,k) \in C_T\}$:`if there is two or more`
  `select one with the smallest` $P_Q(g,g)$
- $C_S = C_S \cup Q(g,g)$
- $C_T = C_T \sim Q(g,g)$
- **case** $P_Q(g,g)$:
    - **2:** `replace` $Q(n,g-1), Q(g+1,m)$ `and` $Q(g,g)$ `at` C_S `by` $Q(n,m)$
    - **1:** `replace` $Q(n,g-1)$ `or` $Q(g+1,m)$ `and` $Q(g,g)$ `at` C_S `by` $Q(n,g)$
      `or` $Q(g,m)$ `at case`

end while

3.3   Prototype Construction

To construct a prototype representing two contours encoded by the chain codes S_1 and S_2 we uses the algorithm to find similar regions and the fusion procedure defined before. First, we get sets C_S, containing those regions meeting the similarity criterion, and C_T which contains dissimilar contour segments. For each $Q(k,l) \in C_S$ get both regions $S_1^{k,l}$ and $S_2^{k,l}$ it determines and compute $S_3^{k,l} = F(S_1^{k,l}, S_2^{k,l})$. To construct $S_3^{g,h}$ from regions at C_T we need its length, which is compute by equation (4), this time, each $S_3^{g,h}[i]$ contains the symbol "?". Finally, we get the prototype concatenating each $S_3^{g,h}$ which have been sorted by g. Now, we illustrate the behaviour of the algorithm by an example:

Be $S_1 = \{2, 2, 5, 1.5, 1.5, 1, 1, 1\}$ and $S_2 = \{3, 2, 1.6, 1.5, 7, 0.3, 0.3\}$; $T = 0.7$. Table 1 shows Q and cost for each edit operation.

Table 1. Minimum Cost Edit Sequence and costs

Q	$w(2,3)$	$w(2,2)$	$w(5,\varepsilon)$	$w(1.5,1.6)$	$w(1.5,1.5)$	$w(1,7)$	$w(1,0.3)$	$w(1,0.3)$
Cost	1	0	2	0.1	0	2	0.7	0.7

It drives to $C_S = \{Q(0,4), Q(6,7)\}$ and $C_T = \{Q(5,5)\}$. From $Q(0,4)$ we get $S_1^{0,4} = \{2,2,5,1.5,1.5\}$; $S_2^{0,4} = \{3,2,1.6,1.5\}$ and by the fusion $S_3^{0,4} = \{2.5,2,1.5,1.5\}$. $Q(6,7)$ turns $S_1^{6,7} = \{1,1\}$; $S_2^{6,7} = \{0.3,0.3\}$ and $S_3^{6,7} = \{0.65,0.65\}$. Putting all $S_3^{0,4}, S_3^{6,7}$ and $S_3^{5,5} = \{\text{"?"}\}$ together we get a prototype: $S_3 = \{3,2,1.6,1.5,?,0.65,0.65\}$.

3.4   Building Prototypes from a Contour Set

Actually our algorithm can handle only two instances at time, thus we need to define an additional procedure if want to get prototypes from a set C_c greater than two objects. To address this problem we iteratively find instances $S_i, S_j \in C_c$ which meet $argmin\{D(S_k,S_l)|S_k,S_l \in C_c\}$, from those instances we build a prototype S_p, which will replace S_i and S_j from C_c. This procedure is repeated while holds:

$$\frac{L_i - C_?(S_i) + L_j - C_?(S_j) - 2C_?(S_p)}{L_i + L_j} \geq P \,. \tag{9}$$

where $C_?(S_x)$ counts the amount of symbols from S_x equals to "?", and P ($0 \leq P \leq 1$), called *persistence factor*, is a measure of how many information haven been lost by the fusion operation.

4   Experimental Results

The proposed algorithm was applied to construct a set of prototypes from a group of contour instances represented by chain codes. Separated experiments where carried with two independent contour subsets, containing digits and letters respectively, from the NIST SPECIAL DATABASE 3 of the National Institute of Standards and Technology. With this subsets we perform a 4-fold crossvalidation where each train and test sets have 60 and 20 instances per class respectively.

First, we classified every instance at test set by the *nearest neighbour rule* and compute the absolute error commited (as percent of wrong classified instances). Later, we use our scheme separately over instances from the same class at the train set to get a new set which will replace the former. We compute a

Table 2. Values for C and ΔE when $T = 0.5$ and $P = 0.1$ (digits experiment)

Fold	C	ΔE
0	52.5	0
1	53.0	0.5
2	54.66	0
3	52.33	2.5
Mean	53.12	0.75

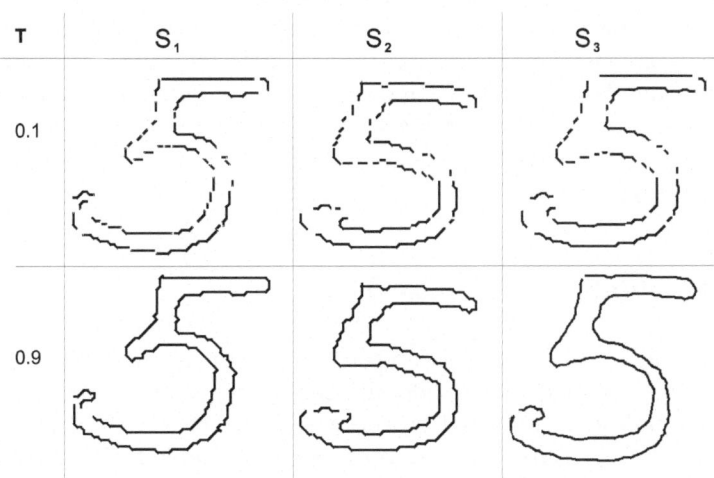

Fig. 2. Each row shows similar segments from two contours S_1 and S_2 and the correspondent ones at the build prototype from different T values

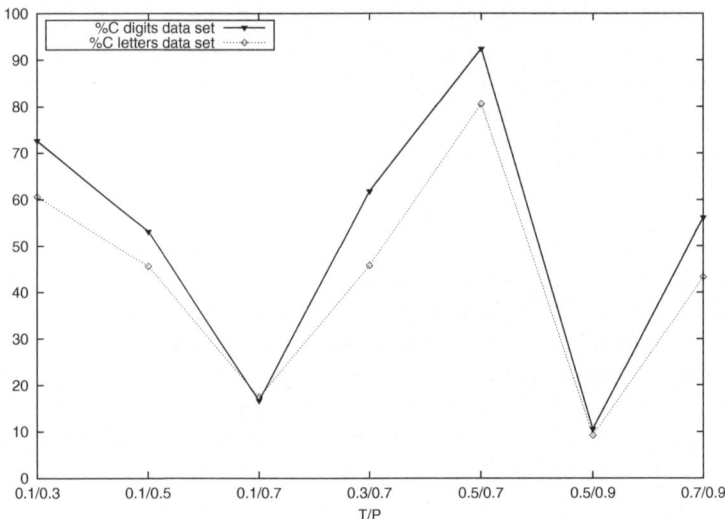

Fig. 3. Values for C through different T and P for digits and letters (*dashed line*) data sets

compression index C that is a measure (as percent) of how much we reduce de original train set, and by classifying again the test set, we get the *error rate variation*. These values characterised the algorithm behaviour since we hope improve the compression index without sensibly increases the classification error.

We try different values for *tolerance* and *persistence* factors to analyse how they affect both compression and error rate. As Table 2 shows, our algorithm performs well for some T and P values. Fig 2 illustrates how this values determines the similar segments from contours. We also are interested into compare how values for T and P determines both compression and error rate variation across different data sets. Graphics at Fig 3 shows our algorithm performs similarly through both databases for the compression index, similar results was obtained for the error rate variation.

5   Conclusions and Future Work

A new method to construct prototypes from a set of contours instances was presented. Our approach lets to identify similar segments through contours by a criterion that can be adjusted by the user, and, from those segments we get the prototypes. Experiments shows our model is suitable for compress contours data sets without affect its representative power. We think our approach can be used for characterise a class of contours and for data compression. Further investigations can be addressed to extend the algorithm to other representations for contours, like cyclic strings.

Acknowledgements

This work is partially supported by the Spanish CICYT under project DPI2006-15542-C04-01 and by the Spanish research programme Consolider Ingenio 2010: MIPRCV (CSD2007-00018).

References

1. Duta, N., Sonka, M., Jain, A.: Learning Shape Models from Examples Using Automatic Shape Clustering and Procrustes Analysis. In: Information Processing in Medical Imaging. LNCS, vol. 1613, pp. 370–375 (2008)
2. Jiang, X., Abegglen, K., Bunke, H., Csirik, J.: Dynamic computation of generalised median strings. Journal Pattern Analysis and Applications 6, 185–193 (2003)
3. Jiang, X., Schiffmann, L., Bunke, H.: Computation of median shapes. In: 4th Asian Conference on Computer Vision (2000)
4. Cárdenas, R.: A Learning Model for Multiple-Prototype Classification of Strings. In: 17th International Conference on Pattern Recognition, vol. 4, pp. 420–442 (2004)
5. Wagner, R., Fischer, M.: The String-to-String Correction Problem. Journal of the ACM 21, 168–173 (1974)
6. Freeman, H.: Computer Processing of Line-Drawing Data. Computer Surveys 6, 57–96 (1974)
7. Chikkerur, S., Wu, C., Govindaraju, V.: A Systematic Approach for Feature Extraction in Fingerprint Images. In: Zhang, D., Jain, A.K. (eds.) ICBA 2004. LNCS, vol. 3072, pp. 344–350. Springer, Heidelberg (2004)
8. Govindaraju, V., Shi, Z., Schneider, J.: Feature Extraction Using a Chaincoded Contour Representation of Fingerprint Images. In: AVBPA, pp. 268–275 (2003)
9. Duta, N., Jain, A., Dubuisson-Jolly, M.: Automatic Construction of 2D Shape Models. IEEE Transactions on Pattern Analysis and Machine Intelligence 23, 433–446 (2001)
10. Rico-Juan, J.R., Mico, L.: Comparison of AESA and LAESA search algorithms using string and tree-edit-distances. Pattern Recognition Letters 24, 1417–1426 (2003)

Cell Division Detection on the Arabidopsis Thaliana Root

Monica Marcuzzo[1], Tiago Guichard[2], Pedro Quelhas[1,2],
Ana Maria Mendonça[1,2], and Aurélio Campilho[1,2]

[1] INEB - Instituto de Engenharia Biomédica
Divisão de Sinal e Imagem, Campus FEUP
[2] Universidade do Porto, Faculdade de Engenharia
Departamento de Engenharia Electrotécnica e Computadores

Abstract. The study of individual plant cells and their growth structure
is an important focus of research in plant genetics. To obtain development
information at cellular level, researchers need to perform *in vivo* imaging of the specimen under study, through time-lapse confocal microscopy.
Within this research field it is important to understand mechanisms like
cell division and elongation of developing cells. We describe a tool to
automatically search for cell division in the *Arabidopsis thaliana* using
information of nuclei shape. The nuclei detection is based on a convergence index filter. Cell division detection is performed by an automatic
classifier, trained through cross-validation. The results are further improved by a stability criterion based on the Mahalanobis distance of the
shape of the nuclei through time. With this approach, we can achieve a
correct detection rate of 94.7%.

1 Introduction

Cellular division is a fundamental process responsible for originating other cell
types in multicellular organisms. In plants, specialized regions, the meristems,
concentrate cellular division. *Arabidopsis thaliana* is a plant with rapid development and with a simple cellular pattern. Due to these characteristics, it is
considered a model organism, widely used in plant research.

The *Arabidopsis* root meristem, located at the tip of the root, is responsible
for perpetuating this pattern by cellular division [1]. However, the control of the
divisions is not completely understood, which motivates *in vivo* analysis of the
Arabidopsis root.

Development biologists studying roots find difficult to cope with the lack of
suitable technology to analyze root growth *in vivo* [1]. The great amount of
data produced leads to the development of image analysis tools to automatically
extract useful information, such as identifying cell division and growth. Some of
these solutions focus on the analysis of *Arabidopsis* development. Cell growth is
analyzed using different approaches, such as mathematical models [2] and motion
estimation methods [3]. The relation between cell division and elongation in the
regulation of organ growth rate is also investigated [4]. These studies show that

H. Araujo et al. (Eds.): IbPRIA 2009, LNCS 5524, pp. 168–175, 2009.

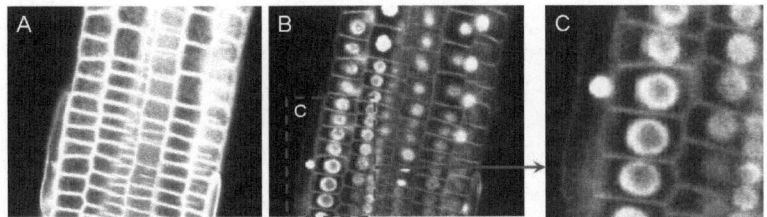

Fig. 1. *In vivo* microscopy image of the Arabidopsis thaliana root. A) image of cell walls marked with green fluorescent protein (GFP). B) image of cell nuclei marked with yellow fluorescent protein (YFP). C) detail of the cell nuclei image (B).

in vivo imaging of the root is a valuable tool. However, none of them provide an automatic way to study the images at a cellular level.

Both the importance of these studies in biology and the lack of automated *in vivo* analysis methods motivate the development of automatic image analysis tools which can extract useful information. Furthermore, other methods which can provide insight about the plant development should be provided, such as cell feature extraction for quantitative and statistical analysis, tracking of individual cells over time, and event coordination.

In most automated cell analysis approaches, the first step is image segmentation, as in approaches described in [5,6]. Unfortunately, segmentation is a difficult problem in computer vision and, in the case of *in vivo* plant imaging, is made worse by image acquisition process, data's variability and noise. These characteristics can lead the segmentation process to produce errors, such as over-segmentation of the cells. This fact, together with the small number of cell divisions, makes the detection of cell division through segmentation an impractical task.

In this work, we introduce a novel approach to cell division detection in plants based on nuclei shape. The nuclei detection is not based on segmentation, but on a convergence index filter. Cell division is then related to nuclei shape by an automatic classifier, trained through cross-validation. The results are further improved by a stability criterion based on the Mahalanobis distance between the shapes of the nuclei through time. The images presented in this paper are of the Green Fluorescent Protein (GFP) marked cell walls and Yellow Fluorescent Protein (YFP) marked cell nuclei. Figure 1 shows the GFP channel (A), the YFP channel (B), and the detail of cell nuclei. However, the methodology in this work is not specific for these images and could be applied to other type of images. This paper is organized as follows: Section 2 describes our approach to detect nuclei and cell division. Section 3 describes the data used and the results obtained. Finally, conclusion is presented in Section 4.

2   Methodology

Our approach is divided into two main steps: nuclei detection and cell division detection. Nuclei detection is based on image filtering and provides the location and shape delimitation of the nuclei. Cell division detection is based on the detected nuclei's shape and the image information within that shape. A further step is introduced to reduce the amount of false detection which is based on the assumption of stability of cells through time (stability which is broken at the division point).

2.1   Nuclei Detection

Most approaches for nuclei detection are based on some segmentation method. These approaches assume that cell nuclei are mostly isolated with few agglomerated cases that must be solved [5,7,8]. However in the case of *in vivo* plant imaging, nuclei are contained in a 3D structure and, as a consequence of image acquisition, nuclei appear superimposed and with different intensities. Also, due to channel cross-talk, the cell walls fluorescence is also visible in the nuclei YFG channel, this renders any segmentation meaningless.

In addition to all the mentioned problems, the protein markers get fixed to the amino acids and this means that the shape that is imaged varies. Marked nuclei appear as rings or circles, or elongated ellipses (Figure 1(C)). This makes it difficult to impose any prior for segmentation.

Our approach to nuclei detection is based on image filter enhancement techniques, which highlight image locations that exhibit a certain characteristic. Since nuclei marked by fluorescent protein have a rounded shape, a filter from the convergence index filter family [9] was selected to perform this enhancement task. Convergence index (CI) filters are based on the maximization the convergence index at each image point of spatial coordinates (x, y), defined by:

$$C(x,y) = \frac{1}{M} \sum_{(k,l) \in R} \cos \theta_i(k,l), \tag{1}$$

where M is the number of points in the filter support region R, θ_i is the angle between the gradient vector calculated for point (k, l) and the direction of the line that connects points (x, y) and (k, l).

The main difference between the distinct members of the CI family is the definition of the support region R, which is formed by radial lines that emerge from the point where the filter result is being calculated, as shown in Figure 2(left). Four filters were evaluated: coin filter (CF), iris filter (IF), adaptive ring filter (ARF) [9,10] and the recently proposed sliding band filter (SBF) [11]. The CF uses a circle with variable radius as support region, the IF maximizes the convergence index by adapting the radius value on each direction and the ARF uses a ring shaped region with fixed width and varying radius. Finally, the SBF combines the basic ideas of IF and ARF by defining a support region formed by a band of fixed width, whose position is changed in each direction to allow the maximization of the convergence index at each point, as defined by:

$$SBF(x,y) = \frac{1}{N} \sum_{i=0}^{N-1} \left(\max_{R_{min} \leq n \geq R_{max}} \left(\frac{1}{d} \sum_{m=n}^{n+d} \cos(\theta_{im}) \right) \right), \tag{2}$$

where N is the number of support region lines that irradiate from (x, y), d is the band width, n is the position of the band in a line that varies from R_{min} to

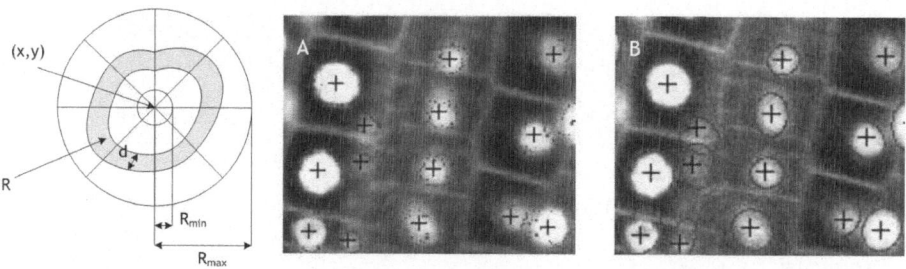

Fig. 2. Sliding band filter (SBF). Support region schematics (left). Filter detections and support points (middle). Estimated ellipses for the detections (right).

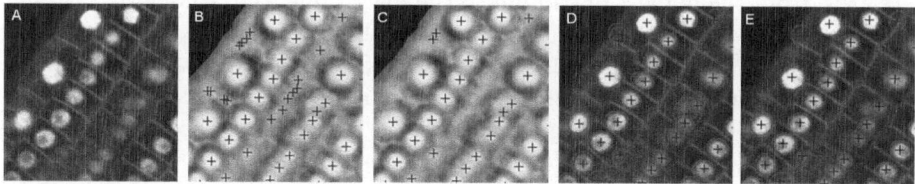

Fig. 3. Cell nuclei detection result: A) original nuclei image; B) full maxima detection in the filter response image; C) filtered detections on walls; D) overlapping ellipses; and E) ellipses representing nuclei detection

R_{max}, and θ_{im} is the angle between the gradient vector and the direction that is currently being analyzed (see Figure 2(left) for filter design schematics). The more generic formulation of the SBF gives a wider detection range of shapes in comparison with other convergence filters. This is desirable for our application due to the distinct shapes that the cell nuclei can exhibit. Testing all the filters we observed that SBF detections are closer to the cell nuclei centers, miss less nuclei and have less false positions.

After the application of the enhancement filter, cell nuclei are associated with the locations of filter maxima response. Low value maxima are ignored, by setting a threshold equal to the mean intensity of the detected local maxima of the enhanced image. However, to avoid eliminating the brighter points of the original image (that are potential nuclei), these points are kept even if their values in the enhanced image are bellow the established threshold.

An additional problem is the filter detections which fall on visible cell walls. To solve this difficulty, cell walls are first located through a phase symmetry filter, as described in [12], and then all the points coincident are eliminated. In each direction of the SBF region of support, the position of the band that maximizes the convergence index response gives an indication of the nucleus border localization in this particular direction. For each local maximum, an ellipse is adapted to the respective band support points, thus forming an initial approximation of the cell nucleus contour (Figure 2(right)). Some of these ellipses have a large overlapping area, either because they correspond to nuclei belonging to distinct layers, or the filtering process resulted in an uneven sliding of the filter band in some directions.

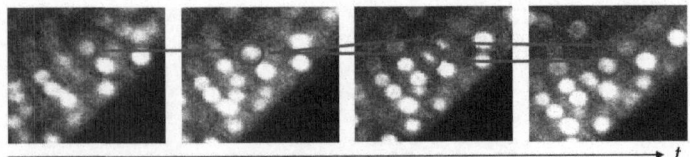

Fig. 4. Illustration of cell division in time. In the second image, amino acids get grouped into an oval shape with high intensity. After that, the nucleus divides itself, giving rise to two nuclei.

To overcome these problems, we select the areas with the highest probability of being nuclei, by ordering the local maxima that correspond to overlaid areas. Afterwards, from the highest maximum to the lowest one, the regions that present an overlap above 50% (using as reference the smallest area) are replaced by a circle with diameter equal to the length of the minor axis of the ellipse, and the common area is once again calculated. If the overlap is still higher than 50%, the point with lowest intensity is discarded. Figure 3 shows the images corresponding to all this process and the ellipses corresponding to the final detection.

2.2 Nuclei Division Detection

Our approach to cell division detection is based on the change of shape that the nuclei suffer during division. Just before a division, cell nucleus amino acids get grouped into a bright oval small shape with high intensity, as shown in Figure 4. This change of shape is what we aim at detecting.

For shape characterization six features were chosen: maximum intensity, mean intensity, compactness, eccentricity, area, and orientation (orientation can only be used after image registration, as described in [12]).

Given the chosen features and labeled examples, we have trained a linear classifier to learn what defines a dividing nucleus. The classifier gives dividing and non-dividing labels for each nucleus in the image, what means that this classification is static and does not use any temporal information.

2.3 Temporal Filtering of False Division Detections

One given property of cells in plants is that their shapes change rather slowly. This means that while not dividing, cell nuclei should have similar shapes. This is of course not the case at the moment of division where nuclei amino acids cause the nuclei image to change.

Given this stability criterion, it is expected that a temporal filtering can be used for improving the detection results. This implies that we must first stabilize the time-lapse image sequence through image registration and then for each cell find the best candidate in the next image based on spatial distance between nuclei center.

After the temporal sequence of nuclei identified, we calculate the Mahalanobis distance between the corresponding nuclei over time, considering just the maximum intensity and the eccentricity features. We found, through a greedy approach, that these two features are the ones that contribute most to the stability criterion. When a considerable change occurs in both features, there is a high probability that a division is about to occur since the shape becomes more elliptical and the nucleus becomes brighter. The other features are more stable or have great variation over time. For instance, the area is not indicative, because when a division is about to occur, nucleus area can remain almost the same, even though shape can suffer significant change. Features like orientation of the nuclei have notable variation over all the sequence due to movement of the root. Therefore, if we have a sequence that verifies the stability criterion, and a division is found using the static approach, this detection is not correct and must be eliminated. Otherwise, it is kept as a true division.

3   Results

To validate our methodology we used images from time-lapse biology experiments. In these experiments, cell walls are marked using GFP and cell nuclei are marked using YFP. We use two sequences of images acquired from two distinct plants. The time-lapse fluorescence microscopy sequences were recorded using a temporal resolution of one image per 15 minutes. Using this time interval, it is possible that certain changes in nuclei shape are missed, as they can occur in less than 15 minutes. The dataset is constituted by 57 images from the two experiments. Visual inspection of the sequences shows that 21 divisions occurred.

Our nuclei detection method (presented in Section. 2.1) found 6183 cells. We used a linear classifier and applied k-fold cross-validation, with $k = 10$, for the approach introduced in Section 2.2. The choice of a linear classifier was motivated by the highly imbalanced set of examples both in the training and test sets. From the total number of detected nuclei, 5730 were considered as non-dividing and 18 as dividing, giving an accuracy of 92.96%. Examples of division detection are shown in Figure 5. In all examples, the division is happening on frame t and the result of division is visible in frame $t + 1$. Cases A and B are correctly classified and cases C and D are misclassified. Apparently the temporal resolution of 15 minutes was not enough to capture the change in shape in these cases. Also, in case B, the nuclei detection method failed because it detected one nucleus instead of two nuclei resulting from the division process.

The temporal filtering approach (Section 2.3) tries to reduce the false positive rate by eliminating false detections over stable sequences. Using this approach, we were able to increase the number of non-dividing nuclei to 5837 and maintain the number of dividing in 18, achieving a final accuracy of 94.7% (reducing in almost 25% the false positive rate). Figure 6 shows one sequence of nuclei over time where two incorrect dividing nuclei (marked in red) were detected using the static approach that were afterwards corrected using the stability criterion. Table 1 resumes all the results obtained using the two cell divisions detection approaches.

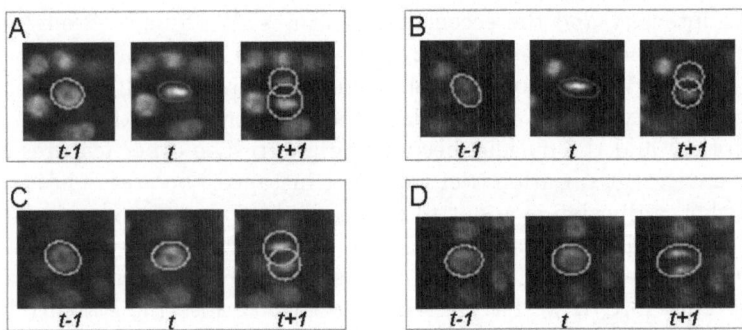

Fig. 5. Classification examples. In all cases, the division is happening in frame t and the result of division is visible in frame $t + 1$. In cases A and B the divisions are correctly detected. Cases C and D are misclassified, probably because no change in shape is noticeable in frame t. In case B, nuclei detection failed also in detecting resulting nuclei division.

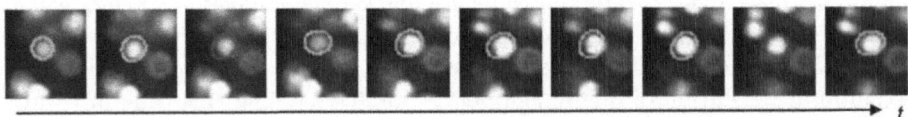

Fig. 6. Temporal filtering. Sequence of nuclei over time, where nuclei divisions detections are represented in red (or dark gray) and non-dividing in cyan (or light gray).

Table 1. Results of the nuclei division detection

	Classification results	Results after stabilization
Accuracy(%)	92.96	94.70
FP rate(%)	7.01	5.27
FN rate(%)	14.29	14.29

4   Conclusion

We introduced an automatic method to detect cell division in *in vivo* time-lapse sequences of growing *Arabidopsis thaliana's* root. The method is based on the nuclei detection through a convergence index filter. Then a classifier is trained to detect nuclei division based on a set of features that characterizes nucleus shape. The results are further improved by a stability criterion based on the Mahalanobis distance of the shape of the nuclei through time.

An initial accuracy of 92.96% was achieved for the static approach but this value was afterwards increased when temporal information was added to the detection procedure, further reducing the false negative rate by 25%.

The future improvements on this approach will include a better evaluation of nuclei detection, since some errors are due to this initial step, and the use of the image's pixel data as an extra source of information.

Acknowledgements

The authors acknowledge the funding of Fundação para a Ciência e Tecnologia, under contract ERA-PG/0007/2006.

References

1. Campilho, A., Garcia, B., Toorn, H., Wijk, H., Campilho, A., Scheres, B.: Time-lapse analysis of stem-cell divisions in the arabidopsis thaliana root meristem. The Plant Journal 48, 619–627 (2006)
2. Iwamoto, A., Satoh, D., Furutani, M., Maruyama, S., Ohba, H., Sugiyama, M.: Insight into the basis of root growth in arabidopsis thaliana provided by a simple mathematical model. J. Plant Res. 119, 85–93 (2006)
3. Roberts, T., Mckenna, S., Wuyts, N., Valentine, T., Bengough, A.: Performance of low-level motion estimation methods for confocal microscopy of plant cells in vivo. In: Motion 2007, p. 13 (2007)
4. Beemster, G., Baskin, T.: Analysis of cell division and elongation underlying the developmental acceleration of root growth in arabidopsis thaliana. Plant Physiology 116, 1515–1526 (1998)
5. Chen, X., Zhou, X., Wong, S.T.C.: Automated segmentation, classification, and tracking of cancer cell nuclei in time-lapse microscopy. IEEE Trans. on Biomedical Engineering 53(4), 762–766 (2006)
6. Mao, K.Z., Zhao, P., Tan, P.: Supervised learning-based cell image segmentation for p53 immunohistochemistry. IEEE Trans. on Biomedical Engineering 53(6), 1153–1163 (2006)
7. Yang, X., Li, H., Zhou, X.: Nuclei segmentation using marker-controlled watershed, tracking using mean-shift, and kalman filter in time-lapse microscopy. IEEE Trans. on Circuits and Systems I-Regul. Papers 53(11), 2405–2414 (2006)
8. Harder, N., M-Bermudez, F., Godinez, W., Ellenberg, J., Eils, R., Rohr, K.: Automated analysis of mitotic cell nuclei in 3d fluorescence microscopy image sequences. In: Workshop on Bio-Image Informatics: Biological Imaging, Computer Vision and Data Mining (2008)
9. Kobatake, H., Hashimoto, S.: Convergence index filter for vector fields. IEEE Trans. on Image Processing 8(8) (1999)
10. Wei, J., Hagihara, Y., Kobatake, H.: Detection of rounded opacities on chest radiographs using convergence index filter. In: Proceedings of the Int. Conference on Image Analysis and Processing, pp. 757–761 (1999)
11. Pereira, C.S., Fernandes, H., Mendonça, A.M., Campilho, A.C.: Detection of lung nodule candidates in chest radiographs. In: Martí, J., Benedí, J.M., Mendonça, A.M., Serrat, J. (eds.) IbPRIA 2007. LNCS, vol. 4478, pp. 170–177. Springer, Heidelberg (2007)
12. Marcuzzo, M., Quelhas, P., Campilho, A., Mendonça, A.M., Campilho, A.: A hybrid approach for cell image segmentation. In: Campilho, A., Kamel, M.S. (eds.) ICIAR 2008. LNCS, vol. 5112, pp. 739–749. Springer, Heidelberg (2008)

HOG-Based Decision Tree for Facial Expression Classification

Carlos Orrite, Andrés Gañán, and Grégory Rogez

Aragon Institute for Engineering Research, University of Zaragoza, Spain
{corrite,aganan,grogez}@unizar.es

Abstract. We address the problem of human emotion identification from still pictures taken in semi-controlled environments. Histogram of Oriented Gradient (HOG) descriptors are considered to describe the local appearance and shape of the face. First, we propose a Bayesian formulation to compute class specific edge distribution and *log-likelihood maps* over the entire aligned training set. A hierarchical decision tree is then built using a bottom-up strategy by recursively clustering and merging the classes at each level. For each branch of the tree we build a list of potentially discriminative HOG features using the *log-likelihood maps* to favor locations that we expect to be more discriminative. Finally, a Support Vector Machine (SVM) is considered for the decision process in each branch. The evaluation of the present method has been carried out on the Cohn-Kanade AU-Coded Facial Expression Database, recognizing different emotional states from single picture of people not present in the training set.

Keywords: Facial expression, HOG, Decision Trees, SVM.

1 Introduction

A facial expression results from several motions or positions of the muscles of the face. It represents an important cue in nonverbal communication as it conveys the emotional state of the individual to observers. Automatic recognition of facial expressions could be very beneficial to human temper (or behavior) analysis systems and advanced Human-Computer Interfaces (HCI).

Over the last few years, different methods have been proposed for facial expression analysis. They can roughly be classified according to the input data used - video sequences or still pictures- and the scope of the analysis -individual facial features extraction or holistic representations of faces- [1]. Expressions are usually better discriminated analyzing the temporal evolution of faces. Therefore facial movements have been characterized analyzing optical flow between frames of video sequences as in [2], [3], tracking facial features [4] or approaching the problem from a sequential point of view, e.g. applying hidden Markov models (HMM) as in [7], and reporting good performance when facial data were correctly extracted.

H. Araujo et al. (Eds.): IbPRIA 2009, LNCS 5524, pp. 176–183, 2009.
© Springer-Verlag Berlin Heidelberg 2009

However, in some cases the analysis of the expression must be done on a single shot. The key point in most recognition process is the appropriate selection of features. Gradients and edges have been reported to be more robust than color-based characteristics with respect to lighting variations. Gabor filters traditionally have been considered among the best discriminative procedures. More recently, Local Binary Patterns (LBP) and Volumetric Local Binary Patterns have reported good results for recognizing facial expressions [6]. Lately, Histograms of Oriented Gradient (HOG) descriptors have received a lot of attention for the purpose of object detection [8].

On the other hand, still pictures include not only emotion information but also physiognomic information. This fact can lead a classifier to take into account the facial features associated with a particular individual instead of focusing on emotion features. To address this problem we proposed a Bayesian formulation to compute edge distribution over the entire training set and favor locations that we expect to be more discriminative between different emotions. Afterwards, a hierarchical tree is built using a bottom-up strategy by recursively clustering and merging the feature classes at each level. At each branch of the tree, we construct intra and interclass probability density maps of edge distributions and the corresponding *log-likelihood maps* that are used to select the appropriate and discriminative HOG blocks. Finally, a different Support Vector Machine (SVM) is trained in each branch of the decision tree.

The evaluation of the present method has been carried out on the Cohn-Kanade AU-Coded Facial Expression Database [9], considering five basic emotions besides the neutral face: happiness, anger, surprise, sadness and disgust.

2 Selection of Discriminative Features

Feature selection if probably the key point in most of the recognition process in computer vision. So, it is very important to select the relevant and most informative features in order to reach a higher recognition rate and, at the same time, to alleviate the effects of the curse of dimensionality. Many different features are used in general recognition problems. Gradients and edges have been reported to be more robust than color-based cues with respect to lighting variations. Recently, HOG descriptors have received a lot of attention for the purpose of object detection. Dalal and Triggs first described HOG descriptors and focused their algorithm on the problem of pedestrian detection in static images [8].

HOG descriptors are considered in this paper to describe the local appearance and shape of the face. Roughly, the implementation of these descriptors can be achieved by dividing the image into small connected regions (cells) for which a histogram of gradient directions (edge orientations) is computed. The combination of these histograms then represents the descriptor. The algorithm involves different steps [10]. The first step is the computation of the gradient values. The second step involves creating the cell histograms. Each pixel within the cell casts a weighted vote for an orientation-based histogram channel based on the values found in the gradient computation. The cells are grouped together into larger, spatially-connected blocks. The HOG descriptor is then the vector that concatenates the components of the normalized histograms from all of the block regions. Here several parameters have to be considered: the size of the cell in pixels, the number of cells per block and the number of orientations bins.

The usage of HOG blocks over the entire image leads to a very large feature vector. Thus an important question is how to select the most informative HOG blocks. In [8], Dalal and Triggs use AdaBoost to keep only the discriminative HOG blocks and train an SVM while in [11], the authors propose to take advantage of the accurate image alignment to locate the most informative HOG blocks for human pose detection.

In this work, we propose an approach, similar in spirit to [11], for facial expression: we study edge distribution over the entire aligned training set p(E), and favor locations that we expect to be more discriminative between different emotions (considered as classes). We thus construct intra and interclass probability density maps of edge distribution that can be used to select the right features: the log-likelihood ratios give information on how discriminative the features are, based on their location. Here we describe a simple Bayesian formulation to compute the log-likelihood ratios which will give us the importance of different regions in the image. Let $C_1, C_2, ..C_n$ be n different classes (in this case, the emotions). Let the probability for the class C_i, given the complete edge map, be $p(C_i|E)$. Using simple Bayes rule we have the following: $p(C_i|E) = p(E|C_i)p(C_i)/p(E)$.

We then introduce the log-likelihood ratio for the $i_t h$ class:

$$L_i = \log(\frac{p(E, C_i)}{p(E)}). \tag{1}$$

We compute $p(E, C_i)$ using the edge maps that correspond only to the training images belonging to class C_i. On the other hand, p(E) is computed using all the

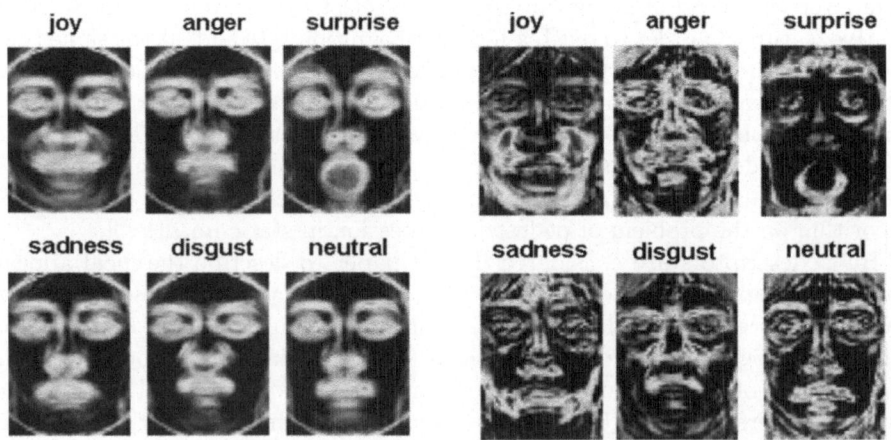

Fig. 1. Mean gradient image (left) and log-likelihood ratios (right) for the 6 facial expressions. Hot colors indicate the discriminative areas for a given emotion.

training images corresponding to classes C_1 to C_n (see Fig. 1). Given this log-likelihood ratio, we can randomly sample boxes from positions where they are expected to be useful and reduce the dimension of the feature space considering only the discriminative HOG blocks. For the example given in Fig. 1, we can easily observe how the space between the eyebrows is a very discriminative region for the anger facial expression.

3   Bottom-Up Hierarchical Tree Learning

A hierarchical tree is built using a bottom-up approach by recursively clustering and merging the classes at each level. This process is based on a similarity matrix, see Table 1, which represents how similar are the different log-likelihood facial expressions. For example, the lowest distance (i.e., 7.94) corresponds to neutral and anger expressions, so both are joined in the same node (i.e., node 1), and so on. The similarity matrix is then recalculated at each level of the tree with the resulting new classes. In this point it is worth mentioning that there are different topologies for the hierarchical tree. After testing several of them, the best results were reached with the structure depicted in Fig. 2.

Once the hierarchical tree has been built, we recalculate the log-likelihood at each node j and for each branch i:

$$L_{i,j} = \log(\frac{\sum_i E_i}{\sum_j E_j}), \tag{2}$$

Table 1. Similarity matrix: Euclidean distance between the log-likelihood maps

Emotion	joy	anger	surprise	sadness	disgust	neutral
joy	0.00	16.21	18.92	17.57	16.28	16.76
anger			13.73	10.26	9.09	7.94
surprise				12.27	15.55	11.53
sadness					13.70	9.40
disgust						11.56
neutral						

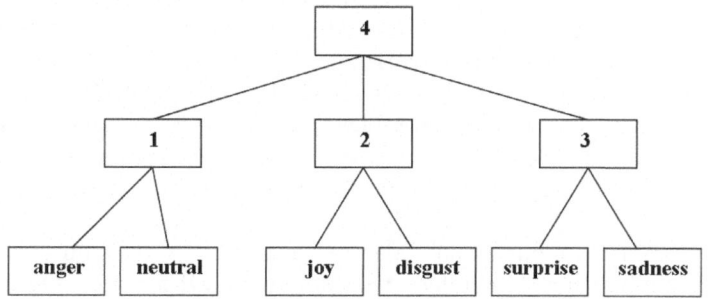

Fig. 2. Hierarchical Decision Tree

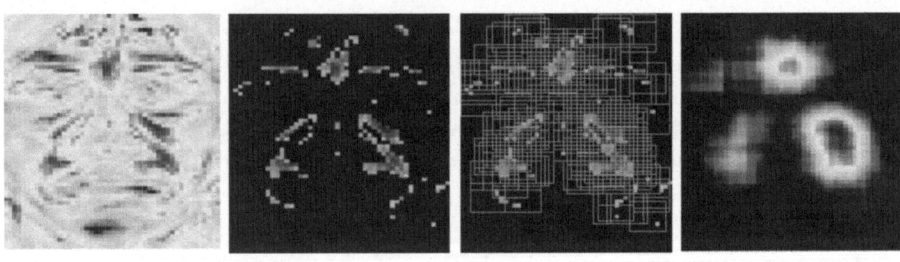

Fig. 3. From left to right: log-likelihood for node 2 (joy and disgust), most discriminative areas after thresholding, extracted HOGs and HOGs density

being E_j the edges maps corresponding to the classes that reach node j and E_i the edges maps corresponding to the classes that pass through branch i.

In Fig. 3a we represent the log-likelihood for node 2 in the previous hierarchical tree, where the facial expressions joy and disgust are merged. After thresholding (Fig. 3b), we obtain the most significant areas where HOG blocks will be extracted (Fig. 3c) to differentiate between joy and disgust expressions. In Fig. 3d, we can see the areas covered by the selected HOG blocks and how the resulting density follows the distribution from Fig. 3b.

For every branch we extract two types of HOGs from the training data set: those which belong to valid images (image that must pass through to a lower node) and those from images that have to be rejected. We then train a Support Vector Machine (SVM) for every branch using the extracted HOGs, thus generating 9 "local" models (one per branch).

4   Results

The proposed method has been tested on the Cohn-Kanade AU-Coded Facial Expression Database [9]. We used a set composed by 20 different individuals acting 5 basic emotions besides the neutral face: happiness, anger, surprise, sadness and disgust, with 3 examples each; 300 pictures all together. All images were normalized, i.e. cropped and manually rectified, in order to make the facial feature extraction easier. It is worth noticing that this is an important issue for a good tree generation, leaving as future work the automatization of this step.

The evaluation was carried out following the leave-one out method. So, 74 images per expression were used for training and 1 for testing. The HOG blocks used were based on square grids with 4 cells per block, 64 pixels per cell, and 8 orientation bins. The results are reported in Table 2. For some cases, an uncertainty is obtained (see 4th column). It happens when an input image reaches more than one leaf (emotion). For instance, the neutral class only obtains a 70.67% of RR but only 8% of FP. It means that 92% of the neutral images have reached the right class but 21.33% also reached another emotion.

Now, we analyze how the different parameters used for the HOG generation affect to the recognition performance, i.e, the size of the cell in pixels, the number of cells per block and the number of orientations per cell histogram. Figure 4a

Table 2. Preliminary results on the Cohn-Kanade AU-Coded Facial Expression Database using square grid HOG blocks with 4 8-pixels cells and 8 orientation bins

Emotion	success	false	indet	RR(%)	FP(%)
joy	70	2	3	93.33	2.66
anger	46	17	12	61.33	22.66
surprise	73	0	2	97.33	0.0
sadness	55	9	11	73.33	12.00
disgust	63	4	8	84.00	5.33
neutral	53	6	16	70.67	8.00

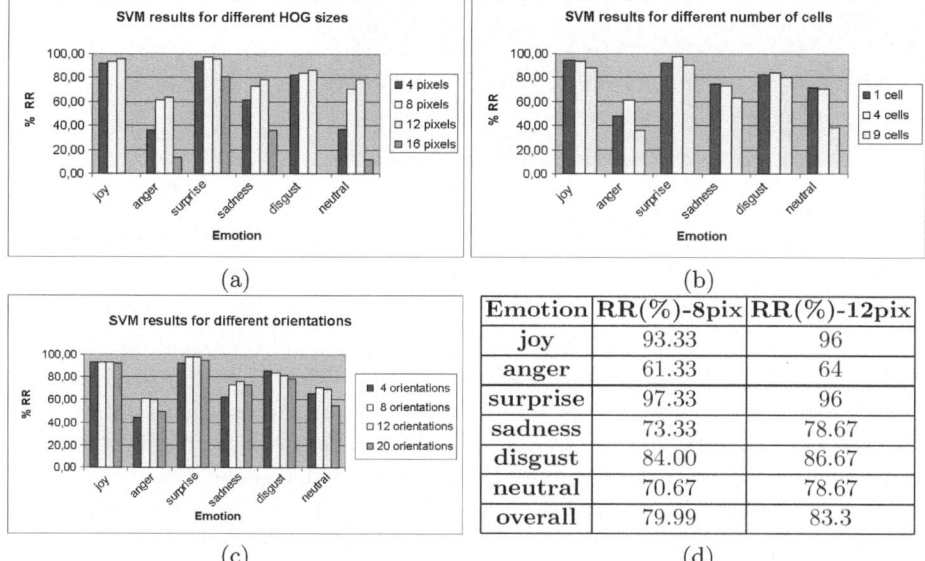

(a)　　　　　　　　　　　　　　　　　(b)

Emotion	RR(%)-8pix	RR(%)-12pix
joy	93.33	96
anger	61.33	64
surprise	97.33	96
sadness	73.33	78.67
disgust	84.00	86.67
neutral	70.67	78.67
overall	79.99	83.3

(c)　　　　　　　　　　　　　　　　　(d)

Fig. 4. Recognition Rate (RR) (a) for different sizes, (b) for different number of cells and (c)different orientations. (d) Improvement when passing from 8 to 12 pixels.

shows the results for different cell sizes. As it can be noticed, in average, a slightly improvement is reached using 12 pixels per cell in relation to the previous size of 8 pixels. On the other hand, quite similar results are obtained with 1 or 4 cells per block, as depicted in Figure 4b. Finally, Figure 4c shows the recognition rate for different number of orientations, where results given when choosing 8 or 12 orientations are the best, being both quite similar.

As a result, we can state that the best average HOG block is that with 12 pixels, 1 or 4 cells per block and 8 or 12 orientation bins, reaching an overall recognition rate of 83.3% (depicted in Fig.4d). Comparing the performance of our approach with others testing on same data set, in [5] the authors used SVM with an overall recognition rate of 87.5%. More recently, Buenaposada et. al. [4], have reported an overall performance of 89.1%. As far as we are concern, the

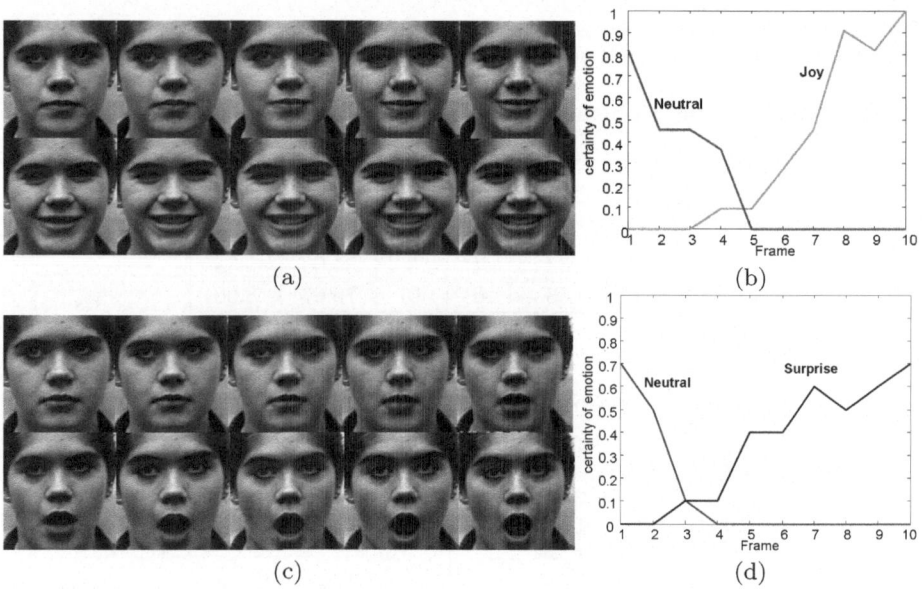

(a)   (b)

(c)   (d)

Fig. 5. (a)Joy sequence, (b)neutral and joy scores varying the degree of emotion, (c)Surprise sequence, (d)neutral and surprise scores varying the degree of emotion

best performance for facial expression has been reached by Zhao et. al. [6], using LBP, obtained an overall score of 96.2%. Obviously, our best approach, with an overall recognition rate of 83.3% does not outperform those previous works in terms of performance, but we should bear in mind that our approach works with still images while the others require the complete video sequences.

We now evaluate the algorithm with several sequences: every sequence is composed of 10 frames running from a neutral face to the maximum expression. Two examples (joy and surprise) are shown in Fig. 5. We show in Fig. 5b and d the average score given by the algorithm for different frames varying the degree of emotion. For instance, in the joy sequence, we can observe that from frames 3 to 7, the system gives a low score for both neutral and joy, which means that there is an uncertainty. It should bear in mind that the system has been trained with images exhibiting a maximum degree of expression (or completely neutral). Finally, the system reaches a high score for expression of joy from frame 8 to 10.

5   Conclusions

The main contribution of this paper is the Bayesian formulation carried out to compute edge distribution over the entire training set and favor locations that we expect to be more discriminative between different emotions.

Another novelty of this work yields on the usage of HOG descriptors to describe the local appearance and shape of the face. We have reported some encouraging results on experiments carried out on the Cohn-Kanade Facial Expression

Database, recognizing different emotional states from people not present in the training set from whom a single picture is available.

We have seen that previous approaches working with video sequences give better recognition rates. However, depending on the applications, it is not always possible to obtain a video sequence and the system can be limited to work with a single snapshot. This is the kind of applications the present work is devised for. And it gives more than acceptable results. Moreover, our method does not return a binary decision: for instance, when the expression is not well defined, e.g. during a transition between emotions, an uncertainty is delivered.

Recent work using LBP has shown very good results with video sequences. In a future work, we will combine our approach for discriminative features selection with this type of features.

Acknowledgments. This work is supported by Spanish Grant TIN2006-11044 (MEyC) and FEDER.

References

1. Fasel, B., Luettin, J.: Recognition of asymmetric facial action unit activities and intensities. In: 15th International Conference on Pattern Recognition (ICPR), vol. 1, p. 5100 (2000)
2. Barlett, M., Viola, P., Sejnowski, T., Larsen, L., Ekman, P.: Classifying facial action. In: Touretzky, D., Mozer, M., Hasselmo, M. (eds.) Advances in Neural Information Processing Systems. MIT Press, Cambridge (1996)
3. Yacoob, Y., Davis, L.S.: Recognizing Human Facial Expressions. Technical Report CAR-TR706, Center for Automation Research, University of Maryland (1994)
4. Buenaposa, J.M., Muñoz, E., Baumela, L.: Recognising facial expressions in video sequences. Pattern Analysis and Applications 11, 101–116 (2008)
5. Michel, P., El Kaliouby, R.: Real time facial expression recognition in video using suport vector machines. In: Proc. Int. Conf. on Multimodal Interfaces, pp. 258–264. ACM, New York (2003)
6. Zhao, G., Piettikäinen, M.: Dynamic texture recognition using local binary patters with an application to facial expressions. IEEE Trans. PAMI 29(6), 915–928 (2007)
7. de la Torre, F., Campoy, J., Ambadar, Z., Cohn, J.: Temporal segmentation of facial behavior. In: International Conference on Computer Vision (October 2007)
8. Dalal, N., Triggs, B.: Histograms of oriented gradients for human detection. In: CVPR (2005)
9. Cohn-Kanade Facial Expression Database,
   http://www.cs.cmu.edu/~face/index2.htm
10. http://en.wikipedia.org/wiki/Histogram_of_oriented_gradients
11. Rogez, G., Rihan, J., Ramalingam, S., Orrite, C., Torr, P.H.S.: Randomized Trees for Human Pose Detection. In: CVPR (2008)

Class Representative Visual Words for Category-Level Object Recognition

Roberto Javier López Sastre[1,*], Tinne Tuytelaars[2],
and Saturnino Maldonado Bascón[1]

[1] University of Alcalá, GRAM
{robertoj.lopez,saturnino.maldonado}@uah.es
[2] K.U. Leuven, ESAT-PSI
Tinne.Tuytelaars@esat.kuleuven.be

Abstract. Recent works in object recognition often use visual words, i.e. vector quantized local descriptors extracted from the images. In this paper we present a novel method to build such a codebook with *class representative* vectors. This method, coined *Cluster Precision Maximization* (CPM), is based on a new measure of the cluster precision and on an optimization procedure that leads any clustering algorithm towards class representative visual words. We compare our procedure with other measures of cluster precision and present the integration of a Reciprocal Nearest Neighbor (RNN) clustering algorithm in the CPM method. In the experiments, on a subset of the the Caltech101 database, we analyze several vocabularies obtained with different local descriptors and different clustering algorithms, and we show that the vocabularies obtained with the CPM process perform best in a category-level object recognition system using a Support Vector Machine (SVM).

Keywords: object recognition, clustering, visual words, class representative.

1 Introduction

A popular strategy to represent images in the context of category-level object recognition is the *Bag of Words* (BoW) approach [1]. The key idea is to quantize the continuous high dimensional space of local image descriptors such as SIFT [2], to get a codebook of so-called visual words. In this philosophy, an image is considered like a text document in which it is possible to find visual *words* to describe its content. A Bag of Words is then built as a histogram over visual word occurrences. This image representation has been shown to characterize the images and the objects within in a robust yet descriptive manner, in spite of the fact that it does not capture the spatial configuration between visual words. It is supposed that if a specific set of visual words appears in an image, there will be a high likelihood of finding the object in it. These BoW systems have

---

* Work performed during stay at Katholieke Universiteit Leuven.

H. Araujo et al. (Eds.): IbPRIA 2009, LNCS 5524, pp. 184–191, 2009.
© Springer-Verlag Berlin Heidelberg 2009

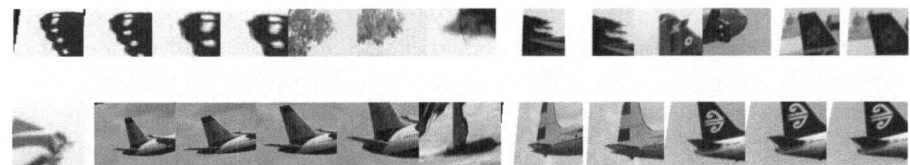

Fig. 1. First row: image patches that have been clustered together. Clearly all come from different object categories and lie on single object instances. Second row: cluster with image patches of the same object category and from different instances of the class, i.e. it contains class representative visual words.

shown impressive results lately, in spite of the simplicity of the scheme [1,3,4]. It is variations on this BoW scheme that have won the recent Pascal Visual Object Classes Challenge on object classification [5].

More precisely, building a BoW representation involves the following steps. First, interest regions are detected, either using a local invariant feature detector [6] or by densely sampling the image. Then, a region descriptor [7] is used to characterize them. After that, a clustering algorithm is run over all these descriptors to perform the vector quantization which finally results in a *visual vocabulary*. The idea is to characterize an image with the number of occurrences of each visual word, so any classifier can then be used for the categorization of this histogram representation.

Different vocabularies can be obtained for the same object class, and their quality depends on several parameters: the number of clusters (frequently fixed empirically), the nature of the descriptor, the chosen distance function to measure the similarity between descriptors, and the clustering algorithm. Our aim in this paper is to describe how to adapt the vector quantization process so as to yield class representative visual words, i.e. how to exploit the information of class labels already during the visual vocabulary construction process.

The main contribution is that we introduce an optimization procedure, the *Cluster Precision Maximization* (CPM), that maximizes the cluster representativeness. High representativeness should be assigned to visual words that generalize well over the within-class variability, yet are discriminative with respect to the object class (between-class variability). The basic idea behind our measure is that a visual word becomes more representative as it is found on a higher number of different instances of the same object class.

Fig.1 shows two examples of clusters of visual words. The first one (upper row) represents a *bad* cluster with visual words that clearly come from different object classes and lie on single object instances, not generalizing well within the class. The second example (lower row), on the other hand, shows a class representative visual word, found almost exclusively on objects of a single class and including different instances of this class. This is the type of cluster we want the CPM to deliver.

Related Work. To date, K-means clustering is still the most widely used vector quantization scheme in this context, in spite of its limitations: it does not take the class-labels into account, its output depends on the initialization, and it is computationally expensive. More efficient and stable alternatives have been proposed. However, here we will focus on work devoted to seeking more class representative visual words. First, there are several works based on frequent itemset mining [8,9,10]. Typically, finding representative visual words then boils down to finding frequent co-occurring groups of descriptors in a transaction database obtained from the training images. Others have tried to add more local geometric information to their codebook generation algorithms. Lazebnik *et al.* [11] constructed a codebook with groups of nearby regions whose appearance and spatial configuration occur repeatably in the training set. In [12] Leibe *et al.* presented how to learn semantic object parts for object categorization. They use what they call co-location and co-activation to learn a visual vocabulary that generalizes beyond the appearance of single objects, and often gets semantic object parts.

Perronnin *et al.* [13] build class representative visual words by enlarging the visual vocabularies, in spite of the increased cost of histograms computations. They propose an approach based on a universal vocabulary plus class specific vocabularies to improve the performance of the recognition system. To get more compact vocabularies Winn *et al.* [14] build an approach based on the bottleneck principle, while Moosmann *et al.* [15] organize the vocabulary using Extremely Randomized Clustering Forests. Finally, Perronnin *et al.* [16] have proposed to use Fisher Kernels, as their gradient representation has much higher dimensionality than a histogram representation, resulting in very compact vocabularies yet highly informative representations.

Closer to our approach are the works of Mikolajczyk *et al.* [17] and Stark *et al.* [18]. In [17] the performance of local detectors and descriptors is compared in the context of the object class recognition problem, and a new evaluation criterion based on the clusters precision is proposed. The problem is that following this approach, many clusters with features from only one object instance get high precision scores. Stark *et al.* [18] decided to give higher scores to feature descriptors that generalize across multiple instances of an object class, and proposed a new cluster precision definition, but their approach gets the best score when each cluster contains only one vector.

Overview. In section 2 we explain the CPM method and the integration of the Reciprocal Nearest Neighbor (RNN) clustering algorithm in it. In section 3 we present results from applying the CPM method to obtain visual vocabularies in a subset of Caltech101 database. Finally, section 4 concludes the paper.

2   Class Representative Visual Words

The main steps of our method can be sketched as follows. First the detection and description of local features for the object classes in the database is done. Then comes the tuning of the clustering algorithm parameters, computing a vocabulary with an efficient vector quantization approach for the obtained local features. The last task is to evaluate the clusters precisions (CP) for every object class, and iterate from the tuning step until the maximum for CP is reached.

There are many different techniques for detecting and describing local image regions [6,7]. Here we briefly describe the detectors and descriptors used in this work[1]. The region detector we use is the Hessian-Laplace [7] that responds to blob-like structures. It searches for local maxima of the Hessian determinant, and selects a characteristic scale via the Laplacian. For the descriptors we experiment with SIFT [2] and Shape Context (SC) [19]. The SIFT descriptor is a 3D histogram over local gradient locations and orientations, weighted by gradients magnitude. SC is based on edge information. For a given interest point, the SC descriptor accumulates the relative locations of nearby edge points in a coarse log-polar histogram.

2.1   Cluster Precision Maximization

Given a set of local features extracted from the images in our database, we could fix the number of clusters we want and apply the clustering algorithm of our choice to obtain a visual vocabulary for the object classes. One strategy to follow is to empirically find the optimal cluster parameters by testing whether this codebook reports an accurate categorization on a validation set. If it does not, we run the algorithm again with different parameters, until we get a codebook casting the lowest empirical risk in categorization. The problem of this kind of approach is that we need to complete the whole pipeline of the system just to validate the clustering.

The Cluster Precision Maximization (CPM) method on the other hand directly searches for class representative visual words, i.e. representative clusters. This new method measures the clusters precisions, so it is not needed to train a classifier and test whether it is accurate enough or not in each iteration. The basic idea behind this approach is that the more images with different object instances contain a particular visual word, the more representative the word is for that object class, and the better the categorization.

Suppose a database $\mathcal{DB}$ which contains N images of M different object classes, $\mathcal{DB} = \{\mathcal{I}_1, \mathcal{I}_2, \ldots, \mathcal{I}_N\}$. For each image in the database we first extract local features f, so an image $\mathcal{I}_i$ can be represented with a set of features $\mathcal{I}_i = \{f_{i_1}, f_{i_2}, \ldots\}$. Note that this will not be a BoW representation until the vector quantization is done using the features from all images in the database. After the clustering, a codebook $\mathcal{W} = \{w_1, w_2, \ldots, w_K\}$ with K words is obtained.

Mikolajczyk $et\ al.$ [17] evaluate the codebook W by computing the average cluster precision for all the object classes. Suppose there are K clusters in the vocabulary, but only K_a in which class a dominates. The average precision defined by Mikolajczyk $et\ al.$ is as follows

$$P_a = \frac{1}{K_a} \sum_{j=1}^{K_a} p_{j_a} \, , \tag{1}$$

where p_{j_a} is the number of features of class a in cluster j, divided by the total number of features in cluster j. In [18] the authors notice the previous definition

---

[1] The binaries have been taken from http://www.robots.ox.ac.uk/~vgg/research/affine/

of cluster precision gets high scores in those clusters that contain features from only a single object instance. They discount such clusters by summing over the fraction of objects of a class a in cluster j instead of individual features, and weight these fractions by cluster sizes, obtaining,

$$ P_a = \left(\sum_{j=1}^{K'_a} s_j \right)^{-1} \sum_{j=1}^{K_a} s_j p_{j_a} , \tag{2} $$

where j now ranges over all K'_a clusters in which objects of class a dominate, and s_j is the total number of features in cluster j. This new cluster precision definition gives higher scores to clusters that generalize across multiple instances of an object class, but it casts the maximum score when each cluster contains only one vector. Because neither of the two cluster precision definitions seem to meet our goal of selecting class representative visual words without artefacts, we propose a new cluster precision, this time summing over the number of objects of class a times the number of features of class a in each cluster. We get

$$ P_a = K \sum_{j=1}^{K} s_{j_a} n_{j_a} , \tag{3} $$

where s_{j_a} is the number of features found in images of object class a in cluster j, n_{j_a} is the number of different objects of class a represented in cluster j, and K is the number of clusters. This cluster precision varies from $S_a \times N_a$ to $S_a{}^2$, where S_a is the total number of features extracted for the object class a, and N_a is the number of different object instances of class a in the database. In each iteration the CPM approach computes the average precision over all object classes, $P = \frac{1}{M} \sum_{m=1}^{M} P_m$, using the definition in equation (3) for P_m, until it gets the maximum value. This maximization leads to the most representative clusters for an object class, and consequently good results in recognition. Any clustering algorithm can be integrated in this methodology. In Algorithm 1 we present in detail how to integrate an efficient average-link agglomerative clustering algorithm based on Reciprocal Nearest Neighbors [20], which has a complexity of $O(N^2 d)$ and only linear space requirements.

3   Experimental Results

For all our experiments we use a subset of the Caltech101 database [21] consisting of 20 classes[2]. The total number of images is 3901. For the classification, 50% of the images of each class are used for training and 50% for testing. The number

---

[2] The classes we use in this paper are: airplanes, bonsai, brain, butterfly, car-side, chandelier, faces-easy, grand-piano, hawksbill, ketch, laptop, leopards, menorah, motorbikes, starfish, sunflower, trilobite, umbrella, watch and yin-yang.

Algorithm 1. CPM for an Average-Link clustering based on RNN.

$CP_{max} = 0$
for $thres = min$ **to** max **do**
$\quad C = \emptyset; \; last \leftarrow 0; \; lastsim[0] \leftarrow 0; \; //C$ *will contain a list with the clusters*
$\quad L[last] \leftarrow v \in V; \; //Start$ *chain L with a random vector v*
$\quad R \leftarrow V \backslash v; \; //All$ *remaining points are kept in R*
$\quad$ **while** $R \neq \emptyset$ **do**
$\quad\quad (s, sim) \leftarrow getNearestNeighbor(L[last], R);$
$\quad\quad$ **if** $sim > lastsim[last]$ **then**
$\quad\quad\quad last \leftarrow last + 1; \; L[last] \leftarrow s; \; R \leftarrow R \backslash \{s\}$
$\quad\quad$ **else**
$\quad\quad\quad$ **if** $lastsim[last] > thres$ **then**
$\quad\quad\quad\quad s \leftarrow agglomerate(L[last], L[last-1]); \; R \leftarrow R \cup \{s\}; \; last \leftarrow last - 2$
$\quad\quad\quad$ **else**
$\quad\quad\quad\quad C \leftarrow C \cup L; \; last \leftarrow -1; \; L = \emptyset;$
$\quad\quad\quad$ **end if**
$\quad\quad$ **end if**
$\quad\quad$ **if** $last < 0$ **then**
$\quad\quad\quad last \leftarrow last + 1; \; L[last] \leftarrow v \in R; \; R \leftarrow R \backslash s$
$\quad\quad$ **end if**
$\quad$ **end while**
$\quad CP \leftarrow getCP(C); \; //Evaluate \; CP$
$\quad$ **if** $CP > CP_{max}$ **then**
$\quad\quad CP_{max} \leftarrow CP; \; C_{optimum} \leftarrow C;$
$\quad$ **end if**
end for

---

of local features used in the experiments varies from 3.000 to 120.000, depending on the number of classes we use.

Fig. 2 shows how the CPM approach is able to find the RNN clustering threshold for which the cluster precision is maximum. We show results computing a vocabulary for 2, 4 and 20 classes in Figure 2(a), and for two descriptors (SIFT and SC). While for SIFT the best threshold for the RNN algorithm does not depend on the number of classes, being always 0.3, for SC descriptor the threshold is between 0.4 and 0.5. Note how for both descriptors the CP quickly drops for suboptimal threshold values. Results from applying an SVM for the category-level object recognition of 4 classes of objects (airplanes, faces, motorbikes and cars) are given in Fig.2(b). For the experiments we have used SVMs with radial basis kernels. The input vectors for the SVMs are the normalized histograms of visual words for each labeled image. We compare the performance of the codebook obtained with a classical BoW approach with Kmeans (K was fixed to 2000 in the experiments), with the vocabularies obtained with the CPM optimization process using RNN. As expected, the SVM trained with the CPM vocabularies outperforms the Bow+Kmeans for all classes. From Table 1 it is clear that good cluster precision is indeed a good prediction for a good classification accuracy: CPM applied to the SC descriptor gets the maximum both with respect to cluster precision and average precision per class.

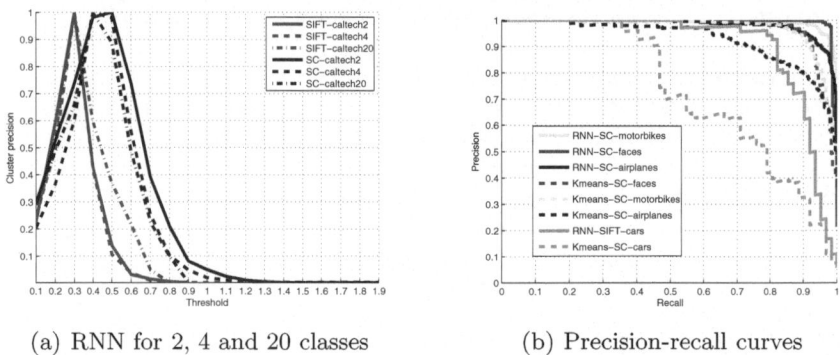

(a) RNN for 2, 4 and 20 classes   (b) Precision-recall curves

Fig. 2. (a) shows the normalized CP running the CPM with different number of object classes (2, 4 and 20). (d) Precision-Recall curves obtained with the classification results.

Table 1. Cluster Precision vs. Average Precision

Clustering	K	CP	airplane	cars	faces	motorbikes
Kmeans-SIFT	2000	4.64e+9	0.88	0.65	0.79	0.92
Kmeans-SC	2000	4.72e+9	0.90	0.70	0.94	0.93
CPM-RNN-SIFT	1527	2.60e+11	0.95	0.88	0.96	0.97
CPM-RNN-SC	3080	**3.46e+11**	0.96	0.87	0.97	0.98

4   Conclusion

In summary, we have introduced an optimization procedure, coined Cluster Precision Maximization, that maximizes the clusters representativeness. The CPM method measures the cluster precision for each class and finds the clustering parameters that cast class representative visual words. A complete description of the method has been given, showing how to integrate a RNN agglomerative clustering algorithm in it. CPM evaluates the intrinsic quality of the clusters for a classification task and as a result, allows to compare the quality of clusters computed with different descriptors, as well as the quality of clusterings with different number of clusters. Results confirm that the vocabularies obtained with CPM get better results.

As future work, we plan to experiment with other descriptors and detectors, as well as with more challenging image databases like the PASCAL VOC challenge data [5]. Also, instead of using a single, global threshold, the method can be extended towards optimizing the threshold for each cluster separately. Another line of research involves bringing local information in the clustering process to discover semantic visual words.

Acknowledgments. We acknowledge support from the Flemish Fund for Scientific Research (FWO) and the Spanish projects MEC TEC2008-02077 and CAM CCG07-UAH/TIC-1740.

References

1. Csurka, G., Dance, C.R., Fan, L., Willamowski, J., Bray, C.: Visual categorization with bags of keypoints. In: Proceedings of the ECCV (2004)
2. Lowe, D.: Object recognition from local scale-invariant features. In: ICCV (1999)
3. Felzenszwalb, P., McAllester, D., Ramanan, D.: A discriminatively trained, multi-scale, deformable part model. In: Proceedings of the CVPR (2008)
4. van de Sande, K., Gevers, T., Snoek, C.: Evaluation of color descriptors for object and scene recognition. In: Proceedings of the CVPR (2008)
5. Everingham, M., et al.: The PASCAL voc 2008 Results (2008), http://www.pascal-network.org/challenges/VOC/voc2008/workshop/index.html
6. Tuytelaars, T., Mikolajczyk, K.: Local invariant feature detectors: A survey. Foundations and Trends in Computer Graphics and Vision 3(3), 177–280 (2008)
7. Mikolajczyk, K., Schmid, C.: A performance evaluation of local descriptors. IEEE Transactions on PAMI 27(10), 1615–1630 (2005)
8. Sivic, J., Zisserman, A.: Video data mining using configurations of viewpoint invariant regions. In: Proceedings of the CVPR, pp. 488–495 (2004)
9. Quack, T., Ferrari, V., Leibe, B., Van Gool, L.: Efficient mining of frequent and distinctive feature configurations. In: Proceedings of the ICCV (2007)
10. Yuan, J., Wu, Y.: Context-aware clustering. In: Proceedings of the CVPR (2008)
11. Lazebnik, S., Schmid, C., Ponce, J.: Semi-local affine parts for object recognition. In: Proceedings of the BMVC (2004)
12. Leibe, B., Ettlin, A., Schiele, B.: Learning semantic object parts for object categorization. Image and Vision Computing 26(1), 15–26 (2008)
13. Perronnin, P., Dance, C., Csurka, G., Bressan, M.: Adapted vocabularies for generic visual categorization. In: Leonardis, A., Bischof, H., Pinz, A. (eds.) ECCV 2006. LNCS, vol. 3954, pp. 464–475. Springer, Heidelberg (2006)
14. Winn, J., Criminisi, A., Minka, A.: Object categorization by learned universal visual dictionary. In: Proceedings of the ICCV (2005)
15. Moosmann, F., Triggs, B., Jurie, F.: Fast discriminative visual codebooks using randomized clustering forests. In: Advances in NIPS (2006)
16. Perronnin, F., Dance, C.: Fisher kernels on visual vocabularies for image categorization. In: Proceedings of the CVPR (2007)
17. Mikolajczyk, K., Leibe, B., Schiele, B.: Local features for object class recognition. In: Proceedings of the ICCV (2005)
18. Stark, M., Schiele, B.: How good are local features for classes of geometric objects. In: Proceedings of the ICCV, pp. 1–8 (2007)
19. Belongie, S., Malik, J., Puzicha, J.: Shape matching and object recognition using shape contexts. IEEE Transactions on PAMI 24(24), 509–522 (2002)
20. Leibe, B., Mikolajczyk, K., Schiele, B.: Efficient clustering and matching for object class recognition. In: Proceedings of the BMVC (2006)
21. Fei-Fei, L., Fergus, R., Perona, P.: Learning generative visual models from few training examples: an incremental bayesian approach tested on 101 object categories. In: Proceedings of the CVPR (2004)

Multi-Scale Image Analysis Applied to Radioastronomical Interferometric Data

Marta Peracaula[1], Joan Martí[1], Jordi Freixenet[1], Josep Martí[2], and Josep M. Paredes[3]

[1] Computer Vision and Robotics Group, Universitat de Girona, Spain
{martapb,joanm,jordif}@eia.udg.es
[2] Grupo de Investigación FQM-322, Universidad de Jaén, Spain
jmarti@ujaen.es
[3] Dept. d'Astronomia i Meteorologia and Institut de Ciències del Cosmos (ICC),
Universitat de Barcelona, Spain
jmparedes@ub.edu

Abstract. Multi-Scale image analysis is specially suited to detect objects in deep wide field radio astronomical images obtained through interferometric aperture synthesis techniques. These images are usually complex and show a diversity of objects that can be characterized at different scales. In this context wavelet decomposition can be a tool to detect and separate the components of the image. However, the presence of very bright sources produce polluting artifacts in the planes of the wavelet decomposition that difficult the analysis. To overcome this problem we propose a hybrid method where in a first stage bright sources are detected through thresholding techniques and a image that does not contain them is created. In a second stage wavelet decomposition is applied to this residual image in order to detect fainter sources. We show the validity of the method using a previously catalogued image.

1 Background

The concept of **multi-scale** is applied in Computer Vision generally when the image we want to segment shows objects with very different sizes or patterns organized in a hierarchical structure [1]. In these cases, there is not an optimal resolution for analyzing the image, and algorithms to process it at different resolutions are needed. Specially suited for this purpose are algorithms that decompose the image through a Wavelet Representation [2], using discrete versions of the Wavelet Transform [3].

Astronomical images display often hierarchically organized structures of objects showing irregular patterns that can be represented at different spatial frequencies. Therefore, their analysis with the purpose of detecting and classifying emitting sources is a clear example where multi-scale methods can be conveniently applied [4]. This is specially noteworthy in the particular case of wide field mosaicked maps produced from Radio interferometric Aperture Synthesis techniques. These images typically contain, on top of some very bright sources,

H. Araujo et al. (Eds.): IbPRIA 2009, LNCS 5524, pp. 192–199, 2009.

a large amount of faint objects and diffuse emission with intensities near to detection levels. The high dynamic range of these kind of images makes it difficult to visualize the full range of intensities of the global map (see for example [5]). On top of that, they typically present a diffuse interferometric pattern and deconvolution artifacts produced by strong sources.

It is in the context of wide field interferometric radio images where we use wavelet decomposition as a tool to detect and separate objects of astronomical interest that can be represented at different spatial frequencies. We try to avoid ringing artifacts created around singularities (strong sources in our case) by previously using thresholding techniques.

The paper is structured as follows: Sect. 2 presents the Wavelet Representation we use and the formulation to obtain it. In Sect. 3 we show how we can apply this wavelet decomposition to a interferometric radio image and what problems can we encounter due to the presence of strong sources that act as singularities. In Sect. 4 we propose a method to overcome these problems and in Sect. 5 we apply the method to the detection of faint compact and semi-compact objects and we compare our results with a previously existing catalogue.

2 Wavelet Representation Using the "à Trous" Algorithm

Multiscale Vision Models [4] decompose an image in J scales or wavelet planes and segment independently each of the images representing a scale. Low index scales emphasize high spatial frequencies whereas high index scales emphasize low spatial frequencies. Since astronomical sources are mostly isotropic (stars, clusters, galaxies, etc) astronomers generally choose to use a wavelet transform that does not privilege any direction in the image and also that maintains the sampling at each scale [6]. For this reason one of the widely used transforms in this field is the Stationary Wavelet Transform (SWT) also called "à Trous" algorithm. The SWT decomposes an image $I(k,l)$ in J scales or wavelet planes $W_j(k,l)$ and a smoothed array $F_J(k,l)$ using a smoothing filter h (associated to the wavelet scaling function) in the following way:

$$I(k,l) = F_J(k,l) + \sum_{j=1}^{J} W_j(k,l) \tag{1}$$

$F_J(k,l)$ and $W_j(k,l)$ are calculated through the following iterative process:

$$\begin{aligned} F_0(k,l) &= I(k,l) \\ F_j(k.l) &= \langle H_j, F_{j-1} \rangle (k,l) \\ W_j(k,l) &= F_{j-1}(k,l) - F_j(k,l) \end{aligned} \tag{2}$$

with $j = 1, ..., J$ and

$$\langle H_j, F_{j-1} \rangle (k,l) \equiv \sum_{n,m} h(n,m) F_{j-1}(k + 2^{j-1}n, l + 2^{j-1}m) \tag{3}$$

The set $W_1, W_2, ..., W_J, F_J$ represents the wavelet transform of the data.

Following Starck & Murtagh (1994) [7] and references therein, in this work we will use as scaling function the B_3-spline function, which is very similar to a Gaussian one. In this way the mask associated to the filter h takes the form:

$$h \equiv \frac{1}{256} \begin{pmatrix} 1 & 4 & 6 & 4 & 1 \\ 4 & 16 & 24 & 16 & 4 \\ 6 & 24 & 36 & 24 & 6 \\ 4 & 16 & 24 & 16 & 4 \\ 1 & 4 & 6 & 4 & 1 \end{pmatrix} \tag{4}$$

3   A Catalogued Radio Image and Its Wavelet Decomposition

The image we use in this paper to illustrate our method is the deep radio map obtained by Paredes et al. 2007 [8] with the Giant Metrewave Radio Telescope (GMRT) covering the TeV J2032+4130 field (Fig. 1). We compare our results with the catalogue produced from this image by Martí et al. 2007 [9].

This image is a paradigmatic test bench for automated detection methods because: 1) It shows a significant amount of detail due to its high spatial dynamic range (over 500), 2) it has a remarkable population of compact sources and shows extended diffuse emission and 3) it shows unwanted interferometric

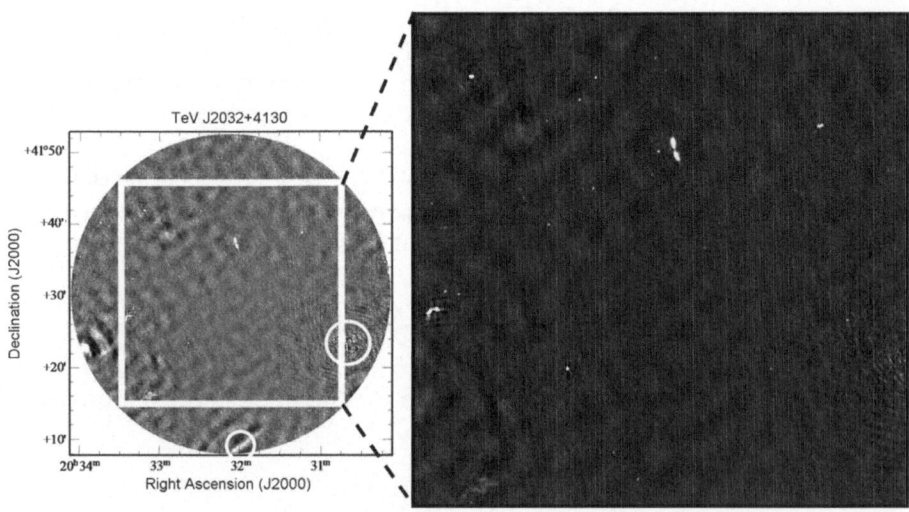

Fig. 1. Wide field radio map of the Cygnus OB2 region based on multi-epoch GMRT observations at 610 MHz frequency [8]. To avoid filtering border effects we use the sub-image contained in the white square overlapped on the observing field and zoomed on the right. The white overlapped circles show the areas excluded by Martí et al. 2007 [9] in their catalogue. This image and all its sub-products shown in this paper have been contrast stretched for a better visualisation of the details.

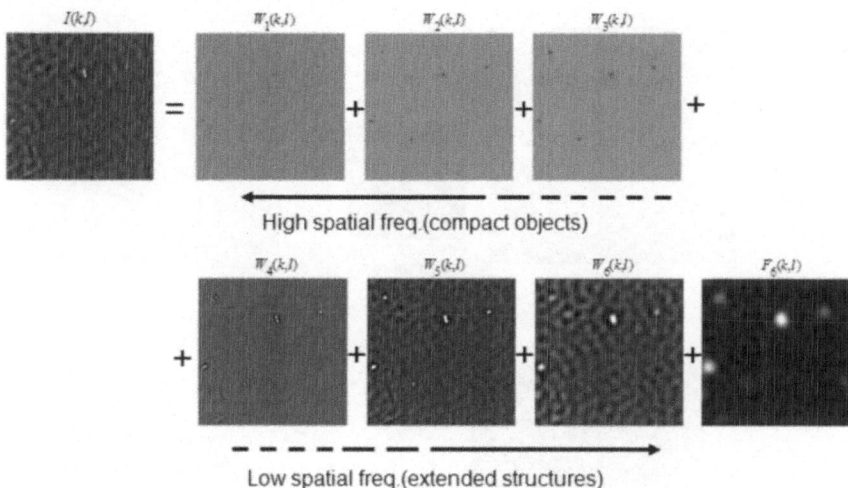

Fig. 2. Decomposition of our image using the "à trous" algorithm and the filter h

pattern mainly caused by deconvolution artifacts and grating rings from strong sources, and possibly some correlator calibration problems.

In Fig. 2 we show the image wavelet decomposition in 6 scales plus the smoothed array using the "à trous" algorithm and the filter h (4).

As we have mentioned before, low index scales emphasize high spatial frequencies, which in this case translates to compact and semi-compact objects in case of true signal. High index scales emphasize low spatial frequencies, in this case diffuse emission and interferometric pattern. Since our aim is the detection of compact sources discarding the diffuse emission and the interferometric pattern, we can select objects coming from the segmentation of the three first scales. The main problem encountered with this approach is the presence at each scale of polluting artifacts created by strong sources (which can be thought as singularities or edges) that complicate the analysis. This is due to the decomposition constraint where the wavelet coefficient mean at each level has to be kept at zero. In the next section we propose a method to overcome this problem in a computationally non-expensive way.

4   Our Proposal

Automated detection of compact objects in wide field astronomical images has classically been produced using thresholding techniques based on local noise estimation. However, since interferometric radio images often contain a remarkable population of faint compact sources with intensities near to noise levels, these can be easily missed by these thresholding techniques.

Therefore, we have a method, local thresholding, that is suitable for the detection of bright sources but misses easily the fainter ones, and another method,

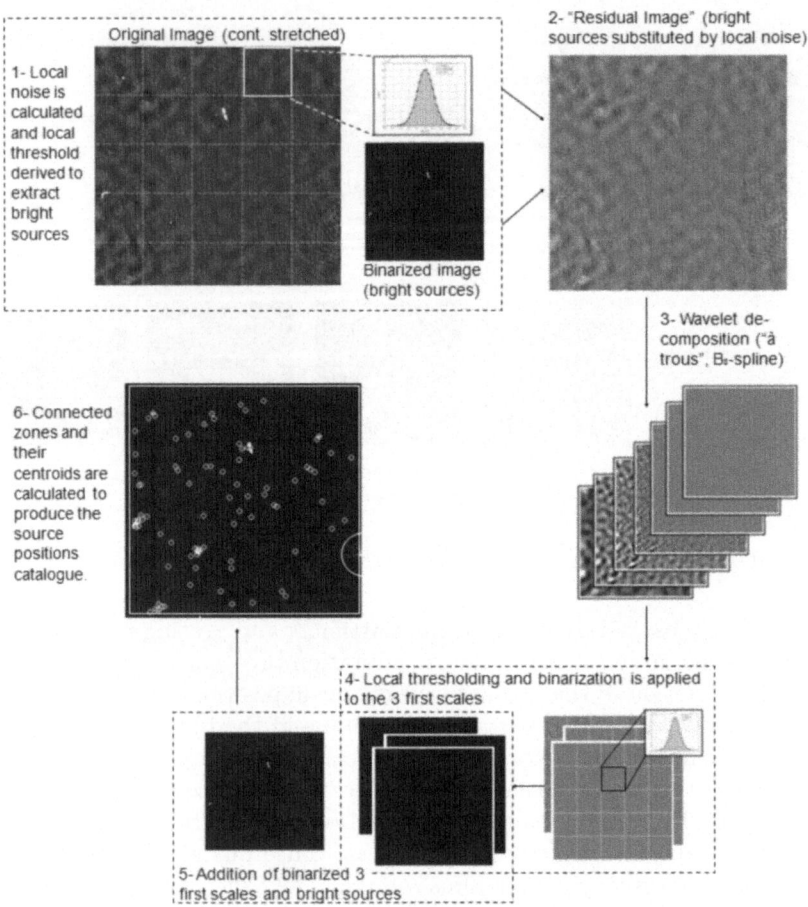

Fig. 3. Schematic view of the algorithm

wavelet decomposition that is not suitable when bright sources (singularities) are present due to the polluting artifacts they create in the decomposition. We propose a hybrid method where both techniques are used at different stages: In a first step bright sources are detected using classical local thresholding and a residual image that does not contain them is produced. In a second step wavelet decomposition is applied to the residual image in order to detect faint compact objects.

The algorithm we follow (shown schematically in Fig. 3) is the next one:

1. We use gaussian fitting of the pixel intensity distribution in subsamples of the original image to calculate local noise and extract bright sources from the derived local threshold.
2. Two images are created: a "residual image" where bright sources have been substituted by local noise, and a binarized image with the bright sources.

3. A 6-scale Wavelet decomposition is applied using the "à Trous" algorithm and a B_3-spline filtering function to the "residual image".
4. Local thresholding and binarization is applied to the 3 first scales.
5. A binary image from the addition of the binarized 3 first scales and the bright sources is created.
6. From this last image connected zones and their centroids are calculated to produce the source positions catalogue.

5   Results and Discussion

Figure 4 shows, on the right of the original image, the result of adding the first 3 wavelet planes from the decomposition of the original image (center) and the result of adding the previously extracted bright sources to the first 3 wavelet planes from the decomposition of the residual image (right). As it can be seen, the central image shows negative ringing artifacts around strong sources. These kind of artifacts actually pollute the whole image which causes the detection of a large number of False Positives (FP). By extracting the bright sources before the decomposition we reduce the FP detected on the right image to more than a half with respect to the one on the center.

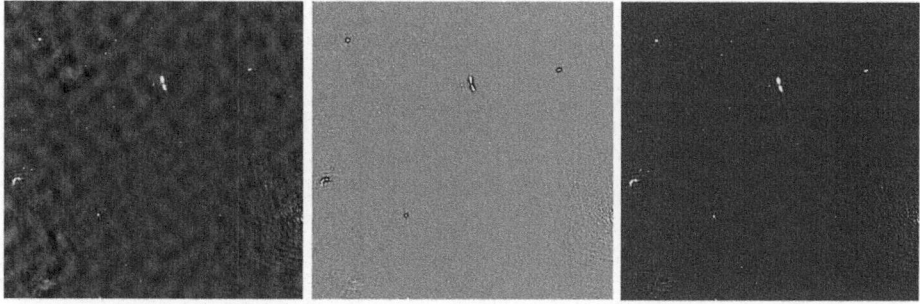

Fig. 4. Left: original image (contrast stretched). **Center:** Addition of the 3 first wavelet planes resulting from the original image decomposition. **Right:** Addition of the subtracted bright sources plus the 3 first wavelet planes resulting from the residual image decomposition.

In Fig. 5 (left) source positions found using our algorithm are displayed on the original sub-image together with the positions found by Martí et al. 2007 [9] using the automated extracting procedure SAD of the AIPS package (based on local thresholding and gaussian fitting of source candidates).

Table 1 shows the symbol code used in the figure and the number of True Positive (TP) and FP detections found in each work (classification of TP and FP detections has been done by close visual inspection of the image by the authors of both works. FP are basically believed to be deconvolution artifacts near bright sources).

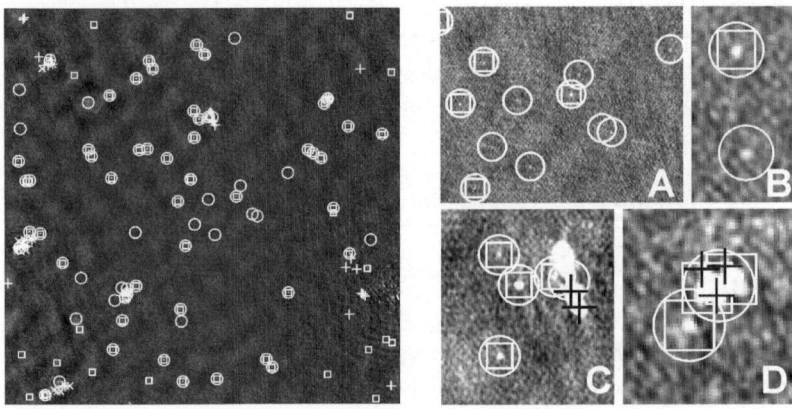

Fig. 5. Left: Location of the detections found using the two methods (see symbol code in Table 1). **Right:** Detailed parts of left image.

Table 1. Number of detections found in each method

Detections	True Positive	False Positive
Present work	○ 71(61c + 10e)	× 15(2c + 13e)
Martí et al. 2007 catalogue	□ 68(63c + 5e)	+ 33(17c + 16e)

(c)Isolated compact source, (e)Extended emission.

The number of TP detections is very similar in both works. However, our method succeeds in reducing the number of FP to less than half with respect to SAD. Most of our FP detections are grouped in zones of extended emission artifacts, while half of the SAD FP detections could be identified as an isolated compact object.

Although both works have almost the same number of TP some of these are not coincident in position: Firstly, 16 of the 68 SAD TP are not found by our method. All of them are located at a large radius from the center (see Fig. 5, left). Secondly, 21 of the present work 71 TP are not found by SAD. Many of them are located near the center (see zoomed parts A and B in Fig. 5, right).

Some of the double bright sources marked with 2 or more detections by SAD are correctly identified as one source in our work (see zoomed parts C and D in Fig. 5, right).

To conclude, we think the performance of our algorithm is very satisfactory, specially near the pointing center. To improve its performance at large radii we need to implement a better noise model according to the instrumental response. The implementation of the algorithm is simple and can be thought as a future automated detection method of faint objects.

Acknowledgments. GMRT is run by the National Centre for Radio Astrophysics of the Tata Institute of Fundamental Research. The authors acknowledge support by DGI of the Spanish Ministerio de Educación y Ciencia (MEC) under grants AYA2007-68034-C03-01, AYA2007-68034-C03-02 AYA2007-68034-C03-03 and TIN2007-60553.

References

1. Mallat, S.G.: Multifrequency Channel Decompositions of Images and Wavelet Models. IEEE Transactions on Acoustics, Speech, and Signal Processing 37(12), 2091–2110 (1989)
2. Mallat, S.G.: A Theory for Multiresolution Signal Decomposition: The Wavelet Representation. IEEE Transactions on Pattern Analysis and Machine Intelligence 11(7), 674–693 (1989)
3. Shensa, M.J.: The Discrete Wavelet Transform: Wedding the À Trous and Mallat Algorithms. IEEE Transactions on Signal Processing 40(10), 2464–2482 (1992)
4. Bijaoui, A., Rué, F.: A multiscale vision model adapted to the astronomical images. Signal processing 46, 245–342 (1995)
5. Taylor, A.R., Gibson, S.J., Peracaula, M., et al.: The Canadian Galactic Plane Survey. Astronomical Journal 125(6), 3145–3164 (2003)
6. Starck, J.L., Murtagh, F.: Astronomical Image and Data Analysis. Springer, New York (2002)
7. Starck, J.L., Murtagh, F.: Image restoration with noise suppression using the wavelet transform. Astronomy & Astrophysics 288(1), 342–348 (1994)
8. Paredes, J.M., Martí, J., Chandra, C.H., Bosch-Ramon, V.: The population of Radio Sources in the Field of the Unidentified Gamma-Ray Source TeV J2032+4130. The Astrophysical Journal 654(2), L135–L138 (2007)
9. Martí, J., Paredes, J.M., Chandra, C.H., Bosch-Ramon, V.: Deep radio images of the HEGRA and Whipple TeVn sources in the Cyngus OB2 region. Astronomy & Astrophysics 472(2), 557–564 (2007)

Robust Statistical Estimation Applied to Automatic Lip Segmentation

B. Goswami, W. Christmas, and J. Kittler

Centre for Vision, Speech and Signal Processing, University of Surrey, Guidford, Surrey, GU2 7XH, United Kingdom

Abstract. Automatic lip segmentation is an indispensable pre-requisite in face-video applications that make use of the mouth-region. Lip segmentation can be treated as a three-stage process: mouth-region detection, separation of the constituent clusters in this region and identification of the cluster containing the lip pixels. This paper describes a novel method of performing automatic, single-frame, chromaticity based lip segmentation with no prior model information or heuristic assumptions. It uses a robust statistical estimator to identify the different regions in the image and then performs post-processing based on cluster colour and shape to identify the lip region.

1 Introduction

Accurate lip segmentation is a pre-requisite in a wide range of applications from video-conferencing to biometrics. The aim of the lip segmentation process is to extract an accurate estimate of the region composed of lip pixels in an image. This region contains the shape, colour and texture information which in turn is used in the above applications. Lip segmentation is a non-trivial process because any system has to be robust to large inter-speaker variations as a result of differences in speaker colour characteristics and image capture conditions. This paper describes an automatic, single-frame based, in-situ process, using statistical estimation to perform lip segmentation.

Some lip segmentation methods use example images to build in-situ lip-models. Lievin [1] uses a spatiotemporal Markov random field on a set of image sequences to label the different regions of the face. Active contours are then used to extract the mouth contour. This method can give good results; however, it uses unconstrained contours and can lead to impossible mouth-shapes. Liew [2] uses an elliptical shape function incorporated into a fuzzy clustering system to iteratively refine a cost function that labels the lip pixels. Both these methods require multi-image training and are likely to be less reliable given a single training image. Sanchez [3] extracts the separable colour clusters in a mouth-region image using a method proposed by Matas [4] and labels the lip pixels using a log-likelihood measure. This method requires manual mouth-region cropping. Sadeghi [5] extends this method by using predictive validation to automatically obtain the number of clusters in the mouth region. While this method is effective, it is slow and can suffer from problems when there are specular reflections.

H. Araujo et al. (Eds.): IbPRIA 2009, LNCS 5524, pp. 200–207, 2009.

Goswami [6] also extends these systems using a robust statistical estimator to extract the skin region in a given mouth-region image. Spatial post-processing is then applied to the remaining data to identify the lip region.

A few methods use contour models to perform lip segmentation. Eveno [7] proposes a method of lip segmentation by extracting key feature points using a chromatic transform followed by gradient-heuristic based edge-finding algorithms. These points are then used with a parametric mouth model to extract the lip contour. The use of heuristic properties of the lip contour makes this method highly error prone. The disadvantages of this are overcome, at the expense of manual intervention, by the use of the system of jumping snakes which help to localise the mouth contour as suggested by Hammal [8].

Lip segmentation can also be performed by building prior global models. Gacon [9] uses a sequence of manually annotated images to build a point distribution model (PDM). Following dimensionality reduction using Principal Components Analysis, this model is then used to generate a series of mouth shape estimates. Lip segmentation then consists of finding the best matching estimate using a Gaussian-local-descriptor-based cost function. Sum [10] uses the system described by Liew [2] to generate a probability map of lip pixel locations. Example lip contours are then generated using a shape model and segmentation is performed by optimising the generated contours to fit the probability map. PDM based methods produce good results but, the model can be restricted by the training data provided. Additionally, the manual annotation of hundreds of images is a tedious and non-trivial task.

If a lip segmentation system is used as a bootstrap mechanism for tracking, it needs to satisfy the following requirements:

- **Single-frame based** - most of the video information needs to be used for tracking. Consequently, multi-frame based segmentation systems (Lievin [1], Liew [2]) are not ideal.
- **Automatic** - lip segmentation systems (Sanchez [3] or Hammal [8]) that make use of manual intervention have obvious efficiency bottlenecks. A desirable property would be to eliminate manual intervention.
- **No global heuristic assumptions or prior models** - prior-model information is only as good as the training data used (Gacon [9]) while heuristic assumptions result in database-specific algorithms instead of problem-specific algorithms (Hammal [8]).

In summary, none of the above methods completely satisfy the requirements posed above. In this paper, we present a system using an iterative, robust statistical estimation method based on the Minimum Covariance Determinant (MCD) algorithm, suggested by Rousseeuw [11] that meets the above requirements. In our evaluation framework, we compare and outperform an adapted benchmark method originally suggested by Sanchez [12] as well as other clustering algorithms (K-means and Fuzzy C-Means, instantiated assuming the mouth-region consists of three clusters).

Automatic lip segmentation can be treated as a three stage process. Initially, an object categorisation system can be used to detect the "mouth-object" in an image as described in Section 2. The detected region is treated as a population of data which is separable based on chromaticity (we shall be using the normalised RG space). Section 3 provides a description of the novel statistical estimation methods employed for cluster separation. Section 4 describes the evaluation framework, followed by the cluster identification method used and the results. The combination of the above three stages leads to a novel lip segmentation system which are evaluated on a test set of 148 images from the XM2VTS database [13]. The conclusions and ideas for future work are presented in Section 5.

2   Mouth-Region Detection

Mouth-region detection can be viewed as an object class detection problem. Thus, a simultaneous recognition and localisation system suggested by Mikolajczyk [14] trained on mouth-region images can provide a satisfactory solution. For recognition, the system uses a novel hierarchical representation of local features based on joint appearance-geometry probability distributions, to model the human mouth. This method is based on shape features and grey level images. The hierarchical representation is constructed during learning with agglomerative clustering and allows for efficient object detection.

Given an image containing a mouth-region, this system provides a location of a cropped window with an associated likelihood of lip presence. The system was trained using 1000 cropped mouth images from the XM2VTS [13] database. For further details of the automatic mouth extraction, refer to [14]. The benchmark method used for comparison is manually cropped rectangular windows containing the mouth-region.

3   Robust Statistical Estimation

The process of mouth-region detection yields a population of data which contains within it separable clusters, one or more of which are composed of lip pixels. This section describes the method used for cluster separation.

This system uses a robust statistical estimator called the Minimum Covariance Determinant estimator (MCD), suggested originally by Rousseeuw [11]. The aim of the MCD estimator is to extract a fraction h of a total population of n samples of p-dimensional data (we use normalised RG values, thus $p = 2$) with the smallest determinant of the covariance matrix. This is performed through iterative refinement of the estimates of mean and location using the Mahalanobis distance of the samples to weight the data, generating the most compact cluster possible for the given hypothesis of h. In lip segmentation, h corresponds to the fraction of data that belongs to a single region (skin, lip etc). The extraction of a single cluster from a given population proceeds as follows:

Elemental Set Generation - a uniformly random set of $p+1$ observations is extracted from the data and a starting estimate of the mean, $\mathbf{T_0}$, and covariance,

$\mathbf{S_0}$, obtained. If the determinant of $\mathbf{S_0}$ is zero, additional samples are extracted until a covariance matrix with a non-zero determinant is obtained.

Iterative refinement - at the rth iteration, we have $\mathbf{T_{r-1}}$ and $\mathbf{S_{r-1}}$ as initial estimates. For each member of the entire data set, the Mahalanobis distance from these estimates is calculated and the resulting set is sorted in increasing order. The first h estimates are then used to calculate the refined values of the mean and covariance $\mathbf{T}_r$ and $\mathbf{S}_r$. At this point, we check for convergence i.e. if $det(\mathbf{S}_r) \simeq det(\mathbf{S}_{r-1})$ or $det(\mathbf{S}_r) = 0$ the process stops. Otherwise, the new estimates are used as inputs to this iterative step. In practice, the system usually converges after 10 iterations.

The MCD algorithm can actually be used, iteratively, in two different ways for lip segmentation either using a fixed value of h or multiple hypotheses of h at each iteration. The two resulting algorithms are described below.

Single Hypothesis, Cascaded MCD (CMCD) - Using a fixed hypothesis that says that h out of n samples of data belong to a cluster, iteratively perform the MCD estimation process. After the ath iteration, we obtain the estimates $\mathbf{T}_a$ and $\mathbf{S}_a$ as well as a corresponding set of h_a pixels. This set of pixels is then removed from the initial population and the process repeated until a minimum sample size is reached. Multiple values of h are used, since it is a heuristic that determines the confidence we have in each cluster's contribution to the total population. Example results, using values of 0.6, 0.75, 0.8 and 0.9 for h are shown in Fig. 1.

Multiple Hypothesis MCD (K-S MCD) - This process is also iterative and is originally suggested in [12]. It is implemented as a nested loop. We have a iterations in total and extract the most compact cluster at each step until a minimum sample size is reached. At each step, we use multiple hypothesis of h and a Gaussian cluster assumption with chi-squared error bounds to extract the "best" cluster as defined by the Kolmogorov-Smirnov test:

- At each iteration, we have a sample population of n_a and want to extract the best cluster using a hypothesis h_a (varying from 0.6 to 0.9 at each iteration) as input to the MCD process to obtain estimates $\mathbf{T^{h_a}}$ and $\mathbf{S^{h_a}}$.
- We perform Kolmogorov Smirnov test on cluster estimates using the observed, $F_{obs}^{h_a}$ (Eqn. 1a), and theoretical, $F_{thr}^{h_a}$ (which is defined implicitly in Eqn. 1b), cumulative distribution functions of the Mahalanobis distances of the points contained inside the cluster. At the ath iteration, for each cluster, we have i members from the data, each with Mahalanobis distance q_i. Thus we define:

$$F_{obs}^{h_a}(i) = \begin{cases} 0 & \text{if } i = 0 \\ \dfrac{\sum_{j=1}^{i} q_j}{\sum_{j=1}^{i_{max}} q_j} & \text{if } 1 \le i \le i_{max} \\ 1 & \text{if } i > i_{max} \end{cases} \qquad \begin{aligned} q_{min[\mathbf{T^{h_a}},\mathbf{S^{h_a}}]}^{(i)} &= \chi_{p,F_{thr}^{h_a}(i)}^{2} \\ i &= 1 \ldots i_{max} \end{aligned}$$

$$(1a,b)$$

where i_{max} is the number of observations for which the Mahalanobis distance is less than $\chi_{p,0.975}^{2}$ and $q_{min[\mathbf{T^{h_a}},\mathbf{S^{h_a}}]}^{(i)}$ is the i−th lowest Mahalanobis distance

in the cluster and is related to $F_{thr}^{h_a}$ because we assume Gaussian clusters. The Kolmogorov Smirnov test produces a quantity $D_{h_a} = sup_i|F_{obs}^{h_a}(i) - F_{thr}^{h_a}(i)|$.
- For all hypothesis of h_a, at each iteration, choose those estimates $\mathbf{T}^{h_a}$ and $\mathbf{S}^{h_a}$ that yield the minimum D_{h_a}. Unless minimum sample size is reached go back to start of the nested loop.

An example result using KS-MCD is shown in Fig. 1(d). The use of iterative algorithms leads to robust identification of clusters in the mouth-region and reduces the dependence on heuristic methods of cluster identification as used in [6]. Fig. 1 shows the clustering results on an example mouth-region image for all the proposed algorithms. For further details of the K-S MCD method, refer [12].

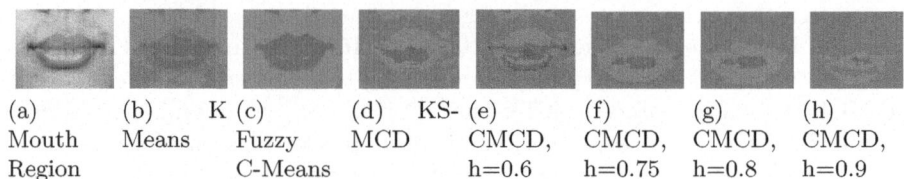

(a)	(b)	K (c)	(d) KS-	(e)	(f)	(g)	(h)
Mouth	Means	Fuzzy	MCD	CMCD,	CMCD,	CMCD,	CMCD,
Region		C-Means		h=0.6	h=0.75	h=0.8	h=0.9

Fig. 1. Results of using various clustering algorithms on a detected mouth-region

4   Cluster Identification and Results

The final stage of automatic lip segmentation is the identification of that cluster which contains the lip-region. This process requires spatial and probabilistic analysis of the labelled cluster data. A cluster grouping method is described in the following section followed by a common evaluation framework.

4.1   Cluster Grouping and Results Using Probabilistic and Spatial Cluster Analysis

Cluster selection involves the identification of the most "lip-like" data, out of a total set of E extracted clusters. The mouth-region image is assumed to consist of two components - the skin and lip regions, which contribute the largest number of samples to the data. Additionally, visual inspection of the clustering results verifies that the skin region is larger than the lip region. Following clustering, we can use the two largest clusters to give us the in-situ statistical estimates of the lip and skin classes. These estimates can be used to establish an objective function based on a log-likelihood ratio that is used to perform Bayesian pixel classification -

$$J(\mathbf{x}) = J_{lips}(\mathbf{x}) - J_{skin}(\mathbf{x})$$
$$\text{where } J_i(\mathbf{x}) = -log|\Sigma_c| - M(\mathbf{x} - \mu_c) \tag{4}$$

$M(\mathbf{x} - \mu_c)$ is the squared Mahalanobis distance of the point $\mathbf{x}$ to the mean of the class c. The objective function assigns the point $\mathbf{x}$ to be in the lip-region,

C_{lip}, ($C_{lip} \subset E$) if $J(\mathbf{x}) > 0$. Probabilistic labelling by itself is insufficient for lip cluster identification unless combined with information about the spatial coherence of the pixels. Hence we perform connected component analysis on the classified lip pixels. The set of lip-like pixels, C_{lip} is spatially disparate. Performing connected components analysis on this set and ordering the resulting sets by decreasing size, we have C^i, such that $i \in \{1 \dots E_{lip}\}$ and $C^i \subset C_{lip}$, where E_{lip} is the number of different spatially disparate, lip-like clusters. The lip-region is chosen to be C^1. This serves to eliminate stray, noisy pixels that might be misclassified as belonging to the lip. This misclassification occurs due to the fact that in normalised RG space, the zero signal point presents a non-removable singularity that cannot be classified reliably. Consequently, "darker" pixels may be misclassified as belonging to the lip class.

4.2 Evaluation Framework

The systems were compared by evaluating the performance of the combination of the three stages. There were two systems for mouth-region detection as described in Section 2. A total of test-set of 148 frontal-face images from the XM2VTS dataset was used. These images were of people from different races and therefore different lip and skin colour characteristics. Note that the test images above and training images used in Section 2 were different.

Given the detected region-of-interest, combinations of cluster separation and cluster identification were used to segment the lip-region. Segmentation quality was measured using the overlap between the segmented and manually labelled ground-truth lip-regions. For a total of N test images, if we considered all the pixels segmented by an algorithm in the nth image ($n \in \{1 \dots N\}$) to be denoted by the set S_n and the lip pixels from the ground truth data to be denoted by the set G_n, then the segmentation quality Q_n was:

$$Q_n = \frac{S_n \cap G_n}{S_n \cup G_n} \qquad (2)$$

A threshold, θ, was used to determine the number of "true" segmentations. For each image, the quality value obtained from Q_n resulted in a binary measure t_n. This formulation allows us to measure the recall of the segmentation, R as shown below:

$$t_n = \begin{cases} 1 & \text{if } Q_n > \theta \\ 0 & \text{otherwise} \end{cases} \qquad\qquad R = \frac{\sum_{i=1}^{N} t_n}{N} \qquad (3a,b)$$

The systems can then be compared quantitatively by varying θ and observing the resultant variation in segmentation quality over the test set, given by R. The system comparison is shown in Fig. 2 and Fig. 3. The quality of each algorithm can be determined by the area under the respective curve in the provided graphs. The results show that the process of lip segmentation using clustering requires the consideration of both the spatial and chromatic properties of the data provided after using statistical estimation to extract the constituent regions

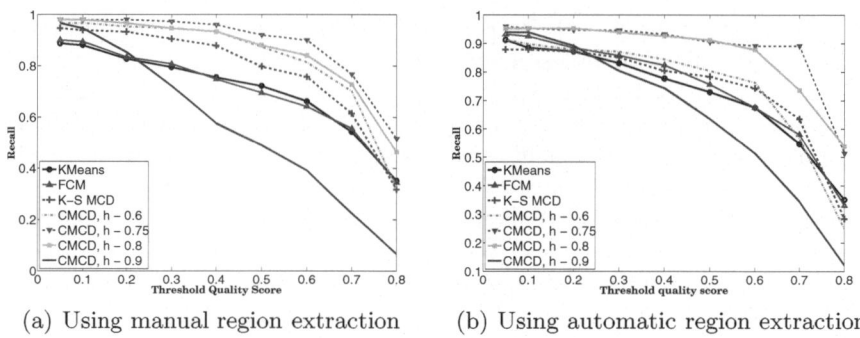

(a) Using manual region extraction   (b) Using automatic region extraction

Fig. 2. Graphical results of the system using probabilistic analysis with shape selection

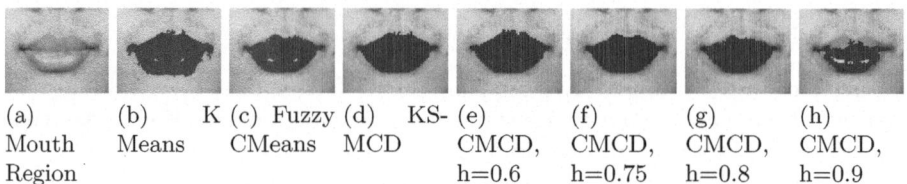

(a)	(b) K	(c) Fuzzy	(d) KS-	(e)	(f)	(g)	(h)
Mouth	Means	CMeans	MCD	CMCD,	CMCD,	CMCD,	CMCD,
Region				h=0.6	h=0.75	h=0.8	h=0.9

Fig. 3. Pictorial results of using probabilistic analysis and shape selection

in a mouth region image. Using our novel, cascaded MCD system yields the best results, with a h measure of 0.75. In all cases, some portion of the lip was successfully and accurately segmented. Segmentation quality however is affected in images with almost no variation in the colour of the lip and skin regions or in images with large specularities in the mouth-region.

The proposed single-hypothesis based cluster extraction system outperforms the benchmark, adapted, multiple-hypothesis based system ([12]) which improved by combining it with the probabilistic and spatial cluster identification technique. This adapted benchmark system, while statistically more accurate, suffers from over-sensitivity especially around the lip-skin boundary where the gradual demarcation leads to noisy cluster extraction.

5   Conclusions and Future Work

The results obtained are of note since using no prior information the system has been able to identify, in-situ the chromatic properties of the skin and lip-regions in a given image. Subsequent, probabilistic pixel-labelling combined with the analysis of connected colour-components have allowed for the reliable identification of the lip-region. Additionally, the system is quick and entirely automatic and does not require any on-line manual intervention. Also, since the system does not make any prior model or heuristic assumptions, it can easily be applied to a wider variety of data. This system can easily be used as a bootstrap mechanism for a general lip-tracking algorithm since it fulfils the requirements stated in Section 1.

Areas for future work include investigating alternative, more descriptive feature vectors to describe the mouth-region data. An improvement to using just colour would be the use of pixel descriptors that implicitly represent the chromatic, spatial and texture properties. The system described here can also be used to form the basis for a colour-trends tracker which adapts to the changes in colour properties to an image on-line in order that it may be used for lip segmentation.

References

1. Liévin, M., Luthon, F.: A hierarchical segmentation algorithm for face analysis. In: ICME, vol. 2, pp. 1080–1088 (2000)
2. Liew, A.W.C., Leung, S.H., Lau, W.H.: Segmentation of color lip images by spatial fuzzy clustering. IEEE Transactions on Fuzzy Systems 11(4), 542–549 (2003)
3. Sanchez, M., Matas, J., Kittler, J.: Statistical chromaticity models for lip tracking with b-splines. In: Bigün, J., Borgefors, G., Chollet, G. (eds.) AVBPA 1997. LNCS, vol. 1206, pp. 69–76. Springer, Heidelberg (1997)
4. Matas, J., Kittler, J.: Spatial and feature space clustering. In: Hlaváč, V., Šára, R. (eds.) CAIP 1995. LNCS, vol. 970, pp. 162–173. Springer, Heidelberg (1995)
5. Sadeghi, M., Kittler, J., Messer, K.: Real time segmentation of lip pixels for lip tracker initialization. In: Skarbek, W. (ed.) CAIP 2001. LNCS, vol. 2124, pp. 317–324. Springer, Heidelberg (2001)
6. Goswami, B., Christmas, W., Kittler, J.: Stastical estimators for use in automatic lip segmentation. In: CVMP, pp. 79–86 (2006)
7. Eveno, N., Caplier, A., Coulon, P.Y.: A parametric model for realistic lip segmentation. In: ICARCV 2002, December 2-5, vol. 3, pp. 1426–1431 (2002)
8. Hammal, Z., Eveno, N., Caplier, A., Coulon, P.Y.: Parametric models for facial features segmentation. Signal Processing 86(2), 399–413 (2006)
9. Gacon, P., Coulon, Y., Bailly, P.G.: Non-linear active model for mouth inner and outer contours detection. In: EUSIPCO (2005)
10. Sum, K.L., Leung, S.H., Liew, A.W.C., Tse, K.W.: A new optimization procedure for extracting the point-based lip contour using active shape model. In: ICASSP, vol. 3, pp. 1485–1488 (2001)
11. Rousseeuw, P., VanDriessen, K.: A fast algorithm for the minimum covariance determinant estimator. Technometrics 41(3), 212–223 (1999)
12. Sánchez, M.U.R.: Aspects of facial biometrics for verification of personal identity. PhD thesis, University of Surrey, UK (2000),
    ftp://ftp.ee.surrey.ac.uk/pub/research/VSSP/papers/ramos-phd00.ps.gz
13. Messer, K., Matas, J., Kittler, J., Luettin, J., Maitre, G.: XM2VTSDB: The extended M2VTS database. In: AVBPA (1999)
14. Mikolajczyk, K., Leibe, B., Schiele, B.: Multiple object class detection with a generative model. In: CVPR, vol. 1, pp. 26–36 (2006)

Textural Features for Hyperspectral Pixel Classification

Olga Rajadell, Pedro García-Sevilla, and Filiberto Pla

Depto. Lenguajes y Sistemas Informáticos
Jaume I University, Campus Riu Sec s/n 12071 Castellón, Spain
{orajadel,pgarcia,pla}@lsi.uji.es
http://www.vision.uji.es

Abstract. Hyperspectral remote sensing provides data in large amounts from a wide range of wavelengths in the spectrum and the possibility of distinguish subtle differences in the image. For this reason, the process of band selection to reduce redundant information is highly recommended to deal with them. Band selection methods pursue the reduction of the dimension of the data resulting in a subset of bands that preserves the most of information. The accuracy is given by the classification performance of the selected set of bands. Usually, pixel classification tasks using grey level values are used to validate the selection of bands. We prove that by using textural features, instead of grey level information, the number of hyperspectral bands can be significantly reduced and the accuracy for pixel classification tasks is improved. Several characterizations based on the frequency domain are presented which outperform grey level classification rates using a very small number of hyperspectral bands.

1 Introduction

Hyperspectral imagery consists of large amounts of channels covering the different wavelengths in the spectrum. These images represent a very rich source of information that allows an accurate recognition of the different areas to be obtained through the use of pattern classification techniques. For this reason, traditionally, this kind of images has been used in remote sensing applications. However, nowadays they are also widely used in medical imaging, product quality inspection or even fine arts. The main problems to deal with hyperspectral images are the high dimension of this data and its high correlation. In the context of supervised classification, an additional problem is the so-called Hughes phenomenon that occurs when the training set size is not large enough to ensure a reliable estimation of the classifier parameters. As a result, a significant reduction in the classification accuracy can be observed [3], [4], [5]. To overcome the Hughes phenomenon the original hyperspectral bands are considered as features and feature-reduction algorithms are applied [11]. They process the original set of features to generate a smaller size set of features with the aim of maximizing the classification accuracy. A particular class of feature reduction methods are band selection methods [9], [10], [7], which select a subset of the original set of bands and discard the remaining to reduce redundant information in the image representation without losing classification accuracy in a significant way. Methods of band selection obtain subsets of relevant bands so as to get the best classification performance. The performance of the

H. Araujo et al. (Eds.): IbPRIA 2009, LNCS 5524, pp. 208–216, 2009.

band selection is usually measured through pixel classification accuracy based on grey level pixel data.

In this paper we propose the use of several frequential texture features to describe each individual pixel. The aim of this characterization is to reduce as much as possible the number of hyperspectral bands required in the global process while keeping the final pixel classification accuracy as high as possible. We start from the band selection scheme described in [7] and compare the classification accuracies obtained using grey level features against textural features. Gabor filters as well as wavelets features are considered in our study. Also, modified versions of Gabor filters are considered with two main objectives: obtaining a more detailed analysis of medium and high frequencies, and, simplifying their computational cost without decreasing their discriminant power.

2 Textural Features

In hyperspectral imaging it is very common to characterize each pixel using a feature vector formed by the grey level values of that pixel in a given set of bands. To measure the performance of a band selection method, a series of pixels are characterized using their grey level values in the selected bands. The rate of correct classification obtained is compared to the classification rate obtained using the whole set of bands, to check the goodness of the selected group of bands as a representation of the entire hyperspectral image.

Now, our purpose is to describe the textural characteristics of a group of selected bands as they are supposed to portray the common features of pixels, that is, the texture they represent. For this reason, we have considered a series of frequential filters in order to extract features from the frequency domain to characterize pixels rewarding their textural features. In all cases, we consider a basic tessellation of the frequency domain taking into account several frequency bands and orientations [8]. A filter mask is applied over each area defined in the tessellation in order to select the frequencies within the chosen area. Then, for each area, we obtain its inverse Fourier transformation into the space domain. The result is an "image" which contains only frequencies in the chosen area, telling us which parts of the original image contain frequencies in this area. Repeating this process for all frequency areas we will have a stack of "images". Therefore, for each pixel we have as many values as frequency areas we used, that is, one value per output "image". This vector of values is used as the frequency signature of each pixel.

The first sort of filters considered are the well known Gabor filters. We construct a basic tessellation of the frequency domain considering several frequency bands and orientations. Each frequency band is double the previous one and a Gaussian mask is applied over each frequency area. Figure 1(a) shows an example of a Gabor filter considered. Figure 1(b) shows the maximum value of all Gabor filters considered for a given tessellation using four frequency bands and six different orientations. As it can be seen in this figure, each individual filter expands far away from the limit of the area defined in the tessellation. For this reason, two variations of these filters

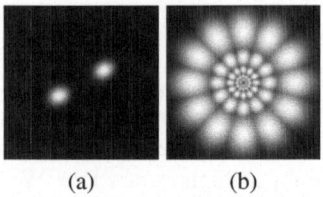

(a)   (b)

Fig. 1. (a) An example of Gabor filter in the frequency domain (b) Maximum value of all Gabor filters considered for a given tessellation using four frequency bands and six different orientation

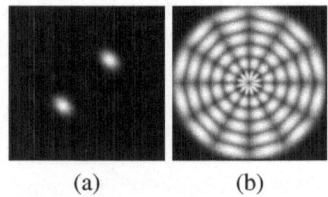

(a)   (b)

Fig. 2. (a) An example of filter keeping constant the width of the frequency band (b) Maximum value of all filters considered for a given tessellation using six frequency bands and six different orientation

(as described in [8]) could also be considered. First, similar Gaussians are applied over each frequency area, but truncating them beyond the limits of the areas in order to eliminate contributions of the same frequencies in different filters. On the other hand, the use of Gaussian masks over the frequency areas leads to the loss of importance of frequencies not lying nearby the center of these areas. That is why, also flat masks covering exactly each frequency area in the tessellation will be considered.

Another disadvantage in the application of Gabor filters using the basic tessellation scheme is that the frequency bands considered are not uniform. In this way, low frequencies are given more importance than middle or high frequencies. However, it is well known that texture information mainly falls in middle and high frequencies [1]. Therefore, we propose a detailed analysis of all frequencies by keeping constant the width of the frequency bands to be analyzed by each filter. Figure 2(a) shows an example of an individual filter using a complete Gaussian mask, while figure 2(b) shows the maximum value of all these filters considered for a given tessellation using six constant frequency bands and six different orientations. Note that, also in this case, truncated Gaussians and flat masks may be used.

Also features derived for each pixel using a wavelet decomposition will be considered. A wavelet decomposition is obtained using two appropriate filters: a low-pass filter L and a high-pass filter H. In this case, we have chosen to use a maximum overlap algorithm, that is, no subsampling is done. Therefore, after applying each filter, an image of the same size of the original image is obtained. Also, a wavelet packet analysis has been used, which means that not only low frequency components will be considered in further levels of analysis. In this case, all components will be taken into account. Figure 3 expresses the wavelet decomposition in the frequency domain for two levels of analysis using the Daubechies-4 filters.

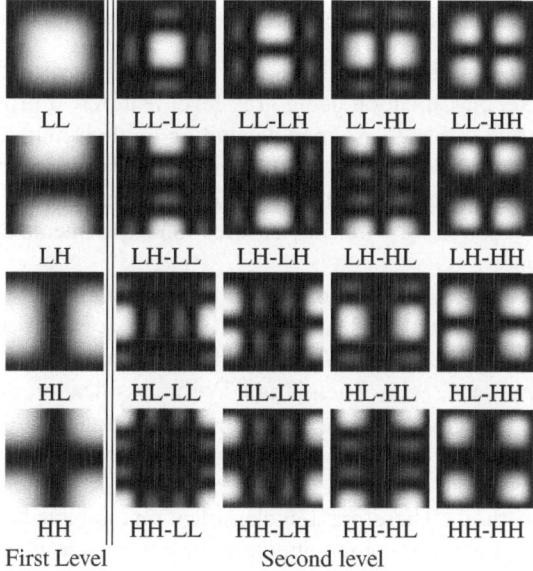

Fig. 3. Wavelet decomposition expressed in the frequency domain for the two levels of analysis using the Daubechies-4 filters

3   Hyperspectral Database

The experimental results will consist of comparing the different characterization methods named above over a widely used hyperspectral database. The 92AV3C source of data corresponds to a spectral image, 145x145 pixel-sized, 220 bands, and 17 classes composed of different crop types, vegetation, man-made structures, and an unknown class. This image is acquired with the Airborne Visible/Infrared Imaging Spectrometer (AVIRIS) data set and collected in June 1992 over the Indian Pine Test site in Northwestern Indiana [2].

4   Experimental Results

Experiments to characterize the texture of each pixel were run using all the textural features described before. For the basic tessellation (where each frequency band is double the other) four different bands and six different orientations (wedges of 30°) were considered, that is, a total of 24 features were used to characterize each pixel. For the constant tessellation, nine frequency bands of the same size and six directions were considered, which provide a total of 54 features for each pixel. These numbers of features are due to the symmetry of the Fourier transform when dealing with real numbers. For the wavelet decomposition, the Daubechies-4 filters were used until three levels of decomposition, providing a total of 84 features per pixel.

4.1 Results Using the Best Band for Grey Level Classification

Let our band selection method be the one in [7], which has already proved its good performance for pixel classification using grey level features. It provides with a series of clusters, that is, sets of bands grouped depending on their mutual information. The bands that composed each set depend on the cluster number as every set by itself represents the best combination for all the possibilities. To test the discriminant power of each set of textural features we will run classification experiments using the only band in cluster number one.

The selection method reported band number 4 for the cluster of size one among the bands which compose the 92AV3C database. The results of all methods of characterization named above can be seen in Table 1. Classification has been performed using the K nearest neighbor rule with 3 neighbors. With classification purposes and due to the massive data that pixel characterization generates, samples have been divided into twenty independent sets keeping the a priori probability of each class and the k-nn rule has been used to classify all sets taken in pairs, one used as training set and the other as test set (1-1 knn3 method). Therefore, ten classification attempts have been performed without data dependencies among the attempts. In this way, a mean rate of all the attempts have been reported.

Table 1. Classification rates (in percentage) for the all characterization methods considered over band number 4 from 92AV3C database

Characterization method		Classification rate
Grey level values		18.85 %
Wavelet packets		27.77 %
Basic tessellation	Gauss	41.58 %
	Truncate	40.07 %
	Flat	41.31 %
Constant tessellation	Gauss	63.77 %
	Truncate	65.05 %
	Flat	65.78 %

Results in table 1 show that all methods outperform grey level classification rates as it was obviously expected due to the higher number of features used. However, the wavelet features were worse than expected. It was the method that used the highest number of features and the percentage of correct classification was just a bit better than the grey level values. The basic tessellation performed significantly better than the wavelet features, using all sort of masks (Gaussian, truncate Gaussian, or flat). Finally, we can note that the constant tessellation outperformed the rest of features. When keeping the frequency band constant, the analysis is equally done for all frequencies bands what seems more appropriate for texture characterization. Moreover, we found that the sort of tessellation used influenced the final results much more that the sort of mask applied. Almost no difference was obtained when different masks were used. This is quite surprising as the used of truncate Gaussian masks should introduce important artifacts in the space domain, even more when the flat masks are considered. However, the classification results are almost the same or even better when the flat masks were used. Perhaps, when Gaussian masks are used, frequencies do not equally contribute to the characterization and some of them lose their characterization significance. Thus, applying flat masks allows all frequencies to contribute equally and uniquely the characterization providing very good results and requiring less computational effort.

4.2 Results Using Individual Bands

Previously, we have seen that using flat filters with a constant tessellation provided the best results of all the characterization methods studied. In consequence, we are now going to test these features for all the bands that make up the 92AV3C database.

Figure 4 shows the maximum, minimum, and mean percentage of correct classification for the same ten independent classification experiments described before run for each band in the database.

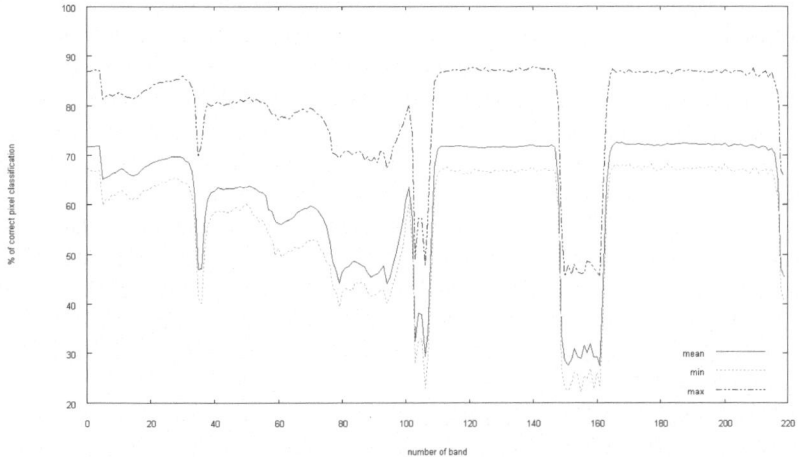

Fig. 4. Classification rates for each band of the 92AV3C database

From figure 4 we can observe that the maximum classification accuracy is not obtained at band number 4 as the chosen band selection method suggested. However, there are several bands, such as 171, that got better performance and consequently are more convenient. These results show that the textural features may be taken into account from the beginning in the band selection process, at least, as a testing criterion.

We can also notice in figure 4 that there are significant differences in the percentage of correct classification between bands. It is well known that several bands in the 92AV3C database are generally dismissed due to their low signal-to-noise ratio. These ranges are known to be bands $0 - 3$, $102 - 109$, $148 - 164$, $216 - 219$, as described in [6]. All these ranges provided the worst classification results, except for the range $0 - 3$ which provided similar results to other bands. If these bands were not considered, even the worst band would provide quite good classification results taking into account that only one band is being used in each case.

4.3   Results for Clusters of Bands

In this section we will show that textural characterization improves itself by using a higher number of bands even when the clusters of bands selected could not be optimal for these features, as it has been previously seen.

When more than one band is considered, all possible pairs of bands will be taken into account and textural features will be derived from them. Taking each pair of bands, a complex band will be formed using one of them as the real part and the other one as the complex part. When the Fourier transform is computed for these complex bands, the symmetric property if no longer fulfilled. Consequently, the number of filters to apply over each complex band doubles since each of the previous filter must be split into two parts due to the non-symmetrical transform.

The feature set obtained for each cluster will be divided into twenty random sets keeping the a priori probability of each class. In first place, as described in the previous sections, classification has been performed with the k-nn rule using 3 neighbors using pairs of sets, one used as training set and the other as test set (1-1 knn3 method). Other classification experiment consists of using each set once as training set whereas all the rest 19 sets are joined together to be used as a test set (1-19 knn3 method). In both experiments, a mean, maximum and minimum rate may be calculated, with ten and twenty independent attempts, respectively. For our current purpose, only the mean will be representative of our results and compared with classification rates reported in [7].

92AV3C database contains 17 different classes of textures, among them, the background class is composed by a heterogenous mixture of non-classified classes. Including this class into the classification process may confuse and decrease the performance rate due to its heterogenous nature, as different characterizations are assigned to the same class. For this reason, the more representative the characterization is of a class the less the classifier will fail, as pixels with a specific class will be properly characterized and so properly fit into its class by the classifier.

Fig. 5(a) shows classification results including the background class while Fig. 5(b) shows similar results without using the background class, in both cases for different numbers of bands in the cluster. It could be noted that textural features reaches

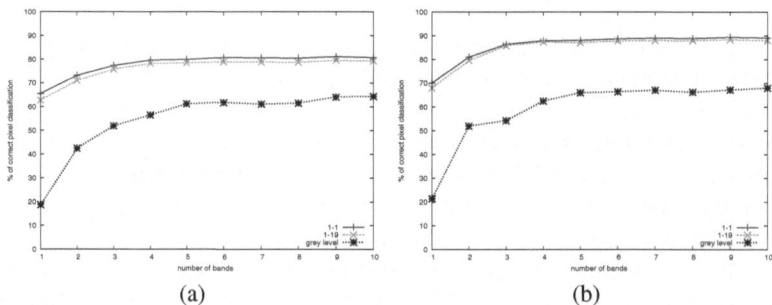

(a)   (b)

Fig. 5. Classification rates for clusters of 92AV3C database, with two methods of classification and compared with grey level characterization (a) taking into account the heterogenous class of background (b) without background class

stability sooner than the old method does, which means that a smaller number of bands is required in the whole process to reach a higher performance. As expected, when background is not taken into account performance enhances since background mistakes are removed (see Fig. 5(b)).

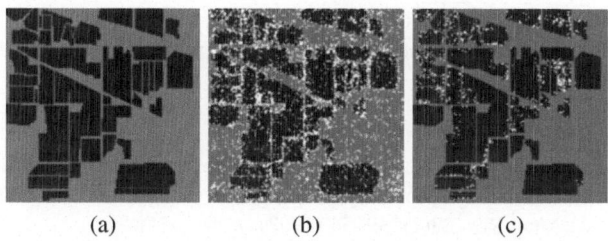

(a)   (b)   (c)

Fig. 6. (a)Ground truth of the 92AV3C database. Localization of classes in the space. (b) Maps of misclassified pixels (in white) using a clusters of 5 bands classified with a 1-1 knn3 method including the background class (c) Same map without the background class.

Fig. 6 presents the classification errors for the cluster composed by 5 bands. It shows misclassified pixels (white) by representing them in the space of the image superposed by the image's ground truth in order to distinguish the original classes recognized in the real image. Notice that the majority of the mistakes will be due to the heterogenous class or the proximity to it (see Fig. 6(b)). To avoid mistakes due to the background class and being able to analyze mistakes of the known classes, the background class may be ignored (observe Fig. 6(c)). In this case, misclassified pixels may be easily recognized and classification rates increase. Note that misclassified pixels fall mainly in the borders of the regions.

5   Conclusions

Results of hyperspectral texture characterization using several frequential filters has been presented in order to test band selection methods and reduce significantly the number of bands required in pixel classification tasks while improve the classification rates. Constant frequency band tessellation performed significantly better than traditional tessellation and the different masks tested performed similarly. We have chosen the flat masks due to its low computational cost. Different classification experiments have shown the stability of the textural features over different spectral bands, as well as when they were obtained from individual bands or from complex bands. Band selection methods usually take grey level pixel characterization as the validation criteria for their selection. We have shown that other validations should be taken into account as better classification rates may be obtained with textural information.

Acknowledgments

This work has been partly supported by Fundació Caixa Castelló-Bancaixa through grant FPI PREDOC/2007/20 and project P1-1B2007-48, project CSD2007 00018 from Consolider Ingenio 2010, and project AYA2008-05965-C04-04 from Spanish CICYT.

References

1. Chang, T., Kuo, C.C.J.: Texture analysis and classification with tree-structured wavelet transform. IEEE Trans. Image Process. 2, 429–441 (1993)
2. Freeware Multispectral Image Data Analysis System,
   `http://dynamo.ecn.purdue.edu/~biehl/MultiSpec`
3. Fukunaga, K.: Introduction to Statistical Pattern Recognition, 2nd edn. Academic, New York (1990)
4. Hughes, G.F.: On the mean accuracy of statistical pattern recognizers. IEEE Trans. Inf. Theory 14(1), 55–63 (1968)
5. Jimenez, L.O., Landgrebe, D.A.: Supervised classification in highdimensional space: Geometrical, statistical, and symptotically properties of multivariate data. IEEE Trans. Syst., Man, Cybern. C, Appl. Rev. 28(1), 39–54 (1998)
6. Landgrebe, D.A.: Signal Theory Methods in Multispectral Remote Sensing. Wiley, Hoboken (2003)
7. Martínez-Usó, A., Pla, F., Sotoca, J.M., García-Sevilla, P.: Clustering-based Hyperspectral Band selection using Information Measures. IEEE Transactions on Geoscience & Remote Sensing 45(12), 4158–4171 (2007)
8. Petrou, M., García-Sevilla, P.: Image Processing: Dealing with Texture. John Wiley & Sons, Chichester (2006)
9. Richards, J., Jia, X.: Remote Sensing Digital Image Analysis, 3rd edn. Springer, Berlin (1999)
10. Serpico, S.B., Bruzzone, L.: A new search algorithm for feature selection in hyperspectral remote sensing images. IEEE Trans. Geosci. Remote Sens. 39(7), 1360–1367 (1994)
11. Shaw, G., Manolakis, D.: Signal processing for hyperspectral image explotation. IEEE Signal Process. Mag. 19(1), 12 (2002)

A New Clustering Algorithm for Color Image Segmentation

Mohammed Talibi Alaoui[1] and Abderrahmane Sbihi[2]

[1] Laboratoire de Recherche en Informatique LARI
Université Mohamed I, FSO, BP. 717, 60000, Oujda, Maroc
[2] Laboratoire Images et Reconnaissance des Formes, LIRF
Université Ibn Tofail, FSK, B.P. 133, 14000, Kénitra, Maroc
talibialaouim@gmail.com

Abstract. In this paper, we present a new data classification algorithm in an unsupervised context, which is based on both Kohonen maps and mathematical morphology. The first part of the proposed algorithm consists to a projection of the distribution of multidimensional data observations onto a Kohonen map which is represented by the underlying probability density function (pdf). Under the assumption that each modal region of this density function has a correspondance with a one and only one cluster in the distribution, the second part of the algorithm consists in partitioning the Kohonen map into connected modal regions by making concepts of morphological watershed transformation suitable for their detection. The classification process is then based on the so detected modal regions. As an application of the proposed algorithm, the sample of observations is constituted by image pixels with 3 color components in the RGB color space. The purpose is to present a new approach for unsupervised color image classification without using any thresholding procedure.

Keywords: Color Image, Kohonen Network, Watershed Transformation, Classification.

1 Introduction

Cluster analysis techniques attempt to separate a set of multidimensional observations into groups or clusters which share some properties of similarity. Many of these techniques are based on mode detection where there is a one-to-one correspondence between the modal regions of the underlying probability density function (pdf) and the clusters [1]. The mapping of multivariate data onto a two-dimensional graphic is a very appealing technique since it takes full advantage of the human skill for organizing the data presented to the eyes of the analyst [2,3,4]. There is a number of methods which permit this mapping by reducing the dimension of the raw data while preserving relationships between data elements. One of the most commonly used among them in an unsupervised context is the Kohonen self organizing feature map [5, 6, 7]. Nevertheless, when using such a map, the analyst has to interactively handle the data. Hence, this technique, when used alone, does not allow to classify the data automatically. To overcome this limitation, we propose a two step methodology.

H. Araujo et al. (Eds.): IbPRIA 2009, LNCS 5524, pp. 217–224, 2009.

2 Self - organising Feature Map and Learning Process

Let $X = \{X_1, ..., X_q, ..., X_Q\}$ be a sample of Q observations X_q in a N-dimensional space where $X_q = [x_{q,1}, ..., x_{q,j}, ..., x_{q,N}]^T$. The Kohonen network is made of a two layers. The first one, or input layer, receives the N attributes of the presented observation. The output layer, or competitive layer, is composed of M units regularly distributed on the map (cf. Figure 1). The neural units of the first layer are connected to the units of the second layer. Each interconnection from an input unit j to an output unit i has a weight W_{ij}. That means that each output unit i has a corresponding weight vector W_i where $W_i = [W_{i1}, ... W_{ij}, ..., W_{iN}]^T$.

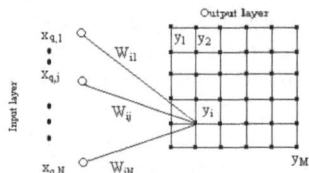

Fig. 1. Kohonen Network

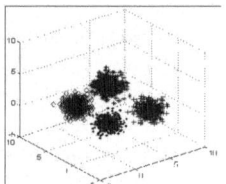

Fig. 2. Generated data

During the training process, when an input X_q is presented to the network, the neural unit whose weight vector is the closest to this observation wins the competition and is allowed to take this input into account in the learning process.

The weight vector of the winning unit and its neighbours are modified according to equations :

$$W_i(t) = W_i(t-1) + a(t).[X_q(t) - W_i(t-1)] \qquad \text{if} \quad i = i*$$
$$W_i(t) = W_i(t-1) + a(t)\, h(i*,t)\, y_i(t)[X_q(t) - W_i(t-1)] \quad \text{if } i \in V(i*, r(t)) \qquad (1)$$
$$W_i(t) = W_i(t-1) \quad \text{if} \quad i \notin V(i*, r(t)) \text{ and } i \neq i*$$

where $i*$ denotes the winning unit defined by :

$$i* = \underset{i}{\text{Arg min}}\ [d(X(t), W_i(t))] \qquad (2)$$

$a(t)$ is the learning coefficient lower than 1. We model it by an exponential function which decreases towards zero proximity when t increases. Let T denote the number of iterations for the learning phase which is adjusted experimentally by defining a number of learning cycles.

$V(i, r(t))$ is the neighbourhood of a unit i, with a radius $r(t)$ defined by :

$$V(i, r(t)) = \left\{ i' \in [0, M[,\ i' \neq i\, /\, d^A(U_i, U_{i'}) \leq r(t) \right\} \qquad (3)$$

where $U_i = (u, v)^T$ and $U_{i'} = (u', v')^T$ denote the position vectors on the map of the i and i' neural units.

$h(i*, t)$ is a neighbourhood function which is used at time t to alter the step size of the ith weight vector. It is a function of the Euclidean distance between its associated neural unit on the lattice and the winning unit $i*$ given by :

$$h\ (i*, t) = \exp\ (-\frac{d^A(U_i, U_{i'})^2}{2\ r(t)^2})\tag{4}$$

where $r(t)$ is the radius which depends on the number t of the iteration. It is decreased every $n_r Q$ iterations, where n_r is the epoch number with a constant radius and Q is the number of observations in the sample. $r(t)$ is defined such as :

$$r(t) = \begin{cases} r(t-1) - 1 & if\ t\ \mathrm{mod}(n\ _rQ) = 0 \ \ and\ \ r(t) > 1 \\ \varepsilon & if\ t\ \mathrm{mod}(n\ _rQ) = 0 \ \ and\ \ r(t) \le 1 \\ r(t) & otherwise \end{cases}\tag{5}$$

At the end of the training phase, the weight vectors of neighboring neural units in the map converge toward the same area in the data space.

3 Proposed Clustering Algorithm

3.1 Principle of the Algorithm

Data projection mapping is done using a Kohonen maps (cf.§ 2.) represented by the underlying pdf. The weight vectors existing in the so-detected modal regions are taken as prototypes for data classification.

3.2 Clustering Algorithm

This algorithm is illustrated using four 3-dimensional artificial Gaussian distributions with 500 observations each (cf. Figure 2), with the statistical parameters given in table 1. The proposed clustering algorithm consists in three basic steps :

Table 1. Statistical parameters of the gaussian distributions

Generated Data				
Clusters	Mean Vectors	Variance Matrix		Probability
1	-0.01409 0.00649 0.02357	0.48587 0.02181 -0.00672 0.02181 0.56119 -0.03122 -0.00672 -0.03122 0.46598		0.25
2	5.99017 0.03629 0.00354	0.47207 -0.00051 0.00742 0.00051 0.58558 -0.00653 0.00742 -0.00653 0.54790		0.25
3	0.01863 0.03123 6.02823	0.52064 - 0.02421 0.01763 0.02421 0.58859 0.00232 0.01763 0.00232 0.55311		0.25
4	-0.04196 6.02157 0.01195	0.49531 0.00951 -0.03312 0.00951 0.44583 0.01832 -0.03312 0.01832 0.48434		0.25

Step 1. The Kohonen map representation

This first step of the process concerns the self-organising and the learning of the network which permit to built the Kohonen map (cf.§ 2.). At the end of the learning phase, the determined weight vectors are used to estimate the underlying probability density function (pdf) in the multidimensional data space. For this purpose, we use the non-parametric Parzen estimate defined by [8,9] :

$$\widehat{p}(W_i) = \frac{1}{Q} \cdot \sum_{q=1}^{Q} \frac{1}{V[D(W_i)]} \cdot \Omega(\frac{W_i - X_q}{h_Q})$$ (6)

with $\Omega(X) = \frac{1}{\sqrt{2\pi}} \cdot \exp(-\frac{1}{2} X^T \cdot X)$

$D(W_i)$ is the domain estimation. When it corresponds to an hypersphere with radius h_Q, and centered at the point defined by W_i, the volume $V[D(W_i)]$ is given by :

$$V[D(W_i)] = \frac{\pi^{\frac{N}{2}}}{\Gamma(\frac{N}{2}+1)} \cdot h_Q^N \quad \text{with} \quad \Gamma(\frac{N}{2}+1) = \frac{(N+1)!\sqrt{\pi}}{2^{(N+1)}(\frac{N+1}{2})!}$$ (7)

and $h_Q = h_0 \sqrt{Q}$

The parameter h_0 has a great effect on the quality of the estimation. If it is large, the little maxima of the pdf are indeterminable. Inversely, if h_0 is too small, we obtain an estimation with a many parasites maxima. The adjustment of h_0 is governed by the concept of cluster stability on the Kohonen map which determine automatically the number of clusters [10].

In figure 4, we can observe that the map is constitued by four regions where the pdf presents high values, separated by valleys where the pdf presents low values.

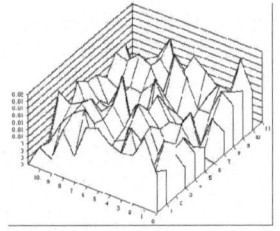

Fig. 3. Representation of the Kohonen map

The following step concerns the problem of modal regions detection in the Kohonen map.

Step 2. Modal regions extraction

The proposed algorithm for modal regions detection which is based on this transformation, consists in two basics phases.

Phase 1. Preprocessing and watershed determination

Prior to mode detection, some kind of pre-processing is needed to smooth the density function by filtering out its small non significant variations (cf. Figure 3). Among several methods for filtering the pdf, the raw estimate is smoothed by a numerical morphological opening (cf. Figure 5). This transformation is a combination of the two basic numerical morphological transformations, which are the numerical dilation and erosion [11, 12].

With the flat 3×3 structuring element H within the square grid (cf. Figure 4), numerical dilation and erosion of $\hat{p}(X)$ representing the pdf function are denoted as :

$$\delta_{\hat{p}}(X) = (\hat{p} \oplus H)(X) = \sup \{ \hat{p}(Y); Y \in H_X \}$$
$$\varepsilon_{\hat{p}}(X) = (\hat{p} \ominus H)(X) = \inf \{ \hat{p}(Y); Y \in H_X \} \qquad (8)$$

H_X denotes the structuring element shifted to the current point X in the map. Let $g(X)$ denote this filtered function.

After this preprocessing, the procedure consists in the localisation of the modal regions of the underlying pdf by means of the watershed algorithm based on homotopic thinnings of the function [11].

This watershed approach allows to determine the so-called catchment basins corresponding to the regional minima of the additive inverse of the pdf, which are the regional maxima of the pdf. The watershed of a function can be constructed through consecutive homotopic thinnings of this function.

1	1	1
1	1	1
1	1	1

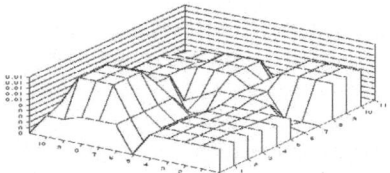

Fig. 4. Configuration of H   **Fig. 5.** Opening smoothing

It has been shown that the sequential thinning converges in a number of iterations that depends on the structure of the function. It is stopped when the idempotence is reached so that two consecutive iterations yield the same result. The final thinned function may present non-significant broken divide lines that do not correspond to the expected closed watershed lines. Fortunately, it is possible to "smooth" these lines by means of a sequential pruning operation. When this sequential pruning operation is iterated until the result does not change, spurious lines are shortened from their free ends, and only what is known to be an acceptable approximation of the true watershed lines remains. As the composition of two idempotent mappings is not necessarely idempotent, the whole process is then iterated until idempotence. Let $w(X)$ be the density function resulting from this idempotent process whose additive inverse is presented in figure 6.

Phase 2. Modal region extraction

Figure 6-a shows that the level of the top of each modal region is constant and two neighbouring modal regions have lower levels than that of the divide separating them. In these conditions, it is evident that performing a dilation with the same structuring element as the one used for the opening operation will modify the value of the additive inverse of the thinned function only at points belonging to the divides separating these modal regions. Hence, the divide set and the modal regions set can be easily extracted from the additive inverse of the thinned function by taking the point-to-point difference between the dilated version and the additive inverse of the thinned function itself (cf. Figure 6-b).

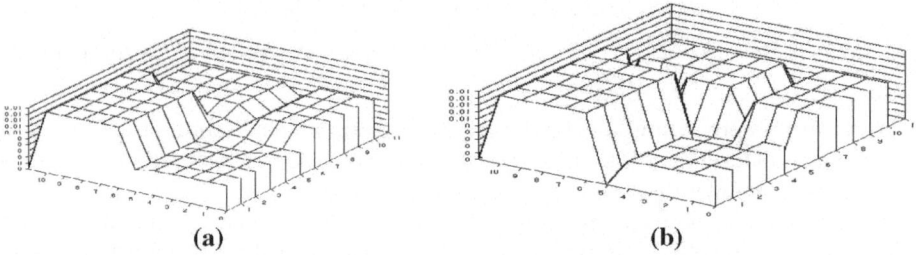

(a)   (b)

Fig. 6. Modal regions of $\hat{p}(X)$ with the watershed algorithm

Step 3. Classification Strategy

Once the different modal domains of the underlying pdf are identified and extracted as connected components, the observations corresponding to them are used as prototypes in the raw space (cf. Figure 7). The data points can finally be assigned to the clusters attached to their nearest neighbour among the prototypes [11].

The classification results are displayed in figure 8. The error rate achieved by the procedure is equal to 2.6 % while the Bayes theoritical minimum error is equal to 1.15 %.

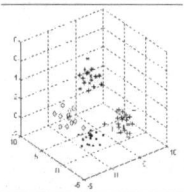

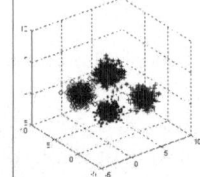

Fig. 7. Prototypes of clusters   **Fig. 8.** Classification Results

4   Application to Color Image Classification

The sample of observations used as application in the proposed algorithm is constituted by color image pixels. The 4096 observations represented in the RGB color space   constitute   for   the   Kohonen   network   the   learning   sample $\Gamma = \{X_1, X_2, ..., X_q, ..., X_{4096}\}$.

Table 2 illustrates the results of applying the proposed algorithm to color image. The result of the watershed transformation (cf. Table 2.) allows to detect and extract the modes from the map. We can see four modal regions 2, 3, 4, and 5 constituted by prototypes which represent the black, green, red and orange balls. The modal region 1 is represented by three under modal regions. All of them represent the bottom of the image. The clustering procedure consists in assigning each pixel to the region whose Euclidean distance between its corresponding mode prototypes is lowest.

Table 2.

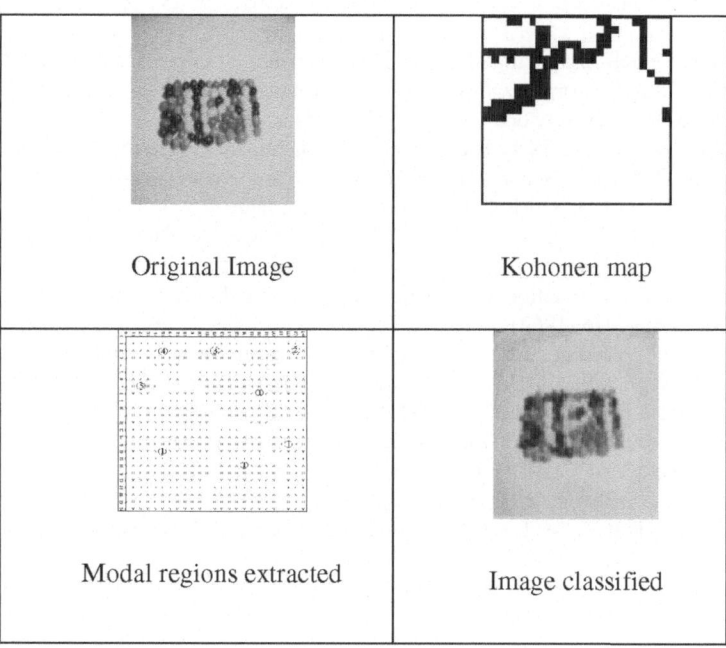

| Original Image | Kohonen map |
| Modal regions extracted | Image classified |

5 Conclusion

In this paper, we have presented a new data clustering scheme in an unsupervised context which is based on both Kohonen map and morphological watershed transformations. Each cluster is associated with a modal region on the Kohonen map where the pdf function is evaluated thanks to the Parzen estimator. Under the assumption that there exists a one to one correspondence between the modal regions of the smoothed pdf function and the catchment basins of its additive inverse, the determination of the watersheds yields the modal regions in the Kohonen map. Thanks to sequential homotopic thinnings, modal regions are detected automatically by the watershed process and are identified as connected components in the map. Each observation of the data is finally assigned to the cluster associated with the appropriate detected modal regions by means of a nearest neighbour classification rule.

References

1. Devijver, P.A.: A statistical Approach. In: Pattern Recognition. Prentice-Hall, Englewood Cliffs (1982)
2. Bow, S.T.: Pattern Recognition, p. 323. Dekker, New York (1984)
3. Delsert, S.: Classification interactive non supervisée de données multidimensionnelles par réseaux de neurones à apprentissage compétitif, Thése de Doctorat, Université de Lille (1996)
4. Betrouni, M., Delsert, S., Hamad, D.: Interactive Pattern Classification by means of Artificial Neural Networks. In: IEEE, Int. Conf. on SMC, vol. IV, pp. 3275–3279 (October 1995)
5. Kohonen, S.: Self-organizing Maps, 2nd extended edn. Springer, Heidelberg (1997)
6. Sadeghi, A.: A Self-organization properly of Kohonen's map with general type of stimuli distribution. Neural Networks, 1637–1643 (1998)
7. Pal, N.R., Bezdek, J., Tsao, E.C.-K., et al.: Generalized Clustering Networks and Kohonen's Self-Organizing Scheme. IEEE Trans. on Neural Networks 4(4), 549–557 (1993)
8. Sbihi, A., Postaire, J.G.: Mode Extraction by Multivalue Morphology for Cluster Analysis. In: Gaul, W., Pfeifer, D. (eds.) From DATA to Knowledge: Theoretical and Practical aspects of classification, pp. 212–221. Springer, Berlin (1995)
9. Parzen, E.: On Estimation of a Probability Density Function and Mode. Ann. Math. Stat. 33, 1065–1076 (1962)
10. Postaire, J.G., Vasseur, C.P.A.: An Approximate Solution to Normal Mixture Identification with Application to Unsupervised Pattern Classification. IEEE Trans. Patt. Anal. & Machine intel. PAMI-3(2), 163–179 (1981)
11. Beucher, S., Lantuejoul, C.: Use of Watersheds in Contour Detection. In: Int. Workshop on Image Processing, CCETT / IRISA, Rennes (September 1979)
12. Postaire, J.-G., Zhang, R.D., Botte-Lecocq, C.: Cluster analysis by binary morphology. IEEE. Trans. Pattern Anal. Machine. Intell. PAMI-15(2), 170–180 (1993)

A Top-Down Approach for Automatic Dropper Extraction in Catenary Scenes

Caroline Petitjean[1], Laurent Heutte[1], Régis Kouadio[1,2], and Vincent Delcourt[2]

[1] Université de Rouen, LITIS, EA 4108
BP 12, 76801 Saint-Etienne-du-Rouvray, France
`caroline.petitjean@univ-rouen.fr`
[2] Direction de l'Innovation et de la Recherche SNCF, 45 rue de Londres, 75379 Paris
Cedex 8, France

Abstract. This paper presents an original system for the automatic detection of droppers in catenary staves. Based on a top-down approach, our system exploits a priori knowledge that are used to perform a reliable extraction of droppers. Experiments conducted on a significant database of real catenary stave images show some promising results on this very challenging machine vision application.

1 Introduction

Overhead wires that are used to transmit electrical energy to trains are called the catenary. The contact wire provides electricity and the carrying wire supports the contact wire. Three vertical elements support the two wires: supporting arms, droppers and droppers with electrical connection. The part of the catenary that is delimited by two supporting arms is called a catenary stave (Figure 1). The number of elements and their location inside a catenary stave are specified in the so-called mounting rules.

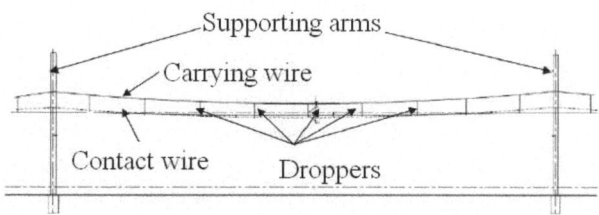

Fig. 1. Perpendicular view of a catenary stave

Maintenance of railway infrastructure consists in checking the presence and the integrity of each element. Today maintenance is carried out by visual inspection. The Innovation and Research Department of the French railways (SNCF) plans to automate this long and fastidious task. A dedicated acquisition system has thus been embedded inside a TGV coach [3]. The speed of the TGV being 320km/h, a high frame acquisition rate is required (53kHz). Thanks to

H. Araujo et al. (Eds.): IbPRIA 2009, LNCS 5524, pp. 225–232, 2009.
© Springer-Verlag Berlin Heidelberg 2009

a regulation of the obturation rate by the train speed, images are not fuzzy. Moreover, filters compensate for bad weather conditions. Images are acquired perpendicularly to the catenary. Their size is 1024x768 pixels and each pixel is coded on an 8-bit-gray level scale. For each image, the acquisition position on the line is provided. Horizontal resolution is 1.8 mm per pixel when the train speed is constant, but the resolution may vary during acceleration or deceleration.

Images represent adjacent segments of the catenary stave. A stave is made of about 40 images. A catenary stave is most often a single stave, with one pair of contact wire and carrying wire (Figure 2).

Fig. 2. Successive images of a single catenary stave

The aim of the study is to conceive and develop an automatic image processing system that allows to identify the catenary elements as described earlier, using the mounting rules. The ultimate goal will then be to detect faults on identified elements (typically, frayed contact wires, unusual objects on the catenary, broken droppers, faulty electrical connection on droppers...). In this paper we will solely focus on the dropper recognition part, as being a preliminary task to the fault detection process. Indeed, droppers are structural elements of the catenary stave and the knowledge of their number and type order is of crucial importance to identify the type of catenary stave we deal with. Conversely, using this knowledge to guide the dropper extraction process would ease the fault detection. Let us stress the fact that such an automatic analysis of the catenary droppers is an original machine vision application which has no equivalent today. To the best of our knowledge, only one similar system has been developed in the world: the work reported in [6] describes an onboard vision system for acquisition of catenary images in which automatic image processing is quite limited in that sense that catenary elements are identified manually before an automatic defect recognition is performed on manually isolated elements.

The remaining of the paper is organized as follows. In section 2 we justify the use of a top-down approach to extract droppers from catenary stave images and give an overview of the proposed system. We detail in section 3 the four steps to detect and classify droppers automatically and show how *a priori* knowledge can be used to perform a reliable detection of droppers; we give some experimental results on a significant database of real catenary stave images. We conclude in section 4 by some future works on this very challenging machine vision application.

2   Overview of the Proposed Approach

Identifying the catenary elements can be seen as a scene analysis problem, for which two main approaches may be used [1]:

- a bottom-up approach: simple, element-independent features are extracted from the image. These features are gathered and knowledge is incorporated into the recognition process in order to finally identify the objects.
- a top-down approach: this approach relies on the hypothesis that the image contains a particular object and thus consists in predicting the presence of features in the image, using high-level *a priori* knowledge.

The model in our application relies on the mounting rules which describe the different types of catenary staves. They indicate, for each type of catenary stave, the number and the order of droppers and droppers with electrical connection as well as the space between them (see for example Figure 4). This *a priori* knowledge can be very useful as it constrains the model that can be used to make the automatic detection of droppers more reliable. However, the model is not always fully applicable, i.e. not applicable on all catenary staves as horizontal resolution of the images may vary during acquisition due to train accelerations and decelerations. For this reason, we had first designed a bottom-up approach in which vertical and horizontal components were first segmented and classified without *a priori* knowledge, then checked and corrected through alignment of the whole stave models [4]. Though providing good results in terms of precision and recall in dropper extraction, this approach suffered from high computation

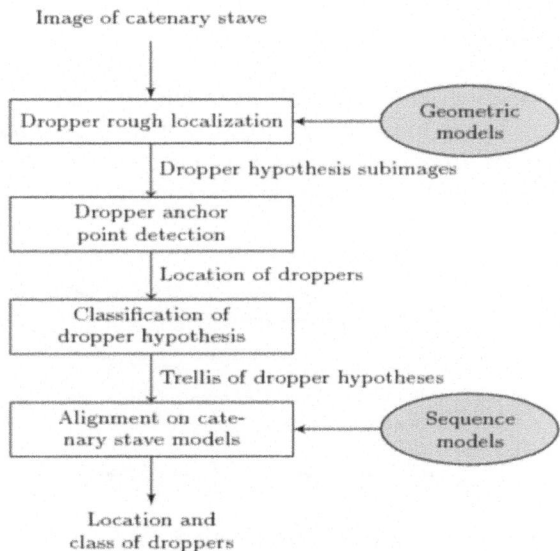

Fig. 3. Overview of the proposed system

time due to the fact that the analysis should necessarily be conducted on the whole image of the catenary stave. Therefore, we have rather turned toward the investigation of the top-down approach we report in this paper, in which *a priori* knowledge is used to guide the dropper extraction process.

An overview of our system is shown in Figure 3. The input of the system is a set of images representing the catenary stave. In this top-down approach, *a priori* knowledge is first used to roughly localize droppers. More precisely, subparts of the whole catenary stave image that may contain droppers are isolated thanks to geometric models. The most likely anchor points of each dropper are then detected on each local binarized image and characterized so as to discriminate between "simple droppers" and "droppers with electrical connections". A trellis of dropper hypotheses (dropper classes along with their probabilities) is then analyzed to search for the most likely path through the alignment of dropper sequence models of catenary staves. The output of the system is a sequence of dropper locations and classes that will be used in a further step for defect detection.

3   Automatic Dropper Detection

We now detail in this section the four steps of our top-down approach to detect droppers. Let us recall that the input of our system is a whole image of a catenary stave obtained from the concatenation of single images. Typically, the whole image is 30000 pixels long made up of the concatenation of about forty 1024x768 images (typically a 1.38m-long subpart of the catenary).

3.1   Dropper Rough Localization

In this first step, *a priori* knowledge about mounting rules is used to limit the search for droppers to the most likely subparts of the whole image and thus to provide hypotheses of dropper locations without needing a "blind" analysis of the whole image. Note that each catenary stave must respect specific mounting

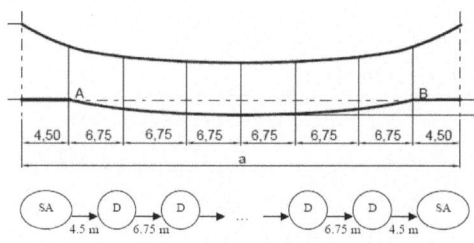

Fig. 4. Mounting rules of a 63m-long catenary stave made up of 7 droppers (D) and its corresponding geometric model defined by the inter-dropper distances between two supporting arms (SA)

rules that set the distance between two consecutive droppers depending on the length of the catenary stave as shown in Figure 4.

The database of catenary models contains 74 types of stave or models ranging from the simplest one made of a sequence of 4 droppers to the most complex made of 15 elements combining droppers and droppers with electrical connections. Therefore, one way to limit the search for droppers is to filter this database of catenary models by estimating the distance between two supporting arms, i.e. the length of the catenary stave [3,4]. This length acts as a discriminative feature that enables to predict roughly the location of dropper hypotheses and thus to segment the whole image of the catenary stave into those subparts of the whole image that contain a dropper. Note that due to small train accelerations and decelerations during image acquisition, width of the subparts of the whole image that will be further analyzed in the next step is chosen large enough to take into account possible variations of horizontal resolution (typically 1500 pixels).

3.2   Dropper Anchor Point Detection

The input of this stage is a subpart (1024x1500 pixels) of the whole image segmented from the dropper rough localization stage, where a dropper is assumed to be present. As the elements of the catenary are quite linear, they may thus be detected by thresholding horizontal and vertical projections of the image. But images are not as straightforward to process as they seem. Indeed, they show inhomogeneous noisy background, that has a poor contrast with the droppers. Droppers are also very thin, only 2 to 3 pixels wide. Furthermore, some objects are darker and some other are lighter than the background. Note that for visualization purposes, all images presented in this paper have been manually contrast-enhanced.

In order to simplify the anchor point detection process, the image is binarized. Because of the background inhomogeneity, binarization is performed using TopHat and BotHat morphological operators. The TopHat (respectively BotHat) operator allows to segment elements which are lighter (respectively darker) than the background [5]. The two structuring elements for these operators are constructed according to the shape and the size of the elements to be detected. They are 10-pixel long horizontal and vertical lines.

Segmentation into vertical and horizontal components is then performed by thresholding the projections of the binarized image along both directions:

- vertically, in order to detect vertical elements (supporting arms, droppers and droppers with electrical connection) ;
- horizontally, in order to detect horizontal elements (contact wire and carrying wire). Since the wire horizontality is not always maintained, the rotation angle is taken into account before projecting the image, by means of a Radon transform.

By intersecting vertical and horizontal elements, two dropper anchor points are thus localized in the binarized image.

3.3   Dropper Classification

To discriminate between simple droppers and droppers with electrical connections, one can observe in Figure 5 that difference between these two elements is simply the presence of a larger area of pixels at wire-dropper intersection in favor of droppers with electrical connections. A 2-feature vector based on pixel densities extracted from the neighborhood of each anchor point seems therefore to be discriminative enough to classify droppers.

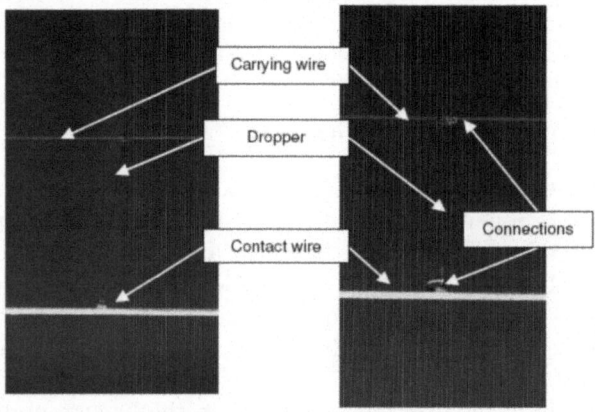

Fig. 5. (left) Simple dropper, (right) Dropper with electrical connections

Classification of droppers is performed by a 2-5-2 MLP. This classifier has been chosen because it is fast in decision, provides good generalization properties, and can output posterior probabilities for sequence model alignment [2]. The output of this stage is finally a sequence of classification hypotheses, each one associated with a posterior probability. The next stage will consist in correcting the possible errors of classification by aligning various models of dropper sequence.

3.4   Alignment on Catenary Stave Models

In a top-down approach, recognition is mainly a verification step that searches for aligning models on observation sequences output by the classification stage. Therefore, the alignment of the catenary stave models consists in searching for the optimal path through dynamic programming for example. In our case, it simply consists in multiplying probabilities provided by the MLP-classifier through model paths. The winner path is that one with the highest final probability as shown in Figure 6.

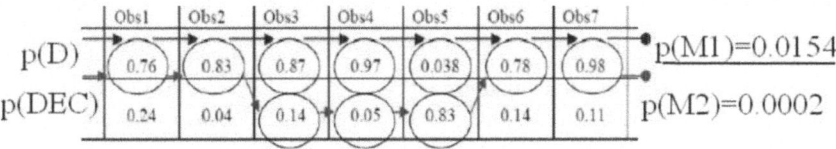

Fig. 6. Alignment on the results of the MLP of two catenary stave models made up of 7 droppers, one with 7 simple droppers (SD), the other with 4 simple droppers (SD) and 3 droppers with electrical connections (CD)

3.5   Experiments and Results

Experiments for dropper detection have been conducted on a database of 689 whole images of catenary staves representing 5161 droppers (simple droppers and droppers with electrical connection) to be detected, for which the ground truth has been obtained by manually tracing a bounding box around the droppers. Two thirds of the elements have been used for training, the last third for testing as shown in Table 1.

Let us stress on the fact that the dropper rough localization succeeds in segmenting the whole images of catenary stave into subparts containing a dropper (either simple or with electrical connection) with a 100% segmentation rate. As for the correct dropper recognition rate is concerned, Table 2 presents the performance of our system before and after model alignment. As one can see, the correct classification rate before alignment (MLP solely) is pretty good for simple droppers but is somehow critical for droppers with electrical connection (DEC). That comes essentially from the binarisation of the segmented subparts of the whole images that introduces some spurious densities of pixels around the anchor points. However, the performance of our system after model alignment are quite satisfying and allow the French Railways to now investigate fault detection on catenary staves.

Recall and precision rates are also two widely used measures for assessing the quality of results of detection and information extraction tasks. Recall is a measure of the ability of the system to localize and recognize all presented droppers. Precision measures the ability of the system to provide only correct hypothesis and thus to limit the number of false alarms. Both rates, as shown in Table 3, are satisfying and show the good performance of our system.

Table 1. Number of images

	Learning base	Test base	Total
Catenary stave	474	215	689
Simple droppers	2752	1262	4014
DEC	803	344	1147
Total droppers	3555	1606	5161

Table 2. Correct classification rate

	Before alignement	After alignement
Simple droppers	99.36%	99.68%
DEC	95.93%	99.13%
Average on droppers	98.62%	99.56%

Table 3. Performance of overall system

Recall	99.06%
Precision	99.06%
F1-measure	99.06%

4   Conclusion and Future Works

We have presented in this paper a top-down approach to automatically extract droppers from catenary stave images and have shown that *a priori* knowledge can be used to perform a reliable detection of droppers. The experimental results obtained on a significant database of real catenary stave images have demonstrated the interest of our approach which is an original and real machine vision application that has no equivalent today. Future works on this very challenging machine vision application will deal now with defect detection particularly some complex tasks such as real-time detection of frayed contact wires, of unusual objects on the catenary, of broken droppers, or of faulty electrical connection on droppers.

References

1. Battle, J., Casals, A., Freixenet, J., Martí, J.: A review on strategies for recognizing natural in colour images of outdoor scenes. Image and Vision Computing 18, 515–530 (2000)
2. Bishop, C.M.: Neural Networks for Pattern Recognition. Oxford University Press, Oxford (1995)
3. Kouadio, R., Delcourt, V., Heutte, L., Petitjean, C.: Video based catenary for preventive maintenance on Iris 320. In: Proc. WCRR 2008, Seoul, Korea (2008)
4. Montreuil, F., Kouadio, R., Petitjean, C., Heutte, L., Delcourt, V.: Automatic extraction of information for catenary scene analysis. In: Proc. EUSIPCO 2008, Lausanne, Switzerland (2008)
5. Lacoste, C., Descombes, X., Zerubia, J., Baghdadi, N.: Unsupervised line network extraction from remotely sensed images by polyline process. In: Proc. EUSIPCO 2004, Vienna, Austria (2004)
6. Richter, U., Schneider, R.: Automatische optische Inspektion von Oberleitungen. Elektrische Bahnen 99, 94–100 (2007)

A Scale Invariant Interest Point Detector for Discriminative Blob Detection

Luis Ferraz[1] and Xavier Binefa[2]

[1] Universitat Autónoma de Barcelona,
Department of Computing Science, Barcelona, Spain
luis.ferraz@uab.es,
[2] Universitat Pompeu Fabra, Department of Information and Communication
Technologies, Barcelona, Spain
xavier.binefa@upf.edu

Abstract. In this paper we present a novel scale invariant interest point detector of blobs which incorporates the idea of blob movement along the scales. This trajectory of the blobs through the scale space is shown to be valuable information in order to estimate the most stable locations and scales of the interest points. Our detector evaluates interest points in terms of their self trajectory along the scales and its evolution obtaining non-redundant and discriminant features. Moreover, in this paper we present a differential geometry view to understand how interest points can be detected. We propose to analyze the gaussian curvature to classify image regions as blobs, edges or corners.

Our interest point detector has been compared with some of the most important scale invariant detectors on infrared (IR) images, outperforming their results in terms of: number of interest points detected and discrimination of the interest points.

Keywords: discriminative features, blob detection, gaussian curvature, blob trajectory.

1 Introduction

Interest point detection algorithms have been shown to be well suited for feature extraction. The main goal of these algorithms is to allow the extraction of features invariant to some viewing conditions. Scale invariant detectors estimate the location and the scale of these features. Different scale invariant detectors have been developed over the past few years and among the most important we can find Laplacian of Gaussian (LoG) [1], Derivative of Gaussian (DoG) [2], Harris-Laplace [3], Hessian-Laplace [3], salient regions [4], Maximally Stable Extremal Regions (MSER) [5] or Speeded-Up Robust Features (SURF) [6].

Typically, detectors are based on a multi-scale analysis of the image [7]. The space-scale can be built using different scale normalized operators, like Laplace filters or difference of Gaussians filters. For these detectors an interest point is detected if a local 3D extreme is present and if its absolute value is higher than a

H. Araujo et al. (Eds.): IbPRIA 2009, LNCS 5524, pp. 233–240, 2009.

threshold. Therefore, blobs at different scales are not related and the same blob can be detected many times along the scale-space. To avoid this problem, our proposal is to estimate the trajectory of blobs along scales and select the scale and location that best represent each blob.

From a differential geometry point of view images can be understood as surfaces with 3 types of regions in function of their gaussian curvature: elliptical regions, parabolic regions and hyperbolic regions. These types of regions allow to see images in a simple way, where elliptical regions can be understood as blobs, parabolic regions as contours or plane regions and hyperbolic regions as corners or saddles.

In order to extract this differential structure we use the full Hessian matrix [8] for each point. This approach outperforms Laplacian based operators more related to obtain rotational invariant information [9].

In this paper we compare LoG, DoG, Harris-Laplace and Hessian-Laplace.Each one construct it scale-space in a different way:

- The LoG filters each scale with a scale adapted Laplacian filter. Blobs are the extremes in its 3D neighborhood (maxima for bright and minima for dark blobs).
- The DoG is a computational cost optimization of LoG, it uses substraction of gaussians with different sigma to approximate the Laplacian filter. Lowe in [2] improve DoG to select blobs with a minimal gray level variation and with a circular shape.
- The Harris-Laplace detector calculates corners at the different scales using a scale adapted Harris operator. After that, locations of detected corners are evaluated with a Laplacian filter in the superior and inferior scales. Interest points correspond to corners with a maximal response of Laplacian filter.
- The Hessian-Laplace detector works in a similar way to Harris-Laplace detector. The main difference is that instead of Harris operator uses the determinant of the Hessian matrix to penalize very long structures.

On the other hand, SURF is an interesting detector because of its low computational cost. However, SURF is quite similar to Hessian-Laplace in its outline and results, for this reason we do not compare this detector. Another interesting detector is MSER. It produces good results in comparison with other detectors but it is not analyzed in this paper because of its bad performance on blurred images [10].

Salient regions detector is not evaluated either because of its excessive computational cost. However, salient detector has been shown as a good discriminative feature extractor [11]. We have designed our detector in this sense. Gaussian curvature can be understood as a saliency measure given that it measures the normal curvatures around each point. On images, normal curvatures measure the variations of the gray level around blobs.

This paper is organized as follows. In section 2 the method to detect interest points by means of curvature analysis is introduced. In section 3 our scale invariant interest point detector is described and finally, in Section 4 we present experimental results.

2   Curvature Analysis on Images

The image behavior in a local neighborhood of a point, uniform and derivable, can be approximated by the Taylor formula. It means that they can be simplified in a expansion of functions. The Taylor expansion of a local neighborhood of a point x_0 is,

$$f(\vec{x_0} + \vec{h}) = f(\vec{x}) = f(\vec{x_0}) + \nabla f(\vec{x_0})\vec{h} + \frac{1}{2!}\vec{h}^T \nabla^2 f(\vec{x_0})\vec{h} + r(\vec{h}) \qquad (1)$$

where $r(\vec{h})$ is a residual.

Differential geometry, in general, allow to extract properties and features of points by means of first and second order terms of the Taylor expansion. First order terms contain information about gradient distribution in a local neighborhood. Second order terms contain information about the local shape.

Each image point is represented by three coordinates $P = (x, y, f(x, y))$. Thus, first order terms from Taylor expansion are the called Jacobian matrix,

$$J = \begin{pmatrix} \frac{\partial P}{\partial x} \\ \frac{\partial P}{\partial y} \end{pmatrix} = \begin{pmatrix} 1 & 0 & f_x \\ 0 & 1 & f_y \end{pmatrix} \qquad (2)$$

The first fundamental form I on an image f is defined as,

$$I = J * J^T = \begin{pmatrix} 1 + f_x^2 & f_x f_y \\ f_y f_x & 1 + f_y^2) \end{pmatrix} \qquad (3)$$

The normal vector $\vec{N}$ associated to each point on an image f is defined as,

$$\vec{N} = \frac{\partial P}{\partial x} \times \frac{\partial P}{\partial y} = \begin{pmatrix} -f_x \\ -f_y \\ 1 \end{pmatrix} \qquad (4)$$

Second order terms from Taylor expansion conform the Hessian matrix H. H for images, is equivalent to the second fundamental form II. The general equation of II is derived from the normal curvature calculation [8] and it is calculated using the second partial derivatives and the normal vector $\vec{N}$ to each neighborhood. Thus, the second fundamental form II for images is defined as,

$$II = \begin{pmatrix} \frac{\partial^2 P}{\partial x^2}\vec{N} & \frac{\partial^2 P}{\partial x \partial y}\vec{N} \\ \frac{\partial^2 P}{\partial x \partial y}\vec{N} & \frac{\partial^2 P}{\partial^2 y}\vec{N} \end{pmatrix} = \begin{pmatrix} (0\ 0\ f_{xx}) \cdot \vec{N} & (0\ 0\ f_{xy}) \cdot \vec{N} \\ (0\ 0\ f_{xy}) \cdot \vec{N} & (0\ 0\ f_{yy}) \cdot \vec{N} \end{pmatrix} = \begin{pmatrix} f_{xx} & f_{xy} \\ f_{yx} & f_{yy} \end{pmatrix} = H \qquad (5)$$

The first and second fundamental forms of a surface determine an important differential-geometric invariant, the Gaussian curvature K. The Gaussian curvature of a point on a surface is the product of their principal curvatures, $K = k_1 k_2$. Gaussian curvature can be expressed as the ratio of the determinants of the second and first fundamental forms,

$$K = k_1 k_2 = \frac{det(II)}{det(I)} = \frac{f_{xx} f_{yy} - f_{xy}^2}{1 + f_x^2 + f_y^2} \qquad (6)$$

The sign of K at a point determines the shape of the surface near that point [8]: for $K > 0$ the surface is locally convex (blob regions) and the point is called elliptic, while for $K < 0$ the surface is saddle shaped (i.e. corners) and the point is called hyperbolic. The points at which K is zero (i.e. contours) are called parabolic. The value of K apart from the type of region in function of the sign offer information about the saliency, this value on images is a measure of the variation of the gray level. An important property of K is that is not singular.

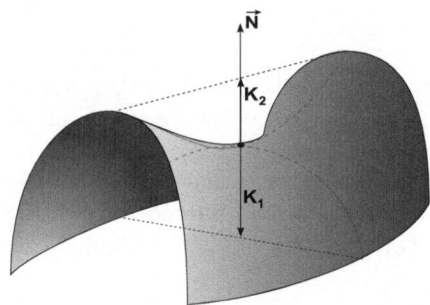

Fig. 1. Saddle surface with its normal curvatures k_1 and k_2

In Fig. 1 is shown the meaning of curvature. Given the normal vector $\vec{N}$ to the point $\vec{x_0}$ and its two principal curvatures k_1 and k_2, Gaussian curvature is defined positive if both curvatures have the same sign, negative if they have different sign and zero if any curvature is zero.

I is positive definite, hence its determinant is positive everywhere. Therefore, the sign of K coincides with the sign of the determinant of II. Assuming that point $\vec{x_0}$ is a critical point (the gradient $\nabla f(\vec{x_0})$ vanishes) the Gaussian curvature of the surface at $\vec{x_0}$ is the determinant of II. So, in this case it is not necessary to calculate I to estimate the Gaussian curvature on $\vec{x_0}$. In the other cases, when the gradient $\nabla f(\vec{x_0})$ do not vanishes, can be shown that $det(II)$ is close to Gaussian curvature. This is due to $det(II)$ usually decreases while $det(I)$ increases. In spite of this appreciation our method uses the complete equation (6) because of we focus on curvature to find the best locations.

It is important to remark that to calculate K with (6) do not increase significantly the computational cost of the method.This is because Hessian matrix can be approximated from the first derivatives.

3   Discriminant Blob Detection Using Trajectories

In this section we propose a new scale invariant interest point detector called Trajectories of Discriminative Blobs (ToDB) based on the analysis of Gaussian curvature of the image along the space-scale representation. Moreover, to obtain more stable interest points the trajectory of each one is extracted.

The evolution of blobs along scales was studied in depth by [12]. Traditionally, the analysis of the behavior of blobs presents severe complications, since it

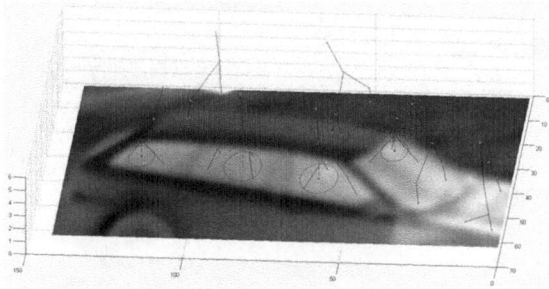

Fig. 2. Trajectories of some blobs along scales (blue lines). Blob movements and blob fusions can be seen. Green points show all the extremes found. Red points are the extremes selected as interest points.

implied a detailed description of the image. However, for our purposes we do not need a precise description and one of the most important contributions of our work is to reduce the detail of the analysis since we only need an approximation of the movement of blobs.

The outline of the algorithm is,

1. To build the scale-space representation with the Gaussian curvature K for pre-selected scales $\sigma_n = \sigma_0 \epsilon^n$. Where ϵ is the scale factor between successive levels and σ_0 is the initial scale.
2. At each level of the representation we extract the interest points by detecting the local maxima in the 8-neighborhood of a point x.
3. Relations between interest points at consecutive levels are extracted.
   For each interest point x_{ij} where j is the level of the representation.
   (a) Search in level $j+1$ using a gradient ascent algorithm the most plausible relation r for the interest point i. x_i in level j must be projected to level $j+1$.
   (b) Save the existing relations $R = \{r_{ik} | exists\ GradientAscent(x_{ij}, x_{k,j+1})\}$
4. By concatenating related relations R, pipes P are build.
5. Each pipe contains the Gaussian curvature of each point that conform it.
6. Finally, interest points are selected as the local maxima along pipes P.

4   Experimental Results

IR images are thermal images that contain a high signal to noise ratio and a lack of contrast, so blurred images are obtained. We have compared our method with four typical interest point detectors that have proved, accordingly to literature, that produce good results in feature extraction tasks: LoG[1], DoG[2], Harris-Laplace[3] and Hessian-Laplace[3].

The experimental results are obtained using an IR database that contains 198 car images. Car images are distributed in 4 classes (4 car models) with 5 different views (rear, rear-lateral, lateral , frontal-lateral and frontal). In Fig. 3 is shown a subset of images of the database.

Fig. 3. Example of database images

To perform a good comparison between the detectors, the same scales have been used to construct the scale-space. Specifically, in this example we have used 12 scales and a scale factor of 1.25. The mean size of car images is 236 x 143 pixels.

To evaluate the detectors an entropy criterion has been used because of it measures the disorder of a local region, so, it is a good measure of discrimination. Thus, entropy allow to perform a non-typical analysis of interest points detected.

In Table 1 is shown that our detector (ToDB) outperforms all the other detectors in terms of discrimination, even DoG. Specifically, our method outperforms in 186% the discrimination of the mean entropy value of all the feasible interest points that could be found on an image. Oddly, Hessian-Laplace and LoG obtain a smaller entropy than all the feasible interest points. An explanation could be the noise sensitivity of these detectors. ToDB avoid the noise sensitivity problem thanks to the trajectories. The trajectories, that force a continuity of each blob along the scales, make a selection of the stable blobs.

Another interesting result, although expected, is that DoG find quite good interest points in front of LoG, Hessian-Laplace or Harris-Laplace. The main idea of DoG is obtaining discriminative regions having in account only the neighborhood information, in Table 1 we have shown that using a high level information as trajectories it is possible to improve its results(ToDB discrimination is a 42% higher than DoG discrimination).

LoG, Hessian-Laplace or Harris-Laplace detectors are more oriented to obtain lots of interest points leaving discrimination in a second term. A typical analysis for these detectors is the repeatability [3]. We have done a very simple comparison of the analyzed detectors on the boat images of [3]. The results show that LoG, Hessian-Laplace and Harris-Laplace obtain very high levels of repeatability (50%-70%) while DoG and ToDB obtain levels around of 35% - 40%.

As a final result, by comparing results shown in Figure 4 seem that ToDB obtains more perceptual interest points than the other ones, even DoG.

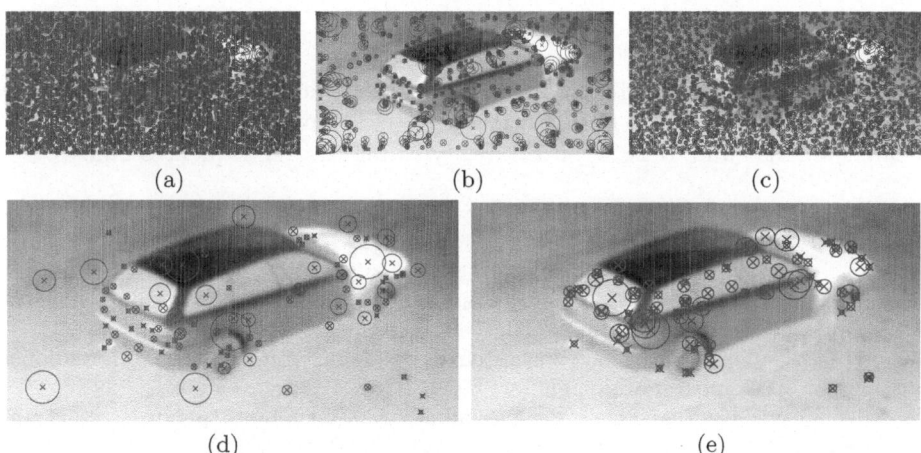

Fig. 4. Example of interest points found using different detectors. (a) Hessian-Laplace (b) Harris-Laplace (c) LoG (d) DoG (e) ToDB.

Table 1. Discrimination index of different detectors

Detector	number of interest points	entropy per interest point	discrimination % taken ToDB as base	outperform (entropy/0.7932)
All points+scale	694384	0.7932	54%	100%
Hessian-Laplace	5077	0.6138	41%	77%
Harris-Laplace	1025	0.9107	62%	115%
LoG	2763	0.7559	51%	95%
DoG	145	1.0410	70%	131%
ToDB	118	1.4764	100%	186%

5   Conclusions

We have presented a powerful mechanism to detect the most stable and discriminative locations of blobs by estimating their trajectories along scales. By means of these trajectories the best locations and scales for each point can easily be selected. Moreover, by using the Gaussian curvature we classify regions on images in a simple way.

By comparing analyzed detectors with our ToDB detector we show that our algorithm outperforms widely all the other ones in function of its discrimination. ToDB opens future research lines around blob trajectories along scales and Gaussian curvature analysis using first and second fundamental forms. Moreover, an extension to the detection of affine blobs could be done by analyzing in depth the normal and geodesic curvature generated around each interest point.

Finally, we want to remark that our detector has been tested mainly on IR images. However, tests done on gray level images have produced similar results.

Acknowledgements

This work was produced thanks to the support of the Universitat Autònoma de Barcelona and the Centro de Investigacion y Desarrollo de la Armada (CIDA). Thanks are also due to Tecnobit S.L. for yielding the car sequences images.

References

1. Lindeberg, T.: Feature detection with automatic scale selection. International Journal on Computer Vision (IJCV) 30, 77–116 (1998)
2. Lowe, D.G.: Distinctive image features from scale-invariant keypoints. International Journal on Computer Vision (IJCV) 60, 91–110 (2004)
3. Mikolajczyk, K., Schmid, C.: Scale & affine invariant interest point detectors. International Journal on Computer Vision (IJCV) 60, 63–86 (2004)
4. Kadir, T., Brady, M.: Saliency, scale and image description. International Journal on Computer Vision (IJCV) 45(2), 83–105 (2001)
5. Matas, J., Chum, O., Urban, M., Pajdla, T.: Robust wide baseline stereo from maximally stable extremal regions. In: British Machine Vision Conference, pp. 384–393 (2002)
6. Bay, H., Ess, A., Tuytelaars, T., Gool, L.J.V.: Speeded-up robust features (surf). Computer Vision and Image Understanding 110(3), 346–359 (2008)
7. Crowley, J.L.: A representation for visual information with application to machine vision. PhD thesis (1982)
8. DoCarmo, M.P.: Differential Geometry of Curves and Surfaces. Prentice-Hall, Englewood Cliffs (1976)
9. Lenz, R.: Group theoretical feature extraction: Weighted invariance and texturle analysis. In: Theory & Applications of Image Analysis: Selected Papers from the 7th Scandinavian Conference on Image Analysis, pp. 63–70 (1992)
10. Mikolajczyk, K., Tuytelaars, T., Schmid, C., Zisserman, A., Matas, J., Schaffalitzky, F., Kadir, T., Van Gool, L.: A comparison of affine region detectors. International Journal on Computer Vision (IJCV) 65, 43–72 (2005)
11. Kadir, T., Zisserman, A., Brady, M.: An affine invariant salient region detector. In: Pajdla, T., Matas, J(G.) (eds.) ECCV 2004. LNCS, vol. 3021, pp. 228–241. Springer, Heidelberg (2004)
12. Lindeberg, T.: Scale-Space Theory in Computer Vision. The International Series in Engineering and Computer Science. Springer, Heidelberg (1993)

Enhancing In-Vitro IVUS Data for Tissue Characterization

Francesco Ciompi[1], Oriol Pujol[1], Oriol Rodriguez Leor[3], Carlo Gatta[2],
Angel Serrano Vida[4], and Petia Radeva[1]

[1] Dep. of Applied Mathematics and Analysis, University of Barcelona, Spain
[2] Computer Vision Center, Campus UAB, Bellaterra, Barcelona, Spain
[3] Hospital Universitari "Germans Trias i Pujol", Badalona, Spain
[4] Hospital General de Granollers, Granollers, Barcelona, Spain
f.ciompi@cvc.uab.es

Abstract. Intravascular Ultrasound (IVUS) data validation is usually
performed by comparing post-mortem (*in-vitro*) IVUS data and corresponding histological analysis of the tissue, obtaining a reliable *ground
truth*. The main drawback of this method is the few number of available study cases due to the complex procedure of histological analysis.
In this work we propose a novel semi-supervised approach to enhance
the *in-vitro* training set by including examples from *in-vivo* coronary
plaques data set. For this purpose, a *Sequential Floating Forward Selection* method is applied on *in-vivo* data and plaque characterization
performances are evaluated by *Leave-One-Patient-Out* cross-validation
technique. Supervised data inclusion improves global classification accuracy from 89.39% to 91.82%.

Keywords: Intravascular Ultrasounds, Plaque characterization, Semi-
supervised learning.

1 Introduction

Coronary plaque rupture is one of the most frequent case of acute coronary
syndromes and it can end in myocardial infarction or sudden cardiac death
[2][8]. An accurate analysis of *in-vivo* plaque composition represents an important task in diagnosis and detection of vulnerable atheroma before plaque
rupture.

IVUS is a powerful imaging technique that gives a detailed cross-sectional
image of the vessel allowing to explore both coronary arteries morphology and
composition. Automatic plaque composition have been performed by texture
analysis on IVUS images [15][17] as well as spectral analysis on raw Radio Frequency (RF) signals [6][11][12][13].

However automatic analysis is hindered by uncontrolled data acquisition with
different imaging system parameters, thus data acquired in different cases are not
comparable.In this work we exploit the RF access to reconstruct IVUS images
with a unique and well controlled parameter set: this process gives us the chance

H. Araujo et al. (Eds.): IbPRIA 2009, LNCS 5524, pp. 241–248, 2009.

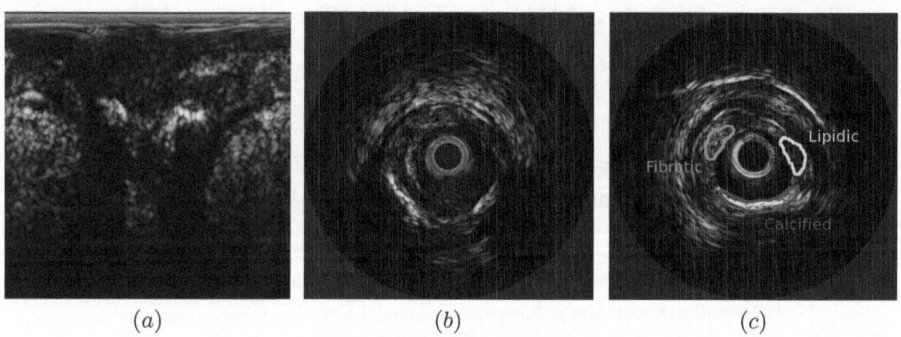

Fig. 1. (a) *In-vivo* IVUS image obtained from RF data and (b) corresponding image in cartesian coordinates; (c) *In-vitro* labeled plaques

to extract normalized features to use in the plaque characterization process, to discriminate among *fibrotic*, *lipidic* and *calcified* tissue.

To achieve a correct IVUS data validation based on tissue-plaque ground truth, a histological analysis of *in-vitro* coronary arteries should be performed. This methodology has the main problem of complicated procedure to obtain *in-vitro* data: scarce artery availability, frequent tissue spoiling during analysis and possible mismatching between IVUS and histological image. As counterpart, provided data are highly reliable. On the other hand, collecting *in-vivo* data is a relatively easy task but the plaques segmentation, performed by expert physicians, cannot be histologically validated.

We propose a method to select plaques from *in-vivo* cases to feed the *in-vitro* training dataset in a supervised manner. The inclusion criterion is based on *Sequential Floating Forward Selection* (SFFS) algorithm [18] and results are computed by *Leave-One-Patient-Out* (LOPO) [4] cross-validation technique. The multiclass classification problem is here solved by adopting the *Error Correcting Output Code* (ECOC) technique [1][7] using AdaBoost on Decision Stumps as basic classifier.

2   Plaque Characterization in Hybrid Data

Since our goal is to fuse *in-vivo* and *in-vitro* data, it is important to consider that the presence of *blood* into *in-vivo* data may modify Ultrasounds response respect to *in-vitro* cases. Our hypothesis is that the two data types could share areas in the feature space, and that *in-vivo* data inclusion, after a proper selection process, could enhance the validated dataset improving classification performances. This fact assumes even more importance since the final application shall detect plaques in *in-vivo* real cases.

Data inclusion process is here formulated as a *semi-supervised learning* problem [20], since *in-vivo* plaques segmentation cannot be validated by histology.

2.1   Data Processing

IVUS RF data (acquired by either *in-vivo* or *in-vitro* cases) are processed to extract textural and spectral features. First, the spatial US attenuation is compensated via *Time Gain Compensation* (TGC). Then the IVUS image is obtained by Band Pass filtering, envelope recovering, normalization, logarithmic compression and Digital Development Process [3]. Classical IVUS image is produced by converting polar data (Figure 1a) in cartesian coordinates (Figure 1b), using linear interpolation and Gaussian smooth filtering.

In order to extract spectral features, we compute the power spectrum by *Auto Regressive Models* (ARM) on the TGC-compensated RF signal. As suggested in [13], the used order is 10. The power spectrum corresponding to each point is then computed by a sliding window as in [3][13]. A typical power spectrum is showed in Figure 2(a).

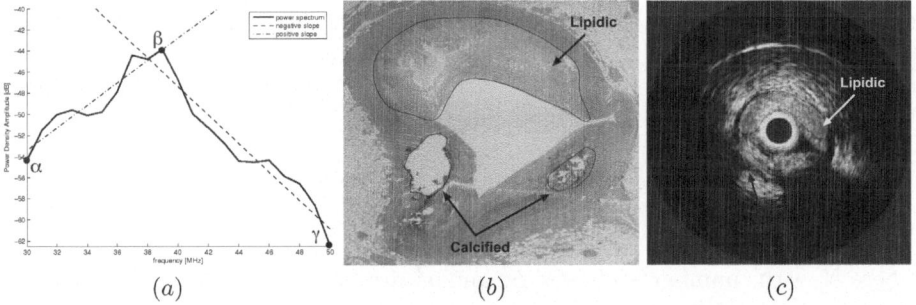

$$(a) \qquad\qquad\qquad (b) \qquad\qquad\qquad (c)$$

Fig. 2. (a) Spectral Features in band B of power spectrum; (b) Atherosclerotic plaques in histological image and (c) corresponding plaques in IVUS image

2.2   Features Extraction

Given the IVUS reconstructed image, we extract a wide set of visual features by applying Gabor filters, Local Binary Patterns and by computing the shading of the polar image, as in [3].

Given the central frequency of the catheter $f_C = 40$ MHz, we consider a 10 MHz band-side, limiting the spectral information to a band $B \in [f_L, f_H]$ ($f_L = 30$ MHz, $f_H = 50$ MHz). Being $S(f)$ the power spectrum function and defining $f_{MAX} = \arg\max_{f \in B}(S(f))$, we compute the straight lines fitting the curves in $[\alpha, \beta]$ and $[\beta, \gamma]$ (Figure 2(a)) and extract corresponding slopes and y-axis-intercept values. We also extract: $S(f_{MAX})$, $S(f_L)$, $S(f_H)$, $S(0)$ values and two other global measures: the *energy of A-line* and the *averaged amplitude of spectral component in B*.

The final feature vector is constructed concatenating textural and spectral features thus providing a description of both spatial and spectral IVUS data.

2.3   Enhancing In-Vitro Data for Tissue Characterization

Sequential Floating Forward Selection has been proposed in [18] as a sub-optimal features selection algorithm. In our case the problem can be formulated as follow: let us call $X = \{x_1, \ldots, x_N\}$ the final training set, initially formed only by plaques from *in-vitro* cases, $Y = \{y_1, \ldots, y_m\}$ the set of frames of *in-vivo* plaques and J_k a parameter related to the classification performance at iteration k.

The algorithm individually includes *in-vivo* plaques from frames $y \in Y$ into the set X while J increases. If $J_{k^*} < J_{k^*-1}$, already added plaques are temporary rested, one by one with re-insertion, and J is computed again. A combination of plaques returning a higher J is kept and temporary rested plaques are permanently discarded. The algorithm stops when $Y = \{\emptyset\}$ or when a certain number K of maximum iterations is reached.

In our method, J is defined as the weighted sensitivity over classes, to avoid the algorithm to improve (or keep constant) global classification quality by growing in sensitivity for some classes while getting worse other classes. For this reason, each weight is inversely proportional to the sensitivity of each class computed at the actual algorithm step k. In this way the class penalized at current iteration will have more weight at next step:

$$J_k = \sum_{l=1}^{N_c} w_k^l S_k^l,$$

where N_c is the number of classes, S_k^l and w_k^l are the sensitivity and the weighting of class l at iteration k, defined as

$$w_k^l = \frac{log\left(\frac{1}{S_k^l}\right)}{\sum_{l=1}^{N_c} log\left(\frac{1}{S_k^l}\right)}.$$

3   Experimental Results

Data acquisition. The IVUS equipment used in this work is a *Galaxy II IVUS Imaging System* (Boston Scientific) with a catheter *Atlantis SR Pro 40 MHz* (Boston Scientific), installed in the Hospital "*Germans Trias i Pujol*" of Badalona (Spain). RF data are collected using a *12-bit Acquiris acquisition card* ($f_s = 200MHz$). In this work we used a rotational catheter, generating 256 A-lines of 1024 samples each one.

In-vivo data are extracted during an hemodynamic intervention procedure. Once the procedure is over an *IVUS Pullback* is acquired by storing data while the probe is *pulled-back* at constant speed[1]. The result is a sequence of images describing the cross-sectional vessel structure in which *in-vivo* plaques can be

---

[1] The catheter is connected to the IVUS equipment by a motorized tool and its position is constantly monitored by X-ray analysis.

labeled by expert physicians according on their professional experience. *In-vivo* data have been taken from 9 patients, plaques have been labeled by two expert physicians resulting in 49 *fibrotic*, 37 *lipidic* and 35 *calcified*: only regions in which both physicians agreed have been considered.

In-vitro data are extracted from a *post-mortem* case. The artery, separated from the heart, is first fixed on a mid-soft plane and filled (by a catheter) with physiological saline solution at constant pressure (around 120 $mmHg$), simulating blood pressure. The probe is then introduced and RF data are acquired in correspondence of plaques: the sampled position is marked on the external part of the artery as reference for histological analysis. When the acquisition is over, the artery can be studied by histological analysis. Observed plaques are then labeled in the corresponding IVUS images. *In-vitro* data have been extracted from 9 *ex-vivo* cases with 26 *fibrotic*, 14 *lipidic* and 31 *calcified* plaques.

Validation methodology. The *in-vitro* data set, enhanced by *in-vivo* selected data, is used to train an Adaboost classifier with up to 50 Decision Stumps [4], in the multiclass framework of Error Correcting Output Codes [1][7] parameterized using a *one-versus-one* coding with Euclidean decoding [5]. Classification performances - plaque sensitivity S and global accuracy A - are evaluated using the *Leave-One-Patient-Out* cross validation technique. Let us call N_p the number of clinical cases: to cross-validate the method, the training set is built taking at each time all *in-vivo* selected frames and all *in-vitro* cases, except one, used as test. The process is repeated N_p times and the confusion matrix C_k is computed at each round k to evaluate classification performance parameters. Global results are computed by averaging the N_p folds.

In our study the amount of *in-vivo* data included in the *in-vitro* dataset is varied from 10% up to 50%. Further inclusion is avoided for the sake of the training set consistency. Including more than 50% in fact could affect too much the validated dataset.

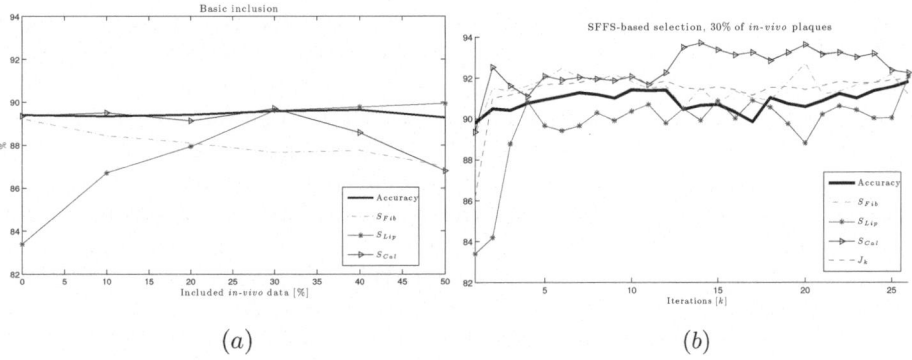

(a)   *(b)*

Fig. 3. (a) Basic-inclusion and (b) SFFS-based inclusion results

Comparisons. The *in-vivo/in-vitro* IVUS data fusion is a novel technique. As such, there are no related methods that directly address this problem. Thus, we compare the method with two plausible approaches. The first one is a *basic inclusion* of the whole *in-vivo* into the *in-vitro* dataset, according to labels given by physicians, at different percentages.

Since the idea of the SFFS-based data fusion is close to the *semi-supervised* learning, the second approach consists in defining an extended training set using the labels provided by means of the *Low Density Separation* (LDS) [19] tecnique. Based on cluster assumption, it essentially trains a *Transductive Support Vector Machine* (TSVM) by gradient descent on a graph-distance derived kernel. The graph is constructed by assigning to each edge a weight given by the Euclidean distance with each other feature point. The main idea is that two points in the same cluster present a continuous connecting curve passing through regions of high density, while two points of different clusters are connected with curves traversing a density valley. The similarity of two points is then defined by maximizing over all continuous connecting curves the minimum density along the connection. MATLAB implementation[2] of the method has been used in this paper.

Both *in-vitro* and *in-vivo* data have been used to construct the distance graph and the TSVM has been trained. *In-vivo* points are added (30%) to the training set according to classification results and performances have been computed by means of the *Leave-One-Patient-Out*. LDS parameters have been set as $(C, \rho) = (850, 0.05)$ by cross-validation.

Figure 3(a) shows the performance measures using *basic inclusion*. Observe that the sensitivity for the lipidic class and global accuracy increase with the amount of *in-vivo* data. However, the classification of *fibrotic* and *calcified* class is poorer. Note that the best performance is achieved when the amount of new included data is around 30%.

Figure 3(b), show the sensitivities and global accuracy for the SFFS-based inclusion method as described in section 2.3 (*in-vivo* plaques are included in the *in-vitro* training set according to segmentation of physicians). The curves in the figure are shown up to the iteration 26, where maximum accuracy is achieved. We can observe how, given initial conditions, plaque sensitivity measure increases up to a stable condition. Note that the lipidic class characterization performance, the most critical one at the initial point, grows as new plaques are added. Different percentages have been tested and 30% resulted to perform better. Observe that the same result is also reported in basic-inclusion approach.

Finally, Table 1 reports classification accuracy and sensitivity for the analyzed approaches, compared with the initial case (*NI*). The *basic-inclusion* only reports poor and unpredictable improvements, mainly due to the unsupervised nature of the data inclusion. The *LDS-based* method (LDS) only results in an improvement in the lipidic class sensitivity. This behavior can be explained by the fact that LDS looks for a minimum density path to cluster data. Since the lipidic plaque is underrepresented in the training set, the improvement in the corresponding

---

[2] http://www.kyb.tuebingen.mpg.de/bs/people/chapelle/lds/

Table 1. Performance of analyzed methods

	NI	BI	LDS	SFFS
A	89.39% (7.33)	89.57% (5.82)	84.96% (7.86)	**91.82% (4.60)**
S_{fib}	89.22% (9.38)	87.66% (8.58)	87.68% (9.53)	**91.73% (7.52)**
S_{lip}	83.38% (14.21)	89.61% (10.86)	89.87% (13.19)	**92.54% (10.51)**
S_{cal}	89.35% (12.85)	89.70% (9.33)	75.98% (22.39)	**92.37% (3.19)**

sensitivity is expected. However, this improvement comes at the cost of hindering *calcified* and *fibrotic* performaces. The proposed *SFFS-based* approach improved all performance parameters of all the classes and outperforms other approaches in all the cases.

4   Conclusions

A framework for IVUS image reconstruction and power spectrum computation from raw radio frequency data extracted and validated from *in-vitro* cases has been presented as well as both textural and spectral features extraction process for robust tissue characterization.

In-vivo data acquisition process has been described and feature extraction has been performed.

It has been demonstrated that the inclusion of selected *in-vivo* data in the *in-vitro* training set by means of SFFS-based method improves both individual sensitivities and overall accuracy.

It has been also showed that the basic formulation of LDS algorithm is not useful to solve our problem, since the cluster assumption seems to be not appropriate to our dataset.

Given the promising results of SFFS-based algorithm, it is worth to study more in depth its potentials by including different classifiers and by comparing it with more semi-supervised learning methods.

Acknowledgment

This work was supported in part by a research grant from projects TIN2006-15308-C02, FIS-PI061290, MI1509-2005 and CONSOLIDER - INGENIO 2010 (CSD2007-00018).

References

1. Allwein, E.L., et al.: Reducing multiclass to binary: A unifying approach for margin classifier. Journal of Machine Learning Research 1, 113–141 (2000)
2. Burke, A.P., et al.: Coronary risk factors and plaque morphology in men with coronary disease who died suddenly. The New England Journal of Medicine 336(18), 1276–1282 (1997)

3. Caballero, K.L., et al.: Using Reconstructed IVUS images for Coronary Plaque Classification. In: Proceedings of the 29th Annual International Conference of the IEEE EMBS
4. Caballero, K.L.: Coronary Plaque Classification Using Intravascular Ultrasound Images and Radio Frequency Signals. Universitat Autónoma de Barcelona (2007)
5. Caballero, K.L., Barajas, J., Pujol, O., Salvatella, N., Radeva, P.I.: In-Vivo IVUS Tissue Classification: A Comparison Between RF Signal Analysis and Reconstructed Image. In: Martínez-Trinidad, J.F., Carrasco Ochoa, J.A., Kittler, J. (eds.) CIARP 2006. LNCS, vol. 4225, pp. 137–146. Springer, Heidelberg (2006)
6. DeMaria, A.N., et al.: Imaging vulnerable plaque by ultrasound. Journal of the American College of Cardiology 47(8), C32–C39 (2006)
7. Dietterich, T.G., Bakiri, G.: Solving multiclass learning problems via error-correcting output codes. Journal of Artificial Intelligence Research 2, 263–286 (1995)
8. Ehara, S., et al.: Spotty calcification typifies the culprit plaque in patients with acute myocardial infarction: An intravascular ultrasound study. Circulation 110, 3424–3429 (2004)
9. Filho, E.D., et al.: A study on intravascular ultrasound image processing (2005)
10. Friedman, J., Hastie, T., Tibshirani, R.: Additive logistic regression: a statistical view of boosting. Annals of Statistics 28(2000) (2000)
11. Moore, M.P., et al.: Characterization of coronary atherosclerotic morphology by spectral analysis of radiofrequency signal: in vitro intravascular ultrasound study with histological and radiological validation. Heart 79, 459–467 (1998)
12. Murashige, A., et al.: Detection of lipid-laden atherosclerotic plaque by wavelet analysis of radiofrequency intravascular ultrasound signals. Journal of the American College of Cardiology 45(12), 1954–1960 (2005)
13. Nair, A., et al.: Coronary plaque classification with intravascular ultrasound radiofrequency data analysis. Circulation 106, 2200–2206 (2002)
14. Proakis, J., Rader, C., Ling, F., Nikias, C.: Advanced Digital Signal Processing. Mc.Millan, NYC (1992)
15. Pujol, O.: A Semi-Supervised Statistical Framework and Generative Snakes for IVUS Analysis. Universitat Autónoma de Barcelona (2004)
16. Schapire, R.E.: The boosting approach to machine learning: An overview (2002)
17. Zhang, X., McKay, C.R., Sonka, M.: Tissue characterization in intravascular ultrasound images. IEEE Transaction on Medical Imaging 17(6), 889–899 (1998)
18. Pudil, P., Ferri, F.J., Kittler, J.: Floating search methods for feature selection with nonmonotonic criterion functions. IAPR, 279–283 (1994)
19. Chapelle, O., Zien, A.: Semi-Supervised Classification by Low Density Separation. In: Proceedings of the Tenth International Workshop on Artificial Intelligence and Statistics, pp. 57–64 (2005)
20. Zhu, X.: Semi-supervised learning literature survey. Computer Sciences Technical Report TR 1530, University of Wisconsin-Madison (2008)

Toward Robust Myocardial Blush Grade Estimation in Contrast Angiography

Carlo Gatta[1], Juan Diego Gomez Valencia[1], Francesco Ciompi[1],
Oriol Rodriguez Leor[2], and Petia Radeva[1]

[1]Computer Vision Center, Campus UAB, Edifici O, 08193, Bellaterra,
Barcelona, Spain
cgatta@cvc.uab.es
[2]Unitat d'hemodinàmica cardíaca hospital universitari Germans Trias i Pujol
Badalona, Spain

Abstract. The assessment of Myocardial Blush Grade after primary angioplasty is a precious diagnostic tool to understand if the patient needs further medication or the use of specifics drugs. Unfortunately, the assessment of MBG is difficult for non highly specialized staff. Experimental data show that there is poor correlation between MBG assessment of low and high specialized staff, thus reducing its applicability. This paper proposes a method able to achieve an objective measure of MBG, or a set of parameters that correlates with the MBG. The method tracks the blush area starting from just one single frame tagged by the physician. As a consequence, the blush area is kept isolated from contaminating phenomena such as diaphragm and arteries movements. We also present a method to extract four parameters that are expected to correlate with the MBG. Preliminary results show that the method is capable of extracting interesting information regarding the behavior of the myocardial perfusion.

Keywords: Medical Imaging, Tracking, Optical Flow, Myocardial perfusion, Myocardial Blush Grade, Primary Angioplasty.

1   Introduction

Primary angioplasty is the most effective way to re-establish a normal flow in an obstructed artery after an acute myocardial infarction. This medical intervention aims at recover a proper coronary flow into the obstructed artery. Physicians localize the artery by visual inspection of a contrast angiography. However, even in a successful primary angioplasty, it can happen that an adequate irrigation on the area subtended by the affected artery is not optimal. In this area, the microcirculation could be not sufficient even after a successful primary angioplasty, thus compromising in a serious way the long term patient survival [1].

The physicians are able to ascertain with enough precision if the normal flow in the unblocked artery has been really recovered by observing pre and post intervention angiographies. To do this, physicians inject a contrast liquid into the

H. Araujo et al. (Eds.): IbPRIA 2009, LNCS 5524, pp. 249–256, 2009.
© Springer-Verlag Berlin Heidelberg 2009

artery that is visible in the x-ray angiography. A major difficult arises when medical doctors try to determinate if the myocardial perfusion has been recovered in a sufficient way or not. The different levels of myocardial perfusion have been standardized using a subjective score called Myocardial Blush Grade (MBG) [1]. The evaluation of the MBG requires the visual assessment of the contrast liquid quantity in the area subtended by the infarcted artery. The assessment of myocardial blush grade is a very difficult task which requires medical doctors with high expertise and training. Only expert medical doctors achieve an observer agreement and a low variability between subjective judgments [2]. The MBG helps to diagnose critical situations that prompt the use of specific drugs and medications [3]. An adequate estimate of the myocardial blush grade can be useful to improve the prognosis of the coronary patients due to its impact on the long term morbidity and mortality [4,5]. Moreover it can be useful for researchers in testing innovative pharmacological approaches and study of new invasive procedures for the myocardial perfusion treatment. In this paper we present and discuss a computer vision methodology for Myocardial Blush Grade **objective** measurement with the aim of creating a tool able to assess the MBG in a semi-automatic way.

2   Previous Work

At the best of our knowledge, only one paper on MBG estimation by means of computer vision has been published. The work in [6] calculates objective descriptors of myocardium staining pattern in order to define an objective score of the myocardial perfusion. The method analyzes image local statistics and tries to discriminate among different phenomena observed in the angiography. The phenomena present in the contrast angiography (contaminating the myocardial perfusion signal) are: x-ray noise, breathing (diaphragm movement) and heartbeat (arteries movement). The method in [6] aims at separate these phenomena by sampling the average gray-scale value of 4 different squares in the angiography video. One square is placed on the blush area, another on a boundary of the diaphragm, the third on a artery and the last one on a noisy area where no other signals are present. In our opinion, the method has several flaws. Firstly, the average gray-scale level measurement is prone to mix different phenomena if the four squares are placed inaccurately; this requires that the user checks the squares positions along the whole video. This tedious procedure cannot be used in real clinic cases and it affects importantly the repeatability of the method. Secondly, the estimation of the MBG is based on spectral analysis on a predefined set of frequency ranges selected with the aim of separate each phenomenon. While this could be reasonable for the diaphragm movement, artery movement and noise, where the signal is expected to be periodic, it is somehow incorrect for the analysis of microcirculation opacity, that is expected to vary in a non periodic way.

3   Proposed Method

The proposed method requires that the physician selects the blush area. Then the method, using an optical flow technique, tracks the blush area during the whole video. On the other side, a simple technique is used to detect the contrast liquid into vessels. This detection is necessary to discard the image pixels that describe the macro-circulation into the arteries, while keeping the information regarding the microcirculation. Once the pixels representing the blush area (but without the vessels) are computed, the method measure the opacity variation by means of the gray level variation during the video. Finally, the method extracts relevant parameters that summarize the behavior of myocardial microcirculation.

3.1   Detection of the Blush Area

Selecting the right blush area into a contrast angiography sequence is a complex task. Physicians must look at the angiography several times to determine the blush area and select the best angiographic projection. For this reason, we do not propose any methodology aimed at automatically detect the blush area. The physician is asked to tag the blush area on only one frame of the angiography sequence (Figure 1 shows an example of tagged blush area).

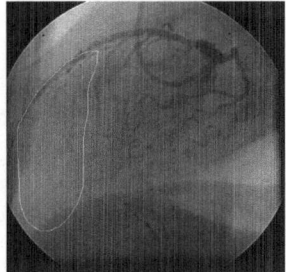

Fig. 1. Frame of the angiography sequence with the blush area duly demarcated by a physician

3.2   Tracking by Optical Flow

To estimate the apparent motion of objects in the angiography video, we use the optical flow technique described in [7]. Using the optical flow technique, we can calculate the displacement field in the angiography (see Figure 2 for an example). Despite the x-ray noise in the angiography video we noticed that the optical flow estimates the diaphragm and heart movements in a consistent way. In this way, we can estimate the position of the blush area on all the frames in the angiography starting from the frame tagged by the physician. This tracking permits to avoid that the diaphragm and coronary artery can enter the blush

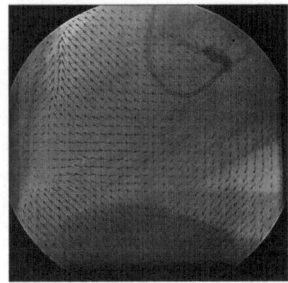

Fig. 2. An example of displacement field obtained using the optical flow technique

area thus corrupting the measurement of blush area opacity. As a consequence, our approach does not have to discriminate between different phenomena using a spectral analysis method on different signals. Moreover, performing the measurement from a wider area (with respect of a small fixed square) gives a more reliable signal that is also less prone to errors induced by the x-ray noise. However, up to now, one limitation of the proposed methods is that the tagged frame should present a blush area isolated from the diaphragm (see Fig. 1). In this unwanted case, the optical flow cannot detect the movement at the blush area boundary because it is located in the internal part of the diaphragm where the apparent movement is almost null.

3.3   Vessel Detection

The vessel detection has been devised using gray-scale morphology. We create a map $M_t(x, y)$ to highlight the vessels as following:

$$M_t(x, y) = (I_t \bullet SE)(x, y) - I_t(x, y) \tag{1}$$

where '$\bullet$' is the gray-scale closing operator and SE is a flat structuring element, more precisely a disk of 8 pixels radius. After this, we define the set $V(t)$ of pixels belonging to a vessel at frame t as following:

$$V(t) = \{(x, y) \mid M_t(x, y) > thr, (x, y) \in \mathcal{I}\} \tag{2}$$

where $\mathcal{I}$ is the spatial support of the image $I_t(x, y)$ and thr is a threshold parameter. The setting of the threshold thr has been done using the method in [8]. An example of this procedure is shown in Figure 3. This vessel detection method is sufficiently accurate. However, the results are not completely satisfactory, thus this point will be further investigated in future papers.

3.4   Measuring Opacity in the Blush Area

After obtaining a good estimation of the blush area on each frame of the video, we can estimate its opacity. The increase of the opacity in the blush area is

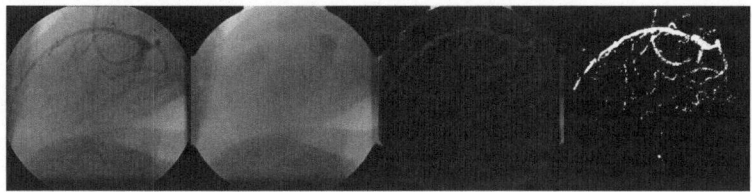

Fig. 3. From left to right: an input frame I_t, the closing of the input image with the structuring element SE, the map $M_t(x, y)$ and finally the map of detected pixels in the set $V(t)$

caused by the flooding of the contrast liquid in the microcirculation. Measuring this opacity is an indirect way to measure how much of the contrast liquid reached the microcirculation thus it is an indirect way to measure the blush grade. Intuitively, the lower the gray value in the angiography, the higher the opacity. We describe the gray-scale value of a frame at time t and at pixel position (x, y) as $I_t(x, y)$. Being $\Omega(t)$ the set of pixels inside the estimated blush area at the frame t, we compute the average gray-scale $g(t)$ during the whole angiography video as following:

$$g(t) = \frac{1}{|\Omega(t) \setminus V(t)|} \sum_{(x,y) \in \Omega(t) \setminus V(t)} I_t(x, y) \qquad (3)$$

The average gray-scale value is computed using the set of pixels in the blush area ($\Omega(t)$) that not belongs to vessels ($V(t)$). This measurement can vary importantly if the settings of the x-ray machine are changed. As an example, if the contrast of the image is enhanced, the variation of $g(t)$ will be higher than in a case in which the x-ray image has a lower contrast. Moreover, the contrast can change during the angiography. We thus compute the standard deviation of the image gray-scale values during the whole video:

$$\sigma(t) = \sqrt{\frac{1}{N} \sum_{(x,y) \in \mathcal{I}} (I_t(x, y) - \overline{I_t})^2} \qquad (4)$$

where N is the number of image pixels and $\overline{I_t}$ is the average gray-scale value of the frame at time t. Finally, we define the normalized gray-scale blush area signal as:

$$ng(t) = g(t)/\sigma(t) \qquad (5)$$

3.5 Extraction of Blush Parameters

In an ideal case, if the medical doctor does not inject the contrast liquid, our measurement $ng(t)$ should be constant. When the medical doctor injects the contrast liquid, in cases in which the microcirculation is sufficiently good, we expect the opacity to increase temporarily and then return to its previous value (when the contrast liquid is not present anymore). This expectation translates to a temporal decrease of the average gray-scale value, followed by an increase to the initial value. Figure 4 (a) shows the ideal expected behavior. Then the question is: how to extract the useful information from $ng(t)$ to infer the MBG? To this aim we describe the expected ideal signal as following:

$$i(t) = k - a \cdot \exp\left(-\frac{(t - t_G)^2}{2\sigma_G^2}\right) \tag{6}$$

where k represents the constant gray-scale value if no contrast liquid is injected; a represents the peak amplitude of the Gaussian, thus the peak of the opacity during the video; t_G represents the center of the Gaussian, thus providing the instant in which the opacity is maximal; finally, σ_G represents the temporal extent of the Gaussian, thus providing information on the duration of the contrast liquid flooding in the microcirculation. Once we obtain the signal $ng(t)$ (as in Figure 4 (c)) we can estimate the parameters by minimizing the L^2 norm between $ng(t)$ and $i(t)$ as following:

$$\{k, a, t_G, \sigma_G\} = \arg\min_{k,a,t_G,\sigma_G} ||i(t) - ng(t)|| \tag{7}$$

Since this minimization requires a non-linear regression [9], the parameter initialization is important. A bad parameter initialization can lead the minimization algorithm to fall in a local minima. Thus we set the initial solution as following:

$$k \equiv \mu(ng(t)) \tag{8}$$
$$a \equiv \mu(ng(t)) - \min_t(ng(t)) \tag{9}$$
$$t_G \equiv \arg\min_t(ng(t)) \tag{10}$$

where $\mu(\cdot)$ is the average operator. Fortunately, once set the above defined three parameters, the standard deviation σ_G is not critical for the convergence of the minimization algorithm to the global minima in equation (7). Figure 4 (d) shows the fitting for the signal in Figure 4 (c); in this case the resulting fitting parameters are $k = 1.35$, $a = 0.13$, $t_G = 2.5s$ and $\sigma_G = 1.17s$.

4   Preliminary Results

To show the advantage of a tracking method for measuring the blush area opacity, in Figure 4(b) we plot the mean gray level temporal variation calculated on the blush area but without applying any optical flow technique. Figure 4(c) shows the measurement obtained for the same video, same blush area, but adapting the blush area during the video according the optical flow based tracking.It is clearly visible that, thanks to the tracking, the artifact induced by the diaphragm movement (which period is of $2.6s$ approximately) has been completely removed while small oscillations are still present, probably due to contrast liquid flow in a vessel inside the blush area that has not been properly detected.

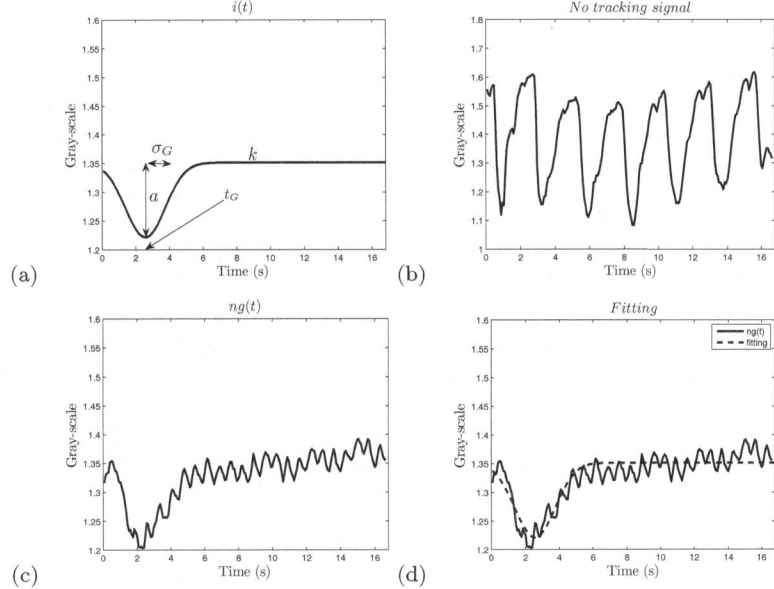

Fig. 4. Gray level variation curve as a descriptor of myocardial staining during an angiography: (a) ideal (b) static blush zone (c) adaptable blush zone using optical flow and (d) curve fitting

5 Conclusion and Future Works

In this paper we proposed a methodology to measure the blush area opacity. To this aim we track the blush area during the video by using an optical flow technique. The vessels are detected and removed not to influence the measurement of microcirculation. This detection has been performed using gray-scale morphology operators. The measured signal is then approximated using a predefined model which parameters summarize the behavior of the contrast liquid in the microcirculation. As above discussed, this paper shows very preliminary results of our research. Future works encompass: (1) the validation of the fitting model and, if necessary, its extension to a more powerful model; (2) the analysis of the correlation between the model parameters and the MBG on a large set of clinical cases; (3) the development of a method to detect and track the diaphragm with the aim of extending the level of automation of the method and, at the same time, increasing the robustness of the whole methodology; (4) refining the vessel detection using more performing algorithms and exploiting the temporal coherence using the displacement field to improve vessel detection.

Acknowledgments

This research is/was supported in part by the projects TIN2006-15308-C02, FIS PI061290, CONSOLIDER-INGENIO 2010 (CSD2007-00018), MI 1509/2005.

References

1. van't Hof, A.W., Liem, A., Suryapranata, H., Hoorntje, J.C., de Boer, M.J., Zijlstra, F.: Angiographic assessment of myocardial reperfusion in patients treated with primary angioplasty for acute myocardial infarction: myocardial blush grade. zwolle myocardial infarction study group. Circulation 97(23), 2302–2306 (1998)
2. Bertomeu-González, V., Bodí, V., Sanchis, J., Núñz, J., López-Lereu, M.P., Peña, G., Losada, A., Gómez, C., Chorro, F.J., Llácer, A.: Limitations of myocardial blush grade in the evaluation of myocardial perfusion in patients with acute myocardial infarction and timi 3 grade flow. Rev. Espa. Cardiol. 59, 575–581 (2006)
3. Henriques, J.P.S., Zijlstra, F., van't Hof, A.W.J., de Boer, M.J., Dambrink, J.H.E., Gosselink, M., Hoorntje, J.C.A., Suryapranata, H.: Angiographic assessment of reperfusion in acute myocardial infarction by myocardial blush grade. Circulation 107(16), 2115–2119 (2003)
4. Gibson, C.M., Cannon, C.P., Murphy, S.A., Ryan, K.A., Mesley, R., Marble, S.J., McCabe, C.H., Van De Werf, F., Braunwald, E.: Relationship of timi myocardial perfusion grade to mortality after administration of thrombolytic drugs. Circulation 101(2), 125–130 (2000)
5. Gibson, C.M., Cannon, C.P., Murphy, S.A., Marble, S.J., Barron, H.V., Braunwald, E., Group, T.I.M.I.S.: Relationship of the timi myocardial perfusion grades, flow grades, frame count, and percutaneous coronary intervention to long-term outcomes after thrombolytic administration in acute myocardial infarction. Circulation 105(16), 1909–1913 (2002)
6. Gil, D., Rodriguez-Leor, O., Radeva, P., Mauri, J.: Myocardial perfusion characterization from contrast angiography spectral distribution. IEEE Trans. Med. Imaging 27(5), 641–649 (2008)
7. Black, M.J., Anandan, P.: The robust estimation of multiple motions: parametric and piecewise-smooth flow fields. Comput. Vis. Image Underst. 63(1), 75–104 (1996)
8. Otsu, N.: A threshold selection method from gray-level histograms. IEEE Transactions On Systems, Man, and Cybernetics 9(1), 62–66 (1979)
9. Coleman, T.F., Li, Y.: An interior trust region approach for nonlinear minimization subject to bounds. SIAM Journal on Optimization 6(2), 418–445 (1996)

Multi-spectral Texture Characterisation for Remote Sensing Image Segmentation

Filiberto Pla[1], Gema Gracia[1], Pedro García-Sevilla[1],
Majid Mirmehdi[2], and Xianghua Xie[3]

[1] Dept. Llenguatges i Sistemes Informàtics, University Jaume I, 12071 Castellón, Spain
{pla,ggracia,pgarcia}@lsi.uji.es
[2] Dept. of Computer Science, University of Bristol, Bristol BS8 1UB, UK
majid@compsci.bristol.ac.uk
[3] Dept. of Computer Science, University of Swansea, Swansea SA2 8PP, UK
x.xie@swansea.ac.uk

Abstract. A multi-spectral texture characterisation model is proposed, the Multi-spectral Local Differences Texem – MLDT, as an affordable approach to be used in multi-spectral images that may contain large number of bands. The MLDT is based on the Texem model. Using an inter-scale post-fusion strategy for image segmentation, framed in a multi-resolution approach, we produce un-supervised multi-spectral image segmentations. Preliminary results on several remote sensing multi-spectral images exhibit a promising performance by the MLDT approach, with further improvements possible to model more complex textures and add some other features, like invariance to spectral intensity.

Keywords: Texture analysis, multispectral images, Texems.

1 Introduction

Multi and hyperspectral sensors acquire information in several spectral bands, which generate hyperspectral data in high dimensional spaces. These systems have tradition-ally been used to perform tasks in remote sensing, and are being introduced and developed in other application fields like medical imaging or product quality assess-ment. Multispectral image data are used in order to estimate and analyze the presence of types of vegetation, land, water and other man made objects, or to assess the quan-tity of substances, chemical compounds, or physical parameters, e.g. temperature, providing a qualitative and quantitative evaluation of those features.

Standard multispectral image interpretation techniques barely exploit the spectral-spatial relationships in the image. The multi-spectral image data is basically treated as a set of independent spectral measurements at each pixel location, without taking into account their spatial relations. In order to exploit hyper-spectral imagery in applica-tions requiring high spatial resolution, e.g., urban land-cover mapping, crops and vegetation mapping, tissues structure identification, it is necessary to incorporate spatial [1], contextual [2] and texture information in the multi-spectral image classifi-cation and segmentation processes.

H. Araujo et al. (Eds.): IbPRIA 2009, LNCS 5524, pp. 257–264, 2009.
© Springer-Verlag Berlin Heidelberg 2009

To the best of our knowledge, there are no texture characterisation methods for mutispectral images with high number of bands. Such methods are unaffordable to be used directly in gray level and colour images due to the increase of dimensionality in texture characterisation. Multi-band images techniques have been traditionally restricted to three-band colour images, by processing each channel independently, taking into account spatial interactions only within each channel [3]. Other approaches decompose the colour image into luminance and chromatic channels, extracting texture features from the luminance channel [4]. There are works that try to combine spatial interaction within each channel and interaction between spectral channels, applying gray level texture techniques to each channel independently [5], or using 3D colour histograms as a way to combine information from all colour channels [6].

Another group of techniques try to extract correlation features between the channels for colour texture analysis, like in [7], where spatial and spectral interactions are simultaneously handled. Such techniques assume the image to be a collection of epitomic primitives, and the neighbourhood of a central pixel to be statistically conditionally independent. A more recent approach based on these premises is the Texem model [8], consisting of a Gaussian mixture model representation for colour images using conditional dependency in neighbouring and cross-channels information. The gray level Texem model assumes spatial conditional dependency within the pixel neighbourhood. The Texem model will be the basis of the work presented in this paper for texture characterisation in multispectral images.

2 The Texem Model

The Texem model [8] is a texture characterisation method that models the image as a generative process where a set of image primitives generate the image by superposition of image patches from a number of texture exemplars, Texems.

This generative model uses a Gaussian mixture to obtain the Texems that have generated an image. The Texems are derived from image patches that may be of any size and shape. In this work, square image patches of size $N = n \times n$ have been considered. The image I is decomposed as a set of $Z = \{Z_i\}_{i=1}^{P}$ patches, each one belonging to any of K possible Texems, $T = \{t_k\}_{k=1}^{K}$. A patch vector at a central pixel location i is defined as $Z_i = (g_{i1}, \ldots g_{iN})$, with the gray level values $g_{ij} = I(x_{ij}, y_{ij})$ at pixel locations $ij = i1, \ldots, iN$ in the patch grid. Each Texem is modelled as a Gaussian distribution, therefore, given the kth Texem t_k, the likelihood of a patch Z_i is expressed as a Normal distribution

$$p(Z_i \mid t_k, \theta_k) = G(Z_i; \mu_k, \Sigma_k) \tag{1}$$

where $\theta_k = (\alpha_k, \mu_k, \Sigma_k)$ is the parameter set defining the Gaussian in a mixture, with the prior probability α_k, mean μ_k and covariance Σ_k, constrained to $\sum_{k=1}^{K} \alpha_k = 1$.

Given a set of sample patches extracted from an image, the generative Gaussian Mixture model of the K Texems that generated that image can be estimated by the Expectation Maximisation (EM) algorithm [9]. Thus, the probability density function of any image patch Z_i will be given by the Gaussian mixture model,

$$p(Z_i \mid \alpha) = \sum_{m=1}^{K} \alpha_m \, p(Z_i \mid t_m, \theta_m) \tag{2}$$

A straightforward way to extend the gray level Texem model to colour images would be consider instead of the image patch $Z_i = (g_{i1}, \ldots g_{iN})$ of N pixel values in a monochrome image, an image patch at pixel i in a three band colour image, e.g. an RGB image, as $Z_i = (g_{i1}^{R}, \ldots g_{iN}^{R}, g_{i1}^{G}, \ldots g_{iN}^{G}, g_{i1}^{B}, \ldots g_{iN}^{B})$. This increases the feature patch dimensionality in a proportional way with respect to the number of bands. In order to avoid the increase in dimensionality of the generative Texem model for colour images, the pixels $i=1,\ldots,N$ within the patch are assumed to be statistically independent within the Texem, with each pixel value following a Gaussian distribution in the colour space [8]. Thus, now the likelihood of a patch Z_i given the kth Texem t_k is expressed as a joint likelihood of the N pixels belonging to the patch, that is,

$$p(Z_i \mid t_k, \theta_k) = \prod_{j=1}^{N} G(Z_{j,i}; \mu_{j,k}, \Sigma_{j,k}) \tag{3}$$

where now the kth Texem parameters $\theta_k = (\mu_{1,k}, \Sigma_{1,k}, \ldots, \mu_{N,k}, \Sigma_{N,k})$ are the mean $\mu_{j,k}$ and covariance $\Sigma_{j,k}$ of the $j=1,\ldots,N$ pixels in the Texem grid. The mean $\mu_{j,k}$ and the covariance $\Sigma_{j,k}$ of each pixel are now defined in the colour space.

3   Segmentation with Inter-scale Post-fusion

In general, to model the texture features of an image appropriately, several Texem sizes are needed. Alternatively, instead of using different Texem sizes to characterise the set of patches that may generate an image, the same Texem size can be used in a multiresolution scheme, assuming each resolution level is generated from a Texem set independently [10]. However, applying multi-resolution to image segmentation needs a fusion process in order to integrate the information across the different image resolution levels, from coarser to finer levels. We follow this approach in this paper.

4   Multi-spectral Local Difference Texems - MLDT

The colour Texem model described in section 2.2 can be easily extended from colour images, usually represented by 3 bands, to any number of bands B. However, multi and hyper-spectral images may contain order of hundred bands to represent each pixel location. This will lead to the estimation of the Gaussian mixtures in very high dimensional spaces, involving more computational complexity issues and to the so-called curse of dimensionality, when having a limited number of samples to estimate the Gaussian mixtures. In order to cope with such a high dimensionality problem, each image patch $\mathbf{Z}_i$ at a pixel location i in a multi-spectral image I with B bands will be defined as follows,

$$\mathbf{Z}_i = (\bar{g}_{i1},...\bar{g}_{iB},d(\mathbf{g}_{i1},\bar{\mathbf{g}}),...,d(\mathbf{g}_{iN},\bar{\mathbf{g}})) \tag{4}$$

where $\bar{g}_{ib}$ is defined as

$$\bar{g}_{ib} = \frac{1}{N}\sum_{j=1}^{N} g_{ijb}; \quad b=1,...,B$$

denoting the mean value of the N pixels in the image patch grid for each band $b=1,...,B$; and

$$d(\mathbf{g}_{ij},\bar{\mathbf{g}}_i) = \frac{1}{B}\sum_{b=1}^{B}|\bar{g}_{ib} - g_{ijb}|; \quad j=1,...,N$$

is the $L1$ norm of the spectral differences between pixels $j=1,...N$ in the image patch $\mathbf{Z}_i$ at pixel location i and the mean spectrum $\bar{\mathbf{g}}_i = (\bar{g}_{i1},...\bar{g}_{iB})$ in the image patch $\mathbf{Z}_i$. In the present work, $L1$ norm has been used, which would represent in a continuous spectral representation the area between two spectral power spectra, although other norms or spectral difference measures could be used. Analogously, instead of the patch mean $\bar{\mathbf{g}}_i$ as the patch spectral reference, other possible spectral image patch representatives could be used, e.g. the median spectral pixel or the spectrum of the central pixel in the patch.

Image patch $\mathbf{Z}_i$ is then a $B+N$ dimensional vector, with B the number of bands and N the number of pixels in the image patch grid. Note that given a patch size N, for any spectral number of bands B, the dimensionality of the texture feature vector has always a fixed part size of N difference terms, and only the mean spectral pixel increases linearly as the number of bands B increases. This is a desirable property of the texture characterisation in the multi-spectral domain, since the complexity of the Texem model is controlled, keeping dimensionality to an affordable way. In addition, if a band reduction technique is used as a previous step [11], the Texem dimensionality can even be kept at a more reduced and affordable level.

The MLDT characterisation captures in a compact way the difference patterns within an image patch in a multi-spectral image, and is thus able to represent the integrated spatial and spectral information in a single representation. Using the image patch representation expressed in (8) will enable the use of the gray level Texem model in section 2.1 directly, keeping spectral and spatial dependencies in the generative model at an affordable feature vector dimensionality.

5 Experimental Data

In order to test the validity of the proposed MLDT characterisation, it has been applied to a set of three hyper-spectral remote sensing images captured with different sensors:

- DAISEX099 project provides useful aerial images about the study of the variability in the reflectance of different natural surfaces. This source of data, referred as HyMap in figures, corresponds to a spectral image of 700×670 pixels and 7 classes of identified crops and other unknown land use class, acquired with the 128-bands HyMap spectrometer during the DAISEX-99 campaign (http:/io.uv.es/projects/daisex/). In this case, 126 bands were used, discarding the lower SNR bands (0, 64). Figure 1 (left) represents a pseudo-colour image composed from three of the 126 bands.

- Satellite PROBA has a positional spectra-radiometric system (CHRIS) that measures the spectral radiance. The images used in this study come from the CHRIS-PROBA mode that operates on an area of 15×15 km, with a spatial resolution of 34m obtaining a set of 62 spectral bands that range from 400 to 1050 nm, 641×617 pixels and 9 classes of identified crop types and other unknown land use classes. In this case, 52 bands were used, discarding the lower SNR bands (25, 33, 36-37, 41-43, 47, 50, 53). Figure 2 (left) represents a pseudo-colour image composed from three of the 52 bands.

- A third multi-spectral image of seven spectral bands and 512×512 pixels, obtained from LandSat-7 of an area around the Kilauea Volcano, in Hawaii. This image will be referred as LandSat-7. Figure 3 (left) represents a pseudo-colour image composed from three of the 7 bands.

Considering multi-spectral images can contain a huge amount of information with a high number of bands, and taking into account that most of these bands are very correlated [11], it seems logical that the dimensionality reduction problem in multi-spectral images has to be linked with the texture characterisation problem, since trying to combine correlations simultaneously in the spectral and spatial domain can be computationally expensive.

In order to exploit inter-band correlation to reduce the multi-spectral band representation, the unsupervised band reduction technique by [11] has been used to reduce the bands of HyMap and CHRIS to the seven most relevant bands. This band reduction technique exploits inter-band correlation to reduce the multi-spectral band representation by means of theoretic information concepts. The seven bands selected by the band selection algorithm for HyMap images have been bands (1, 28, 41, 52, 79, 107, 122), and for CHRIS image, bands (0, 9, 20, 30, 40, 46, 59).

With the selected bands for every image of this dataset, an unsupervised image segmentation algorithm has been applied, based on an EM algorithm for a Gaussian mixture model, fixing the number of Texems as input parameter, and the inter-scale post-fusion strategy pointed out in section 3. The results are discussed in the next section.

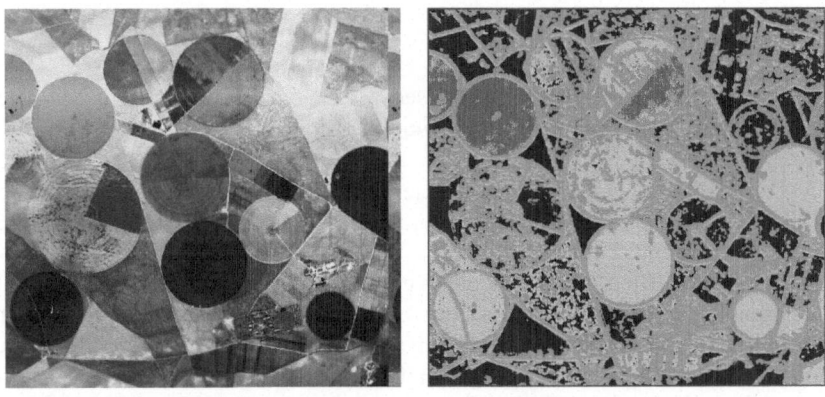

Fig. 1. HyMap pseudo-colour image (left) and its MLDT-based segmentation (right)

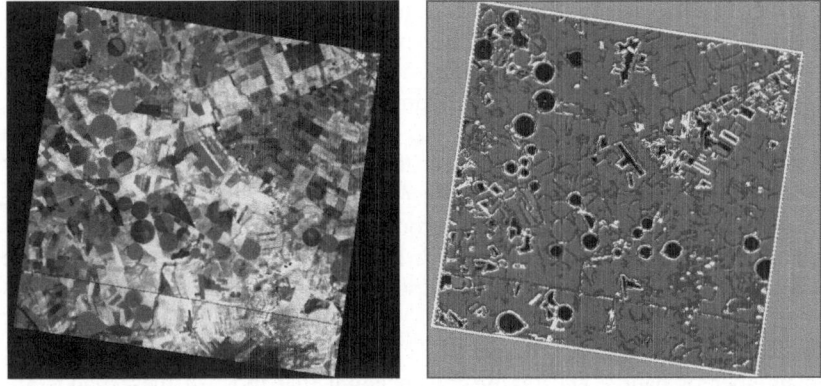

Fig. 2. CHRIS pseudo-colour image (left) and its MLDT-based segmentation (right)

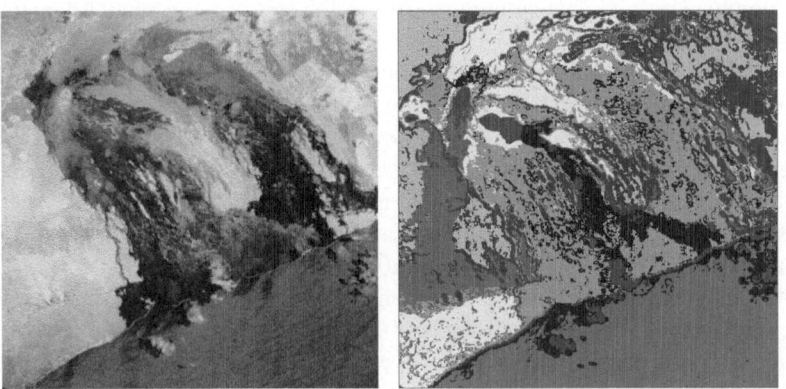

Fig. 3. LandSat-7 pseudo-colour image (left) and its MLDT-based segmentation (right)

6   Results

Figure 1 (right) shows the result of the proposed method to the HyMap multispectral image, using the selected 7 image bands, with L=3 multi-resolution levels, K=12 Texems and N=7×7=49 image patch size. The Texem model was trained with 3000 random image patches in each level. Note how the MLDT multi-spectral characterisation and inter-scale post-fusion segmentation has been able to identify the most important texture types in the image, grouping them in a satisfactory way. Note how the image Texems found model most of the structures of the image, finding the main regions corresponding to the different crop and land uses in the image.

Analogously, Figure 2 (right) shows the result of the algorithm for the CHRIS multispectral image, using the selected 7 image bands, with L=3 multi-resolution levels, K=8 Texems and N=7×7=49 image patch size. The Texem model was trained with 4000 random image patches in each level. In this case, the Texems found correspond to the main three types of land uses. Note how it is also modelled the different types of crop/land borders, where we can distinguish fairly well at least two different border structures modelled by their corresponding Texems.

Finally, Figure 3 (right) shows the result of the algorithm for the LandSat-7 multispectral image, using the 7 image bands, with L=2 multi-resolution levels, K=10 Texems and N=3×3=9 image patch size. The Texem model was trained with 3000 random image patches in each level. The results on this image show how well the different land and water types have been extracted, being able to discriminate even distinct water sediments levels. Another important detail is how the spectral information has also been able to detect the area covered by the smoke from the volcano, which cannot be visually appreciated very well from the pseudo-colour composition, only near the volcano, but the MLDT characterisation has been able to represent.

It is worth noting that when using 7 image bands an a 49 pixel patch size, the MLDT vector has 7+49=56 dimensions, and the Texem model in this case is defined by a single Gaussian of 56 dimensions in a Gaussian mixture model. In the case of a 9 pixel patch size, Texem dimensionality reduces to 7+9=16 dimensions. If the multispectral image had 50 dimensions, the Texem dimensionality for a 3×3=9 patch size would be 50+9=59, which is still affordable.

7   Conclusions

As a final remark, the basis for a multi-spectral texture characterisation technique has been built, with promising results and affordable complexity to deal with the huge amount of data a multi-spectral image may contain, capturing the essential properties of the spatial and spectral relationships.

Possible improvements and variations of the proposed MLDT characterisation can be done in several areas, for instance, if the mean spectra of image patches are dropped, the MLDT vector then reduces considerably and for a given image patch size, the MLDT vector dimension is constant (the image patch size) for any number of bands. This is a particular interesting property to be studied in further work.

Eventually, more tests should also be directed to model Texems as several Gaussian components, as pointed out in [10], exploring some hierarchical clustering structure as in [12], to merge Gaussian modes to form clusters.

Acknowledgments. This work has been partially supported by grant PR2008-0126 and projects ESP2005-00724-C05-05, AYA2008-05965-C04-04/ESP, CSD2007-00018 and PET2005-0643 from the Spanish Ministry of Science and Innovation, and by project P1 1B2007-48 from Fundació Caixa-Castelló.

References

1. Plaza, A., Martínez, P., Plaza, J., Pérez, R.: Dimensionality reduction and classification of hyperspectral image data using sequences of extended morphological transformations. IEEE Transactions on Geoscience and Remote Sensing 37(6), 1097–1116 (2005)
2. Camps-Valls, G., Gomez-Chova, L., Munoz-Mari, J., Vila-Frances, J., Calpe-Maravilla, J.: Composite kernels for hyperspectral image classification. IEEE Geoscience and Remote Sensing Letters (3), 93–97 (2006)
3. Haindl, M., Havlicek, V.: A Simple multispectral multiresolution Markov texture model. In: International Workshop on Texture Analysis and Synthesis, pp. 63–66 (2002)
4. Dubuisson-Jolly, M., Gupta, A.: Color and texture fusion: Application to aerial image segmentation and GIS updating. Image and Vision Computing 18, 823–832 (2000)
5. Palm, C.: Color texture classification by integrative co-occurrence matrices. Pattern Recognition 37(5), 965–976 (2004)
6. Mirmehdi, M., Petrou, M.: Segmentation of color textures. IEEE Transactions on PatternAnalysis and Machine Intelligence 22(2), 142–159 (2000)
7. Jojic, N., Frey, B., Kannan, A.: Epitomic analysis of appearance and shape. In: IEEE International Conference on Computer Vision, pp. 34–42 (2003)
8. Xie, X., Mirmehdi, M.: TEXEMS: Texture exemplars for defect detection on random textured surfaces. IEEE Transactions on Pattern Analysis and Machine Intelligence 29(8), 1454–1464 (2007)
9. Bouman, C.A.: Cluster: An unsupervised algorithm for modelling Gaussian mixtures (April 1997), http://www.ece.purdue.edu/~bouman
10. Xie, X., Mirmehdi, M.: Colour image segmentation using texems. Annals of the BMVA 2007(6), 1–10 (2007)
11. Martinez-Uso, A., Pla, F., Sotoca, J.M., Garcia-Sevilla, P.: Clustering-based Hyperspectral Band Selection using Information Measures. IEEE Transactions on Geoscience & Remote Sensing 45(12), 4158–4171 (2007)
12. Pascual, D., Pla, F., Sánchez, J.S.: Non Parametric Local Density-based Clustering for Multimodal Overlapping Distributions. In: Corchado, E., Yin, H., Botti, V., Fyfe, C. (eds.) IDEAL 2006. LNCS, vol. 4224, pp. 671–678. Springer, Heidelberg (2006)

Texture Measuring by Means of Perceptually-Based Fineness Functions

J. Chamorro-Martínez and P. Martínez-Jiménez[*]

Department of Computer Science and Artificial Intelligence, University of Granada
C/ Periodista Daniel Saucedo Aranda s/n, 18071 Granada, Spain
{jesus,pedromartinez}@decsai.ugr.es

Abstract. Although texture is a widely analyzed property in computer vision, models which relate this feature with human perception are needed. In this paper, a model that associates computational fineness measures with the human perception of this type of texture property is proposed. The fineness perception is collected from human subjects, performing an aggregation of their assessments. Considering a wide variety of measures, a coarseness-fineness function relating these features with the human assesments is obtained as the function which provides the best fit of the collected data.

Keywords: Texture, image features, textural features, human perception, coarseness, fineness.

1 Introduction

Texture is, together with the color and shape, one of the most important features used in the analysis of natural images. It is usual to describe visual textures according to some properties like *coarseness-fineness*, *orientation* or *regularity* [1,2]. From all of them, the *coarseness-fineness* is one of the most popular, being common to associate the presence of texture with the presence of fineness.

Different approaches for texture characterization have been developed over the years [3,4,5]. Haralick [3] proposed a classification of such approaches in two main groups: *statistical methods* (which analyze gray tone spatial distribution by computing some statistics on pixel intensities) and *structural methods* (which characterize texture by means of *texels* arranged in a certain way that is given by a set of rules). However, one of the main drawback of theses methods is that there is not a clear perceptual relationship between the measure value and the way the humans perceive the texture.

One of the first papers where human perception of texture is taken into account was presented by Tamura [2]. However, in Tamura's paper the relationship between the computational measures and the human perception of the different textural features is not learnt, just a rank correlation value is given. More recent approaches perform experiments with humans in order to model human

---

[*] This work was supported by Spanish research programme Consolider Ingenio 2010: MIPRCV (CSD2007-00018).

H. Araujo et al. (Eds.): IbPRIA 2009, LNCS 5524, pp. 265–272, 2009.

perception, but it is usual that the results given by such models just compare two images giving measure of their similarity [6], or only analyze the presence or not of texture without given a measure value [7].

In this paper we face the problem of relating the texture measures with the human perception of texture. Concretely, we focus our study in the coarseness-fineness property, proposing models which relate representative measures of texture (usually some statistic) with its human perception of fineness. For this purpose, a wide variety of measures are analyzed, and human assessments about texture perception are collected. From this data, a functional relationship between the measures and the human assessments is learnt.

The rest of the paper is organized as follows. In section 2 we introduce our methodology to obtain the functions that model the fineness textural property. In section 3 we show the results of applying the models and the main conclusions and future work are sumarized in section 4.

2   Perceptually-Based Fineness Functions

Focusing our study on fineness-coarseness property, there are different measures over the literature that, given an image, capture the fineness (or coarseness) presence in the sense that the greater the value given by the measure, the greater the perception of texture. However two main drawbacks are found: on the one hand, there is no perceptual relationship between that value and the degree that humans perceive the texture; on the other hand, there are no thresholds that, given a certain measure, allow to decide whether there is fine texture, coarse texture or something intermediate (i.e. there are no intervals on the measure domain allowing for textural interpretation).

In this paper, we face the above questions by proposing a function of fineness perception defined on the domain of a given subset of fineness and coarseness measures. Let $\mathcal{P} = \{P_1, \ldots, P_K\}$ be the set of K fineness measures analyzed in this paper (showed in the first column of Table 1), and let $\mathcal{F} = \{F_1, \ldots, F_{K'}\} \subseteq \mathcal{P}$ be a subset of $K' \leq K$ measures selected from $\mathcal{P}$. Thus, we propose to model the fineness perception by means of a function $\mathcal{T}_{\mathcal{F}}$ defined as[1]

$$\mathcal{T}_{\mathcal{F}} : \mathbb{R}^{K'} \to [0, 1] \tag{1}$$

with K' being the cardinality of $\mathcal{F}$. The value given by the function $\mathcal{T}_{\mathcal{F}}$ will indicate how fine or coarse is the texture present in an image. Thus, a value of 1 will mean fineness presence while a value of 0 will mean no fineness presence (i.e. coarseness presence). Therefore, values between 0 and 1 will represent the degree of how fine the image is perceived (the closer the value to 1, the greater the perception of fineness).

In this paper, we propose to obtain $\mathcal{T}_{\mathcal{F}}$ by fitting a suitable function relating fineness measures with the degree of fineness perceived by humans. To learn this

---

[1] Given a set $\mathcal{P}$ of K measures, the function $\mathcal{T}_{\mathcal{F}}$, with $\mathcal{F} \subseteq \mathcal{P}$, could be defined by using all the measures ($K' = K$), or a subset of them ($K' < K$).

Fig. 1. Some examples of images with different degrees of fineness

relationship, a set $\mathcal{I} = \{I_1, \ldots, I_N\}$ of N images covering different degrees of fineness will be used. For each image $I_i \in \mathcal{I}$, we will have (a) a set of fineness values obtained by applying the measures $\mathcal{F}$ to the image I_i and (b) assessments about of the perception of fineness in the image I_i obtained from subjects. To get these assessments, a poll will be performed (section 2.1). Therefore, for each image, we will have pairs of measure-assessment values, so a fitting will be applied in order to obtain a suitable function (section 2.2).

2.1 Assessment Collection

In this section, the way to obtain the fineness assessments from the image set $\mathcal{I}$ will be described. From now on, we will note as $\Gamma = \{v^1, \ldots, v^N\}$ the set of fineness assessment values associated to $\mathcal{I}$, with v^i being the aggregated value representing the degree of fineness perceived by humans in the image $I_i \in \mathcal{I}$.

The texture image set. A set $\mathcal{I} = \{I_1, \ldots, I_N\}$ of $N = 80$ images representative of the *fineness-coarseness* property has been selected. Figure 1 shows some images from the set $\mathcal{I}$. The selection was done satisfying the following properties: (1) it covers the different presence degrees of fineness-coarseness, (2) the number of images for each degree is representative enough, and (3) each image shows, as far as possible, just one degree of fineness. Due to the third property, each image can viewed as "homogeneous" respect to the fineness degree represented, i.e., if we select two random windows (with a dimension which does not "break" the original texture primitives and structure), the perceived fineness will be the same for each window (and also respect to the original image).

As we explained, given an image $I_i \in \mathcal{I}$, a set of measures $\mathcal{F}$ will be applied on it. In fact, and thanks to the third property, we really can apply these measures for each subimage, assuming that the human assessment associated to that subimage will be the human assessment associated to the whole image.

From now on, we will note as $\mathbf{M}_w^i = [m_1^{i,w}, \ldots, m_{K'}^{i,w}]$ the vector of measures for the w-th window of the image I_i, with $m_k^{i,w}$ being the result of applying the measure $F_k \in \mathcal{F}$ to the w-th window of the image I_i. Therefore, and using the previous notation, the set of valid pairs used for the fitting procedure will be given by $\Psi_F = \{(\mathbf{M}_w^i, v^i), i = 1, \ldots, N; w = 1, \ldots, W\}$, with N being the number of images and W the number of windows considered for each image.

The poll. Given the image set $\mathcal{I}$, the next step is to obtain assessments about the perception of fineness from a set of subjects. From now on, we shall denote $\Theta^i = [o_1^i, \ldots, o_L^i]$ the vector of assessments obtained from L subjects for image I_i. To get Θ^i, subjects will be asked to assign images to classes, so that each class has associated a perception degree of texture. In particular, 20 subjects have participated in the poll and 9 classes have been considered. The first nine images in figure 1 show the nine representative images for each class used in this poll. It should be noticed that the images are decreasingly ordered according to the perception degree of fineness.

Assessment aggregation. Our aim at this point is to obtain, for each image $I_i \in \mathcal{I}$, one assessment v^i that summarizes the vector of assessments Θ^i given by the different subjects about the perception degree of fineness. To aggregate opinions we have used an OWA operator guided by the quantifier "the most" [8] which allows to represent the opinion of majority of the polled subjects.

2.2   Fitting the Function

At this point, the aim is to obtain, for a given subset of measures $\mathcal{F} \subseteq \mathcal{P}$, the corresponding function $\mathcal{T}_\mathcal{F}$ by fitting a suitable curve to the set $\Psi_\mathcal{F}$. In this paper, the robust fitting based on M-estimators (a generalization of the least squares fitting)) has been used [15]. For each image $I_i \in \mathcal{I}$, $W = 2000$ subimages of size 32×32 have been considered (so 16000 points have been used for the fitting).

For defining $\mathcal{F}$, we have focused our analysis on the cases of $K' = 1$ and $K' = 2$. The unidimensional case ($K' = 1$) will allow to study each measure separately, comparing its goodness respect to the others. In the bidimensional case ($K' = 2$), we will combine two measures in order to improve the individual ones (all the combinations of two elements have been considered). For higher dimensions ($K' \geq 3$), the fitting based on M-estimators is too complex, so new methods for finding $\mathcal{T}_\mathcal{F}$ need to be considered (for example, some kind of heuristic approaches). The case of $K' \geq 3$ will be considered in future works.

Both the unidimensional and bidimensional fittings are analyzed in the next subsections. In both cases, the following considerations will be taked into account: (1) $\mathcal{T}_F$ should be a monotonic function, and (2) the values $\mathcal{T}_\mathcal{F}(x) = 0$ and $\mathcal{T}_\mathcal{F}(x) = 1$ should be achieved from a certain value. It should be noticed that there is an error related to the fitting, calculated as the mean of the absolute difference between the data points and the curve. This error can also be viewed as a goodness measurement of the measures used in $\mathcal{F}$.

Table 1. Fitting errors related to unidimensional and bidimensional fitting and parameter values for the measures with least error

Unidimensional fitting		Bidimensional fitting		
Measure	Error	Measure x	Measure y	Error
Correlation [3]	0.1466	FD	Amadasun	0.1095
Amadasun [1]	0.1515	Correlation	ED	0.1332
Abbadeni [4]	0.1880	Correlation	Tamura	0.1339
Fractal dim. (FD) [9]	0.1891	Amadasun	Correlation	0.1354
Tamura [2]	0.1994	Abbadeni	Tamura	0.1373
Edge density (ED) [3]	0.2044	Amadasun	ED	0.1431
DGD [10]	0.2120	Correlation	Abbadeni	0.1433
Local Homogeneity [3]	0.2156	Abbadeni	Amadasun	0.1444
Short Run Emphasis [11]	0.2211	Correlation	FD	0.1455
SNE [12]	0.2365	Abbadeni	FD	0.1475
Weszka [5]	0.2383	Tamura	Amadasun	0.1529
Newsam [13], Entropy [3],	WSD	FD	Tamura	0.1634
Uniformity[3], FMPS [14]		ED	Tamura	0.1636
Variance[3]	NR	ED	FD	0.1764
Contrast [3]		Abbadeni	ED	0.1799
Parameters for Correlation:		Parameters for $\{FD, Amadasun\}$:		
a_3=-1.8383, a_2=1.2338, a_1=-1.2079		a_9=1.1169, a_8=-7.60E-4, a_7=0, a_6=-8.53E-3, a_5=-11.388		
a_0=1.0339, α=0.7685, β=0.0289		a_4=6.17E-2, a_3=0.2289, a_2=36.81, a_1=-1.2616, a_0=-34.76		

Unidimensional fitting. Regarding the above properties, in the case of $K' = 1$ we propose to define $\mathcal{T_F}$ as a function of the form[2]

$$\mathcal{T_F}(x; a_n \ldots a_0, \alpha, \beta) = \begin{cases} 0 & x < \alpha, \\ poly1(x; a_n \ldots a_0) & \alpha \leq x \leq \beta, \\ 1 & x > \beta \end{cases} \qquad (2)$$

with $poly1(x; a_n \ldots a_0)$ being a polynomial function

$$poly1(x; a_n \ldots a_0) = a_n x^n + \ldots + a_1 x^1 + a_0 \qquad (3)$$

In our proposal, the parameters $a_n \ldots a_0$, α and β of the function $\mathcal{T_F}$ are calculated by carrying out the robust fitting on $\Psi_{\mathcal{F}}$. For the polynomial function, the cases of n=1,2,3 have been considered.

Table 1 shows, for each measure $F_k \in \mathcal{F}$, the least error obtained in the fitting process (sorted in increasing order of the errors). The parameter values corresonding to the lowest error fitting (correlation) are also shown in Table 1. It should be noticed that we haven't carried out the fitting with six of the measures. Four of them (marked with WSD) are rejected because their values are affected by the window size. The other two (marked with NR) produce a diffuse cloud of points Ψ_F with no representative information.

---

[2] Note that this function is defined for measures that increase according to the perception of fineness. For those that decreases, the function needs to be changed appropriately.

Bidimensional fitting. In the case of $K' = 2$, we define $\mathcal{T}_{\mathcal{F}}$ as a function of the form:

$$\mathcal{T}_{\mathcal{F}}(x, y; a_{(n!+n)} \ldots a_0) = \mathcal{T}_{\mathcal{F}}(x, y; coef) =$$

$$= \begin{cases} 0 & poly2(x, y; coef) < 0, \\ poly2(x, y; coef) & 0 < poly2(x, y; coef) < 1, \\ 1 & poly2(x, y; coef) > 1 \end{cases} \qquad (4)$$

with $poly2(x, y; coef)$ being a polynomial function of two variables

$$poly2(x, y; a_{(n!+n)} \ldots a_0) = \sum_{i=0}^{n} \sum_{j=0}^{i} a_{(i!+j)} x^j y^{i-j}$$

As in the unidimensioanl case, the parameters $a_{(n!+n)} \ldots a_0$ of the function $\mathcal{T}_{\mathcal{F}}$ are calculated by carrying out the robust fitting on $\Psi_{\mathcal{F}}$. For the polynomial function, the cases of n=1,2,3 have been considered.

Table 1 shows the least fitting error obtained for each pair of measures (only the pairs compound by the first six measures in the unidimensional case are shown). It can be noticed that the use of bidimensional functions reduces the error and provides better fineness models than the unidimensional ones. In addition, the combination of two measures improves the results obtained for each measure separately. In our experiments, the pair $\mathcal{F} = \{FD, Amadasun\}$ gives the best results. The parameter values corresponding to this member function are shown in Table 1.

3   Results

In this section, the function $\mathcal{T}_{\mathcal{F}}$ with the least fitting error, corresponding to the pair of measures $\mathcal{F} = \{FD, Amadasun\}$, will be applied in order to analyze the performance of the proposed model.

Let's consider Figure 2(A) corresponding to a mosaic made by several images, each one with a different increasing perception degree of fineness. The fineness of each subimage has been calculated using the proposed model and the results are shown in Figure 2(B), being v the value of the human assessment and f the value computed by our model. It can be noticed that our model captures the evolution of the perception degrees of fineness.

Figure 2(C) shows a mapping from the original image to its fineness values using the proposed model. For each pixel in the original image, a centered window of size 32×32 has been analyzed and its fineness has been calculated. The histogram of this image is shown below, where we can see clearly four differentiated peaks, corresponding to the four different fineness degrees in the image. Figures 2(D) and 2(E) show a mapping from the original image using the Amadasun and FD measures directly. It can be seen that these mappings don't provide as much perceptual information as Figure 2(C). Furthermore, their histograms show that the four peaks can't be obtained with the measures separately.

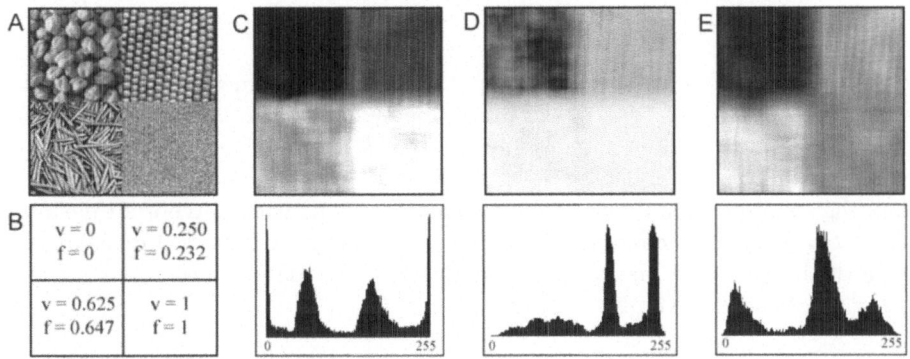

Fig. 2. Results for a mosaic image. (A) Original mosaic image (B) Fineness values obtained with the proposed model for $\mathcal{F} = \{FD, Amadasun\}$, with v being the value of the human assessment and f the value computed by our model (C) Mapping from the original image to its fineness values using the proposed model (D)(E) Mapping using the individual measures Amadasun and FD, respectively.

Figure 3 presents an example where the proposed model has been employed for pattern recognition. Concretely, it shows a microscopy image (Figure 3(A)) corresponding to the microstructure of a metal sample. The lamellae indicates islands of eutectic, which need to be separated from the uniform light regions. The brightness values in regions are similar to the background ones, so texture information is needed for extracting the uniform areas. This fact is showed in Figure 3(B1,B2), where a thersholding on the original image is displayed (homogeneous regions cannot be separated from the textured ones).

Figure 3(C1) shows a mapping from the original image to its fineness values using the proposed model (a window of size 20×20 has been used). It can be noticed that uniform regions correspond to areas with low values of fineness (i.e., high coarseness), so if only the pixels with fineness values lower than 0.1 are selected (which it is equivalent to a coarseness degree upper than 0.9), the uniform light regions emerge with ease (Figure 3(C2,C3)).

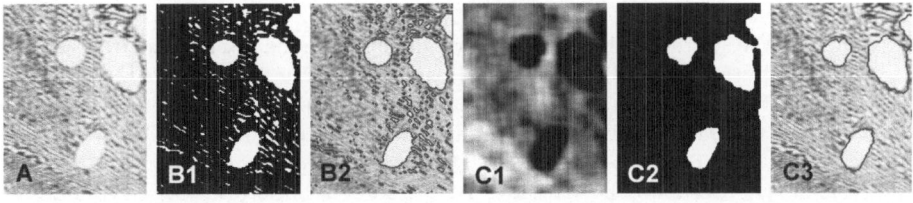

Fig. 3. (A) Original image (B1) Binary image obtained by thresholding the original image (B2) Region outlines of B1 superimposed on original image (C1) Fineness mapping obtained with our model from the original image (C2) Binary image obtained by thresholding C1 (C3) Region outlines of C2 superimposed on original image

4   Conclusions

In this paper, functions relating computational fineness measures with the human perception of this type of texture property have been proposed. In order to obtain assessments about fineness perception, a group of human subjects have been polled. From the collected data, a robust fitting procedure has been applied, resulting unidimensional and bidimensional functions with perceptual meaningful. In our study, the combination of the Amadasum and the FD measures has given the best fitting. The results show a high performance of the model respect to the assessments given by subjects.

References

1. Amadasun, M., King, R.: Textural features corresponding to textural properties. IEEE Transactions on Systems, Man and Cybernetics 19(5), 1264–1274 (1989)
2. Tamura, H., Mori, S., Yamawaki, T.: Textural features corresponding to visual perception. IEEE Trans. on Systems, Man and Cybernetics 8, 460–473 (1978)
3. Haralick, R.: Statistical and structural approaches to texture. Proceedings IEEE 67(5), 786–804 (1979)
4. Abbadeni, N., Ziou, N., Wang, D.: Autocovariance-based perceptual textural features corresponding to human visual perception. In: Proc. of 15th International Conference on Pattern Recognition, vol. 3, pp. 901–904 (2000)
5. Wezska, J., Dyer, C., Rosenfeld, A.: A comparative study of texture measures for terrain classification. IEEE Trans. on SMC 6, 269–285 (1976)
6. Fahmy, G., Black, J., Panchanathan, S.: Texture characterization for joint compression and classification based on human perception in the wavelet domain. IEEE Transactions on Image Processing (2006)
7. Chen, J., Pappas, T., Mojsilovic, A., Rogowitz, B.: Adaptive perceptual color-texture image segmentation. IEEE Transactions on Image Processing (2005)
8. Yager, R.: On ordered weighted averaging aggregation operators in multicriteria decisionmaking. IEEE Trans. on SMC 18(1), 183–190 (1988)
9. Peleg, S., Naor, J., Hartley, R., Avnir, D.: Multiple resolution texture analysis and classification. IEEE Trans. on PAMI (4), 518–523 (1984)
10. Kim, S., Choi, K., Lee, D.: Texture classification using run difference matrix. In: Proc. of IEEE 1991 Ultrasonics Symposium, vol. 2, pp. 1097–1100 (1991)
11. Galloway, M.: Texture analysis using gray level run lengths. Computer Graphics and Image Processing 4, 172–179 (1975)
12. Sun, C., Wee, W.: Neighboring gray level dependence matrix for texture classification. Computer Vision, Graphics and Image Processing 23, 341–352 (1983)
13. Newsam, S., Kammath, C.: Retrieval using texture features in high resolution multi-spectral satellite imagery. In: Data Mining and Knowledge Discovery: Theory, Tools, and Technology VI, SPIE Defense and Security (2004)
14. Yoshida, H., Casalino, D., Keserci, B., Coskun, A., Ozturk, O., Savranlar, A.: Wavelet-packet-based texture analysis for differentiation between benign and malignant liver tumours in ultrasound images. Phy.in Med. Bio. 48, 3735–3753 (2003)
15. Beaton, A., Tukey, J.: The fitting of power series, meaning polynomials, illustrated on band-spectroscopic data. Technometrics 16, 147–185 (1974)

High Performance Circle Detection through a GPU Rasterization Approach[*]

Manuel Ujaldón and Nicolás Guil

Computer Architecture Department, University of Málaga, Spain

Abstract. GPUs have recently attracted our attention as accelerators for a wide variety of algorithms, including assorted examples within the pattern recognition field. After proving the effectiveness of the GPU for computing the Circle Hough Transform [Ujaldon et al. (2008)], we present in this paper a radius compensation method which improves the accuracy and speed-up using the GPU rasterizer. Experimental results confirm a higher precision in circles detection and up to 27% additional savings in the GPU computational time on a GeForce 8800 GTX for a 1024x1024 sample image, thus enhancing the execution of the Circle Hough Transform on a low-cost and emerging architecture like the GPU.

1 Introduction

The performance, use and programming GPUs have greatly improved over the past few years, converting the GPU into an extraordinary resource for implementing general-purpose applications [Owens et al. (2007)]. Among the functional units of the GPU, the rasterizer is responsible for scan conversion as well as the major interpolations required during the generation of graphics. For the purposes of our work, we focus on the rasterizer ability for generating straight lines to the set of input vertices (see Figure 1).

On finite domains, hardware interpolation may be used to estimate information which either is missing or can be generated more easily from a main core available. The central idea is to minimize the computational requirements for

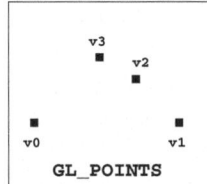 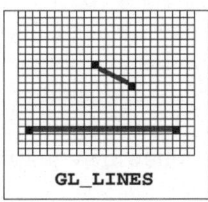 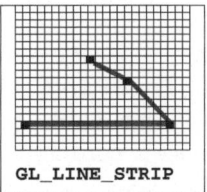 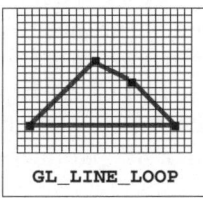

| GL_POINTS | GL_LINES | GL_LINE_STRIP | GL_LINE_LOOP |

Fig. 1. OpenGL assembly primitives used by a GPU rasterizer to interpolate lines from a list of input vertices. Six other alternatives for filling inscribed areas are available as well.

[*] This work was supported by the Junta de Andalucía (Projects PR06-TIC-02109 and PR07-TIC-02800), and the Ministry of Education of Spain (Project TIC2003-06623).

H. Araujo et al. (Eds.): IbPRIA 2009, LNCS 5524, pp. 273–281, 2009.
© Springer-Verlag Berlin Heidelberg 2009

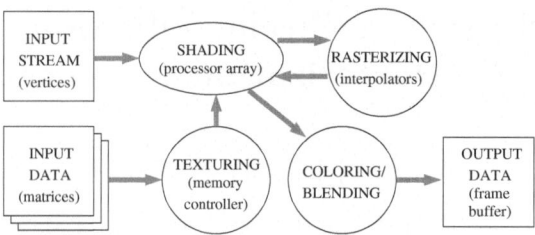

Fig. 2. The graphics pipeline at a glance

the algorithm while maintaining the fidelity for the output results. Our case study for demonstrating the effectiveness of such technique in the past has been the evaluation of the parameter space required by the Hough Transform for detecting circles on images [Ujaldon et al. (2008)]. Prior to using the rasterizer, we also implemented the Circle Hough Transform on the GPU using a standard method with shaders and then validated the output results against a similar algorithm computed on the CPU [Ruiz et al. (2007a)]. Those contributions resulted in a much faster execution without compromising the quality of the results. This paper enables further optimizations for the accuracy of the circles to be recognized and the computational workload required to compute the Hough Transform. We exploit resources provided by the GPU rasterizer from quantitative and qualitative viewpoints, leading to a high-performance execution on a low-cost platform.

Paper contents are organized as follows. Section 2 outlines the Hough Transform and the GPU elements involved during its computation. Section 3 presents our contributions for improving the accuracy and reducing the computational workload. Section 4 compares accuracy and performance on sample images with respect to previous implementations. Section 5 concludes.

2 Improving the Hough Transform on the GPU

The Hough Transform is used to detect lines on an image, where each edge point generates a curve in a two-dimensional parameter space and curves from all edge points are accumulated in the parameter space. The problem of object detection thus becomes the calculation of the maximums accumulated.

The Circle Hough Transform (CHT) is an extension of that basic scheme to detect circular shapes [Yuen et al. (1990)]. Each edge point generates a surface in a 3D parameter space according to the following equation:

$$(x - a)^2 + (y - b)^2 = r^2 \tag{1}$$

With (x, y) as the coordinates for each edge point, (a, b) the circle center and r is radius. If we setup an estimation for the radius based on problem knowledge, the global process becomes a transformation from the (x, y) image space into the (a, b) parameter space with a few equations:

$$a = x - r \cdot cos(t) \qquad b = y - r \cdot sin(t) \qquad t \in [0, 2\pi] \tag{2}$$

The goal is to compute a vote for all (x, y) contour points and t values given a particular radius r, and translate this into a 2D array of cells in the (a, b) parameter space such that the cells receiving more votes are more likely to be the center of a detected circle of radius r in the image holding all contour points. The number of votes generated by each contour point depend on the discretization used for t in equation 2. The increment step, δt, is a key parameter determining the relative weight for each vote as well as the computational workload for the whole algorithm ([Ruiz et al. (2007a)]).

We have recently developed a method to implement, in hardware, most of the evaluations required by the voting process ([Ujaldon et al. (2008)]). Votes are stored as pixel intensities on a 2D texture acting as the required (a, b) parameter space, and the interpolation process carried out by the rasterizer completes the spectrum of votes from a small number of seeds, s, or evaluated points. The more number of seeds, the more accuracy for the interpolation and the less workload for the rasterizer. In this work, we extend our methods to increase accuracy under the same number of seeds, which may lead to keep accuracy within similar ranges while reducing the number of seeds for a faster execution on the GPU.

According to equation 2, all votes for each input (x, y) contour point describe a circle in the (a, b) parameter space after applying all possible instances of the angle $t \in [0, 2\pi]$. Texture resolution and OpenGL assembly primitives affect the way of computing votes within the GPU in different ways. For example, we may use a lower increment step, δt, on **GL_POINTS** to relax the workload, or a greater number of seeds, s, for a better vote precision when using **GL_LINES**.

3   Error Compensation

The total error for an s fraction of the entire circular population of votes is given by the difference between the areas of the corresponding circle portion and the polygon inscribed within (see Figure 3), that is:

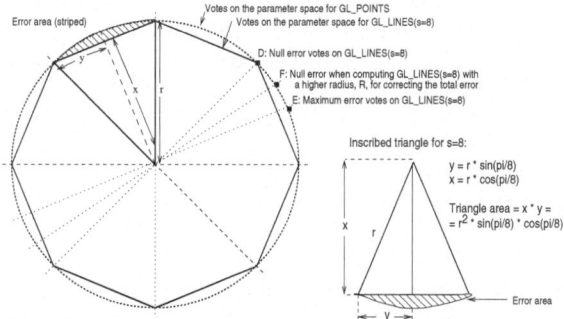

Fig. 3. Calculation of the error incurred when computing the Circle Hough Transform using the GL_LINES primitive under the particular case of $s = 8$

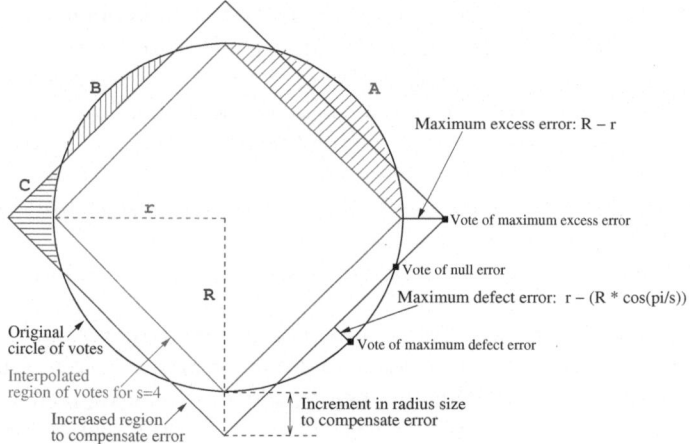

Fig. 4. Error correction when using GL_LINES for interpolating votes under a minimum number of seeds, $s = 4$. The actual radius, r, is increased to an R value for the polygon inscribed so that the error area A (striped diagonally) gets reduced with a larger polygon in B (striped vertically) and compensated by the excess C (striped horizontally).

$$Total \ \ error = (Circular \ sector \ area) - (Inscribed \ triangle \ area) =$$

$$= (\frac{\pi \cdot r^2}{s}) - (r^2 \cdot sin(\frac{\pi}{s}) \cdot cos(\frac{\pi}{s})) = r^2 \cdot (\frac{\pi}{s} - sin(\frac{\pi}{s}) \cdot cos(\frac{\pi}{s})) \qquad (3)$$

The per-vote error is zero on seed points (like D in Figure 3) reaching its maximum value on the equidistant point between two seeds (see E points); overall, each per-vote error can be quantified as the difference between the circle radius and the apothem of the inscribed polygon using s seeds.

Both maximum and mean errors are always defect errors, which can be corrected by increasing the radius we input into the algorithm. That is, we compute Hough for an r value in excess to the actual radius size we want to recognize in the input image, generating errors up to compensate for the down errors. For this compensation to be balanced, we equalize the area of the circular sector for the actual radius, r, with the area of the inscribed triangle for a higher radius, R (see equation 3), and calculate this value out of the resulting relation:

$$\frac{\pi \cdot r^2}{s} = R^2 \cdot sin(\frac{\pi}{s}) \cdot cos(\frac{\pi}{s}) \ \Rightarrow \ R = r \cdot \sqrt{\frac{\pi}{s \cdot sin(\frac{\pi}{s}) \cdot cos(\frac{\pi}{s})}} \qquad (4)$$

where the square root term represents the factor required to increase the actual radius to compensate for errors. This increased radius, R, is illustrated in Figure 4, and for the particular case of $r = 50$ pixels and $s = 16$, it results in a value of 50.65 pixels.

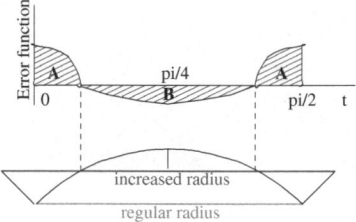

r in	R value (in pixels) for:			
pixels	$s = 4$	$s = 8$	$s = 16$	$s = 32$
20	25.06	21.07	20.26	20.06
50	62.66	52.69	50.65	50.16
100	125.33	105.39	101.30	100.32
200	250.66	210.78	202.60	200.64

Fig. 5. (left) Error area distribution for minimizing the average error when computing the Circle Hough Transform on the GPU. (right) The error in which the rasterizer incurs for a given number of seeds, s, can be corrected by increasing the input radius, r, giving R to minimize the average per-vote error.

Figure 5 provides the shape of the error area distribution as well as the R values for different combinations of r and s. When the number of contour points is big enough (such as required in practice for a circle to be recognized on an input image), their random placement guarantees a similar number of votes with errors down and up, making the R method an unbiased estimation for a given radius size. Moreover, scattered votes can be gathered by applying a convolution operator to the parameter space, which is very fast when implemented on a GPU.

4   Empirical Results

Experiments were driven on a GeForce 8800 GTX GPU using a 1024x1024 sample image containing 500 circles ramdonly placed with a radius size of 50 pixels.

4.1   Qualitative Analysis

Figure 6 depicts the 12x12 neighbourhood area for a single circle center using a 3D chart, with the third dimension being the scaled percentage of votes received by each (x,y) center location on the horizontal plane.

Figure 6.a is the output parameter space for GL_LINES with $s = 16$, that is, using the rasterizer with 16 seeds. The larger amount of votes generated by the rasterizer makes the output image brighter, and the votes concentrate better on each circle center coordinates as compared to the original GL_POINT results obtained without using the rasterizer (see [Ujaldon et al. (2008)]), which leads to a more precise center location.

Figure 6.b is the parameter space for GL_LINES under $s = 16$ with an increased radius size of $R = 50.65$ pixels. We can distinguish the sharpening of the chart for the votes distribution around the circle center, which represents a higher quality parameter space. Also, the better behavior for the error when using R versus r is proven in Figure 7 for a wide range of seeds, s.

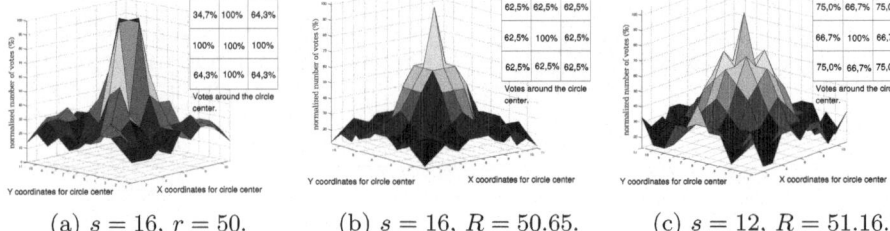

(a) $s = 16$, $r = 50$.   (b) $s = 16$, $R = 50.65$.   (c) $s = 12$, $R = 51.16$.

Fig. 6. Parameter space for the 12x12 neighbourhood area corresponding to a circle center coordinates taken from a sample image where $r = 50$ pixels. The upper right corner on each chart shows a 3x3 grid with the percentage of votes accumulated on each of the 8 neighbour pixels surrounding the one characterizing the circle center (maximum value is taken as 100%). (a) Original GPU computation on the rasterizer using GL_LINES ($s = 16$). (b) Increasing the radius size to minimize the average error. (c) Equivalent to 16 seeds for the subpixel threshold error.

Table 1. Execution times on the GPU for the Circle Hough Transform with a radius size of 50 pixels and a 1024x1024 input image containing 500 circles to be recognized under different computational strategies. The gain factor on the third column is the acceleration versus the reference time given in the second row without using the rasterizer. The 4th column links each execution with the output results that produces, shown in Figure 6. Overall, the reduction in the number of seeds from 16 to 12 for the case of $r = 50$ pixels is translated into additional savings of 17.31% in terms of execution time.

GPU implementation	Exec. time	Gain	Results shown in	Improvement
GL_POINTS($\delta t = 0.02$)	958.47 ms.	-	[Ujaldon et al. (2008)]	Baseline
GL_LINES(s=16), $r = 50$	129.81 ms.	7.38x	Figure 6.a	Speed-up
GL_LINES(s=16), $R = 50.65$	129.81 ms.	7.38x	Figure 6.b	Results
GL_LINES(s=12), $R = 51.16$	107.33 ms.	8.93x	Figure 6.c	Speed-up

4.2   Quantitative Analysis

Table 1 provides the execution times on the GPU for different computational strategies, also connecting those with the actual results shown in Figure 6.

The total CPU time was accelerated around ten times within the GPU under the same number of votes (that is, 314 using $\delta t = 0.02$), even after considering CPU-GPU communication time (see [Ujaldon et al. (2008)]). In both cases, versions with 62 votes were five times faster at the expense of losing accuracy.

The GPU versions involving the rasterizer (that is, using the GL_LINES primitive) spent 129.81 ms using 16 seeds under two different radii: the conventional case, $r = 50$, and the increased radius $R = 50.65$. This represents a 7.38 speed-up factor as compared to the GL_POINTS versions for a even better distribution of votes and a more precise location of the circle centers on the screen where the algorithm output is written.

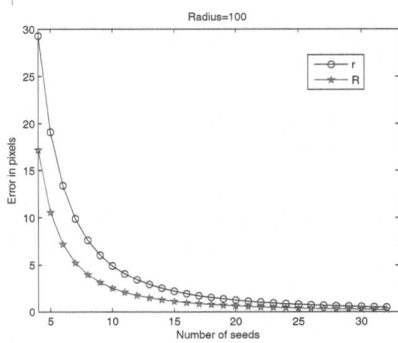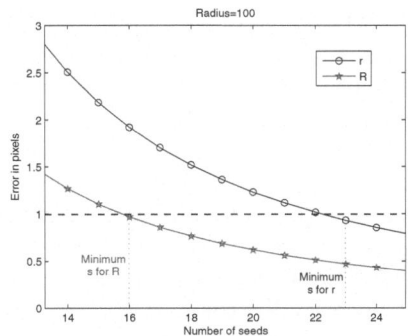

Fig. 7. Maximum error on a vote issued by a GPU rasterizer when increasing the number of seeds, s. The chart on the left corresponds to a circle of radius equal to 100 pixels, and it is zoomed on the right to illustrate the point in which the error crosses the subpixel threshold for two strategies: $r = 100$ (upper values) and $R = 100.97$ (lower values).

Table 2. Minimum number of seeds, s, required to maintain the maximum error below the pixel distance threshold when using the regular and increased radius (second and third rows, respectively) for different radius sizes given in the first row. The savings in the computational workload when using our error correction (R_{max} instead of r for the radius) is shown right after: first, in terms of number of seeds, and then, in execution time for different number of circles to be detected on a 1024x1024 input image.

Radius size (in pixel distance)		$r = 20$	$r = 50$	$r = 100$	$r = 200$
Minimum s using regular radius r		10 seeds	16 seeds	23 seeds	32 seeds
Minimum s using increased radius R		8 seeds	12 seeds	16 seeds	23 seeds
Savings using error correction		2 seeds	4 seeds	7 seeds	9 seeds
Savings in computational time	For 20 circles	1.48%	7.90%	9.75%	10.81%
	For 100 circles	5.24%	10.60%	17.22%	18.94%
	For 500 circles	7.59%	17.31%	24.91%	26.46%

4.3 Computational Savings

Improvements achieved in the output results through the radius increment can be converted into an additional workload reduction when our priority is headed towards faster processing. This reduction can be attained by lowering the number of seeds as long as the per-vote error stays below the one pixel threshold, which is the GPU limitation according to the resolution for the screen holding votes.

In order to maximize this gain, it turns out more profitable to minimize the maximum error for a single vote instead of the average error for the whole population of votes. This results in a new R value, say R_{max}, fulfilling the maximum defect and excess errors depicted in Figure 4 to match. When imposing such condition, we equalize the expressions for both maximum errors, and the formula for R_{max} can be derived as $\frac{2r}{1+\cos\frac{\pi}{s}}$. In example, for $r = 100$ and $s = 16$, R goes to 101.30 exceeding the single pixel threshold $(r + 1)$, whereas the new R_{max} produces 100.97, just below $r + 1$.

Figure 7 represents the behavior of the error in pixels for the new R_{max} as a function of the number of seeds, s, used within the rasterizer. We have also represented the error for the regular radius, r, used by the rasterizer as a departure point for our optimizations. Without the techniques described along this paper, we need to use 23 seeds to keep the error below the one pixel GPU resolution, whereas now 16 seeds suffice.

Conceptually, the new R_{max} reduces the GPU computational workload without penalizing the output results. Table 2 shows the minimum number of seeds required to maintain the error below the one pixel threshold for four different radii $r = 20, 50, 100$ and 200, leading to savings of 2, 4, 7 and 9 seeds, respectively, when using the new radius. This is translated into an additional speed-up for the GPU execution time as outlined in the lower side of the table for different computational workloads of 20, 100 and 500 circles to be recognized in the input image; there, we see solid improvements in a range varying from 5% to 25% without sacrificing accuracy in the computation of the Circle Hough Transform by the GPU rasterizer.

Note that a larger number of seeds always enhances the distribution of rasterizer votes, but Figure 7 reflects how steady improvements are soon converted into modest gains beyond $s = 10$. This confirms that the number of seeds included in the third row of Table 2 becomes a practical number to be used by a rasterizer for each radius size to guarantee satisfactory results combined with high speed-up factors when computing the Circle Hough Transform on the GPU.

5   Summary and Conclusions

We present optimizations for accelerating the execution of the Circle Hough Transform on commodity graphics processors. Under the same number of votes issued by the CPU, the GPU speeds up the code around ten times, with gains varying slightly with the size of the radius and the number of circles detected.

Our optimizations are focused on the functionality of the rasterizer to interpolate the entire spectrum of votes for circle candidates down from a small number of seeds, s. We demonstrate that $s = 10, 16, 23, 32$ for radius sizes of $r = 20, 50, 100, 200$, respectively, obtain a subpixel accuracy and contribute with an additional speed-up factor around 8x on the GPU.

We also evaluate the average error performed by the GPU rasterizer and present methods to minimize it during our executions via a small increment in the radius size. Under this higher radius, the accuracy improves and the computational cost gets reduced around a 25% in the required number of seeds, leading to additional savings around 5-25% in the GPU computational time.

References

[GPGPU (2008)]   A Web page dedicated to the latest developments in general-
                      purpose on the GPU, http://www.gpgpu.org (accessed,
                      February 16 2009)
[Ballard (1981)]   Ballard, D.: Generalized Hough transform to detect arbitrary
                      patterns. IEEE Trans. on Pattern Analysis and Machine In-
                      tel. 13(2), 111–122 (1981)
[Fung et al. (2005)] Fung, J., Mann, S., Aimone, S.: OpenVIDIA: Parallel GPU
                      Computer Vision. In: Proceedings 13th Annual ACM Interna-
                      tional Conference on Multimedia, Singapore, November 6-11
                      (2005)
[Owens et al. (2007)] Owens, J.D., Luebke, D., Govindaraju, N., Harris, M.,
                      Kruger, J., Lefohn, A.E., Purcell, T.J.: A Survey of General-
                      Purpose Computation on Graphics Hardware. Journal Com-
                      puter Graphics Forum 26(1), 80–113 (2007)
[Ruiz et al. (2007a)] Ruiz, A., Ujaldón, M., Guil, N.: Using graphics hardware for
                      enhancing edge and circle detection. In: Martí, J., Benedí,
                      J.M., Mendonça, A.M., Serrat, J. (eds.) IbPRIA 2007. LNCS,
                      vol. 4478, pp. 234–241. Springer, Heidelberg (2007)
[Ujaldon et al. (2008)] Ujaldón, M., Ruiz, A., Guil, N.: On the Computation of the
                      Circle Hough Transform by a GPU Rasterizer. Pattern Rec.
                      Letters 29(2), 319–328 (2008)
[Yuen et al. (1990)] Yuen, H.K., Princen, J., Illingworth, J., Kittler, J.: Compar-
                      ative study of Hough transform methods for circle finding.
                      Image and Vision Computing 8(1), 71–77 (1990)

Appearance and Shape Prior Alignments in Level Set Segmentation

Carlos Platero, Maria C. Tobar, Javier Sanguino, and Jose M. Poncela

Applied Bioengineering Group, Polytechnic University of Madrid, Spain

Abstract. We show a new segmentation technical method that takes shape and appearance data into account. It uses the level set technique. The algorithm merges the edge alignment and homogeneity terms with a shape dissimilarity measure in the segmentation task. Specifically, we make two contributions. In relation to appearance, we propose a new preprocessing step based on non-linear diffusion. The objective is to improve the edge detection and the region smoothing. The second and main contribution is an analytic formulation of the non-rigid transformation of the shape prior over the inertial center of the active contour. We have assumed gaussian density on the sample set of the shape prior and we have applied principal component analysis (PCA). Our method have been validated using 2D and 3D images, including medical images of the liver.

Keywords: segmentation, edge alignment, shape prior, principal component analysis, level set, 3D medical images.

1 Introduction

Image segmentation is a fundamental topic in image analysis. A large variety of segmentation algorithms have been proposed over the last few decades. Earlier approaches were often based on a rather heuristic processing. Optimization methods, more transparent, are now better established. Among them, the level set technique [1], based on variational calculus, has become a popular framework for image segmentation. A review of this technique can be found in Cremers et al[2].

Much research had been developed to integrate prior knowledge into the segmentation task. In this work, we focus on prior knowledge of shape and appearance of the object of interest. We propose a level set approach that incorporates shape priors and appearance data based on a novel nonlinear diffusion preprocessing.

Level set techniques have been adapted to segment images based on numerous low-level criteria such as boundaries to locate in areas of high image gradient [3], uniformity of certain statistical of the image intensity inside and outside the boundary [4] or edge alignment [5]. More recently, shape prior has been integrated into the level set framework. Chen et al [6] introduce an energy term which measures the Chamfer distance between the original active contour and a given prior contour. A variational approach is applied to the rigid transformation

H. Araujo et al. (Eds.): IbPRIA 2009, LNCS 5524, pp. 282–289, 2009.
© Springer-Verlag Berlin Heidelberg 2009

task between two point-sets. Afterwards, Chan and Zhu [7] proposed a variant to compute the dissimilarity of two shapes represented by their embedding level set functions. The idea is to compute the set area symmetric difference. However, this approach needs the registration task since the shape descriptors are not invariants. Finally, Cremers et al [8] performed an invariant approach by means of a set of explicit parameters to take translation and shape scaling into account.

The paper is organized as follows: in section 2, we explain our theoretical framework, which includes functionals that take appearance and shape data into account. In section 3, we show the numerical algorithms for minimizing the functionals. Finally, in section 4, we validate our algorithms using 2D and 3D images, with applications to liver segmentation.

2 Level Set for Segmentation Task

In implicit contour representation, interfaces are defined as the zero level of some embedding function $\phi : \Omega \to \mathbb{R}$, defined over a domain $\Omega \subset \mathbb{R}^m$:

$$C = \partial \omega = \{x \in \Omega / \phi(x) = 0\}; \quad \omega = \{x \in \Omega / \phi(x) > 0\}; \quad \Omega \backslash \bar{\omega} = \{x \in \Omega / \phi(x) < 0\}$$

In a typical level set evolution scheme, the contour evolves by the combination of low-level criteria (dependent on the image data) and shape prior. Such a framework is very popular due to its many advantages. Often, computations can be performed exclusively in the neighborhood of the boundary, getting a high computational efficiency. Furthermore, level set evolution allows a flexible initialization and topological changes.

2.1 Appearance Model

Existing appearance models are validated by means of the edge alignment and homogeneity terms. To improve the segmentation task, the Chan-Vese minimal variance method is combined with the boundary alignment and the geodesic active contours technique [9]. These approaches are based on the fact that the regions are piecewise constant and the borders have high slopes. So edge enhancement and area smoothing are essential. Therefore, we propose a previous image processing step, based on a nonlinear diffusion filter. We have selected a family of diffusivities without control parameters. Based on the analytical formulation, we have experimentally verified stability, consistency and enhancement properties. Using the analytical model, we have determined the relationship between the diffusion time and the gradient module[10].

Starting with an initial image $u_0 : \Omega \to \mathbb{R}$ defined over a domain $\Omega \subset \mathbb{R}^m$, other image $u(x)$ is obtained as solution of a nonlinear diffusion equation with initial and Neumann boundary conditions:

$$u_t = \mathrm{div}\,(g(\|\nabla u\|)\,\nabla u), \quad x \in \Omega, \quad t > 0, \tag{1}$$

with $u(x, 0) = u_0(x)$ when $x \in \Omega$ as initial condition, and $u_n(x) = 0$ for all $x \in \partial \Omega$ as boundary condition, where n is the unit normal vector orthogonal to the boundary. Here $g(\|\nabla u\|) = \frac{1}{\|\nabla u\|^3}$ is the chosen diffusivity function.

Once the image has been filtered obtaining a new image u, our appearance model considers three functionals. The first one has to do with the edge alignment. It is based on the zero crossing detecting of the second-order derivative along the gradient direction. Kimmel and Bruckstein[5] show that the maximization of the functional

$$E_{EDGE}(\phi) = \int_C \nabla u \cdot n \, dx - \int_\omega \text{div}\left(\frac{\nabla u}{\|\nabla u\|}\right) \|\nabla u\| dx \qquad (2)$$

yields the zero crossing detecting. The second functional is the minimal variance term proposed by Chan and Vese[4]. It penalizes the lack of homogeneity inside and outside the evolution contour. It is defined by the weighted formula

$$E_{HOMOGENEITY}(\phi) = \beta_1 \left[\int_\Omega (u - c_{in})^2 H(\phi(x)) dx \right.$$
$$\left. + \int_\Omega (u - c_{out})^2 (1 - H(\phi(x))) dx \right] + \beta_2 \int_\Omega \delta(H(\phi(x))) \|\nabla(\phi(x))\| dx, \qquad (3)$$

where c_{in} and c_{out} are the averages of u inside and outside C respectively, $H()$ denotes the Heaviside step function and $\delta()$ is the Dirac function.

Finally, the third functional has to do with the geodesic active contour. The idea is a minimization of a functional that integrates over an edge indicator function along a contour [3]. It is

$$E_{CONTOUR}(\phi) = \int_\Omega g^*(x)\delta((H(\phi(x)))) \|\nabla(\phi(x)\| dx, \qquad (4)$$

where $g^*(x)$ is an edge indicator function, given, for example, by $g^*(x) = 1/(1 + \|\nabla u\|/k)$, the parameter k used for normalizing the gradient.

The global functional is a weighted sum of the above functionals:

$$E_{appearance}(\phi) = -\alpha E_{EDGE}(\phi) + E_{HOMOGENEITY}(\phi) + \gamma E_{CONTOUR}(\phi) \quad (5)$$

where α, β_1, β_2 and γ are positive constants chosen empirically.

2.2   Shape Model

The first task is to define a distance or dissimilarity measure between shape priors and the contour encoded by the level set function. We compute the dissimilarity of two shapes by calculating their symmetric difference. Given N shape priors $\phi_1, ..., \phi_N$, called templates, and a contour ϕ, an invariant measure is given by[8][11]:

$$d_i^2(\phi, R_i(\phi_i)) = \int_\Omega [H(\phi(x)) - H(\phi_i(R_i^{-1}(x)))]^2 dx \qquad (6)$$

Here R_i is a non-rigid motion, composition of a translation, a rotation and a deformation centered on the inertial center of the contour. Different R_i have been proposed for the registration task. Usually (see [6][7][11]) it is used the variational method, based on the gradient descent of the distance between the shapes. However, this method has several drawbacks[8]. The main problem is to determinate an appropriate time step for each registration parameter, chosen so as to guarantee the stability of the resulting evolution. Experimentally, we found that balancing these parameters requires a careful tuning process. In order to eliminate these difficulties associated with the local optimization for the registration task, we will show that invariance can be achieved analytically by an intrinsic registration process.

Our idea is to build shape statistics which are themselves incorporated into registration and segmentation steps. Let H be the Heaviside function, hence $H(x) = 0$ if $x < 0$ and $H(x) = 1$ if $x \geq 0$. Let $A_i = \{x \in \Omega / \phi_i(x) \geq 0\}$. Then $H(\phi_i(x)) = \chi_{A_i}$, the characteristic function of A_i. For simplification, we assume that the sample sets A_i are given by a Gaussian density function, $f_{A_i}(x) \sim N(\mu_i, \Sigma_i)$, assumption more appropriate if the shape of A_i is oval (see figure 1). Consider the diagonal Jordan canonical matrix D_i for the symmetric matrix Σ_i. The matrix D_i is diagonal, made with the eigenvalues of Σ_i. Let Q_i be the orthogonal matrix whose columns are the eigenvectors of Σ_i. Hence $Q_i^T \Sigma_i Q_i = D_i$. Analogously, for the set A, we have $Q^T \Sigma Q = D$. We perform principal component analysis on A_i, considering three types of transformations: I) Translation according to μ, $T_\mu : \mathbb{R}^m \to \mathbb{R}^m$ $T_\mu(x) = x + \mu$, II) Rotation $Q : \mathbb{R}^m \to \mathbb{R}^m$ and III) Scaling in the principal components $D : \mathbb{R}^m \to \mathbb{R}^m$. Therefore, we propose the following analytic formulation:

$$B_i = T_\mu Q D (T_{\mu_i} Q_i D_i)^{-1} A_i = R_i(A_i) = \{QDD_i^{-1}Q_i^T(x-\mu_i)+\mu \ / \ x \in A_i\}. \quad (7)$$

Since $B_i = R_i(A_i)$, it follows that $\chi_{B_i}(x) = \chi_{A_i}(R_i^{-1}(x)) = H(\phi_i(R_i^{-1}(x)))$, hence the formula (6) is no more than the expression of the symmetric difference of the sets A and B_i:

$$d_i^2(\phi, R_i(\phi_i)) = \int_\Omega [\chi_A - \chi_{B_i}]^2 dx. \quad (8)$$

We observe that the term $(T_{\mu_i} Q_i D_i)^{-1}$ gives the normalization of the shape prior. It is transformed over principal components. Finally, the normalized shape prior is aligned and deformed with respect to the gravity center of ϕ.

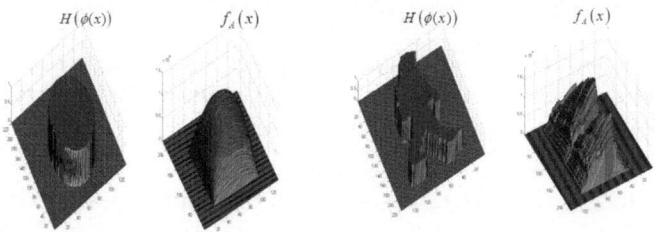

Fig. 1. Shape priors define by means Heaviside function and their density functions of the characteristic sets

The construction of an appropriate shape dissimilarity measure permits to define two goals: 1. To choose the template more similar to the original active contour, and 2. To define a shape energy for the segmentation task. Both of them are supported into the level set domain. Among all the distances d_i^2 between each shape prior and the active contour defined in (6), the minimum distance d_j^2 gives us the correct template ϕ_j to be used:

$$\min_i d_i^2(\phi, R_i(\phi_i)) = d_j^2(\phi, R_j(\phi_j)). \qquad (9)$$

It follows that the shape energy term is given by the formula

$$E_{shape}(\phi) = \zeta \int_\Omega [H(\phi(x)) - H(\phi_j(R_j^{-1}(x)))]^2 dx \qquad (10)$$

where ζ is a positive constant that must be tuned. For other approaches see [8].

3   Numerical Algorithms

We can incorporate shape and appearance data using the following weighted sum for their functionals:

$$E_{total}(\phi) = E_{appearance}(\phi) + E_{shape}(\phi) \qquad (11)$$

In this section, we discuss the numerical algorithms for minimizing this functional. By calculus of variations, the evolution equation $\partial_t \phi = -\partial_\phi E_{total}$ is the gradient flow that minimizes it. The steepest descent process for minimization is:

$$\frac{\partial \phi}{\partial t} = -\delta(\phi)[-\alpha u_{\xi\xi} + \beta_1(u - c_{in})^2 - \beta_1(u - c_{out})^2$$
$$+ \beta_2 \mathrm{div}\left(\frac{\nabla\phi}{\|\nabla\phi\|}\right) + \gamma \mathrm{div}\left(g^* \frac{\nabla\phi}{\|\nabla\phi\|}\right) + 2\zeta(H(\phi) - H(\phi_j(R_j^{-1}(x))))] \qquad (12)$$

where $u_{\xi\xi}$ is the second derivative of u in the gradient direction.

The level set evolution algorithm uses an efficient distance preserving narrow band technique[12]. The reinitialization of the level set is not longer necessary. The algorithm is implemented using a simple finite difference scheme instead of the complex upwind finite difference scheme. It is based on the following internal energy term:

$$\eta \int_\Omega \frac{1}{2}(\|\nabla\phi(x)\| - 1)^2 dx. \qquad (13)$$

Here $\eta > 0$ is a parameter that controls the effect of penalizing the deviation of ϕ from a signed distance function. The resulting evolution of the level set function is the gradient flow that minimizes the overall energy funtional

$$\frac{\partial \phi}{\partial t} = -\delta(\phi)[-\alpha u_{\xi\xi} + \beta_1(u - c_{in})^2 - \beta_1(u - c_{out})^2 + \beta_2 \mathrm{div}\left(\frac{\nabla\phi}{\|\nabla\phi\|}\right) + \gamma \mathrm{div}\left(g^* \frac{\nabla\phi}{\|\nabla\phi\|}\right)$$
$$+ 2\zeta(H(\phi) - H(\phi_j(R_j^{-1}(x))))] - \eta\left[\Delta\phi - \mathrm{div}\left(\frac{\nabla\phi}{\|\nabla\phi\|}\right)\right] \qquad (14)$$

4   Experiments and Applications

For supplying the active contour evolution, 2D and 3D images are filtered by (1). The diffusivity has been regularized with an almost zero positive constant. The non-linear diffusion is implemented using a semi-implicit scheme and extended with an AOS (Additive Operator Splitting) approach [13]. The diffusion time step is calculated in[10]:

$$\Delta t = \frac{\|\nabla u\|_{th}^3}{5 \cdot n_{iter}} \tag{15}$$

where $\|\nabla u\|_{th}$ is the threshold which stars from enhancement is achieved, and n_{iter} denotes the number of iterations. In the experiments carried out, we have employed 10 iterations for 2D and 4 iterations for 3D.

In relation to the narrow band implementation, we have followed Li et al[12] for 2D images and we have extended it for 3D images. In addition, this technique also is an efficient scheme for initializing level set, which uses bi-value region instead of the conventional signed distance function. For this reason, we have used the classic segmentation methods as initialization of our level set algorithm.

In order to determinate the orientations of the principal components, we have applied the condition $diag(Q_i) > 0$. It is based on the fact that the samples are fixed in the first quadrant or octant.

The proposed variational level set method has been applied to a variety of 2D and 3D images; for example, to the case of a partially occluded walking person[14]. Figure 2 shows seven prior templates for this task. We have applied different rotations and scaling over images to check the invariant properties. The first row of figure 3 shows the active contour evolution with only appearance terms. We have observed that the algorithm can not segment the silhouette due to the partial occlusion effect. The rest of the rows shows the evolution of the active contour (painted in red) and the deformable shape prior (painted in green) with different iterations. The control parameters have been tuned with the values $\Delta t = 5s, \alpha = 5, \beta_1 = 1, \beta_2 = 1, \gamma = 1, \zeta = 1$ and $\eta = 0.04$.

Liver segmentation for 3D CT/MRI images is usually the first step in the computer-assisted diagnosis and surgery systems for liver diseases. Algorithms relying solely on image intensities or derived features usually fail. To deal with missing or ambiguous low-level information, shape prior information has been successfully employed. However, the lack of knowledge about the location, orientation and deformation of the liver, due to diseases or different acquisition procedures, adds another major challenge to any segmentation algorithm. In order to address these problems of varying shape, position and orientation, we have applied our framework to liver segmentation. Our algorithm starts with a image preprocessing, following (1) and (15). Then, region growing and 3D edge detector are applied to the filtered image. Morphological post-processing merges the previous

Fig. 2. Walking silhouettes as shape priors

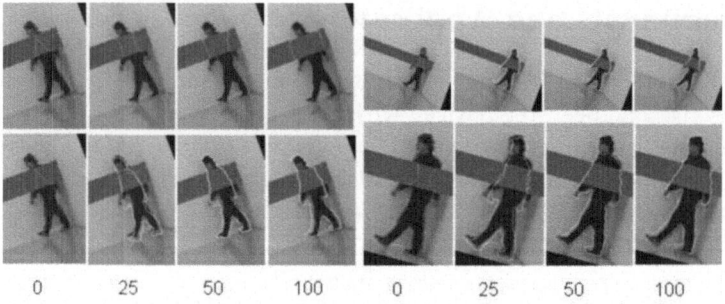

Fig. 3. The evolution of the active contour and the deformable shape prior over the segmentation of a partially occluded human silhouette: a) medium scale, b) small and large scales

Fig. 4. 3D liver model use in the segmentation task

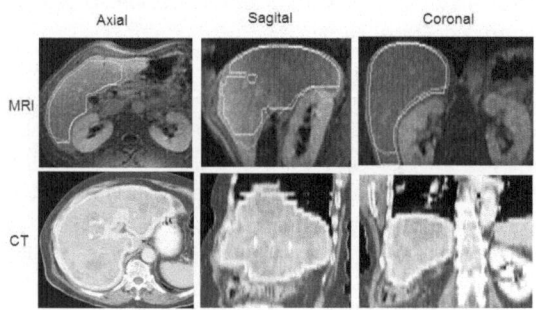

Fig. 5. a)MRI 3D FSPGR 2 mm slice, b)CT 7 mm slice

steps [15], initializing the contour. Subsequently, the surface evolves using our level set algorithm in (14). The shape models have been obtained using several manual segmentations. Figure 4 shows some CT/MRI liver models used in the segmentation task. Finally, figure 5 shows some centered slices of the CT/MRI-livers where the initial contours are in green, the final segmentation in red and the deformable model in blue. For all the cases, we have used the following control parameters: $\Delta t = 2, iter = 50, \alpha = 20, \beta_1 = 15, \beta_2 = 1, \gamma = 2, \zeta = 0.5$ and $\eta = 0.04$.

5   Conclusions

We have developed two contributions. First, we have performed a preprocessing step based on a novel nonlinear diffusion without control parameters. In order to incorporate shape prior data, we have proposed an analytic solution for generating a nonrigid transformation of the shape prior over the active contour. It is based on

PCA over the sample set of the shape priors. Using the proposed nonrigid transformation, a shape dissimilarity measure is defined on the space of level set functions. It allows to choose the template closer to the active contour and it defines a shape energy term. It has been tested on 2D and 3D images for segmentation tasks.

References

1. Osher, S., Sethian, J.A.: Fronts propagating with curvature-dependent speed: algorithms based on Hamilton-Jacobi formulations. Journal of Computational Physics 79, 12–49 (1988)
2. Cremers, D., Rousson, M., Deriche, R.: A Review of Statistical Approaches to Level Set Segmentation: Integrating Color, Texture, Motion and Shape. International Journal of Computer Vision 72, 195–215 (2007)
3. Caselles, V., Kimmel, R., Sapiro, G.: Geodesic Active Contours. International Journal of Computer Vision 22, 61–79 (1997)
4. Chan, T.F., Vese, L.A.: Active contours without edges. IEEE Transactions on Image Processing 10(2), 266–277 (2001)
5. Kimmel, R., Bruckstein, A.M.: Regularized Laplacian Zero Crossings as Optimal Edge Integrators. International Journal of Computer Vision 53(3), 225–243 (2003)
6. Chen, Y., Tagare, H.D., Thiruvenkadam, S., Huang, F., Wilson, D., Gopinath, K.S., Briggs, R.W., Geiser, E.A.: Using Prior Shapes in Geometric Active Contours in a Variational Framework. International Journal of Computer Vision 50(3), 315–328 (2002)
7. Chan, T., Zhu, W.: Level Set Based Shape Prior Segmentation. Computer Vision and Pattern Recognition. In: IEEE Computer Society Conference on Computer Vision and Pattern Recognition. CVPR 2005, vol. 2 (2005)
8. Cremers, D., Osher, S.J., Soatto, S.: Kernel Density Estimation and Intrinsic Alignment for Shape Priors in Level Set Segmentation. International Journal of Computer Vision 69(3), 335–351 (2006)
9. Holtzman-Gazit, M., Kimmel, R., Peled, N., Goldsher, D.: Segmentation of thin structures in volumetric medical images. IEEE Transactions on Image Processing 15(2), 354–363 (2006)
10. Platero, C., Sanguino, J.: Analytical Approximations for Nonlinear Diffusion Time in Multiscale Edge Enhancement. In: International Conference on Computer Vision Theory and Applications (VISAPP 2009), Lisboa, Portugal, February 5-8 (2009)
11. Charpiat, G., Faugeras, O., Keriven, R.: Approximations of Shape Metrics and Application to Shape Warping and Empirical Shape Statistics. Foundations of Computational Mathematics 15(1), 1–58 (2005)
12. Li, C., Xu, C., Gui, C., Fox, M.: Level Set Evolution without Re-Initialization: A New Variational Formulation. In: IEEE Coputer Society Conference on Computer Vision and Pattern Recognition IEEE Computer Society1999, vol. 1, p. 430 (2005)
13. Weickert, J., Romeny, B., Viergever, M.A.: Efficient and reliable schemes for nonlinear diffusion filtering. IEEE Transactions on Image Processing 7(3), 398–410 (1998)
14. Computer Vision Group Bonn,
   http://www-cvpr.iai.uni-bonn.de/index.php?nav=data
15. Platero, C., Poncela, J.M., Gonzalez, P., Tobar, M.C., Sanguino, J., Asensio, G., Santos, E.: Liver segmentation for hepatic lesions detection and characterisation. In: 5th IEEE International Symposium on Biomedical Imaging: From Nano to Macro, 2008. ISBI 2008, pp. 13–16 (2008)

The Diagonal Split: A Pre-segmentation Step for Page Layout Analysis and Classification

Albert Gordo and Ernest Valveny

Computer Vision Center - Computer Science Department
Universitat Autònoma de Barcelona
Spain
{agordo,ernest.valveny}@cvc.uab.es

Abstract. Document classification is an important task in all the processes related to document storage and retrieval. In the case of complex documents, structural features are needed to achieve a correct classification. Unfortunately, physical layout analysis is error prone. In this paper we present a pre-segmentation step based on a divide & conquer strategy that can be used to improve the page segmentation results, independently of the segmentation algorithm used. This pre-segmentation step is evaluated in classification and retrieval using the selective CRLA algorithm for layout segmentation together with a clustering based on the voronoi area diagram, and tested on two different databases, MARG and Girona Archives.

1 Introduction

Document classification is an important task in document management and retrieval. It is usually based on the extraction of some features from the document image. These document features can be of different types. In [4] three categories are proposed (adapted from the four proposed in [5]): *image features*, extracted directly from the image or from a segmented image (e.g. the density of black pixels of a region), *structural features* or relationships between blocks in the page, obtained from the page layout, and *textual features*, based on the OCR output of the image. A classifier may combine these features to get better results.

Structural features are necessary to classify documents with structural variations within a class. Unfortunately, they rely on the results of physical layout analysis, which is complex and error prone. When dealing with simple manhattan layouts, classic approaches like the X-Y cut [10] or the whitespace analysis [3] usually give good results. Harder non-manhattan layouts usually require more complex methods like selective smearing [9], texture analysis [1], kNN analysis [2] or the voronoi area diagram [8]. These complex non-manhattan layouts usually cause lots of merge errors which negatively affect the classification accuracy.

In this paper we present a pre-segmentation step based on a divide & conquer strategy for non-manhattan documents to improve the layout segmentation of the page and decrease the classification and retrieval error rate.

H. Araujo et al. (Eds.): IbPRIA 2009, LNCS 5524, pp. 290–297, 2009.
© Springer-Verlag Berlin Heidelberg 2009

The method tries to find the path of minimum cost traversing the page from one corner to the opposite, where cost is based on the distance to the nearest black pixel. Then, the regions resulting from this division can be used as the input of any page segmentation algorithm. This pre-segmentation step has been applied to the classifcation of pages in two collections of documents using the selective CRLA segmentation algorithm. The results show that, in general, classification error rates decrease when we include the pre-segmentation step.

In section 2 we introduce this method and its formulation. Section 3 deals with the experimentation, and finally, in section 4 we summarize the obtained results.

2   The Diagonal Split

The Diagonal Split follows a divide & conquer strategy to improve the results that a segmentation algorithm would obtain working on a whole non-manhattan page. The idea behind it is to split the image in regions and work on them separately in the same fashion as the X-Y cut algorithm. Unfortunately, most non-manhattan layouts cannot be cut using only straight horizontal or vertical lines without splitting important regions. The Diagonal Split finds the best paths to cross the image from the top-left corner to the bottom-right and from the top-right to the bottom-left while trying to avoid regions with black pixels. These paths are also constrained by the fact that each new step must be closer to its destiny than the previous step. The intersection of these two paths produces up to four simpler non-overlapping regions that can then be segmented with the most suitable segmentation algorithm.

2.1   Formulation

Let I be the binary matrix of size $M \times N$ which represents the original binarized image, and let C be a cost matrix also of size $M \times N$ that represents the intrinsic cost of crossing through certain position in any given time. Then, the cost of the best path from position $(0, 0)$ up to position (y, x) can be recursively defined as

$$D(y,x) = \begin{cases} C(y,x) & \text{if } y = 0 \wedge x = 0, \\ C(y,x) + D(y, x-1) & \text{if } y = 0, \\ C(y,x) + D(y-1, x) & \text{if } x = 0, \\ \min \begin{cases} \sqrt{2}\, C(y,x) + D(y-1, x-1) \\ C(y,x) + D(y-1, x) \\ C(y,x) + D(y, x-1) \end{cases} & \text{otherwise.} \end{cases} \tag{1}$$

and the best path cost from the top left corner up to the bottom right be obtained solving $D(M - 1, N - 1)$. The best path cost from the top right corner up to the bottom left can be analogously obtained. By means of dynamic programming, both equations can be solved in $\mathcal{O}(MN)$ and both paths recovered.

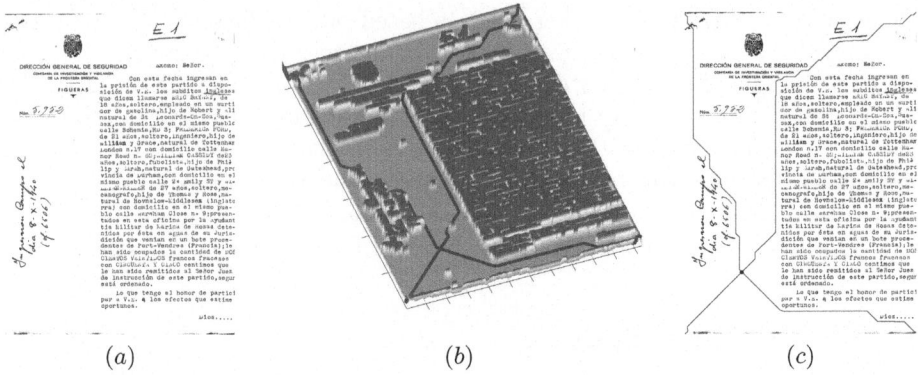

(a)   (b)   (c)

Fig. 1. (a) Original image. (b) Cost map. (c) Diagonal Split paths.

The cost matrix C represents how inconvenient is for the path to cross a given position. Therefore, as we intend to avoid black pixels, these should have a high penalty *BlackPenalty*. Nevertheless, it is important not to give them an infinite penalty, as sometimes going through a black pixel is inevitable. White pixels, on the other hand, should decrease its penalty as we get further from black pixels. A first approach would be to use the inverse distance to the nearest black pixel, but this creates a very abrupt fall that is not appropriate. A better approach is to subtract the distance, possibly scaled by a factor, to the maximum allowed value, i.e. *BlackPenalty*.

We must also ensure that the cost matrix is always not only positive but also greater than zero, as each step must involve a cost. Therefore, the cost matrix C can be defined as

$$C(y, x) = max \begin{cases} 1 \\ BlackPenalty - kDN(y, x) \end{cases} \quad (2)$$

where $DN(y, x)$ represents the distance to the nearest black pixel from position (y, x) and k is a scale factor that represents the slope of the *mountains* of the cost matrix.

Unfortunately, this best path strategy could lead to find typographic rivers of white on text documents. To minimize this effect, a morphological closure is applied to the document before calculating the cost matrix. In figure 1 we can see a sample page with its calculated cost matrix and the resulting Diagonal Split.

3   Experiments and Results

To evaluate the effect of the Diagonal Split in the classification problem two different databases were chosen: The MARG[1] (Medical Article Records Ground-truth) database and the Girona Archives database, both scanned at 300 dpi.

---

[1] http://marg.nlm.nih.gov/index2.ascp

The MARG database contains 1553 images, scanned documents of first pages of different medical journals with a manhattan layout. The database is mostly-text, though some pages contain complex images and tables. This database is divided into nine different categories of documents.

The Girona database consists of border records from the Civil Government of Girona. It contains documents related to people going through the Spanish-French border from 1940 up to 1976 such as safe-conducts, arrest reports, documents of prisoners transfers, medical reports, correspondence, etc. Even if it is a mostly-text database, in this case most of the pages also have images like stamps, signatures, etc in a non-manhattan disposition. Also, even if most of the database is typewritten, some of the pages are handwritten. We have used a subset of the database that contains 690 images and is currently divided in 6 different categories. Some samples of both databases can be seen in figure 2.

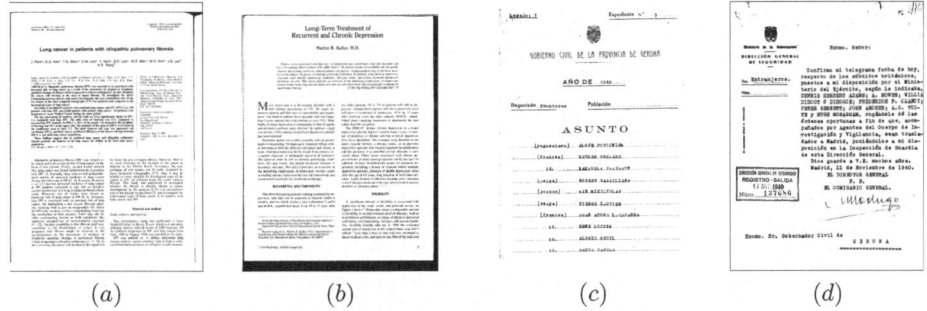

(a)	(b)	(c)	(d)

Fig. 2. (a-b) Samples of MARG database. (c-d) Samples of Girona database.

To test the effect of the Diagonal Split strategy in the classification problem, we will first generate the layout of all the images, both using and not using the Diagonal Split as a first step. Later, we will define a layout distance between pages. Finally, this distance will be used to define a classification strategy to evaluate the quality of the layout obtained.

3.1   Layout Generation

Diagonal Split. As a first step, we will apply the Diagonal Split. Calculating the cost matrix for each image is a heavy task; to speed up the calculus, each image is rescaled to a 50% size before calculating the cost matrix and the borders. As for the parameters, the chosen default values are $k = 4$ and $BlackPenalty = 50$.

Segmentation. For the segmentation, we have chosen the selective CRLA algorithm [9]. This top-bottom algorithm can deal with non-manhattan layouts and also produces a *text* and *non text* separation, which will be useful especially for the Girona database. According to [6], the smearing family also has a low merge error rate, which is again useful for the non-trivial layouts of the Girona database. Finally, the results are not necessarily rectangular but can also be region contours, giving us a more faithful representation of the layout.

Clustering. The selective CRLA produces a line-based segmentation. Therefore, a clustering algorithm must be used to obtain a block-based segmentation as requiered to perform the classification. To do so, we used a clustering based on the voronoi area diagram. The voronoi area diagram [8] is commonly used as a segmentation algorithm [6], just like the selective CRLA. However, it can also be used as a clustering algorithm. Firstly, the voronoi area diagram of the original page must be generated and, secondly, for each of the voronoi regions, we combine the selective CRLA regions that intersect with it. Setting the voronoi area diagram parameters in a rather conservative manner, we can achieve good clustering results.

As the regions are not necessarily rectangular, region merging can be a problem. We have decided to use the bounding box of the union of the regions, but an active contour or even the convex hull could also be feasible alternatives. This decision is partly supported by the fact that the block distance is too computationally expensive when non-rectangular blocks are used. Finally, regarding the *non text* regions, it is not clear *a priori* if they should be clustered or not. Thus, we will try and compare both approaches in our experiments.

3.2   Layout Distance Definition

In order to perform a layout-based classification we must define a layout distance. Based on the results of [11], we have decided to use a block distance consisting of a combination of block overlap and manhattan distance and a page distance based on the Minimum Weight Edge Cover [7] assignment. In our case, though, we have two different kinds of blocks: *text* blocks and *non text* blocks. Therefore, the former block distance may not be accurate when comparing blocks of different types. In this case, we will assign them the maximum possible block distance, i.e., 2.

3.3   Classification and Retrieval

Once a layout distance is defined, we can proceed to classify the pages. We will employ a simple nearest neighbour classifier, and the testing strategy will be Leaving One Out. As one of the main interests is document retrieval, we will also compare the precision and recall results obtained with these approaches.

3.4   Results

Figure 3 shows the effect of applying the Diagonal Split in the classification of each of the databases following a Leaving One out schema and a nearest neighbour classifier. For each one, three different alternatives have been considered regarding the *non-text* regions: Ignore them in the classification, take them into account but do not previously cluster them and, finally, cluster and consider them for the classification. It is interesting how the improvement produced by

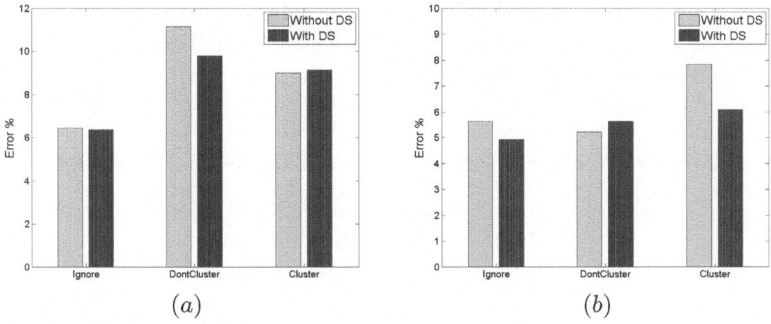

Fig. 3. (a) MARG classification results. (b) Girona classification results.

the Diagonal Split is different depending on the database regarding the clustering of the *non-text* regions. In the case of ignoring them, the Diagonal Split slightly improves the results on both databases, particulary on Girona.

Also interesting is the fact that the best results are systematically obtained when ignoring the *non-text* regions in the classification. In the case of the MARG database, the explanation is simple: there are barely any *non-text* regions in it. Most of the detected *non-regions* are probably false positives, leading to a bad classification. Clustering *non-text* regions decreases the error rate just because there is less penalization in missing one big zone than two small ones. As for the Girona database, the results are more similar as there actually are lots of *non-text* regions. These are already well clustered by the selective CRLA, thus clustering them probably removes zones that were important for the matching. Finally, the fact that ignoring *non-text* regions still leads to better results is probably caused by the fact that the *text / non-text* classifier from the selective CRLA is not accurate enough. It is reasonable to think that a better *text / non-text* classifier would lead to better results when using the unclustered *non-text* regions.

For retrieval we will only use the configuration with the best results at classification, i.e., ignoring the *non-text* regions. We will calculate the precision against recall curve for each query and average the results after resampling to a fixed number of points. The results can be seen in figure 4. For the MARG database, the results are almost equal. In the case of Girona, the curve produced after applying the Diagonal Split is better in the first, and therefore, more relevant retrievals.

This can be quantified using the Average Precision formula

$$AveP = \frac{\sum_{r=1}^{N} (P(r) \times Rel(r))}{\text{Relevant documents}} \tag{3}$$

where N is the total number of documents, $P(r)$ is the precision after retrieving the r *eth* element and the binary function $Rel(r)$ indicates if the r *eth* element is relevant or not.

Table 1 shows the averaged results of this measure. It can be seen that the results for the MARG database are slightly worse with the Diagonal Split while on the Girona database the results are better as expected.

Table 1. Average precision for MARG and Girona databases

	Without DS	With DS
MARG	0.2748	0.2737
Girona	0.5601	0.5630

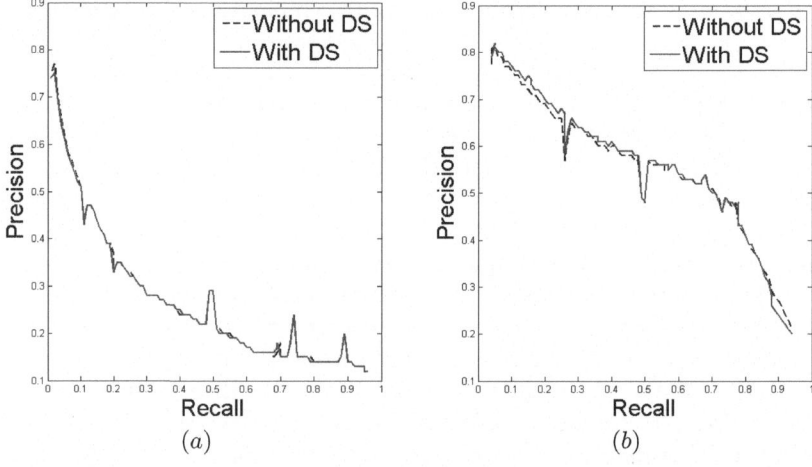

(a)   (b)

Fig. 4. (a) MARG retrieval results. (b) Girona retrieval results.

It should be noted that the selective CRLA parameters have not been tuned for these databases. Tuning the parameters through validation would most likely yield better results in the classification. Moreover, the Diagonal Split approach allows the parameters of the segmentation method to be adapted for each of the different calculated regions. This would allow some algorithms like the document spectrum analysis [2] to work more accurately on pages with different component sizes. In addition, the smearing algorithms have a low merge error ratio[6]. Therefore, the Diagonal Split on other more merge error prone algorithms should make a wider difference.

4   Conclusions

In this paper we have presented a method to improve the segmentation of non-manhattan documents, which can be useful for other tasks, namely classification and categorization of documents. Experimental results show that applying this method to non-manhattan documents using the default parameters increases both the classification and the precision against recall rate. On manhattan documents the classification rates slightly increase while the overall retrieval decreases. Nonetheless, the method can be refined adjusting the parameters k and *BlackPenalty* through validation depending on the database.

References

1. Jain, A.K., Bhattacharjee, S.: Text segmentation using Gabor filters for automatic document processing. Machine Vission Appl. 5, 169–184 (1992)
2. O'Gorman, L.: The Document Spectrum for Page Layout Analysis. IEEE Transactions on Pattern Analysis and Machine Intelligence 15(11), 1162–1173 (1993)
3. Baird, H.S.: Background structure in document images. In: Document Image Analysis, pp. 17–34. World Scientific, Singapore (1994)
4. Chen, N., Blostein, D.: A survey of document image classification: problem statement, classifier architecture and performance evaluation. Int. J. Doc. Anal. Recognit. 10(1), 1–16 (2007)
5. Cesarini, F., Lastri, M., Marinai, S., Soda, G.: Encoding of modified X-Y trees for document classification. In: Proceedings Sixth International Conference on Document Analysis and Recognition, pp. 1131–1136 (2001)
6. Shafait, F., Keysers, D., Breuel, T.M.: Performance Comparison of Six Algorithms for Page Segmentation. In: Bunke, H., Spitz, A.L. (eds.) DAS 2006. LNCS, vol. 3872, pp. 368–379. Springer, Heidelberg (2006)
7. Keysers, D., Deselaers, T., Ney, H.: Pixel-to-Pixel Matching for Image Recognition using Hungarian Graph Matching. In: DAGM 2004, Pattern Recognition, 26th DAGM Symposium, pp. 154–162 (2004)
8. Kise, K., Sato, A., Iwata, M.: Segmentation of page images using the area Voronoi diagram. Comput. Vis. Image Underst. 70(3), 370–382 (1998)
9. Sun, H.: Page segmentation for Manhattan and non-Manhattan layout documents via selective CRLA. In: Proc. Eighth International Conference on Document Analysis and Recognition, vol. 1, pp. 116–120 (2005)
10. Nagy, G., Seth, S.: Hierarchical representation of optically scanned documents. In: Proc. Seventh Int. Conf. Patt. Recogn (ICPR), pp. 347–349 (1984)
11. van Beusekom, J., Keysers, D., Shafait, F., Breuel, T.M.: Distance measures for layout-based document image retrieval. In: Second International Conference on Document Image Analysis for Libraries(DIAL) (2006)

Robust Super-Resolution Using a Median Filter for Irregular Samples

Alfonso Sánchez-Beato[1] and Gonzalo Pajares[2]

[1] Universidad Nacional de Educación a Distancia, Madrid, Spain
abeato@ieee.org
[2] Universidad Complutense de Madrid, Madrid, Spain
pajares@fdi.ucm.es

Abstract. Super-resolution (SR) techniques produce a high resolution (HR) image from a set of low-resolution (LR) undersampled images. Usually, SR problems are posed as estimation problems where the LR images are contaminated by stationary noise. However, in real SR problems is very common to have non-stationary noise due to problems in the registration of the images or outliers. SR methods that address this type of problems are called robust. In this paper we propose a novel robust SR method that employs a median filter directly in the data from the LR images, before proceeding to the interpolation and deblurring steps that are common in SR. We compare this new method with other robust SR methods with synthetic and real data, proving that it outperforms the other methods in both cases.

1 Introduction

Super-Resolution (SR) is a signal processing technique that creates images of bigger resolution and better quality (high resolution images, HR) from a series of images of small resolution and low quality (low resolution images, LR). This problem has been vastly treated in the literature, and there are some good tutorials that provide an excellent introduction to the field, like [1] or [2]. To achieve Super-Resolution there are a few smaller tasks that must be resolved: registration as a first step, interpolation, and restoration (which includes noise reduction and deblurring). In this paper, we will treat specific denoising techniques for super-resolution.

Specific denoising procedures for SR are not numerous. The reason for this is that usually denoising is achieved jointly with data fusion and deblurring. The standard approach for SR is to consider it as an estimation problem where the original signal is embedded in noise [3]. Usually, the problem is discretized and posed as the linear system of equations [4]

$$w = Az + n, \qquad (1)$$

where w and z contain the pixels from the LR images and the pixels from the HR image, respectively, in stacked form, n is additive noise that appears in the

H. Araujo et al. (Eds.): IbPRIA 2009, LNCS 5524, pp. 298–305, 2009.

process of obtaining the LR images, and $\mathbf{A}$ is the system matrix, which produces the geometric warping, blurring and decimation that converts the HR image to the different LR images. In most SR methods, the images are first registered among themselves and then interpolation and restoration steps are performed jointly in an ML or MAP framework, posing a minimization problem of the form

$$\hat{\mathbf{z}} = \arg\min_{\mathbf{z}} \left[\|\mathbf{A}\mathbf{z} - \mathbf{w}\|_{l_p}^{p} + \lambda \Omega(\mathbf{z}) \right], \tag{2}$$

where the l_p norm is used to measure distances, λ, the regularization parameter, is a scalar for properly weighting the first term (similarity cost) against the second term (regularization cost), and Ω is the regularization cost function. The solution to (2), $\hat{\mathbf{z}}$, will be optimal for Gaussian white noise when the norm is l_2 or optimal for biexponentially distributed white noise for norm l_1. When the SR problem is posed differently and the protection against noise is not very strong, specific denoising algorithms have been proposed, as the simple averaging performed after interpolation in [5].

In any case, the denoising in SR has usually assumed stationary noise, while in many real cases this is not enough. Non-stationary noise, like salt and pepper noise, or outliers due to, for instance, registration errors, may appear. The techniques that deal with this kind of noise for image sequences are called robust super-resolution methods. In [6], a method that substituted the mean gradient among the LR images used in iterative solutions of (2) by a median gradient calculated also using the LR images was proposed. Another approach to robust SR was proposed in [7], where instead of using the l_2 norm in (2), the more robust to outliers l_1 norm is employed. In this paper we will propose an alternative approach based on the median filter and the results will be compared with those of the mentioned methods.

The paper is organized as follows. Section 2 describes the proposed median filter for handling non-stationary noise. Section 3 makes a comparison of the proposed method against other robust SR methods. Finally, section 4 exposes the conclusions.

2   Median Filter for Irregular Samples

A median filter applied to N samples first orders the samples in increasing order and then selects the sample in the middle as output, if N is odd. For even N we will select the two samples in the middle and its mean will be selected as output.

When applied to images, the pixels that surround a given pixel are selected and the median filter is applied to them. The selected area is usually rectangular and centered in the output sample coordinates. In some filters, the selected pixels are the center pixel and the pixels that are up, down, left and right of it, five in total. In any case the rectangular grid of the image limits the shape of the area of the selected pixels, which introduces an anisotropy that can produce artifacts in the filter output.

In super-resolution, it makes sense to apply a median filter not in the resampled image, but directly in the LR samples, as the available information is much

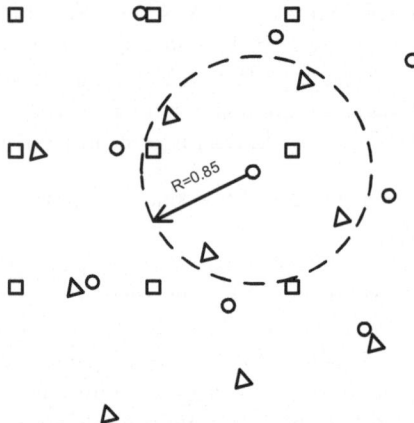

Fig. 1. Median filter for irregular samples. Samples for three different images are represented. The point in the center of the circle is substituted by the median of all points in the circle, including itself. In the figure, the radius of the circle is equal to 0.85 LR pixels.

greater at that moment. The early erasing of non-stationary noise will also help to obtain a better resampled image, as most methods suppose stationary noise. In this way, we can handle both types of noise easily. We propose a median filter for irregular samples, as those coming from the registered LR images in SR, that will have as output locations the same irregular positions as the input samples. To obtain the selected input pixels for a given location, we will simply draw a circumference around that location and all the samples inside that circumference will be the input to the median filter. Note that this area is more regular than that of median filters applied to pixels in a grid, where the area has normally square shape. In Fig. 1 we can see an example where there are three registered LR images. The pixels from each image have a different shape to differentiate among them. The output of the median filter for the location at the center of the circumference in the figure will be the median of the seven LR pixels present in the drawn circle.

As can be easily seen, the radius of the circumference is an important design parameter. There is a trade-off between noise removal and smoothing: for a big radius, we will remove more outliers, but we also will make the output much smoother. In the other hand, a too small radius will make the final HR image sharper, but could also leave artifacts in it due to outliers.

3   Performance Analysis of Robust Noise Removal Methods

In this section we will compare the proposed median filter for irregular samples with different robust super-resolution methods. We will apply our filter and then use the projection method proposed in [8] for resampling in a rectangular grid.

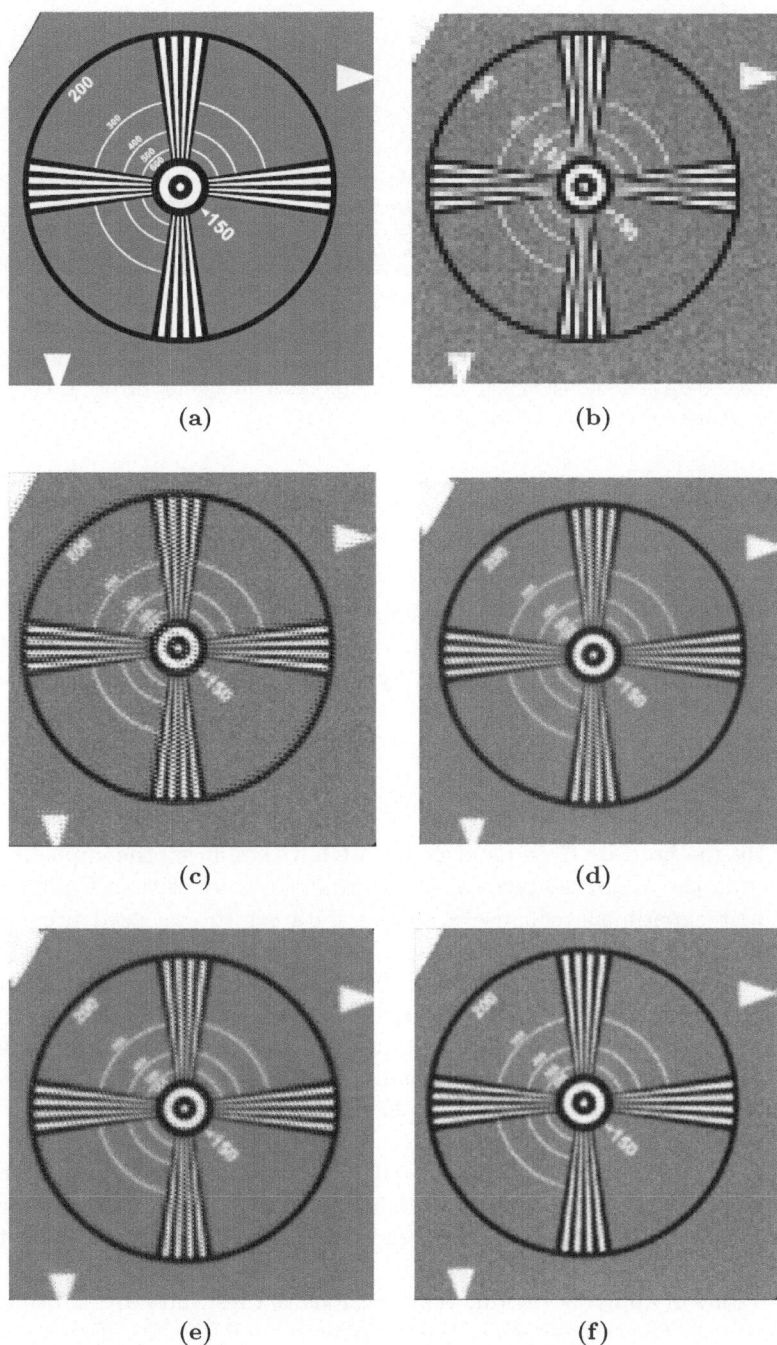

Fig. 2. Chart sequence and generated HR images. (a) The original image for experiment one, (b) a noisy and blurry LR image generated from (a), HR images produced by (c) the projective method from [8], (d) l_1 norm method with bilateral TV regularization, (e) the median gradient method of Zomet with bilateral TV regularization, and (f) the projective method with a previous median filter applied.

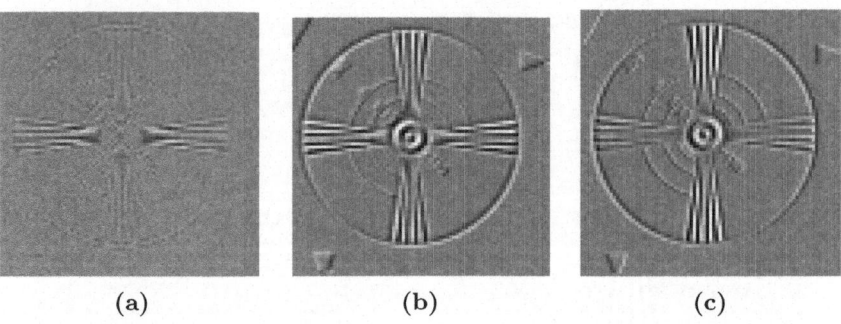

(a)   (b)   (c)

Fig. 3. Simulated registration errors for experiment one. (a) An example difference image when there is no registration error, (b) difference image for error $(1, 1)^T$, and (c) difference image for error $(-1, 0.5)^T$.

We will make two experiments, one with synthetic data and one that uses real data. The methods we will compare to are:

– The plain projective method proposed in [8], to compare with a method that has no protection against non-stationary noise. Among other advantages, this method does not have any adjustable parameters, so it needs no fine-tuning.
– The robust SR method proposed by Farsiu et al. in [7], which is based on using the l_1 norm in (2).
– The robust SR method proposed by Zomet et al. in [6], which is based on using the median of the gradient of the LR images to estimate the gradient used for calculating the next estimation when solving iteratively (2).

To test the methods by Farsiu and Zomet we have employed the implementation contained in the MDSP software package from the University of California [7].

The first experiment will use a similar data set to one used previously in [7]. This data set was generated using a capture of a chart usually employed to measure the resolution of cameras, and then generating 10 low resolution images. Firstly, the original image (see Fig. 2a) is blurred with a Gaussian kernel with variance $\sigma^2 = 1$ and then LR images are generated using random shifts and downsampling the original by four. Finally, white Gaussian noise is added to the LR images until achieving a PSNR of 17 dB. The result can be seen in Fig. 2b. To introduce outliers, we will add errors in the registration step for two of the images, while the registration values will be known for the remaining frames. The vector errors are $(1, 1)^T$ and $(-1, 0.5)^T$, measured in LR pixels. We can see the effect of these errors in the difference images with regard to the reference image of Fig. 3.

The results of applying the different methods to these data are shown in table 1 and in Fig. 2. The table specifies the parameters used for the different methods, which are: λ, the regularization parameter of (2), β, a scale factor defining the step size in the direction of the gradient, the number of iterations for the iterative methods, the radius R of the median filter, and finally the Peak Signal-to-Noise Ratio (PSNR) in dB. No deblurring is made for any of the methods. The

Table 1. Parameter Values and Results for Robust SR Experiment One

Experiment One	λ	β	Iterations	R	PSNR (dB)
Projection	—	—	—	—	16.90
l_1 with bilateral TV	0.005	20	50	—	17.30
Zomet with bilateral TV	0.0005	20	50	—	17.33
Robust Projection	—	—	—	0.35	18.68

Table 2. Parameter Values and Results for Robust SR Experiment Two

Experiment One	λ	β	Iterations	R
Projection	—	—	—	—
l_1 with bilateral TV	0.01	5	50	—
Zomet with bilateral TV	0.0001	1	50	—
Robust Projection	—	—	—	0.25

regularization cost function, Ω, in the Farsiu and Zomet methods is a Bilateral Total Variation (BTV) filter [9]. The parameters needed for the different methods are tuned to maximize the PSNR when compared to the original image. The proposed method achieves the greatest PSNR. Besides this quantitative datum, we can also compare the visual appearance of the output of the different methods in Fig. 2. It is clearly seen that the only method that completely erases the influence of the outliers is the median filter for irregular samples plus projection method. The other robust methods obtain good results when compared to the projection method, but many outliers still remain.

The second experiment has been made using real data, in particular a sequence obtained with low resolution camera. We have used 20 LR images and have multiplied by four the resolution. One of the LR images of the sequence can be seen on Fig. 4a. Again, no deblurring is attempted and the regularization cost function in the Farsiu and Zomet methods is a BTV filter. To register the images among themselves, we have resorted to the multi-resolution approach exposed in [10]. We have tuned the different parameters to obtain the best visual results. The used parameters can be seen in table 2.

We have applied the four SR methods to the sequence, and then zoomed a small part of the resulting HR images to see more clearly the results. These are shown in Fig. 4. The l_1 method and the Zomet method exhibit many artifacts in the edges of the images. The image obtained with the projective method is a bit noisy, as can be seen in the white figures at the left part of the image located in the line in the middle of the clock. The robust method that combines a median filter and the projective method erases all artifacts and is also less noisy than the image obtained just projecting. The price to pay is a bit more blurry image: this can be appreciated in the letters at the right of the image when we compare with Fig. 4b.

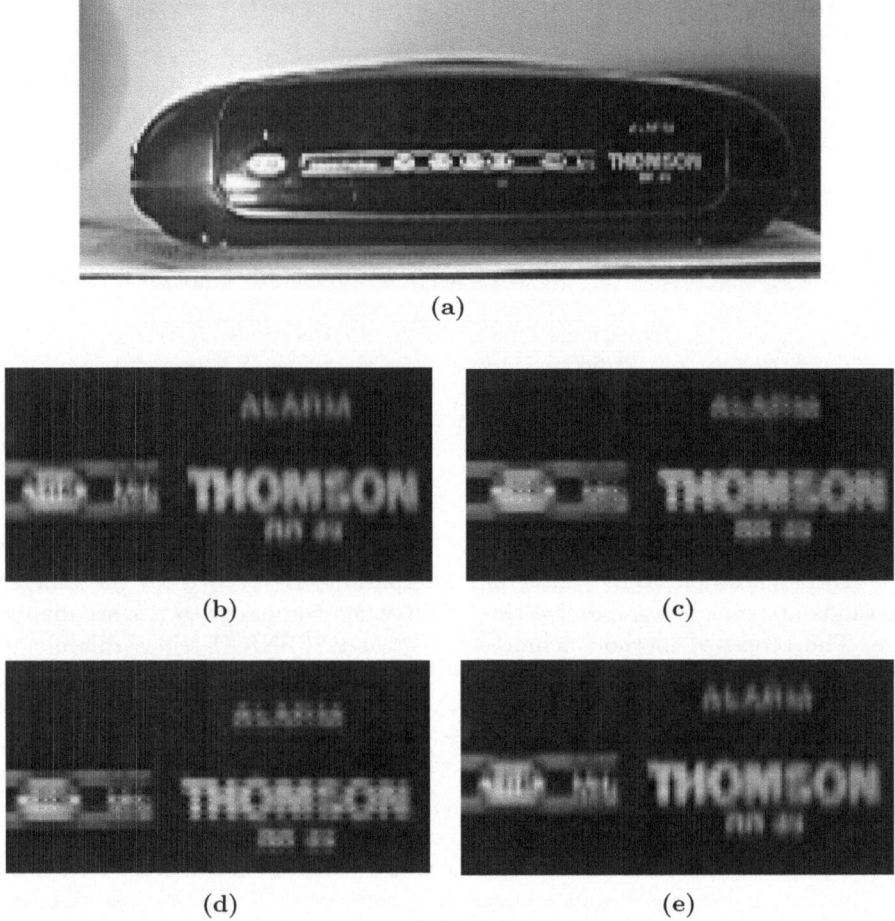

(a)

(b)   (c)

(d)   (e)

Fig. 4. (a) One of the original LR images used for experiment two. (b)–(e) Detail of images from robust methods for clock sequence. (b) The projective method, (c) l_1 norm method with bilateral TV regularization, (d) the median gradient method of Zomet with bilateral TV regularization, and (e) the projective method with a previous median filter applied.

4   Conclusions

In this paper we have studied specific techniques for deblurring and denoising in SR. A novel robust denoising method for SR is proposed. The term "robust" refers to its capability of handling non-stationary noise as the one that appears when outliers are present or for salt and pepper noise. This method is based on a median filter that is applied to an irregular sampling that usually appears in SR. Its performance is checked against other robust methods for SR, outperforming them in the experiments that have been carried out.

References

1. Park, S.C., Park, M.K., Kang, M.G.: Super-resolution image reconstruction: a technical overview. IEEE Signal Processing Magazine 20(3), 21–36 (2003)
2. Farsiu, S., Robinson, D., Elad, M., Milanfar, P.: Advances and challenges in super-resolution. International Journal of Imaging Systems and Technology 14(2), 47–57 (2004)
3. Schultz, R., Stevenson, R.: Extraction of high-resolution frames from video sequences. IEEE Transactions on Image Processing 5(6), 996–1011 (1996)
4. Elad, M., Feuer, A.: Restoration of a single superresolution image from several blurred, noisy, and undersampled measured images. IEEE Transactions on Image Processing 6(12), 1646–1658 (1997)
5. Lertrattanapanich, S., Bose, N.K.: High resolution image formation from low resolution frames using Delaunay triangulation. IEEE Transactions on Image Processing 11(12), 1427–1441 (2002)
6. Zomet, A., Rav-Acha, A., Peleg, S.: Robust super-resolution. In: Proceedings of the 2001 IEEE Computer Society Conference on Computer Vision and Pattern Recognition, vol. 1 (2001)
7. Farsiu, S., Robinson, M.D., Elad, M., Milanfar, P.: Fast and robust multiframe super resolution. IEEE Transactions on Image Processing 13(10), 1327–1344 (2004)
8. Sánchez-Beato, A., Pajares, G.: Noniterative interpolation-based super-resolution minimizing aliasing in the reconstructed image. IEEE Transactions on Image Processing 17(10), 1817–1826 (2008)
9. Tomasi, C., Manduchi, R.: Bilateral filtering for gray and color images. In: Proceedings of the Sixth International Conference on Computer Vision (1998)
10. Bergen, J.R., Anandan, P., Hanna, K.J., Hingorani, R.: Hierarchical model-based motion estimation. In: Sandini, G. (ed.) ECCV 1992. LNCS, vol. 588, pp. 237–252. Springer, Heidelberg (1992)

Left Ventricle Segmentation from Heart MDCT

Samuel Silva, Beatriz Sousa Santos, Joaquim Madeira, and Augusto Silva

DETI / IEETA — University of Aveiro, Aveiro, Portugal
sss@ua.pt

Abstract. A semi-automatic method for left ventricle segmentation from MDCT exams is presented. It was developed using ITK and custom modules integrated in the MeVisLab platform. A preliminary qualitative evaluation shows that the provided segmentation, without any tweaking or manual edition, is reasonably close to the ideal segmentation as judged by experienced radiology technicians.

1 Introduction

Multi-detector row computer tomography (MDCT) systems have been evolving at a fast pace enabling submillimeter spatial resolutions and low exam times, allowing full heart imaging in less than a breath-hold and providing 10+ heart volumes per cardiac cycle. The same data obtained for coronary angiography can be used to perform analysis of left ventricle function and myocardial perfusion with no need of extra radiation exposure, leading to additional information which can help the practitioner to attain a more complete diagnosis. In fact, recent studies (e.g., [1]) comparing data obtained from different imaging modalities, reveal that reliable left ventricle analysis can be performed using MDCT data.

As stated by Cury et al. [2], the full potential of MDCT technology is just beginning to be explored and further advances are essential, concerning not only new automatically computed parameters but also improved tools to enable further insight into the wide range of data now becoming available (e.g., for left ventricle wall motion). At the ground level of such developments are segmentation methods.

Different approaches regarding left ventricle segmentation for a variety of exam modalities have been widely described in the literature in the past years [3] and range from 2D methods (e.g., [4]) to more complex, model-based, approaches (e.g., [5]). Unfortunately, to the best of our knowledge, no off-the-shelf segmentation method is available which could be used as a basis for our work. Therefore, we engaged in the development of a segmentation method which should: 1) be as automatic as possible; 2) segment both left ventricle endocardium and epicardium; 3) provide a segmentation for all cardiac phases included in the MDCT exam; and 4) be validated by radiology technicians to ensure the reliability of the resulting data.

This article describes a semi-automatic left ventricle segmentation method which was implemented using ITK (http://www.itk.org) and custom processing modules integrated in the MeVisLab (http://www.mevislab.de/)

H. Araujo et al. (Eds.): IbPRIA 2009, LNCS 5524, pp. 306–313, 2009.

platform. The results from a qualitative evaluation of the segmentation results, conducted with the collaboration of experienced radiology technicians, are presented and show that the resulting endocardium segmentation (without any parameter tweaking or manual edition) is of good quality, requiring, in general, minimum edition, while the epicardium segmentation performs reasonably but clearly requires further enhancements.

In the next sections the implemented segmentation method is presented followed by a description of the evaluation process and obtained results. Finally, we present some ideas for future work.

2   Left Ventricle Segmentation

Coronary angiography MDCT exams are used (i.e., with contrast agent present [6], mainly in the coronary arteries and left ventricle), containing 10 to 12 heart volumes, along one cardiac cycle, each having a resolution of $512 \times 512 \times 256+$ voxels. To improve image quality before segmentation, two methods are used. First, a minimum intensity filter is applied along the YY axis using a three voxel neighborhood. Then, to partially attenuate noise, a smoothing filter is applied.

The developed segmentation method has four main stages: 1) left ventricle principal axis estimation; 2) reference phase endocardium segmentation; 3) full exam endocardium segmentation; 4) full exam epicardium segmentation. The main aspects of each stage will be explained in the following sections.

2.1   Principal Axis Estimation

Left ventricle axes must be estimated in order to select a proper orientation for the data and segment the left ventricle using slices along its principal axis.

From the 10 to 12 cardiac phases available in each exam, the one corresponding to 60% of the cardiac cycle was chosen for left ventricle principal axis estimation, since it exhibited better image quality. This is due to the fact that it belongs to the diastolic phase of the cardiac cycle where structural motion is less significant and a higher amount of radiation is applied to ensure better image quality. During the remaining phases of the exam the radiation levels are kept to a minimum (to reduce radiation dosage [6]) resulting in images with worse quality.

To estimate left ventricle position a coronal slice at midventricular level is analysed. A threshold is performed and the image is searched from right to left looking for active regions. The first region found with a large area (to exclude regions related with the coronary arteries, lungs, etc.) is considered part of the left ventricle. Region growing is then applied in order to isolate it from all other active regions on the image (including, eventually, portions of the right ventricle where some contrast agent might be present). Finally, the centroid of the segmented region is computed and stored to be used as a reference during the segmentation of the remaining slices.

In order to ease the detection of slices close to the left ventricle apex (where area cannot be used as a detection criteria), 3D region growing is applied to the

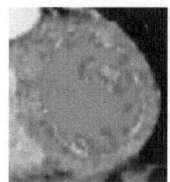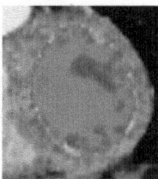

Fig. 1. Slice showing the segmented endocardium not including the papillary muscles (left) and including them in the blood pool (right)

entire set using the previously computed centroid as seed. This will isolate the left ventricle blood pool from other active regions related with the lungs and ribs which might result in classifying a region as part of the left ventricle too early (ribs) or out of place (lungs).

The data set resulting from the previously performed 3D region growing is then processed, slice by slice, along the coronal plane, from the left ventricle apex to its base. Each slice is searched for an active region from right to left. To ensure that none of the possibly remaining regions are misclassified as left ventricle the one closest to the previously computed reference centroid is chosen. It follows region growing to segment that region and hole filling to ensure that holes related with the papillary muscles are closed.

To detect the stopping slice, the leftmost pixel of each segmented region is computed. If a sudden decrease (i.e., it moves to the left of the image) occurs it means that the region where the left ventricle connects with the aorta has been reached (outflow tract). From that moment on, our method looks for a sudden increase in the leftmost pixel of the segmented region which is related with the entrance in the left atrium region and segmentation stops.

Finally, the centroids for the first and last slices are used to compute the left ventricle principal axis.

The exam is then rotated in order to position the left ventricle axis normally to the coronal plane and the remaining processing is performed using this orientation.

2.2   Reference Phase Segmentation

Starting from the 60% phase (due to better image quality), the endocardium is segmented using a method similar to that used to estimate the principal axis. The blood pool centroid and maximum radius are computed at a midventricular slice and 3D region growing is applied using that voxel as seed. The resulting data set is processed, slice by slice, along the coronal plane, from the left ventricle apex to its base. Each slice is searched for an active region from right to left. To ensure that none of the possibly remaining regions are misclassified as left ventricle the one closest to the previously computed reference centroid is chosen. It follows region growing and hole filling to include the papillary muscles in the blood pool (see figure 1).

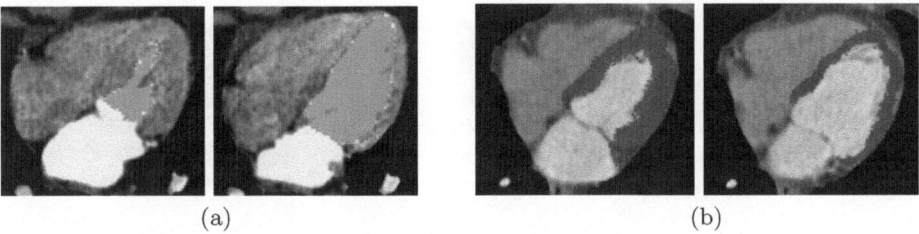

(a)   (b)

Fig. 2. Segmented endocardium (a) and epicardium (b) for end-systolic and end-diastolic phases

The stopping slice (i.e., one desirably at mitral valve level) is detected by a significant change of blood pool radius, when compared with the reference radius obtained earlier (entrance in the outflow tract and left atrium).

2.3   Full Exam Segmentation

After segmenting the endocardium for the reference phase it follows endocardium and epicardium segmentation for all exam phases.

Endocardium. The reference endocardium is scaled (to encompass a slightly larger blood volume for the end-diastolic phase) and used as a mask to isolate the left ventricle blood pool in all exam phases. Next, thresholding is applied followed by hole filling.

Due to left ventricle motion the location of the mitral valve changes. Thus, further processing is necessary to estimate that plane for each phase. A reference blood pool radius is computed for a midventricular slice and the segmentation stopped when blood pool radius significantly exceeds that value (entrance in the left atrium and outflow tract). Figure 2(a) shows two segmentations obtained for end-sistole and end-diastole.

Epicardium. Epicardium segmentation is harder to perform due to poor image quality, including a slight variation of the greylevel interval corresponding to the epicardium along the different exam phases, and due to the existence of pixels inside that interval in adjacent regions such as the right ventricle and liver. To minimize the effects arising from these issues, left ventricle radius is estimated for each phase in order to define a region of interest as narrow as possible and pixels are sampled along the epicardium to help define a suitable greylevel interval for segmentation using thresholding. Figure 2(b) shows two segmented epicardia for end-sistole and end-diastole.

3   Evaluation

At this development stage we opted for a less-costly, preliminary qualitative evaluation that would allow the detection of any serious segmentation problem and inform further fine tuning of the proposed algorithm.

310   S. Silva et al.

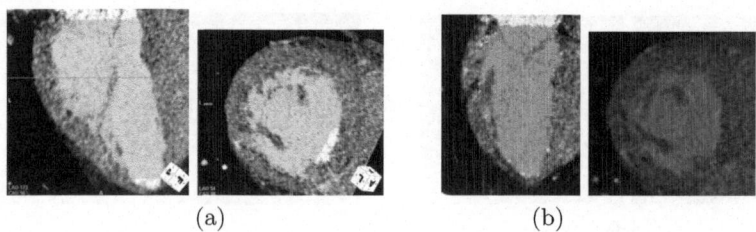

(a)   (b)

Fig. 3. (a) Unedited segmentation results provided by a TeraRecon Aquarius work-station; and (b) unedited segmentation results, for the same exam, provided by our method

Such a preliminary evaluation has been performed with the help of radiology technicians with 3 to 4 years daily experience in analysing MDCT heart images.

3.1   Methods

Eventhough our method segments all exam phases, in this evaluation only three phases were evaluated per exam: the end-systole and end-diastole, which are used to compute important parameters such as the ejection fraction [1], and the 60% phase which was used as a reference for the segmentation of all remaining phases.

An important aspect of every segmentation method is that the resulting first segmentation (i.e, without manual parameter tweaking or edition) should be as accurate as possible in order to minimize correction time. Having that in mind we decided to evaluate the segmentation results using only the standard values for the different parameters (e.g., ratio value between reference endocardium radius and current slice radius to determine mitral valve plane; determined empirically along the development) and no manual edition.

These first segmentations were shown to the technicians and were consid-ered good first approaches with no major abnormalities and comparable to first segmentations (specially for the endocardium) provided, for example, by a Ter-aRecon Aquarius workstation which additionally requires a priori manual align-ment of the data in three different planes. Figure 3 shows an example where, even with the three plane initialization, the TeraRecon workstation provides a worst first segmentation. Notice the segmentation problems in the apex and midventricular slices.

After such preliminary results we decided to perform a more thorough evalu-ation by asking the technicians to classify the resulting segmentations as if they were final.

They were asked to evaluate segmentation results for a set of seven exams taken randomly from that week's exams. Care was only taken to ensure that no serious movement artifacts were present which might influence the results.

Each technician received a grid to guide the evaluation process and where the evaluations should be registered. Regarding the endocardium, the grid considered segmentation evaluation for four anatomical regions deemed of interest: apex, midventricular slices, mitral valve and outflow tract. For each region the segmentation could be generically classified as OK (optimum segmentation), EXCESS (the segmented region is larger than the ideal) and SHORTAGE (the segmented region is smaller than the ideal). For the last two cases, the technician had to classify the severity of the problem using a three-level scale (1 – low significance: the segmentation is very good, although, for the sake of perfectness, it could include/exclude a very small region; 2 – moderate: the segmentation is good but it could be significantly improved by the inclusion/exclusion of a small region; 3 – serious: the segmentation cannot be used without the inclusion/exclusion of important regions). For the epicardium a similar evaluation scale was used and five anatomical regions were considered: apex and the lateral (external) and septal (between ventricles) regions for the midventricular slices and base.

Before evaluating the segmentations for each exam, the technicians were allowed to adjust cutting planes in order to define what they considered the proper 4-chamber (ventricles + atria) and left ventricle short-axis visualizations (which they usually use to analyse the left ventricle). Next, they were presented with those two visualizations of the different exam phases, with the segmentation superimposed onto them, and allowed to scroll along the slices parallel to the cutting planes (which could be changed, at any time, to encompass their needs). The opacity of the segmented regions could be changed in order, e.g., to better examine the regions bellow the segmentation mask. The endocardium and epicardium segmentations could be visualized separately or at the same time. The technicians could take all the time they needed to evaluate each phase and were allowed to alternate between phases for comparison (e.g., in order to assess if the papillary muscles were coherently included/excluded).

3.2   Results

Table 1A shows evaluation results concerning endocardium segmentation. Notice that for most exams and cardiac phases the apex and midventricular slices where considered to be well segmented. Concerning the mitral valve and outflow tract there are different problems with different severities. A worst case example is exam 2 with level 3 problems in four situations. Nevertheless, notice that this just means a segmentation that must be edited before usage and not a completely abnormal segmentation. Figure 4(a) shows the endocardium segmentation for the end-sistole of exam 2 as an example of the worst segmentation found for the mitral valve region. Figure 4(b) shows the corresponding automatic segmentation as provided by a Siemens Circulation workstation with a significant region wrongly segmented inside the left atrium.

Remarkably, during the evaluation, we noticed that two different criteria might be used to evaluate outflow tract segmentation: one considering that the tract should not be included in left ventricle segmentation and another considering that all the tract up to the aortic valve should be considered. This issue requires clarification and a deeper investigation is being carried out.

Concerning epicardium segmentation (evaluation results presented in Table 1B), the technicians found most of the severe problems in the septal sections of both

Table 1. Evaluation results for endocardium and epicardium segmentation

A. Endocardium Segmentation Evaluation

Exam	\multicolumn{4}{End-Sistole} Apex	Mid.	Valve	Tract	End-Diastole Apex	Mid.	Valve	Tract	60% Apex	Mid.	Valve	Tract

Exam	End-Sistole Apex	Mid.	Valve	Tract	End-Diastole Apex	Mid.	Valve	Tract	60% Apex	Mid.	Valve	Tract
1	O	O	-	O	O	O	O	O	O	O	+	O
2	O	O	+++	+++	O	O	++	++	O	O	+++	+++
3	O	O	+	+++	O	O	O	++	O	O	++	++
4	O	O	O	+	O	O	---	O	O	O	--	O
5	-	-	+++	+++	-	O	--	---	-	O	+++	---
6	O	O	++	---	-	O	++	---	-	O	+++	---
7	-	---	---	--	-	---	--	---	--	--	++	---

B. Epicardium Segmentation Evaluation

Exam	End-Sistole Apex	Mid. L	Mid. S	Base L	Base S	End-Diastole Apex	Mid. L	Mid. S	Base L	Base S
1	O	O	+++	O	+++	O	O	+++	O	+++
2	--	O	O	O	+++	--	O	O	O	O
3	-	O	O	O	+	-	-	-	-	-
4	O	-	+++	+++	O	O	-	++	O	O
5	--	--	++	++	++	---	+++	+++	---	---
6	--	--	+++	O	O	--	-	+++	--	O
7	---	---	++	--	--	---	---	-	-	-

O : Optimum
+ : Excess
− : Shortage

Number of symbols conveys severity level, e.g.:
+++ : level 3 excess
-- : level 2 shortage

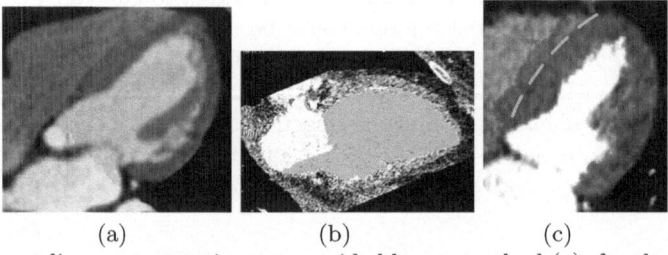

(a)   (b)   (c)

Fig. 4. Endocardium segmentation, as provided by our nethod (a), for the end-distolic phase of exam 2 and corresponding segmentation as provided by a Siemens Circulation workstation (b). In (c), example of epicardium segmentation problem found in the septal section.

midventricular and basal slices. Eventhough our method tries to adapt the threshold interval to each phase and seems to work very reasonably for some exams, the greylevels found in the septal section are, in many exam phases (due to noise and low radiation dosage) similar to those found inside the right ventricle. The initial mask applied to the image, to define a restricted region of interest, is limiting the severity of some of the problems but epicardium segmentation clearly needs further improvements. Figure 4(c) shows an example of a segmentation problem found in the septal section of the midventricular slices. The segmentation should roughly end in the dashed line.

4   Conclusions and Future Work

A semi-automatic left ventricle segmentation method implemented using ITK and custom modules integrated in the MeVisLab platform is presented. A preliminary qualitative evaluation conducted using a set of seven exams evaluated by experienced radiology technicians provided interesting results: the endocardium segmentation (without any parameter tweaking or manual edition) exhibits good quality and epicardium segmentation, although still needing further enhancements concerning the segmentation of the septal section of the ventricle wall, yields promising results.

Motivated by these results the following lines of work are considered relevant:

- Provide a simple editing tool to adjust the resulting segmentation which would easily solve the majority of the segmentation problems found;
- Improve the epicardium segmentation by using more robust statistics to characterize greylevel distribution (e.g., outlier removal), around the endocardium and by defining an improved initial region of interest which better includes the apex;
- Conduct a more elaborate evaluation of the proposed method by asking radiology technicians to manually segment exams for comparison with our segmentations and by comparing our blood volumes and ejection fractions with those obtained using ecocardiography, considered a gold standard for this kind of measures.

Acknowledgments

The authors would like to thank the radiology technicians at the Cardiology Service of Vila Nova de Gaia Hospital Center for their collaboration.

The first author's work is funded by grant SFRH/BD/38073/2007 awarded by the portuguese Science and Technology Foundation (FCT).

References

1. Fischbach, R., Juergens, K., Ozgun, M., Maintz, D., Grude, M., Seifarth, H., Heindel, W., Wichter, T.: Assessment of regional left ventricular function with multidetector-row computed tomography versus magnetic resonance imaging. European Radiology 17(4), 1009–1017 (2007)
2. Cury, R., Nieman, K., Shapiro, M., Nasir, K., Cury, R.C., Brady, T.: Comprehensive cardiac CT study: Evaluation of coronary arteries, left ventricular function, and myocardial perfusion – is it possible? J. of Nuclear Cardiology 14(2), 229–243 (2007)
3. Suri, J.S.: Computer vision, pattern recognition and image processing in left ventricle segmentation: The last 50 years. Patt. Analysis & App. 3(3), 209–242 (2000)
4. Jolly, M.P.: Automatic segmentation of the left ventricle in cardiac MR and CT images. International Journal of Computer Vision 70(2), 151–163 (2006)
5. Zheng, Y., Barbu, B., Gergescu, B., Scheuering, M., Comaniciu, D.: Four-chamber heart modeling and automatic segmentation for 3-D cardiac CT volumes using marginal space learning and steerable features. IEEE Transactions on Medical Imaging, Special Issue on Functional Imaging of the Heart 27(11), 1668–1681 (2008)
6. Pannu, H.K., Flohr, T., Corl, F.M., Fishman, E.K.: Current concepts in multidetector row CT evaluation of the coronary arteries - principles, techniques, and anatomy. Radiographics 23, S111–S125 (2003)

A Comparison of Wavelet Based Spatio-temporal Decomposition Methods for Dynamic Texture Recognition

Sloven Dubois[1,2], Renaud Péteri[2], and Michel Ménard[1]

[1] L3i - Laboratoire Informatique Image et Interaction
[2] MIA - Mathématiques Image et Applications
Avenue Michel Crépeau
17042 La Rochelle, France
{sloven.dubois01,renaud.peteri,michel.menard}@univ-lr.fr

Abstract. This paper presents four spatio-temporal wavelet decompositions for characterizing dynamic textures. The main goal of this work is to compare the influence of spatial and temporal variables in the wavelet decomposition scheme. Its novelty is to establish a comparison between the only existing method [11] and three other spatio-temporal decompositions.

The four decomposition schemes are presented and successfully applied on a large dynamic texture database. Construction of feature descriptors are tackled as well their relevance, and performances of the methods are discussed. Finally, future prospects are exposed.

Keywords: Spatio-temporal wavelets, dynamic textures, feature descriptors, video indexing.

1 Introduction

The last fifteen years have seen the rising of a new issue in texture analysis which its extension to the spatio-temporal domain, called dynamic textures. Dynamic textures are spatially and temporally repetitive patterns like trees waving in the wind, water flows, fire, smoke phenomena, rotational motions ...

The study of dynamic textures has several fields of applications. One of the main topics is the synthesis of dynamic textures [6,12]. Other fields of research are dynamic texture detection [4] or dynamic texture segmentation [2,5]. Our research context is the recognition and description of dynamic textures [8,14]. For a brief survey on this topic, one could refer to [3].

A dynamic texture is composed of motions occurring at several spatio-temporal scales: on figure 1 (a), one can observe the low spatio-temporal motion of the trunk and the high spatio-temporal motion of small branches. An efficient method should then be able to capture this spatio-temporal behavior.

A natural tool for multiscale analysis is the wavelet transform. In the field of image processing, the wavelet transform has been successfully used for characterizing static textures. For instance, gabor wavelets have been used for computing the texture descriptor of the MPEG-7 norm [13].

H. Araujo et al. (Eds.): IbPRIA 2009, LNCS 5524, pp. 314–321, 2009.

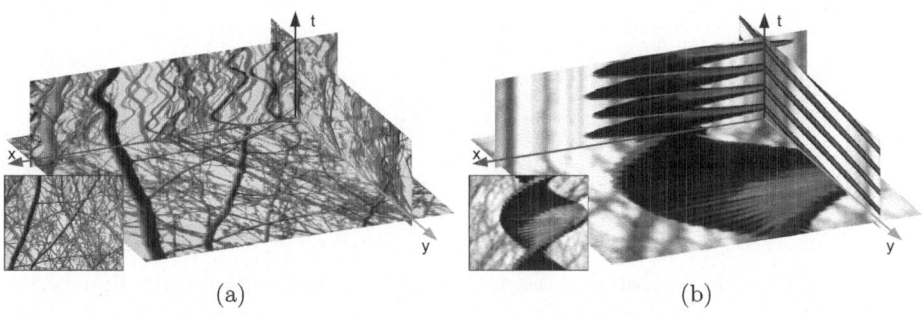

(a)   (b)

Fig. 1. 2D+t slices of two dynamic textures. Here, a dynamic texture is seen as a data cube and is cut at pixel $O(x, y, t)$ for obtaining three planes $(\overrightarrow{x}O\overrightarrow{y})$, $(\overrightarrow{x}O\overrightarrow{t})$ and $(\overrightarrow{y}O\overrightarrow{t})$.

A natural idea is hence to extend the wavelet decomposition to the temporal domain. To our knowledge, the work of [11] has been so far the only spatio-temporal wavelet decomposition method for characterizing dynamic textures. Yet, the authors use a small offline database, which can be a limitation when it comes to study feature relevance and to compare different methods.

In this paper, we present a comparison between this method [11] and three other spatio-temporal wavelet decomposition schemes. Our goal is to study the influence of spatial or temporal variables in the decomposition scheme. For relevant testing purposes, we also aim at computing results on a large online dynamic texture dataset [9].

This article is organized as follows : section 2 recalls how to compute the discrete wavelet transform using filter banks. Section 3 presents four spatio-temporal wavelet decomposition methods which differ from the way space and time variables are treated. In section 4 the construction of texture feature descriptors for each decomposition scheme is presented. Finally, the relevance of each decomposition scheme is tested on a large dataset of dynamic textures [9] and numerical results are presented and discussed.

2   Discrete Wavelet Transform and Filter Banks

For a better understanding of the different decomposition schemes, the discrete wavelet transform (DWT) and its associated filter bank is recalled. For any level j and for any n, we denote:

$$a^j[n] = \langle f, \phi_n^{2^j} \rangle \quad \text{and} \quad d^j[n] = \langle f, \psi_n^{2^j} \rangle \tag{1}$$

with ϕ the scaling function and ψ is the mother wavelet. $a^j[n]$ is the approximation of the signal f and $d^j[n]$ its details at resolution 2^j.

A fast discrete wavelet transform implementation is performed using filter bank [7]. Relations between the decomposition scales are:

$$a^{j+1}[n] = a^j[2n] \otimes \overline{h} \quad \text{and} \quad d^{j+1}[n] = a^j[2n] \otimes \overline{g} \tag{2}$$

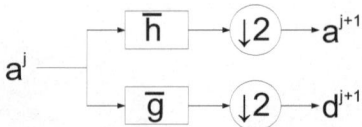

Fig. 2. Scheme of discrete wavelet transform for one level of decomposition where $\boxed{F}$ is the convolution by F and $\downarrow 2$ is the decimation by 2

where $\otimes$ denotes the convolution product, h and g are respectively one-dimensional low-pass and high-pass decomposition filters associated to the scaling function and the mother wavelet, and $\bar{g}[m] = g[-m]$. This filter bank is represented on figure 2. Thereafter in the article, the symbol $\boxed{WT}$ represents the filter bank.

For digital images, the fast wavelet transform is extended to the 2D case using one scaling function and three mother wavelets (see [7]).

At each scale one approximation subband and three detail subbands are obtained using the following filter relations:

$$
\begin{aligned}
a^{j+1}[n,m] &= a^j[2n,2m] \otimes \overline{h_x}\,\overline{h_y} &\text{and}&& d_v^{j+1}[n,m] &= a^j[2n,2m] \otimes \overline{h_x}\,\overline{g_y} \\
d_h^{j+1}[n,m] &= a^j[2n,2m] \otimes \overline{g_x}\,\overline{h_y} &&& d_d^{j+1}[n,m] &= a^j[2n,2m] \otimes \overline{g_x}\,\overline{g_y}
\end{aligned}
\tag{3}
$$

with the notation $hg[n_1,n_2] = h[n_1]g[n_2]$ (hence the associated 2D filters are the matrix product of 1D filters).

3   Video Analysis Using Wavelet Decomposition

In this section, four spatio-temporal decomposition schemes using wavelets are presented. They vary in the way they consider space and time variables in the multiresolution analysis.

3.1   Spatial Wavelet Decomposition

A straightforward approach is to use the wavelet transform image per image. In this case, there is no consideration on the temporal correlation between two successive frames. The first method is summarized figure 3. For each image and for each scale of multiresolution analysis, the approximation subband and three details subbands are computed. The feature descriptors use wavelet subband energies and will be detailed in section 4.

3.2   Temporal Wavelet Decomposition

The first method considers a video image per image, and is thus a purely spatial method. The second natural approach is to perform the multiresolution analysis in the time direction.

Figure 4 shows how the feature descriptors is extracted. For each pixel (x, y) of a dynamic texture video, the temporal profile is extracted and its one dimensional wavelet transform is performed.

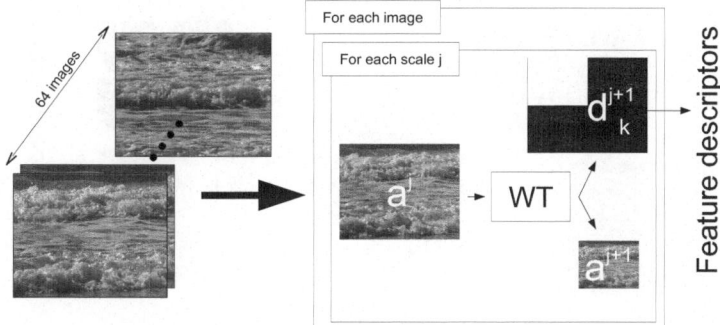

Fig. 3. Spatial wavelet decomposition applied to a sequence of 64 images for obtaining feature descriptors. $\boxed{\text{WT}}$ is the filter bank.

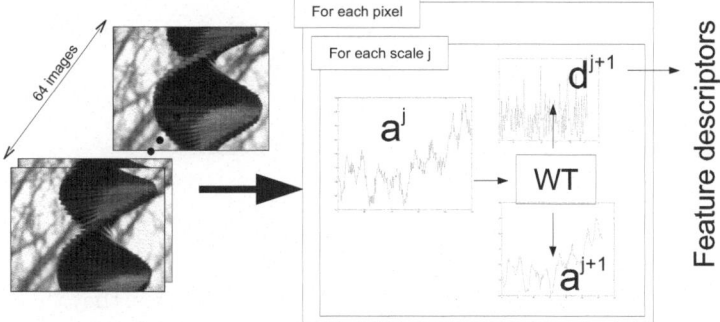

Fig. 4. Temporal wavelet decomposition applied to sequence of 64 images for obtaining feature descriptors. $\boxed{\text{WT}}$ is the filter bank.

The associated filter bank can be written in the same way than in section 2, filters $\overline{h_t}$ and $\overline{g_t}$ being applied in the time direction.

3.3   2D+T Wavelet Decomposition Using Filter Product

Whereas the first method is a purely spatial decomposition and the second one is a temporal decomposition, the third method performs decomposition spatially and temporally.

This extension to the temporal domain of the 2D discrete wavelet transform is done using separable filter banks. As in the 2D case, a separable 3 dimensional convolution can be factored into one-dimensional convolution along rows, columns and image indexes of the video. A cascade of three filters is obtained for each decomposition level and different subbands can be obtained with the following relations:

$$
\begin{aligned}
a^{j+1}[n,m,p] &= a^j[2n,2m,2p] \otimes \overline{h_x}\ \overline{h_y}\ \overline{h_t} & d_t^{j+1}[n,m,p] &= a^j[2n,2m,2p] \otimes \overline{h_x}\ \overline{h_y}\ \overline{g_t} \\
d_h^{j+1}[n,m,p] &= a^j[2n,2m,2p] \otimes \overline{g_x}\ \overline{h_y}\ \overline{h_t} & d_{ht}^{j+1}[n,m,p] &= a^j[2n,2m,2p] \otimes \overline{g_x}\ \overline{h_y}\ \overline{g_t} \\
d_v^{j+1}[n,m,p] &= a^j[2n,2m,2p] \otimes \overline{h_x}\ \overline{g_y}\ \overline{h_t} & d_{vt}^{j+1}[n,m,p] &= a^j[2n,2m,2p] \otimes \overline{h_x}\ \overline{g_y}\ \overline{g_t} \\
d_d^{j+1}[n,m,p] &= a^j[2n,2m,2p] \otimes \overline{g_x}\ \overline{g_y}\ \overline{h_t} & d_{dt}^{j+1}[n,m,p] &= a^j[2n,2m,2p] \otimes \overline{g_x}\ \overline{g_y}\ \overline{g_t}
\end{aligned}
\tag{4}
$$

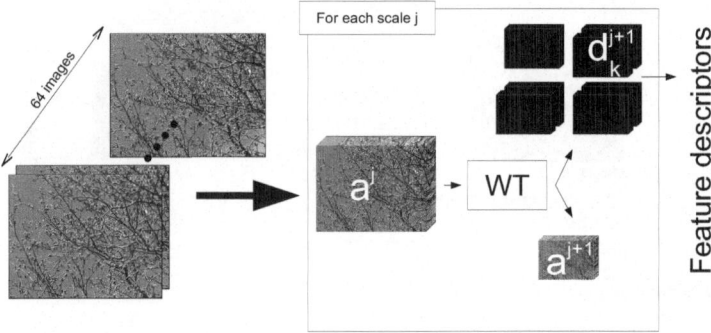

Fig. 5. Simple 3D wavelet decomposition applied to a sequence of 64 images for obtaining feature descriptors. $\boxed{\text{WT}}$ is the filter bank.

Figure 5 shows the third method. For a video of 64 images, seven detail subcubes and one approximation subcube are computed for each scale.

3.4   J. R. Smith *et al.* Wavelet Decomposition

The last decomposition method is the one of Smith *et al.* [11]. This transform is similar to the 2D+T wavelet decomposition, except that the temporal filter is applied two times at each multiresolution step so that the video is decimated twice spatially and twice temporally. For a video of 64 images, they then obtained fifteen detail subcubes and one approximation subcube (see [11] for more details).

For a given resolution 2^j, the filter bank can be written as follows :

$$
\begin{aligned}
a^{j+1}[n,m,p] &= a^j[2n,2m,4p] \otimes \overline{h_x}\,\overline{h_y}\,\overline{h_t}\,\overline{h_t} & d_t^{j+1}[n,m,p] &= a^j[2n,2m,4p] \otimes \overline{h_x}\,\overline{h_y}\,\overline{h_t}\,\overline{g_t}\\
d_h^{j+1}[n,m,p] &= a^j[2n,2m,4p] \otimes \overline{g_x}\,\overline{h_y}\,\overline{h_t}\,\overline{h_t} & d_{ht}^{j+1}[n,m,p] &= a^j[2n,2m,4p] \otimes \overline{g_x}\,\overline{h_y}\,\overline{h_t}\,\overline{g_t}\\
d_v^{j+1}[n,m,p] &= a^j[2n,2m,4p] \otimes \overline{h_x}\,\overline{g_y}\,\overline{h_t}\,\overline{h_t} & d_{vt}^{j+1}[n,m,p] &= a^j[2n,2m,4p] \otimes \overline{h_x}\,\overline{g_y}\,\overline{h_t}\,\overline{g_t}\\
d_d^{j+1}[n,m,p] &= a^j[2n,2m,4p] \otimes \overline{g_x}\,\overline{g_y}\,\overline{h_t}\,\overline{h_t} & d_{dt}^{j+1}[n,m,p] &= a^j[2n,2m,4p] \otimes \overline{g_x}\,\overline{g_y}\,\overline{h_t}\,\overline{g_t}\\
d_{ht}^{j+1}[n,m,p] &= a^j[2n,2m,4p] \otimes \overline{h_x}\,\overline{h_y}\,\overline{g_t}\,\overline{h_t} & d_{htt}^{j+1}[n,m,p] &= a^j[2n,2m,4p] \otimes \overline{h_x}\,\overline{h_y}\,\overline{g_t}\,\overline{g_t}\\
d_{ht}^{j+1}[n,m,p] &= a^j[2n,2m,4p] \otimes \overline{g_x}\,\overline{h_y}\,\overline{g_t}\,\overline{h_t} & d_{htt}^{j+1}[n,m,p] &= a^j[2n,2m,4p] \otimes \overline{g_x}\,\overline{h_y}\,\overline{g_t}\,\overline{g_t}\\
d_{vt}^{j+1}[n,m,p] &= a^j[2n,2m,4p] \otimes \overline{h_x}\,\overline{g_y}\,\overline{g_t}\,\overline{h_t} & d_{vtt}^{j+1}[n,m,p] &= a^j[2n,2m,4p] \otimes \overline{h_x}\,\overline{g_y}\,\overline{g_t}\,\overline{g_t}\\
d_{dt}^{j+1}[n,m,p] &= a^j[2n,2m,4p] \otimes \overline{g_x}\,\overline{g_y}\,\overline{g_t}\,\overline{h_t} & d_{dtt}^{j+1}[n,m,p] &= a^j[2n,2m,4p] \otimes \overline{g_x}\,\overline{g_y}\,\overline{g_t}\,\overline{g_t}
\end{aligned}
\tag{5}
$$

For all four presented methods, feature vectors based on wavelet energies are computed and tested in the next sections.

4   Computing Dynamic Texture Descriptors

In order to characterize a given dynamic texture, subband energies are used. For each decomposition, a family of wavelet coefficients $\{d_k^j\}$ is obtained, k being the direction that depends on the wavelet decomposition scheme (h, v, d, and t). A classical way for establishing feature descriptors is to sum the energy of each subband as follows [11]:

$$E_k^j = \frac{1}{XYT} \sum_x^X \sum_y^Y \sum_t^T |d_k^j|^2 \tag{6}$$

where j denotes the decomposition level, k the direction, X, Y, T are the spatio-temporal dimensions.

The size of feature descriptors depends on the decomposition method. Table 1 gives this size with respect to the method. This table shows that three methods are computed with three decomposition levels and one with five levels.

Table 1. Size of feature descriptors with respect to the wavelet decomposition method

Methods	Spatial Wavelet Decomposition	Temporal Wavelet Decomposition	2D+T Wavelet Decomposition	J. R. Smith *et al.* Wavelet Decomposition
Size	9	5	21	45

5 Results

The feature vectors of the four methods are tested using 83 videos from DynTex [9], a database that provides high-quality videos of dynamic textures. These videos are divided into five classes, representative of different spatio-temporal dynamics. An example for each class can be seen on figure 6.

Dynamic textures of class (a) are composed of low and high frequency motions (for instance a wave motion and sea foam). Class (b) is composed of oscillating motions with different velocities. For example a tree waving in the wind is composed of high oscillations for small branches or leaves and low oscillations for big branches or the trunk. Class (c) is a high frequency motion only, like fountains or wavy water. The class (d) represents a fluid motion, for instance smoke. This is a difficult class of dynamic textures because they can be sometimes partially transparent. The last class (e) is composed of simple translation events like an escalator motion. In order to be in the same testing conditions than [11], the low pass filters and the high pass filters used for all wavelet decomposition methods are the Haar filters.

For studying features pertinence, the "leave-one-out" test is used (see [8] for more details). Feature descriptors are computed on 83 videos and results are summarized in table 2.

Results show that the first method "Spatial Wavelet Decomposition" gives the best classification rate. The main reason is that the four spatio-temporal

(a)   (b)   (c)   (d)   (e)

Fig. 6. Sample for each class

Table 2. Table of results. The first column, presents the class label and its number of videos. The intersection class/method represents the number of well classified videos for each class.

Methods	Spatial Wavelet Decomposition	Temporal Wavelet Decomposition	2D+t Wavelet Decomposition	J. R. Smith *et al.* Wavelet Decomposition
(a) 20	**20**	16	17	16
(b) 20	15	11	**17**	13
(c) 20	**17**	13	13	8
(d) 16	**16**	**16**	12	13
(e) 7	5	4	5	5
Success rate	88%	73%	77%	67%

wavelet decompositions are simple 3D extension of 2D wavelet transform: these decompositions do not fully take benefit of temporal dynamics. These transforms are indeed not adapted to the local motion and create class ambiguities. However for class (b), the 2D+t methods performs better than other methods. This is due to the fact dynamic textures of this class are really 3D textures occurring in all 3 directions of the wavelet transform.

The method "Temporal Wavelet Decomposition" obtains a good classification rate for class (d). Indeed, for most of class (d) videos, the main information is for the time dimension rather than the spatial one.

An observation of all results shows that the number of well classified videos is over 50% except for class (c) with the method of [11]. It could be explained by the fact that their method applies filtering twice in the temporal direction. As this class (c) is composed of high-frequency phenomena, too much temporal information is filtered at each step.

6   Conclusion

This paper presents four methods for characterizing dynamic textures. Our goal is to study the influence of space and time variables in a spatio-temporal wavelet decomposition scheme and to test the extracted features on a significant video database of dynamic texture.

The three wavelet decomposition methods we have proposed already perform better than the only existing method published so far [11]. On a 83 videos database, success rate ranges between 73% and 88% depending on the proposed decomposition method.

When tested on approximately 300 videos where class ambiguity highly increases, the success rate declines of about 20% for each method. It emphasizes the need for the development of more adaptive spatio-temporal wavelet transforms that are able to take into account the motion dynamics. Many dynamic textures are indeed non-stationary and have a privileged motion orientation. Like geometrical wavelets ([1,10]) which are more adapted to the geometrical content of an image than the classical wavelet transform, we are currently working on developing motion tuned wavelet transforms.

References

1. Candes, E., Demanet, L., Donoho, D., Ying, L.: Fast discrete curvelet transforms. Multiscale Modeling & Simulation 5, 861–899 (2006)
2. Chan, A.B., Vasconcelos, N.: Mixtures of dynamic textures. In: Proceedings of Tenth IEEE International Conference on Computer Vision (ICCV 2005), vol. 1, pp. 641–647 (2005)
3. Chetverikov, D., Péteri, R.: A brief survey of dynamic texture description and recognition. In: Proceedings of 4th International Conference on Computer Recognition Systems (CORES 2005), Rydzyna, Poland. Advances in Soft Computing, pp. 17–26. Springer, Heidelberg (2005)
4. Dedeoglu, Y., Toreyin, B.U., Gudukbay, U., Cetin, A.E.: Real-time fire and flame detection in video. In: Proceedings of IEEE International Conference on Acoustics, Speech, and Signal Processing (ICASSP 2005), Philadelphia, PA, vol. II, pp. 669–673 (March 2005)
5. Doretto, G., Cremers, D., Favaro, P., Soatto, S.: Dynamic texture segmentation. In: Proceedings of Ninth IEEE International Conference on Computer Vision (ICCV 2003), vol. 2, pp. 1236–1242 (2003)
6. Filip, J., Haindl, M., Chetverikov, D.: Fast synthesis of dynamic colour textures. In: Proceedings of the 18th IAPR Int. Conf. on Pattern Recognition (ICPR 2006), Hong Kong, pp. 25–28 (2006)
7. Mallat, S.: A theory for multiresolution signal decomposition: The wavelet representation. IEEE Transactions on Pattern Analysis and Machine Intelligence journal (TPAMI) 11(7), 674–693 (1989)
8. Péteri, R., Chetverikov, D.: Dynamic texture recognition using normal flow and texture regularity. In: Marques, J.S., Pérez de la Blanca, N., Pina, P. (eds.) IbPRIA 2005. LNCS, vol. 3523, pp. 223–230. Springer, Heidelberg (2005)
9. Péteri, R., Huiskes, M., Fazekas, S.: Dyntex: A comprehensive database of dynamic textures, http://www.cwi.nl/projects/dyntex/
10. Peyré, G.: Géométrie multi-echelles pour les images et les textures. PhD thesis, Ecole Polytechnique, 148 pages (December 2005)
11. Smith, J.R., Lin, C.Y., Naphade, M.: Video texture indexing using spatio-temporal wavelets. In: Proceedings of IEEE International Conference on Image Processing (ICIP 2002), vol. II, pp. 437–440 (2002)
12. Szummer, M., Picard, R.W.: Temporal texture modeling. In: Proceedings of IEEE International Conference on Image Processing (ICIP 1996), vol. 3, pp. 823–826 (1996)
13. Wu, P., Ro, Y.M., Won, C.S., Choi, Y.: Texture descriptors in MPEG-7. In: Skarbek, W. (ed.) CAIP 2001. LNCS, vol. 2124, pp. 21–28. Springer, Heidelberg (2001)
14. Zhao, G., Pietikainen, M.: Dynamic texture recognition using local binary patterns with an application to facial expressions. IEEE Transactions on Pattern Analysis and Machine Intelligence journal (TPAMI 2007) 6(29), 915–928 (2007)

A Fast Anisotropic Mumford-Shah Functional Based Segmentation

J.F. Garamendi, N. Malpica, and E. Schiavi

Universidad Rey Juan Carlos, Móstoles, Madrid, Spain
{juanfrancisco.garamendi,norberto.malpica,emanuele.schiavi}@urjc.es

Abstract. Digital (binary) image segmentation is a critical step in most image processing protocols, especially in medical imaging where accurate and fast segmentation and classification are a challenging issue. In this paper we present a fast relaxation algorithm to minimize an anistropic Mumford-Shah energy functional for piecewise constant approximation of corrupted data. The algorithm is tested with synthetic phantoms and some CT images of the abdomen. Our results are finally compared with manual segmentations in order to validate the proposed model.

1 Introduction

Image segmentation is a basic step in digital image analysis, and is especially important in the quantification of medical images. Classical segmentation methods include histogram based approaches as well as region and edge based detection. In recent years, active contour methods have become very popular, as they allow to embed both high and low level information into the segmentation process. The first models were curve evolution approaches to edge detection [1,2]. Recently, region based approaches such as the Active Contours without edges [3] have proved very useful in applications were the edges are not clarly defined. These models are normally resolved using level set curve evolution methods. The drawback is that they are normally very slow, which hinders their use in some applications were a fast segmentation is needed.

Fast numerical methods, such as the multigrid method, can be applied to these models [4]. Greater improvements can be obtained by finding equivalent models that allow faster numerical resolutions. Grady et al. reformulated the Mumford-Shah functional on an arbitrary graph and applied combinatorial optimization to produce a fast, low-energy solution [5]. In this paper, we propose a fast resolution of a weighted Mumford-Shah model for digital (binary) image segmentation by demostrating its equivalence to a denoising model.

This paper is organized as follows: in Section 2 we briefly review the classical Rudin-Osher-Fatemi (ROF) denoising model [6] and the Chan-Vese Segmentation model [3], as well as the connection between them proposed by Chambolle [7]. Section 3 introduces the model problem, which is an anisotropic (weighted) version of the popular Mumford Shah model for piece-wise constant approximations, and the link between this model and the ROF model is established.

H. Araujo et al. (Eds.): IbPRIA 2009, LNCS 5524, pp. 322–329, 2009.

This links provides a new relaxation method which allows to solve numerically the segmentation problem in an efficient way. Numerical results are presented in section 4, and discussion and conclusion are presented in Section 5.

2   Material and Methods

2.1   The ROF Denoising Model

The ROF model is a variational method for image denoising which preserves the edges of the image, by regularizing only along (and not through) the image contours. Let $\Omega \subset I\!\!R^2$ be an open, bounded domain (usually a rectangle) where $(x, y) \in \Omega$ denotes pixel location. Image denoising is the process of reconstructing unknown data $u(x, y)$ from observed data $u_0(x, y)$, assuming that $u(x, y)$ has been corrupted by an additive noise $\eta(x, y)$, i.e. $u_0(x, y) = u(x, y) + \eta(x, y)$.

In [6], Rudin, Osher and Fatemi proposed to minimize the following energy functional

$$J(u) = \int_\Omega |\nabla u| dx dy + \frac{1}{2\lambda_{rof}} \int_\Omega (u - u_0)^2 dx dy \tag{1}$$

where λ_{rof} is a parameter which controls the trade off between the Total Variation term $\int_\Omega |\nabla u| dx dy$ (depending on the gradient of the reconstructed image u) and the data fidelity term. Small values of λ_{rof} indicates a strong belief on the data term u_0 while greater values provides strongly denoised versions of the reconstructed image u.

2.2   The Chan-Vese Segmentation Model

The Chan-Vese model for binary segmentation is based on the minimization of an energy functional expressed in terms of a level set formulation. For completeness, we briefly sketch the level set dictionary. Let $\omega \subset \Omega$ be an open, positive measured sub-region of the original domain (eventually not connected). If the curve C represents the boundary of such a segmentation ω then, in the level set formulation, the (free) moving boundary C is the zero level set of a Lipschitz function $\phi : \Omega \to I\!\!R$, that is: $C = \{(x, y) \in \Omega : \phi(x, y) = 0\}$, $C = \partial\omega$ where $\omega = \{(x, y) \in \Omega : \phi(x, y) > 0\}$, $\Omega\backslash\overline{\omega} = \{(x, y) \in \Omega : \phi(x, y) < 0\}$. The level set function ϕ can be characterized as a minimum of the following energy functional:

$$E_{cv}(c_1, c_2, \phi) = \int_\Omega |\nabla H(\phi)| dx dy +$$

$$+ \lambda_{cv} \int_\Omega H(\phi)(u_0 - c_1)^2 dx dy + \lambda_{cv} \int_\Omega (1 - H(\phi))(u_0 - c_2)^2 dx dy \tag{2}$$

where c_1 and c_2 represent the mean value inside and outside the segmented region and λ_{cv} is a weight factor which controls the lenght of the interface defining the two class segmentation. The function $H(x)$ represents the Heaviside function, i.e.: $H(x) = 1$ if $x \geq 0$ and $H(x) = 0$ otherwise, and it allows to express the length of C by

$$|C| = Length(\phi = 0) = \int_\Omega |\nabla H(\phi)| dx dy.$$

2.3   The Link between Chan-Vese and ROF Model

The connection between the Chan-Vese segmentation model and the ROF denoising model was established by Chambolle [7]. Let us consider the minimization problem associated to (2) can be written in geometrical form:

$$\min_{E, c_1, c_2} J_{cv}(E, c_1, c_2)$$

where

$$J_{cv}(E, c_1, c_2) = P(E) + \frac{1}{2\lambda_{cv}} \left(\int_E (u_0 - c_1)^2 dx dy + \int_{CE} (u_0 - c_2)^2 dx dy \right)$$

and $P(E) = \int_\Omega |\nabla \chi_E| dx dy$ denotes (with abuse of notation) the perimeter of the set E and χ_E is the characteristic function of the set E. The proper formalism for BV(Ω) functions can be found in [8].

The key observation was that this minimization problem, embedded in a relaxation scheme, is equivalent to solving the ROF model and thresholding the solution obtained. This is based on the following result [7]:

Lemma 1. *Let u minimize the ROF energy (1) then, for any $s \in \mathbb{R}$, the set $E_s = \{u > s\}$ is a minimizer (over all sets $E \subset \Omega$) of*

$$J(E) = P(E) + \frac{1}{\lambda_{rof}} \int_E (s - f) dx dy$$

Once the λ parameter has been fixed, the relaxation scheme is as follows:

1. Fix an initial partition E^0.
2. Minimize the energy $J_{cv}(E, c_1, c_2)$ w.r.t. the constants c_1 and c_2, i.e. choose c_1 and c_2 like the mean inside E and CE respectively.
3. With c_1 and c_2 fixed by the previous step, minimize the energy $J_{cv}(E, c_1, c_2)$ w.r.t. the set E. This minimization problem has the same minima as [7]:

$$\min_E \left\{ P(E) + \frac{c_1 - c_2}{\lambda_{cv}} \int_E \left(\frac{c_1 + c_2}{2} - f \right) dx dy \right\}$$

By lemma 1, a solution E is given by $E_s = \{u > s\}$, where $s = (c_1 + c_2)/2$ and u minimizes the ROF energy:

$$\int_\Omega |\nabla u| dx dy + \frac{c_1 - c_2}{2\lambda_{cv}} \int_\Omega |u - f|^2 dx dy \qquad (3)$$

4. Go to step 2 until convergence.

Notice that the iterative process generates a sequence of ROF problems with associated parameters $\{\lambda_{rof}^{k}\} = \{\lambda_{cv}/(c_2^{k-1} - c_1^{k-1})\}$, which have to be solved at each iteration. This is a drawback from the numerical point of view, as it slows down the final image segmentation. This introduces the main scope of our technique which is presented in the next section.

3   The Model Problem

3.1   Anisotropic Mumford-Shah Model

Osher and Vese proposed in [9] the following energy functional for image segmentation:

$$J_{ams}(E, c_1, c_2) = |c_2 - c_1|P(E) + \frac{1}{2\lambda}\left(\int_E (u_0 - c_1)^2 dxdy + \int_{CE}(u_0 - c_2)^2 dxdy\right) \tag{4}$$

This energy functional is a modified version of the original Chan-Vese active contours without edges model (2), and represents an anisotropic version of the Mumford-Shah Energy functional, for piecewise constant approximations [10]. If we compare both functionals, (2) and (4), we can notice that the length term $P(E)$ is weighted by the jump $|c_2 - c_1|$. When both models are solved with the same λ parameter, the anisotropic model provides a more detailed segmentation and finer scales are resolved (see figure 2).

3.2   The Link between the Anisotropic Mumford-Shah Model and ROF Model

Our proposal is to apply Chambolle's result described in section 2.3 to the functional (4). This leads to a relaxation scheme in which it suffices to solve the ROF model just once, thus allowing a notable speed-up of the final segmentation.

The presented relaxation scheme is as follows:

1. Initialize c_1 and c_2.
2. Fixed c_1 and c_2 by the previous step, minimize the energy $J_{ams}(E, c_1, c_2)$ w.r.t. the set E. Assume $c_i > c_j$, $i = 1, 2$, $j = 1, 2$, $i \neq j$. It can be shown that this minimization problem has the same minima as:

$$\min_E \left\{|c_i - c_j|P(E) + \frac{c_i - c_j}{\lambda}\int_E \left(\frac{c_i + c_j}{2} - f\right)dxdy\right\} \tag{5}$$

The term $|c_i - c_j|$ can be factorized and as result, the minimization problem (5) has the same minima as:

$$\min_E \left\{P(E) + \frac{1}{\lambda}\int_E \left(\frac{c_i + c_j}{2} - f\right)dxdy\right\} \tag{6}$$

According to lemma 1 showed in section 2.3, a solution E is given by $E_s = \{u > s\}$, where $s = (c_1 + c_2)/2$ is the threshold and u minimizes the ROF energy (1).

3. With E fixed by the previous threshold step, minimize the energy $J_{ams}(E, c_1, c_2)$ w.r.t the constants c_1 and c_2. The minimization leads to the following expressions

$$c_1 = \bar{u}_0^E - \lambda \frac{c_1 - c_2}{|c_1 - c_2|} \frac{P(E)}{|E|} \qquad c_2 = \bar{u}_0^{\mathcal{C}E} - \lambda \frac{c_2 - c_1}{|c_1 - c_2|} \frac{P(\mathcal{C}E)}{|\mathcal{C}E|} \qquad (7)$$

where $\bar{u}_0^E$ and $\bar{u}_0^{\mathcal{C}E}$ are the local averages of the image u_0 on the corresponding regions, and $|E|$, $|\mathcal{C}E|$ are the area enclosed by the regions E and $\mathcal{C}E$.

4. Go to step 2. until stabilization.

Notice that in this iterative process there is only one ROF problem to minimize. The minimum is attained solving the associated elliptic Euler-Lagrange equation with multigrid methods [11].

4   Numerical Results

The relaxation algorithm proposed has been tested on synthetic images with geometrical figures (see figure 1), as well as on medical images with the aim of segmenting the liver in Computerized Tomography (CT) images. In all cases the elliptic Euler-Lagrange equation has been solved following a multigrid scheme [11,12] with maximum final residual below $9 \cdot 10^{-3}$ in the experiments. The multigrid used is composed of a F cycle with 2 and 3 pre and post smoothing iterations respectively. The smoother is a non-linear Gauss-Seidel linewise ω-relaxation with $\omega = 1.3$. The transfers operators are full-weighting for fine-to-coarse interpolation of the residual, inyection for fine-to-coarse interpolation of the solution and linear interpolation for coarse-to-fine interpolation of the error.

We first compared the two models, the Chan-Vese and Anisotropic Mumford-Shah Models. The results, in figure 2, show that for the same value of λ, the anisotropic Mumford-Shah model produces a more detailed segmentation, but similar results can be obtained wit a correctly chosen λ value.

Figure 3 shows the segmentation over the synthetic images. The values of the parameter λ has been set to $\lambda = 0.3$, $\lambda = 0.5$, $\lambda = 1$ and $\lambda = 2$, notice that as in Chan-Vese model, larger values produce a smoother segmentation, .

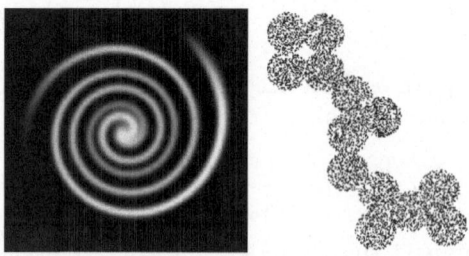

Fig. 1. The synthetic spiral and circles images used on the algorithm tests

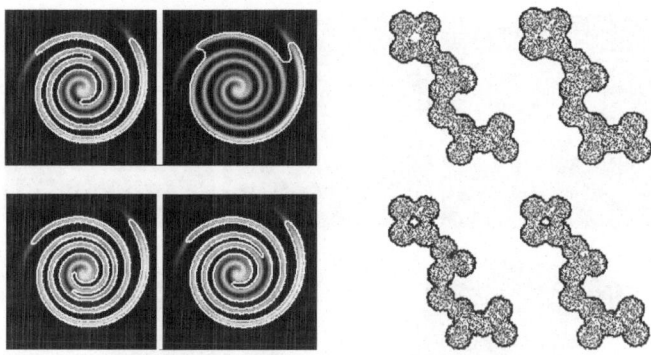

Fig. 2. Comparison between the models of Chan-Vese (first row) and Anisotropic Mumford Shah (second row) solved respectively with Chambolle's relaxation and our proposal. The values of λ are 0.3 for first and third columns and 0.5 for second and four columns.

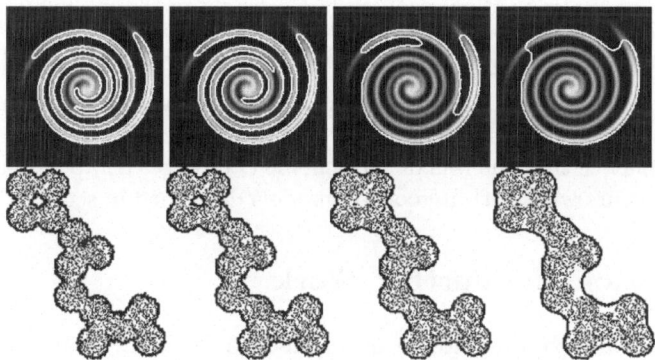

Fig. 3. Effect of λ parameter over spiral and circles images, from left to right the values of λ used has been 0.3, 0.5, 1 and 2

The algorithm has also been tested on several CT data sets series acquired at Fundación Hospital Universitario de Alcorcón, in Madrid (Spain) to segment the liver. The validity of the Chan-Vese and anisotropic Mumford-Shah models to segment the liver in CT images has been previously shown in [13] and [12] respectively. The CT images used were acquired in a General Electric LightSpeed CT scanner. The data sets size is 512x512x40 with spatial resolution 0f 0.74x0.74 mm and with a slice thickness of 5 mm. The automatic liver segmentation has been compared against manually segmented images from an expert radiologist. We use the commercial software Mimics (TM) by Materialise Software to produce a manual segmentation of the liver. Also we loaded the automatic segmentation provided by our method to produces a visual comparative between both segmentations. Figure 4 shows three slices from one data sets and a 3D reconstruction of the automatic segmentation, where de differences between a manual

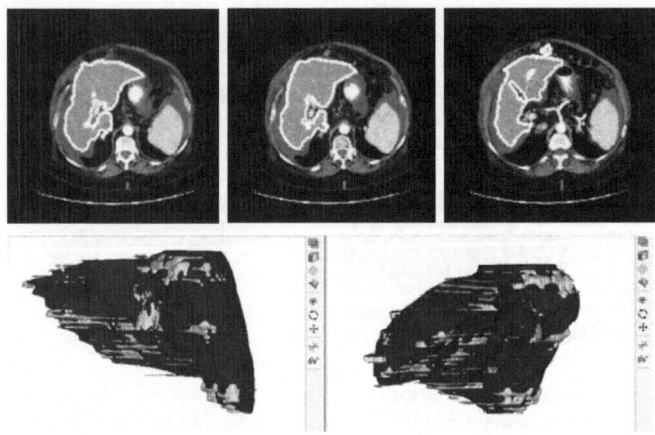

Fig. 4. Automatic liver segmentation done with the proposal method. In the first row, 2D axial views of three slices are shown, and in the second row, two differents views from 3D segmentation loaded in Mimics, where dark color shows the automatic segmentation and light color shows the error with respect manual segmentation.

segmentation are marked in lighter color. It can be shown that the relaxation algorithm works well in most slices, but there are some slices with a significant error, this is consecuence that the relaxation scheme can be get trapped in a local minimum. This occurs with both relaxation models described in sections 2.3 and 3.2.

5   Discussion and Further Work

In this paper we have presented a novel method for fast (binary) digital image segmentation. It is based on a previous method by Chambolle that uses a relaxation scheme in which the ROF equation is solved several times. Our method requires solving the ROF model only once. The preliminary numerical results over synthetic images are promising from both the quantitative and qualitative point of view. In this case, the method works well and finer structures can be recovered tuning the λ parameter. When medical segmentation applications are considered relaxation scheme can converge to a local minimum. The main difference between manual and automatic liver segmentations lies in blood vessels which are wrongly included by our method.

In the way torwards fully automatic liver segmentation, future work will address the above problem following the previous results in [12] where manual selection of the best threshold showed more accurate liver segmentation.

Acknowledgements

This work was partially supported by projects LAIMBIO - PRICIT 05/05 , financed by Comunidad de Madrid, MTM2005-03463 and CCG07-UCM/ESP-2787.

References

1. Kass, M., Witkin, A., Terzopoulos, D.: Snakes: Active Contour Models. International Journal of Computer Vision 1(4), 321–331 (1988)
2. Caselles, V., Catté, F., Coll, B., Dibos, F.: A geometric Model for Active Contours in Image Processing
3. Chan, T.F., Vese, L.A.: Active Contours Without Edges. IEEE Transactions on Image Processing 10(2), 266–277 (2001)
4. Badshah, N., Chen, K.: Multigrid method for the Chan-Vese model in variational segmentation. Commun. Comput. Phys. 4, 294–316 (2008)
5. Grady, L., Alvino, C.: Reformulating and optimizing the Mumford-Shah functional on a graph - A faster, lower energy solution. In: Forsyth, D., Torr, P., Zisserman, A. (eds.) ECCV 2008, Part I. LNCS, vol. 5302, pp. 248–261. Springer, Heidelberg (2008)
6. Rudin, L.I., Osher, S., Fatemi, E.: Nonlinear total variation based noise removal algorithms. Physica D 60, 259–268 (1992)
7. Chambolle, A.: An Algorithm for Total Variation Minimization and Applications. Journal of Mathematical Imaging and Vision 20(1-2), 89–97 (2004)
8. Ambrosio, L., Fusco, N., Pallara, D.: Functions of bounded variation and free discontinuity problems. In: Oxford Mathematical Monographs, pp. xviii+434. The Clarendon Press/ Oxford University Press, New York (2000)
9. Osher, S., Paragios, N.: Geometric Level Set Methods in Imaging, Vision, and Graphics. Springer, Heidelberg (2003)
10. Mumford, D., Shah, J.: Optimal approximations by piecewise smooth functions and associated variational problems. Commun. Pure Appl. Math. 42, 577–685 (1989)
11. Trottenberg, U., Oosterlee, C., Schüller, A.: Multigrid. Academic Press, London (2001)
12. Garamendi, J.F., Malpica, N., Schiavi, E., Gaspar, F.J.: ROF based segmentation of the liver in ct images. In: Congreso Anual de la Sociedad Española de Ingenieria Biomedica (2008)
13. Garamendi, J.F., Malpica, N., Martel, J., Schiavi, E.: Automatic Segmentation of the Liver in CT Using Level Sets Without Edges. In: Martí, J., Benedí, J.M., Mendonça, A.M., Serrat, J. (eds.) IbPRIA 2007. LNCS, vol. 4477, pp. 161–168. Springer, Heidelberg (2007)

Labeling Still Image Databases Using Graphical Models

José I. Gómez[1] and Nicolás Pérez de la Blanca[2]

[1] Dpt. Computer Science, University of Jaen
Campus Las Lagunillas, Jaen, Spain
nacho@ujaen.es
[2] Dpt. Computer Science and Artificial Intelligence, University of Granada
ETSIIT, Granada, Spain

Abstract. Graphical models have proved to be very efficient models for labeling image data. In this paper, the use of graphical models based on Decomposable Triangulated Graphs are applied for several still image databases landmark localization. We use a recently presented algorithm based on the Branch&Bound methodology, that is able to improve the state of the art. Experimental results show the improvement given by this new algorithm with respect to the classical Dynamic Programming based approach.

Keywords: data labeling, graphical models, branch&bound.

1 Introduction

In this paper, graphical models based on Decomposable Triangulated Graphs (DTG) are used to approach the objects landmark localization. Our approach is based on maximizing the likelihood of the probabilistic graphical model from a set of image measurements. Different approaches have been proposed to label or match image data using graphical models [1], [2], [3], [4], [5]. Some of these techniques are very general in the sense that they are applied on any graphical model. However, these approaches are difficult to apply on data with a substantial amount of clutter. Caelli and Caetano [6] compare favorably graphical models with traditional relaxation approaches.

Figure 1 broadly shows an example of the main steps of our approach to label new images from the learned graph models.

We present results on the use of DTG models in the labeling process on several still image databases.

1.1 Related Work

The DTG class [7] is introduced as a simpler graph class to register deformable patterns on static images. More recently, the same graphical model is used to label human body templates in tracking problems [8]. In both approaches, a Dynamic Programming algorithm (DP) was used as the search strategy to find

H. Araujo et al. (Eds.): IbPRIA 2009, LNCS 5524, pp. 330–337, 2009.

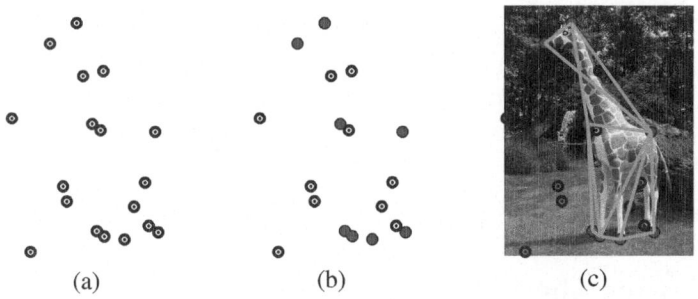

(a)   (b)   (c)

Fig. 1. Overview of the labeling process: (a) input to labeling algorithm: several points are detected from an image; (b) a set of points are selected by the labeling algorithm (red circles represent the selected points); (c) superimposed graph on original image

the best labeling from a learned model [9]. In a DTG, each node represents a landmark of the object with an associated vector of measurements. Although dynamic programming is a very convenient technique to label new sample data from DTG models, this strategy presents three important drawbacks that have been analyzed recently by Gómez et al. [10]. A new Fast and Efficient Pruning (FEP) algorithm is proposed, based on Branch&Bound strategy, that improves the performance of the Dynamic Programming based approach [8]. The FEP algorithm is studied on human motion databases in [10]. Here, we decide to study the performance of the FEP algorithm over several still image databases. In the experimental section 4, we show how this algorithm is able to run in $O(N^2)$ in the most of the tested databases.

Section 2 summarizes the probability model. Section 3 reviews the FEP algorithm. Section 4 shows the experimental results using different still image databases. Section 5 presents our conclusions.

2   The Probability Model

A Decomposable Triangulated Graph (DTG) is a triangle collection where there is a vertex elimination order so that the elimination of each node only affects one triangle. Song et al. [11], [8] propose a greedy algorithm to estimate the probability model associated with a DTG from image data.

Let $S = \{S_1, S_2, ..., S_M\}$ be a set of nodes, and let X_{Si}, $1 \leq i \leq M$ be the measure for each node. The probability model of a DTG describes the conditional dependences and independences of triplets of features associated with the triangles of the DTG:

$$P(X_{S_1}, X_{S_2}, ..., X_{S_M}) = P_{B_T C_T} \cdot \prod_{t=1}^{T} P_{A_t | B_t C_t} \tag{1}$$

where $S = \{A_1, B_1, C_1, A_2, ..., A_T, B_T, C_T\}$; $(A_1, B_1, C_1), (A_2, B_2, C_2), ..., (A_T, B_T, C_T)$ are the triangles, and $(A_1, A_2, ..., A_T)$ is the vertex elimination order. Let $\chi = \{\overline{X}^1, \overline{X}^2, ..., \overline{X}^N\}$ be a set of samples where $\overline{X}^n = \{X^n_{S_1}, ..., X^n_{S_M}\}$,

$1 \leq n \leq N$ represent the labeled data. We have to find the DTG G that maximizes the likelihood of the samples, $P(\chi|G)$, where

$$logP(\chi|G) \simeq -N \cdot h(X_{B_T}, X_{C_T}) - N \cdot \sum_{t=1}^{T} h(X_{A_t}|X_{B_t}, X_{C_t}) \qquad (2)$$

and $h(\cdot)$ is differential entropy or conditional differential entropy [12].

3   Reviewing the FEP Algorithm

Let us assume a DTG model with T triangles and let triangle number T be the base triangle of the model. In order to define a cost for each base edge on each triangle and for each full triangle, the entropy measure associated to the vertexes in each case is used. The goal is to find the labeling minimizing the cost of the DTG. On each iteration, Υ denotes the cost of the best DTG so far and Λ the cost of building the new DTG.

Let us assume N sample data (points), the FEP approach is defined by two basic stages: a) looking for a first solution; and b) improving the current solution. FEP starts by building an ordered list of base edges, using all the possible pairs of nodes, by increasing value of their associated cost. Then each edge is expanded associating to it the ordered list of candidate nodes also by increasing value of their cost. Iterating this process recursively and using a heuristic take-the-first on each expanding list, an initial best solution is obtained. The cost of this initial solution is the Υ initial value.

The improving stage is defined from a prune strategy on the full labeling tree. For each list of candidate nodes to a triangle t is defined a Dynamic Acceptance Threshold, DAT, proportional to the difference between Υ and Λ and inversely proportional to the remaining number of triangles.

The iterative improvement progresses from the initial solution searching for a better solution updating the DAT value on each step and following a branch & bound-like strategy. This process is repeated until no more candidate solutions left or $O(N^3)$ is reached. Figure 2 shows an example about how FEP algorithm works. More details in [10].

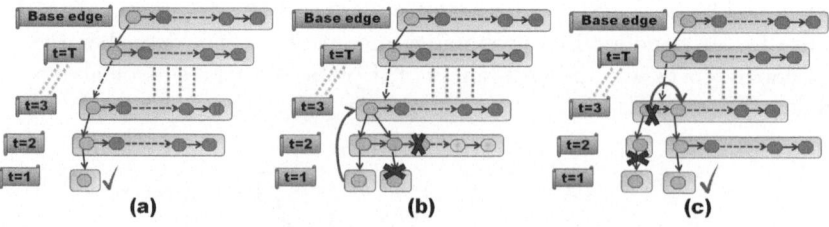

Fig. 2. Algorithm FEP: (a) The initial best solution; (b) Searching for a better solution: if a worse DTG is found the branch is bounded; (c) A better solution is reached

applelogos	bottles	buddhas	giraffes

cows	helicopters	horses

Fig. 3. DTG models associated to still image databases

4   Experiments

4.1   Labeling on Still Image Databases

We have conducted experiments with still image data. In all the cases, we assume that the vector of measurement of each node follows a multivariate Gaussian distribution which substantially simplifies the evaluation of the score measure (see [8]).

In order to validate our algorithm on other still image databases, we have conducted experiments on 546 images of seven databases representing different objects: cows [13], buddhas and helicopters [14], horses [15], giraffes, applelogos and bottles [16].

We have used a different number of labels for making each DTG model depending on the geometric shape to be fitted on each image database. Figure 3 shows the learned DTG models.

The node number for each model is previously set by us: six nodes for bottles, applelogos, buddhas and helicopters, seven for cows, and eight for horses and giraffes. The feature coordinates have been selected by hand. We use the same number of samples for training and testing on each database.

We have tested our experiments without noisy points and with ten noisy points added to each sample. This last test means adding more than twice the number of points defining the models.

The labeling of a sample is considered correct if its cost is lower than the true cost assumed as known (only for the test samples). This criterion unfortunately does not guarantee that the fitted labeling is equal to the true one. It means that, in the case with noisy points added, we could accept a background point as part of the best labeling. This is possible because we are working over still images, so we cannot use information about movement (as happens in the case of human motion [10]). It is not an easy task by using graphical models.

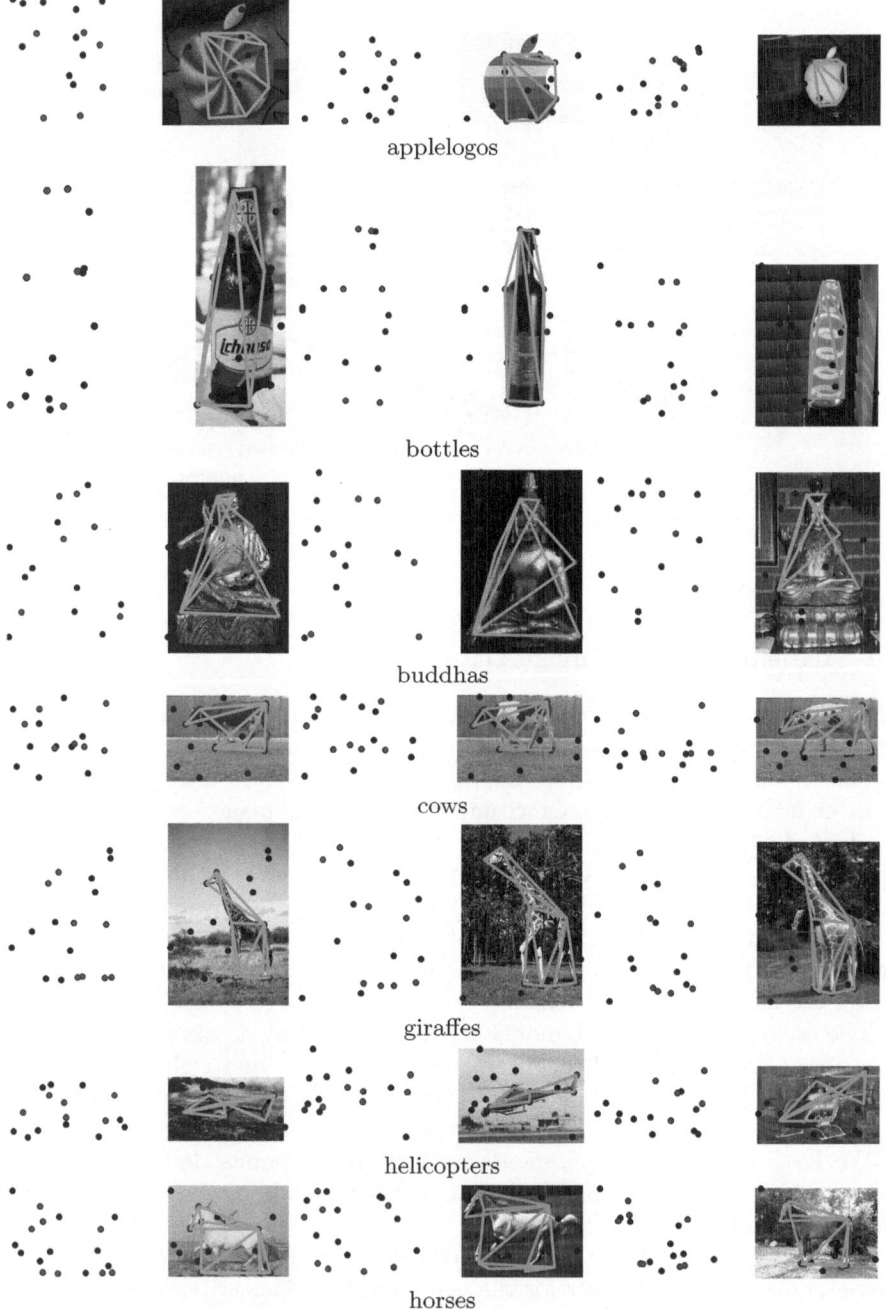

applelogos

bottles

buddhas

cows

giraffes

helicopters

horses

Fig. 4. FEP working over several still image database samples. Two images are shown for each example: first image shows 6, 7 or 8 landmarks (according to the DTG model in Figure 3) plus 10 added noisy points; points selected by FEP are emphasized (filled points in red); second image draws the DTG associated to selected points.

Table 1. This table shows the percentage of times that the best solution is found by DP and FEP on the still image database. For each one, the model shown in Figure 3 has been used. Tests are shown both without noisy points and with ten noisy points added to each sample.

DDBB	Without noisy points		With 10 noisy points	
	% DP	% FEP	% DP	% FEP
applelogos	100%	100%	100%	100%
bottles	100%	100%	100%	100%
buddhas	100%	100%	100%	100%
helicopters	100%	100%	100%	100%
cows	94.0%	100%	100%	100%
giraffes	97.7%	100%	97.7%	95.4%
horses	96.0%	100%	100%	94.0%

Table 2. This table shows the percentage of times that expected and selected labels are coincident. When there are not noisy points it means that some labels have been mistaken amongst themselves.

DDBB	Without noisy points		With 10 noisy points	
	% DP	% FEP	% DP	% FEP
applelogos	100%	100%	100%	100%
bottles	100%	100%	100%	100%
buddhas	100%	100%	100%	100%
helicopters	100%	100%	100%	100%
cows	97.1%	100%	94.3%	94.3%
giraffes	97.5%	97.5%	91.3%	90.0%
horses	96.3%	97.5%	81.3%	76.3%

Table 1 shows the percentage of times that the best solution is found. It can be seen that both FEP and DP achieve a very good general score for all the used databases.

Figure 4 shows some samples of DTG fitted for these still image databases. An example of selected background point as right label is shown in the second sample of buddhas database.

The capacity of finding the right labeling is shown in Table 2. Almost all tests show a percentage higher than 90%, except for the *horses* database when noisy points are added. Nevertheless, Table 1 shows a very good percentage for this database. It means that the selected labeling holds a better cost than the expected labeling. It happens because either some background points have been selected or some landmarks are confused by themselves.

4.2   Evaluating Computational Complexity

In order to evaluate the efficiency of the FEP algorithm, we have calculated the upper bound following the Bachmann-Landau Asymptotic Notation [17]. These

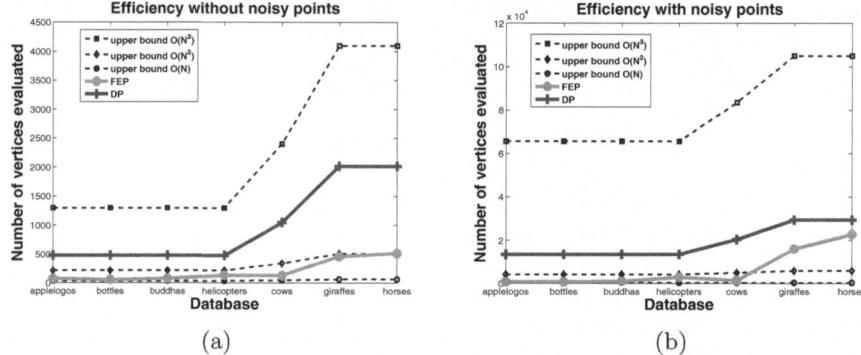

(a)   (b)

Fig. 5. The efficiency is given by the number of vertices evaluated until the best fitting is found. It is shown how FEP algorithm reachs a lower value than DP algorithm for all the databases. While DP algorithm is $O(N^3)$, FEP algorithm gives an $O(N^2)$ efficiency in all the databases except for giraffes and horses databases (only with noisy points added): (a) no noisy points are added; (b) ten noisy points are added.

limits depend on the number of landmarks used by each database. They are shown in Figure 5 using blue dashed lines.

The main difference between the performance of the FEP and DP algorithms on still image databases is in the evaluation of efficiency. It is meassured as the number of vertices evaluated until the best fitting is reached.

DP always evaluates the same number of vertices for fitting a DTG. This value is equal to $T \cdot N \cdot (N - 1) \cdot (N - 2)$, where T is the number of triangles belonging to fitted DTG, and N is the number of points detected on the image (see [7], [8]).

FEP algorithm is able to reach the best fitting in order $O(N^2)$. Figure 5.(a) shows that efficiency is $O(N^2)$ for all the databases. Figure 5.(b) shows how this efficiency is reached too for the most of the databases when ten noisy points are added, except for $giraffes$ and $horses$ databases ($O(N^3)$). However, they both needs to evaluate a lower number of vertices than DP to reach the best fitting.

5   Conclusions

We have shown how a new algorithm (FEP), based on DTG models, is able to find an optimal labeling on several still image databases. The FEP algorithm is faster than the traditional DP algorithm in terms of efficiency, and is able to find a solution of similar quality. We believe that the proposed approach could be generalized to deal with graphical models of higher complexity. This point is the subject of forthcoming research.

Acknowledgements. Thanks to the reviewers for their suggestions. This work was supported by the Spanish Ministry of Science and Innovation under project TIN2005-01665.

References

1. Gold, S., Rangarajan, A.: A graduated assignment algorithm for graph matching. IEEE Trans. Pattern Anal. Mach. Intell. 18(4), 377–388 (1996)
2. Grimson, W.E.L.: Object recognition by computer: the role of geometric constraints. MIT Press, Cambridge (1990)
3. Haralick, R.M., Shapiro, L.G.: Computer and Robot Vision. Addison-Wesley Longman Publishing Co., Inc., Boston (1992)
4. Rangarajan, A., Chui, H., Bookstein, F.L.: The softassign procrustes matching algorithm. In: Duncan, J.S., Gindi, G. (eds.) IPMI 1997. LNCS, vol. 1230, pp. 29–42. Springer, Heidelberg (1997)
5. Ullman, S.: High-level Vision. MIT Press, Cambridge (1996)
6. Caelli, T., Caetano, T.S.: Graphical models for graph matching: Approximate models and optimal algorithms. Pattern Recognition Letters 26(3), 339–346 (2005)
7. Amit, Y., Kong, A.: Graphical templates for model registration. IEEE PAMI 18(3), 225–236 (1996)
8. Song, Y., Goncalves, L., Perona, P.: Unsupervised learning of human motion. IEEE Trans. Patt. Anal. and Mach. Intell. 25(7), 1–14 (2003)
9. Fischler, M.A., Elschlager, R.A.: The representation and matching of pictorial structures. IEEE Trans. Comput. 22(1), 67–92 (1973)
10. Gómez, J.I., Marín-Jiménez, M., de la Blanca, N.P.: Labeling human motion sequences using graphical models. In: International Conf. on Computer Vision Theory and Applications (VISAPP), vol. 1, pp. 488–495 (2009)
11. Song, Y., Feng, X., Perona, P.: Towards detection of human motion. In: IEEE Conference on Computer Vision and Pattern Recognition (CVPR), vol. 1, pp. 810–817 (2000)
12. Cover, T., Thomas, J.: Elements of Information Theory. John Wiley and Sons, Chichester (1991)
13. Leibe, B., Leonardis, A., Schiele, B.: Combined object categorization and segmentation with an implicit shape model. In: ECCV 2004 Workshop on Statistical Learning in Computer Vision, Prague, Czech Republic, pp. 17–32 (2004), http://www.mis.informatik.tu-darmstadt.de/Research/Projects/interleaved/data/
14. Li, F., Fergus, R., Perona, P.: Learning generative visual models from few training examples: An incremental bayesian approach tested on 101 object categories. In: IEEE CVPR Workshop of Generative Model Based Vision (WGMBV) (2004)
15. Borenstein, E., Sharon, E., Ullman, S.: Combining top-down and bottom-up segmentation. In: CVPRW 2004: Proceedings of the 2004 Conference on Computer Vision and Pattern Recognition Workshop (CVPRW 2004), vol. 4, p. 46. IEEE Computer Society, Washington (2004), http://www.msri.org/people/members/eranb/
16. Ferrari, V., Tuytelaars, T., Gool, L.V.: Object detection by contour segment networks. In: Leonardis, A., Bischof, H., Pinz, A. (eds.) ECCV 2006. LNCS, vol. 3953, pp. 14–28. Springer, Heidelberg (2006), http://www.vision.ee.ethz.ch/datasets/
17. Knuth, D.E.: Big omicron and big omega and big theta. SIGACT News 8(2), 18–24 (1976)

AdaBoost Multiple Feature Selection and Combination for Face Recognition

Francisco Martínez-Contreras, Carlos Orrite-Uruñuela,
and Jesús Martínez-del-Rincón

CVLab, Aragon Institute for Engineering Research, University of Zaragoza, Spain
{franjmar,corrite,jesmar}@unizar.es

Abstract. Gabor features have been recognized as one of the most successful face representations. Encouraged by the results given by this approach, other kind of facial representations based on Steerable Gaussian first order kernels and Harris corner detector are proposed in this paper. In order to reduce the high dimensional feature space, PCA and LDA techniques are employed. Once the features have been extracted, AdaBoost learning algorithm is used to select and combine the most representative features. The experimental results on XM2VTS database show an encouraging recognition rate, showing an important improvement with respect to face descriptors only based on Gabor filters.

1 Introduction

Face recognition has become in a relevant biometrics modality due to the broad variety of potential applications in public security, law enforcement, access control and video surveillance. The main two factors that affect to the performance of most current systems are the large variability in facial appearance of a person, due to different poses, lighting and facial expressions, and the high dimensionality of the facial features.

In order to deal with facial expression and illumination, some authors [8,9] propose to use a Gabor wavelet representation. The Gabor wavelet kernels allow to capture salient visual properties such as spatial localization, orientation selectivity, and spacial frequency characteristics.

Recently, others authors [21,22] proposed the use of local oriented Gaussian derivative filters for face identification. The structure of an image can be represented by the outputs of a set of multi-scales Gaussian derivative filters (MGDF) applied to the image as proposed in [15], for the appearance representation in face recognition and image retrieval. More biologically motivated is the use of Steerable Gaussian first order derivative filters as proposed in [4] for detecting facial landmarks from neutral and expressive facial images.

The main drawback when using Gabor or other oriented filter approaches to obtain a new representation of the face is the great redundancy and high dimensionality they exhibit. Recent papers [19,17] have proposed using the AdaBoost learning algorithm presented in [18] to select a small set of filters.

H. Araujo et al. (Eds.): IbPRIA 2009, LNCS 5524, pp. 338–345, 2009.

To cope with this dimensionality problem, some subspace projection techniques to reduce feature dimension are proposed. In addition to the "classical" techniques such as Principal Component Analysis (PCA) and Linear Discriminant Analysis (LDA) or a combination of both (PCA+LDA)(see chapter 7 in [7] for a survey of face recognition in subspaces), recently two discriminant approaches have been proposed in junction with Gabor filters. In [9], the authors apply the Enhanced Fisher linear discriminant Model (EFM). In [16], Shen, at al. propose to transform the Gabor feature space into a General Discriminant Analysis (GDA) space. The mean nearest neighbor rule is used for classification in both methods, using different distance measures(i.e. Euclidean Distance, Mahalanobis Distance or Cosine Similarity).

2   Proposal Overview

Considering the good results given by the Gabor wavelet filters, as well as the multi-scales Gaussian derivative filters, this paper tries to fuse different face representations in order to find the best one among all.

In addition to the previous filters used in face recognition, this paper explores other feature extraction algorithms used in other computer vision applications. For example, Harris corner detector has become a popular interest-point detector due to its strong invariance to rotation, scale, illumination variation and image noise, just the kind of problems found in face recognition.

All these transformations constitute a rich representation of the face, invariant to lighting and facial appearance. However, the final representation of the face may exhibit a great redundancy and high dimensionality.

Let $\boldsymbol{F}$ be an arbitrary filtered image which is projected onto a PCA basis. This image (minus the mean) in the training set can be represented as a linear combination of the best K eigenvectors.

$$\boldsymbol{F} - \boldsymbol{mean} = \sum_{k=1}^{K} w_j a_j, (w_j = a_j^T \boldsymbol{F}) \tag{1}$$

where a_j are called Eigenfilters and w_j are the eigenvalues that can be used as features for the next fusion architecture.

Boosting is considered a powerful technique to combine multiple classifiers producing in this way a form of committee whose performance could be significantly better than that of any of the base classifiers [2]. Here we use a form of boosting called AdaBoost as proposed in [18].

There are several levels at which fusion can take place in a multi-biometric system [6]. In this paper, two different strategies based on AdaBoost algorithm are proposed: feature level fusion and score level fusion. Both approaches use the patterns obtained by applying PCA and LDA to the filtered facial representation after convolving the input image with a kernel filter.

Figure 1 (Left) shows the feature level fusion architecture. In this approach, the AdaBoost algorithm receives as input the eigenvalues w_j set corresponding

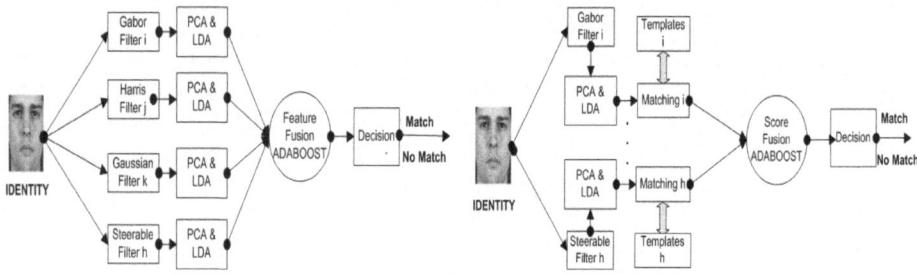

Fig. 1. Feature level fusion(Left) and Score level fusion architectures(Right)

to an Eigenfilter (Fisherfilter) image, together with a group of thresholds. The similarity of two features is defined as a simple subtraction.

In the score level fusion architecture, see Figure 1 (Right), each filter formulates a weak classifier. The decision of acceptance or rejection is based on a measurement of similarity between the filtered face and the template set, with a global threshold. The similarity of two images is defined as the cosine distance. The threshold is selected at the equal error point, EER, at where the False Acceptance Ratio (FAR) is equal to the False Rejection Ratio (FRR) on the evaluation set.

The main contributions of this paper are summarized as follows: 1) Different facial representations are considered to cope with different facial expressions and lighting. 2) Two combination strategies, based on AdaBoost, are proposed in order to select a small set of filters, reducing redundancy and improving at the same time the rates of recognition.

3   Kernel Filters

3.1   Gabor Features for Face Recognition

In the spatial domain, a 2D Gabor filter is a Gaussian kernel function modulated by a sinusoidal plane wave. The equations can be revised in previous experiments [9,19,17,16],in which, the following parameters are used: five scales v and eight orientations u with $\sigma = 2\pi$, $k_{max} = \pi/2$ and $f = \sqrt{2}$. As pointed by [9] the convolution is speeded up by applying the Fast Fourier Transform (FFT).As a result, image $I(z)$ can be represented by a set of Gabor complex coefficients. Like previous works, only magnitudes are used to form the final face representation.

3.2   Differential Features

First order differential features. The structure of an image can be represented by the outputs of a set of multi-scale Gaussian derivative filters. The simplest differential feature is a vector of spatial derivatives [20]. The initial image is incrementally convolved with Gaussians to produce images separated by a constant factor k in scale space. Each octave of scale space (doubling of σ)

is divided into an integer number, s, of intervals, so $k = 2^{1/s}$. In the present approach, the values $\sigma = 1.6$ and $s = 4$ has been used due to empirical experiments. With these values, the number of used scales is seven. The magnitude and the orientation of all the pixels are calculated for all scales.

Oriented Filters. Steerable filters refer to a class of filters in which a filter of an arbitrary orientation is synthesized as a linear combination of a set of "basis filters", see [3]. Following a similar approach as used for Gabor-based feature representation, a bank of filters is adopted, varying the orientations and the frequencies/scales. In this way, oriented edges are extracted by convolving a smoothed image with a set of different kernels. Each kernel is sensitive to a different orientation θ. This paper applies the following values for $\theta = k * 22.5$, $k = 0, \ldots, 7$, the same ones used for Gabor filters, and for $p, q = \{-64, \ldots, 64\}$, in accordance with the size of the image. Two different Steerable filters are tested, one of them is developed in [4]. The value of σ in this case is $2\pi * i$, with $i = \{0.5, 1, 1.5, \ldots, 4\}$. The second kind of Steerable filters are made likeness Gabor filters, with k_v used as scale (eq. 2). In this case, $\sigma=2\pi$, and $k_v = \frac{k_{max}}{fv}$ is the same that in Gabor filters.

$$G_\theta^- = \frac{k_v^2}{2\pi\sigma^2} \cdot e^{-k_v^2 \frac{(p-\sigma\cos\theta)^2+(q-\sigma\sin\theta)^2}{2\sigma^2}} \qquad G_\theta^+ = \frac{k_v^2}{2\pi\sigma^2} \cdot e^{-k_v^2 \frac{(p+\sigma\cos\theta)^2+(q+\sigma\sin\theta)^2}{2\sigma^2}}$$

$$(2)$$

3.3 Harris Corner Detector

The use of local interest points in image matching can be traced back to the work of Moravec [14] on stereo matching using a corner detector. Later, Harris and Stephens [5] improved the Moravec detector making it more repeatable under small image variations and near edges. This work follows an approach similar to that given by Mikolajczyk [12]. The space of scale is a set of images, which are generated convolving the original image by a series of Gaussian kernels with different values of sigma. The sigma increase must be adequately fixed, since a high step would decrease the reliability of finding the most suitable correspondence. The value of an initial sigma is 1.6 and the sigma increase is $k = 2^{1/8}$, and the number of scales used is 5. To work with color images, some authors [13] propose a simple modification of Harris Detector, computing gradients in the RGB space. The parameters obtained by the Harris detector are the magnitude and the orientation and the two Eigenvalues λ_1 and λ_2.

4 Feature Selection and Combination by AdaBoost

4.1 Fusion Architectures

To use AdaBoost in the context of face recognition, the concepts of Intra-personal difference (called positive examples) and Inter-personal (called negative examples) are adopted in order to convert the multi-class problem into a two-class

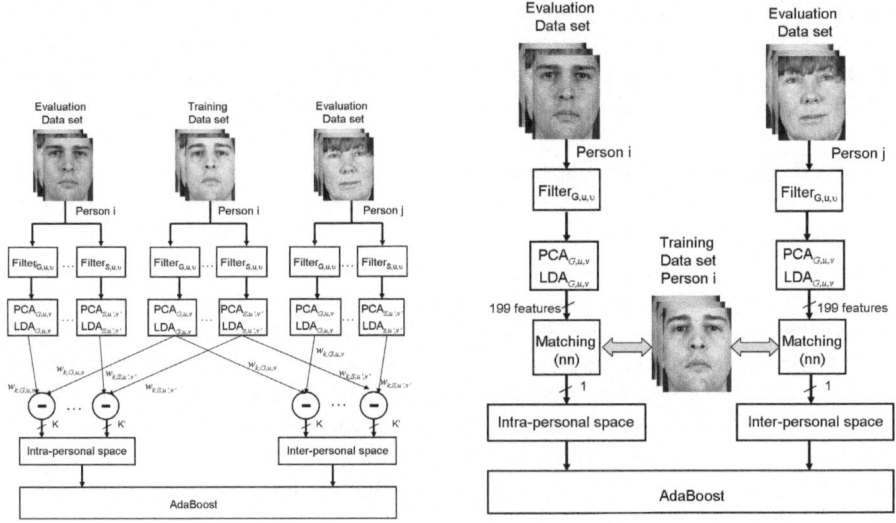

Fig. 2. Flowchart for the face recognition system according to the feature level(Left) and the score level of the fusion architecture(Right)

problem [17]. To accomplish this process, the original database is split into three ones: training, evaluation and test data set. The training data set is applied to obtain the new PCA (LDA) transformation parameters.

Figure 2 (Left) shows the flowchart for the feature level fusion architecture. Given an input image, different filters are applied to obtain a FilterFace representation at different scales and orientations. All the images of the evaluation data set are projected to the new PCA/LDA space. These new features w_k (eq. 1) are then used to generate positive and negative examples in relation to the individuals in the training data set. In this combined strategy, a simple substraction between patterns is done, and the resulting features are introduced into the AdaBoost algorithm. For each feature, the weak learner determines the optimal threshold classification function, such that the minimum numbers of examples are misclassified. The score level fusion architecture is depicted in Figure 2 (Right). The initial stages are the same as far the feature level fusion, but once the K eigenvalues w_k are obtained, a classifier is built based on a measurement of similarity, the nearest neighbor decision rule, between the input and the average of client's training images with a global threshold. The threshold is selected at the equal error point, EER on the evaluation set. The similarity of two features **x**, **y** is given by the cosine distance of its projected vector in PCA (LDA) subspace.

4.2   AdaBoost Algorithm

AdaBoost [18] is an algorithm which obtains a strong classifier from weak classifiers, combining each one of these individual classifiers with different weights to obtain a consensus decision which minimizes the error rate. The weak classifier $h_j(x)$ is composed of one measurement $f_j(x)$ (Cosine Distance or substraction, depending on the fusion architecture), and a threshold Θ_j. If the classifier returns 1, it means that the two patterns belong to the same person.

5   Experiments and Discussion

The proposed methods have been tested on the public XM2VTS face database [1], which contains 2360 images of 295 subjects, with 8 faces for each subject, divided into 4 sessions of 2 images in each one. The testing is performed following the Laussane protocol [11], which splits the database into 3 different sets for training, evaluation and test. Previous works [10] have reported that the configuration II gives lower error rates than configuration I. 200 "clients" and 95 "impostors" have been used.

All images are cropped and rectified according to the manually located eye positions supplied with the XM2VTS data. The normalized images are 128 x 128 pixels. By filtering and normalizing the facial image, a feature vector in a very high dimensionality space is obtained. The use of PCA allows to reduce

Table 1. (Left) FAR and FRR for both fusion architectures using Gabor filters. (Right) Best rates of FAR and FRR obtained with the different filters.

Architecture	FAR	FRR	TER
Score level	1.57	1.25	2.82
Feature level	2.05	1.75	3.80

Label	Filter	In	Out	FAR	FRR	TER
1	Gabor	56	14	1.57	1.25	2.82
2	Harris	20	6	2.28	1.5	3.78
3	Gaussian	14	6	2.65	1.5	4.15
4	Steerable 1	64	12	2.02	1	3.53
5	Steerable 2	64	15	1.98	1.5	3.48

Table 2. Best FAR and FRR obtained by means of the combination of different filters

Combination	FAR(%)	FRR(%)	TER
1+2	2.03	1.25	3.28
1+3	0.93	1.25	2.18
1+4	1.50	0.75	2.25
1+5	1.53	1.5	3.03
2+3	1.15	1.25	2.40
2+4	1.69	0.5	2.19
2+5	1.65	1.75	3.40
3+4	1.78	0.5	2.28
3+5	1.64	1.25	2.89
4+5	1.98	1.5	3.48
1+2+3	0.81	1.25	2.06
1+2+4	1.49	0.5	1.99
1+2+5	1.51	1.5	3.01

Combination	FAR(%)	FRR(%)	TER
1+3+4	1.38	0.5	1.88
1+3+5	1.37	1	2.37
1+4+5	1.60	1.5	3.10
2+3+4	1.47	0.25	1.72
2+3+5	1.57	1.25	2.82
2+4+5	1.67	1.5	3.17
3+4+5	1.60	1.25	2.85
1+2+3+4	1.31	0.5	1.81
1+2+3+5	1.30	1	2.30
1+2+4+5	1.56	1.5	3.06
1+3+4+5	1.60	1.5	3.10
2+3+4+5	1.56	1.25	2.81
1+2+3+4+5	1.26	0.75	2.01

each vector to N-1 dimensions keeping at least 90% of the variance in most of the cases, where N represents the number of classes. Although the reduction is enough, LDA is applied, which gets a better separation among feature vectors of different classes. The dimensionality is maintained after LDA. After that, the size of each pattern, which was initially of 128 x 128 =16384 features, is composed of 199 features (number of clients - 1).

The two fusion architectures explained before are tested using Gabor filters. To measure the performance of the verification system, FAR, FRR and the Total Error Rate (TER), defined as the sum of the FAR and FRR are used.

Table 1 (Left) shows the rates given by both approaches. Clearly, the score level fusion outperforms the feature level fusion in FAR as well as FRR. In addition, the computational cost of the feature level architecture is quite higher than the score level. In this point we took the decision of using the score level fusion architecture for the rest of the facial representation. Table 1 (Right) shows the best results obtained for every facial representation, together with the number of weak classifiers given by the AdaBoost algorithm.

The next step is to combine these filters in order to obtain the best error rates. In total, all combinations of 1-filter, 2-filters, 3-filters, and so on..., have been tested, $C_1^5 + C_2^5 + C_3^5 + C_4^5 + C_5^5 = 31$, where C_i^5 denotes the number of combinations of i filters chosen amongst the possible total number of 5 filters. The results are shown in Table 2. The best combination in order to obtain a lower TER is given by Harris, Gaussian filters and the first Steerable filter proposal, with FAR = 1.47, FRR = 0.25 and TER = 1.72.

6   Conclusions

In this paper, we have presented a novel technique of dimensionality reduction of features for face recognition using the AdaBoost algorithm as a selector of facial representations. We have proposed two different fusion architecture based on score level or feature level fusion. The application of both approaches to the selection of Gabor filters showed that the score level fusion outperforms the feature level one with a lower computational cost.

Besides Gabor features, other kind of facial representations based on Steerable Gaussian first order kernels and Harris corner detector have been tested.

The experimental results on XM2VTS database show that individually, the Gabor filters are the best method for face authentication. The AdaBoost algorithm chooses 14 Gabor representation to give a TER=2.82.

The combination of different filters improves substantially the recognition rate, reaching a TER=1.72 using 16 filters. Surprisingly, Gabor filters are not included in the best combination, unlike other filters with less computational cost.

Acknowledgements

This work is partially supported by grants TIC2003-08382-C05-05 and TIN-2006-11044 (MEyC) and FEDER.

References

1. The xm2vtsdb, http://www.ee.surrey.ac.uk/Research/VSSP/xm2vtsdb
2. Bishop, C.M.: Pattern Recognition and Machine Learning. Springer, Heidelberg (2006)
3. Freeman, W.T., Adelson, E.H.: The design and use of steerable filters. IEEE Trans. Pattern Anal. Mach. Intell. 13(9), 891–906 (1991)
4. Gizatdinova, Surakka: Feature-based detection of facial landmarks from neutral and expressive facial images. Pattern Anal. Mach. Intell. 28(1), 135–139 (2006)
5. Harris, C., Stephens, M.: A combined corner and edge detector. In: 4th ALVEY Vision Conference, pp. 147–151 (1988)
6. ISO/IEC. Technical Report 24722 (2007)
7. Jain, A.K., Li, S.Z.: Handbook of Face Recognition (2005)
8. Krüger, V., Sommer, G.: Gabor wavelet networks for object representation. In: Proceedings of the 10th International Workshop on Theoretical Foundations of Computer Vision, London, UK, pp. 115–128. Springer, Heidelberg (2001)
9. Liu, C., Wechsler, H.: Gabor feature based classification using the enhanced fisher linear discriminant model for face recognition. IEEE Transactions on Image Processing 11(4), 467–476 (2002)
10. Messer, K., Kittler, J., Short, J., Heusch, G., Cardinaux, F., Marcel, S., Rodriguez, Y., Shan, S., Su, Y., Gao, W., Chen, X.: Performance characterisation of face recognition algorithms and their sensitivity to severe illumination changes. In: Advances in Biometrics, International Conference, ICB 2006, pp. 1–11 (2006)
11. Messer, K., Matas, J., Kittler, J., Luettin, J., Maitre, G.: Xm2vtsdb: The extended m2vts database. In: Second International Conference on Audio and Video-based Biometric Person Authentication (March 1999)
12. Mikolajczyk, K., Schmid, C.: Indexing Based on Scale Invariant Interest Points. In: 8th International Conference on Computer Vision (ICCV 2001), pp. 525–531 (2001)
13. Montesinos, P., Gouet, V., Deriche, R.: Differential invariants for color images. In: ICPR 1998:International Conference on Pattern Recognition, vol. 1, p. 838 (1998)
14. Moravec, H.: Rover visual obstacle avoidance. In: International Joint Conference on Artificial Intelligence (IJCAI 1981), pp. 785–790 (1981)
15. Ravela, S., Hanson, A.: On multiscale differential features for face recognition. In: Vision Interface, Ottawa (2001)
16. Shen, L., Bai, L., Fairhurst, M.: Gabor wavelets and general discriminant analysis for face identification and verification. Image Vision Comput. 25(5), 553–563 (2007)
17. Su, Y., Shan, S., Gao, W., Chen, X.: A multiple fisher classifiers combination for face recognition based on grouping adaboosted gabor features. In: Proceeding of British Machin Vision Conference, Oxford, UK, vol. 2, pp. 569–578 (2005)
18. Viola, P.A., Jones, M.J.: Rapid object detection using a boosted cascade of simple features. In: CVPR 2001, pp. 511–518 (2001)
19. Yang, P., Shan, S., Gao, W., Li, S.Z., Zhang, D.: Face recognition using ada-boosted gabor features. In: Sixth IEEE International Conference on Automatic Face and Gesture Recognition (FGR 2004), pp. 356–361 (2004)
20. Yokono, J.J., Poggio, T.: Oriented filters for object recognition: an empirical study. In: Sixth IEEE International Conference on Automatic Face and Gesture Recognition (FGR 2004), pp. 755–760 (2004)
21. Yokono, J.J., Poggio, T.: A multiview face identification model with no geometric constraints. In: FGR 2006: Proceedings of the 7th International Conference on Automatic Face and Gesture Recognition, pp. 493–498 (2006)
22. Zhang, X., Jia, Y.: Face recognition with local steerable phase feature. Pattern Recogn. Lett. 27(16), 1927–1933 (2006)

Median Graph Computation by Means of a Genetic Approach Based on Minimum Common Supergraph and Maximum Common Subgraph

M. Ferrer[1], E. Valveny[2], and F. Serratosa[3]

[1] Institut de Robòtica i Informàtica Industrial, (UPC-CSIC), Spain
mferrer@iri.upc.edu
[2] Centre de Visió per Computador, Universitat Autònoma de Barcelona, Spain
ernest@cvc.uab.cat
[3] Departament d'Informàtica i Matemàtiques, Universitat Rovira i Virgili, Spain
francesc.serratosa@urv.cat

Abstract. Given a set of graphs, the median graph has been theoretically presented as a useful concept to infer a representative of the set. However, the computation of the median graph is a highly complex task and its practical application has been very limited up to now. In this work we present a new genetic algorithm for the median graph computation. A set of experiments on real data, where none of the existing algorithms for the median graph computation could be applied up to now due to their computational complexity, show that we obtain good approximations of the median graph. Finally, we use the median graph in a real nearest neighbour classification showing that it leaves the box of the only-theoretical concepts and demonstrating, from a practical point of view, that can be a useful tool to represent a set of graphs.

1 Introduction

In structural pattern recognition, the concept of median graph [1] has been presented as a useful tool to represent a set of graphs. Given a set of graphs S, the median graph is defined as the graph that minimizes the sum of distances (SOD) to all the graphs in S. It aims to extract the essential information of a set of graphs into a single prototype. Potential applications include graph clustering and prototype learning. For instance, it has been successfully applied to different areas such as image clustering [2], optical character recognition [1] and graphical symbol recognition [3].

Nevertheless, the computation of the median graph is a highly complex task. In the past some exact and approximate algorithms have been developed. Optimal algorithms include a tree search approach called multimatch [4] and a more efficient algorithm which takes advantage of certain conditions about the distance between two graphs [3] . Suboptimal methods include genetic algorithms [1], greedy-based algorithms [2] and spectral-based approaches such that of [3] and [5]. In spite of this wide offer of algorithmic tools, all of them are very limited in their application. They are often restricted to use small graphs and with some particular conditions. None of them have been applied using real data.

H. Araujo et al. (Eds.): IbPRIA 2009, LNCS 5524, pp. 346–353, 2009.

In this paper we tackle the problem of the median graph computation under a particular cost function. Using the results presented in [3], we present a new genetic algorihtm for the median graph computation that allows us to use a real database of 2,430 webpages. Firstly, we assess the accuracy of the median demonstrating that we are obtaining good approximations of the median graph. After that, we try to validate the median graph as a representative of a class of graphs. Up to now, existing algorithms could only be applied to very limited sets of graphs and the median graph could not be evaluated from a practical point of view as a good representative of a class. To that extent, we perform a preliminary classification experiment using the median graph. In some cases, we obtain slightly better results than a nearest-neighbor classifier with a much lower computation time. Thus, we demonstrate, for the first time, that the median graph can be a feasible alternative to represent a set of graphs in real applications.

The rest of the paper is organized as follows. In Section 2, we define the basic concepts used in the paper. Then, in Section 3 the concept of the median graph and its theoretical properties are presented. Section 4 introduces a new genetic algorithm for the median graph computation. Then, Section 5 is devoted to present our experiments and results. Finally, we terminate with some conclusions and possible future research lines.

2   Definitions and Notation

Let L be a finite alphabet of labels for nodes and edges. A **graph** is a four-tuple $g = (V, E, \alpha, \beta)$ where V is the finite set of nodes, E is the set of edges, α is the node labelling function ($\alpha : V \longrightarrow L$), and β is the edge labelling function ($\beta : E \longrightarrow L$). We assume that our graphs are fully connected. Consequently, the set of *edges* is implicitly given (i.e. $E = V \times V$). Such assumption is only for notational convenience, and it does not impose any restriction in the generality of our results. In the case where no edge exists between two given nodes, we can include the special null label ε in the set of labels L to model such situation. Finally, the number of nodes of a graph g is denoted by $|g|$.

Given two graphs, $g_1 = (V_1, E_1, \alpha_1, \beta_1)$ and $g_2 = (V_2, E_2, \alpha_2, \beta_2)$, g_2 is a **subgraph** of g_1, denoted by $g_2 \subseteq g_1$ if, $V_2 \subseteq V_1$, $\alpha_2(v) = \alpha_1(v)$ for all $v \in V_2$ and $\beta_2((u, v)) = \beta_1((u, v))$ for all $(u, v) \in V_2 \times V_1$. From this definition, it follows that, given a graph $g_1 = (V_1, E_1, \alpha_1, \beta_1)$, a subset $V_1 \subseteq V_1$ of its vertices uniquely defines a subgraph. Such subgraph is called the subgraph *induced* by V_2.

Let $S = \{g_1, g_2, ..., g_n\}$ be a set of graphs. A graph $g_m(S)$ is called a **maximum common subgraph of S** if $g_m(S)$ is a common subgraph of $\{g_1, g_2, \cdots, g_n\}$ and there is no other common subgraph of $\{g_1, g_2, \cdots, g_n\}$ having more nodes than $g_m(S)$. In addition, a graph $g_M(S)$ is called a **minimum common supergraph of S** if $\{g_1, g_2, \cdots, g_n\}$ are subgraphs of $g_M(S)$ and there is no other common supergraph of $\{g_1, g_2, \cdots, g_n\}$ having less nodes than $g_M(S)$. We will also denote the $g_m(S)$ and the $g_M(S)$ as $mcs(S)$ and $MCS(S)$ respectively.

The **graph edit distance** [6,7] is commonly used to compute the dissimilarity between graphs. To that extent, a number of distortion or edit operations e, consisting of the insertion, deletion and substitution of both nodes and edges are defined. Then, for every pair of graphs (g_1 and g_2), there exists a sequence of edit operations, or edit path $p(g_1, g_2) = (e_1, \ldots, e_k)$ (e_i denotes an edit operation) that transforms one graph into the other. Several edit paths may exist between two graphs. This set of edit paths is denoted by $\wp(g_1, g_2)$. A cost c is assigned to each edit operation. The edit distance d between two graphs g_1 and g_2 denoted by $d(g_1, g_2)$ is the minimum cost edit path between two graphs.

In this work, we will use a particular cost function where the cost of node deletion and insertion is always 1, the cost of edge deletion and insertion is always 0 and the cost of node and edge substitution takes the values 0 or ∞ depending on whether the substitution is identical or not, respectively. Under this cost function, the edit distance between two graphs can be expressed as [8]:

$$d(g_1, g_2) = |g_1| + |g_2| - 2\,|mcs(g_1, g_2)| = |g_1| + |g_2| - 2\,|g_m| \tag{1}$$

We will use Equation (1) as a distance measure in the rest of the paper.

3   Generalized Median Graph

Let U be the set of graphs that can be constructed using labels from L. Given $S = \{g_1, g_2, \ldots, g_n\} \subseteq U$, the **generalized median graph** $\bar{g}$ of S is defined as $g \in U$ that minimizes the sum of distances (SOD) to all the graphs in S:

$$\bar{g} = arg\,\min_{g \in U} \sum_{g_i \in S} d(g, g_i) = arg\,\min_{g \in U} SOD(g) \tag{2}$$

Note that $\bar{g}$ is not usually a member of S and, in general, more than one generalized median graph can be found for a given set S.

The computation of the generalized median graph is a rather complex task. Both exact [4,3] and approximate algorithms [1,3,5,2] exist, although all of them can only be applied to very limited sets of graphs.

When the computation of the median graph is not possible, the set median graph $\hat{g}$ can be used. While the search space for $\bar{g}$ is U, the whole universe of graphs, the search space for $\hat{g}$ is simply S, the set of graphs in the learning set. The set median graph is usually not the best representative of a set of graphs, but it is often a good starting point towards the generalized median graph.

3.1   Theoretical Properties of the Median Graph

In [3], three new theoretical results, based on the use of the particular cost function presented in Section 2, are shown that can permit to reduce the computation time of the median graph. Basically these properties relate the search space, the size and the SOD of the median graph with the maximum common subgraph ($g_m(S)$) and the minimum common supergraph ($g_M(S)$) of the set of graphs:

- **Search space:** The search space of the median graph of S is composed only of all the induced subgraphs of $g_M(S)$.

- **Size of the median graph:** $0 \leq |g_m(S)| \leq |\bar{g}| \leq |g_M(S)| \leq \sum_{i=1}^{n} |g_i|$

- **Bounds of the SOD:** $SOD(\bar{g}) \leq SOD(g_m(S))$

In the following we will use these results to derive a new genetic algorithm for the median graph computation.

4   A New Genetic Algorithm

In this section we show how the three theoretical results presented in the previous section can be used to develop a new sub-optimal algorithm for the median graph computation. A genetic approach is chosen, since it allows us to easily encode a possible solution and also to explore the search space more efficiently.

In genetic algorithms [9], a possible solution of the problem is encoded using chromosomes, evaluated through a fitness function. Given an initial population of chromosomes, genetic operators, such as mutation or crossover, are applied to alter the chromosomes. This process is repeated until one or more stop conditions are satisfied. In the following we explain our particular implementation.

Chromosome Representation: From the property 1 of Section 2 it follows that a chromosome should be able to encode all the possible subgraphs of $g_M(S)$. Thus, the size of the chromosome is equal to the size of the $g_M(S)$. Each position in the chromosome, is associated to one node of $g_M(S)$, and may store either a value of "1" or a value of "0". Thus, the chromosome specifies which nodes of $g_M(S)$ are present (positions with "1") and which not (positions with "0"), generating an induced subgraph of $g_M(S)$, since a subset of nodes of a given graph uniquely defines a subgraph (Section 2). An example is shown in Figure 1. Assume that the $g_M(S)$ is the graph shown in Figure 1(a). the chromosome (Figure 1(c)) codifies the induced subgraph of $g_M(S)$ shown in Figure 1(b).

Fitness Function: The fitness function of each chromosome c corresponds to the SOD of the induced subgraph g of $g_M(S)$ the chromosome represents.

$$f(c) = SOD(g, S) = \sum_{i=1}^{n} d(g, g_i) = \sum_{i=1}^{n} (|g| - |g_i| - 2|mcs(g, g_i)|) \qquad (3)$$

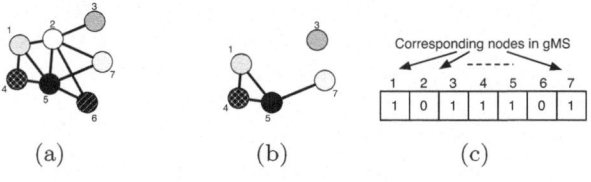

(a)   (b)   (c)

Fig. 1. A graph $g_M(S)$ (a), an induced subgraph g of $g_M(S)$ (b) and the chromosome representing g (c)

The lower its fitness function is, the better the chromosome is. This fitness function implies the computation of the maximum common subgraph of two graphs, which is exponential in the general case. Such computational complexity becomes polynomial when the considered graphs have unique node labels [10].

Genetic Operators: The crossover operator simply interchanges, with a uniform probability, an arbitrary position of two chromosomes. Mutation is accomplished by changing randomly a number in the array with a mutation probability. After the genetic operators have been applied, every chromosome is checked in order to validate whether it fulfils the bounds given in Section 3.1 regarding the size and the SOD of the median graph. If the chromosome is out of such limits, it is randomly altered until it fulfils the conditions. This procedure has two effects. First, we only take into account the induced subgraphs of $g_M(S)$ that fulfils the conditions. In addition, we expect to accelerate the convergence of the algorithm, since non-admissible candidate medians will never appear in the population. To create the descendants, a roulette wheel sampling implementing fitness-proportionate selection is chosen.

Population Initialization: The length of the initial population is set according to a predefined value K (20 in our case), determined empirically. Then, the first n chromosomes (with $n \leq K$) corresponds to the n graphs in S. In this way, we assure that the initial population includes the set median graph, which is a potential generalized median graph. The remaining K-n chromosomes are generated randomly but all of them must fulfil the bounds given in Section 3.

Termination Condition: The population evolution continues until either the maximum number of generations is reached or the best SOD in the population is less than the SOD of the set median graph.

5   Experiments

In this section we present two experiments on real data. The database is composed of 2,430 graphs containing 6 classes, with unique node labels, representing webpages with a mean size of around 200 nodes. In the first one, we evaluate the quality of the median graph according to the SOD. Finally, in a second experiment, we conduct a preliminary classification experiment in order to assess the median as a good representative of a given set of graphs.

Experiment 1. Median Accuracy: This experiment was intended to qualitatively evaluate the median graph computation achieved by the genetic approach. To this end, we computed the median graph of each class using 3, 4, 5, 6 and 7 graphs for each class, randomly selected. Then, we compare the SOD of the median computed using the genetic algorihtm with the SOD of the set median. We do not compare the results of the genetic approach with other methods, because none of them is able to deal with such large sets and graphs. This comparison can give a good idea of whether it is potentially a good median.

Figure 2 show the results of this comparison as a function of the number of graphs in the set S. The results show that we obtain a better SOD with our

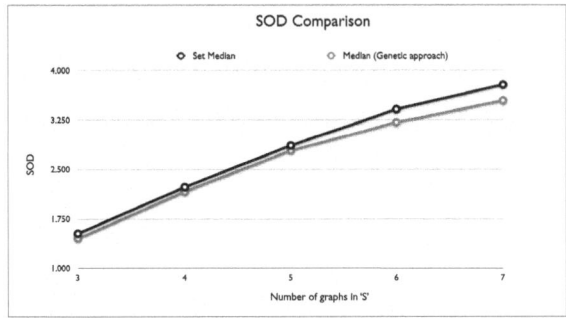

Fig. 2. SOD comparison function of the number of graphs in S

method than with the set median for any number of graphs in the set. What is important in this figure is the tendency in the difference between the set median SOD and the SOD of the approximate median. This difference increases as the number of graphs in S increases. This tendency suggests that the more information of the class the method has (more elements in S), better representations is able to obtain.

With these results at hand, we can conclude that we obtain good approximations of the median graph with this new genetic approach.

Experiment 2. Classification Accuracy: In this experiment, the median graph is used to reduce (filter) the number of classes before the application of an 1NN classifier. That is, firstly, the median is used to obtain the representative of each class using the training set. Then, we compare every element of the test set against the median graph of all the classes. For each element in the test set, we rank all the classes according to the distance to these median graphs. After that, the same element is classified using the 1NN classifier but using only the elements in the training set of the best k classes according to the previous ranking, instead of using all the classes as in the 1NN classical approach. It is clear that, if k is set to 1, then the results are the same as those obtained with the classification using simply the median graph. Conversely, if k is equal to 6, then the results are the same as in the classical 1NN classifier. In order to better generalize the results, we performed 10 repetitions of the classification task. In each repetition, the training set was composed of 36 elements (6 per class), and the test set was composed by 324 elements (54 per class).

Figure 3 shows, for every value of k, the maximum, the average and the minimum classification accuracy achieved along the 10 repetitions of the experiment. An important observation is that, even for $k = 1$ or $k = 2$, the best results using the median graph could outperform the worse results using the 1NN classier. That means that, with the median graph, it is possible to achieve similar results to the 1NN, but using a lower number of comparisons.

Figure 4, shows for every value of k the number of repetitions where this value of k permits to obtain the same or better classification results as in the 1NN classifier. We can see that, in four repetitions (40%), we only need at most 4

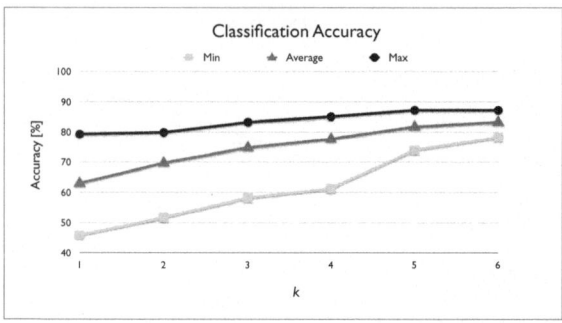

Fig. 3. Maximum, average and minimum classification accuracy for each value of k along the 10 repetitions

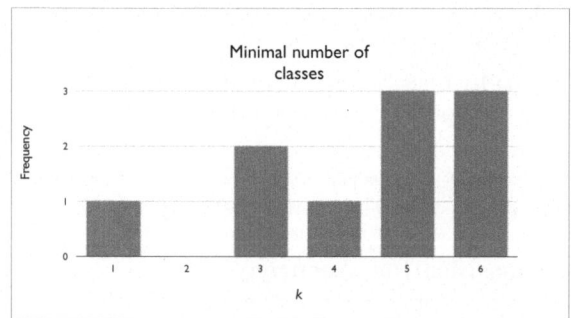

Fig. 4. Minimum number of classes to achieve the same results as in the 1NN classifier

classes ($k = 4$) to obtain better results. That means that, we can obtain the same calssification accuracy of the 1NN classifier with less number of comparisons (for $k = 4$ we need around a 24% less of comparisons than the 1NN classifier). In addition, in 80% of the repetitions, we need at most 5 classes to obtain better results than the 1NN classifier. In this case the reduction is around a 7%. Thus, the median graph can be used in this sense as a representative of a class.

It is important to recall that this is a preliminary experiment with the aim to show that the median graph can be a good representative of a set of graphs. To apply the median graph to real classification problems, further work is required.

6 Conclusions and Future Work

The median graph has been presented as a good alternative to compute the representative of a set of graphs. The existing methods do not permit to use this concept it in real pattern recognition applications.

In this paper we have presented a new genetic algorithm for the median graph computation. With this new algorithm we performed a set of experiments using webpages extracted from real data. The first conclusion of these experiments is that, with this new algorithm, we are able to obtain accurate approximations of the median graph (in terms of SOD) with a computation time that permits to work with sets of graphs composed of around 200 nodes each. Although the applicability of the median graph to real problems is still limited, these results show that the concept of median graph can be used in real world applications. It demonstrates, for the first time, that the median graph is a feasible alternative to obtain a representative of a set of graphs. For instance, we have shown in a preliminary experiment that the classification using the median graph can obtain similar results as a nearest-neighbor classifier but with a lower computation time.

Nevertheless, there are still a number of issues to be investigated in the future. More accurate bounds or properties might be investigated using these new results in order to improve the knowledge of the median graph. Such advances may lead also to obtain more accurate and efficient approximate solutions of the median graph. Applying other optimization algorithms, such as tabu search, remains as an open path to be explored. In addition, the preliminary experiments on classification open the possibility of applying the median graph to classification algorithms where a representative of the set of graphs is required.

References

1. Jiang, X., Münger, A., Bunke, H.: On median graphs: Properties, algorithms, and applications. IEEE Trans. Pattern Anal. Mach. Intell. 23(10), 1144–1151 (2001)
2. Hlaoui, A., Wang, S.: Median graph computation for graph clustering. Soft Comput. 10(1), 47–53 (2006)
3. Ferrer, M.: Theory and algorithms on the median graph. application to graph-based classification and clustering. PhD Thesis, Universitat Autònoma de Barcelona (2008)
4. Münger, A.: Synthesis of prototype graphs from sample graphs. Diploma Thesis, University of Bern (1998) (in German)
5. White, D., Wilson, R.C.: Mixing spectral representations of graphs. In: 18th International Conference on Pattern Recognition (ICPR 2006), Hong Kong, China, August 20-24, 2006, pp. 140–144. IEEE Computer Society, Los Alamitos (2006)
6. Bunke, H., Allerman, G.: Inexact graph matching for structural pattern recognition. Pattern Recognition Letters 1(4), 245–253 (1983)
7. Sanfeliu, A., Fu, K.: A distance measure between attributed relational graphs for pattern recognition. IEEE Transactions on Systems, Man and Cybernetics 13(3), 353–362 (1983)
8. Bunke, H.: On a relation between graph edit distance and maximum common subgraph. Pattern Recognition Letters 18(8), 689–694 (1997)
9. Mitchel, M.: An Introduction to Genetic Algorithms. MIT Press, Cambridge (1996)
10. Kandel, A., Bunke, H., Last, M.: Applied Graph Theory in Computer Vision and Pattern Recognition. Series in Computational Intelligence. Springer, Berlin (2007)

Fatty Liver Characterization and Classification by Ultrasound

Ricardo Ribeiro[1,2,*] and João Sanches[1,3,**]

[1] Institute for Systems and Robotics (ISR)
[2] Escola Superior de Tecnologia da Saúde de Lisboa (ESTeSL)
[3] Instituto Superior Técnico (IST)
Lisbon, Portugal
ricardo.ribeiro@estesl.ipl.pt

Abstract. *Steatosis*, also known as *fatty liver*, corresponds to an abnormal retention of lipids within the hepatic cells and reflects an impairment of the normal processes of synthesis and elimination of fat. Several causes may lead to this condition, namely obesity, diabetes, or alcoholism.

In this paper an automatic classification algorithm is proposed for the diagnosis of the liver steatosis from ultrasound images. The features are selected in order to catch the same characteristics used by the physicians in the diagnosis of the disease based on visual inspection of the ultrasound images.

The algorithm, designed in a Bayesian framework, computes two images: i)a despeckled one, containing the anatomic and echogenic information of the liver, and ii) an image containing only the speckle used to compute the textural features. These images are computed from the estimated RF signal generated by the ultrasound probe where the dynamic range compression performed by the equipment is taken into account.

A Bayes classifier, trained with data manually classified by expert clinicians and used as ground truth, reaches an overall accuracy of 95% and a 100% of sensitivity.

The main novelties of the method are the estimations of the RF and speckle images which make it possible to accurately compute textural features of the liver parenchyma relevant for the diagnosis.

Keywords: Ultrasound, Speckle, Bayesian, Steatosis Diagnosis.

1 Introduction

Fatty infiltration of the liver (*steatosis*), occurs when the fat content of the hepatocytes increases [1,2]. Patients with fatty liver are usually symptom free and the disease is typically detected by chance [1,3]. It is estimate that the prevalence of this disease in the United States and Europe ranges from $14-20\%$ and it is related directly with the obesity, diabetes, or alcoholism [3].

Liver biopsy is the more accurate method to diagnose a fatty liver. However, since it is invasive it is only used when the other non invasive methods fail. Within

---

* Corresponding author.
** Partially supported by FCT, under ISR/IST plurianual funding.

H. Araujo et al. (Eds.): IbPRIA 2009, LNCS 5524, pp. 354–361, 2009.

the non invasive methods, the imaging methods as ultrasound (US), computarized tomography (CT) and nuclear magnetic resonance (MRI) plays a great part in diagnosing and quantifying fatty liver [4]. Diagnosis based on ultrasound images is, among the non invasive methods, the preferred one because it is non-ionizing, non-invasive and is available in most of the medical and clinical facilities.

In general, the diffuse liver diseases appear in the US images with increased echogenicity of the parenchyma and some times, in the pre-cirrhotic stages, with textural changes [2]. In the case of the *fatty liver* this effect are accompanied by an acoustic penetration decreasing and a reduction on the blood vessels and diaphragm definition [5]. However, a simple human visual inspection of the images is not enough to get an accurate diagnosis of the disease stage [6] and highly experimented operators are needed to detect subtle changes on the hepatic texture [5]. In fact, the criteria used to assess this disease by visual inspection are not well defined and the diagnosis is in general highly subjective and operator-dependent [7] (Fig.1). Additionally, the poor quality of the images, the speckle that corrupt them and differences on the tunning parameters of the US scanner prevent the adoption of an unified standard diagnosis procedure [8].

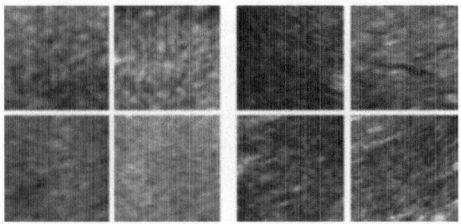

Fig. 1. Liver tissues samples: Steatosis (two left columns) and Normal (two right columns)

Quantitative tissue characterization technique (QTCT) [7], could increase the usefulness of US for the evaluation of diffuse liver disease. QTCT is based on extraction of features from the US images for classification and identification purposes and therefore for diagnosis purposes. The most common features described in the literature are based on the first order statistics [6,5,7], co-occurrence matrix [7,9], wavelet transform [10,9], attenuation and backscattering parameters [7] and backscattering coefficient [7]. [11] proposes a tissue characterization from US images of the thyroid based on features extracted from the Radon transform in order to discriminate pattern directionality characteristics.

In this paper a classifier is proposed for automatic diagnosis of the steatotic disease from ultrasound images of the liver parenchyma. The algorithm is based on the usual criteria used by the physicians in the diagnostic process through visual inspection of the ultrasound images (see Fig. 1). The method uses a Bayes classifier that combines intensity features extracted from the estimated despeckled image and textural features extracted from the estimated speckle image after compensation of the log compression performed by the ultrasound equipment.

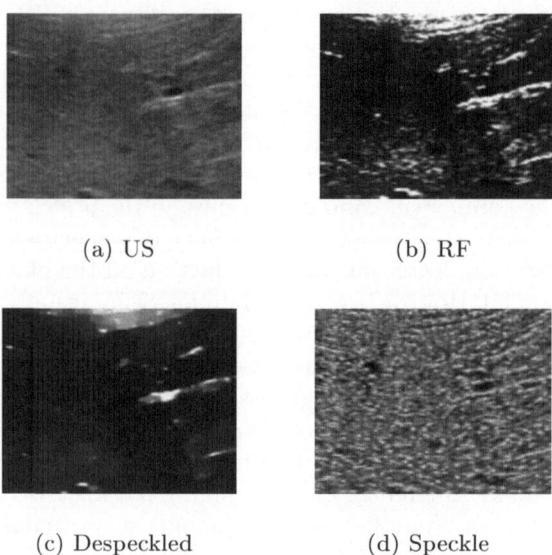

(a) US   (b) RF

(c) Despeckled   (d) Speckle

Fig. 2. Original ultrasound image a), the estimated RF signal b) and the two images from which intensity c) and texture d) features are extracted

The paper is organized as follows: section 2 formulates the problem and characterize the data. In section 3 the classification algorithm is described and in section 4 examples using real data are shown. Section 5 concludes the paper.

2   Problem Formulation

In this paper an objective method is proposed where the observed ultrasound images are pre-processed and the original RF signal generated by the ultrasound probe is estimated, as shown in Fig.2.b). The RF image is used to estimate two images: a despeckled one (see Fig.2.c)) containing the anatomic details from which intensity features are extracted and a second image containing only the speckle (see Fig.2.d)) from which the textural information is obtained. The estimation of the RF signal makes it possible to attenuate the dependence on the the specific tunning parameters of the scanner, such as brightness and contrast, and therefore to reduce the subjective nature of the traditional diagnosis based on visual inspection.

The estimation of the RF and of despeckled anatomic images is performed using the Bayesian methods proposed in [12] and [13] respectively. In these methods the compression operation performed by the ultrasound scanner is modeled by the following logarithmic function

$$\mathbf{Z} = a \log(\mathbf{Y} + 1) + b \tag{1}$$

where $\mathbf{Z}$ is the observed US image and $\mathbf{Y}$ is the RF image to be estimated. The RF image, corrupted by speckle, is described by a Rayleigh distribution

$$p(y_i) = \frac{y_i}{f_i} e^{-\frac{y_i}{2f_i}} \tag{2}$$

where $\mathbf{F} = \{f_i\}$ is the despeckled image and f_i and y_i are the ith despeckled and speckle pixels respectively.

In this paper the estimated noise field is used to extract the textural features needed for the automatic diagnosis of the steatosis. The speckle corrupting the ultrasound images is multiplicative in the sense that its variance depends on the underlying signal $\mathbf{F}$. The image formation model may be formulated as follows:

$$y = \eta\sqrt{f} \tag{3}$$

where f is a pixel intensity of the despeckled image and η is the corresponding noisy intensity. In this model, the noise field, η, is independent of the signal as occurs in the common *additive white Gaussian noise* (AWGN) model where the noisy pixels, $y = f + \eta$, are the sum of two independent terms, f and η. In the case of the multiplicative noise the corruption operation is not additive but multiplicative as shown in (3). The distribution of η is

$$p(\eta) = \left|\frac{dy}{d\eta}\right| p(y) = \eta e^{-\eta^2/2}, \qquad \eta \geq 0 \tag{4}$$

which is a unit parameter Rayleigh distribution independent of f.

3   Classifier

Visual classification of diffuse fatty infiltration disease from US images is usually based on two main features: i) increase in liver parenchyma echogenicity and ii) decreasing on the acoustic penetration with a corresponding visualization loss of the diaphragm and hepatic vessels [2]. In this condition the pixel intensities strongly decay with image depth (y axis).

The feature associated with the intensity decay is obtained by a linear regression computed over the mean values of each line, $h(i) = \frac{1}{M}\sum_{j=1}^{M} f_{i,j}$ of the despeckled image $\mathbf{F}$ where the following cost function is minimized

$$J = \sum_{i=0}^{N} (mi + b - h(i))^2 \tag{5}$$

with N and M being the number of lines and columns respectively and m the slope that is used to quantify the depth decay as displayed in Fig.3.

The textural features are obtained from the speckle image, $\eta_{i,j} = y_{i,j}/\sqrt{f_{i,j}}$ by computing its first Haar wavelet decomposition vertical and horizontal details. The energies of these two images, EdV and EdH respectively, are used as textural discriminant features of healthy and steatotic livers.

A Bayes classifier based on these three features, $\mathbf{x} = \{m, EdV, EdH\}$, is trained with data classified by expert clinicians in two classes, *Normal*, ω_N,

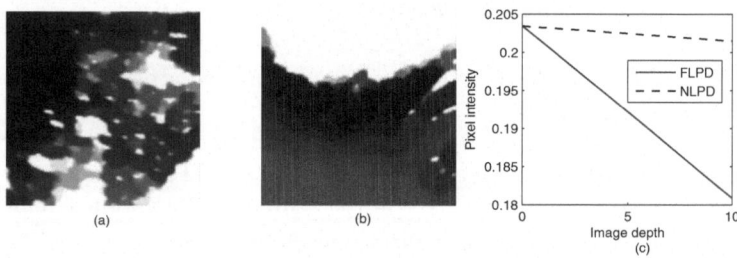

Fig. 3. a) despeckled ultrasound image of a normal liver, b) despeckled ultrasound image of a fatty liver and the c) represents two straight lines with slopes obtained by averaging the m slopes of each set, normal (NLPD) and fatty livers (FLPD), obtained from (5)

and *Fatty*, ω_F. It is assumed that the vector of features are multivariate normal distributed [10,9] with different means, $\{\mu_N, \mu_F\}$ and covariance, $\{\Sigma_N, \Sigma_F\}$, matrices. The linear discriminant functions are

$$g_\tau(\mathbf{x}) = -\frac{1}{2}(\mathbf{x} - \mu_\tau)^T \Sigma_\tau (\mathbf{x} - \mu_\tau) - \frac{1}{2}log |\Sigma_\tau| + logP(w_\tau) \qquad (6)$$

where $\tau \in \{N, F\}$. The classification of a given vector of features $\mathbf{x}$ is performed according with

$$\begin{cases} Fatty & \text{if } g_F(\mathbf{x}) > g_N(\mathbf{x}) \\ Normal & \text{otherwise} \end{cases} \qquad (7)$$

4   Experimental Results

The US images used in this paper were obtained by a common US equipment in a hospital facility and all images were stored in DICOM format. The US equipment settings were not standardize since we estimate the original RF signal and despeckled image.

Two sets of images were stored: normal hepatic parenchyma (10 images) from 5 subjects and fatty hepatic parenchyma (10 images) from 5 subjects. The classification was made manually by the operators and confirmed by indicators obtained from laboratorial analysis.

The training process of the recognition system is operated in two modes: training (learning) and classification (testing) [14]. For each class, w_1=fatty and w_2=normal, the textural features, mean and covariance, were estimated using 10 images with the leave–one–out cross–validation method.

Cross–validation is often used to estimate the generalization ability of a statistical classifier [15]. This method was used due to the lack of enough data for the training and testing procedures.

The classification accuracy were obtained by

$$Ca = 1 - (\text{false-negative } rate + \text{false-positive } rate), \tag{8}$$

where the false-negative rate is defined as the probability that the classification result indicates a normal liver while the true diagnosis is indeed a liver disease and the false-positive is defined as the probability that the classification result indicates a liver disease while the true diagnosis is indeed a normal liver.

Complementary laboratory analysis of the fatty livers are nonspecific but include modest elevations of the aspartate aminotransferase (AST), alanine aminotransferase (ALT), and -glutamyl transpeptidase (GGTP), accompanied by hypertriglyceridemia, hypercholesterolemia [3].

From each image, one ROI of 128 by 128 pixels along the center line have been selected.

The overall accuracy of the Bayesian classifier using the proposed algorithm and combining the features selected was 95%, which is a promising result. In this type of studies one of the most important characteristics is to optimize the sensitivity (conditional probability of detecting a disease while there is in fact a liver disease) and specificity (conditional probability of detecting a normal liver while the liver is indeed normal), in order to reduce the false-negative and the false-positive rate. The false-negative rate, in a first instance, should be completely avoided since it represents a danger to the patient. In this sense, the sensitivity parameter was optimal, since we obtain 100% in the classification process and in terms of specificity of 95%.

The results illustrate a high sensitivity of detecting this type of disease. Also the algorithm proposed apparently is not depending on the place of scanning and on the operator technique, since the results were not influenced by the presence of blood vessel and bile ducts within the liver parenchyma chosen for each ROI, and also by the changes in US image parameters.

As it can be observed in Fig. 4, the results have shown the usefulness of the features in the detection of pathological cases because almost no overlapping is observed between both statistical clouds. The mean cloud parameters for the healthy livers are: Slope (μ=0.8014; σ^2=0.0113); EdH (μ= 0.1997; σ^2= 0.0021); EdV (μ=0.0466; σ^2=2.6068e-04) and for the Fatty livers are: Slope (μ=0.4796; σ^2=0.0337); EdH (μ=0.0979; σ^2=7.1793e-04); EdV (μ=0.0678; σ^2= 2.6477e-04).

As [16] propose, we assume that the physics of US scanning and the speckle is separable into factors arising from orthogonal directions. The x direction will be the transverse (lateral) direction. The z direction will be the range (longitudinal) direction, or the direction of insonification. The physics in the transverse direction is governed by diffraction and interference effects of the coherent pressure (scalar) fields. The physics in the range direction is governed by the shape of the RF pulse that is sent and received. From the analysis of the results obtain by the EdH and EdV it seems that the US images of the liver have different behavior when it is normal or with fatty deposits. Characteristically the normal liver has higher horizontal and lower vertical energy details when compared to the fatty liver. So when the fat content in the liver increases the predominant direction

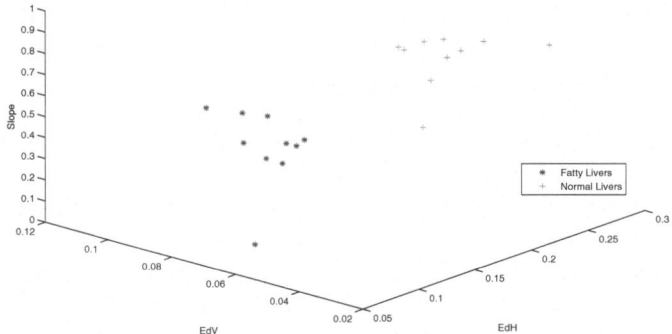

Fig. 4. Distribution of fatty vs normal livers according to the selected features

is z, and in normal livers the predominant direction, according to the textural information of the US image, is x, which is related with the histologic findings in the case of fatty livers (macrovesicular fat).

5   Conclusions

The proposed algorithm, based on the quantification of the visual diagnostic criteria, produces an objective analysis of the liver condition, which could be helpful to aid the diagnosis in this type of diffuse liver disease. The results are very promising in terms of sensitivity and specificity, which could aid in the detection in early stages of this disease, in asymptomatic patients, in order to prevent the progression to major lesions (steato-hepatitis or even cirrhosis). The features used in this paper are mathematical and objective formulations of the criteria used in the subjective and operator dependent traditional procedure based on manual visual inspection.

The RF signal compensation and the separation of the despeckled component from the original one is the key issue for the success of the proposed method.

Further studies in this area are needed. To develop a more robust algorithm, we need to increase the number of patients. Perform the feature extraction methods in the original US images, prior to machine processing. Other classification methods, such as neural network and the support vector machine classifiers should be tested, to optimize the process.

References

1. Sherlock, S., Dooley, J.: Diseases of the liver and Biliary System, 11th edn. Blackwell Science Ltd., Malden (2002)
2. Droga, V., Rubens, D.: Ultrasound Secrets. Hanley and Belfus (2004)
3. Fauci, A., et al.: Harrison's Principles of Internal Medicine, 17th edn. McGraw-Hill's, New York (2008)

 4. Lupsor, M., Badea, R., Nedevschi, S., Mitrea, D., Florea, M.: Ultrasonography contribution to hepatic steatosis quantification. possibilities of improving this method through computerized analysis of ultrasonic image. In: IEEE International Conference on Automation, Quality and Testing, Robotics, vol. 2, pp. 478–483 (May 2006)
 5. Lee, C.H., et al.: Usefulness of standard deviation on the histogram of ultrasound as a quantitative value for hepatic parenchymal echo texture; preliminary study. Ultrasound in Med. & Biol. 32, 1817–1826 (2006)
 6. Maeda, K., et al.: Quantification of sonographic echogenicity with grey-level histogram width: a clinical tissue characterization. Ultrasound in Med. & Biol. 24, 225–234 (1998)
 7. Kadah, Y.M., et al.: Classification algorithms for quantitative tissue characterization of diffuse liver disease from ultrasound images. IEEE Trans. Med. Imaging 15, 466–478 (1996)
 8. Li, G., et al.: Computer aided diagnosis of fatty liver ultrasonic images based on support vector machine. In: 30th Annual International Conference of the IEEE, Engineering in Medicine and Biology Society (EMBS 2008), pp. 4768–4771 (2008)
 9. Yeh, W.-C., et al.: Liver fibrosis grade classification with b-mode ultrasound. Ultrasound in Med. & Biol. 29, 1229–1235 (2003)
10. Mojsilovic, A., et al.: Characterization of visually diffuse diseases from b-scan liver images using non-separable wavelet transform. IEEE Trans. Med. Imaging 17, 541–549 (1998)
11. Savelonas, M.A., et al.: Computational characterization of thyroid tissue in the radon domain. In: Twentieth IEEE International Symposium on Computer-Based Medical Systems (2007)
12. Seabra, J., Sanches, J.: Modeling log-compressed ultrasound images for radio frequency signal recovery. In: 30th Annual International Conference of the IEEE, Engineering in Medicine and Biology Society (EMBS 2008) (2008)
13. Seabra, J., Xavier, J., Sanches, J.: Convex ultrasound image reconstruction with log-euclidean priors. In: 30th Annual International Conference of the IEEE, Engineering in Medicine and Biology Society (EMBS 2008) (2008)
14. Jain, A., et al.: Statical pattern recognition: A review. IEEE Transactions on pattern analysis and machine intelligence 22, 4–37 (2000)
15. Cawley, G., Talbot, N.: Efficient leave-one-out cross-validation of kernel fisher discriminant classifiers. Pattern Recognition 36, 2585–2592 (2003)
16. Wagner, R., et al.: Statistics of speckle in ultrasound b-scans. IEEE Transactions on Sonics and Ultrasonics 30, 156–163 (1983)

Sleep/Wakefulness State from Actigraphy

Pedro Pires[1], Teresa Paiva[2,*], and João Sanches[1]

[1] Institute for Systems and Robotics / Instituto Superior Técnico
[2] Medicine Molecular Institute / Faculdade de Medicina da Universidade de Lisboa
Lisbon, Portugal

Abstract. In this paper a definition of the *activity* (ACT) variable is proposed and a method to estimate it from the noisy *actigraph* output sensor data is described. A statistical model for the *actigraph* data generation process is suggested based on its working physical principles and on physiological considerations about human activity. The *purposeless* nature of the sleeping movements is used to discriminate the *Sleep* and *Wakefulness* (SW) states.

The estimated ACT signal from the *actigraph* output signal is correlated with the data from a *Sleep Diary* to validate the SW oscillations, computed from the ACT. A *Sleep electronic Diary* (SeD) was implemented in the scope of this work to make it possible an accurate register of the patient activities relevant for the diagnosis of sleep disorders.

Examples using real data, illustrating the application of the method, have shown high correlation between the output of the proposed algorithm that characterizes the *activity* and the data registered in the SeD.

Keywords: Statistical Signal Processing, Human Activity, Actigraphy, Sleep Disorder, Sleep Diary, Statistical Mixture.

1 Introduction

Sleeping is a key factor for a healthy condition and the inability to fall asleep or stay asleep has important impacts on people's health [1]. Diabetes, obesity, depression or cardiovascular diseases are associated with sleep disorders. An accurate assessment of the patient activity (ACT) may be very helpful in the diagnosis of pathological sleep disorders. However, an objective and accurate definition of human activity is difficult and depends on each specific application context. *Actigraphy* data may be used to quantify and characterize the ACT variable [2].

The actigraphy data is usually acquired with an *actigraph* sensor that is wrist watch shaped[1]. The actigraph device, containing a three axis accelerometer [3], records the detected acceleration magnitude on the non dominant wrist typically for a period of one week.

The main goal of this technique is to register the activity during the patients daily routine, in their natural environment, without the complexity associated

---

* Partially supported by FCT, under ISR/IST plurianual funding.
[1] In this work a SOMNOwatch^{TM} device from SOMNOmedics GmbH was used.

H. Araujo et al. (Eds.): IbPRIA 2009, LNCS 5524, pp. 362–369, 2009.

with other more sophisticated techniques such as the polysomnography. Despite its simplicity it is able to distinguish sleep form wakefulness states in approximately 80% up to 90% of the cases depending on the algorithm [4,5,6].

In this paper, the analysis of the actigraph output signal has revealed a mixture of two dominant components, one associated with the day life activity and the other associated with the night activity. The evolution of the relative importance of these two components along the circadian cycle have shown a strong correlation with the *Sleep Diary* information for different patients. Therefore, the probability function associated with the actigraph output signal is modeled as a mixture of two distributions modeling the two observed components.

It is thought that the difference in both components reside in the *purposeless* characteristic of the movements during the sleep state. During the wake state the movements are usually purposeful, they are coherent and coordinated which leads to a statistical distribution of the actigraph signal different from the one obtained during the sleep state where the *purposeless* nature of the movements, more impulsive, non coherent and usually more sparsely distributed along the time, induces the generation of an actigraph output signal with different characteristics.

The two distributions used to model the output signal of the actigraph are a shifted Maxwell distribution, prevalent during the wakefulness state and a Poisson distribution prevalent during the sleep state.

The shifted Maxwell distribution arises if the three accelerometer components are *independent and identically distributed* (i.i.d.) non zero mean Gaussian distributed. The Poisson distribution is appropriated when the movements are mainly constituted by short duration and non correlated impulses [7] low pass filtered by the actigraph device and by the window based processing algorithm proposed here. The visual inspection of the histogram of the signal confirms the validity of this model. However, for sake of simplicity, in this paper, the Poisson component is approximated by a normal distribution.

The proposed algorithm estimates the parameters of the mixture at each moment by considering data from a sliding window centered at each sample. The process is repeated for all time instants and regularization and outliers rejection procedures are applied. The overall process is described in the next section.

The ACT signal and the corresponding estimated SW state are compared with the *Sleep Diary* data for validation purposes. A *Sleep Diary* is a registration media where the patient register the events, corresponding time stamps and observations, occurred during the day or night, relevant for the diagnosis of sleep disorders. An electronic *Sleep Diary*, called *Sleep e-Diary* (SeD), was designed and implemented specifically in the scope of this project in order to improve the register accuracy of the data provided by the patient. It is implemented in Python [2] and was designed to run in a mobile phone over the operating system Symbian from Nokia.

---

[2] See Python Programming Language Official Website (http://www.python.org/)

2   Problem Formulation

The main component of the actigraph sensor is a 3D axis accelerometer and the output of the sensor is its acceleration magnitude. Inspection of the experimental data histogram have shown clearly two components, one more important during the day, $p_d(r)$, and the other more important at night, $p_n(r)$.

The first, $p_d(r)$, is modeled as a shifted Maxwell distribution, where the three acceleration components are assumed independent and identically non zero mean Gaussian distributed, $p(a_x) = p(a_y) = p(a_z) = \mathcal{N}(\mu, \sigma^2)$. Under these assumptions the acceleration magnitude, $r = \sqrt{a_x^2 + a_y^2 + a_z^2}$ may be modeled by a shifted *Maxwell* distribution, $\mathcal{M}(c_\mathcal{M}, \sigma_\mathcal{M}^2)$,

$$p_d(r) = \sqrt{\frac{2}{\pi}} \frac{(r - c_\mathcal{M})^2}{\sigma_\mathcal{M}^3} e^{-\frac{(r-c_\mathcal{M})^2}{\sigma_\mathcal{M}^2}} . \tag{1}$$

The second component, $p_n(r)$ is assumed to be generated from involuntary movements, less coordinated and more impulsive [8] [7]. Here, for sake of simplicity, a Gaussian distribution is used to describe this component, $\mathcal{N}(c_\mathcal{N}, \sigma_\mathcal{N}^2)$. Therefore the following mixture is proposed to describe the output signal of the actigraph sensor,

$$p(r, \theta) = \alpha \sqrt{\frac{2}{\pi}} \frac{(r - c_\mathcal{M})^2}{\sigma_\mathcal{M}^3} e^{-\frac{(r-c_\mathcal{M})^2}{\sigma_\mathcal{M}^2}} + \beta \frac{1}{\sqrt{2\pi}} \frac{1}{\sigma_\mathcal{N}} e^{-\frac{(r-c_\mathcal{N})^2}{2\sigma_\mathcal{N}^2}} \tag{2}$$

where the time varying parameter column vector,

$$\theta(n) = \{\underbrace{\alpha(n), \sigma_\mathcal{M}(n), c_\mathcal{M}(n)}_{\theta_\mathcal{M}(n)}, \underbrace{\beta(n), \sigma_\mathcal{N}(n), c_\mathcal{N}(n)}_{\theta_\mathcal{N}(n)}\}^T \tag{3}$$

is estimated to characterize the activity at each discrete instant n.

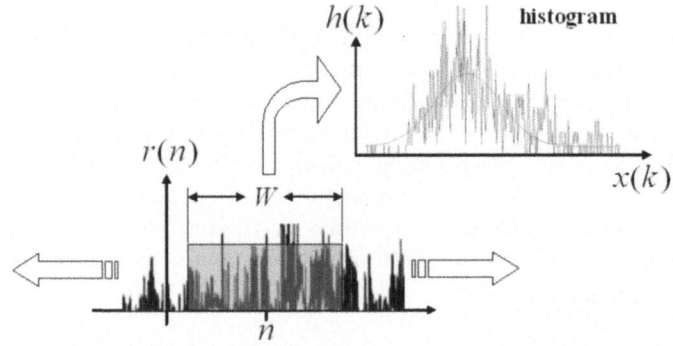

Fig. 1. Windowing parameter estimation with histogram fitting

The estimation of $\theta(n)$ at each instant n is performed by solving the following equation

$$\theta(n) = \arg\min_{\theta} \sum_{k=1}^{L} (h_n(k) - p(x_k, \theta))^2 \tag{4}$$

where $0 < n \leq N$, $\mathbf{h}_n = \{h_n(1), ..., h_n(L)\}$ is the L dimensional histogram, with bins centered at locations $\mathbf{x} = \{x_1, x_2, ..., x_L\}$, computed in a W dimensional window centered at the nth sample and $p(x_k, \theta)$ is the function (2) computed at locations x_k, as shown in Fig.1.

The relative importance of each distribution along the circadian cycle is obtained from the parameters $\alpha(n)$ and $\beta(n)$. In most cases both distributions are present, but in some cases only one of them is present. During the night $p_n(r)$ is prevalent and during the day the more important distribution is usually $p_d(r)$. The multidimensional signal $\theta(n)$, here called *Activity* (ACT), provides a more complete and accurate characterization of the patient activity than the usual simple acceleration magnitude.

The optimization task described in equation (4) is performed by using the function *nlinfit* implemented in MatLab where the unknown parameters are obtained by estimating the coefficients of a nonlinear regression function using the least squares.

This optimization task is an *ill-posed* problem that is iteratively performed after pre-processing the raw data and post processing of the estimated results. Special care must be used with the initialization vector and in the post processing procedure, outliers on the estimated results are removed and replaced by interpolated ones.

3   Sleep/Wakefulness State Estimation

The evolution of the parameters $\theta_{\mathcal{N}}(n)$ and $\theta_{\mathcal{M}}(n)$ along the circadian cycle is used to characterize the type of activity of the patient. Here it is suggested that the relative importance of each distribution seems to be better in the estimation of the *sleep/wakefulness* (SW) state of the patient than the simple actigraph output signal intensity.

The following difference is used to assess the preponderant distribution at instant n

$$sw(n) = \alpha(n) - \beta(n) \tag{5}$$

where $\alpha(n)$ and $\beta(n)$ are the weights associated with $p_d(r)$ (wakefulness) and $p_n(r)$ (sleep) respectively in the mixture.

Let us define the *Sleep/Wakefulness* (SW) binary state variable as follows

$$SW(n) = \begin{cases} 0 & \text{if sleep} \\ 1 & otherwise \end{cases} \tag{6}$$

The state variable $SW(n)$ may be estimated from the noisy (non smoothed) signal $sw(n)$ as follows

$$\hat{\mathbf{SW}} = \arg\min_{\mathbf{SW}} E(\mathbf{sw}, \mathbf{SW}) \qquad (7)$$

where $\mathbf{SW} = \{SW(1), SW(2), ..., SW(N)\}^T$, $\mathbf{sw} = \{sw(1), sw(2), ..., sw(N)\}^T$ and

$$E(\mathbf{sw}, \mathbf{SW}) = \underbrace{\sum_n sw(n)(1 - 2SW(n))}_{\text{binarization}} + \alpha \underbrace{\sum_n |SW(n) - SW(n-1)|}_{\text{regularization}} \qquad (8)$$

where the first term forces the binarization of $sw(n)$ according

$$SW(n) = \begin{cases} 0 & \text{if } sw(n) < 0 \\ 1 & \text{otherwise} \end{cases} \qquad (9)$$

The regularization term based on the L_1 norm is used to force a stepwise constant solution with abrupt transitions by introducing temporal correlation between neighboring samples, $|SW(n) - SW(n-1)|$, where differences between consecutive samples of $\mathbf{SW}$ are penalized by α. As larger α is as the large is the penalization and as stepwise constant is the solution. The value of α is manually chosen in order to keep the significant transitions related with changes on the state of the patient and to eliminate the transition due to the noise present in $sw(n)$.

The minimization of the energy function (8), formulated in (7), is a huge combinatorial optimization problem in the $\{0, 1\}^N$ high dimensional space where N is the length of $\mathbf{SW}$. This minimization is solved by using a *Graph-Cuts* (GC) based algorithm, which is computational efficient providing the global minimum of (8) [9].

4   Experimental Results

In this section an illustrative example using real data is presented. This study was performed for approximately 7 days, comprising about 167 hours. The raw data collected by the actigraph sensor is displayed in Fig.2.a). The six estimated components of $\theta(n)$ are displayed in Fig.2.b).

In this example are visible the 7 periods corresponding to the seven consecutive days that the patient wore the actigraph. The values of $\sigma_{\mathcal{M}}$ range from 0 to 300 mG with $c_{\mathcal{M}}$ ranging between -200 and 200 mG, representing the larger magnitude intensities of the acceleration distribution associated with the Maxwell component. The values associated with $p_n(r)$, are smaller. $\sigma_{\mathcal{N}}$ ranges from 0 to 10 mG and $c_{\mathcal{M}}$ from 0 to 30 mG.

The signal $\alpha(n) + \beta(n)$ is approximately one, with mean 0.98 and standard deviation 0.096, which mean that the mixture is able to describe the data most of the time.

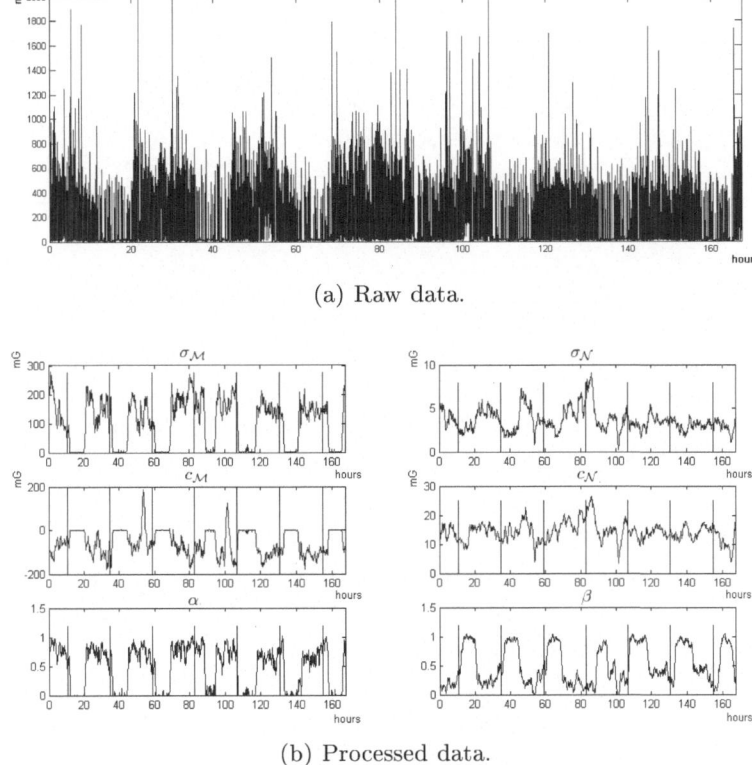

(a) Raw data.

(b) Processed data.

Fig. 2. Real example acquired during 167 hours

Fig.3.a) displays the estimated parameters on a single day between two consecutive midnights extracted from the graphs displayed in Fig.2.b). There are observed changes on the estimated parameters, according to the actions taken by the patient and with the moment that they happened. In these graphs α is very close to zero and β is clearly different from zero between the $"x"$ mark (*go to bed* from the SeD) and the $"o"$ mark (*get out of bed* from the SeD) where the patient is supposed to be sleeping. Out of this interval, at the same day, the situation is reversed, which indicates that the Maxwell distribution is predominant during the day time, while the Normal distribution is predominant during the night.

A relevant detail, observed in Fig.3.a), is the high values of $c_{\mathcal{M}}$ that match the time marked by the subject in the SeD as exercise. This suggests that the signal $\theta(n)$ may be used to detected specific activities or to measure activity intensity levels.

The SW state, estimated by (7), and the SeD data, are overlapped and displayed in the Fig.3.b). Here we can see that the GC method successfully estimates the SW state and that it is well correlated with the SeD data. Other experiments performed with data collected from patients with sleep disorders have shown abnormal patterns on the estimated SW state that may be used in the diagnosis of these disorders.

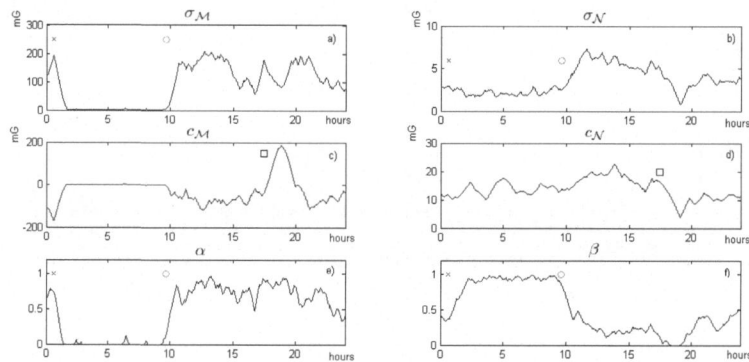

(a) Zoom from Fig.2.b) overlapped with data collected with the SeD. "*x*" and "*o*" marks indicate the "*go to bed*" and the "*get out of bed*" events respectively registered in the SeD. On c) and d), the black square represents the time of exercise.

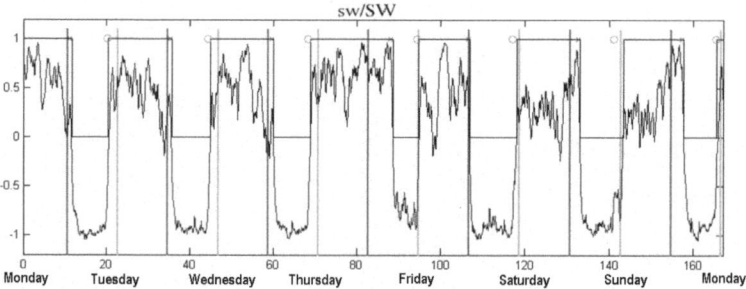

(b) Representation of the *Sleep/Wakefulness* (SW) state. Vertical magenta lines represent the midnight instants and the cyan ones represent the midday. "*x*" and "*o*" marks indicate the "*go to bed*" and the "*get out of bed*" events respectively registered in the SeD.

Fig. 3. Zoom and SW state

5   Conclusions

This paper proposes a new definition and method to estimate the *activity* (ACT) variable from actigraphy data. The *purposeless* nature of the movements during the sleep is the key concept used to model the actigraph sensor output by a mixture of two distributions. During the wakefulness state a Maxwell distribution is prevalent corresponding to movements that are usually coherent and fully purposiveness. During the sleep state the actigraph sensor output signal is better described by a Poisson distribution (here approximated by a Gaussian function) where the movements are impulsive, less coherent and usually *purposeless*.

This paper describes a method where a six dimensional vector of parameters of a two distribution mixture is estimated along the time and is proposed to describe the activity (ACT) that is used to estimate the *Sleep/Wakefulness* (SW) state variable.

An electronic *Sleep Diary*, here called *Sleep electronic Diary* (SeD), was developed in the scope of this work to run in a mobile phone. The goal is the improvement of the information accuracy registered by the patient for sleep disorders diagnosis purposes.

The estimated ACT signal from real patients and the corresponding data registered with the SeD have shown to be highly correlated which strongly suggests the usefulness of the method in the diagnosis of sleep disorders. The estimated SW state in patients with diagnosed sleep disorders have shown abnormal circadian patterns that may be used to identify that disorders without need of other more complex and sophisticated methods such as polysomnography.

Acknowledgments

The authors thank Nokia Portugal S.A. for providing the mobile phones used in this work and to SOMNOmedics for the actigraphy devices used to acquire the actigraphy data.

References

[1] Pandi-Perumal, S.R., Leger, D.: Sleep Disorders: Their Impact on Public Health, Informa Healthcare, UK (December 2006)
[2] Morgenthaler, T.I., Lee-Chiong, T., Alessi, C., Friedman, L., Aurora, R.N., Boehlecke, B., Brown, T., Chesson, A.L., Kapur, V., Maganti, R., Owens, J., Pancer, J., Swick, T.J., Zak, R.: Practice parameters for the clinical evaluation and treatment of circadian rhythm sleep disorders. Sleep 30(11), 1445–1459 (2007)
[3] Motoi, K., Tanaka, S., Nogwa, M., Yamakoshi, K.: Evaluation of a new sensor system for ambulatory monitoring of human posture together with walking speed. Transactions of the Japanese Society for Medical and Biological Engineering: BME 41(4), 273–279 (2003)
[4] Cole, R.J., Kripke, D.F., Gruen, W., Mullaney, D.J., Gillin, J.C.: Automatic sleep/wake identification from wrist activity. Sleep 15(5), 461–469 (1992)
[5] Paquet, J., Kawinska, A., Carrier, J.: Wake detection capacity of actigraphy during sleep. Sleep 30(10), 1362–1369 (2007)
[6] Jean-Louis, G., Kripke, D.F., Cole, R.J., Assmus, J.D., Langer, R.D.: Sleep detection with an accelerometer actigraph: comparisons with polysomnography. Physiology & behavior 72(1-2), 21–28 (2001)
[7] Gimeno, V., Sagales, T., Miguel, L., Ballarin, M.: The statistical distribution of wrist movements during sleep. Neuropsychobiology 38, 108–112 (1998)
[8] Vgontzas, A.N., Kales, A.: Sleep and its disorders. Annual Review of Medicine 50, 387–400 (1999)
[9] Boykov, Y., Veksler, O., Zabih, R.: Fast approximate energy minimization via graph cuts. IEEE Trans. Pattern Anal. Mach. Intell. 23(11), 1222–1239 (2001)

A Random Extension for Discriminative Dimensionality Reduction and Metric Learning[*]

Adrian Perez-Suay, Francesc J. Ferri, and Jesús V. Albert

Dept. Informàtica, Universitat de València. Spain
{Adrian.Perez,Francesc.Ferri}@uv.es

Abstract. A recently proposed metric learning algorithm which enforces the optimal discrimination of the different classes is extended and empirically assessed using different kinds of publicly available data. The optimization problem is posed in terms of landmark points and then, a stochastic approach is followed in order to bypass some of the problems of the original algorithm. According to the results, both computational burden and generalization ability are improved while absolute performance results remain almost unchanged.

1 Introduction

The problem of classifying and/or conveniently representing high dimensional data is of key importance in many different domains across the pattern recognition and image analysis fields. This is specially critical when the objects under study correspond to images or any other kind of visual information. The classical approach for dealing with such high dimensional data is to apply some kind of dimensionality reduction in order to look for either numerical stability, improvement of performance or simply to be able to get results in a reasonable amount of time [1,2].

Dimensionality reduction has been largely studied from different points of view. In particular, linear methods such as Principal Component Analysis (PCA) and Linear Discriminant Analysis (LDA) are very well-known and very often used in practice [1,3]. Particular implementations and extensions of these have been proposed in recent years in particular domains such as face recognition [4,5,6,7].

Most of the linear dimensionality reduction approaches can be conveniently extended to the non linear case by using the ubiquitous kernel trick [8,9] which has now been applied to almost every classical method that involves linear mappings. The vast majority of approaches that propose using either linear or non linear dimensionality reduction to map the original problem into a (usually simplified) representation space, end up using a distance-based method in this target space. The combination of the reduction mapping and distance function can be seen as a composite (and possibly complex) metric in the original space. This puts forward the close relation that exists between dimensionality reduction and metric learning. Metric learning has received recent interest and has been tackled

---

[*] This work has been partially funded by FEDER and Spanish MEC through projects DPI2006-15542-C04-04 and Consolider Ingenio 2010 CSD2007-00018.

H. Araujo et al. (Eds.): IbPRIA 2009, LNCS 5524, pp. 370–377, 2009.

from different viewpoints [10,11,12] using rather different methodologies to learn a convenient metric for a particular problem. Nevertheless, all methods that directly look for a (usually parameterized) distance function follow to some extent the same rationale that guides most (discriminant) dimensionality reduction approaches. This consists of increasing the effective distances between objects from different classes while decreasing the distances among objects of the same class.

This idea has been explicitly used in a recent method that looks for a linear (but kernelizable) mapping that (tries to) make objects from the same class collapse into a single point that is infinitely far away from (collapsed) points of different classes [13]. This method has been named Metric Learning by Collapsing Classes (MCML). Although the idea is basically the same as that used in LDA and other extensions [5,7], it seems that MCML can arrive at more interesting solutions from the point of view of generalization. This method has also been used for learning (linear) combinations of distances for representation problems [14].

Recently, a first attempt at speeding up this algorithm has been presented [15]. In this paper, this extension is taken further by improving not only computational burden but also the generalization ability by following a randomized approach. The proposed extension is implemented, evaluated and compared to the original algorithm for high dimensional and visual data processing. Firstly, the basics of the method is reviewed and the contribution is introduced. The results of a preliminary empirical evaluation using publicly available data are shown. Finally, conclusions of the present work and further research lines are given.

2   Linear Dimensionality Reduction and Metric Learning

Dimensionality reduction or feature extraction in general, that maps a given problem onto a different space, can be considered as a particular case of metric learning by fixing a (simple) metric in the target space. In the particular case of linear feature extraction, a given object, $x \in \mathbb{R}^r$ is mapped onto the new space as Wx. The Euclidean distance between two objects in the target space is given by $d(Wx_i, Wx_j) = (x_i - x_j)^T A(x_i - x_j)$ where $A = W^T W$ is a positive semidefinite matrix. Back into the original space, this distance that will be referred to as $d^A(\cdot, \cdot)$ or $d^W(\cdot, \cdot)$ can be seen as a parameterized distance whose behavior is governed by the matrix A (or W equivalently). This quadratic distance (also referred to as Mahalanobis distance by analogy) is at the root of much recent work on metric learning in which the goal consists of appropriately estimating these matrices.

A recent approach called Maximally Collapsing Metric Learning (MCML) has been proposed to learn these matrices [13]. This approach works by looking for a mapping that makes all classes collapse into a single target point per class (which means null distances) which are infinitely far away from each other.

To construct an appropriate criterion, given a (labeled) training set $X = \{x_i\}_{i=1}^N$, the following normalized function for each object i is considered

$$p^W(j|i) = p^A(j|i) = \frac{1}{Z_i} e^{-d_{ij}^A} = \frac{e^{-d_{ij}^A}}{\sum_{k \neq i} e^{-d_{ik}^A}}$$

where $d_{ij}^A = d^A(x_i, x_j)$. For each i, this is a function of j that can be seen as a discrete probability. In the ideal case of all classes collapsed and infinitely far away, this function would approach the following bi-valued function that can also be seen as a probability:

$$p_0(j|i) \propto \begin{cases} 1 & \text{if } x_i \text{ and } x_j \text{ of the same class} \\ 0 & \text{otherwise} \end{cases}$$

Consequently, the Kullback-Leibler divergence can be used as a convenient measure of how far we are from the goal of having all classes maximally collapsed. The criterion to be minimized is the above mentioned divergence averaged (summed) for all objects i.

Two possibilities arise. Either the sum of divergences is minimized with regard to A (with the constraint of A being PSD) or it is minimized with regard to W. In the first case, the problem can be shown to be convex which adds some guarantees, but managing the constraint can be problematic. Manipulating matrices of the size of A can also be critical for high dimensional data. In the second case, the problem is not convex, and then it is prone to get stuck in local minima. Also, a new parameter is added (the rank of A or size of W) but significantly smaller matrices need to be tackled.

In the two cases, any gradient descent approach can be used. The gradient of the above criterion is given by

$$\nabla f(A) = \sum_{ij} (p_0(j|i) - p^A(j|i))(x_j - x_i)(x_j - x_i)^T$$

$$\nabla f(W) = 2 \sum_{ij} (p_0(j|i) - p^W(j|i))W(x_j - x_i)(x_j - x_i)^T$$

As in the original work [13], we will name MCML the algorithm that uses a gradient descent using $f(A)$ (and enforcing the PSD constraint at each iteration), and MCMLW the algorithm that considers the non convex problem and uses $f(W)$. Both algorithms have pros and cons that will be put forward after the empirical study.

3   MCML with Randomized Landmark Points

One of the problems of MCML algorithms and specially in its convex formulation, is related to the computational cost per iteration. A relatively straightforward way of alleviating this problem while maintaining the rationale of the method consists of considering a convenient set of *landmark* or *anchor* points to which distances are measured instead of the whole training set. This very same idea has been largely used in the literature in different contexts [16,17] and specifically for this very same problem [15].

All above expressions need to be rewritten in terms of a given training set $X = \{x_j\}_{j=1}^N$ and a (reduced) landmark set $Y = \{y_i\}_{i=1}^M$ that can be a subset of X or not. In the particular case of $X = Y$ the original MCML or MCMLW algorithms will be obtained. In the above gradient expressions all terms $(x_j - x_i)$ must be substituted by $(x_j - y_i)$ and the i index now must range over the set Y. If the set Y is small but representative, the new criterion obtained would be a very good approximation of the original one. Even with the smallest possible Y (one per class) it would be possible to obtain good results if there is a projection of the data that can give spherically shaped classes without (significant) overlapping.

Leaving apart the way in which landmark points are selected or generated, our proposal introduces a new parameter into the algorithms: the number (or proportion) of landmark points. For high values, the behavior of the algorithm would be very similar to the original one. On the other hand, the smaller its value, the more efficient the algorithm would be. This will open the possibility of applying this algorithm to larger amounts of higher dimensional data.

On the other hand, different possibilities for selecting appropriate landmark points arise. In a previuous work [15], a k-means algorithm is used to select landmark points and also other possibilities are considered. In this work, another possibility is explored by not fixing a particular set of landmark points. Instead, the training set is subsampled at each particular iteration of the algorithm. As in the case of using landmarks, a new parameter is introduced that directly controls the computational cost of the method. The intended advantage consists of increasing the robustness of the method that will be highly independent on the particular way of selecting landmarks while still allowing a moderate computational cost.

The experiments in the following section have two main goals. Firstly to check the above claims on the quality of the approximation, and secondly and more interestingly, to try to assess how much the new parameter can be decreased without significantly degrading the quality of the approximation.

4   Experimental Results

Several different publicly available databases have been adopted in order to compare the different methods and extensions considered in this work. Firstly, several small size databases from the UCI repository [18] as in the original work [13] have been considered. In particular, Wine, Balance, and Ionosphere have been explicitly used. These have the advantage of being small and consequently allowing an exhaustive and complete tuning of all the parameters of the methods. Data coming from visual data has also been considered. In particular, the well-known AR face database [19] after manually aligning and cropping the images to a 40×40 size.

All databases have been split into train and test data by using the 70/30 rule. Experiments have been repeated 10 times and the results shown are the corresponding average values. In the particular case of the AR database, only 14 images (the ones without occlusions: scarf, glasses, etc.) per individual (20 men and 20 women) have been considered.

The size of the subsampled set used as landmark points for the algorithm is selected as a percentage of the total size of the available training set. The results are compared to a previous proposal [15] in which the set of landmark points is fixed and obtained by applying a standard k-means algorithm with k equal to the number of desired landmark points in each class and with a reduced number of iterations (10). The results will consist basically of measuring the classification error given by the nearest neighbor classifier on the training data and the corresponding computational (training) cost for each value of the parameter.

The methods considered in this work and corresponding extensions have been implemented and experiments have been carried out. MCMLAR and MCML-WAR acronyms will be used to refer to the proposed random extensions to the two original algorithms while MCMLA and MCMLWA will be used to refer to the (fixed) landmark extensions [15]. All parameters of the different methods have been manually tuned taking into account appropriate ranges from each one of them. In particular, rank values (MCMLW), number or percentage of landmark points, learning rate, etc, have been manually set to values that gave quite good results. Only some of them are presented here due to lack of space. Doing a proper (automated) parameter setting for this family of methods is out of the scope of the present work. Nevertheless, the results reported with the experiments carried out can be considered as representative of the differences among the different methods and their corresponding extensions.

It is worth mentioning that the adjustment of the learning rate was in some cases critical for some of the databases but also in the original algorithms. To avoid some of the problems, all databases were centered and normalized (to variance 1 at each dimension) prior to using the algorithms.

Comparative experiments using (convex) MCML and (non convex) MCMLW with different rank values have been carried out. The size of the randomized landmark set is given by a percentage of the available training data. Figures 1 to 3 show the averaged error rates of the different methods along with the standard deviation on the three UCI databases considered in this work.

It is worth noting that the results of non convex algorithms stay at the same for all number of landmarks used. Only the (convex) MCML significantly deviates (in a consistent way, though) as the number of landmarks decreases.

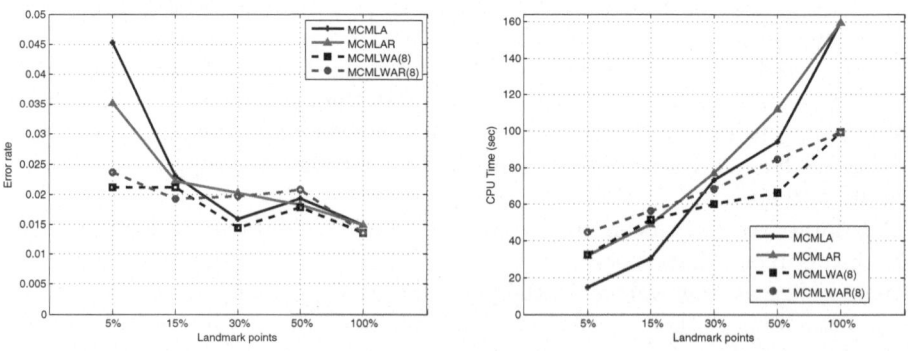

Fig. 1. a) Classification results on the Wine database using both Convex and Non Convex MCML using fixed and randomized sets of landmark points. b) CPU times of the corresponding methods.

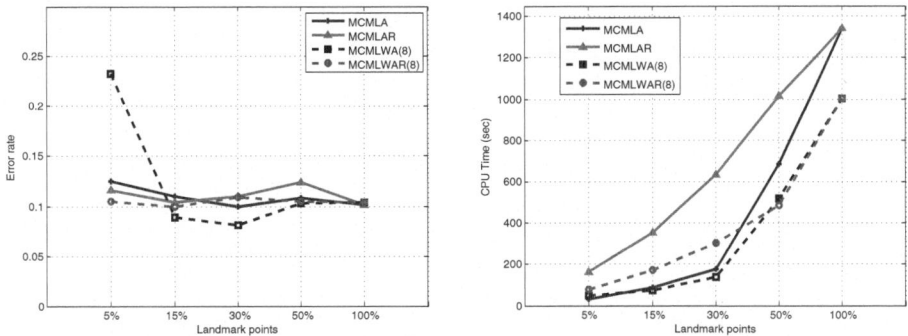

Fig. 2. a) Classification results on the Balance database using both Convex and Non Convex MCML using fixed and randomized sets of landmark points. b) CPU times of the corresponding methods.

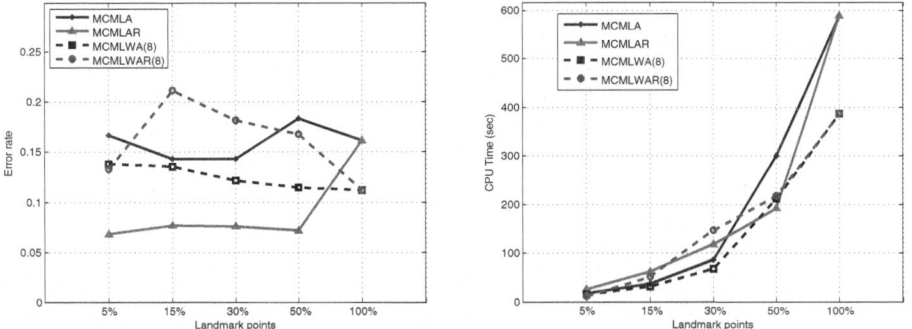

Fig. 3. a) Classification results on the Ionosphere database using both Convex and Non Convex MCML using fixed and randomized sets of landmark points. b) CPU times of the corresponding methods.

Directly tied in with these results are the CPU times shown in the same figures. As can be seen, the MCML is slightly (but significantly) slower than the non convex options. On the other hand, the total savings made by using landmarks can be up to 60%. All MCMLW results were very similar for this data.

The AR database, even after cropping the images is a very high dimensional problem. In order to alleviate the problem for the current experiment, a principal component analysis preserving 99% of data variability is performed prior to any distance learning. Thereafter, all the same algorithms than were in the previous subsection have been used. Appropriate tuning of the most critical parameters has been done manually.

Figure 4 shows the averaged error rates. ranges from 1 to 10. Very similar behavior is observed with this data apart from the fact that MCMLW also degrades when using only 1 landmark per class.

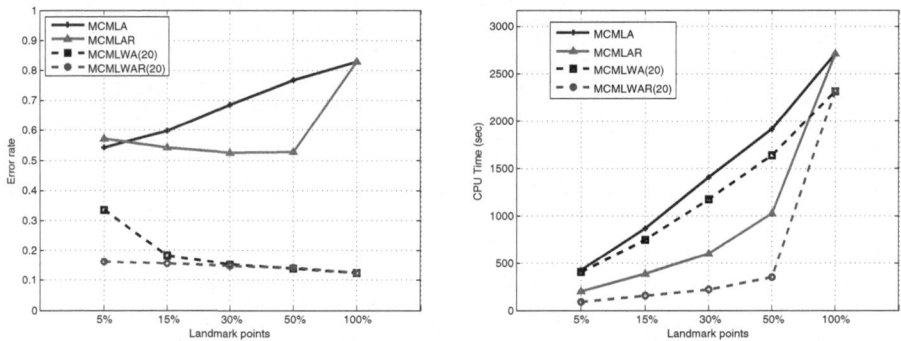

Fig. 4. a) Classification results on the AR database using both Convex and Non Convex MCML using fixed and randomized sets of landmark points. b) CPU times of the corresponding methods.

The corresponding CPU times spent by the different algorithms in these experiments over the AR database are shown in the same figure. As in the previous database, the time spent by the different algorithms consistently increases with M. Also, in this case a more significant difference among convex and non convex (because dimensionality is significantly higher) is observed.

5   Concluding Remarks

An empirical evaluation of different options when implementing both convex and non convex MCML algorithms including using a set of landmark points to speed up the learning process while maintaing or increasing the generalization ability of the methods has been considered.

Some interesting facts and also some critical points have been discovered in this work. Amongst the bad news, the tuning of these methods is not trivial and is not easy to automate. This is in fact the subject of current research. On the other hand, both MCML and MCMLW in its randomized versions do obtain convenient projections that allow for good generalization and representation of the different classes for a wide range of data and specially high dimensional data.

We have introduced the use of a randomized set of landmark points for the MCML and MCMLW algorithms. The preliminary conclusion is that with moderate values of M, the number of landmark points, the behavior is almost indistinguishable from the original algorithms using all training samples. These values can get even smaller in the case of MCMLW. The improvement in cost, as expected, is roughly linear and more important in absolute terms when the dataset is larger.

References

1. Duda, R.O., Hart, P.E., Stork, D.G.: Pattern Classification, 2nd edn. John Wiley and Sons, Chichester (2001)
2. Jain, A.K., Duin, R.P.W., Mao, J.: Statistical pattern recognition: A review. IEEE Trans. Pattern Anal. Mach. Intell. 22, 4–37 (2000)
3. Fukunaga, K.: Introduction to Statistical Pattern Recognition. Academic Press, London (1990)
4. Turk, M., Pentland, A.: Eigenfaces for recognition. Journal of Cognitive Neuroscience 3, 71–86 (1991)
5. Belhumeur, P.N., Hespanha, J.P., Kriegman, D.J.: Eigenfaces vs. fisherfaces: Recognition using class specific linear projection. IEEE Trans. Pattern Anal. Mach. Intell. 19, 711–720 (1997)
6. Chen, L., Liao, H.M., Ko, M., Lin, J., Yu, G.: A new LDA-based face recognition system which can solve the small sample size problem. Pattern Recognition 33, 1713–1726 (2000)
7. Cevikalp, H., Neamtu, M., Wilkes, M., Barkana, A.: Discriminative common vectors for face recognition. IEEE Transactions on Pattern Analysis and Machine Intelligence 27, 4–13 (2005)
8. Scholkopf, B., Smola, A.: Learning with Kernels. MIT Press, Cambridge (2002)
9. Cevikalp, H., Neamtu, M., Wilkes, M.: Discriminative common vector method with kernels. IEEE Transactions on Neural Networks 17, 1550–1565 (2006)
10. Xing, E.P., Ng, A.Y., Jordan, M.I., Russell, S.J.: Distance metric learning with application to clustering with side-information. In: NIPS, pp. 505–512 (2002)
11. Paredes, R., Vidal, E.: Learning weighted metrics to minimize nearest-neighbor classification error. IEEE Trans. Pattern Anal. Mach. Intell. 28, 1100–1110 (2006)
12. Yu, J., Amores, J., Sebe, N., Radeva, P., Tian, Q.: Distance learning for similarity estimation. IEEE Trans. Pattern Anal. Mach. Intell. 30, 451–462 (2008)
13. Globerson, A., Roweis, S.: Metric learning by collapsing classes. In: Neural Information Processing Systems (NIPS 2005), vol. 18, pp. 451–458 (2005)
14. Woznica, A., Kalousis, A., Hilario, M.: Learning to combine distances for complex representations. In: ICML, pp. 1031–1038 (2007)
15. Perez-Suay, A., Ferri, F.: Scaling up a metric learning algorithm for image recognition and representation. In: Bebis, G., et al. (eds.) Advances in Visual Computing. LNCS, vol. 5359, pp. 592–601. Springer, Heidelberg (2008)
16. Micó, L., Oncina, J., Vidal, E.: A new version of the nearest-neighbour approximating and eliminating search algorithm (aesa) with linear preprocessing time and memory requirements. Pattern Recognition Letters 15, 9–17 (1994)
17. Tenenbaum, J.B., de Silva, V., Langford, J.C.: A global geometric framework for nonlinear dimensionality reduction. Science 290, 2319–2323 (2000)
18. Asuncion, A., Newman, D.J.: UCI machine learning repository (2007)
19. Martinez, A., Benavente, R.: The AR face database. Technical Report 24, Computer Vision Center, Barcelona (1998)

Minimum Error-Rate Training in Statistical Machine Translation Using Structural SVMs

Jesús González-Rubio[1], Daniel Ortiz-Martinez[1], and Francisco Casacuberta[2]

[1] Instituto Tecnológico de Informática,
Universidad Politécnica de Valencia, Spain
{jegonzalez,dortiz}@iti.upv.es
[2] Departamento de Sistemas Informáticos y Computación,
Universidad Politécnica de Valencia, Spain
fcn@dsic.upv.es

Abstract. Different works on training of log-linear interpolation models for statistical machine translation reported performance improvements by optimizing parameters with respect to translation quality, rather than to likelihood oriented criteria. This work presents an alternative minimum error-rate training procedure based on structural support vector machines (SSVMs) for log-linear interpolation models which is not limited to the model scaling factors and needs only few iterations to converge. Experimental results are reported on the Spanish–English Europarl corpus.

Keywords: Statistical Machine Translation, Support Vector Machines.

1 Introduction

Log-linear interpolation models, which can be formally derived within the maximum entropy framework [1], are widely applied to statistical machine translation (SMT) [2]. In addition, optimization of interpolation parameters can directly address translation quality, rather than the maximum likelihood criterion [3].

This paper, which is an extension of [4], goes along the direction of [3], and describes an alternative training procedure based on SSVMs [5] that optimize interpolation parameter and also the parameters of the models to be interpolated, requiring only few iterations to converge.

The goal of statistical machine translation (SMT) is to translate a given text in some source language into a target language. Let us assume that we are given a source ('French') sentence $\mathbf{f}$, which is to be translated into a target ('English') sentence $\mathbf{e}$. Among all possible target sentences, we will choose the sentence with the highest probability:[1]

$$\hat{\mathbf{e}} = \underset{\mathbf{e}}{\operatorname{argmax}} \Pr(\mathbf{e}|\mathbf{f}) \ . \tag{1}$$

---

[1] We use the symbol $\Pr(\cdot)$ to denote general probability distributions with (nearly) no specific assumptions and $p(\cdot)$ to denote model-based probability distributions.

H. Araujo et al. (Eds.): IbPRIA 2009, LNCS 5524, pp. 378–385, 2009.

The argmax operation denotes the *search problem*, i.e. the generation of the output sentence in the target language. The decision in Eq. (1) minimizes the number of decision errors. Hence, under a so-called zero-one loss function this decision rule is optimal [6]. Using a different loss function will lead to a different optimal decision rule.

As the true probability distribution $\Pr(\mathbf{e}|\mathbf{f})$ is unknown, we have to develop a model $p(\mathbf{e}|\mathbf{f})$ that approximates $\Pr(\mathbf{e}|\mathbf{f})$. We follow [2] and directly model the posterior probability $\Pr(\mathbf{e}|\mathbf{f})$ by using a log-linear model. In this framework, we have a set of M feature functions $h_m(\mathbf{e}, \mathbf{f})$, $m = 1, \ldots, M$. For each feature function, there exists a model parameter λ_m, $m = 1, \ldots, M$. The direct translation probability is given by:

$$\Pr(\mathbf{e}|\mathbf{f}) \approx p_{\lambda_1^M}(\mathbf{e}|\mathbf{f}) = \frac{\exp[\sum_{m=1}^M \lambda_m h_m(\mathbf{e}, \mathbf{f})]}{\sum_{e_1'^J} \exp[\sum_{m=1}^M \lambda_m h_m(e_1'^J, \mathbf{f})]} . \tag{2}$$

In this framework, the *modeling problem* amounts to developing suitable feature functions that capture the relevant properties of the translation task. The *training problem* amounts to obtaining suitable parameter values λ_1^M. A standard criterion for log-linear models is the maximum mutual information (MMI) criterion, which can be derived from the maximum entropy principle:

$$\hat{\lambda}_1^M = \operatorname*{argmax}_{\lambda_1^M} \left\{ \sum_{s=1}^S \log p_{\lambda_1^M}(\mathbf{e}_s|\mathbf{f}_s) \right\} . \tag{3}$$

The optimization problem under this criterion has very nice properties: there is one unique global optimum, and there are algorithms (e.g. gradient descent) that are guaranteed to converge to the global optimum. Yet, the ultimate goal is to obtain good translation quality on unseen test data, and there is no reason to assume that an optimization of the model parameters using Eq. (3) yields parameters that are optimal with respect to translation quality.

2   Minimum Error-Rate Training

In place of the MMI criterion (Eq. (3)), [3] proposed an alternative training criteria for log-linear SMT models which is directly related to translation quality. In *minimum error-rate training* (MERT), we assume that the best model is the one that produces the smallest overall error with respect to a given error function. Unfortunately, determining the amount of error in a translation is not a well-defined problem with an objective answer, and numerous error metrics have been proposed. However, [3] shows empirically that best results can be achieved for any particular error function when that function is used in our objective function under MERT. This suggests that the accuracy of our SMT systems can be improved simply by devising an error function that more closely corresponds to human judgements of translation error, or with some task-based notion of accuracy. Ideally, this means that SMT researchers can focus on the question of what makes a good translation, instead of what makes a good translation model. With MERT, better evaluation functions should lead directly to better translation.

Formally, we say that if we are given an error function $E(\hat{\mathbf{e}}, \mathbf{e})$ defining the amount of error in some hypothesized translation $\hat{\mathbf{e}}$ with respect to a known good actual translation $\mathbf{e}$, then the objective function is:

$$\hat{\lambda}_1^M = \operatorname*{argmin}_{\lambda_1^M} E(\operatorname*{argmax}_{\hat{e}} p_{\lambda_1^M}(\hat{\mathbf{e}}|\mathbf{f}), \mathbf{e}) \ . \tag{4}$$

The optimization contains an argmax operator, which precludes calculation of a gradient. although there is no way to find a guaranteed optimal solution under these circumstances, we can find a good solution using the method sketched in [3]. In this paper we present a new method to find the solution by using structural support vector machines.

3   Structural Support Vector Machines

Structured output prediction [5] describes the problem of learning a mapping function $g : \mathcal{X} \to \mathcal{Y}$, where $\mathcal{X}$ is the space of inputs, and $\mathcal{Y}$ is the space of outputs. To learn g, we assume that a training sample of input-output pairs $S = ((x_1, y_1), \ldots, (x_n, y_n)) \in (\mathcal{X} \times \mathcal{Y})^n$ is available and drawn from a distribution $\Pr(X, Y)$. For a given hypothesis space $\mathcal{H}$, the goal is to find a function $g \in \mathcal{H}$ that has low prediction error, or, more generally, low risk

$$R_{Pr}^{\Delta}(g) = \int_{\mathcal{X} \times \mathcal{Y}} \Delta(y, g(x)) d\Pr(x, y) \ . \tag{5}$$

$\Delta(y, \overline{y})$ is a loss function that quantifies the loss associated with predicting $\overline{y}$ when y is the correct output value. We follow the Empirical Risk Minimization Principle [7] to infer a function g from the training sample S.

$$R_S^{\Delta}(g) = \frac{1}{n} \sum_{i=1}^{n} \Delta(y_i, g(x_i)) \ . \tag{6}$$

Support vector machines (SVMs) select a $g \in \mathcal{H}$ that minimizes a regularized empirical risk on S. The idea is to learn a discriminant function $l : \mathcal{X} \times \mathcal{Y} \to \mathcal{R}$ over input/output pairs from which one derives a prediction by maximizing l over all $y \in \mathcal{Y}$ for a given input x.

$$g_{\mathbf{w}}(x) = \operatorname*{argmax}_{y \in \mathcal{Y}} l_{\mathbf{w}}(x, y) \ . \tag{7}$$

We assume that $l_{\mathbf{w}}(x, y)$ is a linear function $l_{\mathbf{w}}(x, y) = \mathbf{w}^T \Psi(x, y)$ where $\mathbf{w}^T$ is the transpose of a parameter vector $\mathbf{w} \in \mathcal{R}^N$ and $\Psi(x, y)$ is a N-dimensional feature vector relating input x and output y. Intuitively, $l_{\mathbf{w}}(x, y)$ is a compatibility function that measures how well the output y matches the given input x. The flexibility in designing $\Psi(\cdot)$ allows employing SSVMs for diverse problems.

For training the weights $\mathbf{w}$ of the linear discriminant function, we propose the use of the 1-slack algorithm with margin-rescaling described in [5]. This algorithm is a reformulation of the standard SVM optimization problem [7], where the loss function is introduced into the optimization problem.

Algorithm 1. for training SSVMs (with margin-rescaling) via the 1-slack formulation.

Require: $S = ((x_1, y_1), \ldots, (x_n, y_n)), C, \epsilon$

1: $\mathcal{W} \leftarrow \emptyset$
2: **repeat**
3:    $(\mathbf{w}, \xi) \leftarrow \mathrm{argmin}_{\mathbf{w}, \, \xi \geq 0} \frac{1}{2} \mathbf{w}^T \mathbf{w} + C\xi$
      s.t. $\forall(\bar{y}_1, \ldots, \bar{y}_n) \in \mathcal{W} : \frac{1}{n} \mathbf{w}^T \sum_{1=1}^{n} [\Psi(x_i, y_i) - \Psi(x_i, \bar{y}_i)] \geq \frac{1}{n} \sum_{i=1}^{n} \Delta(y_i, \bar{y}_i) - \xi$
4:    **for** $i = 1, \ldots, n$ **do**
5:       $\hat{y}_i \leftarrow \mathrm{argmax}_{\hat{y} \in \mathcal{Y}} \{ \Delta(y_i, \hat{y}) + \mathbf{w}^T \Psi(x_i, \hat{y}) \}$
6:    **end for**
7:    $\mathcal{W} \leftarrow \mathcal{W} \cup \{ (\hat{y}_1, \ldots, \hat{y}_n) \}$
8: **until** $\frac{1}{n} \sum_{i=1}^{n} \Delta(y_i, \hat{y}_i) - \frac{1}{n} \mathbf{w}^T \sum_{i=1}^{n} [\Psi(x_i, y_i) - \Psi(s_i, \hat{y}_i)] \leq \xi + \epsilon$
9: **return** $(\mathbf{w}, \xi)$

Similar to the cutting-plane algorithms for the formulation in [8] this algorithm iteratively construct a working set of constraints $\mathcal{W}$. In each iteration, the algorithm computes the solution over the current $\mathcal{W}$ (Line 3), find the most violated constraints (Lines 4-6), and add it to the working set. The algorithm stops once no constraint can be found that is violated by more than the desired precision ϵ (Line 8). Using a stopping criterion based on the accuracy of the empirical risk is very intuitive and practically meaningful. Intuitively, ϵ can be used to indicate how close one wants to be to the empirical risk of the best parameter vector.

This algorithm has two interesting properties [5]. First, the upper bound for the number of iterations of the algorithm does not depend on the number of training pairs. Second, the time complexity, when using a lineal kernel, is linear with the number of training pairs.

4   Minimum Error-Rate Training Using SSVMs

To adapt SSVMs to perform MERT we consider all the possible source language sentences as the space of inputs $\mathbf{f} \in \mathcal{X}$ and all the target language sentences as the space of outputs $\mathbf{e} \in \mathcal{Y}$. The feature vector $\Psi_{MERT}(\mathbf{f}, \mathbf{e})$ corresponds to the values of the M different feature functions in a log-linear model.

$$\Psi_{MERT}(\mathbf{f}, \mathbf{e}) = (h_1(\mathbf{f}, \mathbf{e}), \ldots, h_m(\mathbf{f}, \mathbf{e}), \ldots, h_M(\mathbf{f}, \mathbf{e})) \ . \tag{8}$$

To compute the feature vector $\Psi_{MERT}(\mathbf{f}, \mathbf{e})$ we use a yet unpublished extension of the THOT toolkit. THOT [9] is a toolkit for SMT to train phrase-based models. The above mention THOT extension allows to obtain a phrase alignment between a pair of sentences, which maximizes the probability given by a log-linear model [10]. This extension calculates an alignment between two sentences and returns the score of each of the components in the log-linear model given this alignment.

As the loss function we can use any of the several automatic evaluation metrics for MT. We have used the BLEU [11] score and the word error rate (WER) measure. BLEU criterion computes the geometric mean of the precision of n-grams of various lengths between a hypothesis and a (set of) reference translations multiplied by a factor BP that penalizes short sentences:

$$\text{BLEU} = \text{BP} \cdot \exp\left(\sum_{n=1}^{N} \frac{\log p_n}{N}\right). \tag{9}$$

Here p_n denotes the precision of n-grams in the hypothesis translation. We use $N = 4$. WER is an error measure similar to the edit distance used in speech recognition. It computes the minimum number of editions (substitutions, insertions and deletions) needed to convert the hypothesized sentence into the sentence considered ground truth. We have performed experiments using $\Delta(\mathbf{e}, \hat{\mathbf{e}}) = 1 - \text{BLEU}(\mathbf{e}, \hat{\mathbf{e}})$ and $\Delta(\mathbf{e}, \hat{\mathbf{e}}) = \text{WER}(\mathbf{e}, \hat{\mathbf{e}})$ as loss functions.

The argmax operation for prediction (Lines 4-6) of Algorithm 1 is computed via n-best candidate translations. Theoretically we must search, among all possible target sentences, the one with the highest score, but, as there are infinite target sentences, we use the n-best approximation.

5   Experimental Setup

We carried out our experimentation on the second version of the Europarl corpus [12], which is built from the proceedings of the European Parliament. This corpus is divided into three separate sets: one for training, one for development and one for test and was the corpus used in the 2006 Workshop on Machine Translation (WMT) of the ACL conference [13]. We focused on the Spanish–English (Es–En) subcorpora of the Europarl corpus.

Since the original corpus is not sentence-aligned, different corpora are obtained while building the parallel bilingual corpora. The language models used in our experimentation were computed with the SRILM [14] toolkit, using 5-grams

Table 1. Statistics of the Europarl corpus for the Es–En subcorpora. Sent. stands for sentences, OoV for "Out of Vocabulary" words, Perp. for perplexity, K for thousands of elements and M for millions of elements. Perplexity computed with 5-grams.

	Training			Development				Test			
	#Sent.	#Words	Voc.	#Sent.	#Words	OoV	Perp.	#Sent.	#Words	OoV	Perp.
Es	731K	15.7M	103K	2000	61K	208	89.9	2000	60K	207	88.9
En		15.2M	64K		59K	127	89.0		58K	125	90.6

and applying interpolation with the Kneser-Ney discount. The statistics of these corpora and their perplexities according to these language models are displayed in Table 1.

The evaluation was carried out using WER and BLEU measures, following previous works in SMT and for comparison purposes. Moreover, in order to compute time requirements independently from the hardware platform and CPU load, the number of times the full validation corpus is translated during the MERT process was assumed as a reliable measure.

5.1 Baseline System

To perform the experimentation we use a log-linear model with 7 features [15]:

- Target language model score
- Direct and inverse phrase translation scores
- Direct and inverse lexical scores
- Phrase penalty
- Word penalty

We performed monotonous translation, so there was no need for a reordering model. Searching was performed by the MOSES toolkit [16]. MOSES is a decoder based on a beam search algorithm where each target sentence is generated left to right in form of partial translations.

In the following, we will refer to the *baseline* system when uniform parameters are assumed $(\lambda_1, \ldots, \lambda_M = 1)$, i.e. all feature function are equally important.

6 Results

We present monotonous translation results comparing the proposed SSVMs MERT with respect to Powell's algorithm used in [3] and with respect to the baseline system. We want to measure the amount of improvement that is obtained when applying our MERT algorithm with respect to the baseline system (described in section 5.1), and also compare the result of our proposal with respect to the most widespread used MERT algorithm.

Table 2 shows the BLEU and WER scores obtained on the test corpus and the number of times the whole development corpus is translated for four different systems: baseline, Powell's algorithm, our SSVMs proposal optimizing BLEU and our SSVMs proposal optimizing WER.

As expected, best BLEU and WER results were obtained by optimizing parameters with respect to the BLEU and WER measures respectively, but, interestingly, the best WER score corresponds to a low BLEU score. As can be seen on Table 2, optimizing the WER score requires less iterations than optimizing the BLEU score.

Consistent performance improvements were achieved with respect to the baseline system. BLEU score improved 10.9 points while WER score improved 4.1 points. Regarding the Powell's algorithm for MERT, our proposal obtained comparable results for both translation quality and number of iterations.

Table 2. Best monotonous translation results on the Europarl Es→En test set obtained by the baseline system and different MERT algorithms: Powell's algorithm optimizing BLEU, SSVMs optimizing BLEU and SSVMs optimizing WER

Algorithm	Criterion	BLEU	WER	#Translations
Baseline	-	19.8	61.4	–
Powell	BLEU	30.9	58.2	6
SSVMs	BLEU	30.7	58.6	8
	WER	24.0	57.8	4

7   Previous Work and Discussion

Different algorithms to perform MERT have been proposed in the literature. In [3] error minimization relied on the availability of a set of n-best candidate translations for each input sentence. During training, optimal parameters were searched through the Powell's algorithm. In [17] the downhill-simplex algorithm is employed to perform MERT. In this approach, all possible solutions of the search algorithm are exploited, leading to a computationally expensive algorithm.

We measured consistent and stable improvements for two different MT scores with respect to the baseline system, obtaining similar results to those given in [3]. Like [3] we use n-best lists, so our proposal requires a similar number of iterations as the Powell's algorithm needs to converge. In practice $6-10$ iterations of our proposal are enough for convergence instead of the 100 iterations needed in [17]. In addition, the optimization capabilities of the SSVMs are not limited to the model scaling factors as the method described in [3] but they also allow to optimize parameters of the models to be interpolated as in [17].

Acknowledgments. This work has been partially supported by the Spanish MEC under FPU scholarship AP2006-00691, grant Consolider Ingenio 2010 CSD2007-00018 and by the EC (FEDER) and the Spanish MEC under grant TIN2006-15694-CO2-01.

References

1. Klakow, D.: Log-linear interpolation of language models. In: 5th International Conference on Spoken Language Processing, Sydney, Australia, pp. 1695–1699 (1998)
2. Och, F., Ney, H.: Discriminative training and maximum entropy models for statistical machine translation. In: ACL 2002 (2002)
3. Och, F.J.: Minimum error rate training for statistical machine translation. In: Proc. of the ACL, Sapporo, Japan (2003)
4. González-Rubio, J., Ortiz-Martinez, D., Casacuberta, F.: Optimization of log-linear machine translation model parameters using svms. In: Proc. of the 8th Int. Workshop on Pattern Recognition in Information Systems (2008)
5. Joachims, T., Finley, T., Yu, C.N.: Cutting-plane training of structural svms. Machine Learning Journal (to appear)

6. Duda, R., Hart, P.: Pattern Classification and Scene Analysis (1973)
7. Vapnik, V.: Statistical Learning Theory (1998)
8. Tsochantaridis, I., Joachims, T., Hofmann, T., Altun, Y.: Large margin methods for structured and interdependent output variables. Journal of Machine Learning Research (2005)
9. Ortiz-Martínez, D., García-Varea, I., Casacuberta, F.: Thot: a toolkit to train phrase-based statistical translation models. In: 10th MT Summit (2005)
10. Ortiz-Martínez, D., García-Varea, I., Casacuberta, F.: Phrase-level alignment generation using a smoothed log-linear phrase-based statistical alignment model. In: Proc. of EAMT 2008, Hamburg, Germany (September 2008)
11. Papineni, K., Kishore, A., Roukos, S., Ward, T., Zhu, W.: Bleu: A method for automatic evaluation of machine translation. Technical Report RC22176, W0109-022 (2001)
12. Koehn, P.: Europarl: A parallel corpus for statistical machine translation. In: MT Summit (2005)
13. Koehn, P., Monz, C.: Manual and automatic evaluation of machine translation between european languages. In: Proc. of the NAACL, pp. 102–121 (2006)
14. Stolcke, A.: Srilm - an extensible language modeling toolkit. In: Proc. of the Int. Conference on Spoken Language Processing, vol. 2, pp. 901–904 (2002)
15. Koehn, P., Och, F., Marcu, D.: Statistical phrase-based translation. In: Proc. of the NAACL-HLT, vol. 1, pp. 48–54 (2003)
16. Koehn, P., Hoang, H., Birch, A., Callison-Burch, C., Federico, M., Bertoldi, N., Cowan, B., Shen, W., Moran, C., Zens, R., Dyer, C., Bojar, O., Constantine, A., Herbst, E.: Moses: Open source toolkit for statistical machine translation. In: Proc. of the ACL (2007)
17. Cettolo, M., Federico, M.: Minimum error training of log-linear translation models. In: IWSLT 2004, pp. 103–106 (2004)

Morpheme-Based Automatic Speech Recognition of Basque

Víctor G. Guijarrubia, M. Inés Torres, and Raquel Justo*

Departamento de Electricidad y Electrónica
Universidad del País Vasco, Apartado 644, 48080 Bilbao, Spain
{vgga,manes}@we.lc.ehu.es, raquel.justo@ehu.es

Abstract. In this work, we focus on studying a morpheme-based speech recognition system for Basque, an highly inflected language that is official language in the Basque Country (northern Spain). Two different techniques are presented to decompose the words into their morphological units. The morphological units are then integrated into an Automatic Speech Recognition System, and those systems are then compared to a word-based approach in terms of accuracy and processing speed. Results show that whereas the morpheme-based approaches perform similarly from an accuracy point of view, they can be significantly faster than the word-based system when applied to a weather-forecast task.

Keywords: Speech recognition, Morphological operations.

1 Introduction

Highly inflected languages present a large number of word forms per lemma. Therefore, the vocabulary of any application of natural language processing includes a vast variety of word-forms and is higher than in morphologically poor languages. So, it is usual to resort to morphological units to deal with the problems of higher vocabulary sizes, higher perplexities and higher out-of-vocabulary rates.

Basque is a pre-Indo-European language with unknown origin that is, along with Spanish, official language for the 2.5 million inhabitants of the Basque Country. Basque is a highly inflected language in both nouns and verbs.

The novelty of this work lies in the use of morphological units in Automatic Speech Recognition (ASR) of Basque. The use of morphological units has been studied to cope with the peculiarities of other highly inflected languages in ASR [1,2,3,4,5]. In this work we want to use them for Basque, studying how to integrate them in an ASR system and analysing several options that arise during the process, like the smoothing of the morpheme-based language models or the way to generate the word sequences. In Basque there is no freely available linguistic

---

* This work has been partially supported by the University of the Basque Country under grant GIU07/57, by the Spanish CICYT under grant TIN2005-08660-C04-03 and by the Spanish program Consolider-Ingenio 2010 under grant CSD2007-00018.

H. Araujo et al. (Eds.): IbPRIA 2009, LNCS 5524, pp. 386–393, 2009.

tool that splits the words into proper morphemes either. So, for this reason, we have developed some techniques to split words into morpheme-like units by means of data-driven and linguistically motivated techniques. Overall, Basque can be characterised as a suffixing language, meaning that there is a tendency to modify words by appending one or more suffixes. However, it is convenient to keep a low morpheme-to-word ratio. There are many reasons for this. The higher the ratio the bigger the language models (LMs) we need in order to not lose information. The acoustic separability, the word generation or the chances of making incorrect splittings are also highly affected. Therefore, we decided to explore the approximation of decomposing the words, if possible, into two morpheme-like units: a *root* and an *ending* reassembling the suffixes. For that, two different approaches were studied to split the words into that form.

The rest of the paper is organised as follow: Section 2 describes all the information regarding the morphological units: the approximations explored to get the morphological units, the way they are integrated into an ASR system, analysing several ways to smooth the morpheme-based language models, and how to reconstruct the word sequence from the morphemes; Section 3 contains a description of the evaluation database used in the experiments; Section 4 presents the results obtained the different approximations; and Section 5 discusses the conclusions.

2   Morphological Units

2.1   Getting the Morphological Units

Two different approaches were studied to split the words, if possible, into the desired *root - ending* scheme.

Lemma-based approach (LEMMA). This approach has a linguistic motivation since it requires the data to be in not only word form, but also in lemma form. The lemmas are used to get the morphemes, but not directly to get the splittings. The words that make up the vocabulary are grouped according to the lemma. The words belonging to the same group are then analysed to find a common root. Those words are then split into a *common_root - different_ending* form. However there are three particular cases where the word is not split and is left as a full word: a) when the ending is *null* b) when for a specific lemma only one word appears and c) when there are some words for the same lemma, but they do not have a common root, like irregular verbs. So, after applying this procedure, the result is a list of units composed of words, roots and endings. Note also that if a word corresponds to more than one lemma, because it has several different meanings, for each of the cases the word appears in the data, it is split according to the lemma in that particular case.

Morfessor-based approach (MORF). This is a data-driven approach based on unsupervised learning of morphological word segmentation. This approximation requires the use of the Morfessor Categories-MAP software [6]. The tool is capable of segmenting words in an unannotated text corpus into morpheme-like units. It also classifies the resulting units into three categories: prefix (PRE), stem (STM) and suffix (SUF). However, the tool decompose the words into a more complex form than the root-ending one. So, an additional step is required to convert the decompositions into the root-ending form. For that, the following process is applied: all the suffixes at the end of the word are joined to form the ending and the root is built joining all the prefixes, stems and possible suffixes between stems. For example, a Morfessor segmentation like PRE + STM1+ SUF1+STM2+SUF2+SUF3 is converted to the root PRE + STM1+ SUF1+STM2 and the ending SUF2+SUF3. This process is not only interesting because it allows us to get a root and an ending, but also because it makes the resulting morpheme-like units more robust against errors introduced by Morfessor. A particular case appears when the whole word is considered as a root. In this case, that word is considered as a full word and it is not split. So, similarly to the LEMMA approach, the result is a list of units composed of words, roots and endings.

2.2   Using the Morphemes

Morpheme-based ASR for Basque. Most of the ASR systems make use of the Bayes' decision rule to find the best sequence of lexical units for an acoustic observation X.

$$\hat{\bar{u}} = \arg\max_{\bar{u}} P(\bar{u}|X) = \arg\max_{\bar{u}} P(\bar{u})P(X|\bar{u}) \tag{1}$$

where $P(\bar{u})$ is the probability given by the language model for the unit sequence $\bar{u}$, and $P(X|\bar{u})$ is the probability given by the acoustic models for the acoustic observation X given a specific unit sequence $\bar{u}$. Of course, for the word-based systems those units correspond to words and for the morpheme-based ones, to morphemes.

The two procedures described in section 2.1 produce three types of morpheme (m) as mentioned above: full words (w, i.e. words that have not been split), roots (r) and endings (e). Let mention that although other authors [2] have split the full words using a *null* ending, in this work, full words have been left untouched to get better language-modelling coverage. There are some natural restrictions that can be applied. In this work, the following restrictions have been adopted at decoding time:

- e-e transitions (from an ending morpheme to another ending one) are forbidden.
- r-r transitions (from a root morpheme to another root) are forbidden.
- w-e transitions (from a full word to an ending morpheme) are forbidden.
- r-w transitions (from a root morpheme to a full word) are forbidden.
- r-e transitions (from a root morpheme to an ending morpheme) are limited to those observed in training.

With the restrictions established, the *a priori* probability of the sequence of morphemes $m_1^M = m_1 \ldots m_M$ becomes:

$$P(m_1^M) \simeq \prod_{i=1}^{M} p(m_i|m_{i-k_m+1}^{i-1})g(m_i, m_{i-1}) \tag{2}$$

where the weight $g(m_i, m_{i-1})$ is used to represent the restrictions and can be defined as

$$g(m_i, m_{i-1}) = \begin{cases} 1 \text{ if } m_{i-1}m_i \text{ transition is allowed} \\ 0 \text{ otherwise} \end{cases} \qquad (3)$$

A specific probability mass should be reserved to be shared among unseen events. A back-off smoothed LM probability (for a count threshold of 0) can be calculated as follows:

$$p(m_i|m_{i-k_m+1}^{i-1}) = \\ \begin{cases} d_c(m_{i-k_m+1}^i)p_{ML}(m_i|m_{i-k_m+1}^{i-1}) \text{ if } c(m_{i-k_m+1}^i) > 0 \\ \alpha(m_{i-k_m+1}^{i-1})p(m_i|m_{i-k_m+2}^{i-1}) \qquad \text{otherwise} \end{cases} \qquad (4)$$

where $c(m_{i-k_m+1}^i)$ is the count of $(m_{i-k_m+1}, \ldots, m_i)$ in the training data, p_{ML} denotes the maximum-likelihood estimate, d_c represents the discounting factor (Witten-Bell in our experiments) and α is the back-off factor that ensures that the entire distribution still gives the sum of unity. The common way to calculate this factor is as expressed in eq. (5), where some mass probability is derived to all unseen events.

$$\alpha(m_{i-k_m+1}^{i-1}) = \\ = \frac{\left[1 - \displaystyle\sum_{m:c(m,m_{i-k_m+1}^{i-1})>0} d_c(m, m_{i-k_m+1}^{i-1})p_{ML}(m|m_{i-k_m+1}^{i-1})\right]}{\displaystyle\sum_{m:c(m,m_{i-k_m+1}^{i-1})=0} p(m|m_{i-k_m+2}^{i-1})} \qquad (5)$$

However, a new issue arises when the decoding restrictions mentioned above are applied. In this case eq. (5) does not ensure the distribution adds up to unity. Taking the restrictions into account, the denominator of α must be calculated according to eq. (6)

$$\sum_{m:c(m,m_{i-k_m+1}^{i-1})=0 \wedge g(m,m_{i-1})=1} p(m|m_{i-k_m+2}^{i-1}) \qquad (6)$$

As a comparative study, in the experiments we tested the two approaches described here: calculate α according to eq. (5) or using the denominator as in eq. (6). We will denote the former as SM1 from here on, and the latter as SM2.

Word generation. The output of the morpheme-based decoder is a sequence of morphemes. However, we are interested in a sequence of words. Two different approaches to generate the words from the morphemes are proposed. We will refer to the first approach as MARKALL and to the second one as MARKEND.

MARKALL: The three types of units we get through the methodologies described in section 2.1, i.e. (w), (r) and (e), have been marked. Thus, each unit can only be one of the three types of morphemes.

Differentiating them it is easy to generate the words from the morphemes. Due to the decoding restrictions, after any root there is going to be an ending. So, joining them we get the corresponding word.

MARKEND: All the marks proposed in MARKALL are not needed to restore the word sequence. It is also possible marking only the endings or even the roots. This way, we get a vocabulary reduction by means of having some units that can act as two of the three types of morphemes. We will only analyse the "mark ending" option, since it is more interesting and it is also the one resulting in greater vocabulary reduction. The transitions allowed for these units are the those available for the word and the root forms.

Due to the decoding restrictions, the unit appearing before an ending is going to be a unit that can work as a root, even if it is not marked. In this case, we only need to join the ending to the previous unit to get the corresponding word.

3   Task and Corpora

The ASR results obtained in this work correspond to experiments carried out over a specific corpus called METEUS [7]. It consists of a text and speech corpus in Basque of weather forecast reports picked from those published in the Internet by the Basque Institute of Meteorology. This corpus is divided into a training set and an independent test set consisting of 500 sentences. Each sentence of the test was uttered by at least 3 speakers, resulting in a speech evaluation data of 1,800 utterances from 36 speakers (around 3.5 hours of speech).

The main features of the training data of the METEUS database are summarised in Table 1. It includes the features in terms of words, morphemes obtained using LEMMA technique and morphemes by means of MORF.

All the proposed approaches have been evaluated and compared in terms of perplexity. The obtained results are given in Table 2. The standard perplexity (PP) values are not comparable between the different approaches due to the fact that different vocabulary-units or tokens are involved. This drawback can be faced by turning to the normalised perplexity (PP*) [8] which is calculated using the ratio of tokens to words as shown in eq. (7),

$$PP^* = PP^{\frac{N_T}{N_w}} \tag{7}$$

where PP* is the normalised word perplexity, PP is the standard perplexity calculated over the tokens, N_T is the number of tokens and N_w the number of words in the test. Note that the perplexities have been calculated based on a

Table 1. Main features of LM training data of the METEUS Basque corpus in terms or words and morphemes

	WORDS	LEMMA	MORF
# of sentences		14615	
Running units	154,778	247,398	196,340
Vocabulary			
MARKALL	1,097	733 (404(w)+200(r)+129(e))	946 (731(w)+195(r)+20(e))
MARKEND	1,097	591 (404(w)+58(r)+129(e))	798 (731(w)+47(r)+20(e))

Table 2. Perplexity (PP) and normalised perplexity (PP*) values for all the proposed approaches

			PP	PP*
Words (baseline)			8.25	8.25
LEMMA	MARKALL	SM1	4.44	10.83
		SM2	4.38	10.60
	MARKEND	SM1	4.39	10.64
		SM2	4.35	10.48
MORF	MARKALL	SM1	5.49	8.67
		SM2	5.42	8.53
	MARKEND	SM1	5.44	8.57
		SM2	5.39	8.47

3-gram for words and a 4-gram for LEMMA and MORF approaches, since these models achieved the best results and are the ones used in the experiments.

We can see from Table 2 that the differences in PP* are small and more or less the three systems have a similar perplexities. So, we can expect similar performances from all the systems once integrated into an ASR system.

4 Experimental Evaluation

For these experiments, a set of 35 phone-like units was selected to model the Basque sounds. Each unit was modelled by a three-state Hidden Markov Model (HMM), with 32 Gaussian mixtures per state and using 12 Mel-frequency cepstral coefficients with delta and acceleration coefficients, energy and delta-energy as parameters. A phonetically balanced database called EHU-DB16 [9] was used to train those acoustic models using a maximum likelihood criterion. Then, lexical units, both words and morphemes, were modelled by a chain of HMM according to a basic set of transcription rules previously defined for Basque.

The ASR results in terms of Word Error Rate (WER) and decoding time for both the word (baseline) and morpheme based systems, are shown in Table 3. Decoding time is a relative time-cost measure. It was calculated as the time needed to decode the test utterances by the system under consideration relative to the time needed by the baseline system to decode the same test.

From the WER point of view, almost the same results are obtained using either words or morphemes. The task itself is not hard enough and it is equally covered using words and morphemes, accordingly, no significant differences were expected for this task.

As mentioned in Table 2 while for the word-based approach we used just a 3-gram, for the LEMMA and MORF approaches we used a 4-gram LM, since these were the options reporting the best results. This appears to result in smaller WER for the morpheme-based approaches, specially the MORF one. Specifically the *probability of improvement* (poi) [10] of the MORF approaches with respect to the baseline word-based model on the basis of WER scores for 1,000

Table 3. Recognition performance of the word and morpheme based recognition systems

			WER	Time
WORD (baseline)			5.09	1.00
LEMMA	MARKALL	SM1	5.08	0.86
		SM2	5.18	0.91
	MARKEND	SM1	5.12	0.81
		SM2	5.16	0.83
MORF	MARKALL	SM1	4.93	0.92
		SM2	4.98	0.94
	MARKEND	SM1	4.99	0.87
		SM2	4.98	0.91

bootstrap sets reaches values between 85-94%. Using the MORF approach fewer words are split, which might turn to longer history being remembered and better performance.

Comparing the marking and smoothing approaches, Table 3 shows that the differences are negligible. The MARKALL approach uses more specific units at the cost of higher vocabulary sizes and seems to be better for this task. The same can be said about the smoothing approaches. The only difference is the way the unseen words are treated. For this task it seems not to be very relevant: SM1 performs better even if, in principle, SM2 is more adequate.

With regard to the decoding-time, we see that all the morpheme-based systems perform much better than the word based one. Smaller vocabularies and decoding restrictions result in faster decoding. This may be very useful when dealing with bigger tasks. Considering that we do not have any performance lost, having systems that are 6-19% faster results in a significant advantage for ASR. Comparing the two marking approaches, obviously MARKEND one is the best since the vocabulary size is quite smaller. Comparing the two smoothing approximations, SM1 performs better. In this case, as when we use the SM1 approach some probability mass is wasted in unproductive transitions, the LM probabilities are smaller and consequently, the pruning techniques used during decoding act faster and reduce the search space faster, resulting in shorter decoding times.

5   Conclusions

This paper focuses on morpheme-based models for speech recognition of Basque. Different sets of morpheme-like units were tested over a limited-domain speech recognition task. Similar values of normalised perplexities and WER were achieved for both words and morphemes. However, the morpheme-based ASR system has proved to be significantly faster than the word based system. Nevertheless, more significant experiments should be carried out using bigger databases to get some real conclusions regarding the several methodologies explored in this work.

References

1. Kirchhoff, K., Vergyri, D., Bilmes, J., Duh, K., Stolcke, A.: Morphology-based language modeling for conversational Arabic speech recognition. Computer Speech and Language 20, 589–608 (2006)
2. Rotovnik, T., Maučec, M.S., Kačič, Z.: Large vocabulary continuous speech recognition of an inflected language using stems and endings. Speech Communication 49(6), 437–452 (2007)
3. Kirsimäki, T., Creutz, M., Siivola, V., Kurimo, M., Virpioja, S., Pylkkönen, J.: Unlimited vocabulary speech recognition with morph language models applied to Finnish. Computer Speech and Language 20, 515–541 (2006)
4. Arisoy, E., Dutağaci, H., Arslan, L.M.: A unified language model for large vocabulary continuous spech recognition of Turkish. Signal Processing 86, 2844–2862 (2006)
5. Kwon, O.W., Park, J.: Korean large vocabulary continuous speech recognition with morpheme-based recognition units. Speech Communication 39, 287–300 (2003)
6. Creutz, M., Lagus, K.: Inducing the morphological lexicon of a natural language from unannotated text. In: Proceedings of the International and Interdisciplinary Conference on Aadaptive Knowledge Representation and Reasoning (AKRR), Espoo, Finland (June 2005)
7. Pérez, A., Torres, M.I., Casacuberta, F., Guijarrubia, V.: A Spanish-Basque weather forecast corpus for probabilistic speech translation. In: 5th SALTMIL Workshop on Minority Languages, Genoa, pp. 99–101 (May 2006)
8. Kneissler, J., Klakow, D.: Speech recognition for huge vocabularies by using optimized sub-word units. In: Proc. Eurospeech 2001, Aalborg, pp. 69–72 (2001)
9. Guijarrubia, V., Torres, M.I., Rodríguez, L.J.: Evaluation of a spoken phonetic database in Basque language. In: Proceedings of LREC, Lisbon, vol. 6, pp. 2127–2130 (2004)
10. Bisani, M., Ney, H.: Bootstrap estimates for confidence intervals in ASR performance evaluation. In: Proc. IEEE ICASSP, vol. 1, pp. 409–412 (2004)

On a Kernel Regression Approach to Machine Translation

Nicolás Serrano, Jesús Andrés-Ferrer, and Francisco Casacuberta

Instituto Tecnológico de Informática
{nserrano,jandres,fcn}@iti.upv.es

Abstract. We present a machine translation framework based on Kernel Regression techniques. The translation process is modeled as a string-to-string mapping. For doing so, first both source and target strings are mapped to a natural vector space obtaining feature vectors. Afterwards, a translation mapping is defined from the source feature vector to the target feature vector. This translation mapping is learnt by linear regression. Once the target feature vector is obtained, we use a multi-graph search to find all the possible target strings whose mappings correspond to the "translated" feature vector. We present experiments in a small but relevant task showing encouraging results.

1 Introduction

Machine translation deals with the problem of mapping sentences x from a source language X^* to a target language Y^*. Due to the complexity of the translation problem, the relationships between these two languages cannot be properly enumerated as a set of rules. Consequently, several authors have approached this problem as a statistical pattern recognition problem [1]. However, we present a new method for machine translation based on the work in [2], where a regression framework for learning transductions is proposed. Similar methods have been applied to many fields such as text categorization [3] or machine translation [4].

In our approach, both source and target strings are mapped to natural feature vectors. Then a *translation mapping* is learnt between feature vector domains. Given a source string x, the translation process consists in mapping it to a feature vector u and then, mapping this vector u to its corresponding target feature vector v. The latter mapping, the so-called translation mapping is learnt by regression techniques. Finally, the pre-image set for the target feature vector v must be found. This problem is referred as the "Pre-image" problem. The focus of this paper is to solve this problem in a regression-based machine translation framework.

Some previous works such as [4], have explore the idea of learning the translation as a regression problem. These works do not handle the pre-image problem directly but use the model as a score to the standard statistical machine translation systems. Specifically, they use a phrased-based statistical machine translation model [5] and use the kernel regression model as an additional score to the

H. Araujo et al. (Eds.): IbPRIA 2009, LNCS 5524, pp. 394–401, 2009.

phrased-based search. This approach does not make the best of the regression approach, as proposed in [2], losing some of its main advantages.

On the contrary, the pre-image search proposed in [6] is adapted in this work to the peculiarities in the machine translation problem. This aim is achieved by building the DeBruijn Graph [7] for a target feature vector and then finding eulerian paths within it. Nevertheless, due to the high dimensionality of the feature vectors, severe problems arise.

2   The Training Process

The aim of machine translation is to learn a mapping from a source language $X^\star$ to a target language $Y^\star$, i.e. $f : X^\star \to Y^\star$, where X is the source vocabulary and Y is the target vocabulary. In statistical machine translation the optimal translation function f is designed based on Bayes' decision theory [1]

$$f(\boldsymbol{x}) = \arg\max_{\boldsymbol{y} \in Y^\star} p(\boldsymbol{y}|\boldsymbol{x}) \tag{1}$$

where $p(\boldsymbol{y}|\boldsymbol{x})$ is approximated by

$$p(\boldsymbol{y}|\boldsymbol{x}) = \frac{\exp(C(\boldsymbol{x}, \boldsymbol{y}))}{\sum_{\boldsymbol{y}' \in Y^\star} \exp(C(\boldsymbol{x}, \boldsymbol{y}'))} \tag{2}$$

since the exponential function is monotonically increasing, Eq. (1) simplifies to

$$f(\boldsymbol{x}) = \arg\max_{\boldsymbol{y} \in Y^\star} C(\boldsymbol{x}, \boldsymbol{y}) \tag{3}$$

where $C(\boldsymbol{x}, \boldsymbol{y})$ is a score function, which is modelled by a feature set $\{h_k\}_1^K$ of theoretically and heuristically motivated functions [8]

$$C(\boldsymbol{x}, \boldsymbol{y}) = \sum_k \lambda_k h_k(\boldsymbol{x}, \boldsymbol{y}) \tag{4}$$

where λ_k are the model parameters that weight the feature function relevance. In state-of-art translation systems [9], these feature functions are mainly modelled by logarithms of probability models, such as the phrase-based models [5].

However, we propose a method for learning the translation function f based on regression techniques. In order to configure the regression framework, the source strings $\boldsymbol{x} \in X^\star$ are mapped to the natural domain $\boldsymbol{u} \in U \subset \mathbb{N}^{D_1}$ via a source mapping function ϕ_X, i.e. $\boldsymbol{u} = \phi_X(x)$. Similarly, the target strings $y \in Y^\star$ are mapped to another natural domain, $v \in V \subset \mathbb{N}^{D_2}$, via a target mapping function ϕ_Y, i.e. $\phi_Y(y)$. Although both source and target mappings are not required to be of the same type, we will henceforth assume so. Then, we define the mappings, ϕ_X and ϕ_Y, as the function, ϕ_n, that generates a n-gram count vector from a given string, $\boldsymbol{x}$ and $\boldsymbol{y}$ respectively. More accurately, $\phi_n(x) = \{|x|_{\boldsymbol{u}_1}, \ldots, |x|_{\boldsymbol{u}_n}\}$ with $\boldsymbol{u}_i$ standing for the i-th n-gram in lexicografic order of the vocabulary X, and $|x|_u$ is the number of occurrences of u in x. For instance, the string $x = "aaabb"$ of the language $X^* = \{a, b\}^*$ will correspond to the bigram mapping output $u = \phi_2(x) = (2, 1, 0, 1)$.

The feature vector mapping $u \in U \subset \mathbb{N}^{D_1}$ is useful when comparing strings, since it helps to define a kernel between strings as follows

$$K_n(x, x') = \phi_n(x)\phi_n(x')^T = \sum_{u \in \Sigma^n} |x|_u |x'|_u \qquad (5)$$

where $K_n(x, x')$ ranges from the number of common n-grams if both strings are equal, to zero if they totally differ.

Once the string-to-vector mapping is defined, the training problem is restated as a regression problem where a source-to-target mapping must to be found, i.e. finding the translation mapping $h : U \rightarrow V$. Given such a mapping h and two sentences, a source sentence x and its translation y; we define a string to target feature mapping, $g : X^* \rightarrow V$, as follows

$$g(x) = h(\phi_X(x)) = \phi_Y(y) \qquad (6)$$

Given a source string x, the proposed translation method consists in mapping it to U via $\phi_X(x)$ and then, mapping it to V with the translation function $h(x)$. Afterwards, given the target feature vector v obtained from the translation mapping, we compute its pre-image set $\phi_Y^{-1}(v)$. Figure 1 depicts a general scheme of the whole translation process.

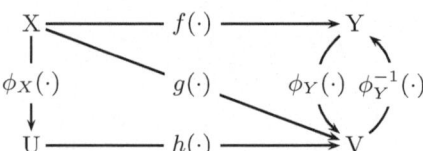

Fig. 1. Machine translation kernel regression scheme

2.1 The Linear Regression

The function h maps between two natural domains $h : \mathbb{N}^{D_1} \rightarrow \mathbb{N}^{D_2}$. Since discrete regression problems yield complicated training algorithms, we learn an extension of this function $\bar{h}$ that approximates the natural domains by real domains, i.e. $\bar{h} : \mathbb{R}^{D_1} \rightarrow \mathbb{R}^{D_2}$. We further assume that our regression problem is linear, that is to say, that the mapping function $h(u)$, and hereby its extension $\bar{h}$, can be aproximated with a linear function, i.e. $\bar{h}(u) = \mathbf{W}u$. Note that in this case the string-to-feature vector mapping g, is simplified to $g(x) = \mathbf{W}\phi_X(x)$. Given a set of sentences, $(x_m, y_m)_1^M$, we can learn the optimal $\hat{\mathbf{W}}$ matrix using the regularised least square as follows

$$\hat{\mathbf{W}} = \arg\min_W \sum_{m=1}^{M} ||\mathbf{W}\phi_X(x_m) - \phi_Y(y_m)||^2 + \gamma||\mathbf{W}||_F^2 \qquad (7)$$

where $|| \cdot ||_F$ refers to the Frobenius norm and where $\gamma > 0$ is the regularization term. The aim of the regularisation term is to avoid the weights matrix $\mathbf{W}$ to contain large weights, which is a clear evidence of overtraining.

The solution to Eq. (7) is unique and is found by differentiating the expression and equaling it to zero

$$\hat{\mathbf{W}} = \mathbf{M}_Y(\mathbf{K}_X + \gamma\mathbf{I})^{-1}\mathbf{M}_X^T \tag{8}$$

where $\mathbf{M}_Y = [\phi_Y(y_1), \ldots, \phi_Y(y_M)]$ is the $D_2 \times M$ matrix of which j-th column vector is $\phi_Y(y_j)$, where $\mathbf{M}_X = [\phi_X(x_1), ..., \phi_X(x_M)]$ is the analogous for the source strings, and where $\mathbf{K}_X$ is the Gram matrix associated to the kernel K_n applied to the source samples, i.e. $[\mathbf{K}_X]_{ij} = K_n(\boldsymbol{x}_i, \boldsymbol{x}_j)$ for all i, j such that $1 \leq i, j \leq M$.

3   The Decoding Problem

In the proposed framework, the regression output for a given source string $\boldsymbol{x}$, is a feature vector $\boldsymbol{v}$ which represents the occurrence counts of each target n-gram in its respective target translation $\boldsymbol{y}$. Any target string $\boldsymbol{y}$, that produces the same count vector $\boldsymbol{v}$ by means of the target mapping $\phi_Y(\boldsymbol{y})$ is regarded as a possible translation of the source sentence $\boldsymbol{x}$. Therefore, the decoding problem or the pre-image problem is theoretically constrained to a subdomain of Y^*.

The decoding or pre-image problem is stated as the problem of finding which target sentences are represented as given a feature vector, i.e., to find the set $\phi_Y^{-1}(g(\boldsymbol{x}))$. The pre-image of $g(\boldsymbol{x})$ is not unique since each reordering of the same counts leads to the same target feature vector $\boldsymbol{v}$. To further understand the problem we give a simple example. We assume the target language in the example is given by $Y^* = \{a, b\}^*$ and that the mapping function is ϕ_2, i.e. counting the number of possible bigrams. This implies that the count vector has four dimensions, one for each of the possible bigrams $\{aa, ab, ba, bb\}$. Since the dimensions are sorted in lexicographic order, the first dimension v_1 represents the occurrences of the bigram aa, the second dimension v_2, the occurrences of ab; and so on. If the regression output for a source sentence $\boldsymbol{x}$ is $\boldsymbol{v} = g(\boldsymbol{x}) = \{2, 1, 1, 0\}$, then its pre-image set is $\phi_Y^{-1}(\boldsymbol{v}) = \{aaaba, aabaa, baaab\}$.

When dealing with natural feature vectors the pre-image problem has a well-known solution [7]. First, it is needed to build the so-called DeBruijn graph as follows: all the $(n-1)$-gram sequences represent a different node in the graph, and edges are added going from a node, $a_1a_2 \ldots a_{n-1}$, to a node, $a_2 \ldots a_{n-1}a_n$, if they have a positive weight, which is the count of the n-gram $a_1 \ldots a_n$ in $\boldsymbol{v}$. In this graph, each Eulerian path[1] corresponds to a target string in the pre-image set. The DeBruijn graph of the proposed example is shown Fig. 2.

At this point several problems arise in practice

- The translation regresion is real-valued $\bar{h}$ instead of natural-valued h. Eulerian paths are not correctly defined in this case, since the DeBruijn technique cannot be directly applied in real-valued feature vectors.

---

[1] A path inside a graph visiting each edge the number of times indicated by its weight.

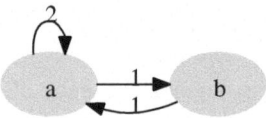

Fig. 2. A DeBruijn graph for bigrams and the feature vector $v = \{2,1,1,0\}$

- There are unknown source and target n-grams, those not appearing at the training samples. This makes the target feature vector v not to define a unique connected DeBruijn graph, but one with multiple isolated connected components.
- Even if we obtain all the possible eulerian paths within the graph, that represents all the possible translation, there is no way to select the proper translation corresponding to the source string.

3.1   The Aliasing Problem

The result obtained from the regression is a real-valued g function where the meaning of each of the target vector dimensions v_k is not clear. For instance, we take the example in which the target vocabulary is given by $Y^* = \{a, b\}^*$ and a bigram mapping is used $\phi_2(\cdot)$. In this example, the obtained target feature vector for a given source string could be $v = (1.2, 0.5, 0.8, 0.25)$ instead of the perfect regression $v' = (2, 1, 1, 0)$.

For deeply understanding the implication of any approximation, we must analyse the effect of variations in the natural-valued feature vector. Assuming that the correct regresion is given by $v = (2, 1, 1, 0)$ then the pre-image set is $\phi^{-1}(v) = \{abaa, aaba, baaab\}$. In the case in which the regresion produces $v = (2, 1, 1, 1)$, the pre-image set changes to $\phi^{-1}(v) = \{abbaa, aabba, baaabb, bbaaab\}$. Therefore, adding (or subtracting) 1 to any count dimension incurs in one extra (or less) word.

The search method originally proposed in [2] is to round the real vector and then, build a DeBruijn graph from it and search eulerian paths within the graph. However, the best solution takes into account the previously discussed regression errors. For this aim we define the *Levensthein loan*[2] as the real increment or decrement that must be added to a given real vector in order to convert it to the natural domain. The Levensthein loan can be understood as the average Levensthein error of correct hypothesis with respect to the unknown reference.

In order to find the pre-image for real-valued feature vectors, we build a weighted graph in a similar way the DeBruijn graph is built. The edges represent the real count of each n-gram according to the real-valued feature vector, instead of actual natural counts. During the search, the Levensthein loan is used to add or substract any necessary amount to the eulerian path simulating, in this way, a natural vector. In summary, the search algorithm looks for a path that uses the more of the weights in the graph and ask for the lowest possible loan.

---

[2] Named after the Levensthein distance [10].

3.2   The Unknown n-Grams Problem

In practice, it is common to find unknown n-grams when mapping strings to the feature vector count domain. This problem is stressed as the n becomes larger. Usually, this leads to DeBruijn graphs with isolated connected components and without eulerian paths covering the full sentence.

A way to amend the problem is to apply "backing-off" to lower order models during the search. That is to say, when searching for a path, the search is simultaneously performed in different l-gram graphs ($1 \leq l \leq n$). Higher values of l are more restrictive during the search and also capture more structural dependencies but more number of parameters must be estimated in the regression. When the search at the highest order graph cannot continue building an eulerian path, the search backs off one order level with a penalisation factor, similarly to backing-off smoothing in language modeling [11]. This process goes on recursively until the unigram level if needed.

3.3   Adding Scores to the Search

Lenvensthein loan score is not enough to select just one target string from the real-valued feature vector. Recall that even in the theoretical situation this would not be possible since several sentences can be built from different reordering of the same n-gram counts. These sentences have the same loan and therefore, we have no way to discriminate among them.

Obviously, this problem is solved by adding an additional score to the target string y and consequently to each path in the pre-image search. Although, several scores can be proposed such as the probability given by statistical translations models, we have adopted in this first work a language model probability, specifically the n-gram language model [11]. In summary, the score in Eq. (3) for a given pair (x, y) is defined as follows for the proposed kernel regression model

$$C(x, y) = \left(\sum_{i=1}^{N} \lambda_i \, \mathrm{sc}_i(x, y) \right) + \lambda_{lm} p_n(y) + \lambda_l \exp^{(-|y|\alpha)} \tag{9}$$

where sc_i is the Levensthein loan for the target string y at the i-th level graph; $p_n(y)$ is the language probability model for the target sentence y, and the last term represents a word-bonus score to counteract the language model bias towards short sentences.

4   Experimental Results

We have carried out experiments on the categorized EuTrans corpus [12]. This corpus comprises tourist requests at hotel front desks. Categorized EuTrans consists in 13000 pair of sentences divided into three sets: 9000 sentences to train, 1000 sentences were left out for validation and 3000 sentences for testing. There are 420 source and 230 target categories. The corpora perplexity is 3.95 and 4.73 for the target and source language respectively.

Table 1. Results on categorized EuTrans. N stands for the order of the kernel whilst the LM order row stands for the order of the n-gram language model (0 no LM).

Model	$N = 2$					$N = 3$					$N = 3 + (N = 2)$ Backoff				
LM order	0	2	3	4	5	0	2	3	4	5	0	2	3	4	5
BLEU	86.8	93.4	94.1	**95.0**	94.8	94.0	**94.4**	93.8	94.1	94.3	95.3	**95.5**	95.5	95.5	95.4

Three kernel n-gram models where trained: one built from bigrams consisting on 2145 source bigrams and 929 target bigrams, another built from trigrams consisting on 5048 source trigrams and 2102 target trigrams; and the concatenation of both as described in 3.2. We trained increasing sizes of n-gram language models from 2 to 5 estimated by the SRILM toolkit [13]. The score weights, λ, in Eq. (9) were adjusted by the Downhill Simplex algorithm [14] for optimizing the BLEU score [15] on the validation set. The proposed system was compared with the Moses [9] baseline system, in which we have limited the phrase length to 7 allowing reordering and optimizing the parameters on a validation set. The Moses baseline system scored 92.3 points of BLEU compared to the 95.5 points of our best system. A practical behaviour analysis of the proposed method is enclosed in the table 1. The results on this simple task are encouraging since almost all results surpass the baseline system. It can be observed that adding language information considerably improves the bigram system. However the trigram system is not benefited from the language model information, probably because of the corpus simplicity. Finally as expected, the search smoothing with "back-off" improves the results.

5   Conclusions and Future Work

Kernel regression models are a new and encouraging approach to the machine translation field. In this work we have proposed a complete regression framework to machine translation by proposing a regression-based search. In contrast, other works perform the search by means of a phrase-based decoding. In addition, we have explored the idea of adding language information to rank the target strings among all the pre-image set. In a future work, different models apart from the n-gram language model will be added to rank the target strings, such as IBM word models and phrased-based models.

Nevertheless several problems arise when complex corpus are used. To deal with them, further optimizations such as perform the model estimation through Cholesky incomplete decomposition or subset selection techniques are left for further research. Other possible improvements in the process would be using different kernel functions for comparing strings and use quadratic regression instead of linear regression as the regression model.

Acknowledgments. This work has been supported by the Spanish MEC under FPU scholarship AP2007-02867, the valencian "Conselleria d'Empresa i Ciència" grant CTBPRA/2005/004, grant Consolider Ingenio 2010 CSD2007-00018 by the EC (FEDER) and the Spanish MEC under grant TIN2006-15694-CO2-01.

References

1. Brown, P.F., et al.: The mathematics of statistical machine translation: Parameter estimation. Computational Linguistic 19(2), 263–311 (1993)
2. Cortes, C., Mohri, M., Weston, J.: A general regression technique for learning transductions. In: Proc. of the 22nd international conference on Machine learning (2005)
3. Cancedda, N., Gaussier, E., Goutte, C., Render, J.: Word-Sequence Kernels. Journal of Machine Learning Research 3, 1059–1082 (2003)
4. Wang, Z., Shawe-Taylor, J.: Kernel Regression Based Machine Translation. In: NAACL HLT 2007, Companion Volume, pp. 185–188 (2007)
5. Koehn, P., Och, F.J., Marcu, D.: Statistical phrase based translation. In: Proceedings of HLT/NACL (2003)
6. Cortes, C., Mohri, M., Weston, J.: A General Regression Framework for Learning String-to-String Mappings. In: Predicting Structured Data. MIT Press, Cambridge (2007)
7. Gross, J.L., Yellen, J.: Handbook of Graph Theory, pp. 253–260. CRC Press, Boca Raton (2004)
8. Och, F.J., Ney, H.: The alignment template approach to statistical machine translation. Computational Linguistics 30(4), 417–449
9. Koehn, P., Hoang, H., Birch, A., Callison-Burch, C.: Moses: Open Source Toolkit for Statistical Machine Translation. In: Proc. of ACL 2007, pp. 177–180 (2007)
10. Levenshtein, V.I.: Binary codes capable of correcting deletions, insertions, and reversals. Soviet Physics Doklady 10, 707–710 (1966)
11. Goodman, J.T.: An empirical study of smoothing techniques for language modelling. In: Proc. of ACL 1996, pp. 310–318 (1996)
12. Casacuberta, F., et al.: Some approaches to statistical and finite-state speech-to-speech tranlation. Computer Speech and Language 18, 25–47 (2004)
13. Stolcke, A.: SRILM - An Extensible Language Modeling Toolkit. In: Proc. Intl. Conf. Spoken Language Processing, Denver, Colorado (September 2002)
14. Nelder, J.A., Mead, R.: A Simplex Method for Function Minimization. The Computer Journal 7, 308–313 (1965)
15. Papineni, K., Roukos, S., Ward, T., Zhu, W.J.: BLEU: a method for automatic evaluation of machine translation. In: ACL 2002, pp. 311–318 (2002)

Experimental Analysis of Insertion Costs in a Naïve Dynamic MDF-Tree

Luisa Micó and Jose Oncina

Departamento de Lenguajes y Sistemas Informáticos
Universidad de Alicante
P.O. box 99, E-03080 Alicante, Spain
{mico,oncina}@dlsi.ua.es
http://www.dlsi.ua.es

Abstract. Similarity search is a widely employed technique in Pattern Recognition. In order to speed up the search many indexing techniques have been proposed. However, the majority of the proposed techniques are static, that is, a fixed training set is used to build up the index. This characteristic becomes a major problem when these techniques are used in dynamic (interactive) systems. In these systems updating the training set is necessary to improve its performance. In this work, we explore the surprising efficiency of a naïve algorithm that allows making incremental insertion in a previously known index: the MDF-tree.

1 Introduction

In the area of similarity search techniques, the metric space searching is an arising general approach that has received special attention. In this work we are interested in the most general case, when no assumption about the structure of the prototypes (points) is made. Some examples are protein sequences (represented by strings), skeleton of images (represented by trees or graphs), histograms of images, etc.

Actually, many techniques have been proposed based on this approach (some reviews can be found in [3][8][15]). These techniques, based on the use of any of the elementary types of similarity queries, have been used in many applications. For example, content based image retrieval [7], person detection or automatic image annotation [13], texture synthesis, image colourisation or super-resolution [1]. However, most of the existing techniques are static [14][2][10][11]. Then, the insertion or deletion of one object in the index that has been built up in a preprocessing step, requires a complete rebuild that is very expensive.

In recent years, an increasing attention on interactive systems has been observed in the information technology society. In particular, during an interactive operation, new samples (new information) should be added in an on-line training process adapting the model to the present situation.

Some methods to speed up insertion/deletion points have been proposed. Some of them are focused in dynamic indexing in secondary memory ([4]) and

H. Araujo et al. (Eds.): IbPRIA 2009, LNCS 5524, pp. 402–408, 2009.

others are focused to work in main memory [12]. In some cases, the dynamic approaches have been proposed based as modifications of a previous existing static indexing algorithm but there are also techniques devised from the beginning as dynamic such as the M-tree [5].

In this paper we analyse experimentally a naïve strategy to insert new samples in the *Most Distant from the Father tree* (MDF-tree). This type of structure have been used in several hierarchical search procedures ([9],[6]) but no dynamic approach has been proposed up to now for it.

2   New Incremental Indexing Approximation

The MDF-tree is a binary indexing structure proposed and used in [9][6] based on a hyperplane partitioning approach. The main characteristic of the method is related to the selection of the representatives for the next partition. To build up the tree, firstly a pivot is randomly selected as the root of the tree (first level). After that, a new pivot, the most distant from the root, is selected and the space is divided according the distances to both pivots. On the following levels the space is recursively divided between the current pivot of the subspace represented by the node and the most distant pivot in the subspace. This procedure is repeated until each internal node has only one object.

For each node, a representative (the pivot) and the covering radius (the distance from the pivot to the most distant point in the subspace) is computed and stored in the respective node. This procedure is described in the algorithm 1.

The function build(ℓ, S) takes as arguments the future representative of the root node and the set of objects to include in the tree (excluding ℓ), and returns the MDF-tree that contains $S \cup \{\ell\}$. The first time that build(ℓ,S) is called, ℓ is a random object. In the algorithm M_T represents the representative of T, r_T the covering radius, and T_L (T_R) the left (right) subtree of T.

Although several similarity search strategies can be applied, in this work we are focused in nearest neighbour search. The search procedure consists on a first-depth traversal through the tree, looking for the nearest neighbour. Given a node in the tree, the search continues through the child node whose representative is nearest to the query. Using different types of elimination rules, some branches of the tree are bounded and the search ends when no more possibilities to explore in the tree are possible. The last candidate is selected as the solution.

2.1   Rebuilding the Tree

In this work we focus on a procedure to obtain incrementally the exact structure that will be obtained if a complete rebuild of the tree was made. Note that in such case the performance of the algorithm when searching is exactly the same as in the static case. Then no further research in search degradation performance is needed.

We are going to study a naïve approach. When a new object is inserted first we search the position where object should appear as pivot in a static built tree. Then, the affected part of the tree is completely rebuilt.

Algorithm 1. build(ℓ, S)

Data:
   $S \cup \{\ell\}$: set of points to include in T
   ℓ: future left representative of T
create MDF-tree T
if S *is empty* **then**
 | $M_T = \ell$
 | $r_T = 0$
 | **return** T
end
$r_T = \max_{x \in S} d(\ell, S)$
$r = \text{argmax}_{x \in S} d(\ell, S)$
$S_\ell = \{x \in S | d(\ell, x) < d(r, x)\}$
$S_r = \{x \in S | d(\ell, x) \geq d(r, x)\} - \{r\}$
$T_L = \text{build}(\ell, S_\ell)$
$T_R = \text{build}(r, S_r)$
return T

Algorithm 2. insert(T, x)

Data:
   T: MDF-tree
   x: object to insert in T
if $d(M_T, x) > r_T$ **then**
 | **return** build($M_T, \{s | s \in T\} \cup \{x\} - \{M_T\}$)
end
if T_L *is empty* **then**
 | **return** build($M_T, \{x\}$)
end
$d_\ell = d(M_{T_L}, x)$ // this distance computation can be avoided
$d_r = d(M_{T_R}, x)$
if $d_\ell < d_r$ **then**
 | $T_L = \text{insert}(T_L, x)$
end
$T_R = \text{insert}(T_R, x)$
return T

This may seems a quite expensive strategy, but as the pivots are very unusual objects (the farthest of its sibling pivot), big reconstructions of the tree happens with a very low probability compensating its high cost.

Let T be the MDF-tree built using a sample set S. Let x be the new object we are interested to include in the index, and let T' the MDF-tree built using the sample set $S \cup \{x\}$. The algorithm works rebuilding the subtree of T that is different from T'.

Let we denote by M_T the representative of the root node of the MDF-tree T, r_T be its covering radius, and T_L (T_R) the left (right) MDF-subtrees of T.

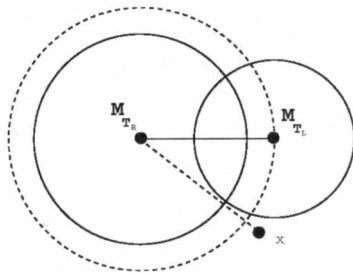

Fig. 1. Case when a complete rebuilt is needed

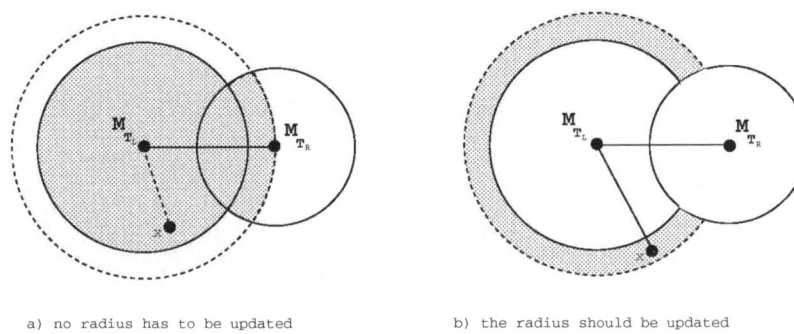

a) no radius has to be updated   b) the radius should be updated

Fig. 2. Location of the inserted object

We have several cases:

- If $d(M_T, x) > r_T$, T' differs from T in the root node because the object x is selected in T' as the representative of the right node. Then the whole tree T is rebuilt in order to include x (see fig. 1).
- Otherwise, the roots of the trees T and T' are identical. Then we have two cases (see fig. 2):
  - if $d(M_{T_L}, x) < d(M_{T_R}, x)$ the object x should be inserted in the left tree T_L and then the tree T'_R is identical to T_R.
  - Conversely if $d(M_{T_L}, x) \geq d(M_{T_R}, x)$ the object should be inserted in T_R and the tree T'_L is identical to T_L.

Algorithm 2 shows the insertion procedure.

3 Experiments

Some experiments have been developed in order to study the performance of the new approach.

The experiments where performed by extracting 5, 10 and 15 dimensional points from the unit hypercube with a uniform distribution.

First, in order to study the distribution of the number of distance computations when a new point is inserted, 10000 insertions of one point over a fixed

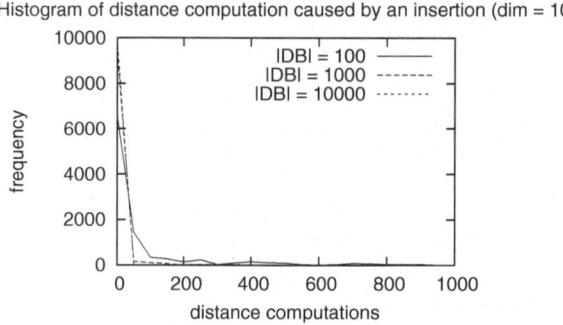

Fig. 3. Histogram of the distance computations caused by an insertion for 100, 1000, and 10000 database sizes in dimension 10

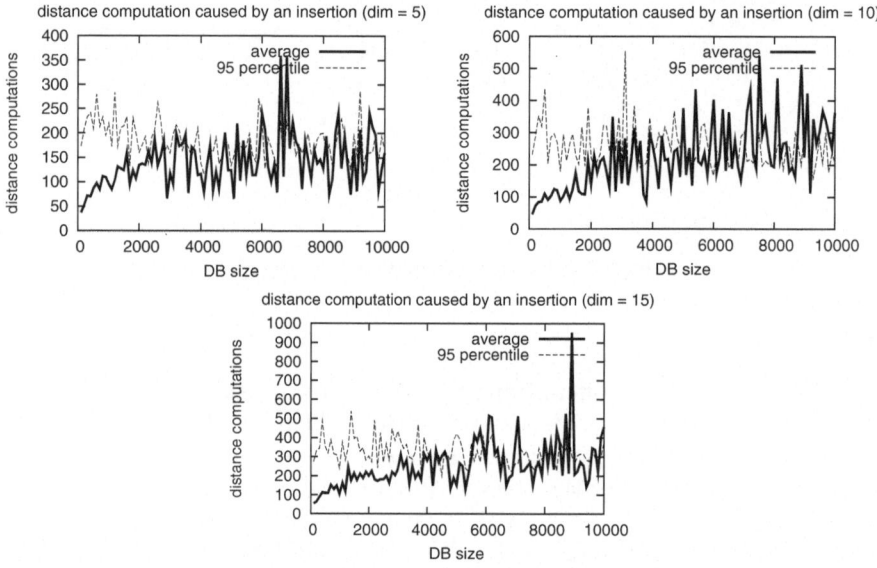

Fig. 4. Average distance computations caused by an insertion for increasing size database sets and for dimensions 5, 10, 15

MDF-tree with sizes 100, 1000, and 10000 was made. The number of distance computations were counted and its histogram was depicted in figure 3. We show only the case for dimension 10, the other cases are similar.

It can be observed that, as expected, almost all the insertions causes very few distance computations and, conversely, there are very few insertion that causes a big number of distance computations.

It can also be observed that this figure is very far of a normal distribution, then on the following experiments instead of using the variance we used the 95 percentile.

In the next experiment we have depicted the expected number of distance (over 1000 repetitions) for inserting a point when the databases grows from 100 to 10000 in steps of 100. The 95 percentile is also depicted (fig. 4). That means that although the expected number of distance computations is the line showed by the average, in the 95% of the cases the number of distance computations is bellow the line of the 95 percentile.

Although these results are quite preliminary, it can be seen that the distance computations caused by an insertion seems to grow very slowly with the database size.

4   Conclusions

We have proposed a naïve algorithm that allows the insertion in MDF-trees avoiding (with high probability) a complete rebuilt of the tree. We have also performed several artificial experiments to support this assertion.

In the future we plan to make more extensive experimentation and develop some ideas in order to have a theoretical support of this result.

We also plan to relax the condition on maintaining the same tree as if all the objects were inserted at once with the hope to decrease the number of distance computations and the stability of the algorithm.

Acknowledgements

This work has been supported in part by grants DPI2006-15542-C04-01 from the Spanish CICYT (Ministerio de Ciencia y Tecnología), the IST Programme of the European Community, under the Pascal Network of Excellence, IST-2002-506778, and the program CONSOLIDER INGENIO 2010 (CSD2007-00018).

References

1. Battiato, S., Di Blasi, G., Reforgiato, D.: Advanced indexing schema for imaging applications: three case studies. Image Processing, IET 1(3), 249–268 (2007)
2. Brin, S.: Near neighbor search in large metric spaces. In: Proceedings of the 21st International Conference on Very Large Data Bases, pp. 574–584 (1995)
3. Chávez, E., Navarro, G., Baeza-Yates, R., Marroquin, J.L.: Searching in metric spaces. ACM Computing Surveys 33(3), 273–321 (2001)
4. Chee Fu, A.W., Chan, P.M.S., Cheung, Y.l., Moon, Y.S.: Dynamic vp-tree indexing for n-nearest neighbor search given pair-wise distances. VLDB Journal 9, 154–173 (2000)
5. Ciaccia, P., Patella, M., Zezula, P.: M-tree: An efficient access method for similarity search in metric spaces. In: Proceedings of the 23rd International Conference on VLDB, Athens, Greece, pp. 426–435. Morgan Kaufmann Publishers, San Francisco (1997)
6. Gómez-Ballester, E., Micó, L., Oncina, J.: Some approaches to improve tree-based nearest neighbour search algorithms. Pattern Recognition 39(2), 171–179 (2006)
7. Giacinto, G.: A nearest-neighbor approach to relevance feedback in content based image retrieval. In: CIVR 2007: Proceedings of the 6th ACM international conference on Image and video retrieval, pp. 456–463. ACM, New York (2007)

8. Hjaltason, G.R., Samet, H.: Index-driven similarity search in metric spaces. ACM Trans. Database Syst. 28(4), 517–580 (2003)
9. Micó, L., Oncina, J., Carrasco, R.C.: A fast branch and bound nearest neighbor classifier in metric spaces. Pattern Recognition Letters 17, 731–773 (1996)
10. Micó, L., Oncina, J., Vidal, E.: A new version of the nearest-neighbour approximating and eliminating search algorithm (aesa) with linear preprocessing time and memory requirements. Pattern Recognition Letters 15, 9–17 (1994)
11. Navarro, G.: Searching in metric spaces by spatial approximation. VLDB Journal 11(1), 28–46 (2002)
12. Navarro, G., Reyes, N.: Dynamic spatial approximation trees. J. Exp. Algorithmics 12, 1–68 (2008)
13. Torralba, A., Fergus, R., Freeman, W.T.: 80 million tiny images: A large data set for nonparametric object and scene recognition. IEEE Transactions on Pattern Analysis and Machine Intelligence 30(11), 1958–1970 (2008)
14. Yianilos, P.N.: Data structures and algorithms for nearest neighbor search in general metric spaces. In: Proceedings of the ACM-SIAM Symposium on Discrete Algorithms, pp. 311–321 (1993)
15. Zezula, P., Amato, G., Dohnal, V., Batko, M.: Similarity Search: The Metric Space Approach. Springer, Heidelberg (2006)

An Approach to Estimate Perplexity Values for Language Models Based on Phrase Classes

Raquel Justo and M. Inés Torres*

Departamento de Electricidad y Electrónica
Universidad del País Vasco, 48940 Leioa, Spain
{raquel.justo,manes.torres}@ehu.es

Abstract. In this work we propose an approach to estimate perplexity values for complex language models such as a language model based on phrase classes. The perplexity values obtained by using this method are compared to other typically employed approaches and to the perplexity obtained without any simplification. Experiments over two different corpora were carried out and it can be concluded that the proposed approach provides a good estimation of the perplexity while reduces the computational cost.

Keywords: Language Model, Perplexity, Automatic Speech Recognition.

1 Introduction

Language Models (LMs) are broadly used in different areas of Natural Language Processing such as, machine translation, information retrieval, automatic speech recognition (ASR),... Within the framework of language modeling for ASR systems, two approaches based on phrase classes were proposed and formulated in previous works [1]. In this work, we would like to compute the Perplexity (PP) value for such complex LMs. However, these calculations could involve a high computational cost, thus, alternative approaches are adopted in other author's works [2,3]. In the same way, we propose a new method to estimate PP values and we compare it to classical approaches employed in the works mentioned above and to the real value of PP. Experimental evaluation was carried out over two different corpora in order to asses the effectiveness of the proposed method. The obtained results show that the proposed approach provides a good estimation of PP.

2 Description of Language Models

In this Section different LMs, that were used in the presented work, are described and formulated. Some of these models are based on the combination of several

* This work has been partially supported by the University of the Basque Country under grant GIU07/57, by the Spanish CICYT under grant TIN2008-06856-C05-01 and by the Spanish program Consolider-Ingenio 2010 under grant CSD2007-00018.

H. Araujo et al. (Eds.): IbPRIA 2009, LNCS 5524, pp. 409–416, 2009.

simpler models. Thus, a syntactic framework that allows the use of Stochastic Finite State Automata (SFSA) was used in this work. Specifically, we chose k-Testable in the Strict Sense (k-TSS) LMs [4] that are considered the syntactic approach of the well known n-gram models. In this way, the whole LM is represented as a combination of several SFSA that can be easily integrated into the ASR system at decoding time.

Moreover, the required smoothing, needed to deal with unseen events, is carried out for each simple model by interpolating K k-TSS models, where $k = 1, \ldots, K$ into a unique smoothed SFSA under a backing-off structure [5].

First of all, two baseline LMs are described in Section 2.1. Then, the LMs based on phrase classes are also briefly described in Section 2.2.

2.1   Baseline Language Models

First of all a classical word k-TSS LM (M_w) is considered. The probability of a word sequence, $\bar{w} = w_1, \ldots, w_N$, using this model is given in Equation 1, where $(k_w - 1)$ stands for the maximum length of the word histories considered.

$$P(\bar{w}) \simeq P_{M_w}(\bar{w}) = \prod_{i=1}^{N} P(w_i | w_{i-k_w+1}^{i-1}) \tag{1}$$

Then a classical class k-TSS LM is considered, M_c. Using such a model the probability of a word sequence $\bar{w}$ is given by Equation 2, where $\mathcal{C}$ is the set of all the possible sequences of classes ($\bar{c}$) generated using a previously defined set of N_c classes of words. ($k_c - 1$) is the maximum length of the class histories and the restriction that each word belongs to a single class was assumed.

$$P(\bar{w}) = \sum_{\forall \bar{c} \in \mathcal{C}} P(\bar{w}|\bar{c})P(\bar{c}) \simeq$$
$$\simeq P_{M_c}(\bar{w}) = \prod_{i=1}^{N} P(w_i|c_i)P(c_i|c_{i-k_c+1}^{i-1}) \tag{2}$$

2.2   LMs Based on Phrase Classes

Finally, two different approaches to LMs based on phrase classes were considered. These two approaches were proposed and properly described and formulated in [1]

- In the first approach, M_{sw}, classes are made up of phrases constituted by not linked words. The probability of a sequence of words, using the M_{sw} model, can be computed by means of Equation 3:

$$P(\bar{w}) = \sum_{\forall \bar{c} \in \mathcal{C}} \sum_{\forall s \in \mathcal{S}_{\bar{c}}(\bar{w})} P(\bar{w}|s, \bar{c})P(s|\bar{c})P(\bar{c}) \tag{3}$$

being $\mathcal{C}$ the set of all the possible sequences of classes , given a predetermined set of classes C. The classes in C are made up of phrases constituted by not linked words. $\mathcal{S}_{\bar{c}}(\bar{w})$ is a set of segmentations (s) of the word sequence $\bar{w}$, which were compatible with the possible sequences of classes ($\bar{c}$) associated with each sequence of words. Then, assuming the following approaches: a k-TSS model to estimate the term $P(\bar{c})$, $P(s|\bar{c}) \simeq \alpha$ and $P(\bar{w}|s,\bar{c})$ estimated with zero order models, Equation 3 is rewritten as Equation 4

$$P(\bar{w}) \simeq P_{M_{sw}}(\bar{w}) = \alpha \sum_{\forall \bar{c} \in \mathcal{C}} \sum_{\forall s \in \mathcal{S}_{\bar{c}}(\bar{w})} \prod_{i=1}^{T}$$
$$\left[\left[\prod_{j=a_{i-1}+1}^{a_i} P(w_j|w_{j-k_{cw}+1}^{j-1}, c_i) \right] P(c_i|c_{i-k_c+1}^{i-1}) \right] \tag{4}$$

In the second approach, M_{sl}, classes are made up of phrases constituted by linked words, $\bar{l}$. The probability of a word sequence using this model is given by Equation 5, being $\mathcal{C}$ the set of all the possible sequences of classes, given a predetermined set of classes C. $\mathcal{L}_{\bar{c}}(\bar{w})$ is the set of all the possible sequences of phrases compatible with the given sequence of words and the possible sequences of classes. Assuming that $P(\bar{c})$ is estimated using a k-TSS model, that $P(\bar{l}|\bar{c})$ is estimated using zero-order models and finally, $P(\bar{w}|\bar{l},\bar{c})$ is equal to 1 for $\bar{l} \in \mathcal{L}_{\bar{c}}(\bar{w})$, and 0 otherwise, then Equation 5 is rewritten as Equation 6 considering that $P(\bar{w}) \simeq P_{M_{sl}}(\bar{w})$.

$$P(\bar{w}) = \sum_{\forall \bar{c} \in \mathcal{C}} \sum_{\forall \bar{l} \in \mathcal{L}_{\bar{c}}(\bar{w})} P(\bar{w}|\bar{l},\bar{c})P(\bar{l}|\bar{c})P(\bar{c}) \tag{5}$$

$$P_{M_{sl}}(\bar{w}) = \sum_{\forall \bar{c} \in \mathcal{C}} \sum_{\forall \bar{l} \in \mathcal{L}_{\bar{c}}(\bar{w})} \prod_{i=1}^{T} \left[P(l_i|c_i)P(c_i|c_{i-k_c+1}^{i-1}) \right] \tag{6}$$

3   Estimating PP Value

The PP gives an idea of the predictive capability of LMs and it is typically employed to measure the performance of them. Thus, it is desirable to obtain the PP value for the LMs described above. It is calculated by using Equation 7.

$$\text{PP} = e^{-\frac{1}{W}log(\prod_{\forall \bar{w}} P(\bar{w}))} \tag{7}$$

where W is the total number of words in the test set and $P(\bar{w})$ is the probability of a word sequence $\bar{w}$ using the language model of choice.

When M_w model is considered, the PP value is easily obtained by introducing the $P_{M_w}(\bar{w})$ value of Equation 1 in the term $P(\bar{w})$ of Equation 7. The same happens with M_c model since each word belongs to an only one class. Nevertheless, when the LMs based on phrase classes are considered, M_{sw} and M_{sl}, all the possible class sequences and all the possible segmentations associated with each sequence of classes, $\bar{c}$, are needed for each sequence of words $\bar{w}$ to obtain the $P_{M_{sw}}(\bar{w})$ and $P_{M_{sl}}(\bar{w})$ values, as shown in Equations 4 and 6. When the number of segmentations associated with each word sequence increases a lot (due to very long sentences in the test corpus for instance) this method (baseline case) could result in a very high computational cost, thus, alternative approaches could be considered in order to avoid this problem.

3.1   Approach1

In several author's work [2,3], the maximum is considered as an approach to the sum over all the probabilities when dealing with the computation of PP. In such cases only the segmentation and classification choice that provides the maximum probability is considered. The $P(\bar{w})$ term to be introduced in Equation 7 is calculated using Equation 8 for M_{sw} and Equation 9 for M_{sl} model. It must be taken into account that the maximization is globally done, that is, considering the whole sequence. Therefore, the probability associated with all the possible s and $\bar{c}$ must be calculated, thus, although it is not necessary to save in memory all the probabilities but only the best one, a high computational cost is still associated to this process. In this work we use the results obtained with this approach for comparison purposes.

$$P_{M_{sw}}(\bar{w}) \simeq \alpha \max_{\forall \bar{c} \in \mathcal{C}} \max_{\forall s \in \mathcal{S}_{\bar{c}}(\bar{w})} \prod_{i=1}^{T} \left[\left[\prod_{j=a_{i-1}+1}^{a_i} P(w_j | w_{j-k_{cw}+1}^{j-1}, c_i) \right] P(c_i | c_{i-k_c+1}^{i-1}) \right] \tag{8}$$

$$P_{M_{sl}}(\bar{w}) \simeq \max_{\forall \bar{c} \in \mathcal{C}} \max_{\forall \bar{l} \in \mathcal{L}_{\bar{c}}(\bar{w})} \prod_{i=1}^{T} \left[P(l_i | c_i) P(c_i | c_{i-k_c+1}^{i-1}) \right] \tag{9}$$

3.2   Approach2

In this work, we propose a new method where an only one segmentation and classification are considered for each sequence of words by employing a dynamic programming algorithm that carries out the maximization locally (Viterbi algorithm). In this case, the obtained result is not the one with the highest probability, a suboptimal result is obtained, but the computational cost is significantly reduced.

Thus, $\bar{w}$ is considered to be produced by a Markov chain, where its p_i states correspond to the SFSA associated with the LM of choice (M_{sw} for the Equation 10). The specific segmentation and classification for a word sequence $\bar{w}$ according to the Viterbi algorithm is given by the Equation below.

$$[\hat{s}, \hat{\bar{c}}] = \arg\max_{\forall \bar{c} \in \mathcal{C}, \forall s \in \mathcal{S}_{\bar{c}}(\bar{w})} P(\bar{c}, s) P(\bar{w} | \bar{c}, s) = \arg\max_{\forall \bar{c} \in \mathcal{C}, \forall s \in \mathcal{S}_{\bar{c}}(\bar{w})} P(s | \bar{c}) P(\bar{c}) P(\bar{w} | \bar{c}, s) \tag{10}$$

where $P(\bar{w} | \bar{c}, s) = \sum_{p_0^N} P(\bar{w}, p_0^N | \bar{c}, s)$, N is the number of words in $\bar{w}$ and $p_i^{i+j} = p_i, \ldots, p_{i+j}$ represents a sequence of p_i states.

Using the Viterbi algorithm the obtained $\hat{\bar{c}}$ and $\hat{s}$ are not the most likely segmentation and class sequence, but they correspond to the best sequence of

Table 1. Features of DIHANA and WSJ corpora

		DIHANA	WSJ
Training	Sentences	8,606	298,574
	Different sent.	5,590	283,674
	Words	77,476	5,724,701
	Vocabulary	865	4,954
	Audio Length	8.5 h.	~ 60 h.
Test	Sentences	1,349	215
	Words	12,365	4,064
	Vocabulary	503	1,030

p_i states of the decoding network. The probability for M_{sw} and M_{sl} models are then given in Equations 11 and 12 respectively, being L the no. states needed to reach the end of the word sequence in M_{sl}.

$$P_{M_{sw}}(\bar{w}) \simeq \max_{\forall \bar{c} \in \mathcal{C}} \max_{\forall s \in \mathcal{S}_{\bar{c}}(\bar{w})} \left[P(\bar{c}, s) \max_{p_0^N} P(\bar{w}, p_0^N | \bar{c}, s) \right] \tag{11}$$

$$P_{M_{sl}}(\bar{w}) \simeq \max_{\forall \bar{c} \in \mathcal{C}} \max_{\forall \bar{l} \in \mathcal{L}_{\bar{c}}(\bar{w})} \left[P(\bar{c}, \bar{l}) \max_{p_0^L} P(\bar{w}, p_0^L | \bar{c}, \bar{l}) \right] \tag{12}$$

4   Experimental Results

The experiments were carried out over two different corpora. The first one is a task-oriented corpus that consists of human-machine dialogues in Spanish, DI-HANA [6], acquired by a Consortium of Spanish Universities. In this corpus 225 speakers ask by telephone for information about long-distance train timetables, fares, destinations and services. Since DIHANA is a corpus of a limited size and highly irregular due to the spontaneity of the speech, Wall Street Journal (WSJ) corpus was also used to carry out experiments. The WSJ1 with 5K vocabulary training set was employed to build the LMs and HUB2 test set was employed for evaluation. Features of the different corpora are given in Table 1.

The PP values for the LMs described in Section 2 were calculated making use of the three methods detailed in Section 3. When dealing with the DIHANA corpus the following models were generated: M_w, M_c, M_{sw} and M_{sl}. For the M_w model a value of $k_w = 2$ was selected and for all of the class-based models a value of $k_c = 2$. Regarding M_c model different sets of 100, 200, 300 and 400 statistical classes
made up of single words were obtained making use of *mkcls*. *mkcls* is a free tool that provides a set of statistical classes by using a clustering algorithm based on a maximum likelihood approach and developed by [7]. M_{sw} and M_{sl} were built employing different sets of 100, 200, 300 and 400 statistical classes made up of phrases. The set of phrases was selected using a statistical criterion (as describes [8]) and the set of classes by means of *mkcls* again. The obtained results are shown in Table 2.

Table 2. PP results obtained with the three methods (Baseline, Approach1 and Approach2) and WER over DIHANA

			PP DIHANA			WER
			Base.	App 1	App 2	
M_w			22.20			21.69
M_c	no. classes	100	21.01	21.01	21.01	19.77
		200	20.17	20.17	20.17	
		300	20.51	20.51	20.51	(200 clas.)
		400	20.81	20.81	20.81	
M_{sw}	no. classes	100	18.25	18.73	18.40	18.46
		200	17.08	17.42	17.21	
		300	17.12	17.36	17.23	(200 clas.)
		400	17.56	17.76	17.63	
M_{sl}	no. classes	100	18.10	18.54	18.53	18.15
		200	16.90	17.24	17.24	
		300	16.92	17.15	17.15	(200 clas.)
		400	17.38	17.57	17.57	

When dealing with WSJ the same models were generated using here values of $k_w = 3$ and $k_c = 3$. In this case M_c model was built using different sets of 3,000, 4,000, 4,500 and 4,954 classes. Alternatively, M_{sw} and M_{sl} were built employing different sets of 3,000, 4,000, 4,500 and 5,000 classes of phrases. The sets of classes and phrases were obtained by employing the aforementioned statistical methods again. The results are given in Table 3.

Regarding PP results obtained with both, DIHANA and WSJ corpora, if we compare the values obtained with the different approaches for M_{sw} and M_{sl} models, it can be seen that Approach1 provides slightly higher PP values than the baseline case, as it was expected. However, the obtained results are quite similar and the rate between the two values remains constant, so Approach1 could be considered as a good approach and it is used in other author's work as mentioned above. Nevertheless, the computational cost of this calculation could result still high. Regarding the results obtained with the proposed method (Approach2), the achieved PP values are very similar to those obtained with Approach1 for both M_{sw} and M_{sl} models and using both DIHANA and WSJ corpora. Thus, it can be concluded that Approach2, being the one that has the lower computational cost (the processing time is reduced 60 times with regard to the Approach1) provides a good estimation of the PP value.

Comparing the PP results obtained for the different LMs using the DIHANA corpus, Table 2 shows that M_{sw} and M_{sl} models provide better PP values than M_w and M_c and that the best PP values are achieved with 200 classes for all the models. Moreover, the same PP values were calculated over WSJ that is a higher sized corpus with more regular sentences. The results shown in Table 3 show that M_{sw} and M_{sl} models provide, also in this case, values of PP significantly lower than M_c and M_w models. The best PP values are obtained with 4,500 classes for all of the evaluated models.

Table 3. PP results obtained with the three methods (Baseline, Approach1 and Approach2) and WER results over WSJ

	no. classes	PP WSJ Base.	App 1	App 2	WER
M_w		64.79			18.21
M_c	3000	64.5	64.5	64.5	19.90
	4000	64.33	64.33	64.33	
	4500	64.15	64.15	64.15	(4,500 clas)
	4954	64.79	64.79	64.79	
M_{sw}	3000	61.34	61.45	61.46	18.82
	4000	60.11	60.21	60.22	
	4500	60.01	60.11	60.12	(4,500 clas)
	5000	60.59	60.69	60.72	
M_{sl}	3000	61.64	61.73	61.73	18.25
	4000	60.66	60.76	60.76	
	4500	60.08	60.19	60.19	(4,500 clas)
	5000	60.71	60.81	60.81	

Table 4. Total no. phrases in different corpora and the no. phrases having 5, 4, 3, 2 and 1 words

		no. phrases DIHANA	WSJ
phrase vocab.		1288	5302
no. words in a phrase	5	35 (%2.7)	6 (%0.1)
	4	46 (%3.6)	21 (%0.4)
	3	107 (%8.3)	93 (%1.7)
	2	184 (%14.3)	228 (%4.3)
	1	916 (%71.1)	4954 (%93.4)

Finally, we chose the optimum number of classes achieved in the evaluation (in terms of PP) and we integrated those models into an ASR system. WER results were obtained. Regarding DIHANA corpus the best results were achieved with the M_{sl} and M_{sw} models (see Table 2). That is, PP improvements are translated into WER improvements. However, when dealing with WSJ corpus although PP improvements achieved with LMs based on phrase classes are noticeable, the improvement in terms of WER is not so significant. Moreover the M_w model provides similar or even better WER values (see Table 3). This could be owing to the fact that the number of phrases having more than a word, relative to the total number of phrases, is much smaller in this corpus than it was in DIHANA corpus as Table 4 shows. This effect can also be noticed analyzing carefully the PP results. The PP values obtained with the proposed Approach2 for M_{sw} and DIHANA corpus are slightly lower than those obtained with Approach1. This happens because, due to the nature of this model, it can provide new segmentations, sometimes with higher probabilities, that are not considered when the defined set of phrases is taken into account. Let us show an example of a specific class c = { "de ida", "billete de ida y vuelta", "billete"} and a word sequence ($\bar{w}$ = billete de ida). Considering a 2-TSS model inside the classes of the M_{sw} model, "billete de ida" could be considered because the bigrams "billete de" and "de ida" are possible although they are not in the set of phrases, when the Viterbi algorithm is used. In the WSJ corpus this effect is not noticeable because the relative number of phrases having more than a word is much smaller. For further work we propose to explore a new set of phrases for WSJ, with a higher number of multi-word phrases.

5 Conclusions

In this paper an approach that considers the Viterbi algorithm is proposed to estimate PP value for complex models based on phrase classes. The obtained results over two different corpora are compared to other approaches and to the real value of PP. It can be concluded that the proposed method provides a good estimation of the PP value while reduces the computational cost. The evaluation of the models in terms of PP is also employed to choose the optimum number of classes for class-based models. Thus, those models were integrated into an ASR system in order to evaluate them in terms of WER.

References

1. Justo, R., Torres, M.I.: Phrase classes in two-level language models for ASR. Pattern Analysis and Applications Journal (in press) (2008)
2. Yamamoto, H., Isogai, S., Sagisaka, Y.: Multi-class composite n-gram language model. Speech Communication 41(2-3), 369–379 (2003)
3. Zitouni, I.: A hierarchical language model based on variable-length class sequences: the mcni approach. IEEE Trans. on Speech and Audio Proc. 10(3), 193–198 (2002)
4. García, P., Vidal, E.: Inference of k-testable languages in the strict sense and application to syntactic pattern recognition. IEEE Trans. Pattern Anal. Mach. Intell. 12(9), 920–925 (1990)
5. Torres, I., Varona, A.: k-tss language models in speech recognition systems. Computer Speech and Language 15(2), 127–149 (2001)
6. Benedí, J., Lleida, E., Varona, A., Castro, M., Galiano, I., Justo, R., López, I., Miguel, A.: Design and acquisition of a telephone spontaneous speech dialogue corpus in Spanish: DIHANA. In: Proc. of LREC 2006, Genoa, Italy (May 2006)
7. Och, F.J.: An efficient method for determining bilingual word classes. In: Proceedings of the ninth conference on European chapter of the ACL, Bergen, Norway, pp. 71–76 (1999)
8. Justo, R., Torres, M.I.: Two approaches to class-based language models for asr. In: IEEE Workshop on MLSP, Thessaloniki, Greece, August 27-29 (2007)

An Adaptive Approach for Affine-Invariant 2D Shape Description

A. Bandera[1], E. Antúnez[2], and R. Marfil[1]

[1] Grupo ISIS, Dpto. Tecnología Electrónica
University of Málaga, Spain
{ajbandera,rebeca}@uma.es
[2] PRIP, Vienna University of Technology, Austria
eortiz@prip.tuwien.ac.at

Abstract. In this paper, a new algorithm for 2D shape characterization is proposed. This method characterizes a planar object using a triangle-area representation obtained from its closed contour. As main novelty with respect to previous approaches, in our approach the triangle side lengths at each contour point are adapted to the local variations of the shape, removing noise from the contour without missing relevant points. This representation is invariant to affine transformations, and robust against noise. The performance of our proposal is demonstrated using a standard test on the well-known MPEG-7 CE-shape-1 data set.

1   Introduction

The increasing number of applications which relies on multimedia databases has motivated that object representation and recognition will be the subject of much research. Among other image features which are used to achieve this goal, like colour or texture, shape is commonly considered the most promising tool to represent and identify objects [1]. Among other shape descriptors [2], this paper is focused on those techniques which attempt to represent shapes using the curvature of their outer boundaries.

For continuous curves, the curvature is an unambiguously defined concept that admits precise analytical formulations involving the first and second order directional derivatives of the plane curve coordinates. However, this is not the same in the case of computational analysis, where the plane curve is represented in a digital form [2]. The literature on curvature estimators for digital curves is relatively huge. Thus, there are interpolation-based curvature estimators which approximate the plane curve coordinates [3], and approaches that employ an alternative measure of curvature [4,1,5,6]. Most of these approaches remove the plane curve noise by specifying a region-of-support for each curve point where a local measure of curvature will be estimated. However, if this region-of-support presents a fixed size, this process implies to filter the curve descriptor at a fixed cut frequency (*single-scale methods*). As features appear at different natural scales, single scale methods only detect the features unaffected by this filtering process. To avoid this problem, *multi-scale methods* have been

H. Araujo et al. (Eds.): IbPRIA 2009, LNCS 5524, pp. 417–424, 2009.
© Springer-Verlag Berlin Heidelberg 2009

proposed. These approaches typically use iterative feature detection for different sizes of the region-of-support, i.e. different cut frequencies. Thus, a popular solution is the curvature scale space (CSS) [3], which filters the curve descriptor with a Gaussian kernel and imparts smoothing at different levels of scale (the scale being proportional to the width of the kernel). Instead of these iterative approaches, a more computationally cheap solution is to adapt the cut frequency of the filter at each curve point as a function of the local properties of the shape around it (*adaptive methods*), e.g. using a Gaussian filter of variable bandwidth [7].

In this paper, a new adaptive algorithm for measuring the curvature of the outer boundary of digitized closed curves is presented. The proposed algorithm approximates the curvature at each shape point by the area of a triangle whose vertices depend on the local region-of-support of this point. In order to calculate this region-of-support, the normalized area of the region delimited by the arc and the chord is monitored at both sides of every contour point. The region-of-support continues to grow from each side of the point as long as this normalized area remains below a threshold, which is set according to the area of the whole shape. The main advantage of the proposed approach is that the process to determine the region-of-support as well as the shape descriptor are invariant under general affine transformations. Section 2 presents the proposed method. Experimental results revealing the efficacy of the method are described in Section 3. The paper concludes along with discussions and future work in Section 4.

2   Proposed Method

2.1   Adaptive Estimation of the Region-of-Support

Teh and Chin [8] pointed out that the estimation of the shape curvature relies primarily on the precise calculation of the region-of-support associated to each contour point. Thus, they estimated the region-of-support for each point based on the chord length and the perpendicular distance to the chord. The region-of-support is extended from each boundary point outwards until certain conditions are violated [8]. Following this proposal, Bandera et al [6] propose to monitor the normalized difference between the arc and chord lengths. The region-of-support continues to grow from each side of the point of interest as long as this ratio remains below a fixed threshold, which is set to provide a more robust shape representation in presence of noise. In order to estimate the region-of-support at each boundary point, Marji and Siy [2] propose to maximize the difference between the chord length and the sum of the squared perpendicular distances from the boundary points to the line segment that defines the chord. Wu [9] proposes to determine the region-of-support of each point looking for the neighbor point which maximizes the k-cosine between both points.

As it can be noted, most of the approaches proposed to estimate the region-of-support are based on criteria which employ the Euclidean distance between points to compute, by example, the chord length or the k-cosine. Therefore, under general affine transformations, these criteria could generate regions which are not covariant with this transformation. In order to ensure that the region-of-support of every contour point remains covariant under general affine transformations, we will define a criterion to define the size of this region which is based on the area of triangles inner to the shape. The area of any triangle is relatively affine invariant and the ratios of such areas are affine invariant [10].

Let each contour point be represented by its x and y coordinates. Then, separated parameterized contour sequences x_n and y_n are obtained and re-sampled to N points. To specify the region-of-support associated to the point i of the shape contour, the algorithm must determine the maximum length of shape contour presenting no significant discontinuities on the right and left sides of the point i, $t_f[i]$ and $t_b[i]$, respectively. To estimate the $t_f[i]$ value, the algorithm firstly computes two set of triangles, $\{t_j^a\}_{j=i}^{i+t_f[i]-1}$ and $\{t_j^c\}_{j=i}^{i+t_f[i]-1}$ (see Fig. 1). The area of the triangle t_j^a is defined as

$$|t_j^a| = \frac{1}{2} \begin{vmatrix} x_j & x_c & x_{j+1} \\ y_j & y_c & y_{j+1} \\ 1 & 1 & 1 \end{vmatrix} \tag{1}$$

where (x_j, y_j) and (x_{j+1}, y_{j+1}) are the arc points j and $j+1$ and (x_c, y_c) is the area centre of gravity of the shape R, $\mathbf{x}_c$. This is a geometric primitive covariant with affine transformations which can be calculated as [11]

$$\mathbf{x}_c = \frac{1}{|R|} \int_R \mathbf{x} dR \tag{2}$$

where $|R|$ is the area of the shape R.

The area of the triangle t_j^c is defined as

$$|t_j^c| = \frac{1}{2} \begin{vmatrix} x_j^p & x_c & x_{j+1}^p \\ y_j^p & y_c & y_{j+1}^p \\ 1 & 1 & 1 \end{vmatrix} \tag{3}$$

where (x_j^p, y_j^p) is the intersection of the line that joins (x_j, y_j) and (x_c, y_c) with the chord which joins the contour points i and $i + t_f[i]$.

If $T_{i,t_f[i]}^a$ and $T_{i,t_f[i]}^c$ are equal to $\sum_{j=i}^{i+t_f[i]-1} |t_j^a|$ and $\sum_{j=i}^{i+t_f[i]-1} |t_j^c|$, respectively, then $t_f[i]$ will be defined by the largest value that satisfies

$$((T_{i,t_f[i]}^a \cup T_{i,t_f[i]}^c) - (T_{i,t_f[i]}^a \cap T_{i,t_f[i]}^c)) < U \tag{4}$$

The threshold U has been set as a percentage of the area of the shape. In Section 2.3, it is shown that the area of a transformed shape, $S' = \mathbf{A}S + \mathbf{t}$ equals $|\mathbf{A}|$ times the area of the original shape S. Then, this threshold will change covariantly with the affine transform. Fig. 1 shows the process to extract one $t_f[i]$ value. $t_b[i]$ is also set according to the described scheme, but using $i - t_b[i]$ instead of $i + t_f[i]$.

The correct selection of the U value is very important. Thus, if the value of U is large, $t_f[i]$ and $t_b[i]$ tend to be large and contour details may be missed and, if it is small, $t_f[i]$ and $t_b[i]$ are always very small and the resulting function

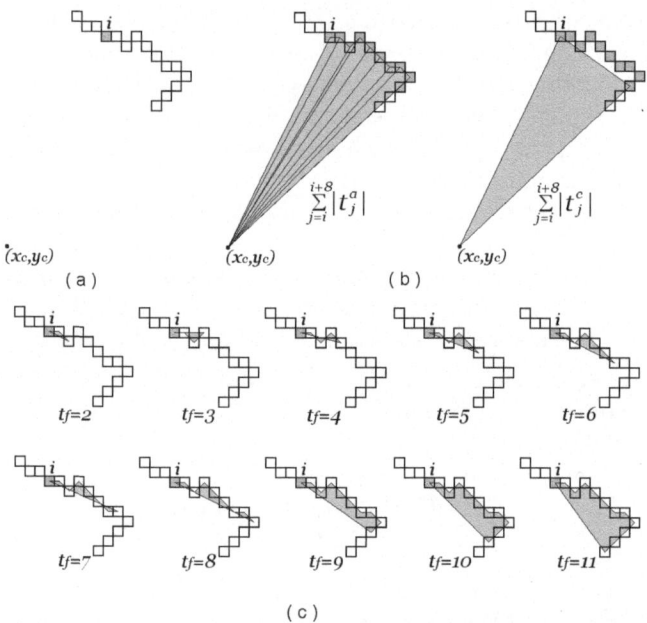

Fig. 1. Calculation of the maximum length of contour presenting no significant discontinuity on the right side of point i ($t_f[i]$): a) Part of the shape contour and point i; b) one example of estimation of $\sum_{j=i}^{i+t_f[i]-1} |t_j^a|$ and $\sum_{j=i}^{i+t_f[i]-1} |t_j^c|$ for $t_f[i]=9$; and c) evolution of the area delimited by the arc and the chord $((\sum_{j=i}^{i+t_f[i]-1} |t_j^a| \cup \sum_{j=i}^{i+t_f[i]-1} |t_j^c|) - (\sum_{j=i}^{i+t_f[i]-1} |t_j^a| \cap \sum_{j=i}^{i+t_f[i]-1} |t_j^c|))$. It can be noted that this area suffers a sharp increasing when $t_f[i] \geq 8$. This change allows to estimate the correct $t_f[i]$ value and it will be detected in our approach using the Eq. (4) (in this case, $t_f[i]=8$).

is noisy. In this work, the fixed U value provokes a slightly smoothing of the contours. This will be interesting to match noisy shapes with the original one in the shape retrieval framework where the proposed approach will be tested.

2.2 Affine-Invariant Shape Descriptor

The area of the triangle formed by the outer boundary points can be used as the basis for shape representations [1]. The proposed shape recognition system employs a curvature estimator to characterize the shape contour which is based on this triangle-area representation (TAR). Given a shape and, once our proposal have determined the local region-of-support associated to every point of its contour, the process to extract the associated TAR consists of the following steps:

1. Calculation of the local vectors $\boldsymbol{f_i}$ and $\boldsymbol{b_i}$ associated to each point i. These vectors present the variation in the x and y axis between points i and $i+t_f[i]$, and between i and $i-t_b[i]$. If (x_i, y_i) are the Cartesian coordinates of the point i, the local vectors associated to i are defined as

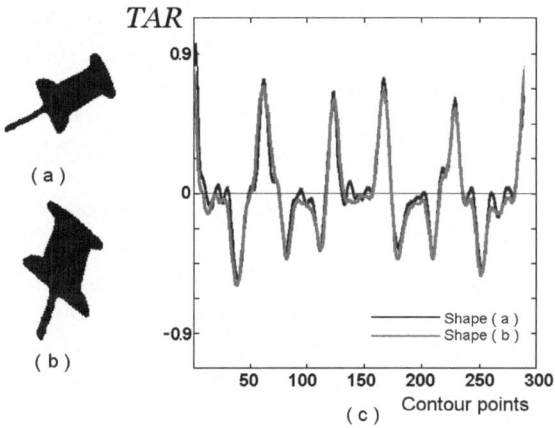

Fig. 2. a) Shape #1; b) shape #2; and c) adaptive TARs associated to a) and b)

$$\boldsymbol{f_i} = (x_{i+t_f[i]} - x_i, y_{i+t_f[i]} - y_i) = (f_{x_i}, f_{y_i})$$
$$\boldsymbol{b_i} = (x_{i-t_b[i]} - x_i, y_{i-t_b[i]} - y_i) = (b_{x_i}, b_{y_i}) \tag{5}$$

2. Calculation of the TAR associated to each contour point. The signed area of the triangle at contour point i is given by [1]:

$$\kappa_i = \frac{1}{2} \begin{vmatrix} b_{x_i} & b_{y_i} & 1 \\ 0 & 0 & 1 \\ f_{x_i} & f_{y_i} & 1 \end{vmatrix} \tag{6}$$

3. TAR Normalization. The TAR of the whole contour, $\{\kappa_i\}_{i=1}^N$, is normalized by dividing it by its absolute maximum value.

When the contour is traversed in counter clockwise direction, positive, negative and zero values of TAR mean convex, concave and straight-line points, respectively. Fig. 2 shows two shapes. The shape at Fig. 2b has been obtained by transforming (translation, scaling, skewing and rotation) the shape at Fig. 2a. Fig. 2c presents the TARs associated to Figs. 2a-b. They have been resized to the same value. It can be noted that the representations are practically equal.

2.3   Our Shape Descriptor under General Affine Transformations

Let $\{x_i, y_i\}_{i=1}^N$ be the Cartesian coordinates of the shape contour. If this shape is subjected to an affine transformation, the relation between the original and the distorted contour representations is given by

$$\begin{bmatrix} \hat{x}_i \\ \hat{y}_i \end{bmatrix} = \begin{bmatrix} a & b \\ c & d \end{bmatrix} \begin{bmatrix} x_i \\ y_i \end{bmatrix} + \begin{bmatrix} t_1 \\ t_2 \end{bmatrix} \tag{7}$$

where $\{\hat{x}_i, \hat{y}_i\}_{i=1}^N$ is the affine distorted representation of the shape contour, a, b, c and d represent scale, rotation and shear and t_1 and t_2 represent translation.

Lemma 1. *Let $\{x_i, y_i\}_{i=1}^N$ and $\{\hat{x}_i, \hat{y}_i\}_{i=1}^N$ be the Cartesian coordinates of a shape contours S and its affine transformed version S'. If $S' = \mathbf{A}S + t$, then the area of S' is $|\mathbf{A}|$ times the area of S, $|S'| = |\mathbf{A}||S|$.*

Proof. The shape S' is formed by the points $\{\hat{\mathbf{x}} | \hat{\mathbf{x}} = \mathbf{A}\mathbf{x} + t; \mathbf{x} \in S\}$. Hence, the area of S' is [11]

$$|S'| = \int_{S'} dS' = \int_S |\mathbf{A}| dS = |\mathbf{A}||S'| \tag{8}$$

Lemma 2. *Let $\{x_i, y_i\}$ be the Cartesian coordinates of a shape contour point of S. Let C be the shape formed by the maximum set of consecutive points $\{\{x_i, y_i\}, \{x_{i+1}, y_{i+1}\}...\{x_{i+t_f}, y_{i+t_f}\}\}$ whose area is less than $U = k|S|$, $|C| < k|S|$. If $\{\hat{x}_i, \hat{y}_i\}$ is the corresponding affine transformed version of $\{x_i, y_i\}$ on S' and the number of points of S and S' are the same, then the set of consecutive contour points $\{\{\hat{x}_i, \hat{y}_i\}, \{\hat{x}_{i+1}, \hat{y}_{i+1}\}...\{\hat{x}_{i+\hat{t}_f}, \hat{y}_{i+\hat{t}_f}\}\}$ conforms the bigger shape C' which is less than $U' = k|S'|$ iff t_f is equal to $\hat{t}_f$.*

Proof. If $S' = \mathbf{A}S + t$, then $|S'| = |\mathbf{A}||S|$. Besides, if $U = k|S|$ is the threshold used to find the $\{t_f, t_b\}$ values on S, then $U' = k|S'| = k|\mathbf{A}||S|$ is the threshold which will be used to find the $\{\hat{t}_f, \hat{t}_b\}$ values. As the shapes C and C' are related by $C' = \mathbf{A}C + t$ and $|C| < k|S|$, then $|C'| = |\mathbf{A}||C| < |\mathbf{A}|k|S| = k|S'|$.

Lemma 3. *The TAR representations associated to a shape contours S and its affine transformed version S' are equal.*

Proof. According to Lemma 2, given a shape contours S and its affine transformed version S', if both shapes have the same number of points N, then the $\{\hat{t}_f, \hat{t}_b\}$ values associated to each point i of S' will be equal to the $\{t_f, t_b\}$ values associated to its corresponding point i of S. By substituting the expressions for $\{\hat{x}_i, \hat{y}_i\}_{i=1}^N$ into Eq. (5), we obtain

$$\begin{aligned}
f_{\hat{x}_i} &= \hat{x}_{i+\hat{t}_f[i]} - \hat{x}_i = \hat{x}_{i+t_f[i]} - \hat{x}_i = a(x_{i+t_f[i]} - x_i) + b(y_{i+t_f[i]} - y_i) = af_{x_i} + bf_{y_i} \\
f_{\hat{y}_i} &= c(x_{i+t_f[i]} - x_i) + d(y_{i+t_f[i]} - y_i) = c \cdot f_{x_i} + d \cdot f_{y_i} \\
b_{\hat{x}_i} &= a(x_{i-t_b[i]} - x_i) + b(y_{i-t_b[i]} - y_i) = a \cdot b_{x_i} + b \cdot b_{y_i} \\
b_{\hat{y}_i} &= c(x_{i-t_b[i]} - x_i) + d(y_{i-t_b[i]} - y_i) = c \cdot b_{x_i} + d \cdot b_{y_i}
\end{aligned} \tag{9}$$

Then, if we substitute (9) into (6), it is obtained that $\hat{\kappa}_i = (ad - bc)\kappa_i$, where $\hat{\kappa}_i$ is the affine transformed version of κ_i. As $\{\kappa_i\}$ is normalized, then its maximum value is 1.0 and the maximum value of $\{\hat{\kappa}_i\}$ will be $(ad - bc)$. If $\{\hat{\kappa}_i\}$ is also normalized by this maximum, then both representations will be equal.

3   Experimental Results

In order to test the proposed shape representation into a more general shape retrieval framework, it is also needed to address the problem of comparing the current shape with a set of stored ones. This matching stage must take into

Fig. 3. Some example of shape images from the MPEG-7 CE-shape-1

Table 1. Comparison of the results of different curvature-based approaches on the MPEG-7 CE-shape-1 part B (Bull's Eye test). It must be noted that the percentage retrieval for our proposal is similar to the state-of-the-art but it is faster (see text).

CSS	AM	BAS	Proposed	MCC	DSW
81.12 %	81.73 %	82.37 %	84.97 %	84.93 %	85.03 %

account the different boundary lengths of the shapes to compare. In our case, the dynamic time warping (DTW) has been employed to find the best alignment between two shape representations.

The performance of the shape descriptor is demonstrated using a standard experiment on the well-known MPEG-7 CE-shape-1 database [4]. This data set contains 1400 silhouette images semantically classified into 70 classes. Each class has 20 different shapes. Fig. 3 shows several shape images.

Specifically, the retrieval performance of the proposed descriptor is evaluated using the MPEG-7 CE-shape-1 part B test. The total number of images in the database was used here. Each class was used as a query, and the number of similar images (which belong to the same group) was counted in the top 40 matches (Bull's Eye score). As it has been mentioned in previous works [4,1], 100% retrieval is not possible, since some groups contain objects whose shape is significantly different so that is not possible to classify them into the same group using only shape information. In order to evaluate the performance of the proposed method, the results of several curvature-based approaches on this same test has been compared. The chosen approaches are the dynamic space warping (DSW) [1]; the multi-scale convexity concavity (MCC) representation [4]; the beam angle statistics (BAS) [5]; the curvature scale space (CSS) [3]; and the adaptive approach (AM) [6]. All these methods use dynamic programming to compare the shape descriptor with the ones stored in the databases. Table 1 presents the results of these methods on the MPEG-7 CE-shape-1 part B test. Our results are better than the ones provided by the CSS and BAS approaches and similar to the ones provided by the DSW and MCC methods. However, the reported complexities of these last two multi-scale approaches for shape description (i.e., not taken into account the matching process), when they are applied to a contour length of N points, are $\mathcal{O}(N^2)$ for the DSW and $\mathcal{O}(N^3)$ for the MCC [1]. On the contrary, the complexity of our approach is $\mathcal{O}(N)$, as it is directly related to the contour length.

4   Conclusions

In this paper, an affine-invariant closed-contour shape representation that employs the triangle-area representation to measure the convexity/concavity of each contour point is described. The proposed method uses an adaptive algorithm to determine the region-of-support associated to every contour point. This algorithm allows to define a region-of-support which changes covariantly with the affine transform. The proposed shape descriptor is invariant to translation, rotation and scaling and it is also robust against moderate amounts of noise.

Acknowledgements

This work has been partially granted by the Spanish Junta de Andalucía project P07-TIC-03106 and by the Austrian Science Fond under grants P18716-N13 and S9103-N13.

References

1. Alajlan, N., El Rube, I., Kamel, M., Freeman, G.: Shape retrieval using triangle-area representation and dynamic space warping. Pattern Recognition 40, 1911–1920 (2007)
2. Marji, M., Siy, P.: A new algorithm for dominant points detection and polygonization of digital curves. Pattern Recognition 36, 2239–2251 (2003)
3. Mokhtarian, F., Bober, M.: Curvature Scale Space Representation: Theory, Applications, and MPEG-7 Standardization. Kluwer Academic Publishers, Dordrecht (2003)
4. Adamek, T., O'Connor, N.: A multiscale representation method for nonrigid shapes with a single closed contour. IEEE Trans. Circuit Syst. Video Technol. 14, 742–753 (2004)
5. Arica, N., Vural, F.: Bas: a perceptual shape descriptor based on the beam angle statistics. Pattern Recognition Letters 24, 1627–1639 (2003)
6. Bandera, A., Urdiales, C., Arrebola, F., Sandoval, F.: Corner detection by means of adaptively estimated curvature function. Electronics Letters 36, 124–126 (2000)
7. Ansari, N., Delp, E.: On detecting dominant points. Pattern Recognition 24, 441–451 (1991)
8. Teh, C., Chin, R.: On the detection of dominant points on digital curves. IEEE Trans. on Pattern Anal. Machine Intell. 11, 859–872 (1989)
9. Wu, W.: An adaptive method for detecting dominant points. Pattern Recognition 36, 2231–2237 (2003)
10. Shen, D., Ip, H., Teoh, E.: Affine invariant detection of perceptually parallel 3D planar curves. Pattern Recognition 33, 1909–1918 (2000)
11. Obdrzálek, S., Matas, J.: Object recognition using local affine frames on maximally stable extremal regions. In: Ponce, J., Hebert, M., Schmid, C., Zisserman, A. (eds.) Toward Category-Level Object Recognition. LNCS, vol. 4170, pp. 83–104. Springer, Heidelberg (2006)

Towards Real-Time Human Action Recognition

Bhaskar Chakraborty, Andrew D. Bagdanov, and Jordi Gonzàlez

Departament de Ciències de la Computació and Computer Vision Center
Universitat Autonoma de Barcelona,
Campus UAB Edifici O
08193 Bellaterra, Spain
bhaskar@cvc.uab.es

Abstract. This work presents a novel approach to human detection based action-recognition in real-time. To realize this goal our method first detects humans in different poses using a correlation-based approach. Recognition of actions is done afterward based on the change of the angular values subtended by various body parts. Real-time human detection and action recognition are very challenging, and most state-of-the-art approaches employ complex feature extraction and classification techniques, which ultimately becomes a handicap for real-time recognition. Our correlation-based method, on the other hand, is computationally efficient and uses very simple gradient-based features. For action recognition angular features of body parts are extracted using a skeleton technique. Results for action recognition are comparable with the present state-of-the-art.

Keywords: Human detection, Action recognition, Correlation, Skeletonization.

1 Introduction

Visual recognition and understanding of human actions are among the most important research areas in computer vision [15]. Good solutions to these problems would yield huge potential for many applications such as the search and the structuring of large video archives, video surveillance, human-computer interaction, gesture recognition and video editing. Human detection and action recognition are extremely challenging due to the non-rigid nature of humans in video sequences due to changes in pose, changing illumination conditions, and erratic, non-linear motion. Most state-of-the-art techniques apply sophisticated feature extraction and classification techniques to the problem, creating a barrier to real-time detection and action recognition in realistic scenarios.

In our proposed approach, human detection is done prior to action recognition. The process of human detection is realized by computing the correlation of a test region with components obtained from training images of humans in different poses. Gradient-based features are extracted to build different pose correlation masks. A test region is considered to be human if the computed correlation coefficient is maximum among all regions in the image. Once human detection

H. Araujo et al. (Eds.): IbPRIA 2009, LNCS 5524, pp. 425–432, 2009.

is done, skeletonization is applied to extract straight-line estimations of limbs, from which we compute angular changes in a sequence of images. These angular features are used to learn different action classes and a simple Euclidean distance measure is used to classify actions.

The performance is close to real-time due to the fact that the method of correlation, the skeletonization process and angular feature extraction are very simple, yet robust, techniques and have low run time complexity. We demonstrate the effectiveness of our approach on three different types of actions chosen from a standard human action database [17]. The recognition rate is compared with current state of the art [17].

In the next section we review relevant work in the literature. Section 2.2 describes our approach to human detection and in section 2 the technique for human action recognition is described. Section 4 reports some preliminary experimental results of the overall approach on a standard human action database. In section 5 we conclude with some discussion and indications of future research.

1.1   Related Work

Human detection based action recognition has become an important area of research in recent years. Many approaches can be found in the literature [15], but most current methods are based on holistic body parts. In the work of Ahmad et al. [1], action recognition is done using human body silhouette features and the Cartesian component of optical flow velocity. Human action models are created in each viewing direction for some specific actions using a Hidden Markov Model (HMM). Classification is done by feeding a given test sequence in any viewing direction to all the learned HMMs and employing a likelihood measure to declare the action performed in the image sequence.

In [13], action recognition is performed by learning motion features and projecting them onto lower-dimensional manifold. Motion information is computed using an Infinite Impulse Response filter, similar to Davis and Bobick [7]. Principal Component Analysis (PCA) is used for dimensionality reduction of features.

Authors like Gorelick et al. [9] use space-time features such as time saliency, action dynamics, shape structure and orientation for action recognition. This approach is based on the observation that in video sequences a human action generates a space-time shape in the space-time volume. Some techniques recognize human actions using an HMM based on a contour histogram of the full body [14]. The approach in [2] combines shape information and optical flow based on the silhouette to recognize actions, and the authors of [18] likewise use the sum of silhouette pixels.

The key drawback of whole-body, silhouette-based approaches is that body parts and their influence on action interpretation are not explicitly modeled. We demonstrate in this paper that when knowledge of body part detection is applied to action recognition, high detection rates can be achieved with less computational effort.

Most of the approaches cited perform action recognition without explicitly applying human detection. Background subtraction is typically used for human

Fig. 1. Extraction of human contour from training image. The training images are taken from the KTH database.

identification, which has several disadvantages due to ghosting and the camouflage problem, and is not applicable in many situations such as when pan-tilt-zoom cameras are used [4]. Our approach is similar to the work of [3], but instead of using background subtraction, a correlation-based method is used for human detection which does not require any *a priori* background modeling. Human detection in video and images is also an active area of research [16]. Approaches are mainly divided into two categories: methods based on back- ground subtraction and the methods based on direct detection. The work of [19] uses background subtraction with colour information and human detection is done using extracted colour and contour features. Yoon et al. [20] also use back- ground subtraction and motion, colour and geometric features are used to detect humans. The work of Jiang et al. [11] uses fusion of infrared and colour features to identify humans in a scene.

On the other hand, methods like [8,5] use an explicit model of humans incorporating periodic motion and shape templates. Human detection is performed by classifying motion similarity and chamfer distance to known motion and shape templates. Some methods use shape and motion features for human modeling and cascaded Adaboost classifier for detection [12].

Recently, Dalal and Triggs [6] proposed the histogram of oriented gradients (HOG) features and a Support Vector Machine (SVM) to detect human. Our human detection method is similar in that it uses gradient features similar to the HOG, but we use a much simpler and less computationally demanding feature extraction and classification techniques.

2 Human Detection

Our overall approach to action recognition first requires robust, view- and pose-invariant human detection. To address this, we sample the four major pose angles: left profile, right profile, frontal and backward view.

We do not perform any background subtraction, but images are first preprocessed to extract the contour of the human. This is done by applying a Sobel operator to compute the gradient of the image, and then applying a threshold learned empirically from the statistics of the training sample. Figure 1 gives and example of such a contour image.

2.1   Feature Extraction

After contour extraction, four images are formed corresponding to the four major directions i.e. 0 , $\frac{\pi}{4}$, $\frac{\pi}{2}$ and $\frac{3\pi}{4}$:

$$I_0(x,y) = I(x+1,y)$$
$$I_{\frac{\pi}{4}}(x,y) = I(x+1,y+1)$$
$$I_{\frac{\pi}{2}}(x,y) = I(x,y-1)$$
$$I_{\frac{3\pi}{4}}(x,y) = I(x-1,y-1).$$

Difference images are then computed which constitute a gradient feature space restricted to contours:

$$\delta_\theta(x,y) = I_\theta(x,y) - I(x,y) \text{ for } \theta \in \{0, \frac{\pi}{4}, \frac{\pi}{2}, \frac{3\pi}{4}\}$$

These difference images are averaged over all training samples to form a mean difference image representing the patterns of directional correlation in each cardinal direction. The directional average difference images are denoted as $\bar{\delta}_\theta$.

2.2   Correlation-Based Human Detection

Our human detection technique is based on the correlation between the difference images I and a region I^{test} moved over a test image preprocessed with gradients and contour extraction as described above. The correlation coefficient ρ_{test} of I^{test} is computed as:

$$\rho_{test} = \prod_{\theta \in \{0, \frac{\pi}{4}, \frac{\pi}{2}, \frac{3\pi}{4}\}} \bar{\delta}_\theta I_\theta^{test}$$

From the maximum value of ρ_{test} the region with human to be found.

3   Action Recognition

The main focus of this paper is to select simple but robust features from the detected human and apply them to action recognition. Human body motion is the combined movement of different body parts and connected joints. The angles subtended by these joints with the vertical axis change in a periodic way while performing actions. We measure these angles for the body parts corresponding to the legs of detected humans.

We first pre-process regions containing identified humans by extracting the skeleton of the contour corresponding to the human. Skeletonization has been used extensively in human motion analysis to extract a skeletonized image of the human subject or to generate stick figure models. Bharatkumar et al. [4] used the medial axial transformation to extract stick figures and compared the two-dimensional information obtained from stick figures with that obtained from anthropometric data. Guo et al. [10] also used skeletonization on the extracted human silhouette to yield stick figure models. Skeletonization is useful to obtain the different angles imposed by lower body parts.

3.1   Computation of Component Angles

To compute the angles subtended by body parts and the vertical axis, we fit a straight-line model to the lower part of the extracted skeleton. The skeleton bounding box is divided into two horizontal parts based on the center of mass. The lower half is divided into four parts: two vertical parts based on the original centre of mass of the skeleton and two horizontal parts based on the centre of mass of the lower part. A χ-square line fitting algorithm is used to obtain best line which approximates the skeleton parts. From the lower four parts, i.e. the two vertical and two horizontal parts, the best two straight lines are estimated and three angles are computed corresponding to the angles subtended by the vertical axis and the straight line of upper half skeleton and the two straight lines from the lower halves. This three-angle vector is denoted $(\theta_1 , \theta_2 , \theta_3)$.

Assuming there are N of training sequences, each with n images in the sequence, for each action a_i . From each training sequence the standard deviation of the angular features is computed:

$$(\sigma_{\theta_1}^{a_i}, \sigma_{\theta_2}^{a_i}, \sigma_{\theta_3}^{a_i})$$

where,

$$\sigma_{\theta_j}^{a_i} = \left(\frac{1}{n}\right) \sum_{l=1}^{n} (\theta_{jl}^{a_i} - \mu_{\theta_j}^{a_i})^2 \text{ for } i \in \{1, 2, ..., N\} \text{ and } j \in \{1, 2, 3\}$$

and finally the *mean* of these standard deviations:

$$(\mu_{\sigma_{\theta_1}^{a_i}}, \mu_{\sigma_{\theta_2}^{a_i}}, \mu_{\sigma_{\theta_3}^{a_i}})$$

where,

$$\mu_{\sigma_{\theta_j}^{a_i}} = \left(\frac{1}{N}\right) \sum_{l=1}^{N} (\sigma_{\theta_{jl}}^{a_i}) \text{ for } i \in \{1, 2, ..., N\} \text{ and } j \in \{1, 2, 3\}$$

is taken to represent one action class. The Euclidean distance is used to recognize the action class of an unknown sequence.

4   Experimental Results

The KTH database [17][1] was used for all experiments on human detection and action recognition. In the KTH database there are several different types of actions: walking, jogging, boxing, hand waving etc. These actions were performed by 25 different people in four different scenarios: outdoors, outdoors with scale variation, outdoors with different clothes and indoors. For every kind of action there are 100 different sequences.

---

[1] http://www.nada.kth.se/cvap/actions/

Fig. 2. Performance of human detection in the image sequences of KTH database

For our experiments on human detection we select 20% of the sequences from the KTH dataset for training. The remaining 80% of the sequences are used for evaluating the system performance. Detection was been done using four viewpoints: frontal, backward, left and right profiles. We use a fixed size detection window (134 x 400), but images sequences were scaled to several sizes to make the detection process scale independent.

The correlation-based human detection procedure described in Section 2.2 performed well on the test sequences, with a detection rate of 94%. Figure 2 shows a variety of correct detections from the test dataset. Note that humans are detected correctly despite variations in pose and posture.

For action recognition, we consider the classes of walking, jogging and running actions. To learn the angular change model described in Section 2 we randomly selected 20 sequences from each of the three action classes for training. Another 25 sequences different from these were selected for testing. Table 1 shows the confusion matrix for action recognition on the independent test dataset for these action classes. Table 2 shows a comparison of action recognition rate with [17]. Our method performs well for jogging and running. But for walking we have a slightly lower recognition rate. It is interesting to note that all the running

Table 1. Confusion matrix of action recognition using the proposed method. Walking, jogging and running actions are considered on 25 test sequences from the KTH database.

	Walking	Jogging	Running
Walking	**19**	6	0
Jogging	4	**20**	1
Running	0	0	**25**

Table 2. Comparison of action recognition rates with the local feature based SVM approach [17]

	SVM [17]	Ours
Walking	83.8	**76.0**
Jogging	60.4	**80.0**
Running	54.6	**100.0**

actions were successfully detected. There are some misclassified walking and jogging sequences. This is due to the fact that we only take angle information of legs into consideration. Since walking and jogging are quite similar in nature, this angular change sometimes cannot distinguish between these two actions.

Our approach is able to detect humans in image sequences at approximately 33 frames per second and to extract angular features at approximately 21 frames per second. The combined detection and action recognition procedure runs at about 18 frames per second (i.e. when a human is detected and angular features must be extracted). The current implementation is in Matlab 7.2.0.232(R2006a) and timings were computed on an Intel(R) Core(TM)2 CPU 6400 @ 2.13GHz with 2GB of RAM.

5   Conclusions

In this paper we presented a simple but robust human detection and action recognition techniques. Correlation-based human detection has advantages since it works close to real time. On the other hand it is not robust when detecting humans against complex backgrounds. The correlation-based method also has a problems obtaining the gradient feature space images, since it requires all training images to be aligned and centered in a common coordinate frame.

The performance of action recognition technique using angle features is encouraging, but improvements can be made in noise removal after skeletonization. More angles can be computed corresponding to different body components in order to add more robustness to the current technique. This method can be equally applicable towards hand related actions where angle from the upper half of the body become important.

The computational efficiency of our unoptimized Matlab implementation is very encouraging, and there is every reason to believe that an optimized version will run in at more than 25 frames per second.

Acknowledgements

This work is supported by EC grants IST-027110 for the HERMES project and IST-045547 for the VIDI-video project, and by the Spanish MEC under projects TIN2006-14606 and CONSOLIDER-INGENIO 2010 MIPRCV CSD2007-00018.

References

1. Ahmad, M., Lee, S.: Hmm-based human action recognition using multiview image sequences, Hong Kong, China, vol. 1, pp. 263–266 (August 2006)
2. Ahmad, M., Lee, S.: Human action recognition using multi-view image sequence features. In: 7th International Conference on Automatic Face and Gesture Recognition, Southampton, UK, pp. 10–12 (April 2006)
3. Ali, A., Aggarwal, J.K.: Segmentation and recognition of continuous human activity. Event, 28 (2001)

4. Cucchiara, R., Grana, C., Piccardi, M., Prati, A.: Detecting moving objects, ghosts and shadows in video streams. IEEE Transactions on Pattern Analysis and Machine Intelligence 25, 1337–1342 (2003)
5. Cutler, R., Davis, L.: Robust real-time periodic motion detection, analysis, and applications. IEEE Transactions on Pattern Analysis and Machine Intelligence 22, 781–796 (2000)
6. Dalal, N., Triggs, B.: Histogram of oriented gradients for human detection, San Diego, CA, USA, vol. 2, pp. 886–893 (June 2005)
7. Davis, J.W., Bobick, A.F.: The representation and recognition of human movement using temporal templates. IEEE Transactions on Computer Vision and Pattern Recognition, 928–934 (June 1997)
8. Gavrila, D.M., Giebel, J.: Shape-based pedestrian detection and localization. In: IEEE Intelligent Vehicle Symposium, Versailles, France, vol. 1, pp. 8–14 (June 2002)
9. Gorelick, L., Blank, M., Shechtman, E., Irani, M., Basri, R.: Actions as space-time shapes. IEEE Transactions on Pattern Analysis and Machine Intelligence 29, 2247–2253 (2007)
10. Guo, Y., Xu, G., Tsuji, S.: Understanding human motion patterns. In: 12th IAPR Conference on Computer Vision and Image Processing, Jerusalem, Israel, pp. 325–329 (1994)
11. Jiang, L., Tian, F., Shen, L.E., Yao, S., Lu, Z., Xu, L.: Perceptual-based fusion of ir and visual images for human detection. In: International Symposium on Intelligent Multimedia, Video and Speech Processing, pp. 514–517 (2004)
12. Jones, M., Viola, P.: Detecting pedestrians using patterns of motion and appearance. In: IEEE International Conference on Computer Vision, Nice, France, pp. 734–741 (2003)
13. Masoud, O., Papanikolopoulos, N.P.: A method for human action recognition, vol. 21, pp. 729–743 (August 2003)
14. Mendoza, M.A., Pérez de la Blanca, N.: Hmm-based action recognition using contour histograms. In: Martí, J., Benedí, J.M., Mendonça, A.M., Serrat, J. (eds.) IbPRIA 2007. LNCS, vol. 4477, pp. 394–401. Springer, Heidelberg (2007)
15. Moeslund, T.B., Hilton, A., Krüger, V.: A survey of advances in vision-based human motion capture and analysis. Computer Vision and Image Understanding 8, 231–268 (2006)
16. Ogale, N.A.: A survey of techniques for human detection from video, USA, Department of Computer Science, University Of Maryland, College Park
17. Schuldt, C., Laptev, I., Caputo, B.: Recognizing human actions: a local svm approach. In: International Conference on Pattern Recognition, Cambridge, UK, pp. 32–36 (August 2004)
18. Sundaresan, A., RoyChowdhury, A., Chellappa, R.: A hidden markov model based framework for recognition of humans from gait sequences. In: International Conference on Image Processing, Barcelona, Catalunia, Spain, pp. 93–96 (September 2003)
19. Wren, C., Azarbayejani, A., Darrell, T., Pentl, A.: Pfinder: Real-time tracking of the human body. IEEE Transactions on Pattern Analysis and Machine Intelligence 19, 780–785 (1997)
20. Yoon, S.M., Kim, H.: Real-time multiple people detection using skin color, motion and appearence information. In: International Workshop on Robot and Human Interactive Communication, Kurashiki, Okayama Japan, pp. 331–334 (2004)

Using One-Class Classification Techniques in the Anti-phoneme Problem

Gábor Gosztolya, András Bánhalmi, and László Tóth

MTA-SZTE Research Group on Artificial Intelligence
of the Hungarian Academy of Sciences and University of Szeged
H-6720 Szeged, Aradi vértanúk tere 1., Hungary
{ggabor,banhalmi,tothl}@inf.u-szeged.hu

Abstract. In this paper we focus on the *anti-phoneme modelling* part of segment-based speech recognition, where we have to distinguish the real phonemes from anything else which may appear (like parts of phonemes, several consecutive phonemes and noise). As it has to be performed while only having samples of the correct phonemes, it is an example of one-class classification. To solve this problem, first all phonemes are modelled with a number of Gaussian distributions; then the problem is converted into a two-class classification task by generating counter-examples; this way some machine learning algorithm (like ANNs) can be used to separate the two classes. We tested two methods for a counter-example generation like this: one was a solution specific to the anti-phoneme problem, while the other used a general algorithm. By making modifications to the latter to reduce its time requirements, we were able to achieve an improvement in the recognition scores of over 60% compared to having no anti-phoneme model at all, and it performed considerably better than the other two methods.

Keywords: speech recognition, one-class classification, counter-example generation, Artificial Neural Networks, Gaussian Mixture Models.

1 Introduction

One-class classification is an area of Artificial Intelligence where the task is to characterize one given class to distinguish it from anything else [1]. In this area examples of just this class are given; thus, in contrast with the conventional classification problem, there are no examples from any other class. An area where this kind of problem arises is the segment-based approach of speech recognition, where we have to determine whether speech segments correspond to a correct phoneme or not. To do this, we have a large number of examples of correct segments in the form of a hand-labelled corpus, but there are no given counter-examples which contain anything else that could occur in a sound recording (various noise, segments longer or shorter than one phoneme, etc.). These excerpts are called "anti-phonemes" [2] and the whole problem is called the "anti-phoneme problem".

H. Araujo et al. (Eds.): IbPRIA 2009, LNCS 5524, pp. 433–440, 2009.

This problem can be solved in three entirely different ways: we can use a tool which models all the positive examples as a distribution, we can generate counter-examples in a task-specified way (using excerpts of multiple phonemes) and separate the two classes via some machine-learning method, or we can utilize a general counter-example generator algorithm (and then use the same machine-learning method). One good aspect about this problem is that the results will not be mere classification scores: a good one-class modelling method will lead to an improvement in a real application (in the accuracy of speech recognition).

2   Segment-Based Speech Recognition

In the speech recognition problem we are given some speech signal A and a list of possible words W, and our task is to find the most probable word $\hat{w} \in W$ via

$$\hat{w} = arg \max_{w \in W} P(w|A). \tag{1}$$

Using Bayes' theorem and noting that $P(A)$ is the same for all w's, we have that

$$\hat{w} = arg \max_{w \in W} P(A|w)P(w). \tag{2}$$

Now there are two distinct factors: the first describes the relation between the word and the speech signal, while the second simply states how probable the given word is. We will consider $P(w)$ as given, supplied by some *language model*, and concentrate on $P(A|w)$. In the segment-based approach we will assume that the signal A can be divided into non-overlapping segments, each of which corresponds to one of the o_j phonemes of the word $w = o_1, \ldots, o_n$. As the correct segmentation of A is not known, it appears as a hidden variable S:

$$P(A|w) = arg \max_{s \in S} P(A, s|w). \tag{3}$$

There are several ways of decomposing $P(A, s|w)$ further, depending on our modelling assumptions. What is common in all the derivations is that they trace the global probability back to the probabilities associated with the segments. The segments are usually assumed to be independent, so the corresponding local probability values will simply be multiplied. Glass et al. employ the formula [2]

$$\prod_{j=1}^{n} \frac{P(A_j|o_j)}{P(A_j|\alpha)} P(s_j|o_j), \tag{4}$$

where $P(s_j|o_j)$ is a duration model, A_j is the feature set extracted from the jth segment, and α denotes the "anti-phoneme" – a class that covers all the possible signal samples that are not real phonemes. Tóth et al. propose the formula [3]

$$\prod_{j=1}^{n} \frac{P(o_j|A_j)P(\overline{\alpha}|A_j)}{P(o_j)}, \tag{5}$$

where $P(\overline{\alpha}|A_j)$ denotes the probability that the given segment is *not* an anti-phoneme. The main difference between the two models is that in the former the acoustic observations are conditioned on the class labels (or the anti-phone), while in the latter it is the other way round. So in practice the components of the first formula are modelled by generative techniques, while discriminative ones are more straightforward for the latter. But as the posterior and class-conditional probabilities can always be easily converted to each other by Bayes' formula, these derivations do not limit us when choosing the machine-learning algorithm. In this paper we will focus on the anti-phoneme component $P(A_j|\alpha)$ or $P(\overline{\alpha}|A_j)$.

3   The Anti-phoneme Problem

Now we have examples for real phonemes, and we want to somehow distinguish them from any other speech segments that might appear. There are two main approaches for solving such a one-class classification problem: using a method which can model all these examples, or taking the actual occurrences of phonemes as positive examples and somehow creating anti-phonemes as negative ones. Then these two classes can be separated by classification methods like Artificial Neural Networks (ANNs) [4] or Support Vector Machines (SVM) [5]. But we have no training examples for the anti-phonemes, thus this generation is not trivial. We shall describe a solution for one-class modelling, and two approaches for automatic counter-example generation: a speech recognition-specific method [3] and the use of a general-purpose algorithm [6]. For the latter we also propose some modifications which have a surprisingly good effect on its running speed.

3.1   Modelling All Phonemes with Gaussians

Perhaps the most straightforward idea for describing all phonemes is to convert their occurrences to a probability distribution over the feature space, and model them with the sum of Gaussian curves. This is what Gaussian Mixture Models (GMM) [7] do: after the feature extraction part a clustering is performed on the set of resulting d-dimensional vectors (the positive examples) to divide them into n distinct subsets. Then a d-dimensional Gaussian is placed over every subset by calculating the mean and variance values of its elements.

3.2   The Incorrect Segment Sampling Algorithm

Tóth introduced a method for generating "incorrect" segments [3], based on the idea that the negative examples are probably parts of speech with incorrect segmentation bounds (they commence and/or end at positions where there is no real bound between phonemes). If we know the real phonetic boundaries – which is the case for any training database –, then it is easy to generate negative examples by choosing incorrect phoneme boundaries for the start and/or end segment bound. In the actual solution six anti-phonemes are generated for each phoneme by placing one or both phoneme boundaries earlier or later by δ milliseconds. In this method choosing the counter-examples is done *before* feature extraction.

3.3   Using General Counter-Example Generation

Another option is to use a general counter-example generation algorithm: in this case we take all our examples (all the phonemes *after* the feature extraction part) as the elements of one class, and generate a number of counter-examples. The input will be a set of d-dimensional vectors $(X, |X| = N)$, while the output will be also a set of d-dimensional vectors somehow representing the opposite of our examples. Bánhalmi introduced such a counter-example generation algorithm [6], which will be briefly described in the following. The main idea here is to project each positive example $x \in X$ outside X. To do this, first the set of boundary elements is calculated, then each positive example is projected beyond the closest boundary point, producing N negative examples for N positive ones.

Determining the Boundary Points. First the boundary points B of the original example set are calculated $(B \subseteq X)$. For an $x \in X$ first we place the k closest points into a set K, then an approximated center vector x_{center} is calculated from these elements: for each dimension, the lowest and the highest coordinates are added up after subtracting the appropriate coordinate of x from both of them. Then, for each $x_i \in K$, we calculate

$$\cos(\varphi_i) = \frac{(x_i - x)^T x_{center}}{\|x_i - x\| \, \|x_{center}\|}. \tag{6}$$

If all these values are nonnegative – so the angles between the vectors to the k nearest neighbors and the center vector are acute angles –, then x is added to the set of boundary points B. As this condition is only a sufficient one for being a boundary point, this method supplies only a subset of the real boundaries. An exact solution for this task is also given by attempting to separate x from the elements of K via an SVM [5]. If it is successful, x is a boundary element; but as this process is very slow, we used the one described above.

Projecting Beyond the Closest Boundary Point. After the set of boundary points B has been calculated, each element $x \in X$ is projected beyond the closest boundary point $x_b \in B$, resulting in a new point (hopefully) outside the region of positive examples. Besides x and x_b, it uses the center vector for x_b obtained earlier. There are two further parameters: *dist* sets the distance between the new point and the boundary point, while *curv* controls the curvature of the resulting hyper-surface. Fig. 1 shows a few examples with different *dist* and *curv* values.

Is It Really an Outlier? When the new point is determined, finally we check to see whether it is indeed an outer point, which is done in the same way as the boundary points were detected. If it is not an inner point, then it is added to the set of counter-examples; otherwise x_b is removed from the set of correct boundaries, and the whole transformation process has to be repeated with the now-closest boundary point $x_b' \in B$. In the end this algorithm will generate N counter-examples for a positive dataset of N data samples: one negative example for each positive one.

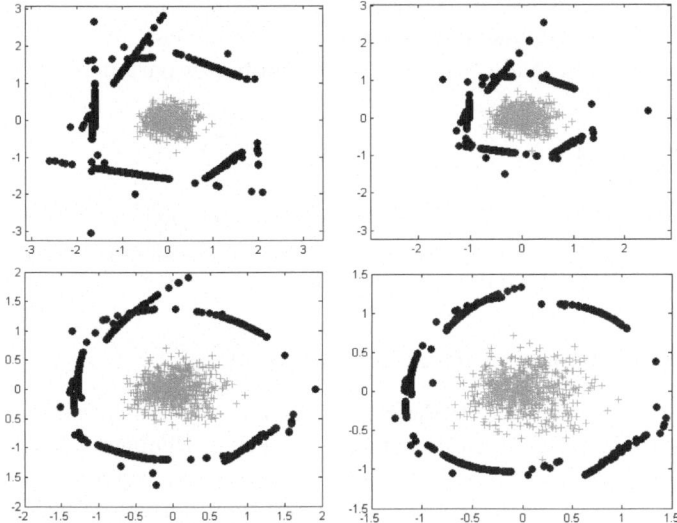

Fig. 1. Some counter-examples with different settings. Left to right: 1st: $(dist, curv) = (1, 0)$, 2nd: $(dist, curv) = (0.4, 0)$, 3rd: $(dist, curv) = (1, 0.5)$, 4th: $(dist, curv) = (1, 1)$.

Suggested Improvements of the Method. The obvious weakness of this algorithm is its time requirement: it is $o(kN^2 \log N)$ for the boundary point detection and $o(|B|Nk)$ for the projection for N positive examples and k neighbors. In our case large datasets were used (so N was quite big), thus executing this algorithm with different $dist$ and $curv$ parameters took a long time: even for one configuration the counter-example generation ran for a week on our test machine, making thorough testing practically impossible.

We found, however, that this algorithm can be divided into two distinct parts: the first one calculates the boundary points and the center vectors, while the second one carries out the actual counter-example generation. Luckily the first part uses most of the CPU time, while the $dist$ and $curv$ parameters appear only in the second part. Thus, regardless of the number of parameter combinations tested, the first and much slower part has to be computed just once. But the second part could be divided up further: for each element $x \in X$, before doing the actual projection, first the closest boundary point has to be found. The varying parameters also have no effect on this procedure, hence it can be separated from the projection and computed just once (although strictly after determining B).

With these modifications we reduced the running time of this method for a parameter pair to one day. (Of course it involves only the projection of points.) But in the last part, after the projections, the resulting point is checked to see whether it is an outer point for the positive examples. It is done in the same way as in the first part (finding the k closest points, calculating $\cos(\varphi_i)$s, etc.), so it is rather slow; and it cannot be pre-calculated since it is done on the newly generated counter-examples. We found, however, that this check is not always needed: for larger $dist$ values (in our tests $dist \geq 1.5$) the projected point lies too far from X to be an inner point. Omitting this condition leads to an overwhelming speed-up, causing the run to finish in just 15 minutes. Applying this last modification made testing a large number of parameter pairs possible.

4   Experiments

At this point, having described the problem and the methods we used, we turn to testing. We describe the speech recognition environment briefly, discuss the testing methodology of each method applied, then present the results obtained.

4.1   The Speech Recognition Environment

Testing was done within our OASIS Speech Laboratory, which, due to its module-based structure, is quite suitable for experimenting. Phoneme classification was done by an ANN with one hidden layer, using typical segment-based features: they were averages of the 12 MFCC values and their derivates over specific parts of the segment. These ANNs were trained on a large, general database: 332 people of various ages spoke 12 sentences and 12 words each. The task was sentence recognition on medical reports with automatically generated phoneme labelling and segmentation. A simple word 2-gram was used as the model, i.e. the likelihood of a word only depended on it and the previous word; the vocabulary size was around 2,500. The tests were carried out on 150 sentences; the performance was measured via the widely-used accuracy and correctness values. Using no anti-phoneme model led to scores of 88.17% and 88.53% for (word-level) accuracy and correctness, respectively.

4.2   Testing

Testing the Gaussian Mixture Models was a rather straightforward task. Treating all phonemes as members of just one class, we did tests with 10, 15 and 20 Gaussian components. Since the GMM training procedure is not deterministic due to the initial clustering part, we performed three tests for each configuration, and averaged their results. Testing the Incorrect Segment Sampling Algorithm was also straightforward: for each correct phoneme, all six anti-phonemes were generated, and a feed-forward ANN was trained on this set with 100 hidden neurons. During evaluation the value of the appropriate output neuron served as an approximation of $P(\overline{a}|A_j)$. As the standard neural net training procedure is a nondeterministic one, we compensated for it by performing the training three times; then all three nets were tested and their performance score was averaged.

Testing the General Counter-example Generation Method was the most complicated part as we sought to test several $dist$ and $curv$ pairs. First the promising region of these parameters was determined by preliminary tests, then this region was examined more closely: we performed tests with $1.0 \leq dist \leq 4.0$ and $0.0 \leq curv \leq 0.4$, of course, applying the proposed speed-up modifications. For one such parameter pairing an ANN was trained, just like in the previous case.

Table 1. Test results for the GMM and the Incorrect Segment Sampling method

Method	Accuracy		Correctness	
	Value	RER	Value	RER
GMM with 10 Gaussians	91.05%	24.60%	91.48%	25.72%
GMM with 15 Gaussians	90.98%	24.01%	91.58%	26.59%
GMM with 20 Gaussians	91.12%	25.19%	91.80%	28.51%
Incorrect Segment Sampling	91.97%	32.35%	92.62%	35.66%
No anti-phoneme modelling	88.17%	—	88.53%	—

Table 2. Accuracy scores for different *dist* and *curv* parameter values for the general counter-example generation method, averaged from three tests. Notably high values are highlighted in **bold**. With no anti-phoneme model, it results in a score of 88.17%.

		dist						
		1.0	1.5	2.0	2.5	3.0	3.5	4.0
	0.0	**93.91%**	**95.58%**	93.19%	90.32%	90.44%	91.52%	**93.67%**
	0.1	**93.91%**	93.31%	90.80%	90.68%	90.08%	89.13%	87.69%
curv	0.2	90.56%	91.40%	90.92%	89.25%	91.88%	89.13%	89.37%
	0.3	91.64%	92.47%	90.20%	91.88%	**94.03%**	92.35%	89.73%
	0.4	91.87%	92.59%	**93.43%**	91.16%	90.80%	91.87%	91.28%

Table 3. Correctness scores for different *dist* and *curv* parameter values for the general counter-example generation method, averaged from three tests. Notably high values are highlighted in **bold**. With no anti-phoneme model, it results in a score of 88.53%.

		dist						
		1.0	1.5	2.0	2.5	3.0	3.5	4.0
	0.0	**94.26%**	**95.82%**	93.55%	90.68%	90.80%	91.88%	**94.03%**
	0.1	**94.15%**	93.67%	91.16%	91.04%	90.44%	89.49%	88.05%
curv	0.2	91.75%	92.35%	91.28%	89.73%	92.48%	89.49%	89.73%
	0.3	92.83%	93.67%	90.80%	92.47%	**94.38%**	92.71%	90.56%
	0.4	93.31%	93.91%	**94.02%**	91.63%	91.75%	92.35%	92.11%

4.3   Results

Table 1 shows our results using GMMs. The performance scores improved only slightly, but it is quite insensitive to the number of Gaussians used: a relative error reduction (RER) of about 25% was achieved. The Incorrect Segment Sampling Algorithm proved to be more effective (see Table 1 again): the RER scores of 32% and 35% are quite good. Although this method is a little more complicated, we recommend it in place of GMMs. Overall, the General Counter-example Generation Method yielded the best results (see tables 2 and 3). Hardly any *dist-curv* pair made the recognition scores worse, but usually performance remained at the level of GMMs. At certain points, however, even the method of incorrect segment sampling was significantly outperformed; with $dist = 1.5$ and $curv = 0.0$ we attained scores of 95.58% and 95.82% (accuracy and correctness, respectively), which values, coming from averaging three ANNs, cannot be due to mere chance. It means a surprisingly large (over 60%) score of relative error reduction compared to having no anti-phoneme model. Of course, testing numerous *dist-curv* pair values would not be possible without our proposed speed-up improvements, which are clearly useful in other tasks too. Lastly, we would like to stress that the actual *curv* and *dist* values are of little importance; it is the improvements in the recognition scores, which were achieved by setting them.

5   Conclusions and Future Work

In this study we investigated several strategies for tackling the anti-phoneme problem in segment-based speech recognition. As in this task we have to characterize the "phone-ness" of a part of speech knowing only correct phonemes, methods appropriate for one-class classification should be considered. Apart from the traditional GMM we tested two methods which generate counter-examples for the given examples: one especially designed for the anti-phoneme problem and one of a general type. By introducing speed-up modifications for the latter one, we achieved a big reduction in the error rates, significantly outperforming the other two techniques. This result justifies our efforts of applying this generation method, and our modifications could be used in other one-class learning tasks as well. There are other methods for one-class modelling like one-class SVM, as well as ones for separating the two classes of examples like SVM [5]; as they could also work well here, it will be the subject of a future study.

References

1. Tax, D.M.J.: One-class classification; Concept-learning in the absence of counter-examples. PhD thesis, Delft University of Technology (2001)
2. Glass, J.R.: A probabilistic framework for segment-based speech recognition. Computer Speech and Language 17(2), 137–152 (2003)
3. Tóth, L., Kocsor, A., Gosztolya, G.: Telephone speech recognition via the combination of knowledge sources in a segmental speech model. Acta Cybernetica 16(4), 643–657 (2004)
4. Bishop, C.M.: Neural Networks for Pattern Recognition. Clarendon Press, Oxford (1995)
5. Schölkopf, B., Platt, J.C., Shawe-Taylor, J., Smola, A.J., Williamson, R.C.: Estimating the support of a high-dimensional distribution. Neural Computation 13(7), 1443–1471 (2001)
6. Bánhalmi, A., Kocsor, A., Busa-Fekete, R.: Counter-example generation-based one-class classification. In: Kok, J.N., Koronacki, J., Lopez de Mantaras, R., Matwin, S., Mladenič, D., Skowron, A. (eds.) ECML 2007. LNCS, vol. 4701, pp. 543–550. Springer, Heidelberg (2007)
7. Duda, R., Hart, P.: Pattern Classification and Scene Analysis. Wiley & Sons, New York (1973)

Index of Balanced Accuracy: A Performance Measure for Skewed Class Distributions*

V. García[1,2], R.A. Mollineda[2], and J.S. Sánchez[2]

[1] Lab. Reconocimiento de Patrones, Instituto Tecnológico de Toluca
Av. Tecnológico s/n, 52140 Metepec, México
[2] Dept. Llenguatges i Sistemes Informàtics, Universitat Jaume I
Av. Sos Baynat s/n, 12071 Castelló de la Plana, Spain

Abstract. This paper introduces a new metric, named *Index of Balanced Accuracy*, for evaluating learning processes in two-class imbalanced domains. The method combines an unbiased index of its overall accuracy and a measure about how dominant is the class with the highest individual accuracy rate. Some theoretical examples are conducted to illustrate the benefits of the new metric over other well-known performance measures. Finally, a number of experiments demonstrate the consistency and validity of the evaluation method here proposed.

1 Introduction

Many learning approaches assume that the problem classes share similar prior probabilities. However, in many real-world tasks this assumption is grossly violated. Often, the ratios of prior probabilities between classes are significantly skewed. This situation is known as the imbalance problem. A two-class data set is said to be imbalanced when one of the classes (the minority one) is heavily under-represented as regards the other class (the majority one) [6]. This topic is particularly important in those applications where it is costly to misclassify examples from the minority class. Because of examples of the minority and majority classes usually represent the presence and absence of rare cases, respectively, they are also known as positive and negative examples.

As pointed out by many authors, the performance of a classification process over imbalanced data sets should not be expressed in terms of the plain accuracy and/or error rates [2, 3, 4, 8, 9]. The use of these simple measures might produce misleading conclusions since they do not take into account misclassification costs, are strongly biased to favor the majority class, and are sensitive to class skews.

Alternative measures have been proposed to evaluate classifiers in imbalanced scenarios. Some widely-known examples are Receiver Operating Characteristic (ROC) curve, the area under the ROC curve (AUC) [1], the geometric mean of class accuracies [7] and the f-measure [3]. Another measure, less renowned but possibly more powerful than those previously cited, refers to the optimized precision [9]. All these measures are combinations of error/accuracy rates measured separately on each class, thus alleviating biased results of the classification performance. Nevertheless, most of

---

* Partially supported by grants DPI2006–15542 and CSD2007–00018 from the Spanish Ministry of Education and Science, and P1–1B2007–60 from Fundació Caixa Castelló - Bancaixa.

H. Araujo et al. (Eds.): IbPRIA 2009, LNCS 5524, pp. 441–448, 2009.

these measures do not consider how dominant is the accuracy on an individual class over another. Hence their results do not reflect the contribution of each class to the overall performance. In some cases, it could be interesting (and complementary) to know whether the accuracies on each class are balanced and if not, to find out which is the 'dominant class' (the class with the highest accuracy rate).

This paper introduces a new method to evaluate the performance of a classification system in two-class imbalanced data sets. It quantifies a trade-off between an unbiased measure of overall accuracy and an index of how balanced are the two class accuracies. This relationship is represented by means of a two-dimensional graph whose axes correspond to the square of the geometric mean of class accuracies and the signed difference between the accuracies on positive and negative classes. The second term is intended to favor those cases with higher accuracy rate on the positive class. Some illustrative examples are simulated to better explain the differences between the measure here proposed and other well-known metrics. Final experiments on real-world problems are designed to demonstrate the consistency and validity of the new performance evaluation method here introduced.

2   Evaluation of Classifier Performance in Imbalanced Domains

Typical metrics for measuring the performance of learning systems are classification accuracy and/or error rates, which for a two-class problem can be easily derived from a 2×2 confusion matrix as that given in Table 1. These measures can be computed as $Acc = (TP+TN)/(TP+FN+TN+FP)$ and $Err = (FP+FN)/(TP+FN+TN+FP)$.

However, empirical evidence shows that these measures are biased with respect to the data imbalance and proportions of correct and incorrect classifications. Shortcomings of these evaluators have motivated search for new measures.

Table 1. Confusion matrix for a two-class problem

	Predicted positive	Predicted negative
Positive class	True Positive (TP)	False Negative (FN)
Negative class	False Positive (FP)	True Negative (TN)

Some straightforward examples of alternative measures are: (i) *True positive rate* (also referred to as *recall* or *sensitivity*) is the percentage of positive examples which are correctly classified, $TPrate = TP/(TP + FN)$; (ii) *True negative rate* (or *specificity*) is the percentage of negative examples which are correctly classified, $TNrate = TN/(TN + FP)$; (iii) *False positive rate* is the percentage of negative examples which are misclassified, $FPrate = FP/(TN + FP)$; (iv) *False negative rate* is the percentage of positive examples which are misclassified, $FNrate = FN/(TP + FN)$; (v) *Precision* (or *purity*) is defined as the percentage of samples which are correctly labeled as positive, $Precision = TP/(TP + FP)$.

One of the most widely-used techniques for the evaluation of classifiers in imbalanced domains is the ROC curve, which is a tool for visualizing, organizing and selecting classifiers based on their trade-offs between benefits (true positives) and costs (false positives). Furthermore, a quantitative representation of a ROC curve is the area under it, which is known as AUC [1, 5]. When only one run is available from a classifier, its AUC can be computed as $AUC = (TPrate + TNrate)/2$ [10].

Kubat et al. [7] use *the geometric mean* of accuracies measured separately on each class, $Gmean = \sqrt{TPrate \cdot TNrate}$. This measure is associated to a point on the ROC curve, and the idea is to maximize the accuracies of both classes while keeping them balanced.

Both AUC and Gmean minimize the negative influence of skewed distributions of classes, but they do not distinguish the contribution of each class to the overall performance, nor which is the prevalent class. This means that different combinations of TPrate and TNrate produce the same value of the corresponding metric (AUC or Gmean).

More recently, Ranawana and Palade [9] proposed a new measure called *optimized precision* which is computed as $OP = Acc - (|TNrate - TPrate|/(TNrate + TPrate))$. This represents the difference between the global accuracy and a second term that computes how balanced the two class accuracies are. High OP performances require high global accuracies and balanced class accuracies. Nevertheless, it has to be pointed out that it can be strongly affected by the biased influence of the global accuracy.

3   The New Performance Evaluation Method

This section introduces a new measure, named *Index of Balanced Accuracy* (IBA), whose expression results from the computation of the area of a rectangular region in a two-dimensional space here called *Balanced Accuracy Graph*. This space is defined by the product of the accuracies on each class ($Gmean^2$), which is a suitable measure of the overall accuracy in imbalanced domains, and by a new simple index here introduced, the *Dominance*, which measures how prevalent is the dominant class rate with respect to the other. A final simulated example illustrates the benefits of the IBA with respect to some well-known classifier performance metrics.

3.1   The Dominance Index

As previously pointed out, AUC and Gmean are unable to explain the contribution of each class to the overall performances, giving the same result for many different combinations of $(TPrate, TNrate)$.

A new simple index called *Dominance* is here proposed for evaluating the relationship between the TPrate and TNrate. The expected role of this index is to inform about which is the dominant class and how significant is its dominance relationship. The *Dominance* can be computed as follows:

$$Dominance = TPrate - TNrate \qquad (1)$$

This measure can take on any value between -1 and $+1$, since both the TPrate and the TNrate are in the range $[0, +1]$. A Dominance value of $+1$ represents a situation of perfect accuracy on the positive class, but failing on all negative cases; a value of -1 corresponds to the opposite situation. The closer the Dominance is to 0, the more balanced both individual rates are. In practice, the Dominance can be interpreted as an indicator of how balanced the TPrate and the TNrate are.

3.2 The Balanced Accuracy Graph

In order to take advantage of the good properties of the Gmean and the Dominance and to avoid their shortcomings, this section introduces the *Balanced Accuracy Graph* (BAG) as a tool to visualize and measure the behavior of a classifier from the joint perspective of global accuracy and Dominance. With the aim of simplicity, $Gmean^2$ is used instead of Gmean.

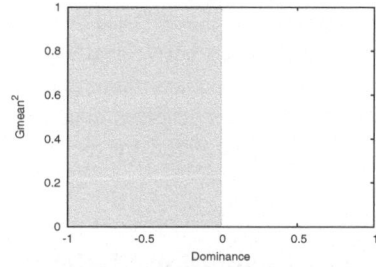

Fig. 1. The balanced accuracy graph. The plot represents the optimal point ($Dominance = 0$ and $Gmean^2 = 1$), producing the maximum area.

Fig. 1 illustrates the BAG as a two-dimensional coordinate system where the X axis corresponds to Dominance and the $Gmean^2$ is plotted on the Y axis. The BAG depicts relative trade-offs between Dominance and $Gmean^2$. The performance of a classifier measured as a pair ($Dominance$, $Gmean^2$) corresponds to a single point in this graph. The upper central point $(0, +1)$ represents a perfect classifier where $TPrate = TNrate = 1$, while points $(-1, 0)$ and $(+1, 0)$ match with the useless cases of $TPrate = 0, TNrate = 1$ and $TPrate = 1, TNrate = 0$, respectively.

The upper left $(-1, +1)$ and upper right $(+1, +1)$ points correspond to 'unfeasible cases' because when Dominance is -1 or $+1$, one of the two class rates is 0 what makes impossible for the Gmean to achieve values greater than 0. Actually, there is an infinite number of points in the BAG which represents unfeasible cases.

3.3 Index of Balanced Accuracy

Given a point (d, g) in a BAG, it would be interesting to quantify the trade-off between Dominance and $Gmean^2$ represented by that point. To this end, we propose to use the rectangular area whose vertices are at points $(-1, 0)$, $(-1, g)$, (d, g) and $(d, 0)$ (see

Fig. 1 for the case with $d = 0$ and $g = 1$). The area of such a rectangle is here named *Index of Balanced Accuracy* (IBA), which can be formalized as:

$$IBA = (1 + Dominance) \cdot Gmean^2 \qquad (2)$$

When substituting Dominance and Gmean^2, the resulting function provides useful details for a better understanding about how IBA supports the trade-off. Besides, we add $0 \leq \alpha \leq 1$ to weight the value of Dominance. Significant effects are obtained for $\alpha \leq 0.5$. However, note that if $\alpha = 0$, the IBA turns into the Gmean^2.

$$IBA_\alpha = (1 + \alpha \cdot (TPrate - TNrate)) \cdot TPrate \cdot TNrate \qquad (3)$$

The IBA can take on any value between 0 and +1, which is the area of the greatest possible rectangle, that is, the one corresponding to a point with Dominance= 0 and Gmean^2 = 1 (optimal classification). Fig. 2 illustrates the surface of the IBA (with $\alpha = 1$) as a function of TPrate and TNrate, showing that its maximum is +1 and that it occurs for $TPrate = TNrate = 1$. These facts can also be demonstrated by analytically optimizing the mathematical expression of IBA (Eq. 3).

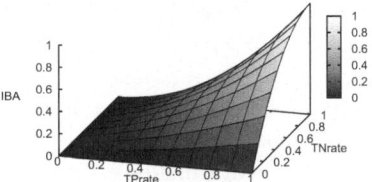

Fig. 2. The IBA function ($\alpha = 1$)

3.4   A Theoretical Example

Finally, a theoretical example is designed to clear up the benefits/advantages of the IBA with respect to other well-known metrics for classifier evaluation.

Let $f(\theta)$ be a classifier that depends on a set of parameters θ. Suppose that θ should be optimized so that $f(\theta)$ can discriminate between the two classes of a particular imbalanced problem (with a ratio 1:10). Let T and V be the training and validation sets, respectively. During learning, four possible configurations (θ_1, θ_2, θ_3, θ_4) have been obtained from T, and then the corresponding classifiers $f(\theta_i)$ have been run over V. Table 2 reports the results of several performance measures used to evaluate each particular classifier $f(\theta_i)$. The last step in learning should be to pick up the best configuration θ^* according to the performance measure adopted.

First of all, note that configurations θ_1 and θ_4 correspond to cases with a clearly biased behavior, whereas θ_2 and θ_3 produce less differences between TPrate and TNrate. Both accuracy and AUC would select one of those biased θ_1 and θ_4. In the case of accuracy, this is because it strongly depends on the majority class rate. The geometric mean and OP suggest one of the moderate configurations θ_2 and θ_3, ignoring the fact that the minority class is usually the most important. While the former does not distinguish between them, OP would prefer θ_2 rather than θ_3 because its computation is affected

Table 2. Several performance measures for the theoretical example (highlighted are the best results for each metric)

	TPrate	TNrate	Acc	Gmean	AUC	OP	IBA_1	$IBA_{0.5}$	$IBA_{0.1}$
θ_1	0.550	0.950	**0.914**	0.723	**0.750**	0.647	0.314	0.418	0.502
θ_2	0.680	0.810	0.798	**0.742**	0.745	**0.711**	0.479	0.515	0.544
θ_3	0.810	0.680	0.692	**0.742**	0.745	0.605	0.622	0.587	**0.558**
θ_4	0.950	0.550	0.586	0.723	**0.750**	0.320	**0.732**	**0.627**	0.543

by the accuracy. These drawbacks can be overcome when using the IBA measure by appropriately tuning the parameter α (see Eq. 3). One can see that $IBA_{0.1}$ selects θ_3, which corresponds to the moderate case with the highest TPrate.

4   Experiments

In this section we present an experiment with the aim of validating usefulness and consistency of the IBA measure. To this end, we will compare IBA with a number of representative metrics: accuracy, geometric mean, AUC, and optimized precision. The experiment is carried out on 17 real data sets taken from the UCI Machine Learning Database Repository (http://archive.ics.uci.edu/ml/) and a private library (http://www.vision.uji.es/~sanchez/Databases/). All data sets were transformed into two-class problems by keeping one original class and joining the objects of the remaining classes. From these databases, here we have included the results of the four cases representing the most diversity of situations. The majority/minority ratio for each of these databases is: Breast (2.42), Glass (11.59), Satimage (9.28), and Laryngeal-2 (12.06). The results for the rest of databases are available at (http://www.vision.uji.es/~sanchez/Results).

For each database, we have estimated the performance measures mentioned above by repeating 5 times a 10–fold cross–validation when using different classifiers: the nearest neighbor (1-NN) rule, a multi-layer perceptron (MLP), a support vector classifier (SVC), the naïve Bayes classifier (NBC), a decision tree (J48), and a radial basis function network (RBF).

4.1   The Results

For each database, the six classifiers have been used and their results (TPrate and TNrate) have been evaluated in terms of the five performance metrics. From this, each measure will suggest the best classifier. Our study will consist of judging the decision inferred from each measure with the aim of remarking the merits of IBA when compared to other metrics.

From results in Table 3, some preliminary conclusions can be drawn. In general, as expected, accuracy appears ineffective in imbalanced domains. IBA usually chooses the classifier with the highest TPrate, demonstrating to be robust as regards to the parameter α. The rest of measures are usually affected by high TNrates, thus undervaluing the relevance of TPrate. Focusing on each particular database, some comments can be remarked:

Table 3. Experimental results (highlighted are the best results for each metric)

Breast									
	TPrate	TNrate	Acc	Gmean	AUC	OP	IBA_1	$IBA_{0.5}$	$IBA_{0.1}$
1NN	0.454	0.761	0.671	0.588	0.608	**0.419**	**0.240**	**0.293**	**0.335**
MLP	0.368	0.845	0.705	0.558	0.606	0.312	0.163	0.237	0.296
SVC	0.328	0.864	0.708	0.533	0.596	0.258	0.132	0.208	0.269
NBC	0.402	0.865	**0.730**	**0.590**	**0.634**	0.365	0.187	0.268	0.332
J48	0.321	0.891	0.724	0.535	0.606	0.254	0.123	0.204	0.270
RBF	0.390	0.867	0.728	0.582	0.629	0.348	0.177	0.258	0.322
Glass									
	TPrate	TNrate	Acc	Gmean	AUC	OP	IBA_1	$IBA_{0.5}$	$IBA_{0.1}$
1NN	0.318	0.948	0.898	0.549	0.633	0.400	0.111	0.206	0.282
MLP	0.141	0.969	0.903	0.370	0.555	0.157	0.024	0.080	0.125
SVC	0.000	0.991	**0.912**	0.000	0.495	-0.088	0.000	0.000	0.000
NBC	0.753	0.444	0.468	0.578	0.598	0.210	**0.437**	**0.386**	**0.344**
J48	0.353	0.963	0.915	**0.583**	**0.658**	**0.451**	0.132	0.236	0.319
RBF	0.000	0.999	0.920	0.000	0.499	-0.080	0.000	0.000	0.000
Satimage									
	TPrate	TNrate	Acc	Gmean	AUC	OP	IBA_1	$IBA_{0.5}$	$IBA_{0.1}$
1NN	0.705	0.960	**0.935**	0.823	0.833	0.782	0.504	0.591	0.660
MLP	0.637	0.966	0.934	0.785	0.802	0.729	0.413	0.515	0.596
SVC	0.000	1.000	0.903	0.000	0.500	-0.097	0.000	0.000	0.000
NBC	0.870	0.815	0.820	**0.842**	**0.843**	**0.788**	**0.749**	**0.729**	**0.713**
J48	0.550	0.959	0.919	0.726	0.755	0.648	0.312	0.420	0.506
RBF	0.000	1.000	0.903	0.000	0.500	-0.097	0.000	0.000	0.000
Laryngeal-2									
	TPrate	TNrate	Acc	Gmean	AUC	OP	IBA_1	$IBA_{0.5}$	$IBA_{0.1}$
1NN	0.694	0.970	0.949	0.821	0.832	0.783	0.488	0.581	0.655
MLP	0.770	0.979	**0.963**	0.868	0.875	**0.844**	0.596	0.675	0.738
SVC	0.672	0.942	0.922	0.796	0.807	0.754	0.462	0.547	0.616
NBC	0.943	0.844	0.851	**0.892**	**0.894**	0.796	**0.875**	**0.836**	**0.804**
J48	0.638	0.980	0.954	0.791	0.809	0.742	0.411	0.518	0.604
RBF	0.558	0.985	0.952	0.742	0.772	0.676	0.316	0.433	0.526

Breast: 1NN and NBC provide similar results in terms of TPrate and TNrate. However, OP and IBA suggest 1NN because its performances on both classes are more balanced. In contrast, the other measures select NBC, where the overall error is lower due to a greater bias to the majority class.

Glass: IBA prefers NBC because the TPrate is clearly the best and even it is higher than the TNrate. Gmean, AUC and OP choose J48 because they are strongly affected by the overall error, despite the low performance on the minority class makes this classifier useless.

Satimage: This is a straightforward case, in which all measures (except accuracy) give NBC as the best classifier. Both TPrate and TNrate are high enough and they are sufficiently balanced.

Laryngeal-2: Gmean, AUC and IBA select NBC, which seems to be the classifier with the best performance. The fact that OP prefers MLP is because it depends on the overall accuracy (here particularly affected by a significant imbalance ratio).

5   Conclusions and Further Extensions

In this paper, we have introduced a new method to evaluate the performance of classification systems in two-class problems with skewed data distributions. It is defined as a trade-off between a global performance measure (Gmean^2) and a new proposed signed index to reflect how balanced are the individual accuracies (Dominance). High values of the new measure IBA are obtained when the accuracies of both classes are high and balanced. Unlike most metrics, the IBA function does not take care of the overall accuracy only, but also intends to favor classifiers with better results on the positive class (generally the most important class). The most closely related measure to IBA is the optimized precision, although this is biased to the majority class.

Theoretical and empirical studies have shown the robustness and advantages of IBA with respect to some other well-known performance measures. Future work will primarily be addressed to extend the combination of Dominance with other global metrics especially useful for certain real-world applications. Also, this kind of performance evaluation methods could be designed to include misclassification costs.

References

1. Bradley, P.W.: The use of the area under the ROC curve in the evaluation of machine learning algorithms. Pattern Recognition 30, 1145–1159 (1997)
2. Chawla, N.V., Japkowicz, N., Kotcz, A.: Editorial: special issue on learning from imbalanced data sets. SIGKDD Exploration Newsletters 6, 1–6 (2004)
3. Daskalaki, S., Kopanas, I., Avouris, N.: Evaluation of classifiers for an uneven class distribution problem. Applied Artificial Intelligence 20, 381–417 (2006)
4. Elazmeh, W., Japkowicz, N., Matwin, S.: Evaluating misclassifications in imbalanced data. In: Proc. 17th European Conference on Machine Learning, pp. 126–137 (2006)
5. Huang, J., Ling, C.X.: Using AUC and accuracy in evaluating learning algorithms. IEEE Trans. on Knowledge and Data Engineering 17, 299–310 (2005)
6. Japkowicz, N., Stephen, S.: The class imbalance problem: a systematic study. Intelligent Data Analysis 6, 40–49 (2002)
7. Kubat, M., Matwin, S.: Adressing the curse of imbalanced training sets: one-sided selection. In: Proc. 14th Intl. Conf. on Machine Learning Nashville, TN, pp. 179–186 (1997)
8. Provost, F., Fawcett, T.: Analysis and visualization of classifier performance: Comparison under imprecise class and cost distributions. In: Proc. 3rd Intl. Conf. on Knowledge Discovery and Data Mining Newport Beach, CA, pp. 43–48 (1997)
9. Ranawana, R., Palade, V.: Optimized Precision - A new measure for classifier performance evaluation. In: Proc. IEEE Congress on Evolutionary Computation, pp. 2254–2261 (2006)
10. Sokolova, M., Japkowicz, N., Szpakowicz, S.: Beyond Accuracy, F-Score and ROC: A family of discriminant measures for performance evaluation. In: Sattar, A., Kang, B.-h. (eds.) AI 2006. LNCS, vol. 4304, pp. 1015–1021. Springer, Heidelberg (2006)

Chromatographic Pattern Recognition Using Optimized One-Class Classifiers

António V. Sousa[1,2], Ana Maria Mendonça[1,3], and Aurélio Campilho[1,3]

[1] Instituto de Engenharia Biomédica
Rua Roberto Frias, 4200-465 Porto, Portugal
[2] Instituto Superior de Engenharia do Porto
Rua Dr. António Bernardino de Almeida 431, 4200-072 Porto, Portugal
ats@isep.ipp.pt
[3] Faculdade de Engenharia da Universidade do Porto
Rua Roberto Frias, 4200-465 Porto, Portugal
{amendon,campilho}@fe.up.pt

Abstract. This paper presents a method for automating the selection of the rejection rate of one-class classifiers aiming at optimizing the classifier performance. These classifiers are used in a new classification approach to deal with class imbalance in Thin-Layer Chromatography (TLC) patterns, which is due to the huge difference between the number of normal and pathological cases, as a consequence of the rarity of Lysosomal Storage Disorders (LSD) diseases. The classification is performed in two decision stages, both implemented using optimized one-class classifiers: the first stage aims at recognizing most of the normal samples; the outliers of this first decision level are presented to the second stage, which is a multiclassifier prepared to deal with both pathological and normal patterns. The results that were obtained proved that the proposed methodology is able to overcome some of the difficulties associated with the choice of the rejection rate of one-class classifiers, and generally contribute to the minimization of the imbalance problem in TLC pattern classification.

1 Introduction

In classification applications where the number of samples of one given class is very low when compared with the total number of available samples, an additional difficulty appears in the implementation of the classifier, known as class imbalance problem, [1, 2]. Some of the techniques used for dealing with this problem are based on balancing the training set either by under-sampling or by over-sampling, or even by generation of new synthetic data. The imbalance problem has also been studied through specialized recognition algorithms, namely the one-class classifiers [3]. This kind of classifier learns with the training samples of the most frequent class, or target class, looking for natural groups of objects of this class and rejecting all the samples that are not adjusted to the learned examples.

The classification of chromatographic patterns corresponding to Lysosomal Disorders (LSD) is a clear example of class imbalance; LSD are exceptionally rare diseases that result in serious situations of nervous degeneration and mental retardation, and even causing precocious death, and, fortunately, the number of pathological cases is

H. Araujo et al. (Eds.): IbPRIA 2009, LNCS 5524, pp. 449–456, 2009.
© Springer-Verlag Berlin Heidelberg 2009

much lower than the normal situations [4]. The first phase of LSD diagnosis is performed by Thin-Layer Chromatography (TLC) analysis of the patient urine sample on silica gel plates [5], and the generated chromatographic patterns are afterwards visually inspected and compared with previously classified patterns by specialists.

Most of the solutions presented for automatic TLC pattern classification use a chromatographic profile as a direct input for the classifier. The discriminant analysis based on the chromatographic profile is supported by dissimilarity measures between pairs of samples and specific classifiers that are able to deal with this type of information. Two main reasons favour the use of this type of methodology: one is that all the information from the profile is integrated by the classifier; the other is the fact that the use of dissimilarities is also considered an essential factor in the human process of classification and recognition [6]. The most common approaches for TLC pattern classification were compared in [7], and our main conclusion was that dissimilarity-based representation for the data is the most adequate for this kind of application.

In a previous work [8] we proposed a methodology to deal with the class imbalance in TLC profile identification based on the use of a classification system with two decision stages: the first one was implemented by a one-class classifier aiming at recognizing most of the normal cases; the second stage was prepared to deal with the remaining samples, which were likely to contain all the pathological and a small percentage of normal samples, thus expecting a negligible effect from class imbalance in the final classification results. In that work, one of the main difficulties was related with the selection of the rejection rate parameter of the one-class classifier in the first stage, as a low rejection rate caused an unacceptable situation of several pathological samples being classified as normal, while a high value of this parameter had as consequence a very large number of normal samples being passed to the second level.

This paper presents a method for automating the selection of the rejection rate of one-class classifiers aiming at optimizing the classifier performance. These classifiers are used in a new classification approach to deal with class imbalance in TLC patterns. The classification is performed in two decision stages, both implemented using optimized one-class classifiers: the first stage aims at recognizing most of the normal samples; the outliers of this first decision level are presented to the second stage, which is a multiclassifier prepared to identify both pathological and normal patterns.

The layout of this paper is as follows: section 2 is devoted to the description of the proposed methodology for one-class classifiers optimization that supports the classification approach detailed in section 3. Some results and conclusions are presented in sections 4 and 5, respectively.

2   One-Class Classifier Optimization

One-class classifiers learn only with samples of one class, the target class. Afterwards, when an unseen sample is available for classification, the result of its comparison with the learned class is a dissimilarity measure, which can be either a distance or a probability, and that is used for accepting or rejecting the unseen sample as a member of the class that the classifier is prepared to recognize. As during the training phase only samples of the target class are presented to the classifier, the identification of the elements that do not belong to the target class (outliers) is based on the definition of a rejection threshold which is determined from the target samples in the training phase. The percentage of target samples that are rejected during training is a parameter of the one-class classifier, and this value is usually empirically established as 5% or 10% of the number of elements of the training set [3]. However, the frontier of the class thus formed can be inadequate for posterior classification tasks, if it does not guarantee a balance between a high acceptance rate of target samples and a high rejection rate of outliers. In order to achieve the required balance, we need to establish criteria for the optimization of the rejection rate threshold. The method that we have developed for this particular purpose, based on Receiver Operating Characteristic (ROC) curves and classifier performance functions, is described in the following subsections.

2.1 Classifier Performance Assessment Using ROC Analysis

A ROC curve pictures the percentage of correctly classified target samples as a function of the percentage of outliers that are erroneously considered as belonging to the target class, hence implicitly combining the information concerning the distribution of the classification error between the target and outlier classes. As each curve point is associated with a particular value of the rejection rate of the one-class classifier, the curve can be obtained after marking several operating points, which are afterwards linked by line segments, starting at point (0,0) and ending at (1,1).

Since distinct classifier types generate distinct ROC curves, the area under the curve is commonly used to evaluate and compare the performance of the individual classifiers. Nevertheless, the ROC area is a global measure that congregates all possible operating points of a particular classifier type, and it is not interesting in what concerns the selection of the parameter that maximizes the classifier performance. A one-class classifier with a specific rejection rate corresponds to a specific ROC curve point, and the selection of the threshold that warranties the best performance for a particular application is an essential step in the classifier specification process.

Figure 1a presents the ROC curve for a one-class classifier trained with the 50 target samples shown in the dispersion diagram of figure 1b, where other 50 outliers are also depicted. The frontiers of the target class generated by distinct values for the rejection rate parameter, ranging from 10% (outer frontier) to 50% (inner frontier), are also shown. From the analysis of this diagram, we can conclude that the establishment of the decision threshold that optimizes the classifier performance is a difficult task.

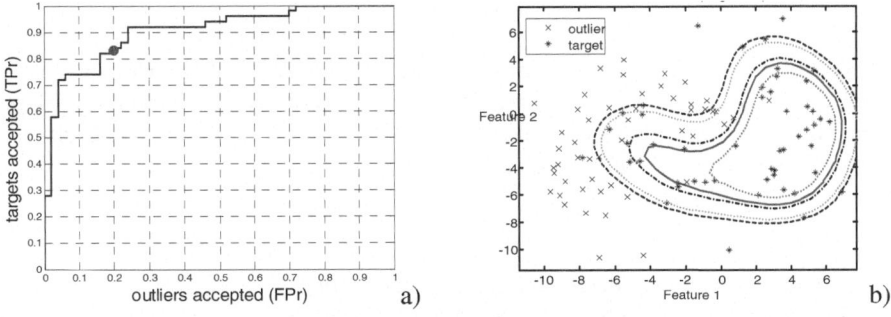

Fig. 1. a) ROC curve for a one-class classifier trained with the 50 target samples; b) dispersion diagram depicting 100 samples (50 target and 50 outliers)

2.2 Automatic Estimation of the Rejection Parameter

A classification matrix shows the final results of a particular classification task, and its elements can be used for calculating some performance measures relating the number of correctly and incorrectly classified samples. The matrix associated with the operating point marked on the ROC curve of figure 1a is presented in Table 1. The definitions and values of some of the performance measures that are most commonly calculated from this matrix, namely the true positive rate (*tpr*), the false positive rate (*fpr*), Recall (*R*) and Precision (*P*), are also shown.

Table 1.

True Labels	Estimated Labels		
	Outlier	Target	TOTAL
Outlier	TN = 40	FP = 10	Neg = 50
Target	FN = 9	TP = 41	Pos = 50
TOTAL	49	51	100

$$R = tpr = \frac{TP}{Pos} = 0.820$$

$$fpr = \frac{FP}{Neg} = 0.200$$

$$P = \frac{TP}{TP + FP} = 0.804$$

An efficient classifier must generate high values both for *R* and *P*. However, as it is not possible to guarantee the simultaneous increase of these two measures, it is common to use another performance measure, the F_β function (equation 1), which combines the values of *R* and *P* in a harmonic average such that high values for F_β always correspond to high values of *R* and *P*. β is a parameter that establishes the relative weights of *R* and *P*.

$$F_\beta = \frac{(\beta^2 + 1) RP}{\beta^2 P + R} \tag{1}$$

In order to relate the values of F_β with those presented on the ROC curve, we can state *P* as a function of *tpr* and *fpr* (equation 2), and obtain the new expression for the F_β function shown in equation 3.

$$P = \frac{tpr}{tpr + c \cdot fpr}, \quad c = \frac{Neg}{Pos} \tag{2}$$

$$F_\beta = \frac{(\beta^2 + 1) tpr}{\beta^2 + tpr + c \cdot fpr} \tag{3}$$

When the value of F_β is set equal to a constant *k*, the resulting isometric curve, $F_\beta = k$, can be overlapped on the corresponding ROC (equation 4). If this procedure is repeated for *k* within a specific range, the optimal operating point of the classifier belongs to the isometric curve tangent to the ROC.

$$tpr = \frac{k \cdot c}{\beta^2 + 1 - k} \left[fpr + \frac{\beta^2}{c} \right] \tag{4}$$

As an alternative to the described procedure, equation 3 can be used for calculating directly the curve that characterizes the F_β measure. The *tpr* and *fpr* values corresponding to the maximum of F_β allow the direct determination of the optimal operating point, which corresponds to the optimal rejection rate, T_{Rej}, of the classifier.

$$T_{Rej} = 1 - tpr \tag{5}$$

The methodology just described was used for obtaining the F_β curve depicted in fig. 2a, where the maximal value for this performance measure is also marked. In figure 2b some isometric F_β curves are overlapped on the original ROC of figure 1a; in this figure, the maximum of F_β corresponds to the isometric curve which is tangent to the ROC, and the tangency point is the optimal operating point of the classifier. As can be observed in fig. 2, the same value for the *fpr* is determined from the two graphs.

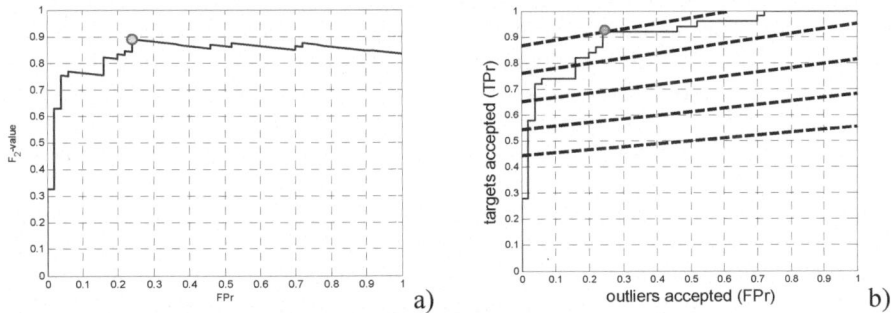

Fig. 2. a) F_β curve with the point corresponding to function maximum marked; b) ROC curve with isometric F_β curves

3   Recognition of Chromatographic Profiles Using One-Class Classifiers

This paper proposes a new approach to deal with the class imbalance in TLC patterns based on the use of one-class classifiers, structured in two decision stages: the first one is implemented by a classifier aiming at recognizing most of the normal samples; the outliers of this first stage are then presented to the second decision level, which is a multiclassifier prepared to deal with both pathological and normal classes.

As class distribution is unknown, we have selected Parzen one-class classifiers which are easily adapted to almost all types of distributions and have already demonstrated to be adequate for the recognition of chromatographic patterns [8].

The chromatographic patterns are initially processed in order to generate chromatographic profiles that are representative of the pathological and normal classes. This data was afterwards converted to the dissimilarity representation proposed by Pekalska [6] as described in [7].

The one-class classifier of the first stage was trained with half normal samples randomly selected. The optimization phase followed the procedure described in the previous section, and the dataset used for the determination of the F_β function maximum consisted of the remaining normal samples and a set of outliers formed by synthetic pathological samples.

In the second decision level, the multiclassifier is defined by a voting scheme based on the highest *a posteriori* probability that uses the results of four optimized one-classifiers, three for recognizing each of the pathological classes while the fourth one is prepared to identify the remaining normal samples. The datasets used for the training and optimization steps were oversampled with the introduction of synthetic pathological samples, as described in [9].

4 Experimental Results

The proposed classification approach was evaluated with images of TLC plates containing urine chromatograms of individuals suspicious of suffering from a LSD disease. The dataset is formed by samples from four classes, three corresponding to LSD diseases and one normal, with the following distribution: 14 classified as Gangliosidosis (GM1), 8 as Hurler syndrome (HUR), 17 as Alpha-Mannosidosis (MAN) and the remaining 996 labeled as normal. This uneven distribution of samples among the classes clearly defines this classification problem as a highly imbalanced problem.

Figure 3 shows the classification matrices obtained for the first decision level using the optimized one-class classifier (left) and the non-optimized one-class classifier (right) presented in [8]. From these results, it is worth mentioning that classifier optimization allows a significant decrease of the number of misclassified pathological patterns, even though a global increase of the number of outliers is also observed. To deal with this situation, the multiclassifier in the second stage, besides being designed with three classifiers optimized to recognize each of the pathological classes, also includes a one-class classifier trained with samples considered as outliers in the first level, but that are effectively typical normal patterns.

Figure 4 presents the classification matrices for two forests of 15 two-stage classifiers: the results on the left were obtained with the solution proposed in this paper using only optimized one-class classifiers; the values on the right were obtained with the two-stage classifier presented in [8]. All values were obtained with leave-one-out cross validation method. For F_β calculation we considered $\beta=2$, as we are mainly interested in the detection of the pathological cases, which justifies the higher significance given to recall when compared to precision [10]. The classification

True	Estimated Labels		
Labels	Outlier	Target	TOTAL
Outlier	37	2	39
Target	356	643	996
TOTAL	390	645	1035

True	Estimated Labels		
Labels	Outlier	Target	TOTAL
Outlier	35	4	39
Target	206	790	996
TOTAL	241	794	1035

Fig. 3. Classification matrices for the optimized one-class classifier (left) and the non-optimized one-class classifier (right)

True Labels	Estimated Labels				
	GM1	HUR	MAN	NOR	Total
GM1	13	0	0	1	14
HUR	0	5	0	3	8
MAN	0	0	13	4	17
NOR	0	8	0	988	996
Total	13	13	13	996	1035

	GM1	HUR	MAN	NOR
R	0.93	0.63	0.76	0.99
P	1.00	0.38	1.00	0.99
F_2	0.94	0.56	0.8	0.99

True Labels	Estimated Labels				
	GM1	HUR	MAN	NOR	Total
GM1	13	0	0	1	14
HUR	0	4	0	4	8
MAN	0	0	15	2	17
NOR	5	12	10	969	996
Total	18	16	25	976	1035

	GM1	HUR	MAN	NOR
R	0.93	0.50	0.88	0.97
P	0.72	0.25	0.60	0.99
F_2	0.88	0.42	0.81	0.98

Fig. 4. Classification matrix for the two-stage classifier using optimized one-class classifiers on the two levels of decision (left) and classification matrix for the two-stage classifier combining a non-optimized one-class classifier (1st stage) and hierarchical classifier (2nd stage) presented in [8]

results and performance measure values presented in figure 4 demonstrate that both approaches are adequate for dealing with the high imbalance between the normal and pathological classes in TLC pattern classification. Nevertheless, with the exception of a slight decrease in performance for the MAN class, we can conclude that the solution based on optimized classifiers is globally superior.

5 Conclusions

This paper presented a method for the optimization of one-class classifiers based on the automatic selection of the classifier rejection rate. These classifiers are the basis for a novel classification approach to deal with class imbalance in TLC patterns recognition, which is due to the huge difference between the number of normal and pathological cases, as a consequence of the rarity of LSD diseases. The classification is performed in two decision stages, both implemented using optimized one-class classifiers: the first stage aims at recognizing most of the normal samples; the outliers of this first decision level are presented to the second stage, which is a multiclassifier prepared to deal with both pathological and normal patterns.

The proposed classification approach was evaluated with chromatographic profiles derived from images of TLC plates, using samples from the normal and three pathological classes. The use of an optimized classifier in the first decision level reduced the number of pathological samples that are erroneously classified as normal, but was still able to recognize most of the normal samples, thus avoiding the need of undersampling strategies for this class. We can also conclude that the proposed solution produced a global increase of the final performance measures when compared with previous results for the same dataset, except for the slight decrease observed for the MAN class. However, it is worth mentioning that the use of optimized classifiers in the second stage of classification was able to produce a significant decrease of the number of false positives.

References

[1] Skurichina, M., Raudys, S., Duin, R.P.W.: K-Nearest Neighbors Directed Noise Injection in Multilayer Perceptron Training. IEEE Transactions on Neural Networks 11 (2000)

[2] Chawla, N.V., Japkowicz, N., Kolcz, A.: Editorial: Special Issue: Learning from Imbalanced Data Sets. Sigkdd Explorations 6, 1–6 (2004)

[3] Tax, D.M.J.: One-class Classification; Concept-learning in the Absence of Counterexamples. Ph.D. thesis: Delft University of Technology (2001)

[4] Durand, G., Seta, N.: Protein Glycosylation and Diseases: Blood and Urinary Oligosaccharides as Markers for Diagnosis and Therapeutic Monitoring. Clin. Chem. 46, 795–805 (2000)

[5] Sewell, A.C.: Urinary Oligosaccharides. Techniques in Diagnostic Human Biochemical Genetics, pp. 219–231 (1991)

[6] Pekalska, E., Duin, R.P.W.: Dissimilarity Representations Allow for Building Good Classifiers. Pattern Recogn. Lett. 23, 943–956 (2002)

[7] Sousa, A.V., Mendonça, A.M., Campilho, A.: Dissimilarity-based Classification of Chromatographic Profiles. Pattern Analysis and Applications 11(3-4), 409–423 (2008)

[8] Sousa, A.V., Mendonça, A.M., Campilho, A.: Minimizing the Imbalance Problem in Chromatographic Profile Classification with One-class Classifiers. In: Campilho, A., Kamel, M.S. (eds.) ICIAR 2008. LNCS, vol. 5112, pp. 413–422. Springer, Heidelberg (2008)

[9] Sousa, A.V., Mendonça, A.M., Campilho, A.: Chromatographic Pattern Classification. IEEE Trans. on Biomedical Engineering 55(6), 1687–1696 (2008)

[10] Visa, S., Ralescu, A.: Learning Imbalanced and Overlapping Classes Using Fuzzy Sets. In: Workshop on Learning from Imbalanced Datasets II, ICML, Washington DC (2003)

Variable Order Finite-Context Models in DNA Sequence Coding

Daniel A. Martins*, António J.R. Neves, and Armando J. Pinho

Signal Processing Lab, DETI / IEETA
University of Aveiro, 3810–193 Aveiro, Portugal
dam@ua.pt, an@ua.pt, ap@ua.pt

Abstract. Being an essential key in biological research, the DNA sequences are often shared between researchers and digitally stored for future use. As these sequences grow in volume, it also grows the need to encode them, thus saving space for more sequences. Besides this, a better coding method corresponds to a better model of the sequence, allowing new insights about the DNA structure. In this paper, we present an algorithm capable of improving the encoding results of algorithms that depend of low-order finite-context models to encode DNA sequences. To do so, we implemented a variable order finite-context model, supported by a predictive function. The proposed algorithm allows using three finite-context models at once without requiring the inclusion of side information in the encoded sequence. Currently, the proposed method shows small improvements in the encoding results when compared with same order finite-context models. However, we also present results showing that there is space for further improvements regarding the use variable order finite-context models for DNA sequence coding.

1 Introduction

The complete human genome has about 3 000 million bases [1] and the genome of the wheat has nearly 16 000 million [2]. These two examples show that DNA sequences can have very large sizes when stored or transmitted without any kind of encoding.

DNA is a language written with an alphabet of four different symbols (usually known as nucleotides or bases), namely, Adenine (A), Cytosine (C), Guanine (G), and Thymine (T). Therefore, without compression, it takes approximately 750 MBytes to store the human genome (using $\log_2 4 = 2$ bits per base) and 4 GBytes to store the genome of the wheat.

Besides this motivation, DNA compression can play an important role in providing new insights regarding the underlying information source. This is due to the models associated to each compression technique: the closer the model to the DNA information source, the better the resulting encoding will be.

---

* This work was supported in part by the FCT (Fundação para a Ciência e Tecnologia) grant PTDC/EIA/72569/2006.

H. Araujo et al. (Eds.): IbPRIA 2009, LNCS 5524, pp. 457–464, 2009.

In the last years, finite-context models (FCM) have been used for DNA sequence compression as secondary, fallback, mechanisms [3,4,5,6,7,8]. The FCM's used in these cases are usually of low-order (typically, 1 to 3) and are used only when the main encoding algorithm produces bad results.

In order to improve the encoding results that depend on these low-order FCM's, we developed an algorithm capable of choosing between models of different orders. This method allows to encode DNA sequences using FCM's with different orders as it was a single model. The improvements attained with this approach are due to the use of multiple models of different orders, without needing to include side information. This reduces the average number of bits per base (bpb) necessary for encoding the sequences, therefore improving the encoding result.

This paper contains six sections. We start by introducing the finite-context models and their relevance in current DNA encoding techniques (Section 2). In Section 3, we briefly explain the concept of variable order finite-context models (VOFCM) and we introduce the proposed prediction function. The tree representation of the VOFCM is presented in Section 4. Finally, we present experimental results in Section 5 and draw some conclusions in Section 6.

2   Low Order Finite-Context Models

Consider an information source that generates symbols, s, from a finite alphabet $\mathcal{A}$. At time t, the sequence of outcomes generated by the source is $x^t = x_1 x_2 \ldots x_t$. The proposed algorithm relies on a VOFCM that generates probability estimates that are then used for driving an arithmetic encoder [9]. The VOFCM collects statistical information from a context of depth M_{vofcm}, which is also the maximum order of the VOFCM. At time t, we represent the conditioning outcomes by $c^t = x_{t-M_{\text{vofcm}}+1}, \ldots, x_{t-1}, x_t$. Note that the total number of conditioning states of a VOFCM with maximum context depth M_{vofcm} is $\frac{|\mathcal{A}|^{M_{\text{vofcm}}+1}-1}{|\mathcal{A}|-1}$. In the case of DNA, $|\mathcal{A}| = 4$. In Fig 1 and 2 we show an example of a FCM and a VOFCM, respectively.

From the most recent algorithms for DNA compression, we can conclude that there is a common interest in using several competing encoding techniques. This is due to the fact that different regions in the DNA sequences are better encoded with different algorithms. Knowing this property, it is possible to use a fallback algorithm when the primary algorithm produces bad results.

Regardeless of the main encoding method, the fallback algorithm is most of the cases a low-order FCM. Some of the DNA compression algorithms that use FCM's as a fallback mechanism are:

- *Biocompress-2* [3];
- *GenCompress* [4,5];
- *DNA2* and *DNA3* [6];
- *GeNML* [7];
- *DNAEnc* [8].

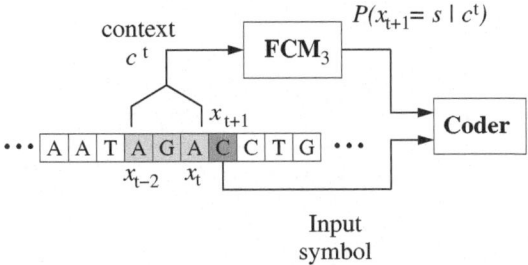

Fig. 1. Example of an order-3 finite-context model, used for estimating the probabilities. The probability of the next outcome, x_{t+1}, is conditioned by the last 3 outcomes.

Using a FCM, we can model the DNA sequence by counting the occurrences of each symbol given a certain past (see Fig. 1). Encouraged by the overall acceptance as a fallback encoding algorithm, we went from this fixed low-order FCM to a variable low-order FCM, as described in Section 3.

3   Variable Order Finite-Context Models

In this paper, we present a technique capable of improving the compression rates produced by low-order FCM's. This is achieved by allowing the encoding system to use a FCM with variable order (VOFCM). In fact, this VOFCM is a group of three fixed low-order FCM's, being the order of the FCM decided automatically, avoiding the need to pass information (overhead) of the chosen FCM to the decoder. This way, the proposed algorithm acts like a single FCM model, making its use transparent to the encoder and decoder. This VOFCM is also known as a *Variable Length Markov Chain* (VLMC) [10].

In order to choose which FCM order is used, we developed a function that automatically tries to select the best order for each symbol being encoded. The developed function, called *Efficiency*, is in fact a simple prediction system that decides which FCM to use, taking into account the following statistics:

- the entropy associated to the FCM;
- the probability associated to the last outcome symbol in the FCM;
- the FCM associated *Bonus*.

The *Bonus* is a function with range $[0, 1]$, that increases if the last occurred symbol was the most probable to appear and decreases otherwise. Next we define the proposed *Efficiency* function (1), and the *Bonus* function (2):

$$E(k, t) = \frac{P(x_t|\text{FCM}_k)B(k, t)}{H(k, t)}, \tag{1}$$

$$B(k, t) = \begin{cases} B(k, t-1) - (1 - B(k, t-1)) \log P(x_t|\text{FCM}_k) \\ B(k, t-1) + B(k, t-1) \log P(x_t|\text{FCM}_k) \end{cases}, \tag{2}$$

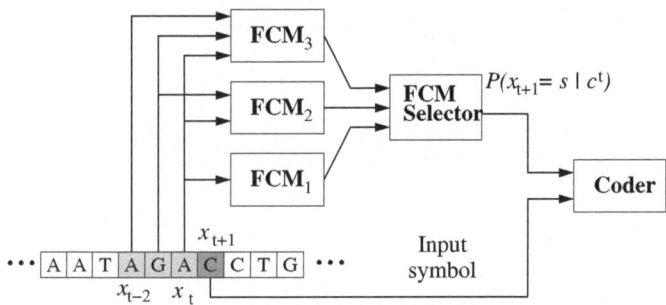

Fig. 2. Example of the proposed approach, where the variable low-order FCM is composed by 3 fixed low-order FCM of order 1, 2 and 3. The next input symbol probability is conditioned by the last 3 outcomes and the *Efficiency* function.

where the first member of (2) is used when

$$P(x_t|\text{FCM}_k) = \max P(x|\text{FCM}_k), \quad x \in \{A, C, T, G\},$$

and where k represents the order of the FCM, $H(k,t)$ is the entropy of FCM_k at time t, and $P(x_t|\text{FCM}_k)$ is the conditional probability of the last symbol calculated according to a FCM of order k.

4   Tree-Structured Representation of VOFCM

Inspired by the work of J. Rissanen [11], also considered in [10], we implemented a tree representation for the statistical information collected from the DNA sequence. Note that we do not use the *Context Gather* algorithm described in Section III of [11], but, instead, we developed a greedy algorithm to create the tree.

Basically, each level of the tree corresponds to a position of a context symbol. For example, a tree with a depth 3 corresponds to an order-3 context model. Each node of the tree is constructed the first time that the symbol appears in the corresponding position of the context. Note that by *context* we refer to a ordered group of outcome symbols.

Each node of the tree contains the probabilistic information about a specific model and each branch represents a past outcome symbol. For example, the root node has 4 branches, each one representing the last outcome symbol. Furthermore, with this representation we have easy access to all the FCM's. In fact, as we visit the tree, from the root to the leaves, we are visiting the different FCM's from a specific context.

Fig. 3 shows an example of the tree-structured representation of the VOFCM. In this example, it is possible to see that the tree has not yet reached its full extension. The *TREE* block has the tree basic information like number of nodes and maximum FCM order (*maxDepth*). From the *TREE* block it grows two nodes. On the left node, we have the next outcome (*NEXT*) and the current

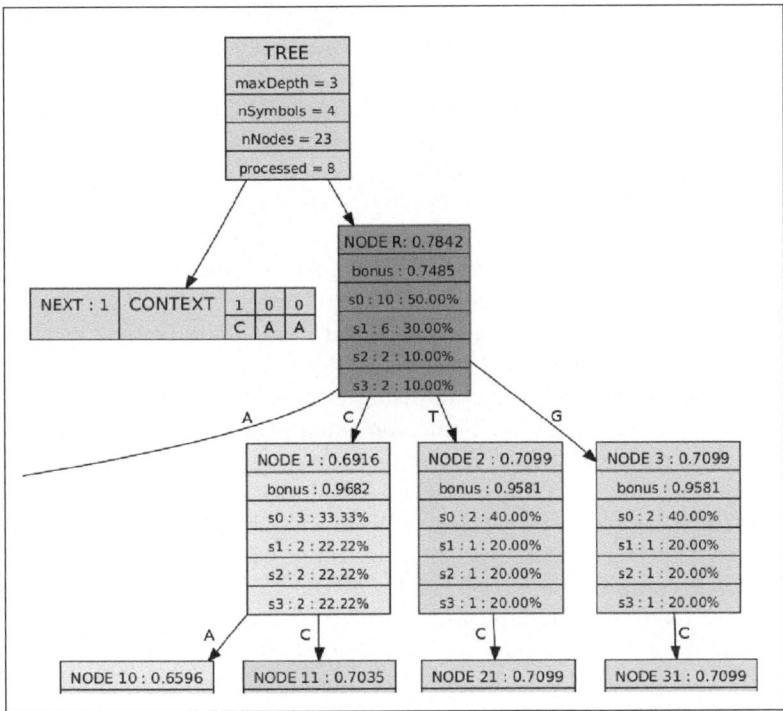

Fig. 3. Detail of a tree-structured VOFCM. In the figure, it is possible to see the tree details along with the context and the root node.

context (*CONTEXT*). The right node (*NODE R*) is the root node of the tree. In each node, we have the statistical information about each symbol, the *Bonus* and the *Efficiency* values. The efficiency value is presented in the first row of each node. Still in Fig. 3, the yellow and green nodes represent the current context, the green node being the one that presents higher *Efficiency*.

5 Experimental Results

In order to present a first approach to the lower bound of encoding using low-order FCM's, we compare the difference between encoding using a fixed order FCM and encoding using a variable order FCM (always choosing the best order for each symbol being encoded). Afterwards, we tested the proposed method using the *Efficiency* function presented in Section 3.

The results are presented in Table 1 in the *Test 1* columns. The first and second columns of the table contain the name and size (in number of bases) of the DNA sequences. In the *FCM* columns it is presented the encoding results (in bpb) of the DNA sequences using the fixed low-order FCM, for orders 1, 2 and 3.

In the *FCM Limit* column it is presented a lower bound of the encoding results using the variable low-order FCM. These results were obtained choosing the best from the three models in each symbol to be encoded. Because this choice was made by comparing the encoding results from the three models, the results provided in the column *FCM Limit* are to be taken as a lower limit comparison, as they don't include the necessary overhead to signal which was the selected FCM for each symbol. Doing so would make the encoder unusable, as the necessary overhead would increase the resulting bpb value drastically.

Finally, the column *FCM Eff* presents the results from the proposed algorithm using the *Efficiency* function to decide which order of the FCM to use. Note that in columns 6 and 7 we use a VOFCM with maximum order 3 as this is only intended to use in fallback low-order FCM algorithms.

In [8] it is presented some results using arithmetic encoding with FCM's as primary and fallback methods. Using the same primary encoding method, i.e., a FCM with the same order than the presented in [8], we tested the proposed VOFCM method as the fallback method. To do so, we replaced the fixed order FCM used in [8] (an order-3 FCM) as fallback encoding by the VOFCM proposed in this paper. The results are presented in Table 1 in the *Test 2* columns.

The *DNA3* column shows the results of the DNA3 compressor of Manzini *et al.* [6], to allow some comparison with other existing methods. The *FCM-IR* columns show the order of the primary FCM that was obtained using a "brute force" approach [8] and the corresponding encoding results in bpb. The columns *VOFCM* show the order of the primary FCM (that is equal to the used in *FCM-IR*) and the encoding results in bpb. In the *Total* row it is possible to notice that the results obtained in *VOFCM* are globally slightly better.

6   Conclusions

According to Table 1, we can see the benefits of using the proposed method, as the bpb necessary to the encoding reduce. In columns *Test 1* of Table 1, we show the potential gain of using the proposed method versus the use of a fixed order FCM. Besides the improvements of the encoding results, the proposed method allows using three FCM's with different orders at the same time. Recall that the FCM model is chosen by the *Efficiency* function on an symbol by symbol basis.

From columns *Test 2*, we conclude that it is possible to bring improvements to the overall encoding results, replacing the fallback mechanism by the proposed VOFCM with the *Efficiency* function. Furthermore, we can take advantage of using more than one FCM without having to conduct a "brute force" search for the FCM with best encoding results.

In *Test 1*, the improvements provided by the use of the VOFCM are more visible than in *Test 2*, because, in the latter, the proposed algorithm is only used when the primary encoding method fails, making the improvements less notable in the results. Nevertheless, the proposed method brought better overall results to the DNA encoding technique that uses low-order FCM's. Moreover, the results from column *FCM Limit* show that the use of VOFCM with a predictive system

Table 1. Test 1: Encoding results using low-order FCM with fixed and variable order. In column *FCM* the encoding is done using fixed order FCM, in *FCM Limit* it is chosen the best order for each encoding symbol (used as a lower bound for comparison) and in *FCM Eff* we have the results using the proposed VOFCM. The best average results are presented in bold. **Test 2**: Comparison of encoding results using the proposed VOFCM as fallback method. Column *DNA3* and *FCM IR* show results from [6] and [8], respectively. Column *VOFCM* shows the result of the same method applied in *FCM-IR*, but using the proposed VOFCM as fallback method.

Name	Size	Test 1					Test 2				
		FCM			FCM	FCM	DNA3	FCM-IR		VOFCM	
		1	2	3	Limit	Eff	bps	Order	bpb	Order	bpb
y-1	230 203	1.958	1.954	1.950	1.862	1.951	1.871	11	1.909	11	1.913
y-4	1 531 929	1.947	1.944	1.939	1.867	1.944	1.881	12	1.910	12	1.918
y-14	784 328	1.953	1.949	1.945	1.870	1.950	1.926	12	1.938	12	1.946
y-mit	85 779	1.590	1.568	1.542	1.411	1.605	1.523	7	1.479	7	1.478
Average	–	1.938	1.934	**1.929**	1.852	1.935	**1.882**	–	1.904	–	1.912
m-7	5 114 647	1.933	1.924	1.922	1.837	1.917	1.835	12	1.835	12	1.833
m-11	49 909 125	1.935	1.925	1.923	1.828	1.918	1.790	13	1.778	13	1.776
m-19	703 729	1.944	1.932	1.928	1.828	1.920	1.888	10	1.873	10	1.869
m-x	17 430 763	1.921	1.913	1.911	1.827	1.911	1.703	13	1.692	13	1.691
m-y	711 108	1.918	1.910	1.909	1.826	1.907	1.707	11	1.741	11	1.742
Average	–	1.931	1.922	1.920	1.828	**1.916**	1.772	–	1.762	–	**1.761**
at-1	29 830 437	1.928	1.923	1.920	1.843	1.919	1.844	13	1.878	13	1.881
at-3	23 465 336	1.931	1.927	1.923	1.846	1.922	1.843	13	1.873	13	1.875
at-4	17 550 033	1.929	1.925	1.921	1.844	1.919	1.851	13	1.878	13	1.880
Average	–	1.929	1.925	1.921	1.844	**1.920**	**1.845**	–	1.876	–	1.879
h-2	236 268 154	1.924	1.916	1.913	1.819	1.910	1.790	13	1.734	13	1.731
h-13	95 206 001	1.918	1.910	1.907	1.816	1.906	1.818	13	1.759	13	1.760
h-22	33 821 688	1.942	1.929	1.922	1.806	1.915	1.767	12	1.710	12	1.703
h-x	144 793 946	1.922	1.914	1.911	1.821	1.910	1.732	13	1.666	13	1.665
h-y	22 668 225	1.918	1.910	1.908	1.812	1.900	1.411	13	1.579	13	1.577
Average	–	1.923	1.915	1.912	1.818	**1.909**	1.762	–	1.712	–	**1.710**
Total	–	1.925	1.917	1.914	1.822	**1.911**	1.772	–	1.735	–	**1.734**

can bring even better encoding results. To explore this potentiality, we pretend to further explore the use the VOFCM using other predictive and cost functions and apply them to higher order FCM's.

References

1. Rowen, L., Mahairas, G., Hood, L.: Sequencing the human genome. Science 278, 605–607 (1997)
2. Dennis, C., Surridge, C.: A. thaliana genome. Nature 408, 791 (2000)
3. Grumbach, S., Tahi, F.: A new challenge for compression algorithms: genetic sequences. Information Processing & Management 30(6), 875–886 (1994)

4. Chen, X., Kwong, S., Li, M.: A compression algorithm for DNA sequences and its applications in genome comparison. In: Asai, K., Miyano, S., Takagi, T. (eds.) Genome Informatics 1999: Proc. of the 10th Workshop, Tokyo, Japan, pp. 51–61 (1999)
5. Chen, X., Kwong, S., Li, M.: A compression algorithm for DNA sequences. IEEE Engineering in Medicine and Biology Magazine 20, 61–66 (2001)
6. Manzini, G., Rastero, M.: A simple and fast DNA compressor. Software—Practice and Experience 34, 1397–1411 (2004)
7. Korodi, G., Tabus, I.: An efficient normalized maximum likelihood algorithm for DNA sequence compression. ACM Trans. on Information Systems 23(1), 3–34 (2005)
8. Pinho, A.J., Neves, A.J.R., Ferreira, P.J.S.G.: Inverted-repeats-aware finite-context models for DNA coding. In: Proc. of the 16th European Signal Processing Conf., EUSIPCO 2008, Lausanne, Switzerland (August 2008)
9. Salomon, D.: Data compression - The complete reference, 2nd edn. Springer, Heidelberg (2000)
10. Bühlmann, P., Wyner, A.J.: Variable length Markov chains. The Annals of Statistics 27(2), 480–513 (1999)
11. Rissanen, J.: A universal data compression system. IEEE Trans. on Information Theory 29(5), 656–664 (1983)

Characterizing Graphs Using Spherical Triangles

Hewayda ElGhawalby[1,2] and Edwin R. Hancock[1,*]

[1] Department of Computer Science, University of York,
YO10 5DD, UK
[2] Faculty of Engineering, Suez Canal university, Egypt
{howaida,erh}@cs.york.ac.uk

Abstract. In this paper the Hausdorff distance, and a robust modified variant of the Hausdorff distance are used for the purpose of matching graphs whose structure can be described in terms of triangular faces. A geometric quantity from the geodesic triangle and the corresponding Euclidean triangle is deduced and used as a feature for the purposes of gauging the similarity of graphs, and hence clustering them. we experiment on sets of graphs representing the proximity image features in different views of different objects from the CMU, MOVI and chalet house sequences. By applying multidimensional scaling to the Hausdorff distances between the different object views, we demonstrate that this representation is capable of clustering the different views of the same object together.

1 Introduction

Graph embeddings have found widespread use in machine learning and pattern recognition for the purposes of clustering, analyzing and visualization relational data. However, they have also proved to be useful as a means of graph characterization. The idea here is to embed the nodes of a graph on a manifold in a vector space, and to use the geometric properties of the resulting point-set as a graph characteristic. Using the heat kernel of a graph to construct the embedding, Xiao and Hancock [8] have shown how both moments of the embedded point-sets can be used as effective characteristics for graph clustering. However, this picture can be taken further if we view the nodes of a graph as residing on a manifold. In this case, we can associate curvatures with the edges of the graph since these can be viewed as geodesics on the manifold. In a recent paper [5], we have explored this characterization and have shown how graphs can be matched by computing the Hausdorff distance between the curvatures of sets of edges. In [4] our goal was to undertake analysis of the embedding of a graph using the Gauss-Bonnet theorem to link the topological structure of a graph to the geometry of the embedding. In this paper and as an intermediate step we have turned our attention to the geodesic triangles resulting from the embedding of first-order cycles. We show how to compute the areas of geodesic and Euclidean triangles, and use the area

---

* The authors acknowledge the financial support from the FET programme within the EU FP7, under the SIMBAD project (contract 213250).

H. Araujo et al. (Eds.): IbPRIA 2009, LNCS 5524, pp. 465–472, 2009.

ratio as an invariant for the purposes of matching. Experiments reveal that this is one of the most effective characterizations available.

2   Graphs Embedded into Manifolds

In this work we will study the manifold embedding of graphs resulting from the Young-Householder decomposition of the heat kernel [9]. We commence by letting the graph under study to be denoted by $G = (V, E)$ where V is the set of nodes and $E \subseteq V \times V$ is the set of edges. The elements of the adjacency matrix A of the graph G is defined by:

$$A(u, v) = \begin{cases} 1 & if (u, v) \in E \\ 0 & otherwise \end{cases} \tag{1}$$

To construct the Laplacian matrix we first establish a diagonal degree matrix D with elements $D(u, u) = \sum_{v \in V} A(u, v) = d_u$ From the degree and the adjacency matrices we can construct the Laplacian matrix $L = D - A$, that is the degree matrix minus the adjacency matrix.

$$L(u, v) = \begin{cases} d_u & if u = v \\ -1 & if (u, v) \in E \\ 0 & otherwise \end{cases} \tag{2}$$

The normalized is given by $\widehat{L} = D^{-1/2} L D^{-1/2}$. The spectral decomposition of the normalized Laplacian matrix is $\widehat{L} = \Phi L \Phi^T = \sum_{i=1}^{|V|} \lambda_i \phi_i \phi_i^T$ where $|V|$ is the number of nodes and $\Lambda = diag(\lambda_1, \lambda_2, ..., \lambda_{|V|}), (0 < \lambda_1 < \lambda_2 < ... < \lambda_{|V|})$ is the diagonal matrix with the ordered eigenvalues as elements and $\Phi = (\phi_1 | \phi_2 | ... | \phi_{|V|})$ is the matrix with the eigenvectors as columns. The heat kernel plays an important role in spectral graph theory. It encapsulates the way in which information flows through the edges of graph over time under the heat equation, and is the solution of the partial differential equation

$$\frac{\partial h_t}{\partial t} = -\widehat{L} h_t \tag{3}$$

where h_t is the heat kernel and t is the time. The solution is found by exponentiating the Laplacian eigenspectrum as follows

$$h_t = \exp[-\widehat{L} t] = \Phi \exp[-t\Lambda] \Phi^T \tag{4}$$

The heat kernel can be used to embed the nodes of a graph in a vector space. The matrix of embedding coordinates Y (i.e. the matrix whose columns are the vectors of node coordinates), is found by performing the Young-Householder decomposition $h_t = Y^T Y$ as a result the matrix of node embedding coordinates is

$$Y = (y_1 | y_2 | ... | y_{|V|}) = \exp[-\frac{1}{2} t \Lambda] \Phi^T \tag{5}$$

where y_u is the coordinate vector for the node u. In the vector space, the Euclidean distance between the nodes u and v of the graph is

$$d_e^2(u, v) = (y_u - y_v)^T(y_u - y_v) = \sum_{i=1}^{|V|} \exp[-\lambda_i t](\phi_i(u) - \phi_i(v))^2 \qquad (6)$$

When a pair of nodes are connected by an edge, then $d_G(u, v) = 1$. Assuming that the geodesic between the pair of nodes can be approximated by a segment of circle whose arc-length is the geodesic distance and whose chord-length is the Euclidean distance, if the radius of the circle is $R_s(u, v)$ and that the tangent vector to the circle arc undergoes a change in direction of $2\theta(u, v)$, then we have

$$d_g(u, v) = 2r_s(u, v)\theta(u, v) \qquad (7)$$

and

$$d_e(u, v) = 2r_s(u, v)\sin\theta(u, v) \qquad (8)$$

3   Geometric Preliminaries

Let M be a triangulation of a smooth surface S in $\Re^3$, A_g be the area of a geodesic triangle on S with angles $\{\alpha_i\}_{i=1}^3$ and geodesic edge lengths $\{d_{gi}\}_{i=1}^3$, and A_e be the area of the corresponding Euclidean triangle with edge lengths $\{d_{ei}\}_{i=1}^3$ and angles $\{\varphi_i\}_{i=1}^3$. Assuming that each geodesic is a great arc on a sphere with radius R_i, $i = 1, 2, 3$ corresponding to a central angle 2θ, and that the geodesic triangle is a triangle on a sphere with radius $R = \frac{1}{3}\sum_{i=1}^3 R_i$, with the Euclidean distance between the pair of nodes to be $d_e = \frac{1}{3}\sum_{i=1}^3 d_{ei}$. Considering a small area element on the sphere given in spherical coordinates by $dA = R^2 \sin\theta d\theta d\varphi$, the integration of dA bounded by 2θ gives us the area of the geodesic triangle

$$\begin{aligned} A_g &= R^2 \int_0^{2\theta} \int_0^{2\theta} \sin\theta d\theta d\varphi \\ &= R^2(2\theta)(1 - \cos(2\theta)) \\ &= R^2(2\theta)(2(\sin(\theta))^2) \\ &= \frac{1}{2R}(2R\theta)(2R\sin(\theta))^2 \end{aligned}$$

Substituting from (7) and (8) into (9), we obtain

$$A = \frac{1}{2R}(d_g)(d_e)^2 \qquad (9)$$

Since for an edge of the graph $d_g = 1$, we have

$$A = \frac{1}{2R}d_e^2 \qquad (10)$$

where d_e^2 is computed from the embedding using (6). Then we compute the curvature as the ratio $k = \frac{A_g}{A_d}$. Where $A_d = (1/2)d_{ei}d_{ej}\sin(\varphi_{ij})$ and φ_{ij} is the turning angle of the geodesic. We can now describe the data and model graphs in terms of triangular faces and assign to each face a curvature ratio k.

4   Hausdorff Distance

The Hausdorff distance has been used for a number of matching and recognition problems. It provides a means of computing the distance between sets of unordered observations when the correspondences between the individual items are unknown. In its most general setting, the Hausdorff distance is defined between compact sets in a metric space. Given two such sets, we consider for each point in one set is the closest point in the second set. Hausdorff distance is the maximum over all these values. More formally, the classical Hausdorff distance (HD) [6] between two finite point sets A and B is given by

$$H(A,B) = \max(h(A,B), h(B,A)) \tag{11}$$

where the directed Hausdorff distance from A to B is defined to be

$$h(A,B) = \max_{a \in A} \min_{b \in B} \|a - b\| \tag{12}$$

and $\|.\|$ is some underlying norm on the points of A and B (e.g., the L2 or Euclidean norm). Regardless of the norm, the Hausdorff metric captures the notion of the worst match between two objects. The computed value represents the largest distance between a point in one set and a point in the other one. Several variations of the Hausdorff distance have been proposed as alternatives to the maximum of the minimum approach in the classical one. These include Hausdorff fraction, Hausdorff quantile [6] and Spatially Coherent Matching [1]. A robust modified Hausdorff distance (MHD) based on the average distance value instead of the maximum value was proposed by Dubuisson and Jain [3], in this sense they defined the directed distance of the MHD as

$$h(A,B) = \frac{1}{N_A} \sum_{a \in A} \min_{b \in B} \|a - b\| \tag{13}$$

For this paper we will consider the classical and the modified Hausdorff distances. Using these ingredients we can describe how Hausdorff distances can be extended to graph-based representations. To commence let us consider two graphs $G_1 = (V_1, E_1, T_1, k_1)$ and $G_2 = (V_2, E_2, T_1, k_2)$, where V_1, V_2 are the sets of nodes, E_1, E_2 the sets of edges, T_1, T_2 are the sets of triangles, and k_1, k_2 the sets of Area ratio between the geodesic triangles and the corresponding Euclidean triangles defined in the previous section. We can now write the distances between two graphs as follows:

1) The classic Hausdorff distance (HD) is

$$h_{HD}(G_1, G_2) = \max_{i \in V_1} \min_{j \in V_2} \|k_2(j) - k_1(i)\| \tag{14}$$

2) The modified Hausdorff distance (MHD) is

$$h_{MHD}(G_1, G_2) = \frac{1}{|V_1|} \sum_{i \in V_1} \min_{j \in V_2} \|k_2(j) - k_1(i)\| \tag{15}$$

5   Multidimensional Scaling

For the purpose of visualization, the classical Multidimensional Scaling (MDS) [2] is a commonly used technique to embed the data specified in the matrix in Euclidean space. Given that H is the distance matrix with row r and column c entry H_{rc}. The first step of MDS is to calculate a matrix T whose element with row r and column c is given by $T_{rc} = -\frac{1}{2}[H_{rc}^2 - \widehat{H}_{r.}^2 - \widehat{H}_{.c}^2 + \widehat{H}_{..}^2]$ where $\widehat{H}_{r.} = \frac{1}{N}\sum_{c=1}^{N} H_{rc}$ is the average value over the rth row in the distance matrix, $H_{.c}$ is the similarly defined average value over the cth column and $\widehat{H}_{..} = \frac{1}{N^2}\sum_{r=1}^{N}\sum_{c=1}^{N} H_{rc}$ is the average value over all rows and columns of the distance matrix. Then, we subject the matrix T to an eigenvector analysis to obtain a matrix of embedding coordinates X. If the rank of T is k; $k \leq N$, then we will have k non-zero eigenvalues. We arrange these k non-zero eigenvalues in descending order, i.e., $l_1 \geq l_2 \geq ... \geq l_k \geq 0$. The corresponding ordered eigenvectors are denoted by u_i where l_i is the ith eigenvalue. The embedding coordinate system for the graphs is $X = [\sqrt{l_1}u_1, \sqrt{l_2}u_2, ..., \sqrt{l_k}u_k]$ for the graph indexed i, the embedded vector of the coordinates is $x_i = (X_{i,1}, X_{i,2}, ..., X_{i,k})^T$.

6   Experiments

In our experiments we use the standard CMU,MOVI and chalet house sequences as our data set [7]. These data sets contain different views of model houses from equally spaced viewing directions. From the house images, corner features are extracted, and Delaunay graphs representing the arrangement of feature points are constructed. Our data consists of ten graphs for each of the three houses. To commence, we compute the Euclidean distances between the nodes in each graph based on the heat kernel with the values of $t = 10.0, 1.0, 0.1$ and 0.01. Then we compute the area of each geodesic triangle and that of the corresponding Euclidean triangle and compute the ratio between these two values. From the area ratios, we compute the distance matrices for the thirty different graphs using the classical Hausdorff distance and the modified Hausdorff distance. Finally, we subject the distance matrices to the Multidimensional Scaling (MDS) procedure to embed them into a 2D space. Here each graph is represented by a single point. Figure 1 shows the results obtained using the classical Hausdorff distance. The subfigures are ordered from left to right and from top to bottom, using $t = 10.0, 1.0, 0.1$ and 0.01 in the heat kernel. Figure 2 shows the corresponding results obtained when the modified Hausdorff distance is used.

When the Euclidean distances are computed directly from the Laplacian embedding (i.e. $Y = \sqrt{\Lambda}\Phi^T$), the results shown in Figure 3 are obtained.

To investigate the results in more detail table 1 shows the rand index for the distance as a function of t. This index is computed as follows: We compute the mean for each cluster, then Compute the distance from each point to each mean. If the distance from correct mean is smaller than those to remaining means,then classification is correct, if not then classification is incorrect.Then compute the value (incorrect/(incorrect+correct)).

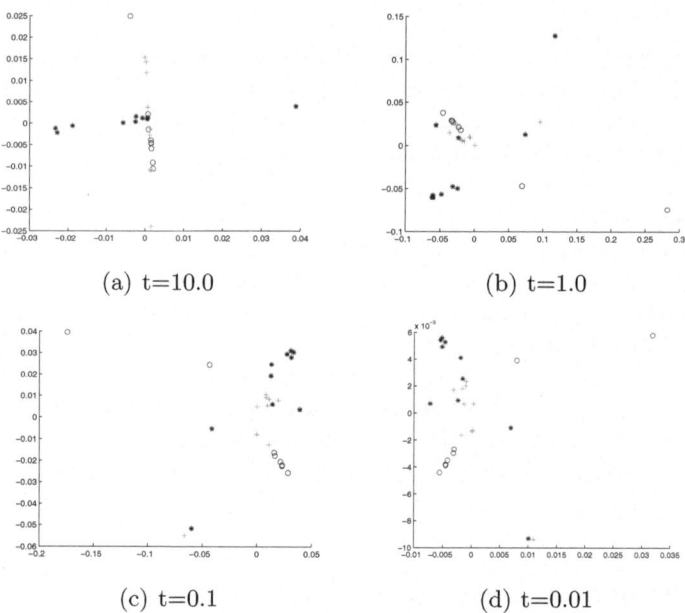

Fig. 1. MDS embedding obtained using HD for the houses data

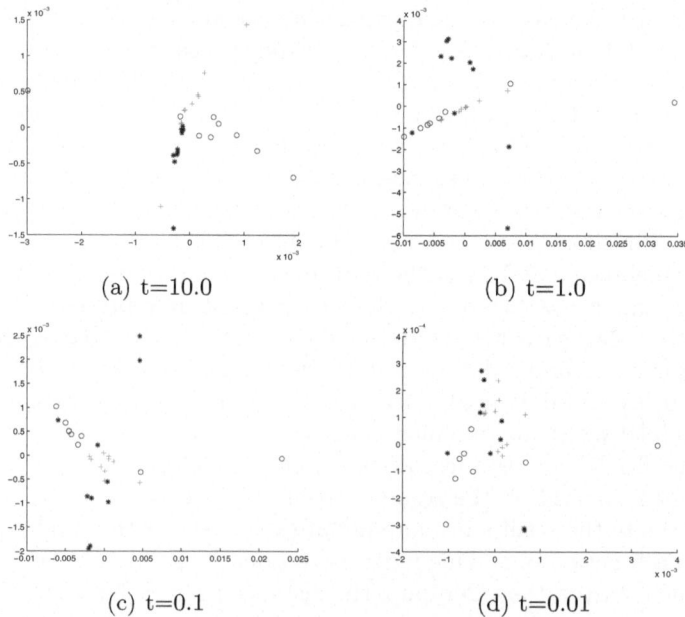

Fig. 2. MDS embedding obtained using MHD for the houses data

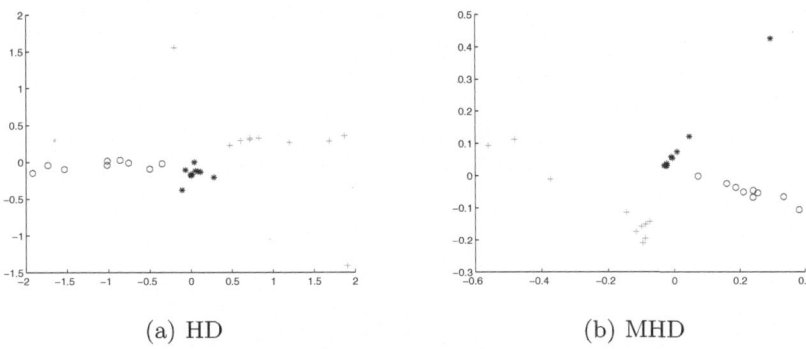

(a) HD   (b) MHD

Fig. 3. MDS embedding obtained using HD (to the left) and MHD (to the right) when d_e computed from the Laplacian embedding

Table 1. A rand index vs. t

	lap	t=10	t=1.0	t=0.1	t=0.01
HD	0.0667	0.4667	0.4333	0.5667	0.3667
MHD	0.0333	0.1333	0.3667	0.4333	0.3333

Table 2. A rand index vs. t. induced when the curvature was used.

	lap	t=10	t=1.0	t=0.1	t=0.01
HD	0.2333	0.1000	0.1667	0.4333	0.0333
MHD	0.100	0.1333	0.2333	0.1333	0.0333

There are two conclusions that can be drawn from this experimental study. First, the Laplacian eigenmap distinguishes the different classes better than the heat kernel embedding. Second, MHD gives better clusters than HD.

In previous work [5], we used the sectional curvature associated with the embedding as feature for the purposes of gauging the similarity of graphs, and hence clustering them. The table 2 shows the rand index for the results obtained as a function of t.

A comparison shows that the curvature attributes give a better clusters than those obtained by contrast when using the heat kernel embedding, better results are obtained when using the Laplacian eigenmap. In future work we will investigate a combination of these two attributes.

7   Conclusion and Future Work

In this paper we used a geometric quantity deduced from the area ratio of the geodesic and Euclidean triangles on a sphere as a means of computing graph-similarity. By computing the modified Hausdorff distances between sets of ratios we are able to gauge the similarity of graphs, and by applying MDS to these similarities we are able to cluster graphs into different object categories. A comparison shows that the curvature attributes computed from the heat kernel embedding give better clusters than those obtained from the Laplacian eigenmap specially when $t = 0.01$.

For future we intend to investigate whether we can use a formula of both the sectional curvature and the ratio between the area of the geodesic and Euclidean triangles can be used to characterize the graph.

References

1. Boykov, Y., Huttenlocher, D.: A new bayesian framework for object recognition. In: Proceeding of IEEE Computer Society Conference on CVPR, vol. 2, pp. 517–523 (1999)
2. Cox, T., Cox, M.: Multidimensional Scaling. Chapman-Hall, Boca Raton (1994)
3. Dubuisson, M., Jain, A.: A modified hausdorff distance for object matching, pp. 566–568 (1994)
4. ElGhawalby, H., Hancock, E.R.: Graph characteristic from the gauss-bonnet theorem. LNCS, vol. 5342, pp. 207–216 (2008)
5. ElGhawalby, H., Hancock, E.R.: Measuring graph similarity using spectral geometry. In: Campilho, A., Kamel, M.S. (eds.) ICIAR 2008. LNCS, vol. 5112, pp. 517–526. Springer, Heidelberg (2008)
6. Huttenlocher, D., Klanderman, G., Rucklidge, W.: Comparing images using the hausdorff distance. IEEE. Trans. Pattern Anal. Mach. Intell. 15, 850–863 (1993)
7. Luo, B., Wilson, R.C., Hancock, E.R.: Spectral embedding of graphs. Pattern Recogintion 36, 2213–2230 (2003)
8. Xiao, B., Hancock, E.R.: Heat kernel, riemannian manifolds and graph embedding. In: Fred, A., Caelli, T.M., Duin, R.P.W., Campilho, A.C., de Ridder, D. (eds.) SSPR&SPR 2004. LNCS, vol. 3138, pp. 198–206. Springer, Heidelberg (2004)
9. Young, G., Householder, A.S.: Disscussion of a set of points in terms of their mutual distances. Psychometrika 3, 19–22 (1938)

Score Fusion by Maximizing the Area under the ROC Curve*

Mauricio Villegas and Roberto Paredes

Instituto Tecnológico de Informática
Universidad Politécnica de Valencia
Camino de Vera s/n, Edif. 8G Acc. B 46022 Valencia, Spain
{mvillegas,rparedes}@iti.upv.es

Abstract. Information fusion is currently a very active research topic aimed at improving the performance of biometric systems. This paper proposes a novel method for optimizing the parameters of a score fusion model based on maximizing an index related to the Area Under the ROC Curve. This approach has the convenience that the fusion parameters are learned without having to specify the client and impostor priors or the costs for the different errors. Empirical results on several datasets show the effectiveness of the proposed approach.

1 Introduction

Biometrics is currently a very active area of research due to the numerous applications it offers. By biometrics it is meant the automatic identification of a person by means of an anatomical or behavioral characteristic such as a facial image or a fingerprint. A method for improving the performance of biometric systems is to fuse information from several sources. This information can be fused at different levels, which can be at the sensor, feature, match score or decision levels. This work is focussed at match score fusion.

In the literature numerous score fusion approaches have been proposed. These can be categorized into two groups, which are the non-training based methods and the training based methods [1]. The non-training methods assume that the output of the individual matchers are the posterior probabilities that the pattern belongs to the claimed identity. Because this assumption is not generally true a previous normalization step is required [2]. The training based methods as the name suggest requires a training step. Among these are all of the methods which treat the fusion as a classification problem [3,4,5].

A significant drawback that the classification approach to score fusion has, is that these methods tend to minimize the classification error. However, the standard way of comparing biometric systems is by using a ROC curve. This way it is not necessary to specify which are the client and impostor priors or what are the costs for each of the possible errors of the system, values which are

---

* Work supported by the Spanish projects DPI2006-15542-C04 and TIN2008-04571 and the Generalitat Valenciana - Consellería d'Educació under an FPI scholarship.

H. Araujo et al. (Eds.): IbPRIA 2009, LNCS 5524, pp. 473–480, 2009.
© Springer-Verlag Berlin Heidelberg 2009

difficult to estimate and vary depending on the application. From this perspective, minimizing the classification error may not improve the performance in the practice. The Area Under the ROC Curve (AUC) summarizes the ROC curve, and this can be a better measure for assessing biometric systems without having to specify the priors or costs [6]. Motivated by this idea, in this work we propose to learn the parameters of a score fusion model by maximizing the AUC. In the literature there are several works on maximizing the AUC, due to lack of space we limit ourselves to referencing a few [7,8,9].

The rest of the paper is organized as follows. The next section defines a score fusion model and derives an algorithm which optimizes the model parameters by maximizing the AUC. The experimental results are presented in section 3 and the final section draws the conclusions and directions for future research.

2   Score Fusion by Maximizing the AUC

As was explained in the previous section, the AUC is an adequate measure to assess the quality of a biometric system without having to specify the client and impostor priors or the costs for the different errors. Motivated by this evidence, we propose to derive an algorithm that learns the parameters of a score fusion model by maximizing the AUC. In order to do this we have to address two tasks, the first one is to define a model that fuses scores according to some parameters, and second is to optimize the parameters of the model so that the AUC is maximized.

To choose the model for score fusion we have taken into account the following criteria. The model should be capable of weighting the different scores giving more or less importance to each of them. Also, the model should be able to handle scores with arbitrary input ranges. Finally the model should have few parameters so that they can be well estimated evading the small sample size problem. A simple method that fulfills the previous requirements is to first normalize the scores so that they are all in a common range and afterwards combine linearly the normalized scores.

2.1   Score Normalization

In the literature several methods for score normalization can be found, for a review of the most used ones in biometric fusion refer to [2]. The normalization we have chosen is based on the *tanh-estimators* which is somewhat insensitive to the presence of outliers [2]. This normalization is a nonlinear transformation of the score using a sigmoid function and it depends on two parameters, the sigmoid slope and its displacement. The slope determines how fast is the transition from zero to one, and the displacement indicates at what value the sigmoid is in the midpoint of the transition. The sigmoid normalization is given by

$$\phi_{u,v}(z) = \frac{1}{1 + \exp[u(v - z)]} \ , \tag{1}$$

where u and v are the slope and the displacement of the sigmoid respectively.

2.2   Score Fusion Model

To be able to represent the model mathematically first we need to state some definitions. Let $\mathbf{z}$ be an M-dimensional vector composed of the M scores we want to fuse $z_1, \ldots, z_M$. Furthermore let $\boldsymbol{\Phi}_{\mathbf{u}, \mathbf{v}}(\mathbf{z})$ be a vector composed of the normalized scores $\phi(z_1, u_1, v_1), \ldots, \phi(z_M, u_M, v_M)$ and the vectors $\mathbf{u}$ and $\mathbf{v}$ be a more compact representation of the sigmoid slopes $u_1, \ldots, u_M$ and displacements $v_1, \ldots, v_M$. As mentioned earlier, the model is a linear combination of the normalized scores, then we denote the score weights by $w_1, \ldots, w_M$ which are also represented more compactly by the vector $\mathbf{w}$.

The input scores can be either similarity or distance measures, however the sigmoid normalization can transform all of the scores to be similarity measures by having a positive or negative slope. Given that all the normalized scores are similarity measures, if they contain discriminative information then they should have a positive contribution to the final score, otherwise they should not have any contribution. Therefore without any loss of generality we can restrict the weights to being positive, $w_m \geq 0$ for $m = 1 \ldots M$. On the other hand, scaling the fused score does not have any effect on its discrimination ability, thus we can further restrict the weights so that their sum equals the unity, $\sum_{m=1}^{M} w_m = 1$. Note that given the two restrictions, the fused score has the nice property of being a value between zero and one.

The score fusion model is given by:

$$f_{\mathbf{u}, \mathbf{v}, \mathbf{w}}(\mathbf{z}) = \mathbf{w}^T \boldsymbol{\Phi}_{\mathbf{u}, \mathbf{v}}(\mathbf{z}) \ . \tag{2}$$

The parameters of the model are $\mathbf{u}, \mathbf{v}, \mathbf{w} \in \mathbb{R}^M$, which means that in total there are $3M$ parameters that need to be estimated.

2.3   AUC Maximization

Although there are few parameters to be estimated in the score fusion model (2), it can be highly computationally expensive to obtain an adequate estimation and clearly brute force is not advisable. Therefore our aim is an index that is directly related to the AUC and use an optimization procedure to maximize it.

Among the different alternatives to compute the AUC the one that lends itself for the simplest optimization process is the one known as the Wilcoxon-Mann-Whitney statistic:

$$\mathcal{A} = \frac{1}{PN} \sum_{p=1}^{P} \sum_{n=1}^{N} \mathcal{H}(x_p - y_n) \ , \tag{3}$$

where P and N are the number of client and impostor samples respectively, and $\mathcal{H}()$ is the Heaviside step function which has a value of zero or one for negative and positive numbers respectively, and a value of $1/2$ at zero.

The expression in equation (3) is not differentiable, therefore inspired on the same ideas as in [10,11], the Heaviside step function can be approximated using a sigmoid function. Doing this approximation and using the score fusion model (2), leads to the following optimization index:

$$J(\mathbf{u}, \mathbf{v}, \mathbf{w}) = \frac{1}{PN} \sum_{p=1}^{P} \sum_{n=1}^{N} S_\beta \left(\mathbf{w}^T \left(\hat{\mathbf{x}}_p - \hat{\mathbf{y}}_n \right) \right), \tag{4}$$

where the hat indicates that the sore is normalized, i.e. $\hat{\mathbf{x}}_p = \Phi_{\mathbf{u},\mathbf{v}}(\mathbf{x}_p)$ and $\hat{\mathbf{y}}_n = \Phi_{\mathbf{u},\mathbf{v}}(\mathbf{y}_n)$, and the sigmoid function is defined by

$$S_\beta(z) = \frac{1}{1 + \exp(-\beta z)} . \tag{5}$$

Care must be taken not to confuse this sigmoid function, which is used for AUC maximization, with the sigmoid used for score normalization from equation (1).

To maximize the index (4) we propose to use a batch gradient descent procedure. To this end, we take the partial derivatives of the index with respect to the parameters obtaining:

$$\frac{\partial J}{\partial \mathbf{u}} = \mathbf{w} \bullet \frac{1}{PN} \sum_{p=1}^{P} \sum_{n=1}^{N} S'_\beta \left(\mathbf{w}^T \left(\hat{\mathbf{x}}_p - \hat{\mathbf{y}}_n \right) \right) \bullet$$
$$\left((\mathbf{x}_p - \mathbf{v}) \bullet \Phi'(\mathbf{x}_p) - (\mathbf{y}_n - \mathbf{v}) \bullet \Phi'(\mathbf{y}_n) \right) ;$$

$$\frac{\partial J}{\partial \mathbf{v}} = \mathbf{w} \bullet \mathbf{u} \bullet \frac{1}{PN} \sum_{p=1}^{P} \sum_{n=1}^{N} S'_\beta \left(\mathbf{w}^T \left(\hat{\mathbf{x}}_p - \hat{\mathbf{y}}_n \right) \right) \bullet \tag{6}$$
$$\left(\Phi'(\mathbf{y}_n) - \Phi'(\mathbf{x}_p) \right) ;$$

$$\frac{\partial J}{\partial \mathbf{w}} = \frac{1}{PN} \sum_{p=1}^{P} \sum_{n=1}^{N} S'_\beta \left(\mathbf{w}^T \left(\hat{\mathbf{x}}_p - \hat{\mathbf{y}}_n \right) \right) \left(\hat{\mathbf{x}}_p - \hat{\mathbf{y}}_n \right) .$$

The big dot $\bullet$ indicates a Hadamard or entry-wise product, $S'_\beta()$ is the derivative of the sigmoid function (5) and the elements of the vectors $\Phi'(\mathbf{x}_p)$ and $\Phi'(\mathbf{y}_n)$ are given by

$$\phi'(z) = \frac{\exp[u(v - z)]}{(1 + \exp[u(v - z)])^2} . \tag{7}$$

Finally the corresponding gradient ascend update equations are

$$\mathbf{s}^{(t+1)} = \mathbf{s}^{(t)} + \gamma \frac{\partial J}{\partial \mathbf{s}}^{(t)} , \tag{8}$$

where $\mathbf{s} = \{\mathbf{u}, \mathbf{v}, \mathbf{w}\}$ and γ is the learning rate. After each iteration the weights are renormalized so that the restrictions of being positive and sum to unity are met.

This approach to maximization of the AUC has been previously mentioned in the work of Yan et al. [7], however they report having significant numerical problems for values of $\beta > 2$, in which case the sigmoid function is a poor estimate of the step function. Our experience differs completely from this notion, being the optimization quite stable for higher values of β on several data sets.

2.4   Notes on the Implementation of the Algorithm

The algorithm has a very high computational cost which makes it unpractical for large datasets. However there are several approaches that can be used to speed up the computation without sacrificing performance. For most of the client and impostor score pairs the derivative of the sigmoid function is practically zero. Therefore in each iteration a large amount of pairs can be discarded depending on their relative difference. Another approach could be to use the stochastic gradient ascend instead of the batch. This reduces significantly the amount of iterations that the algorithms needs to converge.

2.5   Extensions of the Algorithm

An initial clarification must be made. Although in this paper a score fusion model is defined and optimized, the maximization by AUC is a general approach which can be applied to other models and other problems different from score fusion. Furthermore the proposed score fusion model is very simple and linear and therefore it is unable to handle complex distributions. Depending on the problem, improvements to the model must be made.

Up to this point, the proposed model has very few parameters, and it is a simple linear combination of normalized scores. The algorithm can be extended to be nonlinear, it is as straight forward as adding new virtual scores which are a nonlinear combination of the original scores. This nonlinear extension can also be useful to increase the number of parameters of the score fusion model and thus it increases its representation capability.

Along with the research on biometric score fusion there is another related topic. This topic is the use of quality measures to determine how confident a biometric score is. This information can greatly improve the recognition accuracy of the systems if they are taken into account during the fusion. An approach to integrate the quality measures into the proposed model could be to include these values as if they were other scores like it is done in [12]. However the quality values can mean different things under different circumstances [5], making this approach unsatisfactory. A simple and better approach would be to include the quality measures as scores but removing the restriction of the weight being positive. This way the quality can reward or penalize the final score depending on the circumstance.

3   Experiments

The proposed approach was evaluated using three publicly available datasets. The first dataset was the LP1 set of scores obtained from the XM2VTS face and voice multimodal database [13]. This dataset includes eight biometric scores per claim, five for face images and the remaining three for speech. The experimentation protocol for this dataset is clearly defined, first there is an evaluation set, which is used to optimize the fusion parameters, and then there is a test set which is used to assess the performance. In total the evaluation set has 600 client and 40k impostor claims, and the test set has 400 client and around 112k impostor claims.

The other two datasets used in the experiments were the Multimodal and the Face datasets from the NIST Biometric Scores Set - Release 1 (BSSR1) [14]. The Multimodal dataset is composed of four scores per claim, two correspond to face matchers and the other two to the right and left index fingerprints for the same matcher. This dataset has 517 client and around 267k impostor claims. Finally the Face dataset is composed of two scores per claim, each one for a different face matcher. In this case there are 6k client and 1.8M impostor claims. For these datasets there is no experimentation protocol defined. In our experiments we did a repeated hold-out using half of the data for training and the other half for test, and repeated 20 times.

The results of the experiments for the test sets are summarized in the table 1. For each dataset three results are presented. The first one is for the single matcher which obtained the best result without doing score fusion. The second result is the best one obtained by trying among several baseline techniques. The baseline techniques tried were the sum, product, min and max rules, each one either with z-score or maxmin normalization. The final result is for our technique (SFMA). For each dataset and method the table presents three performance measures, the AUC given as a percentage of the total area, the Equal Error Rate (EER) and the Total Error Rate at a False Acceptance Rate of 0.01% (TER@FAR=0.01%). The 95% confidence intervals are included for the BSSR1 datasets.

On biometric research papers it is common to plot either a ROC or a DET curve to compare various systems. Nonetheless these curves do not take into account how the thresholds are selected, making the comparison of systems somewhat unreliable. In this paper we have opted to use the Expected Performance

Table 1. Summary of score fusion results on different datasets

Dataset	Method	AUC (%)		EER (%)		TER@ FAR=0.01% (%)	
XM2VTS (LP1)	Best Matcher	99.917		1.14		15.0	
	Sum Rule/z-score	99.973		0.56		3.0	
	SFMA	**99.997**		**0.28**		**1.0**	
BSSR1 (Multimodal)	Best Matcher	98.84	±0.10	4.67	±0.23	26.8	±1.07
	Sum Rule/z-score	**99.99**	±0.00	**0.50**	±0.07	3.2	±0.41
	SFMA	**99.99**	±0.00	**0.50**	±0.18	**1.5**	±0.25
BSSR1 (Face)	Best Matcher	65.39	±1.07	5.26	±0.05	28.9	±0.27
	Sum Rule/z-score	98.62	±0.03	5.09	±0.03	**24.2**	±0.31
	SFMA	**99.07**	±0.03	**4.25**	±0.05	25.3	±0.33

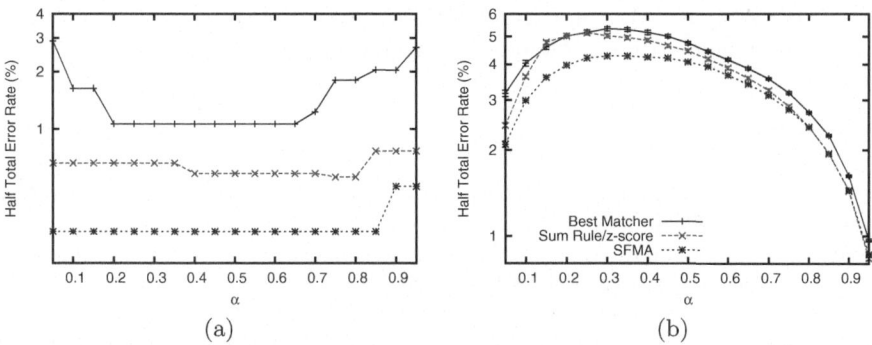

Fig. 1. Expected Performance Curves of the fusion algorithms for (a) XM2VTS LP1 and (b) BSSR1 Face

Curves (EPC) [15], which plots the HTER using a threshold $(\hat{\theta}_\alpha)$ obtained on a development set by $\arg\min(\theta_\alpha) = \alpha\mathrm{FAR} + (1 - \alpha)\mathrm{FRR}$. The parameter α is a value between zero and one which weights the importance of the errors. The EPC curves for two of the datasets are presented in figure 1.

The results for the proposed technique are very promising. In all of the datasets SFMA improves the AUC even though the maximization was done on the training set, this suggests that the technique has good generalization capability. Only the TER@FAR=0.01% for the BSSR1 Face dataset is slightly worse than Sum Rule with z-score, however this is an extreme operating point. For this dataset the improvement is significant for a wide range of operating thresholds as can be observed on its EPC curve.

4 Conclusions

This paper presented a novel method for optimizing the parameters of a score fusion model based on maximizing an index related to the Area Under the ROC Curve (AUC). A score fusion model based on a linear combination of normalized scores was chosen and the AUC optimization procedure was derived for it.

The proposed algorithm was empirically evaluated using three publicly available datasets, the XM2VTS LP1, the BSSR1 Multimodal and the BSSR1 Face. The results show that the technique works as expected. The AUC is iteratively improved by the algorithm and the result generalizes well to new data. Also, by maximizing the AUC, specific operating points on the ROC curve also improve without having to choose which one will be used in the final system.

Several research topics are left for future work. One topic is to analyze the computational cost of the algorithm. To speedup the algorithm some approximations can be made and a stochastic gradient ascend procedure can be employed. Therefore the question remains about how much time is required by the algorithm and how much do the approximations affect the results. For future work also is how to integrate quality measures into the score fusion model and how does the algorithm perform using this type of information. Another topic to work on is using the AUC maximization for other problems, such as biometric verification or biometric sample quality estimation.

References

1. Toh, K.A., Kim, J., Lee, S.: Biometric scores fusion based on total error rate minimization. Pattern Recognition 41(3), 1066–1082 (2008)
2. Jain, A., Nandakumar, K., Ross, A.: Score normalization in multimodal biometric systems. Pattern Recognition 38(12), 2270–2285 (2005)
3. Gutschoven, B., Verlinde, P.: Multi-modal identity verification using support vector machines (svm). In: Proceedings of the Third International Conference on Information Fusion. FUSION 2000, vol. 2, pp. THB3/3–THB3/8 (July 2000)
4. Ma, Y., Cukic, B., Singh, H.: A classification approach to multi-biometric score fusion. In: Kanade, T., Jain, A., Ratha, N.K. (eds.) AVBPA 2005. LNCS, vol. 3546, pp. 484–493. Springer, Heidelberg (2005)
5. Maurer, D.E., Baker, J.P.: Fusing multimodal biometrics with quality estimates via a bayesian belief network. Pattern Recogn. 41(3), 821–832 (2008)
6. Ling, C.X., Huang, J., Zhang, H.: Auc: a statistically consistent and more discriminating measure than accuracy. In: Proc. of IJCAI 2003, pp. 519–524 (2003)
7. Yan, L., Dodier, R.H., Mozer, M., Wolniewicz, R.H.: Optimizing classifier performance via an approximation to the wilcoxon-mann-whitney statistic. In: Machine Learning, Proceedings of the Twentieth International Conference (ICML 2003), Washington, DC, USA, pp. 848–855. AAAI Press, Menlo Park (2003)
8. Marrocco, C., Molinara, M., Tortorella, F.: Exploiting auc for optimal linear combinations of dichotomizers. Pattern Recogn. Lett. 27(8), 900–907 (2006)
9. Marrocco, C., Duin, R.P.W., Tortorella, F.: Maximizing the area under the roc curve by pairwise feature combination. Pattern Recogn. 41(6), 1961–1974 (2008)
10. Paredes, R., Vidal, E.: Learning prototypes and distances: a prototype reduction technique based on nearest neighbor error minimization. Pattern Recognition 39(2), 180–188 (2006)
11. Villegas, M., Paredes, R.: Simultaneous learning of a discriminative projection and prototypes for nearest-neighbor classification. In: IEEE Conference on Computer Vision and Pattern Recognition. CVPR 2008, pp. 1–8 (2008)
12. Nandakumar, K., Chen, Y., Dass, S.C., Jain, A.: Likelihood ratio-based biometric score fusion. IEEE Transactions on Pattern Analysis and Machine Intelligence 30(2), 342–347 (2008)
13. Poh, N., Bengio, S.: A score-level fusion benchmark database for biometric authentication. In: Kanade, T., Jain, A., Ratha, N.K. (eds.) AVBPA 2005. LNCS, vol. 3546, pp. 1059–1070. Springer, Heidelberg (2005)
14. National Institute of Standards and Technology: NIST Biometric Scores Set - Release 1 (BSSR1) (2004),
    http://www.itl.nist.gov/iad/894.03/biometricscores/
15. Bengio, S., Mariéthoz, J., Keller, M.: The expected performance curve. In: Proceedings of the Second Workshop on ROC Analysis in ML, pp. 9–16 (2005)

Gender Recognition from a Partial View of the Face Using Local Feature Vectors

Yasmina Andreu, Ramón A. Mollineda, and Pedro García-Sevilla

Dpto. Lenguajes y Sistemas Informáticos
Universidad Jaume I. Castellón de la Plana, Spain
{yandreu,mollined,pgarcia}@uji.es

Abstract. This paper proposes a gender recognition scheme focused on local appearance-based features to describe the top half of the face. Due to the fact that only the top half of the face is used, this is a feasible approach in those situations where the bottom half is hidden. In the experiments, several face detection methods with different precision levels are used in order to prove the robustness of the scheme with respect to variations in the accuracy level of the face detection process.

Keywords: Gender recognition, Face image analysis, Local features.

1 Introduction

Automatic gender recognition is an emerging issue in the face analysis area. A number of fields can benefit from the application of this technique, for example, demographic data acquisition, access control and other face analysis tasks such as age, ethnic or face recognition. In the latter cases, the prior prediction of the gender can reduce the search space to approximately half.

Some recent papers have addressed this problem, most of them proposing solutions based on descriptions of full faces [1,2,3]. This holistic representation is undoubtedly the most useful one for discriminating between genders when a frontal view of the whole face is available. The reasons for this are obvious: along with all the parts of the face, this description contains the structural relationships between parts that also contribute to discriminating between genders [4].

However, in the real world faces can usually be partially covered by accessories such as scarves, hats, veils and other objects. In these situations, the use of local approaches seems to be a suitable choice.

Furthermore, the unconstrained problem of face recognition and analysis is far from solved. A general solution should deal with a wide diversity of poses, lighting conditions, hidden areas, facial expressions, image resolutions and many other factors. One of the most ambitious works is [5], where a face recognition task is carried out on test faces that are imprecisely localized, partially occluded and with no restrictions on their expressions, while using a single training sample per class. In the case of gender recognition, as far as we know, no previous efforts in similar conditions have been reported.

H. Araujo et al. (Eds.): IbPRIA 2009, LNCS 5524, pp. 481–488, 2009.

This paper proposes a gender classification scheme based on the combination of several appearance-based local descriptions of the top half of the face. This approach can handle situations where this part of the face is available, while the bottom half could be hidden. The method applied to locally extract features from the images is similar to that used in [6].

In our experiments, the top half of the face was detected using two methods: in the first method the exact coordinates of the eyes were used to extract an accurate subimage, whereas in the second one the top half of the face was automatically detected using the face image as the only input. Additionally, experiments in which the area that contains the face was intentionally shifted were carried out.

The experiments demonstrate that the classification method based on local features used to recognize gender from the top half of the face is robust to the accuracy level of face detection.

The experiments were defined for the FERET database [7] and a 1-NN classifier.

The rest of this paper is organized as follows. Section 2 presents the methodology used to extract local features of the faces and also the classification technique implemented. Section 3 presents the description of the image database as well as the experiments and the discussion of their results. Finally, Section 4 summarizes the conclusions and future work.

2   Methodology

2.1   Feature Extraction

Given a greyscale image of a frontal view of a face, this section explains how the features that describe the face are extracted (see Fig. 1 for a graphical explanation). As a general overview, the process detects the face in the image and extracts the top half of that face. Then several vectors of local features are obtained from the extracted area using a window that enables us to locally select the features. Finally, the features are filtered in order to reduce complexity and to discard the information that is not very relevant.

This process can be divided in the following steps:

1. **Face detection**

   Two different approaches have been used to detect the face in the image. In the first method the face is detected using the exact coordinates of the two eyes, which are available for each image in the database, while in the second one the detection is completely automatic.

   The process followed in the first approach is based on an empirical rule about the ideal balance of a human face sketched by Leonardo da Vinci [8,9]. The division points are automatically computed from the knowledge of the coordinates of the eyes and the distance between them. For the automatic method, the Viola and Jones algorithm [10] implemented in the OpenCV library [11] is used. On the left, Fig. 2 shows the areas obtained after applying

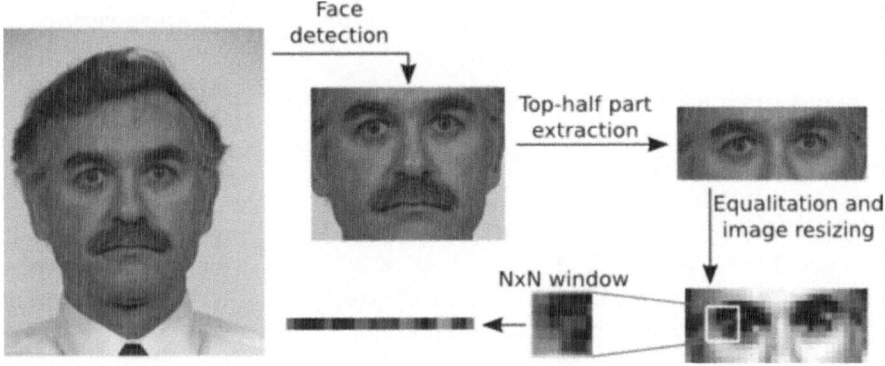

Fig. 1. Feature extraction process. Firstly, the face is detected and the top half is extracted, equalized and resized. Then the image is scanned with an $N \times N$ window to obtain a set of local feature vectors.

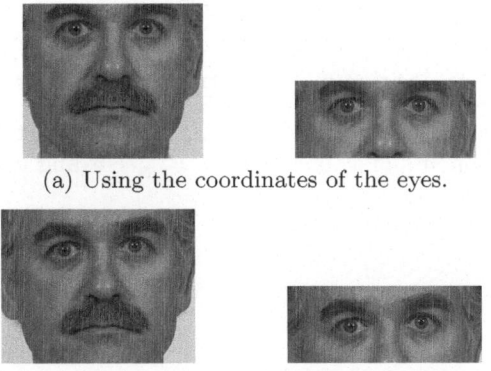

(a) Using the coordinates of the eyes.

(b) Using the Viola and Jones algorithm.

Fig. 2. Facial area and the top half of a face detected using two different methods

each face detection method to the same image and on the right, it shows the top half used in the experiments.

2. **Image pre-processing**

Given the coordinates of the face in the image, a subimage containing the top half of that face is extracted (see right side of Fig. 2) and it is resized to a given width. A three-lobed Lanczos windowed sinc function [12] is used in the interpolation process required for the resizing step. Finally, histogram equalization is applied to improve contrast and to make lighting conditions more uniform.

3. **Local features extraction**

The basic idea is similar to that introduced in [6]. It consists of a window of some moderate size $N \times N$ that is scanned across the image. From each window position, a vector containing all the grey level values of the pixels within the window is built. As a result, a set of local feature vectors that describe the image are extracted.

4. **From grey levels to numeric labels**

In order to obtain vector descriptions that are more robust to illumination changes, grey levels are substituted by their internal ranking position within each vector. In other words, each grey level is replaced by a numeric label that represents its position in the sorted list of all grey values in ascending order. Moreover, for moderate values of N, the size of the new attribute space ($N \times N$) is smaller than the 256 possible grey levels, which can also contribute to making vector representations more general. This codification process can be detailed as follows:

(a) Let $x = (x_1, x_2, ..., x_{N \times N})$ be a vector of grey-level components

(b) Let G be a threshold that represents the maximum difference between two grey levels to consider them equal

(c) Compute the ordered version of x, $x' = (x_{i_1}, x_{i_2}, ..., x_{i_{N \times N}}), x_{i_j} \le x_{i_{j+1}}$, where i_j is the position of x_{i_j} in the original vector x

(d) Build a parallel vector $r' = (r_1, r_2, ..., r_{N \times N})$ with the ranking positions of the components of x as regard to x', according to the algorithm:

$k = 1$
$ranking = 1$
for $j = 1 : N \times N$ do,
  if $x_{i_j} - x_{i_k} > G$,
    $k = j$
    $ranking = ranking + 1$
  $r'_j = ranking$

(e) Let r be the re-sorted vector r' with regard to the original positions of the components in x

for $j = 1 : N \times N$ do,
  $r_{i_j} = r'_j$

This process is shown graphically in Fig. 3.

5. **Reducing the size/complexity of the problem**

The goal of this step is to reduce the complexity of the problem. In order to achieve this goal, the vectors where the number of different numeric labels is lower than a threshold T are ruled out. These vectors match with those regions with low contrast, which are assumed to not provide too much discriminant information.

This step is optional so it was not used in experiments unless this is remarked on the experiments section.

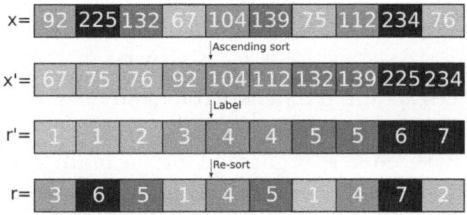

Fig. 3. Example of the transformation of a grey level vector into a ranking vector with $G = 8$. Two grey levels with a difference lower than or equal to 8 are considered similar, resulting in the same ranking position.

2.2 Classification

Applying the feature extraction process explained in Sect. 2.1 several vectors are extracted to describe the same face, so a particular classification process should be used to obtain only one class label per face from those vectors.

Firstly in the classification process, the nearest neighbour of each vector extracted from the test images is computed and its class label is assigned to the corresponding vector. Then the class assigned to each test image is the one obtained by majority voting of its vectors.

The metric used to compute the nearest neighbour is $\sum_{i=1}^{n} |v_i - w_i|$, where v and w are vectors extracted from a training image and a test image respectively.

3 Experiments

The experiments were designed to prove that the gender recognition method presented is robust to inaccuracies in the detection of top half of the face. To this end, two different face detection algorithms were used. The first one uses the exact coordinates of the eyes obtained from the face database as input information whereas the second one is completely automatic. Different combinations of these algorithms were applied to the training and test image sets leading to the following experiments:

Experiment 1 : Training set: based on the exact coordinates; test set: based on the exact coordinates.

Experiment 2 : Training set: based on the exact coordinates; test set: automatic method.

Experiment 3 : Training set: automatic method; test set: automatic method.

In addition to these experiments another one (**Experiment 4**) where the coordinates of the area that contains the face were randomly shifted in all directions between 0 to 15 pixels was performed. In this case, the method that detects the face from the exact coordinates of the eyes was used.

Two series of these four experiments were carried out. In the first series all the feature vectors extracted from the images were used and in the other series the number of feature vectors was reduced before the classification process took place (see step 5 in Sect. 2.1).

3.1   Description of the Database

The experiments are based on the well-known FERET database of face images [7]. It contains human faces acquired in a controlled environment with no restrictions such as age, race, or facial expressions. There are several images of each person, which are replicated in three sizes organized into as many collections. Only faces in a frontal pose without glasses were used, because glasses could strongly distort the effectiveness of the top half of the face in the gender recognition task. The experiments involved 2147 medium-sized images of 256×384 pixels from 834 subjects separated into 842 female faces and 1305 male faces.

3.2   Description of Experiments

The images used in the experiments were divided into two sets: training and test, consisting of 60% and 40% of the total amount of images respectively. As there are several images per subject, this division was carefully implemented in order to assign all the images of the same subject to the same set.

Each of the top half faces used was resized to obtain images of 30 pixels in width using a resizing process that maintains the aspect ratio of the original image.

The feature extraction process uses a window of size 9×9 (see step 3 in Sect. 2.1). As a result, vectors of 81 components each were obtained and the number of vectors extracted from each face was usually 110, since the top half of the faces used had the same width-height ratio in most cases.

For the process that transforms the grey level vectors into numeric label vectors, the threshold used to consider two grey levels equal was $G = 8$, so 32 different numeric labels are possible since 256 grey levels exist (see step 4 in Sect. 2.1).

For the process of reducing the complexity of the data, a threshold $T = 16$ was used (only in the second series of experiments) to rule out those local feature vectors with poor information for discriminating between genders (see step 5 in Sect. 2.1). It is worth noting that due to the fact that the threshold T was set to 16 and G set to 8, the discarded vectors are those whose number of different label values is at most 16 (which is half the total amount of labels).

Table 1. Recognition rates for both series of experiments

	Tra and Tst coordinates (Exp. 1)	Tra coordinates Tst auto detection (Exp. 2)	Tra and Tst auto detection (Exp. 3)	Shifting the area of the face (Exp. 4)
1st series	79.55%	83.16%	82.57%	79.21%
2nd series	81.07%	82.30%	88.51%	83.06%

 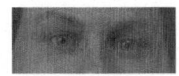   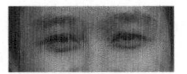 

(a) Males classified as females.   (b) Females classified as males.

Fig. 4. Misclassified subjects

3.3   Discussion of Results

Table 1 shows the recognition performance for the experiments that use all the features extracted from the images (first series of experiments) and the rates from the experiments where the complexity of the problem was reduced (second series of experiments) respectively.

All the results obtained are very close to or higher than 80% despite the fact that the system does not have any restriction on how accurate the detection of the face should be.

In the first series of experiments, the best recognition rates were achieved when the face was automatically detected in the test images or in both sets. This could be explained because this automatic method provides a wider area that contains more of the face and the method that uses the coordinates of the eyes obtains a smaller region that provides less information.

As expected, the recognition rates achieved for the second series of experiments are higher than those obtained in the first series. Taking into account that in this case a lower number of vectors, which were (hopefully) the most discriminant, were used to describe the faces, it is possible that those vectors that were ruled out were the ones that provided information that confused the classifier.

As a further benchmark to assess the results of this work, work of paper [13] is considered. It also focuses on the task of gender classification over the FERET database. Its experiments were based on the full face, the internal face (which excludes hair, ears and facial contour) and the eyes, and other parts of the face. The feature extraction process was executed using the coordinates of the eyes to accurately locate the facial region of interest. Under such controlled conditions, the best recognition rates were 95.21%, 92.37% and 85.47% using the full face, the internal face and the eyes respectively. The best rate in this paper is 88.51%, which unlike the results in [13] was achieved from the completely automatic extraction of the top half of the face, so it is more suitable for use in real situations.

Fig. 4 shows some misclassified faces. It could be that these are somehow confusing even for human beings, since in these cases there is little information to enable us to guess the gender of these people.

4   Conclusions

This paper has proposed a gender recognition scheme based on local feature descriptions from the top half of the face, which makes it suitable for use in real situations where the bottom half is hidden. As the experiments demonstrate this method is robust to variations in the accuracy of face detection, since the classification results obtained from the intentional shift of the face regions produced similar results to those achieved under normal conditions.

Future lines of research may include the definition of methodologies for learning the model parameters, the comparison of the local feature vectors used in this paper with other local representations such as Local Binary Patterns and the design of more powerful classifiers to handle the gender recognition task.

Acknowledgments

This work was partially funded by Projects CSD2007-00018 and DPI2006-15542 from the Spanish Ministry of Science and Innovation, and P1·1B2007-60 from the Fundació Caixa Castelló-Bancaixa.

References

1. Lapedriza, A., Marín-Jiménez, M., Vitrià, J.: Gender recognition in non controlled environments. In: Proc. of 18th ICPR. IEEE, Hong Kong (2006)
2. Moghaddam, B., Yang, M.: Learning gender with support faces. IEEE Trans. on PAMI 24(5), 707–711 (2002)
3. Wu, J., Smith, W., Hancock, E.: Learning mixture models for gender classification based on facial surface normals. In: Martí, J., Benedí, J.M., Mendonça, A.M., Serrat, J. (eds.) IbPRIA 2007. LNCS, vol. 4477, pp. 39–46. Springer, Heidelberg (2007)
4. Burton, A., Bruce, V., Dench, N.: What's the difference between men and women? evidence from facial measurement. Perception 22(2), 153–176 (1993)
5. Martínez, A.: Recognizing imprecisely localized, partially occluded and expression variant faces from a single sample per class. IEEE Trans. on PAMI 24(6), 748–763 (2002)
6. Paredes, R., Pérez-Cortes, J.C., Juan, A., Vidal, E.: Local representations and a direct voting scheme for face recognition. In: PRIS 2001: Proceedings of the 1st International Workshop on Pattern Recognition in Information Systems, pp. 71–79. ICEIS Press (2001)
7. Phillips, H., Moon, P., Rizvi, S.: The FERET evaluation methodology for face recognition algorithms. IEEE Trans. on PAMI 22(10) (2000)
8. Nainia, F.B., Mossb, J.P., Gillc, D.S.: The enigma of facial beauty: Esthetics, proportions, deformity, and controversy. American Journal of Orthodontics and Dentofacial Orthopedics 130(3), 277–282 (2006)
9. Oguz, O.: The proportion of the face in younger adults using the thumb rule of Leonardo da Vinci. Surgical and Radiologic Anatomy 18(2), 111–114 (1996)
10. Viola, P., Jones, M.J.: Robust real-time face detection. Int. J. Comput. Vision 57(2), 137–154 (2004)
11. Bradski, G.R., Kaehler, A.: Learning OpenCV. O'Reilly (2008)
12. Turkowski, K.: Filters for common resampling tasks, 147–165 (1990)
13. Andreu, Y., Mollineda, R.A.: The role of face parts in gender recognition. In: Campilho, A., Kamel, M.S. (eds.) ICIAR 2008. LNCS, vol. 5112, pp. 945–954. Springer, Heidelberg (2008)

Melodic Track Identification in MIDI Files Considering the Imbalanced Context*

Raúl Martín, Ramón A. Mollineda, and Vicente García

Department of Programming Languages and Information Systems
University Jaume I of Castellón, Spain
{martinr,mollined,vgarcia}@uji.es

Abstract. In this paper, the problem of identifying the melodic track of a MIDI file in imbalanced scenarios is addressed. A polyphonic MIDI file is a digital score that consists of a set of tracks where usually only one of them contains the melody and the remaining tracks hold the accompaniment. This leads to a two-class imbalance problem that, unlike in previous work, is managed by over-sampling the melody class (the minority one) or by under-sampling the accompaniment class (the majority one) until both classes are the same size. Experimental results over three different music genres prove that learning from balanced training sets clearly provides better results than the standard classification process.

Keywords: Melody finding, music information retrieval, class imbalance problem, classification.

1 Introduction

This paper aims to solve the problem of automatic identification of the melodic line from a polyphonic MIDI file. A MIDI file is a kind of digital score as MusicXML and other XML music formats. It consists of a set of tracks where usually only one of them is the melodic track while the remaining tracks contain the accompaniment of that melody. An effective solution to this problem could be of interest for a large number of applications. For example, it could be used to retrieve a MIDI file whose melodic line matches with a hummed or whistled melody [1] from a multimedia database, to recommend songs similar to a given one by comparing their melodies, and for many other similar uses. Another application could be plagiarism detection in the field of copyright management by identifying a percentage of the melody of one song in another one.

The automatic identification of the melodic line can be modelled as a two-class problem involving the melody class and the accompaniment (or non-melody) class. The first one can be considered as the minority class because the number of samples in it, usually one track per MIDI file, is much lower than that for

---

* We would like to acknowledge the *Pattern Recognition and Artificial Intelligence Group* at the University of Alicante who provided us with the datasets used in this paper.

H. Araujo et al. (Eds.): IbPRIA 2009, LNCS 5524, pp. 489–496, 2009.

the non-melody class, which contains many accompaniment tracks per MIDI. Therefore, this ratio generally results in a class-imbalance problem.

Some previous papers have addressed the main goal of this work but ignored the imbalance nature. Most of them [2,3,4] represent a track by a vector of low-level statistical descriptors of its musical content, which are then used in a common learning/classification process. Another different approach follows a structural paradigm by coding the sequence of notes as strings or trees [5].

This paper deals with the automatic identification of the melodic line in MIDI files but, unlike in previous work, it considers the imbalance of the classes and provides results for more than one classifier. The imbalance is managed by re-sampling classes in the training set as a preprocessing stage prior to classifier learning. This process balances the sizes of both classes by either over-sampling the minority class or under-sampling the majority class. Experiments are performed over corpora of MIDI files belonging to three different musical genres, crossing them over for training and testing purposes. Most of the classification results obtained from resampled training sets were significantly better than those derived from the corresponding original imbalanced training set.

2   Methodology

An overview of the solution is shown in Fig. 1 where the four main steps are remarked. Then the following subsections explain these steps.

2.1   Track Feature Extraction

This step creates vector representations for all tracks of the MIDI files included in both the training and test corpora. As a result, two related sets of track vectors are obtained for training and testing purposes. Tracks are described using 38 features (many of them also used in [2,3]) that summarize their musical content and by a class label indicating whether the track contains the melody or not. All of these features (see Table 1) are preprocessed by filling the missing values with the corresponding mean (it is necessary to apply SMOTE -see Sect. 2.2-)

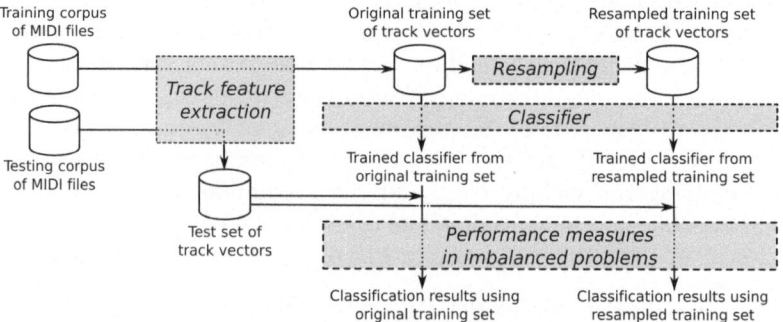

Fig. 1. Architecture of the solution

Table 1. Set of track features

− *Global properties*	− *Absolute intervals*	− *Non-diatonic notes*
• Song identifier	• Highest	• Count
• Number of notes	• Lowest	• Average
• Track duration	• Range	• Standard deviation
• Polyphony rate	• Average	• Average relative
• Occupation rate	• Standard deviation	− *Rests*
− *Pitch*	• Average relative	
	• Most repeated	• Number of significant
• Highest	• Number of distinct	• Number of non-significant
• Lowest		
• Range	− *Note duration*	• Shortest duration
• Average		• Longest duration
• Standard deviation	• Shortest	• Duration range
• Average relative	• Longest	• Average duration
	• Range	• Standard deviation duration
− *Syncopation*	• Average	
	• Standard deviation	• Average relative duration
• Number of syncopated notes	• Average relative	

and finally, they are normalized in the range [0,1]. The *Song identifier* feature, which indicates the MIDI file that a track belongs to, is only used in testing to assess the effectiveness of the MIDI classification process.

2.2 Resampling

As mentioned above, the original training set of track vectors is a two-class imbalance problem because the number of melodic tracks is much lower than the number of non-melodic tracks. One possible solution to imbalance at a data level is to resample the original training set either by over-sampling the minority class or by under-sampling the majority class until the class sizes are similar. In this work, one method with each strategy has been applied: *Synthetic Minority Oversampling TEchnique (SMOTE)* for over-sampling and *Random Under-Sampling (RUS)* for under-sampling the training set.

SMOTE [6] is a method that generates new synthetic samples in the minority class from a number of instances that lie together. For each sample in the minority class, this algorithm computes the k intra-class nearest neighbours and several new instances are created by interpolating the focused sample and some of its neighbours, which are randomly selected. Its major drawback is an increase in the computational cost of the learning algorithm. In contrast, *RUS* [7] is a non-heuristic method that aims to balance class distributions by randomly discarding samples of the majority class. Its major drawback is that it can ignore potentially useful data that could be important in the learning process.

2.3 Classifiers

The aim of the classification stage is to identify the melodic track in each MIDI file. This process is made up of two decision levels: i) *track level*, where individual tracks are classified into either melodic or accompaniment classes and ii) *MIDI file level*, in which identification of the melodic track of a MIDI file is carried out based on results at track level. The training process at track level is based on both the original and the resampled training sets of track vectors (see Fig. 1). As regards the set used for training (original or resampled), the effectiveness of the detection of the melodic track at MIDI file level is evaluated. A detailed description of this process is as follows:

Track level

1. Given a track, a classifier assigns probabilities of membership of both classes (melody and accompaniment)
2. Tracks are discarded when one of the following two conditions is satisfied:
   - the difference between both probabilities is lower than 0.1
   - the probability of being melody is higher than the non-melody probability, but lower than 0.6

MIDI file level

1. Given all non-discarded tracks from the same MIDI file, the one with the highest positive difference between the two probabilities of being melody and accompaniment respectively, is selected as the melodic track
2. The decision is considered a *hit* if
   - *True Positive*: the selected track is originally labelled as melody, or
   - *True Negative*: in a file with no track labelled as melody, all the tracks have been discarded or they have negative differences between their probabilities
3. The decision is considered a *miss* if
   - *False Positive*: the selected track is originally unlabelled or labelled as accompaniment, or
   - *False Negative*: in a file with at least one track labelled as melody, all its tracks have been discarded or they have negative differences between their probabilities

The base classifiers used at track level are the k-Nearest Neighbour (k-NN), a Support Vector Machine (SVM), a Multi-Layer Perceptron (MLP) and a Random Forest (RF). They were chosen due to their diversity in terms of the geometry of their decision boundaries. In this paper, the experimental results are obtained by using the classifier implementations included in the WEKA toolkit[1] with their default parameters. In addition, k-NN is performed with $k = 1$ and $k = 5$, and RF (a weighted combination of decision trees) is configured with 10 trees, each of them using five randomly selected features.

2.4   Performance Measures in Class Imbalance Problems

A typical metric for measuring the performance of learning systems is classification accuracy rate, which for a two-class problem can be easily derived from a 2×2 confusion matrix defined by i) TP (True positive) and ii) TN (True Negative), which are the numbers of positive and negative samples correctly classified, respectively, and iii) FP (False positive) and iv) FN (False Negative), which are

---

[1] http://www.cs.waikato.ac.nz/ml/weka/

Table 2. Corpora used in the experiments

| CorpusID | Music Genre | Midi Files | | Tracks | | |
		Total number	without melody tracks	non-melody	melody	unlabelled
CL200	Classical	200	1%	489	198	16
JZ200	Jazz	200	1.5%	561	197	11
KR200	Popular	200	20.5%	1171	159	338
CLA	Classical	131	35.88%	284	84	265
JAZ	Jazz	1016	0.98%	3131	1006	71
KAR	Popular	1358	8.18%	9416	1247	858

the numbers of misclassified negative and positive samples, respectively. This measure can be computed as $Acc = (TP + TN)/(TP + FN + TN + FP)$.

However, empirical evidence shows that this measure is biased with respect to the data imbalance and proportions of correct and incorrect classifications [8]. Shortcomings of these evaluators have motivated a search for new measures. Some straightforward examples of these alternative measures used in this work are: (i) *True positive rate* (also referred to as *recall*) is the percentage of positive examples which are correctly classified, $TPr = TP/(TP + FN)$; (ii) *Precision* (or *purity*) is defined as the percentage of samples which are correctly labelled as positive, $Precision = TP/(TP+FP)$; and (iii) *F-measure* combines TPr and Precision, $F\text{-}measure = (2 * TPr * Precision)/(TPr + Precision)$.

3 Experimental Results

3.1 Datasets

Experiments involve six datasets of track vectors obtained from the same number of corpora of MIDI files created in [2,3]. These corpora contain MIDI files of three different music genres: classical music (CL200 and CLA), jazz music (JZ200 and JAZ) and popular music in karaoke format (KR200 and KAR). A more detailed description of these corpora is shown in Table 2. From each corpus, a corresponding dataset of 38-dimensional track vectors is available (see Sect. 2.1) where each vector has been manually labelled by a trained musicologist as melody, non-melody or unlabelled.

These corpora can be divided into two groups with regard to their data complexity and also mainly due to their sizes. A first group can include CL200, JZ200 and KR200, and they have in common the number of MIDI files (200). Moreover, most of them have well-defined melodic tracks which make them suitable for training purposes. In contrast, CLA, JAZ and KAR are more heterogeneous corpora and, consequently, lead to more challenging tasks [2,3].

3.2 Experimental Design

In the following experiments, different combinations of CL200, JZ200 and KR200 are employed for training, whereas CLA, JAZ and KAR are used as three separated test sets. In a first series, the classifier is trained with two music genres (from among CL200, JZ200 and KR200) and is tested with the remaining one (from among CLA, JAZ and KAR). In the second experiment, only one training set, here named ALL200, is built from the union of CL200, JZ200 and KR200. The rationale of this experimental design is to find out whether the melodic track identification in a music genre depends on including samples of the same music genre in the training set. Unlike in previous work [2,3], conclusions are provided from the analysis of the results of more than one classifier (see Sect. 2.3).

In addition to the previous objective, this work also aims to study the advisability of managing the imbalanced nature of the training sets. Table 2 shows the imbalance between the distributions of both the melody and non-melody classes in all corpora. In order to evaluate the relevance of imbalance in classification results, all previous experiments were performed on three versions of each training set: i) the imbalanced original set, ii) a version balanced by SMOTE, and iii) a version balanced by RUS (see Sec. 2.2).

Due to the random behaviour of SMOTE and RUS, each experiment on the balanced training sets was performed 10 times and the results were averaged. In the case of the RF classifier, which selects random features, the experiments were also repeated 10 times on the original imbalanced training set.

For each experiment the Accuracy (Acc) was computed taking into account all MIDI files. However, TPr, Precision (Prec) and Fmeasure (Fm) ignored the MIDI files without melody tracks (see Table 2) as was stated in previous related works [2,3]. Note that this affects the calculation of TN and FP (see Sect. 2.3).

3.3   Experiment I

This experiment evaluates the effectiveness of detecting the melodic track in MIDI files of a specific music genre, when no samples of this genre have been used in the training stage. In particular, the following three pairs of training and test sets were considered: i) (JZ200+KR200, CLA), ii) (CL200+KR200, JAZ) and iii) (CL200+JZ200, KAR). Its results are shown in Table 3.

This experiment can be analysed in two ways. Firstly to compare classification results with regard to the music genres used for training and testing, and secondly in relation to the evaluation of the influence of managing imbalance before classification.

In terms of the analysis among the music styles, all classifiers except SVM seem to be sensitive to the genres used for training and testing both in imbalanced and balanced contexts. The most robust classifier is SVM, which obtained steady and high rates on the positive class (TPr, Prec and Fm). The worst results belong to RF with low values in all measures, probably because its random behaviour is more sensitive to the lack of samples of the test genre in the training set. In the case of Acc, its low values can be explained by the fact that the accuracy considers those test MIDI files without any melodic track, with the number of these shown in Table 2.

In regard to the influence of managing imbalance, most of the classifiers operating in the balanced contexts improve their results over the original imbalanced context. This effect is accentuated in the case of JAZ, where measures in the imbalanced scenario are, in general, the lowest among the three genres. The results

Table 3. Averaged results of Experiment I

Training strategy	Classifier	Train: JZ200+KR200 Test: CLA				Train: CL200+KR200 Test: JAZ				Train: CL200+JZ200 Test: KAR			
		Acc	TPr	Prec	Fm	Acc	TPr	Prec	Fm	Acc	TPr	Prec	Fm
Original	1-NN	0.53	0.65	0.93	0.76	0.62	0.64	0.96	0.77	0.73	0.92	0.84	0.88
	5-NN	0.58	0.67	0.96	0.79	0.61	0.62	0.97	0.76	0.71	0.98	0.78	0.86
	SVM	0.69	0.95	0.99	0.97	0.87	0.89	0.99	0.94	0.85	0.97	0.94	0.96
	MLP	0.62	0.96	0.94	0.95	0.56	0.57	0.96	0.72	0.67	0.97	0.74	0.84
	RF	0.45	0.18	1	0.3	0.05	0.04	0.78	0.08	0.47	0.95	0.52	0.67
SMOTE	1-NN	0.57	0.73	0.97	0.83	0.74	0.76	0.97	0.85	0.74	0.94	0.84	0.89
	5-NN	0.64	0.84	0.97	0.9	0.84	0.87	0.97	0.92	0.73	0.99	0.8	0.88
	SVM	0.67	0.99	0.99	0.99	0.94	0.96	0.99	0.98	0.86	0.98	0.95	0.97
	MLP	0.63	0.87	0.94	0.91	0.68	0.71	0.94	0.81	0.41	0.77	0.49	0.6
	RF	0.43	0.23	1	0.38	0.06	0.05	0.8	0.09	0.59	0.95	0.66	0.78
RUS	1-NN	0.6	0.84	0.96	0.89	0.83	0.86	0.98	0.91	0.8	0.98	0.89	0.93
	5-NN	0.63	0.79	0.97	0.87	0.79	0.81	0.98	0.89	0.76	0.98	0.84	0.9
	SVM	**0.67**	**0.99**	**1**	**0.99**	**0.95**	**0.97**	**0.99**	**0.98**	**0.88**	**0.99**	**0.96**	**0.98**
	MLP	0.66	0.96	0.94	0.95	0.84	0.89	0.95	0.92	0.62	0.99	0.67	0.8
	RF	0.51	0.5	0.95	0.66	0.26	0.27	0.86	0.41	0.44	0.93	0.49	0.64

Table 4. Averaged results of Experiment II

Training estrategy	Classifier	Train: ALL200 Test: CLA				Train: ALL200 Test: JAZ				Train: ALL200 Test: KAR			
		Acc	TPr	Prec	Fm	Acc	TPr	Prec	Fm	Acc	TPr	Prec	Fm
Original	1-NN	0.64	0.88	0.97	0.92	0.89	0.91	0.99	0.95	0.73	0.92	0.84	0.88
	5-NN	0.66	0.87	0.97	0.92	0.91	0.92	1	0.96	0.63	0.88	0.74	0.81
	SVM	0.63	0.99	0.99	0.99	0.89	0.9	1	0.94	0.85	0.95	0.96	0.96
	MLP	0.61	1	0.94	0.97	0.87	0.88	0.99	0.93	0.53	0.75	0.69	0.72
	RF	0.63	0.82	0.9	0.86	0.71	0.73	0.97	0.83	0.56	0.76	0.73	0.75
SMOTE	1-NN	0.67	0.94	0.97	0.96	0.92	0.93	0.99	0.96	0.82	0.98	0.91	0.94
	5-NN	0.68	0.98	0.98	0.98	0.93	0.95	0.99	0.97	0.77	0.99	0.84	0.91
	SVM	0.64	1	0.99	0.99	0.93	0.94	1	0.97	0.91	1	0.99	0.99
	MLP	0.6	0.84	0.96	0.89	0.89	0.9	0.99	0.94	0.59	0.8	0.73	0.76
	RF	0.64	0.91	0.93	0.92	0.82	0.84	0.98	0.9	0.73	0.9	0.85	0.88
RUS	1-NN	0.7	0.98	1	0.99	0.93	0.94	0.99	0.97	0.84	0.99	0.92	0.95
	5-NN	0.67	0.99	0.9	0.8	0.94	0.95	0.99	0.97	0.71	1	0.77	0.87
	SVM	0.64	1	**0.99**	**0.99**	**0.94**	**0.95**	**0.99**	**0.97**	**0.91**	1	0.99	1
	MLP	0.63	0.99	0.95	0.97	0.91	0.93	0.98	0.96	0.67	0.96	0.74	0.84
	RF	0.62	0.92	0.94	0.93	0.86	0.89	0.98	0.93	0.75	0.97	0.82	0.89

of SVM obtained from both SMOTE and RUS are the highest and very similar, which suggests, for this problem, the use of RUS is most appropriate because it significantly reduces the complexity of the training set. Taking into account TPr, Prec and Fm, which only considers MIDI files with a melodic track, RUS+SVM achieved results greater than 95%, most of them being greater or equal to 99%.

3.4 Experiment II

The second experiment involves the same task as the first one but in this case the training set contains samples of all music genres. The training set is ALL200 (see Sect. 3.2) and the test sets are again CLA, JAZ and KAR. The results of this experiment are shown in Table 4.

As in the first experiment, the classification results based on balanced training sets are better than those obtained from the original training set. Moreover, most of the classifiers clearly improve on their behaviour in the previous series.

This effect is highlighted in the case of RF due to its previous poor results. In contrast, the improvement of SVM is negligible because its previous results were very high. However, the RUS+SVM combination remains the best choice and its results slightly improve on those reported in previous work [2,3], although these were obtained with fewer features in an imbalanced scenario.

4   Conclusions and Future Work

This paper deals with the problem of identifying the melodic track in a MIDI file considering the imbalanced context. This task is supported by a primary decision problem consisting of the classification of tracks either in the melody or in the accompaniment class. The higher number of accompaniment tracks compared to melody tracks defines a two-class imbalance problem. Unlike in previous related work, imbalance is managed in these experiments by resampling before learning and several classifiers are used to draw the conclusions. Experiments study the melodic track identification within a music genre depending on the inclusion or not of samples of the same music style in the training set, in both balanced and imbalanced contexts. Most of the results obtained from resampled training sets were significantly better than those derived from the corresponding original imbalanced training set. The best solution based on SVM provides high results that are independent of the music genres used for training and testing.

Future lines of work could involve feature selection or extraction, and the segmentation of tracks in pieces that better match with the melody along with the corresponding labelling at piece level. This approach may be more suitable when the melody line moves across tracks.

References

1. Shen, H.C., Lee, C.: Whistle for music: using melody transcription and approximate string matching for content-based query over a midi database. Multimedia Tools Appl. 35(3), 259–283 (2007)
2. Rizo, D., Ponce de León, P., Pérez-Sancho, C., Pertusa, A., Iñesta, J.: A pattern recognition approach for melody track selection in midi files. In: Proc. of the 7th ISMIR, Victoria, Canada, pp. 61–66 (2006)
3. Rizo, D., Ponce de León, P., Pertusa, A., Iñesta, J.: Melodic track identification in midi files. In: Proc. of the 19th Int. FLAIRS Conf. AAAI Press, Menlo Park (2006)
4. Madsen, S.T., Widmer, G.: Towards a computational model of melody identification in polyphonic music. In: IJCAI, pp. 459–464 (2007)
5. Habrard, A., Iñesta, J.M., Rizo, D., Sebban, M.: Melody recognition with learned edit distances. LNCS, vol. 5342, pp. 86–96 (2008)
6. Chawla, N.V., Bowyer, K.W., Hall, L.O., Kegelmeyer, W.P.: Smote: Synthetic minority over-sampling technique. J. Artif. Intell. Res. (JAIR) 16, 321–357 (2002)
7. Kotsiantis, S.: Mixture of expert agents for handling imbalanced data sets. Annals of Mathematics, Computing & TeleInformatics 1, 46–55 (2003)
8. Provost, F., Fawcett, T.: Analysis and visualization of classifier performance: Comparison under imprecise class and cost distributions. In: Proc. of the 3rd ACM SIGKDD, pp. 43–48 (1997)

Bernoulli HMMs at Subword Level for Handwritten Word Recognition*

Adrià Giménez and Alfons Juan

DSIC/ITI, Univ. Politècnica de València,
E-46022 València, Spain
{agimenez,ajuan}@dsic.upv.es

Abstract. This paper presents a handwritten word recogniser based on HMMs at subword level (characters) in which state-emission probabilities are governed by multivariate Bernoulli probability functions. This recogniser works directly with raw binary pixels of the image, instead of conventional, real-valued local features. A detailed experimentation has been carried out by varying the number of states, and comparing the results with those from a conventional system based on continuous (Gaussian) densities. From this experimentation, it becomes clear that the proposed recogniser is much better than the conventional system.

Keywords: HMM, Subword, Bernoulli, Handwritten word recognition.

1 Introduction

Hidden Markov models (HMMs) have received significant attention in off-line handwriting recognition during the last few years [2,3]. As in speech recognition [6], HMMs are used to model the probability (density) of an observation sequence, given its corresponding text transcription or simply its class label.

Observation sequences typically consist of fixed-dimension feature vectors which are computed locally, using a sliding window along the handwritten text image. In [1], we explored the possibility of using raw, binary pixels as feature vectors. This was done with two ideas in mind. On the one hand, this guarantees that no discriminative information is filtered out during feature extraction. On the other hand, this allows us to introduce probabilistic models that deal more directly with the object to be recognised [4,7]. This lead us to the study of Bernoulli HMMs, that is, HMMs in which the state-conditional probabilities are governed by multivariate Bernoulli probability functions.

The direct method to model handwritten words with Bernoulli HMMs is to use an independent, separate Bernoulli HMM for each word. We did it in [1], where successful results were obtained in a task of word classification with a moderate number of (word) classes. However, this direct approach is no longer applicable in

* Work supported by the EC (FEDER) and the Spanish MEC under the MIPRCV "Consolider Ingenio 2010" research programme (CSD2007-00018), the iTransDoc research project (TIN2006-15694-CO2-01), and the FPU grant AP2005-1840.

H. Araujo et al. (Eds.): IbPRIA 2009, LNCS 5524, pp. 497–504, 2009.

the case of classification tasks involving a large number of classes since, typically, most classes do not have enough examples for reliable parameter estimation. As in continuous handwritten text recognition, which can be considered the extreme case of unlimited number of classes, this problem can be alleviated by using subword (character) HMMs; that is, all word classes (sentences) are modelled by concatenation of subword (character) HMMs, and thus only one HMM per character has to be trained. This is precisely what we do in this work. Empirical results are reported in which Bernoulli HMMs at subword level are compared with both, independent Bernoulli HMMs, and conventional (Gaussian) HMMs at subword level [3].

The paper is organised as follows. We first review basic HMM theory in Sections 2 and 3, mainly to fix notation. Then, in Section 4, the previous basic HMM theory is particularised to case of Bernoulli HMMs. Experiments are described in Section 5, while concluding remarks and future work are discussed in Section 6.

2   Hidden Markov Models

HMMs are used to model the probability (density) of an observation sequence. In a way similar to [6], we characterise an HMM as follows:

1. M, the number of states in the model. Individual states are labelled as $\{1, 2, \ldots, M\}$ and we denote the state at time t as q_t. In addition, we define the special states I and F for *start* and *stop*.
2. The state-transition probability distribution, $A = \{a_{ij}\}$, where

$$a_{ij} = P(q_{t+1} = j \mid q_t = i), \qquad 1 \leq i, j \leq M,\ i = I,\ j = F. \qquad (1)$$

   For convenience, we set $a_{IF} = 0$.
3. The observation probability (density) function, $B = \{b_j(o)\}$, in which

$$b_j(o_t) = P(o_t \mid q_t = j), \qquad (2)$$

   defines the probability (density) function in state j, $j = 1, 2, \ldots, M$.

For convenience, the specification of an HMM can be compacted as

$$\lambda = (A, B). \qquad (3)$$

Therefore, the probability (density) of an observation sequence $O = o_1, \ldots, o_T$ is given by:

$$P(O \mid \lambda) = \sum_{I, q_1, \ldots, q_T, F} a_{I q_1} \left[\prod_{1 \leq t < T} a_{q_t q_{t+1}} \right] a_{q_T F} \prod_{t=1}^{T} b_{q_t}(o_t). \qquad (4)$$

Maximum likelihood estimation of the parameters governing an HMM can be carried out using the EM algorithm for HMMs; i.e. using Baum-Welch re-estimation formulae. Assume that the likelihood is calculated with respect to

N observation sequences $O_1, \ldots, O_N$; with $O_n = (o_{n1}, \ldots, o_{nT_n})$. In the E step (at iteration k), the forward probability for each sample n, state i and time t, $\alpha_{nt}(i) = P(o_{n1}, \ldots, o_{nt}, q_{nt} = i \mid \lambda)$, is calculated as:

$$\alpha_{nt+1}^{(k)}(j) = \begin{cases} a_{Ii}^{(k)} b_i^{(k)}(o_{n1}) & 1 \le i \le M, t = 0 \\ \left[\displaystyle\sum_{i=1}^M \alpha_{nt}^{(k)}(i) a_{ij}^{(k)} \right] b_j^{(k)}(o_{nt+1}) & \begin{array}{l} 1 \le j \le M \\ 1 \le t < T_n \end{array} \end{cases} , \qquad (5)$$

while the backward probability, $\beta_{nt}(i) = P(o_{nt+1}, \ldots, o_{nT_n} \mid q_{nt} = i, \lambda)$, is:

$$\beta_{nt}^{(k)}(i) = \begin{cases} a_{iF}^{(k)} & 1 \le i \le M, t = T_n \\ \displaystyle\sum_{j=1}^M a_{ij}^{(k)} b_j^{(k)}(o_{nt+1}) \beta_{nt+1}^{(k)}(j) & \begin{array}{l} 1 \le i \le M \\ 1 \le t < T_n \end{array} \end{cases} . \qquad (6)$$

The probability (density) of an observation can be calculated using forward probabilities:

$$P(O_n \mid \lambda) = \sum_{i=1}^M \alpha_{nT_n}(i) a_{iF} . \qquad (7)$$

In the M step (at iteration k), the transition parameters are updated as follows:

$$a_{ij}^{(k+1)} = \begin{cases} \dfrac{1}{N} \displaystyle\sum_n \dfrac{\alpha_{n1}(j)^{(k)} \beta_{n1}(j)^{(k)}}{P(O_n \mid \lambda)^{(k)}} & \begin{array}{l} i = 1 \\ 1 \le j \le M \end{array} \\[3ex] \dfrac{1}{\gamma(i)} \displaystyle\sum_n \dfrac{\sum_{t=1}^{T_n-1} \alpha_{nt}^{(k)}(i) a_{ij}^{(k)} b_j^{(k)}(o_{nt+1}) \beta_{nt+1}^{(k)}(j)}{P(O_n \mid \lambda)^{(k)}} & 1 \le i, j \le M \\[3ex] \dfrac{1}{\gamma(i)} \displaystyle\sum_n \dfrac{\alpha_{nT_n}^{(k)}(i) \beta_{nT_n}^{(k)}(i)}{P(O_n \mid \lambda)^{(k)}} & \begin{array}{l} 1 \le i \le M \\ j = F \end{array} \end{cases} , \qquad (8)$$

where $\gamma(i)$ is:

$$\gamma(i) = \sum_n \dfrac{\sum_{t=1}^{T_n} \alpha_{nt}^{(k)}(i) \beta_{nt}^{(k)}(i)}{P(O_n \mid \lambda)^{(k)}} . \qquad (9)$$

3   Subunit Models Based on HMMs

HMMs are often used in classification tasks to model the conditional probability of an observation sequence given a class label. A large number of classes involves a huge number of parameters; more precisely, one independent, complete HMM per class. Nevertheless, if the classes are in fact symbol sequences of a given alphabet $\{1, \ldots, C\}$, this problem can be alleviated by instead defining an HMM for each symbol of the alphabet $\{\lambda_1, \ldots, \lambda_C\}$. Therefore, for each class label we have a virtual HMM by concatenating the HMMs related to the class symbols.

The concatenation is done by joining the state F of an HMM with the state I of the next HMM. Thus, the probability of an observation sequence $o_1, \ldots, o_T$ given a symbol sequence $s_1, \ldots, s_L$, where $L \leq T$, is:

$$P(o_1^T \mid s_1^L, \lambda_1^C) = \sum_{\substack{I, q_1, \ldots, q_{e(1)}, Q_1, \\ q_{b(2)}, \ldots, q_{e(2)}, Q_2 \\ \cdots \\ q_{b(L)}, \ldots, q_T, F}} \prod_{l=1}^{L} P(o_{b(l)}^{e(l)}, q_{b(l)}^{e(l)}, Q_l \mid \lambda_{s_l}, Q_{l-1}), \qquad (10)$$

where $e(l)$ and $b(l)$ are the positions of the first and the last observations generated by λ_{s_l} respectively, $Q_l = I_{s_{l+1}} = F_{s_l}$, and:

$$P(o_{b(l)}^{e(l)}, q_{b(l)}^{e(l)}, Q_l \mid \lambda_{s_l}, Q_{l-1}) = a_{s_l I q_{b(l)}} \left[\prod_{t=b(l)}^{e(l)-1} a_{s_l q_t q_{t+1}} \right] a_{s_l q_{e(l)} F} \prod_{t=b(l)}^{e(l)} b_{s_l q_t}(o_t). \quad (11)$$

As in the previous section, the parameters can be estimated using the EM algorithm. Consider the calculation of the likelihood function with respect to N pairs of sequences $(O_1, S_1), \ldots, (O_N, S_N)$; with $O_n = (o_{n1}, \ldots, o_{nT_n})$ and $S_n = (s_{n1}, \ldots, s_{nL_n})$, where $L_n \leq T_n$. In the E step, the forward probabilities are calculated as:

$$\alpha_{nlt+1}^{(k)}(j) = \begin{cases} a_{s_{n1}Ij}^{(k)} b_{s_{n1}j}^{(k)}(o_{n1}) & \begin{array}{l} l = 1, t = 0 \\ 1 \leq j \leq M_{s_{n1}} \end{array} \\[2em] \left[\displaystyle\sum_{\substack{1 \leq i \leq M_{s_{nl}} \\ i = I_{s_{nl}}}} \alpha_{nlt}^{(k)}(i) a_{s_{nl}ij}^{(k)} \right] b_{s_{nl}j}^{(k)}(o_{nt+1}) & \begin{array}{l} 1 \leq l \leq L_n \\ 1 \leq t < T_n \\ 1 \leq j \leq M_{s_{nl}} \end{array} \\[2em] \displaystyle\sum_{i=1}^{M_{s_{nl}}} \alpha_{nlt+1}^{(k)}(i) a_{s_{nl}iF}^{(k)} & \begin{array}{l} 1 \leq l \leq L_n \\ 0 \leq t < T_n \\ j = F_{s_{nl}} \end{array} \\[2em] \alpha_{nl-1t+1}^{(k)}(F_{s_{nl-1}}) & \begin{array}{l} 1 < l \leq L_n \\ 0 \leq t < T_n \\ j = I_{s_{nl}} \end{array} \\[1em] 0 & \text{otherwise} \end{cases} \qquad (12)$$

Similarly, the backward probabilities are given by:

$$\beta_{nlt}^{(k)}(i) = \begin{cases} a_{s_{nL_n}iF}^{(k)} & \begin{array}{l} l = L_n, t = T_n \\ 1 \leq i \leq M_{s_{nL_n}} \end{array} \\[1.5em] a_{s_{nl}iF}^{(k)} \beta_{nlt}^{(k)}(F_{s_{nl}}) & \begin{array}{l} 1 \leq l \leq L_n \\ 1 \leq t < T_n \end{array} \\[1em] \quad + \displaystyle\sum_{j=1}^{M_{s_{nl}}} a_{s_{nl}ij}^{(k)} b_{s_{nl}j}^{(k)}(o_{nt+1}) \beta_{nlt+1}^{(k)}(j) & \begin{array}{l} 1 \leq i \leq M_{s_{nl}} \\ i = I_{s_{nl}} \end{array} \\[1.5em] \beta_{nl+1t}^{(k)}(I_{s_{nl+1}}) & \begin{array}{l} 1 \leq l < L_n \\ 1 \leq t < T_n \\ i = F_{s_{nl}} \end{array} \\[1em] 0 & \text{otherwise} \end{cases} \qquad (13)$$

Using the forward probabilities, the probability of an observation can be computed as:
$$P(O \mid S, \lambda_1^C) = \alpha_{LT}(F_{s_L}). \tag{14}$$

In the M step, transition parameters of λ_c are updated for all i ($1 \le i \le M_c$ and $i = I_c$) as:

$$a_{cij}^{(k+1)} = \frac{1}{\gamma_c(i)} \begin{cases} \sum_n \dfrac{\sum_{l:s_{nl}=c} \sum_{t=1}^{T_n-1} \alpha_{nlt}^{(k)}(i) a_{cij}^{(k)} b_{cj}^{(k)}(o_{nt+1}) \beta_{nlt+1}^{(k)}(j)}{P(O_n \mid S_n, \lambda_1^C)} & 1 \le j \le M_c \\[3ex] \sum_n \dfrac{\sum_{l:s_{nl}=c} \sum_{t=1}^{T_n} \alpha_{nlt}^{(k)}(i) a_{ciF}^{(k)} \beta_{nlt}^{(k)}(F_c)}{P(O_n \mid S_n, \lambda_1^C)} & j = F_c \end{cases}, \tag{15}$$

where:

$$\gamma_c(i) = \sum_n \frac{\sum_{l:s_{nl}=c} \sum_{t=1}^{T_n} \alpha_{nlt}^{(k)}(i) \beta_{nlt}^{(k)}(i)}{P(O_n \mid S_n, \lambda_1^C)}. \tag{16}$$

4 Bernoulli HMM

Let $O = (o_1, \ldots, o_T)$ be a sequence of D-dimensional binary observation vectors. A Bernoulli HMM is an HMM in which the probability of observing o_t, when $q_t = j$, is given by multivariate Bernoulli probability function for the state j:

$$b_j(o_t) = \prod_{d=1}^{D} p_{jd}^{o_{td}} (1 - p_{jd})^{1-o_{td}}, \tag{17}$$

where p_{jd} is the probability for bit d to be 1 when the observation vector is generated in the state j. Note that (17) is just the product of state-conditional unidimensional Bernoulli variables. The parameter vector associated with the state j, $p_j = (p_{j1}, \ldots, p_{jD})^t$, will be referred to as the prototype of the Bernoulli distribution in the state j.

Using the EM algorithm, the Bernoulli prototype corresponding to the state j of λ_c has to be updated as:

$$p_{cj}^{(k+1)} = \frac{1}{\gamma_c(j)} \sum_n \frac{\sum_{l:s_{nl}=c} \sum_{t=1}^{T_n} \alpha_{nlt}^{(k)}(j) o_{nt} \beta_{nlt}^{(k)}(j)}{P(O_n \mid S_n, \lambda_1^C)}, \tag{18}$$

where $\gamma_c(j)$ is defined in (16).

Note that the time required for an EM iteration over a single sequence is $O(TM^2D)$ ($M = \sum_{l=1}^{L} M_{s_l}$ in the case of subunit HMMs), which reduces to $O(TMD)$ in the usual case of simple, linear HMM topologies. This time cost does not differ from that of continuous (Gaussian) HMMs (with diagonal covariance matrices).

In order to avoid 0 probabilities at Bernoulli prototypes, these are smoothed by a linear interpolation with a flat (uniform) prototype, **0.5**,

$$\tilde{p} = (1 - \xi) p + \xi\, 0.5, \tag{19}$$

where typically $\xi = 10^{-6}$.

5 Experiments

The experiments have been carried out using the IAM database [5]. This corpus contains forms of unconstrained handwritten English text. All texts were extracted from the LOB corpus. A total of 657 writers contributed. Different datasets were obtained by using segmentations techniques, in particular we have used the handwritten words dataset. More precisely, we have selected those samples in this dataset that are marked as correctly segmented in the corpus, and which belong to a word with at least 10 samples.

All input gray level images were preprocessed before transforming them into sequences of feature vectors. Preprocessing consisted of three steps: gray level normalisation, deslanting, and size normalisation of ascenders and descenders. See [3] for further details.

Selected samples were randomly splitted into 30 80%-20% training-test partitions at the writer level to ensure writer-independent testing. This means about 59000 samples for training and 14000 for testing. The lexicon comprises 1117 different words and the alphabet is composed by 71 characters (upper and lowercase letters, punctuation signs, digits, etc.). This task is similar to that described in [2].

For the Bernoulli system, feature extraction has been carried out by rescaling the image to height 30 while respecting the original aspect ratio, and applying an Otsu binarisation to the resulting image. Therefore, the observation sequence is in fact a binary image of height 30. In the Gaussian case, feature vectors are of dimension 60, where the first 20 values are gray levels, and the other 40 are horizontal and vertical gray level derivatives [3]. In this case, we used the well-known HTK software [8].

Experiments have been carried out by varying number of states, $Q \in \{4, 6, 8, 10, 12\}$, and comparing our Bernoulli system to a conventional system based on Gaussian HMMs. Both systems have been initialised by first segmenting the training set using a "neutral" model, and then using the resulting segments to perform a Viterbi initialisation. The model has been trained with 4 EM iterations, and the recognition has been performed using the Viterbi algorithm. Figure 1 shows the results, where each point is the average of 30 repetitions (30 random splits). Vertical bars denote ± standard deviation.

The results obtained with the Bernoulli system are much better than those given by the Gaussian system. In particular, the best result for the Bernoulli system is a 44.0% classification error, obtained with $Q = 10$. In contrast, the best result for the Gaussian system is a 64.2% classification error, obtained with $Q = 8$.

We have extended the experiment by using a different number of states for each HMM. For this purpose, the training set was first aligned and segmented. Then, for each HMM, the number of states was calculated as the average length of the segments multiplied by a predefined *load factor, f*. This load factor indicates the number of observations that a state generates on average. We have tried several load factors $\{0.1, 0.2, 0.3, 0.4, 0.5, 0.6\}$. The results obtained are very similar to those reported above; i.e. the Bernoulli system outperforms the

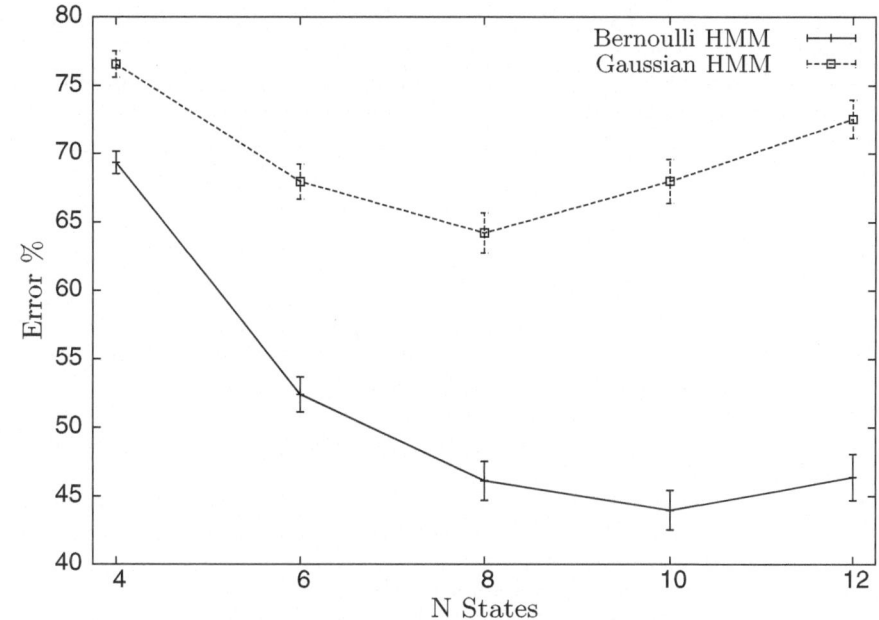

Fig. 1. Classification error (in %) as a function of the number of states for the Bernoulli HMM system and the conventional, Gaussian HMM system

Gaussian system with error rates similar to those in Figure 1. In both systems the best results are obtained with $f = 0.4$.

We concluded the experiments by repeating those shown in Figure 1, but using one Bernoulli HMM per word instead of one Bernoulli HMM per character while (approximately) keeping the same number of parameters. Using Bernoulli HMMs at word level and $Q = 1$ (1117 Bernoulli prototypes) a classification error of 89.3% was achieved, while with Bernoulli HMMs at subword level and $Q = 10$ (710 Bernoulli prototypes) we had a classification error of 44.0%. Moreover, using Bernoulli HMMs at word level and $Q = 10$ (11170 Bernoulli prototypes) the classification error is 64%; that is, it is still not better than that obtained with Bernoulli HMMs at subword level.

6   Concluding Remarks and Future Work

Bernoulli HMMs at subword (character) level has been studied and empirically tested on a task of handwritten word classification from the IAM database. We have obtained a classification error of 44.0%, which is 20 points better than the best result obtained with a conventional, Gaussian-based HMM system. It is also worth noting that the proposed system works with less features and parameters than the conventional system (30 vs 60 and half of the parameters). On the other hand, the proposed system has been also compared with Bernoulli HMM-based classifier at word level. As expected, the advantage of using subword models has been clearly confirmed.

For future work, we plan to try Bernoulli mixtures instead of a single Bernoulli at each state. We also plan to use the ideas reported in [7] for explicitly modelling of invariances in Bernoulli mixtures, and to extend the experiments to general handwritten text recognition.

References

1. Giménez-Pastor, A., Juan-Císcar, A.: Bernoulli HMMs for Off-line Handwriting Recognition. In: Proc. of the 8th Int. Workshop on Pattern Recognition in Information Systems (PRIS 2008), Barcelona, Spain, pp. 86–91 (June 2008)
2. Günter, S., Bunke, H.: HMM-based handwritten word recognition: on the optimization of the number of states, training iterations and Gaussian components. Pattern Recognition 37, 2069–2079 (2004)
3. Gadea, M.P.: Aportaciones al reconocimiento automático de texto manuscrito. PhD thesis, Dep. de Sistemes Informàtics i Computació, València, Spain. Advisors: Vidal, E., Tosselli, A.H. (October 2007)
4. Juan, A., Vidal, E.: Bernoulli mixture models for binary images. In: Proc. of the 17th Int. Conf. on Pattern Recognition (ICPR 2004), Cambridge, UK, vol. 3 (August 2004)
5. Marti, U.V., Bunke, H.: The IAM-database: an English sentence database for offline handwriting recognition. 5(1), 39–46 (2002)
6. Rabiner, L., Juang, B.-H.: Fundamentals of speech recognition. Prentice-Hall, Englewood Cliffs (1993)
7. Romero, V., Giménez, A., Juan, A.: Explicit Modelling of Invariances in Bernoulli Mixtures for Binary Images. In: Martí, J., Benedí, J.M., Mendonça, A.M., Serrat, J. (eds.) IbPRIA 2007. LNCS (LNAI), vol. 4477, pp. 539–546. Springer, Heidelberg (2007)
8. Young, S., et al.: The HTK Book. Cambridge University Engineering Department (1995)

Simultaneous Identity and Expression Recognition Using Face Geometry on Low Dimensional Manifolds

Pedro Martins and Jorge Batista*

Institute of Systems and Robotics
Dep. of Electrical Engineering and Computers
University of Coimbra - Portugal
{pedromartins,batista}@isr.uc.pt

Abstract. A solution for simultaneous identity and expression recognition is proposed. The proposed solution starts by extracting face geometry from input images using Active Appearance Models (AAM). Low dimensional manifolds were then derived using Laplacian EigenMaps resulting in two types of manifolds, one for model identity and the other for expression. Respective multiclass Support Vector Machines (SVM) were trained. The recognition is composed by a two step cascade, where first the identity is predicted and then its associated expression model is used to predict the facial expression. For evaluation proposes a database was build consisting on 6770 images captured from 4 people exhibiting 7 different emotions. The identity overall recognition rate was 96.8%. Facial expression results are identity dependent, and the most expressive individual achieves 76.8% of overall recognition rate.

Keywords: Active Appearance Models, Laplacian EigenMaps, Support Vector Machines, Identity and Expression Manifolds.

1 Introduction

Facial expression is one of the most powerful, natural and immediate means for humans to share their emotions and intentions. Psychological studies focus on the interpretation on this mean to interact and describe that there are six basic emotions universally recognized [1], namely: joy, sadness, surprise, fear, anger and disgust. An automatic, efficient and accurate facial expression extraction system would thus be a powerfull tool assisting in these studies, allowing also other kinds of applications such as Human Computer Interface (HCI), smart interactive systems, video compression, etc. The proposed simultaneous identity and facial expression recognition it is based on the idea that it is straightforward for a human to capture the emotion and consequently the identity of a mimic actor our someone known using makeup. Humans can understand both the identity/expression based only in facial motion. This guidance idea lead to

---

* This work was funded by FCT grant SFRH/BD/45178/2008.

H. Araujo et al. (Eds.): IbPRIA 2009, LNCS 5524, pp. 505–512, 2009.

face geometry used to recognize the identity and facial expression (focusing on the six basic emotions plus the neutral one). Laplacian EigenMaps [2] are non-linear dimension reduction techniques that derive a low dimensional manifold lying in a higher dimensional more complex manifold. An identity/facial expression manifold is derived by embedding image data into a low dimensional space, where a image sequence is then represented as a trajectory in the parameter space. Learning a manifold of this nature require to derive a discriminative facial representation from raw images, in fact face images are represented by a set of sparse 2D feature point and the identity/expression manifolds were learned in a facial geometric feature space. The recognition has a feature extracting mechanism and a two stage cascade of multiclass Support Vector Machines (SVM) [3] classifiers trained with low dimensional manifold data of face geometry. Discriminative facial representation from raw images was achieved using Active Appearance Models (AAM) [4] that is an effective way to locate facial features, modeling both shape and texture from an observed training set, being able to extract relevant face information without background interference. For an input image, the AAM fitting framework extracts facial geometry related features, and the first SVM stage predict the identity, on the second SVM stage it is loaded the correspondent expression model for the predicted identity and the current expression is also predicted.

2   Active Appearance Models

Active Appearance Models (AAM) [4] are generative nonlinear parametric models of shape and texture, commonly used to model faces. These adaptive template matching methods, learn offline the variability of shape and texture, that is captured from a representative training set, being able to fully describe with photorealistic quality the trained faces as well as unseen.

2.1   Shape and Texture Models

The shape of an AAM is defined by the vertex locations of a 2D triangulated mesh. Mathematically, the representation used for a single v-point shape is a $2v$ vector given by $\mathbf{s} = (x_1, y_1, \ldots, x_v, y_v)^T$. The AAM training data consists of a set of annotated images with the shape mesh marked (usually by hand). The shapes are then aligned to a common mean shape using a Generalised Procrustes Analysis (GPA), removing location, scale and rotation effects. Principal Components Analysis (PCA) are then applied to the aligned shapes, resulting on the parametric model

$$\mathbf{s} = \mathbf{s}_0 + \sum_{i=1}^{n} p_i \mathbf{s}_i \tag{1}$$

where a new shapes, $\mathbf{s}$, are synthesised by deforming the mean shape, $\mathbf{s}_0$, using a weighted linear combination of eigenvectors, $\mathbf{s}_i$. n is the number of eigenvectors that holds a user defined variance, typically 95%. p_i is a vector of shape

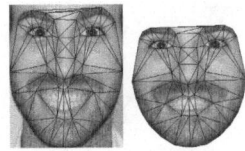

Fig. 1. On left the Original Image I, on right the Warped Image $I(\mathbf{W}(\mathbf{x};\mathbf{p}))$

parameters which represents the weights. Building a texture model, requires warping each training image so that the control points match those of the mean shape, $\mathbf{s}_0$. The texture mapping is performed, using a piece wise affine warp, i.e. partitioning the convex hull of the mean shape by a set of triangles using the Delaunay triangulation. Each pixel inside a triangle is mapped into the correspondent triangle in the mean shape using barycentric coordinates, see figure 1. This procedure removes differences in texture due shape changes, establishing a common texture reference frame. A texture model can be obtained by applying a low-memory PCA on the normalized textures. Defining pixel coordinates as $\mathbf{x} = (x,y)^T$, the appearance of the AAM is an image, $A(\mathbf{x})$, defined over the pixels $\mathbf{x} \in \mathbf{s}_0$ such as $A(\mathbf{x}) = A_0(\mathbf{x}) + \sum_{i=1}^{m} \lambda_i \mathbf{A}_i(\mathbf{x})$, $\quad \mathbf{x} \in \mathbf{s}_0$. The appearance $A(\mathbf{x})$ can be expressed as a base appearance $A_0(\mathbf{x})$ plus a linear combination of m appearance images $A_i(\mathbf{x})$ (EigenFaces). The coefficients λ_i are the appearance parameters.

2.2   Model Fitting

Fitting an AAM is usually formulated [5] as minimizing the texture error, in the least square sense, between the model instance $A(\mathbf{x})$ and the input backwarped image onto the base mesh $I(\mathbf{W}(\mathbf{x};\mathbf{p}))$,

$$\sum_{\mathbf{x}\in\mathbf{s}_0} \left[A_0(\mathbf{x}) + \sum_{i=1}^{m} \lambda_i A_i(\mathbf{x}) - I(\mathbf{W}(\mathbf{x},\mathbf{p})) \right]^2 . \tag{2}$$

In eq. 2 the warp $\mathbf{W}$ is the piecewise affine warp from the base mesh $\mathbf{s}_0$ to the current AAM shape $\mathbf{s}$, see figure 1. Hence, $\mathbf{W}$ is a function of the shape parameters $\mathbf{p}$. Notice that, the shape normalization on the model building process (Procrustes Analysis) the AAM do not model similarity transformations to the target image. Refer to [5] where is shown how to include it on the warp $\mathbf{W}(\mathbf{x};\mathbf{p})$.

The Simultaneous Inverse Compositional (SIC) [6] which minimize eq. 2 by performing a Gauss-Newtow gradient descent optimization simultaneously on the warp parameters $\mathbf{p}$ and the appearance parameters $\boldsymbol{\lambda}$ with respect to $\Delta\mathbf{p}$ and $\Delta\boldsymbol{\lambda}$, updating the warp by inverse composition: $\mathbf{W}(\mathbf{x};\mathbf{p}) \leftarrow \mathbf{W}(\mathbf{x};\mathbf{p}) \circ \mathbf{W}(\mathbf{x};\Delta\mathbf{p})^{-1}$ and the appearance parameters additively: $\boldsymbol{\lambda}\leftarrow\boldsymbol{\lambda}+\Delta\boldsymbol{\lambda}$. Denoting, $\mathbf{q} = \begin{pmatrix} \mathbf{p} \\ \boldsymbol{\lambda} \end{pmatrix}$, i.e. $\mathbf{q}$ is an $n+m$ dimensional vector containing the warp parameters $\mathbf{p}$ and the appearance $\boldsymbol{\lambda}$. The $m+n$ Steepest Descent images [6] are of the form

$$\mathbf{SD}_{SIC}(\mathbf{x}) = \left(\nabla A \frac{\partial \mathbf{W}}{\partial p_1}, \cdots, \nabla A \frac{\partial \mathbf{W}}{\partial p_n}, A_1(\mathbf{x}), \cdots, A_m(\mathbf{x}) \right) \qquad (3)$$

where ∇A is defined as $\nabla A = \nabla A_0 + \sum_{i=1}^{m} \lambda_i \nabla A_i$. The parameters update is computed as

$$\Delta \mathbf{q} = -H_{SIC}^{-1} \sum_{\mathbf{x} \in \mathbf{s}_0} \mathbf{SD}_{SIC}^T(\mathbf{x}) E(\mathbf{x}), \quad H_{SIC} = \sum_{\mathbf{x} \in \mathbf{s}_0} \mathbf{SD}_{SIC}^T(\mathbf{x}) \mathbf{SD}_{SIC}(\mathbf{x}), \quad (4)$$

where H_{SIC} is the Gauss-Newtow approximation of the Hessian. The error image, $E(\mathbf{x})$, is defined as

$$E(\mathbf{x}) = I(\mathbf{W}(\mathbf{x}; \mathbf{p})) - \left[A_0(\mathbf{x}) + \sum_{i=1}^{m} \lambda_i A_i(\mathbf{x}) \right]. \qquad (5)$$

The Simultaneous Inverse Compositional when compared with other fitting approaches, such as the Project-Out [5] or the precomputed numerical estimate [4], work rather slow, since the Steepest Descent images depend on the appearance parameters and they have to re-computed in every iteration. By the other hand, SIC achieves the better fitting performance which is desirable for our proposes. Starting with a given estimate for the model, $\mathbf{q}_0$, and a rough estimate of the location of the face (provided by AdaBoost [7] method), an AAM model can be fitted with SIC following the algorithm 1. Figure 2 shows an example of AAM fitting into a target image.

Algorithm 1. Simultaneous Inverse Compositional Image Alignment

1: Evaluate the gradients ∇A_0 and ∇A_i for $i = 1, \cdots, m$
2: Evaluate the Jacobian of the warp $\dfrac{\partial \mathbf{W}}{\partial \mathbf{p}}$ at $(\mathbf{x}; 0)$
3: **while** MaxIterations reached or $|\Delta \mathbf{q}| < \varepsilon$ **do**
4:    Warp I with $\mathbf{W}(\mathbf{x}; \mathbf{p})$ to compute $I(\mathbf{W}(\mathbf{x}; \mathbf{p}))$
5:    Compute the error image, $E(\mathbf{x})$, using eq. 5
6:    Compute the Steepest Descent images, $\mathbf{SD}(\mathbf{x})$, using eq. 3
7:    Compute the Hessian matrix, H, eq. 4
8:    Compute the parameters updates, $\Delta \mathbf{q}$, with eq. 4
9:    Inverse Compose the Warp $\mathbf{W}(\mathbf{x}; \mathbf{p}) \leftarrow \mathbf{W}(\mathbf{x}; \mathbf{p}) \circ \mathbf{W}(\mathbf{x}; \Delta \mathbf{p})^{-1}$
10:    Update the appearance parameters $\lambda \leftarrow \lambda + \Delta \lambda$
11: **end while**

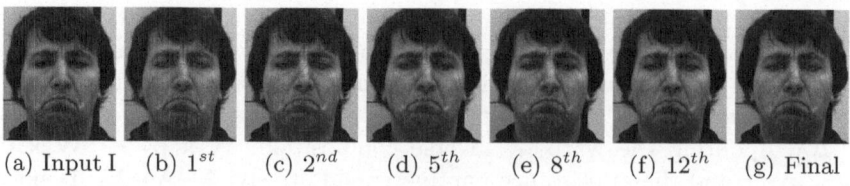

(a) Input I   (b) 1st (c) 2nd (d) 5th (e) 8th (f) 12th (g) Final

Fig. 2. AAM fitting

3   Laplacian EigenMaps

Laplacian EigenMaps [2] are nonlinear dimension reduction techniques that derive a low dimensional manifold lying in a higher dimensional more complex manifold. The Laplacian EigenMaps builds a graph that incorporates neighborhood information of the dataset and using the notion of the Laplacian of the graph, computes a low dimensional representation that optimally preserves local neighborhood information. Given k feature points $\mathbf{x}_1, \cdots, \mathbf{x}_k \in \Re^l$, a weighted graph with k nodes is build, one for each point, with a set of edges connecting neighboring points. The embedding map is found by computing the eigenvectors of the graph Laplacian [2]. See algorithm 2 where this method is described. Finding such embedding map, $\varPhi$, requires tuning n nearest neighbors for graph building and select the number of dimensions, m, where the input features were projected into.

Algorithm 2. Laplacian EigenMaps

- Build the Adjacency Graph:
Nodes i and j (or j and i) are connected by an edge to the n nearest neighbors.
- Choosing the weights W_{ij}: (if i and j are connected by an edge) then $W_{ij} = 1$
- Build EigenMaps:
Compute eigenvalues and eigenvectors for the generalized eigenvector problem

$$L\mathbf{f} = \lambda D\mathbf{f} \qquad (6)$$

where $D_{ii} = \sum_j W_{ji}$ is a diagonal weight matrix and $L = D - W$ is the Laplacian matrix. Let $\mathbf{f}_0, \cdots, \mathbf{f}_{k-1}$ be the solutions of eq. 6 order by eigenvalues $\lambda_0 = 0 \leq \lambda_1 \leq \cdots \leq \lambda_{k-1}$). Leaving out the eigenvector $\mathbf{f}_0$ corresponding to eigenvalue 0, the embedding m-dimensional Euclidian space is given by $\varPhi = [\mathbf{f}_1 | \mathbf{f}_2 | \cdots | \mathbf{f}_m]$.

---

4   Simultaneous Identity and Facial Expression Recognition

The proposed solution models both identity and facial expression in independent low dimensional manifolds. The system performs simultaneous identity and facial expression recognition by building different manifolds that were derived from embedding image data into a low dimensional subspace using Laplacian EigenMaps [2]. In order to learn these manifolds it is necessary to derive discriminative facial representation from raw images. This process it is done by the AAM fitting framework, see figure 2, where face images are represented by a set of sparse 2D feature point. As discriminatory features, insted of (x, y) feature points, were used AAM related geometric features, i.e. regarding eq. 1 the shape parameters, $\mathbf{p}$, provide the same geometric information but using lower dimensional features ($n << 2v$). All faces were normalized by selecting only shape parameters that model only deformation (ignoring the 4 similarity parameters, refer to [5]). Both identity and expression manifolds were then learnt in a facial geometric feature space. One image sequence from a test subject describing a facial emotion is represented as a trajectory in the learnt manifold acquired from the parameter space of the AAM.

See figure 4. These manifolds were build using Laplacian EigenMaps representations for the shape parameters (that are related to face geometry). This approach maps the dimensionality of **p** into a less dimensional space where the mapped features acquire a huge discrimination power. Two kinds of Laplacian EigenMaps were build. The first type of EigenMap (lets call it identity manifold) finds the lower dimensional manifold using data from all individuals, see figure 3. The second type, the expression manifold, uses data only from a single individual, that maps data emphasising the differences in individual facial motion of the different expressions, see figure 4. This system holds an indentity manifold and expression manifold for each of the individuals in the training set. For recognition proposes, several muticlass Support Vector Machines (SVM) [3] classifiers were build, where the low dimensional identity and expression manifolds, provide the training data in these models. Summarizing, the simultaneous identity/expression recognition has a feature extracting mechanism and a two stage cascade of SVM classifiers trained with embedded manifold data. For an input image, the AAM fitting framework extracts the normalized shape parameters, **p**, and the first SVM stage predict the identity for these parameters. On the second SVM stage it is loaded the correspondent expression model for the predicted identity and the current expression is predicted also.

5   Experimental Results

For the purpose of this work, a Facial Dynamics Database was built. It consists of 4 individuals, in a frontal position, showing 7 different facial expressions, namely: neutral expression, happiness, sadness, surprise, anger, fear and disgust. All facial emotions were taken by starting and ending on the neutral expression. Each individual repeated all facial emotions four times. The dataset is formed

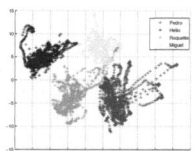

	Person1	Person2	Person3	Person4
Person1	**98.11**	0.09	1.79	0
Person2	1.32	**98.67**	0	0
Person3	2.93	0.29	**94.50**	2.27
Person4	1.29	0.13	2.32	**96.25**

Overall recognition rate = 96.88%

Fig. 3. Left - Identity manifold learnt with geometric AAM related features for 4 persons. Right - Confusion matrix for the identity manifold.

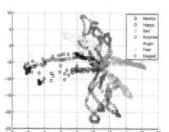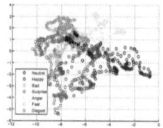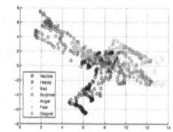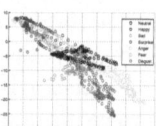

Fig. 4. Low dimensional manifolds learnt with geometric AAM related features for 4 persons exhibiting 7 expressions several turns each. Left-to-right figures represents the expression models for person 1, 2 ,3 and 4 respectively.

Table 1. Expression model confusion matrices for each one of the individuals

Person 1

	Neut	Happ	Sad	Surp	Ang	Fear	Disg
Neut	**69.85**	9.16	2.29	0	0.76	1.14	16.79
Happ	0	**84.58**	3.33	10.41	1.66	0	0
Sad	0	0	**100**	0	0	0	0
Surp	0.66	0	0	**99.33**	0	0	0
Ang	2.3952	0	0.89	0.59	**84.43**	0.29	11.37
Fear	0	0.74	0	38.66	0	**60.59**	0
Disg	2.54	0	0	37.57	20.70	0	**39.17**

Overall recognition rate = 76.85%

Person 2

	Neut	Happ	Sad	Surp	Ang	Fear	Disg
Neut	**67.78**	0	6.37	0	0	25.83	0
Happ	1.14	**78.70**	0	17.11	0	3.04	0
Sad	1.73	0	**86.85**	5.53	0	0	5.88
Surp	0.76	25.95	0.76	**41.60**	0	26.71	4.19
Ang	1.38	0	1.84	0	**79.26**	0.46	17.05
Fear	2.86	0	2.04	57.37	0	**33.61**	4.09
Disg	1.62	17.26	3.58	22.80	1.62	2.93	**50.16**

Overall recognition rate = 62.56%

Person 3

	Neut	Happ	Sad	Surp	Ang	Fear	Disg
Neut	**43.71**	0	20.10	25.62	0	10.55	0
Happ	3.89	**80.52**	0.43	6.49	0	3.89	4.76
Sad	8.29	0	**72.48**	0	10.48	2.62	6.11
Surp	5.31	6.91	0	**65.95**	0	21.80	0
Ang	4.28	0.47	25.71	0	**61.90**	0.95	6.66
Fear	21.25	23.13	0	18.75	0	**23.13**	13.75
Disg	10.13	2.02	37.16	10.81	5.40	2.02	**32.43**

Overall recognition rate = 54.30%

Person 4

	Neut	Happ	Sad	Surp	Ang	Fear	Disg
Neut	**52.50**	17.50	0	18.00	0	0	12.00
Happ	4.67	**90.19**	0	3.73	0	1.14	0
Sad	2.01	12.56	**42.71**	0	0	0	42.71
Surp	1.86	2.80	0	**56.54**	0	32.71	6.07
Ang	2.19	0	0	0	**55.70**	0	42.10
Fear	1.43	3.34	0	16.26	0	**75.60**	3.34
Disg	0.49	6.46	0	0	0.99	0	**92.03**

Overall recognition rate = 66.47%

by a total of 6770 images (640 × 480). The AAM model was build using a total of 28 images (7 images for each of the 4 person). Since the AAM will be used to fit every frame of the captured database, it should held as much shape variation possible. The training images were then composed by the most expressive images of the 7 emotions (from a random repetition sequence). These training images were hand annotated using 58 landmarks ($v = 58$). Training the model holding 95% of shape and appearance variance produces an AAM with 18 shape parameters, ($n = 18$), and 29 EigenFaces, ($m = 29$). All the 6770 frames of the Facial Dynamics Database were then fitted using the AAM model, retrieving the shape parameters, **p**, for each frame. Two main schemes were used for the manifold building: setting data for identity and setting the data for the expressions of each individual. A total of 5 manifolds were constructed (one model for identity plus 4 for each person expressions). These Laplacian EigenMaps were build with both the number of adjacency graph neighbours, and the number of dimensions where the input features were projected into, found by cross-validation. Figure 3 and 4 shows the manifolds produced for the identity and expressions respectively. Five multiclass SVM models were trained (again 1 for identity + 4 for expression). The multiclass SVM classication was achieved using one-against-all voting scheme with a Gaussian Radial Basis Function (RBF). The kernel parameters and the missclassification penalty, were found also by cross-validation. To evaluate the performance of the system the dataset was divided into 4 fold for cross validation F1, F2, F3 and F4, that matches to the 4 repetitions of all expressions that each subject was made. The results shown are confusion matrices that were obtained from the cross-validation of the 4 folds ([test F1, train F2,F3,F4]; [test F2, train F1,F3,F4;] ...). Identity and expression models were evaluated independently. Figure 3-left displays results for the identity recognition and table 1 shows results for the expression models for each person in the dataset. Regarding figure 4 it is noticed that person 1 (figure 4-most-left) is the most expressive. All facial emotions start and end from the neutral expression, which explains the high concentration of projected points over the neutral cluster. Experiments also shown that during the evolution of an emotion over time, due noise and the effect of confusion bettween expressions, the ground truth emotion is sometimes misclassified, i.e. the test point falls into other nearby cluster. This problem could be reduced by including facial dynamics constraints. Since our system only uses static based recognition, an improvement is expected by changing the way expressions are validated, that will be regarded in a near future work.

6   Conclusions

Simultaneous identity and expression recognition were achieved using a two stage classifier using high discriminative, low dimensional, geometric based features. Identity and expression of each individual were learn independently deriving a low dimensional manifold using Laplacian EigenMaps. Face geometric data was extracted using Active Appearance Models (AAM). For each image the AAM fitting framework provide normalized geometric related features and derived an identity manifold and expressions manifolds for each one of the individuals. Respective multiclass Support Vector Machines (SVM) were trained providing a two step classifier cascade where the first stage predicts identity. On second the expression model for the predicted identity is loaded and the expression is also predicted. For evaluation proposes an database was build having 6770 images captured from 4 people exhibiting 7 different emotions. Our 4 fold cross-validation results show that the system is able to recognize an overall 96.8% in the identity. The facial expression is very depend for each individual. In our dataset the most expressive individual achieves an overall recognition rate of 76.8% and the less expressive 54.3%.

References

1. Handbook of Cognition and Emotion. John Wiley & Sons Ltd., Chichester (1999)
2. Niyogi, P., Belkin, M.: Laplacian eigenmaps for dimensionality reduction and data representation. Neural Computation (2003)
3. The Nature of Statistical Learning Theory. Springer, New York (1995)
4. Edwards, G.J., Cootes, T.F., Taylor, C.J.: Active appearance models. IEEE Transactions on Pattern Analysis and Machine Intelligence (2001)
5. Matthews, I., Baker, S.: Active appearance models revisited. International Journal of Computer Vision (2004)
6. Matthews, I., Baker, S., Gross, R.: Lucas kanade 20 years on: A unifying framework: Part 3. Tech. Rep., Carnegie Mellon University Robotics Institute (2003)
7. Viola, P., Jones, M.: Rapid object detection using a boosted cascate of simple features. Computer Vision and Pattern Recognition

Author Index